PERSPECTIVES ON AN EVOLVING CREATION

PERSPECTIVES *on an* EVOLVING CREATION

Edited by

Keith B. Miller

WILLIAM B. EERDMANS PUBLISHING COMPANY
GRAND RAPIDS, MICHIGAN / CAMBRIDGE, U.K.

Wm. B. Eerdmans Publishing Co.
2140 Oak Industrial Drive N.E., Grand Rapids, Michigan 49505 /
P.O. Box 163, Cambridge CB3 9PU U.K.

Printed in the United States of America

12 11 10 09 08 07   7 6 5 4 3 2

Library of Congress Cataloging-in-Publication Data

Perspectives on an evolving creation / edited by Keith B. Miller.
      p.   cm.
Includes bibliographical references.
ISBN 978-0-8028-0512-6 (pbk.: alk. paper)
1. Creationism.   2. Evolution (Biology) — Religious aspects — Christianity.
I. Miller, Keith B.

BS651.P45   2003
231.7′652 — dc21
2003045403

www.eerdmans.com

To my parents:

Elizabeth G. Miller and John C. Miller

Contents

Preface

This book developed as an expression of two quite different personal desires. As a geologist and paleoecologist with interests in reconstructing Earth and life history, I want to share the excitement and challenge of current evolutionary research. New discoveries and theoretical advances are being made at a bewildering pace. Furthermore, I am convinced that science is not only a profession but also a Christian vocation, and part of that vocation is using scientific knowledge to deepen our understanding of God and of our calling as Creation's stewards. Secondly, having become deeply frustrated with the often fruitless and divisive nature of much of the "creation/evolution" debate within the evangelical Christian community, I hope to move the conversation in a more positive direction. The popular discussion of evolution has been carried out largely in ignorance both of the extensive body of scientific research, and of the scholarly Christian commentary on it. Productive interaction on the issues raised by evolutionary theory begins with becoming well-informed concerning current scientific practice and evidence.

The objective of this book is thus to provide a wide-ranging and authoritative evaluation of evolutionary theory from those with an orthodox Christian perspective. To that end, contributors were recruited from a variety of disciplines — astronomy, geology, paleontology, anthropology, biochemistry, genetics, philosophy, theology, and the history of science — to address specific issues. The assembly of the volume was motivated by the conviction that any Christian theology which hopes to compete in the world of ideas must take seriously the conclusions of modern science just as it must take seriously contributions from all other areas of human knowledge.

The phrase "evolving creation" in the title was chosen to communicate a view of God's creative activity that has received little attention within the evangelical community outside of academic circles. Much of the literature approaching evolution from a Christian perspective occurs in specialized journals or in books that do not have a broad evangelical readership. Unfortunately, evolution is widely perceived as being in conflict with a Christian faith that maintains a high view of Scripture. Most people know virtually nothing about the long history of Christian reflection on evolution. The general "conflict" mode of thinking in many cases effectively excludes integrative views from the discussion. There is thus a great need to have the concept of an "evolving creation" be made available to the larger Christian community for serious exploration.

Our scientific and technological society is in desperate need of a theological foundation which can give it purpose and moral guidance. Some people, both theists and non-theists, favor a view of complete independence and separation between theological and scientific perspectives concerning the natural world. However, although science and theology clearly occupy different realms of experience and thought, they do touch and impact one another. Both conflict and independence approaches to science and theology are doomed to failure, because in neither case is a real dialogue established. What is needed are efforts to achieve an integrated Christian worldview which take seriously both scriptural revelation and the testimony of the created universe. I think it is vital for both the health of the Christian community and science that more Christians become aware that evolution and God's creative activity are not inherently antithetical concepts. Only then will constructive engagement with the scientific community, and positive influence on the important theological and ethical issues involved be possible. It is hoped that this series of papers reflecting on evolutionary theory from clearly articulated orthodox Christian perspectives will have a significant impact on the quality of the Christian response to current scientific understanding.

This book should be a valuable resource for anyone interested in science/faith issues — particularly those surrounding evolution. It provides access to perspectives and data from a wide range of disciplines, as well as an entry into an extensive and, for the most part, little-known literature. The book should be an especially important resource for Christian college and university students. Often students are seriously challenged with evolutionary concepts for the first time in their college classes. This can be a crisis experience for students who do not have any Christian models of faith/science integration to draw from.

The book is organized topically with three main divisions. The first part provides the needed biblical, historical and scientific context for the discussions which follow. Conrad Hyers lays out the foundation for one commonly-used hermeneutic with which to interpret the biblical texts. Well-known historians of science Ted Davis, David Livingstone and Mark Noll set the historical context for the current "evolution/creation" conflict. Finally, a review of the nature and limitations of scientific investigation, including a discussion of the relationships between scientific and theological descriptions of natural processes, is presented by Loren Haarsma.

The second part of the book lays out the scientific evidence for an evolving creation. Specialists in a variety of fields summarize how our current evolutionary view of cosmic, Earth and biological history was constructed. Beginning with the origin and evolution of the universe, the focus of the essays progresses logically to biological evolution and human origins. Astronomers Deborah Haarsma and Jennifer Wiseman present evidence for an evolving cosmos. The dynamic and evolving Earth system reconstructed by geology, and discussed by Jeff Greenberg, provides the context for biological evolution. The evidence from the fossil record is discussed in essays by David Campbell and myself. The anthropological and genetic evidence for Human evolution, often the focus of arguments against an evolutionary view, is discussed by James Hurd and David Wilcox. This second section ends with two essays by Terry Gray and Loren Haarsma that tackle issues in biochemistry, developmental biology, and the origin of biological complexity.

The third part focuses on philosophical and theological issues commonly raised in connection with evolution. Howard Van Till, who has written widely on the nature of God's creative action, explores the significance of a "gapless creation" for the doctrine of creation. In his essay, Bob Russell, director of the Center for Theology and Natural Science, develops his idea of non-interventionist divine providence using genetic mutation as an example. George Murphy, a physicist and Lutheran pastor, sees the theology of the cross as the fundamental starting point for developing a coherent Christian understanding of evolution. Essays by Jeffrey Greenberg and Laurie Braaten consider how our understanding of Earth's ancient and dynamic biological system can inform our stewardship of Creation. The critical issues of animal suffering and the meaning of original sin in the context of an evolving Creation are addressed by John Munday and Robin Collins. Concluding the volume is an essay by Warren Brown that tackles the problem of developing a unified conception of the "soulishness" of humanity that is workable in both a biblical and scientific context.

While all are orthodox Christians with a high view of Scripture, the contributors to this volume represent a relatively diverse range of theological views. There are significant differences of opinion among us. The views expressed by any individual author thus do not necessarily represent the views of all, or even the majority of, those Christians who accept an evolutionary description of Earth and life history. But they all represent well-informed and thoughtful integrations of science and faith that respect the authority of Scripture and the integrity of the scientific enterprise. My hope is that each reader will be challenged to think more deeply about the very substantive issues addressed.

In the process of putting together this volume, I have received the enthusiastic support of individuals too numerous to mention. I extend my deep appreciation to all of the volume authors who have given of their time and energy over an extended period of time. The interaction I have had with these Christian colleagues has been most rewarding. Ted Davis and Loren Haarsma in particular were a great encouragement during the early stages of assembling contributors and developing a framework for the project. I also want to acknowledge my indebtedness to the many individuals (scientists, pastors and friends) with whom I have discussed these matters over many years. They have both stimulated my personal intellectual and spiritual growth, and given me hope that thoughtful reflection and respectful dialogue are indeed possible.

KEITH B. MILLER
Department of Geology
Kansas State University

I PROVIDING A CONTEXT

1

An Evolving Creation:
Oxymoron or Fruitful Insight?

KEITH B. MILLER

Before discussing how the relationship of "creation" and "evolution" might be best understood, it is useful first to define the terms. In my discussion below, "evolution" refers to the descent with modification of all living things from a common ancestor. That is, the history of life can be envisioned as a branching tree of life in which all living things are linked together in a genealogical relationship that extends back to the first living cells. Understood in this way, the word "evolution" includes any of a number of proposed mechanisms by which evolutionary change occurred. Furthermore, evolutionary theory does not address whether, or how, God might act to guide such processes. "Creation" refers to everything to which God has given being. As a verb, "creation" refers to the past and continuing action of God to bring into existence all that is and has been. A closely related theological concept is that of "providence." This doctrine includes several distinct aspects: God's sustaining and upholding of creation; divine cooperation with creaturely action; and the governance of creation toward God's desired ends.[1] As thus defined, are the concepts of evolution and creation really antithetical as often portrayed? Is the idea of an evolving creation truly an oxymoron, or might it just prove to be a fruitful source of theological reflection?

Much of the public controversy over evolution and creation seems to rest firmly on the widely held view that the conclusions of the historical sciences are in essential conflict with a Christian faith that holds Scripture in high regard. Current scientific and theological descriptions are often seen as being mutually exclusive and contradictory. This conflict model is given legitimacy by persistent misconceptions of the nature and limitations of scientific and theological inquiry perpetuated by the rhetoric of some scientists as well as nonscientists, of some theists as well as nontheists. The task of correcting these misconcep-

---

1. See Benjamin Wirt Farley, *The Providence of God* (Grand Rapids: Baker, 1988).

3

tions is made more difficult by the frequent lack of an awareness of the historical context of the current debates.

The conflict or "warfare" view of science and faith entered historical and scientific lore largely on the popularity of two 19th-century works — John William Draper's *History of the Conflict between Religion and Science* (1874), and Andrew Dickson White's *A History of the Warfare of Science with Theology in Christendom* (1896).[2] However, this simplistic warfare metaphor has been thoroughly discredited by both theological and historical scholarship. Christian theologians (including evangelicals) have long recognized that a faithful reading of Scripture does not demand a young Earth nor does it prohibit God's use of evolutionary mechanisms to accomplish his creative will. Many evangelical Christians at the time of Darwin found no inherent conflict between evolution and Scripture. In fact, several of the authors of the "Fundamentals" (the set of volumes that gave us the term "fundamentalist") accepted some form of evolutionary theory. Even B. B. Warfield, who argued forcefully for biblical inerrancy, accepted the validity of evolution as a scientific description of origins. The primary advocates of Darwin's theory in America included Asa Gray, George Frederick Wright, and James Dana — all committed evangelical Christians.[3]

Evolution has been viewed by many theologically orthodox Christians, since the publication of *The Origin of Species*, as a positive contribution to understanding God's creative and redemptive work. For many, important theological truths concerning the nature of humanity, the goodness of creation, God's providence, and the meaning of the cross and suffering find renewed significance and amplification when applied to an evolutionary view of God's creative work. The integration of an evolutionary understanding of Earth and life history with theological understandings of God's creative and redemptive activity have yielded important insights.[4] The fruits of these efforts need to be more widely known and discussed.

---

2. The historical context of these two influential works is discussed by James R. Moore in *The Post-Darwinian Controversies* (Cambridge: Cambridge University Press, 1979). Moore seeks to dispel the hold of this metaphor on the public consciousness by detailing the responses of a variety of Christian theologians and scientists in the years following the publication of the *Origin*.

3. The Christian evangelical response to Darwin's ideas is well documented in: David N. Livingstone, *Darwin's Forgotten Defenders: The Encounter Between Evangelical Theology and Evolutionary Thought* (Grand Rapids: Eerdmans, 1987); and in David N. Livingstone, D. G. Hart, and Mark A. Noll, eds., *Evangelicals and Science in Historical Perspective* (New York: Oxford University Press, 1999).

4. There are several excellent reviews of ways in which science and religious faith can be related: Ian Barbour, *Religion in an Age of Science* (San Francisco: Harper San Francisco, 1990); Alister E. McGrath, *Science & Religion: An Introduction* (Oxford, U.K. and Malden, Mass.: Blackwell, 1999); and Richard H. Bube, *Putting It All Together: Seven Patterns for Relating Science*

Despite the long theological dialogue with evolutionary theory, many people continue to view evolution as inherently antitheistic and inseparably wedded to a worldview that denies God and objective morality. Although this understanding of the meaning of evolutionary theory is widely promoted by individuals both inside and outside of the scientific community, its conflation of a metaphysical naturalism with evolution should be rejected on philosophical, theological, and historical grounds. The equation of evolutionary theory with a philosophy that denies the reality of anything beyond matter and energy not only is false but is an impediment to quality scientific and theological thinking.

Interpreting Scripture and Nature

One consequence of the conflict view is that scientific and theological descriptions are often viewed as mutually exclusive. Complete scientific explanations for natural phenomena are seen as excluding divine action. There is not a large step from this to the perception that science's focus on natural cause-and-effect explanations is a thinly disguised effort to promote a godless worldview.

The perceived tension between scientific description and divine action also derives in part from expectations concerning the purpose and meaning of the scriptural texts. Conflicts are bound to result if Scripture and science are understood to be addressing the same issues in the same sort of way. Appeals to the "plain meaning" of Scripture and an emphasis on personal interpretation divorced from its historical, cultural, and literary context encourage Scripture to be read from a modern Western scientific outlook. However, does this way of reading Scripture do it justice? To answer this question, our hermeneutic — the

---

and the Christian Faith (Lanham, Md.: University Press of America, 1995). A selection of recent works that integrate an evolving creation with Christian theology are: John Polkinghorne, *Science and Providence: God's Interaction with the World* (Boston: Shambhala, 1989); Jürgen Moltmann, *God in Creation* (Minneapolis: Fortress, 1993); Howard J. Van Till, *The Fourth Day* (Grand Rapids: Eerdmans, 1986); Nancey Murphy, *Reconciling Theology and Science: A Radical Reformation Perspective* (London: Pandora, 1997); George L. Murphy, *The Trademark of God: A Christian Course in Creation, Evolution and Salvation* (Harrisburg, Pa.: Morehouse-Barlow, 1986); Denis Edwards, *The God of Evolution* (New York: Paulist, 1999); John F. Haught, *God After Darwin: A Theology of Evolution* (Boulder, Colo.: Westview, 2000); and Robert J. Russell, William R. Stoeger, and Francisco J. Ayala, eds., *Evolutionary and Molecular Biology: Scientific Perspectives on Divine Action* (Rome: Vatican Observatory and the Center for Theology and the Natural Sciences, 1998). My own personal synthesis is summarized in the article "Theological Implications of an Evolving Creation" which appeared in *Perspectives on Science and Christian Faith* 45 (1993): 150-60.

assumptions we apply in the interpretation of Scripture — must be subject to critical evaluation. It thus becomes imperative that we first evaluate the appropriateness of our hermeneutic before we set out to deal with supposed conflicts.[5]

Just as there is no such thing as an objective reading of the Bible (it must be filtered through some interpretive framework), there is also no such thing as pure inductive Baconian science. Rather, science works by proposing hypotheses, generating predictions by deduction, and then testing those predictions against new observations. The construction of hypotheses takes place within an interpretive framework that includes philosophical and cultural assumptions of which the investigator is often unaware. However, those hypotheses are subject to test and will not become widely held by the scientific community unless their predictions are fruitful.

Theoretical inquiry is the essence of science. By contrast, the public perception is often that science consists primarily of a body of "proven fact." However, the acceptance of a theory by the majority of the scientific community does not mean that it is "proven." No scientific theory can be proven in the sense of a logical or mathematical proof. The purpose of theories is to integrate disparate observations of the natural world and make them understandable. They provide the predictions that suggest new observations and drive new discovery. The history of our changing scientific understanding of the universe, with new theories replacing old and previously accepted models being overturned by new discoveries, can be puzzling to those who have learned science as a collection of unchanging "facts." Furthermore, uncertainty and sharp disagreement within the scientific community are often seen as weaknesses and failings of scientific knowledge. Rather, the exact opposite is the case. It is the dynamic, changing, self-correcting nature of science that is its very strength. The less science is seen as a body of established knowledge, the more inherently interesting and exciting it becomes. Science is not primarily the mastery of a body of knowledge but a way of inquiry about our physical environment.

Many theories may be proposed to explain the same set of observations. However, not all theories are given equal weight by the scientific community. Some are rejected by the preponderance of practicing scientists, and others remain at the fringes provoking critical examination. How do we distinguish a

5. Some good discussions of the hermeneutics of the Genesis texts include: Henri Blocher, *In the Beginning: The Opening Chapters of Genesis* (Downers Grove, Ill.: InterVarsity, 1984); Conrad Hyers, *The Meaning of Creation: Genesis and Modern Science* (Atlanta: John Knox, 1984); John H. Stek, "What Says the Scripture?" in *Portraits of Creation*, ed. Howard J. Van Till et al. (Grand Rapids: Eerdmans, 1990); and Meredith G. Kline, "Space and Time in the Genesis Cosmogony," *Perspectives on Science and Christian Faith* 48 (1996): 2-15.

good theory from a bad one? How do we establish relative confidence in theories? Criteria for a good scientific theory include: (1) explanatory power; (2) predictive power (testable expectations); (3) fruitfulness (ability to generate new questions and new directions of research); and (4) aesthetics (e.g., beauty, simplicity, symmetry). Many past theories in the historical sciences have been discarded with the accumulation of new observations and the development of new theories of greater explanatory power. The reason evolutionary theory (descent with modification of all living things from a common ancestor) is a powerful theory is that it makes sense of an incredible variety of observations and continues to generate fruitful and testable hypotheses.

Science is a methodology, a limited way of knowing about the natural world. Scientific research proceeds by the search for chains of cause-and-effect and confines itself to the investigation of "natural" entities and forces. This self-limitation is sometimes referred to as "methodological naturalism." Science restricts itself to proximate causes, and the confirmation or denial of ultimate causes is beyond its capacity. Science does not deny the existence of a creator — it is simply silent on the existence or action of God. The term "methodological naturalism" is intended to communicate that only natural (as opposed to supernatural) causes can in principle be investigated using scientific methodologies. Methodological naturalism describes what empirical inquiry is — it is certainly not a statement of the nature of cosmic reality.[6] Science pursues truth within very narrow limits. Our most profound questions about the nature of reality (questions of ultimate meaning, purpose, and morality), while they may arise from within science, are theological or philosophical in nature, and their answers lie beyond the reach of science.

While some scientists have tried to use science to promote an atheistic philosophy, such attempts step clearly outside of the realm of scientific inquiry. The scientific enterprise is no more based on a philosophy that denies God than is plumbing or auto mechanics. Science works, it is productive and fruitful, because it is religiously neutral. As a result, scientists representing widely different cultures and religious and nonreligious beliefs can communicate and productively pursue questions about the physical universe. Theological perspectives can provide a context for understanding and integrating scientific understanding with a broader view of reality. However, that synthesis is not itself a scientific conclusion.

Those of us in the scientific disciplines engage in our scientific activity as

---

6. For a longer discussion of the issue of "methodological naturalism" see my essay "Design and Purpose within an Evolving Creation," in *Darwinism Defeated?* ed. Phillip E. Johnson, Denis O. Lamoureux, et al. (Vancouver: Regent College, 1999).

whole integrated beings, and our scientific work is inextricably tied into a particular cultural, political, philosophical, and theological context. While distinct, our scientific and theological understandings must inform each other if we are to be intellectually whole persons. They should not be kept in hermetically sealed mental compartments. It is our obligation and calling as Christians to strive to attain an integrated whole picture of reality. However, we are actually better able to integrate different types of knowledge when we maintain clear definitions. When we confuse philosophical naturalism with evolutionary theory, we actually inhibit the productive interaction between the sciences and Christian theology. We do this by injecting into a scientific theory a metaphysical worldview that is simply not a necessary component of the theory.

Important Theological Issues

One commonly held perspective that tends to reinforce a conflict view of science and faith is that God's action or involvement in creation is confined to those events that lack a scientific explanation. Meaningful divine action is equated with breaks in chains of cause-and-effect processes. This view has been called a "God-of-the-gaps" theology. God's creative action is seen only, or primarily, in the gaps of human knowledge where scientific description fails. With this perspective, each advance in scientific understanding results in a corresponding diminution of divine action, and conflict between science and faith is assured. However, this is a totally unnecessary state of affairs. God's creative activity is clearly identified in Scripture as including natural processes. According to Scripture, God is providentially active in all natural processes, and all of creation declares the glory of God. The evidence for God's presence in creation, for the existence of a creator God, is declared to be precisely those everyday "natural events" experienced by us all. Thus Christians should not fear causal natural explanations. Complete scientific descriptions of events or processes should pose no threat to Christian theism. Rather, each new advance in our scientific understanding can be met with excitement and praise at the revelation of God's creative hand.

Another common confusion is over the meaning of "chance" or "random." Chance or random processes are often seen as antithetical to God's action. Many people understand "chance" as implying a purposeless, meaningless, and accidental event. However, scientifically, chance events are simply those whose occurrence cannot be predicted based on initial conditions and known natural laws. Such events are describable by probabilistic equations. This understanding of chance is not in any way in conflict with God's creative action. The Bible, in fact, describes a God who is sovereign over all natural events, even those we attribute to chance such as the casting of lots or tomorrow's weather. This perspective has been placed into a modern scientific context by some theologians who see God's action exercised through determining the indeterminacies of natural processes. God is thus seen as affecting events both at the quantum level and at the level of large chaotic systems.[7] Regardless of how one understands the manner in which God exercises sovereignty over natural process, chance events certainly pose no theological barrier to God's action in and through the evolutionary process.

A very common argument against evolution as God's means of actualizing his creative will is the central role of death in the evolutionary process. The theological problem of pain and suffering in nature is an ancient one, but it is given additional significance in an evolutionary context. The apparent conflict between God's goodness and the presence of pain and suffering is made especially acute when we consider the nonhuman creation. How can we accommodate the death and suffering of animals within a theology that declares both God's omnipotence and goodness? This is hardly a new issue. The problem of death, pain, and suffering in the natural world, what has been referred to as "natural evil," has been the focus of much theological and philosophical debate within the Christian church since the 1st century. Developing a theology of "natural evil" requires an understanding of God's immanence in creation as well as God's transcendence, of God's providence as well as sovereignty. It bears on questions of God's purposes for, and participation in, human and natural history.[8] For many Christians an evolutionary understanding of God's creative activity has provided a useful context within which to approach these ancient theological questions. Efforts toward reconciling the existence of pain and suffering with divine goodness in an evolving creation have encouraged renewed contemplation of the doctrines of providence, incarnation, redemption, and the centrality of the cross.

Other important theological issues are brought into sharp focus by evolutionary theory. The doctrine of the fall and original sin would seem to be challenged by the proposal that humans bear a genetic and physical continuity with the rest of the animal creation. Similarly the meaning of mankind's cre-

---

7. These ideas have been explored extensively by John Polkinghorne. See also the essay by Robert Russell in this volume.

8. An excellent summary of the history of theological thought on the problem of evil is John Hick, *Evil and the God of Love,* rev. ed. (New York: HarperCollins, 1977). An equally thorough and valuable review of the place of nature in Christian theology is H. Paul Santmire, *The Travail of Nature: The Ambiguous Ecological Promise of Christian Theology* (Philadelphia: Fortress, 1985).

ation in the "image of God" is seen by some as being undermined by the acceptance of human evolution. While these questions have not received the attention their importance requires, particularly within the evangelical theological community, that which has been written provides a valuable foundation for further contemplation.[9] This work shows that the central Christian doctrines of the universality of human sin and the necessity of the cross are not compromised by an evolutionary view of human origins.

Scientific Issues

In addition to the theological issues relevant to an evolutionary view of God's creative activity, some have raised questions about the scientific support for evolutionary theory. The scientific issues raised range from questioning the existence of transitional fossil species and critiquing the evolutionary interpretation of genetic data, to claims that complex organ and cellular structures could not arise via evolutionary mechanisms.

In order to address these scientific issues it must first be recognized that biological evolution is part of, and embedded in, the evolution of the cosmos and of our planet Earth. Biological evolution is made possible by the preceding physical and chemical evolution of the cosmos. Furthermore, the evolution of life is both a response to and a cause of the evolving physical environment of the Earth. What we actually see in the geologic record is a concordance between sometimes dramatic changes in the Earth's oceans, atmosphere, climate, and geography and changes in the Earth's biosphere from the scale of individual species to entire ecosystems.

There are numerous lines of evidence from a wide range of scientific disciplines that together make a very strong case for the reality of common descent.[10] (1) The sequence of fossil species in the geologic record is consistent on

9. Two examples of recent efforts to consider the nature and fall of humanity within the context of an evolving creation are: Jerry D. Korsmeyer, *Evolution & Eden: Balancing Original Sin and Contemporary Science* (New York: Paulist, 1998); and Warren S. Brown, Nancey Murphy, and H. Newton Malony, eds., *Whatever Happened to the Soul? Scientific and Theological Portraits of Human Nature* (Minneapolis: Fortress, 1998).

10. There are many quality resources that summarize the scientific evidence for common descent. An excellent historical review of how our current understanding of the fossil record emerged is presented in Martin J. S. Rudwick, *The Meaning of Fossils* (Chicago: University of Chicago Press, 1985). A detailed but popular historical account of the reconstruction of the human fossil record is Ian Tattersall, *The Fossil Trail* (New York: Oxford University Press, 1995). Robert L. Carroll's *Patterns and Processes of Vertebrate Evolution* (Cambridge, U.K. and New

a worldwide basis. That is, fossil species follow the same pattern of relative order of appearance. The order of fossil species was determined before the existence of any technique to date the age of rocks. Yet, when those dating methods were developed, they confirmed the order of fossils (and geologic events) already determined. (2) The order of appearance of higher taxa in the geologic record is broadly consistent with the evolutionary sequence inferred from the anatomical data and from DNA. (3) Fossils with transitional anatomical features are common within the fossil record. Such transitional forms commonly possess a mixture of traits considered characteristic of different groups (genera, orders, classes, etc.). They may also possess particular anatomical characters that are themselves in an intermediate state. (4) The geographic distribution of fossil species is consistent with common descent and with independent geological reconstructions of the Earth's changing geography over time. That is, common descent makes sense of the locations in which specific fossil (and living) species are found. (5) The fossil record of changing species over time yields a comprehensive picture of ecological and environmental change. Species changes do not occur randomly but rather are part of the evolution of communities and entire ecosystems. Predators evolve with their prey, parasites evolve with their hosts, herbivores evolve with the plant communities, and so forth. We thus not only can reconstruct the changes in particular lines of descent, but can reconstruct changing ecosystems.[11]

It is the comprehensiveness and integrated nature of the evidence that becomes overwhelming. There simply is no other way to make sense of this immense body of data than as the record of a very ancient evolving biological and environmental system.

Recently, objections to evolution have appeared which do not attack the

---

York: Cambridge University Press, 1997) is an up-to-date detailed discussion of both theoretical issues and fossil evidence, and Simon Conway Morris's *The Crucible of Creation* (New York: Oxford University Press, 1998) discusses the "Cambrian explosion." Two recent publications dealing with diverse aspects of the evidence for evolution and designed as teaching resources are: Patricia H. Kelley, Jonathan R. Bryan, and Thor A Hansen, eds., *The Evolution-Creation Controversy II: Perspectives on Science, Religion, and Geological Education,* Paleontological Society Papers, vol. 5 (1999); and Judy Scotchmoor and Dale A. Springer, eds., *Evolution: Investigating the Evidence,* Paleontological Society Special Publication, vol. 9 (1999).

11. Anna K. Behrensmeyer et al., eds., *Terrestrial Ecosystems through Time* (Chicago: University of Chicago Press, 1992) provides an overview of the evolution of entire ecosystems through time and shows the way in which organisms evolve with their physical and biological environments. The ways in which various ecological relationships (predator/prey, plant/herbivore, etc.) have impacted the evolution of individual species and biological communities are discussed in Geerat J. Vermeij, *Evolution and Escalation: An Ecological History of Life* (Princeton: Princeton University Press, 1987).

current reconstructions of the history of life, but rather claim the inadequacy of natural mechanisms to account for them. Some of these critiques make arguments that the origin and subsequent evolution of life are effectively impossible statistically. For example, it has been argued that the probability of a certain specified sequence of amino acids (i.e., a protein) being assembled by chance is impossibly small. This argument, however, assumes that evolution demands that such a protein must have been assembled, without precursors, by chance processes alone. This assumption ignores much of what has been learned about prebiotic chemistry and evolution. The assembly of functional macromolecules is not a pure chance phenomenon but occurs, like biological evolution, within a selective environment. In fact, the process of random mutation and selection has actually been used in the laboratory to synthesize highly functional organic compounds by trial and error.[12]

Another approach is the attempt to empirically recognize "design" within the biological world through the identification of structures of "specified small probability" or with "irreducible complexity."[13] This form of argumentation is central to the critiques of evolution made by advocates of "intelligent design" (ID). It is important to realize that the way "design" is used in these arguments is not the same as the theological understanding that creation has a divine purpose and plan — that it was intelligently conceived. Rather, the objective of ID is to identify aspects of the biological world that cannot be accounted for by the action of natural processes. However, these lines of criticism face several significant objections. For example, the appeal to irreducible complexity is an attempt to find criteria that exclude the possibility that a given complex biological structure or system could have been assembled in a series of functional steps. A major error in this approach is the failure to consider how complex biological systems can be built up by the modification and/or duplication of preexisting biochemical or genetic components. A common pattern in the history of life is the co-opting of preexisting biological structures, biomolecules, and DNA sequences to serve new functions. Despite claims to the contrary, plausible, and

12. A. D. Keefe and J. W. Szostak, "Functional Proteins from a Random-Sequence Library," *Nature* 410 (2001): 715-18. E. H. Ekland, J. W. Szostak, and D. P. Bartel, "Structurally Complex and Highly Active RNA Ligases Derived from Random RNA Sequences," *Science* 269 (1995): 364-70. G. F. Joyce, "Directed Molecular Evolution," *Scientific American* 267, no. 6 (1992): 90-97.

13. Two important works by intelligent design advocates are: William A. Dembski, ed., *Mere Creation: Science, Faith & Intelligent Design* (Downers Grove, Ill.: InterVarsity, 1998); and Michael J. Behe, *Darwin's Black Box: The Biochemical Challenge to Evolution* (New York: Free Press, 1996).

entirely functional, sequential steps have been proposed for a number of highly complex biochemical systems and biological structures.[14]

Critics of evolution often discuss design as though God's action is analogous to the work of an engineer or artisan. Such human action involves the imposing of form on preexisting materials. What the engineer or artisan can do is limited by the nature of those materials. By contrast, a divine creator brings into existence the very materials themselves. God creates the substance as well as the form. Perhaps we should expect nature to have been created with the inherent capabilities to bring forth what God desires without violating its integrity.[15] That is, God may act continually within creation by drawing out the creaturely potentialities already present. I believe that such a perspective is much more consistent with the continuity of processes in the physical universe than is an engineering view of God's action. It makes the discovery of each new natural capability, or each new link in the history of creation, an opportunity for the praise of God rather than being perceived as another obstacle to faith or challenge to the doctrine of creation.

The doctrine of creation really says nothing about "How" God creates. It does not provide a basis for a testable theory of the mechanism of change. If it does not address this issue, then it does not contribute anything to a specifically *scientific* description of the history of life. I believe that all of creation is designed by God and has its being in God, but that does not give me any insights into the processes by which God brought that creation into existence. That is the role of scientific investigation, a vocation in which I find great excitement and fulfillment.

Science is still far from having all the answers to how evolution proceeded during the 3.5 billion years during which life has existed on Earth. However, it is these very unanswered questions, and the apparent conflicts and contradictions in our current understanding, that drive new inquiry and discovery. The last decade has seen incredible advances in scientific fields as diverse as biochemistry, genetics, developmental biology, and paleontology. These discoveries and theoretical advances have closed previous gaps in our understanding, overturned past views, and provided promise of new breakthroughs. Some progress is being made even in such long-unresolved and seemingly intractable prob-

14. Kenneth R. Miller (*Finding Darwin's God: A Scientist's Search for Common Ground Between God and Evolution* [New York: HarperCollins, 1999]) provides extended rebuttals to many of the arguments presented by advocates of intelligent design.

15. This inherent capability of the creation to accomplish God's creative will has been termed "creation's functional integrity" by Howard J. Van Till. This perspective is outlined in Van Till's chapter "The Fully Gifted Creation," in *Three Views on Creation and Evolution*, ed. J. P. Moreland and John Mark Reynolds (Downers Grove, Ill.: InterVarsity, 1999).

lems as the origin of life.[16] It is the continuing success of scientific research to resolve previous questions about the nature and history of the physical universe, and to raise new and more penetrating ones, that drives the work of individual scientists. For the theist this simply affirms that, in creating and preserving the universe, God has endowed it with contingent order and intelligibility, and given us as bearers of the divine image the capability to perceive that order.

Looking Forward

In conclusion, biological evolution is an extremely well-supported and fruitful theory that provides a basis for understanding and synthesizing an amazing range of observations of our natural world. There is no other conceptual framework that has been proposed that provides anything like the explanatory and predictive power of evolutionary theory. The evangelical Christian community must thus pursue the integration of an evolutionary understanding of Earth and life history with theological understandings of God's creative and redemptive activity if we wish to effectively impact our increasingly technological and scientific society. In reality, many Christian scientists and theologians have productively engaged evolutionary ideas since the time of Darwin.

There is a desperate need to diffuse the heated conflict that has grown up around the issue of evolution. The evolution/creation "warfare" view has effectively inhibited productive popular dialogue on important theological issues. Furthermore, it has driven an unnecessary wedge between the Christian and scientific community, and has generated division and personal attack within the body of Christ. It is my sincere hope that this volume will be a significant step toward opening doors through the wall that now separates evolutionary science and Christian faith in the minds of many — a wall constructed diligently by theists as well as nontheists, scientists as well as nonscientists.

---

16. Recent discoveries have opened up whole new theoretical and research possibilities in approaching the problem of the origin of life. See the following sources for discussions of this ongoing work: C. Ponnamperuma and J. Chela-Flores, eds., *Chemical Evolution: Origin of Life* (Hampton, Va.: A. Deepak, 1992); N. G. Holm, ed., *Marine Hydrothermal Systems and the Origin of Life* (Dordrecht: Kluwer Academic, 1992); M. P. Bernstein, S. A. Sanford, and L. J. Allamandola, "Life's Far-Flung Raw Materials," *Scientific American* 281, no. 1 (1999): 42-49. An excellent summary of our current understanding of conditions on Earth during the origin and early evolution of life is E. G. Nisbet and N. H. Sleep, "The Habitat and Nature of Early Life," *Nature* 409 (2001): 1083-91.

Worshipping the God of Providence

DEBORAH HAARSMA

Every Sunday, Christians worship God for his character and his great acts of salvation. But how often do we worship God for one of his most amazing acts — the creation of the entire universe over billions of years? Scripture calls us to respond to the natural world in two ways: stewardship, which includes both care of the creation and scientific study, and worship. By worship, I mean our praise of God in response to his power, beauty, creativity, faithfulness, and immensity as displayed in his handiwork, and our submission to him as the Creator and Source of the physical universe. If we encounter the natural world only on a scientific level and do not pause in worship of its Maker, we ignore an important part of God's will. While it is appropriate when studying the intersection of science and the Christian faith to examine the arguments and evidence on an intellectual level, seeking a reasoned conclusion that unites good science with sound theology, we must not stop there. We must also consider how that conclusion affects our spiritual lives and our worship attitudes.

As Christians, we should praise God whenever we read in the newspapers about exciting new discoveries in cosmology, paleontology, neuroscience, and other sciences. The worship response, however, is often discouraged by the way the media tends to mix overtones of atheism in with the scientific results (such as "science can now explain what was once the realm of religion"). Such popular presentations seem to offer a simplistic choice: either believe in atheism or disbelieve the scientific result.

Churches should counter this portrayal of science by occasionally presenting scientific discoveries in a context that allows for worship. Unfortunately, in many churches science is mentioned only in the context of the origins debate. Science is sometimes openly portrayed as the "bad guy," out to prove atheism and disprove the Bible (although it cannot do either). Other churches avoid the origins issue, and thus all mention of science, entirely. Rarely is science presented as a call to joyful worship.

In my own life of faith, it took time to develop an appropriate worship response to science. As I grappled intellectually with the origins debate, I found that the theological arguments and scientific evidence supported the evolutionary creation view of origins (as presented in this book). But after reaching that intellectual conclusion, it took a few years to re-pattern my worship habits to match it. During my whole upbringing, I had envisioned the six-day young-earth creation during worship, with God creating each bird, flower, and mountain with a separate, special miracle. But if God made birds and mountains using ordinary processes like evolutionary biology and tectonic plate motion, what do we praise God for?

In this book, we offer many answers to that question. In the evolutionary creation picture, the amazing results of science point us to the amazing character of the Creator, but perhaps in ways different than you are used to thinking. We offer you the opportunity to respond to scientific discoveries in worship by setting them in a worshipful context, including beautiful images, Scripture, and a meditation. These devotionals are interleaved throughout the book. We invite you to pause, amid the intellectual arguments, to consider the many calls to praise God within the evolutionary creation framework.

Universal Language

Psalm 19

I magine David as he composed this Psalm over three thousand years ago — sitting on a hillside in Judea, gazing at the brilliant stars strewn across the sky with the bright band of the Milky Way running through them. Without the pollution of modern city lights, he had a view of the stars that most of us see only when traveling far from home. But perhaps you have been camping, hiking, or visiting a remote seashore and have seen the same beautiful sight. The brilliant night sky evokes in most people a deep emotional and spiritual response, just as it did for David. Some may feel dwarfed by the size of the universe, others may get a sense that an intelligent presence of some kind is behind it all, and others

Southern Cross and Milky Way
Image courtesy of Greg Bock, Southern Astronomical Society, Queensland, Australia, March 1996

may simply be overwhelmed by its beauty. For people of faith, these feelings are naturally redirected into praise of their God, the Creator of the universe. But nearly all people, regardless of creed or culture, feel *something* — the beauty of creation is truly a universal voice which "goes out into all the earth." And it is a patient voice — "day after day they pour forth speech, night after night they display knowledge," and through their message God speaks to people in all times and places.

Most of my astronomer colleagues share this sense of wonder when viewing the Milky Way, and enjoy each opportunity to visit telescopes in remote places (where the view is magnificent). In addition, however, we get a similar sense of wonder under rather different circumstances: when analyzing data with the computer, completing an experiment in the lab, or reading a recent result in a journal. The joy of discovering something new about the natural world, or the wonder of seeing a complicated mathematical model that exactly predicts events in the real world, can evoke a similar emotional and spiritual response. Not only does the night sky "proclaim the work of his hands," but the discoveries of modern telescopes, microscopes, and supercomputers "declare the glory of God."

2 Comparing Biblical and Scientific Maps of Origins

CONRAD HYERS

In the last five hundred years two main areas of contention between religion and science have been *space* and *time*. Controversies over the spatial character of the universe came first with challenges to the earth-centered, flat-earthed, domed-stadium picture of the cosmos. This cosmology had become so universally accepted and so tightly interwoven with the Church's faith and doctrine that it seemed that the new scientific views were a profound threat to the grand medieval synthesis. Gradually, however, the new views of space were accommodated to the point that it would be rare indeed today to find defenders of geocentricity and a flat Earth within scientific or religious communities.

As issues of spatial relations were being resolved, issues of time spans and development over the new time horizons began to arise as a result of early discoveries and theories in geology, paleontology, and biology. Time scales that had been worked out on the basis of biblical lists and ages (e.g., Archbishop Ussher giving the creation as 4004 B.C.) were hardly adequate to accommodate the accumulating evidence that suggested ever larger time spans for everything from rock strata to fossil remains to life forms, and from the solar system to galaxies of stars — along with seemingly infinite change and diversity.

The central thesis of this study is that the same general approach taken in resolving alleged conflicts between science and religion over *space* may be used relative to *time*. As an example of an early effort to resolve apparent conflicts over space I will take John Calvin, writing in the 16th century. Calvin argued that alleged conflicts arose because of linguistic and literary confusions. Biblical references to nature were not scientific statements, which then might be said to be in conflict with scientific data, observations, and theories. The Bible uses the common, everyday, universal language of appearances. If matters were otherwise, in order to be successful in harmonizing the Bible with the science of any particular people and generation, the Bible would necessarily be placed out of harmony with every other people and generation.[1]

Phenomenal Language

In this phenomenal use of language, it appears that the Sun rises and sets, and, like the Moon, orbits the earth. It appears that the earth is flat and is the center of the universe. It appears that the stars and planets orbit about us, and that the directions of north, south, east and west, as well as zenith and nadir, have a fixed rather than relative meaning. It appears that the sky is domed above us and an underworld lies beneath us. It appears that everything in the natural order is centered in and focused upon us. Calvin pointed out, for example, that the biblical statement that the Sun and Moon are the two great lights of the heaven (if construed as a scientific statement) is in error since "the star of Saturn, which, on account of its great distance, appears the least of all, is greater than the moon."[2] But, Calvin argued (rather tartly): "Nothing is here treated of but the visible form of the world. He who would learn astronomy, and other recondite arts, let him go elsewhere."[3] Or again, "Moses does not speak with philosophical acuteness on occult mysteries, but relates those things which are everywhere observed, even by the uncultivated, and which are in common use."[4]

Calvin's observations were applied to the growing controversies over space. Controversies over time did not begin in earnest until two centuries later. Nevertheless the same approach is applicable. In fact, those who accept modern views of space and not modern views of time are inconsistent, both scientifically and religiously. Space and time are coordinates as in our measurement of spatial distances in light years, and ironically the same kinds of arguments have been used against modern views of time as were used formerly to dismiss modern views of space. Both lines of argument assume that biblical statements about nature are of the same order as modern scientific statements, as if both were operating on the same tracks and with the same destinations.

Or, to use an analogy from cartography rather than railroading, a certain

1. For a discussion of early evangelical responses to growing scientific evidences for evolution, and to Darwinism in particular, see David N. Livingstone, *Darwin's Forgotten Defenders* (Grand Rapids: Eerdmans, 1987).

2. John Calvin, *Commentaries on the First Book of Moses Called Genesis,* trans. John King (Grand Rapids: Eerdmans, 1948), 1:85.

3. Calvin, *Commentaries,* 1:79.

4. Calvin, *Commentaries,* 1:84.

territory (in this case the universe in space and time) may be mapped in a variety of quite different ways. One might map the United States for state boundaries, location of rivers and lakes, topography, climate, roadways, or rail lines. All these mappings can be true simultaneously, because they serve different purposes. No one map can contain the sum total of truth and no one way of mapping is necessarily in conflict with any other, unless they are confused. One could, for example, draw up a map of all churches in a given area, and the same for all saloons, but it would be best not to interchange them. One might even color in all states with different colors for the purpose of easy distinction, without taking the coloration literally and expecting the grass to change color when crossing state lines.

Now, the biblical accounts of creation in Genesis are different ways of mapping origins than those to which we who have been schooled in science are accustomed. In fact, even the two accounts of creation in Genesis 1 and 2 (the six-day account and the Adam-and-Eve account) have significant differences, reflecting the significant differences between the two cultural traditions in ancient Israel, the agricultural/urban and the shepherd/nomadic. Genesis 1 is a mapping of creation using the imagery, terminology, and perspectives of agricultural/urban Israel; and Genesis 2, of pastoral/nomadic Israel.

The Two Creation Accounts

We immediately recognize this difference in biblical language and usage elsewhere, as among the prophets and psalmists, to depict God's relationship to the world and to humanity. Isaiah, for example, goes back and forth between these two sets of imagery, as in Isaiah 40.[5] On the one hand, Isaiah draws upon agricultural/urban imagery, as he speaks of God surveying the universe ("who has measured the waters in the hollow of his hand, and marked off the heavens with a span," v. 12), or God laying a foundation ("Have you not understood from the foundations of the earth," v. 21). But Isaiah also draws on shepherd/nomadic imagery: "He stretches out the heavens like a curtain, and spreads them like a tent to dwell in" (v. 22), or "He will feed his flock like a shepherd, he will gather the lambs in his arms" (v. 11). Shepherds would speak naturally in terms of tents, curtains, sheep, garden oases, and the simple life of nomads. Farmers and city-dwellers would speak naturally in terms of foundations, pillars, boundaries, the sedentary life, and cosmic and social order.

---

5. Biblical quotations here and throughout are from the Revised Standard Version, Old Testament Section, Copyright 1952 by the Division of Christian Education of the National Council of the Churches of Christ in the United States of America.

What we are given in the first chapters of Genesis are two distinct accounts of creation, the first using the language, imagery, and concerns of the agricultural/urban tradition in Israel, and the second using those of the pastoral/nomadic tradition. This observation helps to explain the inevitable problems in a literal/historical approach to harmonizing the two accounts of creation, as well as, in turn, trying to harmonize both of them with modern scientific accounts of origins. The order of events in the Adam and Eve version in Genesis 2, for example, is quite different from the six-day account with which Genesis begins.

Genesis 1-2:4a	Genesis 2:4b-24
(Water and Formless Earth)	(Heavens and Earth Presupposed)
Light (day 1)	Water (mist)
Firmament (day 2)	Adam
Earth and Vegetation (day 3)	Vegetation
Sun, Moon, and Stars (day 4)	Rivers
Fish and Birds (day 5)	Land Animals, Birds (no fish)
Land Animals, Humans (day 6)	Eve

In Genesis 2, instead of humans created (both male and female) at the end of the process, Adam is created not only before Eve but before vegetation, rivers, animals, and birds. Further, the two accounts begin at opposite poles: Genesis 1 begins with the problem of a watery chaos, engulfing the earth, while Genesis 2 begins with the absence of water, which twice needs to be introduced to the barren landscape. In Genesis 1 the waters of the deep need to be separated into the waters above and the waters below (day 2). The waters below can then be gathered into one place so that the dry land might appear and vegetation be created (day 3). In Genesis 2 the earth is originally dry and in need of water: "For the Lord God had not caused it to rain upon the earth . . ." (Gen. 2:5). So in the first case the chaotic threat is depicted as a universe filled with water, while in the second case the initial problem is barrenness into which water must be brought.

The attempt to interpret these materials as literal, chronological accounts of origins runs into enormous difficulties internally, well before modern scientific scenarios are introduced. Despite valiant efforts by clever exegetes, the two biblical accounts cannot be reconciled, as long as the assumption is made that they are intended to be read as comparable to a natural history. The clue to the differences is to be found within Israel itself where, broadly speaking, there were two main traditions: the pastoral/nomadic and the agricultural/urban. Genesis 1 has drawn upon the imagery and concerns of the farmers and city-dwellers who inhabited river basins prone to flooding, while Genesis 2 has drawn upon the experiences of shepherds, goat-herders, and camel-drivers who lived on the semiarid fringes of the fertile plains, around and between wells and oases. For the pastoral nomads and desert peoples the fundamental threat to life was dryness and barrenness, whereas for those agricultural and urban peoples in or near flood plains the threat was too much water, and the chaotic possibilities of water. It is also revealing that Genesis 2 does not mention a creation of fish, whereas fish in abundance are prominent in Genesis 1 (fish occupy half of day five, with "swarms of living creatures").[6]

This interpretive approach also helps explain why the two versions of creation present such different — nearly opposite — views of human nature. In Genesis 1 human beings are pictured in the lofty terms of royalty, taking dominion over the earth and subduing it — imagery and values drawn from the very pinnacle of ancient civilizations, which Israel itself achieved in the time of Solomon. In Genesis 2, however, Adam and Eve are pictured as *servants* of the garden, living in a garden oasis: essentially the gardener and his wife. And while Genesis 1 refers to humans as made in "the image and likeness of God," in the continuation of the garden story in Genesis 3 the theme of godlikeness is introduced by the *serpent* who tempts Eve with the promise that by eating of the fruit of the Tree of Knowledge, they would be "like God," knowing good and evil. Celebrants of science and technology beware!

Thus, while Genesis 1 is comfortable with the values of civilization and the fruits of its many achievements and creations, Genesis 2 offers a humble view of humanity, a reminder of the simple life and values of the shepherd ancestors, before farming, and even before shepherding, in an Edenic state of food gathering and tending. In this manner these two views of human nature are counterbalanced. They are not contradictory but complementary. Any celebration of human creation and its achievements is tempered by warnings concerning overweening pride and claims to godlikeness. Our heads at times may be in the clouds, but our feet walk on the Earth and are made of clay.

The two accounts of creation in Genesis are contradictory only if taken as

---

6. This approach to the creation accounts does not depend upon or argue for any version of the "documentary hypothesis." Whatever position may be taken on this complex of issues, it is still the case that the two accounts of creation offer these very different images of creation, which may be understood in terms of their two cultural traditions and heritages. Whether one takes the traditional view of Mosaic authorship or locates these materials in the post-Davidic era, it is significant that both Moses and David had substantial experiences in both traditions: Moses going from the pinnacle of Egyptian civilization to tending sheep and wandering in the wilderness, while David goes from shepherd boy to Saul's palace and ultimately to his own reign.

literal history, rather than recognizing that they are operating *analogically,* using the contrasting imagery and concerns of the two main traditions in ancient Israel. The biblical accounts are also not in contradiction with modern scientific accounts either, because (again) the biblical accounts are interpreting origins analogically (albeit using very different sets of analogy), not geologically or biologically. To cite Calvin again: "The Holy Spirit had no intention to teach astronomy, and, in proposing instruction meant to be common to the simplest and most uneducated persons, he made use by Moses and the other prophets of popular language, that none might shelter himself under the pretext of obscurity."[7] Thus it may be said that biblical affirmations of creation are in harmony with the science of any age and culture, not because they have been harmonized by clever argument, but because they have little to do with such concerns.

Numbers and Numerology

Focusing on Genesis 1, which has seemed to many to be the more modern of the two biblical accounts — and perhaps comparable to modern scenarios — the first question to ask is, What were the issues for those writing, hearing, and reading this account of origins? Certainly modern theories of evolution and their vast scales of space and time were not a point of contention. So what were the concerns of ancient cosmologies as they depicted spatial relationships, and cosmogonies as they presented the origins of things? And what were the concerns in ancient Israel in particular, relative to these other accounts? To fail to raise these kinds of questions from the start is to open up the Genesis materials to the assumption that they share our interests, forms of discourse, types of investigation and modes of expression — that is, a modernistic approach which tells us much about ourselves but little about ancient peoples and the messages they were concerned to convey.

Part of the overall structure of the first account of creation in Genesis is the use of an analogy with a seven-day week, common among Semitic peoples, and with a seventh day of rest, of specific interest to Hebrew life. Instead of being something we might recognize as a scientific model of origins, this is obviously a calendrical model that uses the six days of work and a seventh day of rest as an analogy for interpreting divine work in creation.

The use of the analogy of a divine rest on a cosmic Sabbath also introduces the number seven to the equation. The significance of the number seven

---

7. John Calvin, *Commentary on the Book of Psalms*, trans. James Anderson (Grand Rapids: Eerdmans, 1949), 5:184.

is easily missed in that almost the entirety of our modern use of numbers is numerical, whereas in the ancient world, especially in religious texts, numbers were often understood numerologically. Their symbolic value was what was of importance, not their position in a numerical sequence. This was a sacred use of numbers as distinct from a secular use of numbers in counting. Numbers were understood as having or giving access to profound symbolic meaning and power. One of the few vestiges of this way of thinking is in our modern aversion to the number thirteen. Even at the Mayo Clinic, where we expect to encounter the cutting edge of modern medical science, there is a building without a thirteenth floor. Here the numerical value of the number thirteen is sacrificed to its numerological meaning, in this case negative and to be avoided. In the one use of numbers it is important that the numbers add up to the correct number numerically, in which case we would insist that there has been an error in numbering. In the other case, it is of paramount importance that the numbers add up to the correct number symbolically.

The fact that the first account of creation depicts the origins of all things as completed by the end of the sixth day is transparently a numerological use of numbers, controlled both by the analogy with the work week and Sabbath and by the symbolism of the number seven. Seven has the meaning of completeness, wholeness, and totality. This derives from a combination of two other numbers with the same meaning in more limited form: three and four. The number three corresponds to the three main zones of the cosmos pictured vertically (heavens above, Earth below, and the underworld floating on a cosmic ocean beneath). The number four corresponds to the four zones of the cosmos pictured horizontally (the four directions, four corners of the earth, and four quarters). Most suggestive of completeness, wholeness, and totality would then be to put the vertical three and the horizontal four together — hence, the number seven as the more powerful and "complete" number for completeness. Similarly, the number twelve is given the same meaning through multiplying three times four. It is no coincidence that the most commonly used numbers in the Bible are three, four, seven, and twelve. Seven, for example, appears over five hundred times.

The intent of the use of a seven-day week in discussing origins is not to provide numerical, chronological, and historical information — in which case these materials might be said to be in conflict with modern scientific accounts — but to make the religious affirmation that the totality of the universe has its origin in God, who is the one supreme power behind and within the universe, and whose works are (as the text concludes) "very good." The number that corresponds to this affirmation of totality and "very goodness" is the number seven. If the account had concluded on some other day, say day five or eleven or thirteen, it would have been very jarring, and there would be a contradiction between what is being said in words and what is being said in numbers.[8]

The number twelve is also worked into the structure in that on each of the six days of creating there are two main divisions: light and dark, waters above and below, seas and dry land, Sun and Moon and stars, birds and fish, land animals and humans. Six days, multiplied by two groupings each day, realizes twelve regions of the cosmic totality. Twelve creative acts are completed by the end of the sixth day, and God rests on the seventh day.

Chaos and Cosmos

The number three is also very prominent in the account, and its special use gives further clues as to the ways in which the biblical cosmogony is mapped out. In some respects Genesis structures its cosmogony in a way that was common to ancient cosmogonies, and that is by a pattern of movement from chaos to cosmos. Order and the threat of disorder were central concerns for sedentary peoples as they sought to avoid chaos, maintain order, and place themselves in harmony with the forces of cosmos. Thus, after an introductory affirmation ("In the beginning God created the heavens and the earth"), the account commences by identifying the forces of chaos that must be controlled: "The earth was without form and void, and darkness was upon the face of the deep, and the Spirit of God was moving over the face of the waters" (Gen. 1:2).

Three forces of chaos are thus presented: formless earth, darkness, and the primeval sea. These are three common threats to an orderly environment, and the first three days of creation solve these threats by the creation of counter forces. On the first day light is created; on the second day a firmament is placed in the sky to separate the waters into those above and below; and on the third day the waters below are separated into their proper bounds so that dry land might appear. The three forces of chaos are not destroyed but given their boundaries and turned to positive functions in a new orderly cosmos.

In the second set of three days, creatures are made and brought in to populate the established regions of the first three days. On the fourth day the Sun, Moon, and stars are created to dwell in the spaces of light and darkness. On the fifth day the birds and fish are created to inhabit the sky above and waters below, made possible by the firmament of day two. And on the sixth day land ani-

---

8. For an extensive discussion of biblical uses of numbers, see Lloyd R. Bailey, *Genesis, Creation, and Creationism* (Mahwah, N.J.: Paulist, 1993).

mals and humans are created to dwell on the dry land that came into being on the third day, along with vegetation for food.

We are thus presented with three sets of three: three forces of chaos are brought under control and placed in an orderly cosmos by the creations of the first three days, making possible the introduction of the inhabitants of the second three days. Now, this is not the way in which modern scientific accounts of origins get organized. But that does not mean that one mapping of the cosmos is right and another wrong, unless it can be demonstrated that both approaches to origins are mapping the same things.

To follow the lead of Calvin again, when Genesis discusses the "separating" of the waters by the "firmament" into the waters above (rain, snow, hail) and the waters below (lakes, rivers, oceans), or speaks of a "gathering" of the waters below to allow dry land to appear, astronomical or geological terms are not being used, but rather popular expressions that draw upon common observations of and speech about nature. Similarly, the phrase "each according to its own kind," which refers to the observable hereditary distinctions among plants and animals, is not the language of geneticists discussing the "fixity of species," but reflects everyday, phenomenal observations of an orderly cosmos. Modern controversies over gradual evolution, punctuated equilibrium, macro and microevolution, and so forth are just that — modern. These are not the issues, context, or linguistic usage of the Genesis materials.

Interpretation by Analogy: Creator, Ruler, Architect

We find further clues as to the character of the biblical cosmogony by observing the various kinds of analogy being used to interpret origins. In addition to the overall structure derived from the analogy of a divine work week and Sabbath rest, we find three main analogies being employed: creator, ruler, and architect. The first is the most obvious. The account begins and ends with the image of God as creator of the heavens and the earth. God is specifically referred to as making the various creations of days four through six: Sun, Moon, and stars; birds and fish; land animals and humans.

The second analogy — God the ruler — is apparent in two ways. Throughout the account God is pictured as like a divine emperor issuing decrees: "And God said, 'Let there be light/Let there be a firmament/Let the waters under the heaven be gathered together/Let the earth put forth vegetation/Let there be lights/Let the waters bring forth/Let the earth bring forth/Let us make man.'" All things come into being by the authority and power and command of the divine Word, and they are controlled and guided by divine laws giving order and rationality to the cosmos.

The theme of ruling is also prominent in that the Sun and Moon are said to be created to "rule" the day and might, while humans are given the royal attributes of having "dominion" over all living things and of "subduing" the earth. Such analogies are obviously drawn from the common sociopolitical order of the day. Emperors ruled over, and in part by means of, lesser kings or governors who had been conquered or appointed. Using this analogy, God is the supreme ruler and force in the universe as "King of Kings and Lord of Lords," with the Sun and Moon as subordinate rulers of the regions of light and darkness, and human beings given dominion over the animals and the task of subduing the earth.

The third analogy being used is that of divine architect. The universe has a fundamental structure, organization, and design. It is not merely "an accidental collocation of molecules," as Bertrand Russell put it. Nor is it fundamentally irrational and chaotic. Even the wild and negative forces are turned to useful purposes, as darkness, water, and formless earth are shaped, separated, and limited. The use of an architectural analogy sheds further light on some of the — to modern readers — peculiarities in the ordering of events. We might feel comfortable with the first day of creation, commencing with, "Let there be light," since that may seem to resemble our "big-bang" theories of origin. Yet before there is light (v. 3), already present is a formless earth engulfed in darkness and a watery abyss (v. 2).

If one were going to treat these materials as in any way comparable to modern scientific theories of origin, one would not have a big-bang theory but a "big-splash" theory! There is also the problem that, while light comes into existence on the first day, the Sun, Moon, and stars are not created until the fourth day; indeed the stars are mentioned *after* the creation of the Sun and Moon. And, finally, vegetation appears on the third day, before the creation of the Sun or stars.

A great deal of effort has been expended by creationists to explain these peculiarities. Yet if one recognizes that a central analogy in depicting origins in Genesis 1 is that of a divine architect, they are perfectly consistent and rational. The six days of creation are arranged in the way an architect might think and proceed; they are thus consistent with the analogy being employed. The first thing an architect does before creating a building is to consider the potential threats to the building, such as tornadoes, earthquakes, and floods. A good architect will accommodate these threats in the design before and during construction. Here God, as the architect of the universe, is being depicted as, first of all, identifying the three main forces of chaos that would threaten a habitable cosmos: darkness, water, and formless earth.

And the earth was without form and void, and darkness was upon the face of the deep; and the Spirit of God was moving over the face of the waters. (Gen. 1:2)

These threats are then resolved by the activities of the first three days, which are laid out in parallel with the three chaotic forces: the creation of light and separation from darkness of day one; the creation of a firmament and its separation of the waters into those above and below on day two; and the separation of the earth from the waters below on day three so that the earth may take shape and be dry.

Now that the cosmos is constructed and secured, the inhabitants can then be brought into the three regions of the universe. The Sun, Moon, and stars of day four are placed in the regions of light and darkness established on day one. The birds and fish of day five can occupy the air and water, made possible by the separation of the firmament on day two. And the land animals and humans created on day six can be introduced to the secure and dry land of day three. Vegetation has also been provided for food on day three.

While this is not the way in which the natural sciences might reconstruct the origins of the universe or life forms or humanity, it is a perfectly rational way of organizing the subject of origins, and completely consistent with the analogy of a divine architect. Though it is not geological logic or biological logic or chronological logic, it is quite logical in its own terms as analogical logic, using the analogies of divine architect, ruler, and creator, along with numerological logic employing numbers three, seven, and twelve.

Theological Logic

The point that Genesis represents a theological use of logic should properly have been discussed first, since this is primarily a religious text. Yet we are so used to thinking in terms of science and history that it takes special effort to seek out the issues, concerns, and thought forms that would have been the preoccupation of the day in the ancient world. Every group of people in this historical context had generated or borrowed or modified a cosmogony. Even the cosmogony of Genesis has affinities with surrounding cosmogonies. The decisive difference, and the theological bone of contention, was that the Israelite cosmogony is monotheistic whereas everyone else's cosmogony was polytheistic. Regardless of the extent to which the Israelite cosmogony has connections with those of surrounding peoples, the point is that these other forms are being emptied of their polytheistic content and filled with monotheistic meaning.

Much of the cosmogonic material of other ancient peoples was literally

Chaos to Cosmos to Habitation

Problem	Preparation	Population
(verse 2)	*(days 1-3)*	*(days 4-6)*
darkness	1 a. creation of light (day) b. separation from darkness (night)	4 a. creation of Sun b. creation of Moon, planets and stars
watery abyss	2 a. creation of firmament b. separation of waters above from waters below	5 a. creation of birds b. creation of fish
formless earth	3 a. separation of earth from the sea b. creation of vegetation on dry land	6 a. creation of land animals b. creation of humans
without form *(tohu)* and void *(bohu)*	*tohu* is formed	*bohu* is filled

cosmogonic: a birthing of the cosmos. For in polytheism the origins of the main elements of the universe were commonly understood in terms of the births of gods and goddesses and their subsequent power struggles, jealousies, and conflicts. All the regions of what we today call nature were understood as supernatural. The forces of chaos (darkness, earth, water) were gods and goddesses. There were gods and goddesses of light, sky, and vegetation; Sun, Moon, and stars were divine; and pharaohs and kings were often counted as sons of gods.

The paramount reason for the Genesis account being structured as it is — and it is a theological reason — is that it rejects the polytheistic reading of the cosmos and restructures the cosmogonic form and content to read monotheistically. "In the beginning God" — the one God, the only God, the God who is not to be identified with any part of the furniture of the universe, is the beginning and end of all things. The gods and goddesses, however, are not divinities at all but creatures, creations of this God. They are simply aspects of the natural order and are not to be worshipped, feared, or supplicated. To worship them, no matter how great the forces they represent, is idolatry.

Identifying these theological concerns helps to explain further (to moderns) the peculiarities of the account. On day four, the stars are mentioned last, after the Sun and Moon, three days after the coming of light, and a day after the appearance of vegetation. The stars are hardly mentioned at all: "He made the stars also." Indeed the Hebrew word lumps stars and planets together. Why such short shrift, especially when we consider what a large part of the universe we are talking about?

The treatment of the subject is, however, quite logical theologically. In the world of ancient civilizations one of the burgeoning religious occupations was astrology. Both Egypt and Mesopotamia were leaders in astrology. And astrology was a true mixing of science and religion, the numerical and the numerological. Not only were the stars seen as divinities, but human fates and fortunes were read as being intimately tied to the heavenly bodies.

In biblical monotheism, however, the planets and stars were awarded no special powers, beyond those powers that were theirs as part of the natural order. They were not to be feared, solicited, or consulted. To underline that concern, the stars and planets are mentioned at the last possible moment (before the birds and fish), in the most minimal manner, and appearing as an afterthought, as if to say, "This is all the religious importance to be granted the planets and stars." This, then, is not being offered as a scientific statement to be debated by astronomers, but is an anti-astrological statement. As Deuteronomy states it: "And beware lest you lift up your eyes to heaven, and when you see the sun and the moon and the stars, all the host of heaven, you be drawn away and worship them and serve them . . ." (4:19).

Another peculiarity of the Genesis account is the summation found in chapter 2 verse 4a. After such careful structuring of the account in terms of six days, concluding each day with "and the evening and the morning were the . . . day" (even on the first three days in which there were light and darkness, but no Sun, Moon, planets, or stars), the account concludes with the term "generations" *(toledoth)* instead of "days." "These are the generations of the heavens and the earth when they were created" (2:4a). Why the sudden leap from "days" to "generations"? Is this is to be interpreted as some sort of scientific statement of chronological events? At the minimum, both statements cannot be taken literally.

The answer may again lie in the theological context of competing cosmogonies. The polytheistic cosmogonies were commonly structured around genealogies of the gods and goddesses. If one were to ask most ancient peoples how the various forces of "nature" were related to one another, one would be given a divine family tree. The Mesopotamian cosmogony in the *Enuma Elish* begins with Abzu, god of the sweet waters (streams), mating with Tiamat, the goddess of the salt waters, and begetting the divinities of silt, Lahmu and Lahamu, with further matings bringing other cosmic features.[9]

Hesiod's *Theogony* ("birth of the gods") of the 8th century B.C. attempts

---

9. See Samuel Noah Kramer, *Sumerian Mythology: A Study of Spiritual and Literary Achievement in the Third Millennium B.C.*, rev. ed. (New York: Harper & Brothers, 1961). Also James B. Pritchard, ed., *Ancient Near Eastern Texts Relating to the Old Testament*, 3rd ed. (Princeton: Princeton University Press, 1969).

to sort out the myriad divinities of ancient Greece into the interactions within and among various divine family trees. Such cosmogonies were theogonies and would conclude, in effect: "These are the generations of the heavens and the earth when they were *procreated*." The use of the word "generations" in the conclusion of the Genesis account offers a kind of pun on the whole interpretation of nature in terms of genealogies of the gods: "These are the generations of the heavens and earth when they were *created*." Clearly the target of these verses is not a latter-day theory of the evolution of nature but the prevailing myths of the evolution of the gods and goddesses.[10]

Conclusions

When we examine the Genesis account of origins in its own terms and its own historical context, it becomes apparent that we have something that is considerably different from that of the natural sciences. It has a theological agenda aimed at affirming a monotheistic reading of the cosmos and rejecting the prevailing polytheistic reading. None of its phrasing or organization or use of numbers corresponds to the methods and materials of the natural sciences. This does not imply that Genesis is to be seen as unscientific or antiscientific or even prescientific, as if superseded by better methods of understanding the world. The materials of Genesis 1 are nonscientific; they offer a different kind of map of the universe and our place within it.

In literary terms, Genesis 1 is not employing a narrative similar to the narratives of a modern natural history. The fact that Genesis uses a narrative of days of creation is easily misread by interpreters twenty-five to thirty-five hundred years later as comparable to a historical narrative. This leap from narrative form to natural history and scientific "fact" is a mistake commonly made — as in the thesis of "scientific creationist" Henry Morris: "The biblical record, accepted in its natural and literal sense, gives the only scientific and satisfying account of the origin of all things. . . . The creation account is clear, definite, sequential, and matter-of-fact, giving every appearance of straightforward historical narrative."[11]

Yet there are many kinds of narrative that use the same general form and all "tell a story": history, biography, chronology, parable, allegory, novel, short

---

10. For a fuller discussion of the issues summarized in this essay see Conrad Hyers, *The Meaning of Creation: Genesis and Modern Science* (Atlanta: John Knox, 1984).

11. Henry M Morris, *The Remarkable Birth of Planet Earth* (San Diego: Creation-Life, 1972), pp. vii, 84.

story, fable, fairytale, legend, epic, saga, myth, and — as we have just discussed — cosmogony. Even instructional manuals and jokes use the narrative form. The identification of Genesis 1 as a narrative tells nothing in itself about the specific type of narrative form being used. Careful consideration of the text itself in its historical and theological context indicates that it employs a very different kind of narrative form and linguistic usage than those found in modern natural histories. The *form* is cosmogonic narrative. However, it is a cosmogony whose content is radically different from the cosmogonies of surrounding peoples, replacing a polytheistic content with a monotheistic reading.

> To whom then will you compare me,
>   that I should be like him? says the Holy One.
> Lift up your eyes on high and see:
>   who created these?
> He who brings out their host by number,
>   calling them all by name. (Isa. 40:25-26)

Having said this, we have a clearer way to discuss what the real issues are — and have been all along — in the relationship between science and religion: the natural and the supernatural, chance and law, freedom and determinism, unpredictability and predictability, randomness and intelligent design, materialistic and theistic interpretations of nature, and so forth. For too long and too often we have been sidetracked in favor of issues that were not the issues in biblical times, and should not be today.

Additional Bibliography

Barth, Karl. *Church Dogmatics,* vol. 3: *The Doctrine of Creation.* Trans. G. W. Bromiley and R. J. Ehrlich. Edinburgh: T. & T. Clark, 1960.

Frye, Roland Mushat, ed. *Is God a Creationist? The Religious Case against Creation Science.* New York: Charles Scribner's Sons, 1983.

Livingstone, David N. *Darwin's Forgotten Defenders.* Grand Rapids: Eerdmans, 1987.

Miller, Kenneth R. *Finding Darwin's God.* New York: Harper Collins, 1999.

Peacocke, Arthur. *Creation and the World of Science.* Oxford: Clarendon, 1979.

Pennock, Robert T. *Tower of Babel: The Evidence against the New Creationism.* Cambridge, Mass.: MIT Press, 1999.

Spong, John S. *Rescuing the Bible from Fundamentalism.* San Francisco: Harper and Row, 1991.

Van Till, Howard J. *The Fourth Day: What the Bible and the Heavens Are Telling Us about the Creation.* Grand Rapids: Eerdmans, 1986.

3 The Word and the Works:
Concordism and American Evangelicals

EDWARD B. DAVIS

About an hour by rail east of Manhattan, just off the coast of Long Island Sound, lies the upscale suburb of Westport, Connecticut. Today a prestigious bedroom community for successful professionals and wealthy artists, in the last century Westport was a quiet, rural New England town of tidy frame houses, enough still standing to retain a sense of charm in spite of the strip malls, split levels, and traffic lights that have since appeared among them. My great-great-grandfather, Ebenezer Banks Adams, built one of those stately homes in 1838, his first year as master of the Adams Academy, where for three decades before suffering a debilitating injury he prepared hundreds of boys to attend Yale College in nearby New Haven.[1] When I visited the house for the last time several years ago — it is no longer in the family[2] — I spent a pleasant hour or two browsing in Mr. Adams' library, shelved in a small room over the front door at the top of the stairs. Among several hundred Greek and Roman classics, grammars for various ancient and modern languages, histories of the world, and treatises on theology and moral philosophy, were about a dozen scientific texts, among them David Brewster's *Optics,* John Torrey's *Botany,* and John Lee Comstock's *Chemistry.* Then I spied a copy of the second (1833) American edition of Robert Bakewell's *An Introduction to Geology.* Although I was hardly surprised to find it — like the others, Bakewell was a standard work for the period — I immediately felt a sublime, controlled pleasure, not unlike that engendered by a sudden encounter with an old and dear friend. Forgetting the others,

---

1. Classes were held from 1838 to 1867 in a one-room building that is now a museum of the Westport Historical Society.

2. The Adams homestead, called "the Bird's Nest," was bought, completely renovated, and resold by Martha Stewart, who has written about it in *Martha Stewart's New Old House* (New York: Potter, 1992).

I lifted it gently out of its place, puffed away layers of dust, and promptly turned to the back of the book.

And there it was, just as I knew it should be: the famous appendix on the "Consistency of Geology with Sacred History," an attempt to relate recent geological conclusions to the early chapters of Genesis by Benjamin Silliman (1779-1864), the first professor of chemistry and natural history at Yale and the most influential science teacher in antebellum America. Yet, in the midst of my joy at seeing Silliman's piece and cradling it in my hands in a most appropriate setting, I was also profoundly sorry, for the distance separating Silliman's world from mine was all too apparent. The inclusion of a large amount of explicitly theological material in a standard scientific text was commonplace in his day, owing at least in part to his own considerable influence, yet today it would almost certainly invite puzzlement if not scorn. If modernity has encroached on Westport, it has positively overwhelmed institutions like the Adams Academy and the college it served with a profound secularism, so much so that few tasks are more difficult to justify today to the broader culture than efforts like Silliman's to bring Christianity and science together. Our goals in this chapter are to outline the history of this change, to identify some of the causes, and to comment briefly on the contemporary situation in light of the past.

Background: Concordism in the 17th Century

During the early years of the scientific revolution, as natural philosophers turned their attention increasingly to the book of nature itself and gave less deference to the books of traditional authorities, a new model for the relation between Christianity and science rose to prominence, challenging the traditional view that science is merely a "handmaiden" to theology — a view ultimately derived from the great Hellenistic Jewish philosopher, Philo of Alexandria (fl. 1st century A.D.), and later used by leading Christian writers such as Clement of Alexandria, Augustine, and Bonaventure. The catalyst for this change was the gradual acceptance of Copernican astronomy, which seemed to challenge the very words of Scripture by affirming the motion of the earth rather than the Sun. (In several places, the Bible speaks of the motion of the Sun through the sky, as if it were a real motion rather than an apparent one, or else of the stability of the earth.)[3] Johannes Kepler (1571-1630) and Galileo Galilei (1564-1642) showed how the new hypothesis could be reconciled with the Bible. In the pref-

---

3. For example, see Josh. 10:12-14; Job 9:7; Ps. 19:4-6; 93:1; 104:5; Eccles. 1:5; Isa. 38:8; and Hab. 3:11, among others.

ace to his most important book, *The New Astronomy* (1609), Kepler used the Augustinian principle of accommodation to justify the figurative interpretation of biblical references to the motion of the Sun. The Bible, he noted, speaks in a very human way about ordinary matters in a manner that can be understood, using ordinary speech to convey loftier theological truths. Thus the literal sense of texts making reference to nature should not be mistaken for accurate scientific statements. Probably influenced by Kepler, Galileo made an identical argument just a few years later in his *Letter to the Grand Duchess Christina* (1615): their respect for the ignorance of the vulgar "made the sacred authors accommodate themselves (in matters unnecessary for salvation) more to accepted usage than to the true essence of things."[4]

Although Catholic scientists were almost immediately silenced by an injunction that placed Copernicus's book on the Index of Prohibited Books — it was not a good time for a Catholic like Galileo to behave like a Protestant, interpreting the Bible for himself and suggesting to the theologians that they might follow his lead — many Protestant scientists openly and eagerly accepted the arguments of Kepler and Galileo. And by using the principle of accommodation to gain acceptance for the new astronomy in spite of biblical passages that seem to contradict it, they were implicitly raising the status of science from that of an obedient handmaiden to something more like an equal partner in the search for truth. Consider Galileo's premise that the meaning of Scripture is often ambiguous, owing to the various meanings of human language, whereas nature speaks clearly and decisively in the divine language of mathematics. In order for both books to agree, therefore, the theologian must allow a certain latitude of interpretation to biblical texts about nature. Once the truth about nature has been determined by sense experience and reason, the exegete can then apply the principle of accommodation to say that the true meaning of an otherwise contrary passage is theological rather than scientific. Because the inerrant Bible is for the vulgar no less than the learned, it employs the (technically erroneous) language of ordinary appearances rather than the (technically correct) language of theoretical science. In the case of heliocentrism, then, the scientists showed the theologians how they had to interpret the Bible, if a contradiction between the two truths was to be avoided.

Yet the principle of accommodation was hardly new. The scientists did not invent it, nor was it crafted to meet a particular challenge from science. Galileo mentions explicitly Augustine's treatise *On the Literal Interpretation of Genesis,* a work about the larger subject of biblical hermeneutics written long

4. Quoting the translation by Stillman Drake, *Discoveries and Opinions of Galileo* (Garden City, N.Y.: Doubleday, 1957), p. 200.

before the controversy over the motion of the earth. John Calvin (1509-64), almost certainly writing without any knowledge of the new astronomy, stated in the century before Galileo that "the Holy Spirit had no intention to teach astronomy; and in proposing instruction meant to be common to the simplest and most uneducated persons, he made use by Moses and other prophets of popular language that none might shelter himself under the pretext of obscurity."[5] Elsewhere, Calvin allowed that the Bible might even contain erroneous statements, if they reflect common beliefs and are used to make correct theological points.[6]

In context, then, the effort to reinterpret the Bible in light of Copernicanism must be seen as part of a broader issue of interpretation, arising out of the fundamental theological problem of understanding how the infinite God speaks to finite human beings in imperfect human language. The resources were already there for Kepler and Galileo to draw on, yet the fact remains that the acceptance of the new astronomy underscored this problem and ultimately brought from theologians the admission that *scientific* conclusions could bear directly on biblical interpretation — something most thoughtful Christians take for granted today, but at the time a controversial idea.

Other factors were also leading to a reevaluation of the status of science, especially the desire by many scientists and intellectuals to see science become the engine of technological, medical, and social progress. A crucial figure here was the English statesman and essayist, Francis Bacon (1561-1626), another principal contributor to what is often called the "harmony" or "concordist" model of the relation between Christianity and science, which we diagram here (see figure 1). According to this model, the book of Scripture and the book of nature cannot conflict, since both have the same author, but they are about substantially different things and should be read separately whenever possible. Galileo later said as much in his famous letter to Christina de' Medici,[7] but for a definitive (though strongly gendered) statement we quote two passages from Bacon's *Advancement of Learning* (1605), written several years earlier and deeply influential on English and American science for the next two and a half centuries:

5. Calvin, *Commentary on the Psalms,* ed. James Anderson (Grand Rapids: Baker, 1981), pp. v, 184-85.

6. See, for example, his comments on Ps. 58:4-5, where he doubts that snake charming is genuine, although those verses liken the wicked to deaf adders that do not respond to the charmers. On Calvin's views generally, see R. Hooykaas, *Religion and the Rise of Modern Science* (Grand Rapids: Eerdmans, 1972), pp. 117-22.

7. Galileo quoted Cesare Cardinal Baronio, the Vatican librarian, to this effect: "The intention of the Holy Ghost is to teach us how one goes to heaven, not how heaven goes" (Drake, *Discoveries and Opinions,* p. 186).

Let no man upon a weak conceit of sobriety or an ill-applied moderation think or maintain, that a man can search too far, or be too well studied in the book of God's word, or in the book of God's works, divinity or philosophy; but rather let men endeavor an endless progress or proficience in both; only let men beware . . . that they do not unwisely mingle or confound these learnings together.[8]

. . . our Saviour saith, "You err, not knowing the scriptures, nor the power of God"; laying before us two books or volumes to study, if we will be secured from error; first the scriptures, revealing the will of God, and then the creatures expressing his power; whereof the latter is a key unto the former: not only opening our understanding to conceive the true sense of the scriptures, by the general notions of reason and rules of speech; but chiefly opening our belief, in drawing us into a due meditation of the omnipotency of God, which is chiefly signed and engraven upon his works.[9]

Two things are important to notice here. First, Bacon places natural philosophy on the same level as theology: both are equally worthy of study, according to Christ himself (in Bacon's peculiar interpretation of Matt. 22:29), and indeed the study of nature can help us "conceive the true sense of the scriptures." Second, we must avoid "unwisely mingling or confounding" the two together. However there is a significant exception, an area of overlap that presumably betokens wisdom rather than confusion. Because the study of nature can "open our belief" by "drawing us into a due meditation of the omnipotency of God," the doing of natural theology is an integral part of natural philosophy. Bacon did not mean that reason could lead a person into Christian faith; elsewhere he expressly declared it impossible "to deduce the truth of the Christian religion from the principles of the philosophers, and to confirm it by their authority," and he regarded attempts to replace biblical religion with science as "disparaging things divine by mingling with things human."[10] He meant only that it was a proper goal of science to confute "atheism."[11]

8. Bacon, *The Advancement of Learning*, book I, sec. I, para. 3.

9. Bacon, *The Advancement of Learning*, book I, sec. VI, para. 16.

10. Bacon, *Novum Organum* (1620), book I, aphorism lxxxix.

11. See esp. *The Advancement of Learning*, book III, sec. II. The precise meaning of "atheism" as Bacon and other early modern thinkers identified it is difficult to define. Genuine philosophical atheism was rare at that time, but what Henry More and Robert Boyle called "practical atheism," living as if there were no God to whom one is accountable, was commonplace.

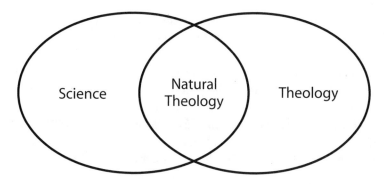

Figure 1
The Relation of Science and Theology according to Francis Bacon

Concordism in New England Geology

Because it offered relative autonomy for science without detracting from the legitimate authority of theology, the Baconian model dominated Anglo-American thinking through the middle of the 19th century. Robert Boyle (1627-91) epitomized the harmony model in its purest Baconian form by aggressively pursuing an extensive program of natural theology while generally avoiding the use of the Bible as a scientific text. More than a century later, however, adherents of this model were much less reluctant to cite Scripture on scientific matters, no doubt because the age and origin of the earth had become frequent topics of scientific discussion. Three evangelical geologists from New England were perhaps the most enthusiastic, and surely the most influential, proponents of the harmony model in antebellum America: Benjamin Silliman (1779-1864), Edward Hitchcock (1793-1864), and James Dwight Dana (1813-95).

Born in North Stratford (now Trumbull), Connecticut, during the American Revolution, Benjamin Silliman was the second son of General Gold Silliman of the Continental Army, who was at the time of his son's birth held prisoner on Long Island. After graduating from Yale College in 1796, Silliman ran the family farm and taught school briefly before entering Yale Law School. Then, one morning in July 1801, Silliman happened upon his father's friend Timothy Dwight, the evangelical president of Yale College, who asked him on the spot to become Yale's first professor of chemistry and natural history, a post he assumed in September 1802. Although some other scientific subjects had been taught at

Yale in the 18th century,[12] Dwight recognized the importance of natural history and desired to fill the position with a person of solid Christian character, who would view science as an ally of faith.[13] To prepare himself for the job, Silliman studied chemistry and medicine at the University of Pennsylvania Medical School and attended lectures in chemistry at Edinburgh University, where he met Robert Darwin (father of Charles Darwin). In later years he was influenced by the "concordist" approach to Genesis and geology advocated by Edinburgh geologist Robert Jameson. At Yale, Silliman enjoyed a long, distinguished career as a highly influential teacher (many leading American scientists were his former pupils), founding editor of the *American Journal of Science and the Arts* (known in its early years as "Silliman's Journal"), and president of the Association of American Geologists, which in 1848 became the American Association for the Advancement of Science. His reputation was only enhanced by marrying Harriet Trumbull, daughter of Connecticut governor Jonathan Trumbull. He was perhaps best known to the general public, however, as a popular lecturer throughout the length and breadth of the early republic, in which connection he captivated audiences with his love of science coupled with his obvious love of God. "Admiring as we do the perfection of science exhibited continually by the lecturer," commented a Boston reporter who had heard him give a lecture in 1843, "we have yet a higher love and reverence for that beautiful exhibition of divine truth to which Mr. Silliman constantly alludes." This, he added, "is the source of our respect for this accomplished Professor, in comparison with which our admiration for his scientific attainments sinks into insignificance."[14]

Edward Hitchcock was also the son of a Revolutionary War veteran, a pious but impoverished farmer and hatter from Deerfield, Massachusetts. In his twenty-first year, the younger Hitchcock suffered a serious attack of mumps that left him with impaired vision, broken health, and a profound sense of his own mortality for the rest of his days. This experience led him to abandon his early interest in Unitarianism and return to his father's Congregationalism. As he recalled many years later,

12. See Louis W. McKeehan, *Yale Science: The First Hundred Years, 1701-1801* (New York: Henry Schuman, 1947), and Theodore Hornberger, *Scientific Thought in the American Colleges, 1638-1800* (Austin: University of Texas Press, 1945).

13. This theme is stressed by John C. Greene, "Protestantism, Science, and American Enterprise: Benjamin Silliman's Moral Universe," in *Benjamin Silliman and His Circle: Studies in the Influence of Benjamin Silliman on Science in America*, ed. Leonard G. Wilson (New York: Science History Publications, 1979), pp. 11-27. Wilson's biographical sketch in the same volume is also helpful.

14. From the *Boston Transcript*, 30 March 1843, quoted by George P. Fisher, *Life of Benjamin Silliman*, 2 vols. (New York: Scribner and Company, 1866), vol. 1, p. 398.

Providence first struck down my ability to study . . . and thus by cutting off my worldly prospects led me to inquire on what foundation I was building for eternity, and a prayerful study of the inspired volume forced me to give up inch by inch the ground on which I tried to stand and brought me into the belief which became cordial as soon as I understood it, of the plain old-fashioned doctrines of the Puritans.[15]

Shortly after this he became preceptor of Deerfield Academy, where he had attended himself. A few years later, he entered Yale to prepare for the ministry, but while there he made a point of attending Silliman's geology lectures. From 1821 to 1825 he was pastor of a Congregational Church in Conway, Massachusetts, before ill health forced his dismissal. Following four months studying with Silliman, he became professor of chemistry and natural history — later professor of geology and natural theology as well as president — at Amherst College, where he remained until his death. Appointed geologist for the states of Massachusetts and Vermont, his *Report on the Geology, Mineralogy, Botany, and Zoology of Massachusetts* (1833) is the first of its kind. Soon afterward, Hitchcock reported on the first dinosaur tracks ever found, though he and others (including Silliman) mistook them for the tracks of ancient birds. Hitchcock served as first president of the Association of American Geologists and was a founding member of the National Academy of Sciences. His textbook, *Elementary Geology*, was reprinted at least 30 times after the first edition of 1840, and *The Religion of Geology* (1851), his most complete statement of natural theology — the subject closest to his heart — was widely read on both sides of the Atlantic.[16]

The eldest of ten children of a merchant from Utica, New York, James Dwight Dana graduated from Utica High School, where he was well grounded in natural history before matriculating in 1830 at Yale, where he went specifically in order to study with Silliman — whose third daughter, Henrietta, he married many years later (in June 1844). After graduation Dana taught mathematics on a naval vessel in the Mediterranean, observing natural phenomena and collecting specimens of shells, plants, and minerals whenever possible. Upon his return, Silliman made Dana his assistant to help prepare samples for

15. Edward Hitchcock, *Reminiscences of Amherst College* (Northampton: Bridgman & Childs, 1863), p. 283.

16. No full biography of Hitchcock exists. For good short accounts, see Gloria Robinson, "Edward Hitchcock," in *Benjamin Silliman and His Circle*, pp. 49-83; Philip J. Lawrence, "Edward Hitchcock: The Christian Geologist," *Proceedings of the American Philosophical Society* 116 (1972): 21-34; Stanley M. Guralnick, "Geology and Religion Before Darwin: The Case of Edward Hitchcock, Theologian and Geologist," in *Science in America Since 1820*, ed. Nathan Reingold (New York: Science History Publications, 1976), pp. 116-30.

his geology lectures, a post that left considerable time for Dana to carry out his own research, culminating in his first book, *A System of Mineralogy* (1837), a great work that remains in use today. Two momentous events in 1838 altered the course of his life and work. First, he was appointed geologist (with a very good salary) on a scientific exploration to the South Pacific on the *U.S.S. Wilkes*, a four-year voyage around the world that gave Dana an experience highly similar to that enjoyed by Charles Darwin on the *H.M.S. Beagle* only a few years before. Indeed Dana was able to confirm and extend Darwin's first important scientific contribution, his theory of coral reef formation, and in so doing he earned a considerable reputation for himself. The second event occurred just prior to the voyage, while Dana was still living in New Haven. Reflecting on the dangers that lay ahead and on reports of a religious revival back home in Utica, Dana underwent a conversion of his own — the details are unclear, but the result was, in the words of historian Margaret Rossiter, that "his religious views were to become much more noticeable in his scientific work and correspondence."[17] In future years he would find Silliman's work very helpful as he, too, sought to defend the harmony of science and religion, most visibly in the four editions of his *Manual of Geology* (1862) but also in popular and religious magazines, such as *Bibliotheca Sacra*. As first occupant of the Silliman Professorship of Natural History at Yale (starting in 1848), Dana was a worthy successor to his father-in-law.

Silliman, Hitchcock, and Dana saw in the books of nature and Scripture essentially the same story, going beyond the general but vague assumption of harmony to endorse a strong concordism, arguing for close, specific parallels between the text of Genesis and the conclusions of geology. Seemingly ignoring Bacon's warning not to mingle the two books unwisely, they produced detailed schemes of harmonization, such as the one reproduced here (see figure 2),[18] which Silliman borrowed from Robert Jameson and included in his appendix, in which the various creative acts of God are matched with specific geological evidence. Silliman's basic strategy, later employed by Dana, was to interpret the days of Genesis as creative periods of indeterminate length, thus giving geologists the vast quantities of time they were demanding; this is often called the "day-age" view. His former pupil Hitchcock preferred the more "literal" approach to the creation days often called the "interval" view at the time, later

17. Margaret Rossiter, "A Portrait of James Dwight Dana," in *Benjamin Silliman and His Circle*, pp. 105-27, quoting p. 110.

18. I have used the 5th London and 3rd American edition (New Haven, 1839) of Bakewell, in which the chart appears on pp. 562-63. I have made available a lengthy excerpt from Silliman's appendix, along with excerpts from several other texts cited in this essay, at http://www.messiah.edu/HPAGES/FACSTAFF/TDAVIS/texts.htm.

called the "gap theory" or the "creation-restitution" view. According to this interpretation, which had been endorsed by the Scottish theologian Thomas Chalmers (1780-1847) and the English geologist William Buckland (1784-1856), a period of unknown length separated the original creation of the universe described in the first verse of the Bible from the subsequent creation of all present forms of life in six literal days, about 6,000 years ago.[19]

Both Silliman and Hitchcock, like Galileo before them, believed that theologians simply could not interpret the Bible correctly without input from scientists, and many theologians shared their view.[20] As Charles Hodge (1797-1878) saw it three decades later, "we only interpret the Word of God by the Word of God when we interpret the Bible by science."[21] For concordists the principal point of contact between geology and the biblical story of creation was the fact that the earth was much older than 6,000 years; thus they had to confront the crucial theological problem of explaining the existence of animal death before the fall of Adam. This very issue is still at the heart of young-Earth creationism in our own day, motivating its adherents perhaps more than any other issue to reject old-Earth interpretations of Genesis.[22] Hitchcock dealt with this forthrightly in a fascinating section, entitled "Connection between Geology and Natural and Revealed Religion," in *Elementary Geology;* his comments in the eighth (1847) edition are especially interesting. "Not only geology," he noted, "but zoology and comparative anatomy, teach us that death among the inferior animals did not result from the fall of man, but from the original constitution given them by their Creator. One large class of animals, the carnivores, have organs expressly intended for destroying other classes for food." Even herbivores

19. For an extensive treatment (from the point of view of a young-Earth creationist) of this position and its history, see Weston W. Fields, *Unformed and Unfilled: A Critique of the Gap Theory* (Nutley, N.J.: Presbyterian and Reformed, 1976). For comments on modern adherents, see Tom McIver, "Formless and Void: Gap Theory Creationism," *Creation/Evolution* 24 (Fall 1988): 1-24.

20. Rodney L. Stiling stresses this particular point in his essay, "Scriptural Geology in America," in *Evangelicals and Science in Historical Perspective,* ed. David N. Livingstone, D. G. Hart, and Mark A. Noll (New York: Oxford University Press, 1999), pp. 177-92. Though this essay is based on my own study of Silliman and Hitchcock, it overlaps somewhat with Stiling's account and might be read in parallel with it.

21. Charles Hodge, "The Bible in Science," *New York Observer,* 26 March 1863, pp. 98-99, reprinted in Charles Hodge, *What Is Darwinism?* ed. Mark A. Noll and David N. Livingstone (Grand Rapids: Baker, 1994), pp. 53-56, on p. 54.

22. A good recent example is the following quotation, from the Answers in Genesis webpage (http://www.christiananswers.net/q-aig/aig-c005.html): "This reinterpretation [of the Bible in terms of an old earth] also means having to accept that there were billions of years of death, disease, and bloodshed before Adam, thus eroding the creation/Fall/restoration framework within which the gospel is presented in the Bible."

Table of Coincidences between the Order of Events as described in Genesis, and that unfolded by Geological Investigation

In Genesis	No.	Discovered by Geology
Gen. 1.1, 2. In the beginning God created the heavens and the earth. And the earth was without form and void; and darkness was upon the face of the deep; and the Spirit of God moved upon the face of the waters.	1	It is impossible to deny, that the waters of the sea have formerly, and for a long time, covered those masses of matter which now constitute our highest mountains;
3, 4, 5. *Creation of Light.* 6, 7, 8. *Creation of the expansion or atmosphere.* 9, 10. Appearance of the dry land.	2	and, further, that these waters, during a long time, did not support any living bodies — *Cuvier's Theory of the Earth, sect. 7.*
11, 12, 13. Creation of shooting plants, and of seed-bearing herbs and trees.	3	1. Cryptogamous plants in the coal strata. — *Many observers.* 2. Species of the most perfect developed class, the Dicotyledonus, already appear in the period of the secondary formations, and the first traces of them can be shown in the oldest strata of the secondary formation; while they uninterruptedly increase in the successive formations. — *Prof. Jameson's remarks on the Ancient Flora of the Earth.*
14 to 19. *Sun, moon, and stars made to be for signs, and for seasons, and for days, and for years.*		
20. Creation of the inhabitants of the waters.	4	Shells in Alpine and Jura limestone. — *Humboldt's tablets.* Fish in Jura limestone. — *Do.* Teeth and scales of fish in Tilgate sandstone. — *Mr. Mantell.*
Creation of flying things.	5	Bones of birds in Tilgate sandstone. — *Mr. Mantell, Geological Transactions,* 1826. Elytra* of winged insects in calcareous slate, at Stonesfield. — *Mr. Mantell.*
21. The creation of great reptiles.	6	It will be impossible not to acknowledge as a certain truth, the number, the largeness, and the variety of the reptiles, which inhabited the seas or the land at the epoch in which the strata of Jura were deposited. — *Cuvier's Ossem. Foss.* There was a period when the earth was peopled by oviparous quadrupeds of the most appalling magnitude. Reptiles were the lords of Creation. — *Mr. Mantell.*
24, 25. Creation of the mammalia.	7	Bones of mammiferous land quadrupeds, found only when we come up to the formations above the coarse limestone, which is above the chalk.† — *Cuvier's Theory, sect.* 20.
26, 27. Creation of man.	8	No human remains among extraneous fossils. — *Cuvier's Theory, sect.* 32. But found covered with mud in caves of Bize. — *Journal.*
Genesis, VII. The flood of Noah, 4200 years ago.	9	The crust of the globe has been subjected to a great and sudden revolution, which cannot be dated much farther back than five or six thousand years ago. — *Cuvier's Theory,* 32, 33, 34, 35, *and Buckland's Relig. Dilvr.*

* *Sheaths.*

† *One solitary exception is since discovered, in the calcareous slate of Stonesfield, in the bones of a didelphia, an opossum, a tribe whose position may be held intermediate between the oviparous and mammiferous races.*

Figure 2

Coincidences between the Bible and geology, from Silliman (1833)

"must have destroyed a multitude of insects, of which several species inhabit almost every species of plant," not to mention the destruction of "millions of animalcula [microscopic organisms], which abound in many of the fluids which animals drink, and even in the air which they breathe." "In short," he added (almost prophetically, if one thinks of scientific creationists today), "death could not be excluded from the world, without an entire change in the constitution and course of nature; and such a change we have no reason to suppose, from the Mosaic account, took place when man fell." Furthermore, on biblical grounds alone one might have to allow animal death before the fall. Not only does Romans 5:12 explicitly limit the scope of death to humanity; unless Adam himself had seen death, how could the threat of death for disobedience have real force?[23] Therefore Hitchcock believed that the fall introduced humans to spiritual death, not animals to physical death.

The harmony model was not without critics, among them Thomas Cooper (1759-1839), an immigrant from England who, as president and professor of chemistry at the College of South Carolina, issued a wholesale attack on the Mosaic authorship and divine inspiration of the Pentateuch in the form of an open letter to Silliman, whom he saw as bending over backwards to satisfy the theologians. Cooper was responding to Silliman's claim (in the first version of his appendix), following Buckland, that "geology fully confirms the scripture history" of Noah's flood.[24] Cooper hotly disputed this, noting that "no well informed geologist of Europe or this country" would agree, and adding that "hardly a single Divine of reputation in Europe, now believes that the book of Genesis, as we possess it, was written by Moses, or by any one else, under divine inspiration." Cooper concluded that, in the absence of any positive geological evidence, the biblical flood could certainly not be asserted on Moses' authority. Although Silliman never accepted Cooper's view of the Bible and continued to believe in the historicity of the flood, he did change his mind about its geological significance, toning down his comments considerably in later editions of the appendix. Here he undoubtedly followed the lead of several English diluvialists who altered their position in the early 1830s; Buckland himself altered his position in his Bridgewater treatise of 1836.

Some leading American biblical scholars were also critical of Silliman, though for quite different reasons. Moses Stuart (1780-1852), professor of sacred literature at Andover Seminary, had written Silliman with objections to the

23. Edward Hitchcock, *Elementary Geology,* 8th ed. (New York: Newman, 1847), pp. 299-300.

24. "Outline of the Course of Geological Lectures Given in Yale College," appended to Robert Bakewell, *An Introduction to Geology,* 3rd London and 1st American ed. (New Haven: Hezekiah Howe, 1829), p. 7.

concordist approach as early as 1824, but first stated his views publicly in his *Hebrew Chrestomathy* (1829). The day-age view was simply unacceptable, he argued, for "to violate the laws of exegesis in order to accommodate a geological theory . . . is not acting in accordance with the precepts of Scriptural Hermeneutics." Exhibiting a contempt for science that was probably not representative of the bulk of his professional colleagues, Stuart conceded that the geologists might someday "deserve more serious consideration," but for the time being they could not even agree on how the earth was formed, and their knowledge of the earth's interior was no more than a mile deep.[25] Seven years later, Stuart made similar points, responding this time to Hitchcock's gap theory, in the *American Biblical Repository*. After attacking the exegetical basis for Hitchcock's interpretation, Stuart concluded with further digs at the incomplete knowledge of feuding geologists and a telling shot: "The digging of rocks and the digging of Hebrew roots are not as yet precisely the same operation."[26] But Hitchcock's colleague J. L. Kingsley had the last word, showing that Stuart actually violated his own principle, by reinterpreting Moses' statements about the firmament in light of modern astronomy![27]

Yet another exchange between the geologists and the philologists took place two decades later, when Union College classicist Tayler Lewis (1802-77) raised similar concerns in *The Six Days of Creation* (1855). Although he accepted the day-age view and noted the existence of certain obvious parallels between Genesis and geology — indeed at times Lewis sounds almost like Dana — he nonetheless poured contempt on the idea that scientific theories ought to be used to interpret Scripture. The Bible, Lewis claimed, should be interpreted on its own terms as a literary text, without regard for the conclusions of scientists, which were only transitory truths in any case. Echoing Augustine, he called the creative days *dies ineffables*, that is, unknowable days, "incommensurable by any estimates we could apply." The geologist "talks very flippantly, and very ignorantly, of millions and billions of years."[28] In one respect Lewis's objections

25. Moses Stuart, *A Hebrew Chrestomathy* (Andover: Flagg and Gould, 1829), p. 118, quoted by John H. Giltner, "Genesis and Geology: The Stuart-Silliman-Hitchcock Debate," *The Journal of Religious Thought* 23 (1966-67): 3-14, on p. 7.

26. Moses Stuart, "A Critical Examination of Some Passages in Gen. I; with Remarks on Difficulties That Attend Some of the Present Modes of Geological Reasoning," *American Biblical Repository* 7 (1836): 46-105, p. 103, quoted by Giltner, "Genesis and Geology, " pp. 11-12. Stuart refers to alternative schools of geology, known as Vulcanists (who emphasized the agency of heat in forming the earth's surface) and Neptunists (who emphasized water).

27. Kingsley's rebuttal appeared in *American Journal of Science and Arts* 30 (1836): 114-30. See Conrad Wright, "The Religion of Geology," *The New England Quarterly* 14 (1941): 335-58, p. 345.

28. Tayler Lewis, *The Six Days of Creation, or, The Scriptural Cosmology with the Ancient*

(and those of Stuart) have a surprisingly modern ring:[29] most contemporary biblical scholars and scientists would agree that the meaning of a biblical text has little or nothing to do with scientific matters. But Dana, the leading American geologist of the generation following Silliman (his father-in-law) and Hitchcock, took Lewis's book personally as a frontal attack on his profession — each man called the other an "infidel," though they were apparently reconciled many years later — and replied in a series of four articles published in *Bibliotheca Sacra* over the next two years. Summing up his belief in the importance of drawing theological conclusions from geology, he wrote, "This placing in antagonism God's word and his works, is only fitted to make the young scout the former; for they know the latter has its great truths, having the best of all evidence."[30]

Dana was a classical concordist who viewed Genesis as a broadly historical account of the origin of the world. "The record in the Bible," he wrote in 1874, is "profoundly philosophical in the scheme of creation it presents." Since the Bible is "both true and divine," there is no "real conflict between the two Books of the GREAT AUTHOR. Both are revelations made by Him to Man."[31] Because Dana remained a concordist for many years after Darwin's theory of evolution made inroads in America, we should look more closely at his views on this subject. For a succinct statement of his mature reflections, we refer to his "Observations on Geological History," part of a popular treatment of geology from 1876. In several places, including the following passage, he sounded very much like a theistic evolutionist:

> With every step there was an unfolding of a plan, and not merely an adaptation to external conditions. There was a working forward according to pre-established methods and lines up to the final species, Man, and according to an order so perfect and harmonious in its parts, that the progress is rightly pronounced a development or evolution. Creation by a divine method, that is, by the creative acts of a Being of infinite wisdom, whether

---

Idea of Time-Worlds in Distinction from Worlds in Space (Schenectady, N.Y.: G. Y. Debogert, 1855), p. 163.

29. This point is stressed (for Stuart, not Lewis) by Wright, "Religion of Geology," pp. 344-45.

30. James D. Dana, "Science and the Bible: A Review of 'The Six Days of Creation' of Prof. Tayler Lewis," *Bibliotheca Sacra* 13 (1856): 80-129, quoting p. 91. My interpretation of this debate follows Morgan B. Sherwood, "Genesis, Evolution, and Geology in America Before Darwin: The Dana-Lewis Controversy, 1856-1857," in *Toward a History of Geology*, ed. Cecil J. Schneer (Cambridge, Mass.: MIT Press, 1969), pp. 305-16.

31. James D. Dana, *Manual of Geology*, 2nd ed. (New York: Ivison, Blakeman, Taylor and Co., 1874), p. 770.

through one fiat or many, could be no other than perfect in system, and exact in its relations to all external conditions, — no other, indeed, than the very system of evolution that geological history makes known.

Elsewhere, however, he seemed to qualify his position — or, perhaps, to explain it more clearly. This is most evident in what he said about "Man, the last and highest being in the system of life," whose superior brain and erect stature give exalted status: "Thus, by an abrupt transition, he stands apart from the ape and all brute races." Furthermore, Dana held that a fully evolutionary origin of all living things had not yet been demonstrated from the fossil record. "This is admitted by all," he stated, "even by those who believe that the transitions were gradual. Geology has brought to light fewer examples of gradual transition than occur among living species." Although some "intermediate species" had been discovered "from time to time," such as that bridging "the interval between the Elephant and the Mastodon, and for that between the Horse of modern time and the Tapir-like animals of the early Tertiary," nevertheless "the idea of *abruptness between species* is not yet set aside by geological evidence," though the fossil record "is unquestionably very imperfect." Dana especially emphasized the absence of "intermediate species" between "Man and the Man-Ape," supporting his conclusion that "Man is not of Nature's making," but "owes his existence to the special act of the Infinite Being whose image he bears."[32]

Yet even before this passage was penned, confidence in the harmony model had begun to wane, as evolution gained acceptance in American colleges and universities. Harvard botanist Asa Gray (1810-88), the first public defender of Darwinism in America, expressed his dissent in his anonymous 1863 review of the first edition of Dana's *Manual of Geology*, which contained a short section on cosmogony. Dana's cosmogony, Gray noted,

> is merely a summary of the views of [geologist Arnold] Guyot, looking to a harmony of the Mosaic cosmogony with modern science, — views which Professor Dana has adopted and maintained elsewhere more in detail, and which, under the circumstances, are naturally enough here reproduced. We regard them with curious interest, but without much sympathy for the anxious feeling which demands such harmonies. We have faith in revelation,

32. James D. Dana, *The Geological Story Briefly Told* (New York and Chicago: Ivison, Blakeman, Taylor, and Company, 1876), pp. 243-44, 249, 250 (his italics), and 252-53. He held to this position to the end; in the final (4th) edition of his *Manual of Geology* (New York, 1895), he stated (p. 1036) "that the intervention of a Power above Nature was at the basis of Man's development." For a clear review of Dana's view on evolution, see William F. Sanford, Jr., "Dana and Darwinism," *Journal of the History of Ideas* 21 (1965): 531-46.

and faith in science, in each after its kind; but, as respects cosmogony, we are not called upon to yield an implicit assent to any proposed reconciliation of the two.[33]

This passage, I believe, is crucial for understanding the subsequent history of the harmony model. Gray was both an evolutionist and a Christian committed to a high Augustinian view of God's relation to the world. The strong concordism for which he had little sympathy cries out for a nonevolutionary view of human origins: if the Bible really is a reliable source about the early history of the planet, as Dana and the other concordists assumed, then it is difficult to see how a fully evolutionary position could be acceptable; thus concordism had become outmoded. Addressing the students at Yale Divinity School nearly twenty years later, after noting the influence of "Professor Silliman's transparent Christian character," Gray recalled a time

> when schemes for reconciling Genesis with Geology had an importance in the churches, and among thoughtful people, which few if any would now assign to them; when it was thought necessary — for only necessity could justify it — to bring the details of the two into agreement by extraneous suppositions and forced constructions of language, such as would now offend our critical and sometimes our moral sense. The change of view which we have witnessed amounts to this. Our predecessors implicitly held that Holy Scripture must somehow truly teach such natural science as it had occasion to refer to, or at least could never contradict it; while the most that is now intelligently claimed is, that the teachings of the two, properly understood, are not incompatible. We may take it to be the accepted idea that the Mosaic books were not handed down to us for our instruction in scientific knowledge, and that it is our duty to ground our scientific beliefs upon observation and inference, unmixed with considerations of a different order. Then, when fundamental principles of the cosmogony in Genesis are found to coincide with established facts and probable inferences, the coincidence has its value; and wherever the particulars are incongruous, the discrepancy does not distress us, I may add, does not concern us. I trust that the veneration rightly due to the Old Testament is not impaired by the ascertaining that the Mosaic is not an original but a compiled cosmogony. Its glory is, that while its materials were the earlier property of the race, they were in this record purged of polytheism and Nature-worship, and impregnated with ideas which we suppose the world will never outgrow. For its funda-

33. [Asa Gray,] "Review of Dana's *Geology*," *North American Review* 97 (1863): 372-86, quoting p. 375.

mental note is, the declaration of one God, maker of heaven and Earth, and of all things, visible and invisible, — a declaration which, if physical science is unable to establish, it is equally unable to overthrow.[34]

For Gray, then, concordism was based upon a faulty view of Genesis itself: for all of their Galileian statements that the Bible was not a science book, the concordists had continued to treat it as if it were, anxiously showing how the details of geology supported the words of Scripture.

Instead of concordism, Gray clearly held a compatibilist or complementarian view of theology and science, according to which the Bible teaches truths of a wholly different order than the truths of science, so that it is impossible to confirm or disconfirm Christianity by appealing to science. "I accept Christianity on its own evidence," Gray confessed, "and I am yet to learn how physical or any other science conflicts with it any more than it conflicts with simple theism. I take it that religion is based on the idea of a Divine Mind revealing himself to intelligent creatures for moral ends." Revelation culminated "in the advent of a Divine Person, who, being made man, manifested the Divine Nature in union with the human," and "this manifestation constitutes Christianity." The incarnation was for Gray "the crowning miracle," attended by other miracles he also accepted. Thus Gray was able consistently to affirm his acceptance of Darwin alongside his faith in Christ, even a very traditional faith whose "essential contents" were "briefly summed up" in the Apostles' and Nicene creeds.[35]

From Harmony to Conflict in the Early 20th Century

It was evidently lectures like Gray's, at institutions like Yale, that in December 1891 led Dana's former student, geologist William North Rice (1845-1928), to speak the following words to the American Society of Naturalists, words published thirteen months later in the conservative theological journal, *Bibliotheca Sacra*: "The curriculum of an orthodox theological seminary is hardly regarded as complete today without a course of lectures in the consistency of Evolution with theistic philosophy."[36] The same words were quoted again in 1954, this time by the late Baptist theologian Bernard Ramm (1916-92), in his seminal study, *The Christian View of Science and Scripture*. "Theistic evolution had be-

34. Asa Gray, *Natural Science and Religion: Two Lectures Delivered to the Theological School of Yale College* (New York: Scribner's, 1880), pp. 6 and 7-9.

35. Gray, *Natural Science and Religion*, pp. 106 and 108-9.

36. William N. Rice, "Twenty-Five Years of Scientific Progress," *Bibliotheca Sacra* 50 (1893): 1-29, on p. 28.

come so popular by the end of the nineteenth century," Ramm commented, "that some writers voiced their opinion that the controversy was over with. They did not reckon with the Fundamentalist movement in the twentieth century and its dynamic, militant attack upon evolution and theistic evolution."[37] In the preface to his book, Ramm was even more specific, identifying "two traditions in Bible and science" at the end of the 19th century. One, the "noble" tradition established by people such as Dana and Gray (among others), "is the tradition of the great and learned evangelical Christians who have been patient, genuine, and kind and who have taken great pains to learn the facts of science and Scripture." The "ignoble" tradition, on the other hand, "has taken a most unwholesome attitude toward science, and has used arguments and procedures not in the better traditions of established scholarship." His observation on the state of affairs among evangelicals at mid-century is telling:

> Unfortunately the noble tradition which was in ascendency in the closing years of the nineteenth century has not been the major tradition in evangelicalism in the twentieth century. Both a narrow evangelicalism, and its narrow theology, buried the noble tradition. The sad result has been that in spite of stout affirmations that true science and the Bible agree and do not conflict, science has repudiated the ignoble tradition.[38]

Ironically, the one person whom Ramm most had in mind as representative of the "ignoble" tradition — self-educated evangelist Harry Rimmer (1890-1952), author of *The Harmony of Science and Scripture* (1936) and several other works that led fundamentalists to view him as a genuine "authority" on science — was himself a staunch defender of a concordist interpretation of Scripture, the gap theory; on one occasion Rimmer even bested fellow fundamentalist William Bell Riley (1861-1947) in a debate in which Rimmer defended the gap theory and Riley argued for the day-age view.[39] Rimmer's ad-

37. Bernard Ramm, *The Christian View of Science and Scripture* (Grand Rapids: Eerdmans, 1954), p. 284 and note on the same page; citing the 4th printing (1962); pagination is not identical in all printings.

38. Ramm, *Christian View*, n.p. In the 10th printing (1976), the second sentence reads: "A narrow bibliolatry, the product not of faith but of fear, buried the noble tradition." And a final sentence has also been added: "It is our wish to call evangelicalism back to the noble tradition of the closing years of the nineteenth century." Ramm's comments have recently been echoed by Mark A. Noll, *The Scandal of the Evangelical Mind* (Grand Rapids: Eerdmans, 1994).

39. *A Debate: Resolved, That the Creative Days in Genesis were Aeons, Not Solar Days* (Glendale, Calif.: Research Science Bureau, 1930). On Rimmer, see Edward B. Davis, ed., *The Antievolution Pamphlets of Harry Rimmer*, Creationism in Twentieth-Century America, vol. 6 (New York: Garland, 1995), pp. ix-xxviii.

vocacy of the gap theory derived from the endorsement it had received from
C. I. Scofield (1843-1921) in his famous "reference" edition of the Bible, probably the most widely used Bible among fundamentalists in the first half of the
20th century.[40] Indeed, various concordist interpretations of Genesis were the
principal options available to even the most conservative Christians up
through the 1960s.

What made fundamentalist appeals to the language of two books so different from those of the classical concordists — what made them "ignoble"
rather than "noble" — was the overall attitude they took toward the science of
their own day. Where Silliman and his followers did their best to relate Scripture to the views of the larger scientific community, Rimmer and his followers
clung to an outmoded notion of science as containing only established matters
of fact, not the theories that explain those facts, and they poured scorn on any
scientific conclusions that contradicted their literalistic interpretations of Genesis. Rimmer's pamphlet, "Modern Science and the Youth of Today," printed in
the year of the Scopes trial, illustrates this well. "True" science, as Rimmer defined it, "is a correlated body of absolute knowledge," whereas "modern" science "is so largely speculation and theory."[41] Rimmer and other fundamentalist
commentators on science, including William Jennings Bryan (1860-1925), saw
Genesis as a scientifically accurate description of the origin of the cosmos and
emphasized the absolute dominance of scriptural "truths" over the "mere theories" of "agnostic" and "atheist" scientists. They stressed the wholly subservient
role of science to theology, including the value of using what they considered to
be the "facts" of "true science" rather than the "guesses" of "science falsely so
called" for apologetic purposes, to uphold the reliability of the Bible against
evolutionists and biblical critics and to convince unbelievers to accept the gospel.[42] As Bryan saw it, "the word hypothesis is a synonym used by scientists for
the word guess," and thus the theory of evolution was no better than "guesses

40. C. I. Scofield, *The Holy Bible containing the Old and New Testaments: Authorized version with a new system of connected topical references to all the greater themes of Scripture, with
annotations, revised marginal renderings, summaries, definitions, chronology, and index, to which
are added, helps at hard places, explanations of seeming discrepancies, and a new system of para-
graphs* (New York: Oxford University Press, 1909).

41. Harry Rimmer, "Modern Science and the Youth of Today" (Los Angeles: Research Science Bureau, 1925), pp. 1-2; see Davis, *The Antievolution Pamphlets of Harry Rimmer*, pp. 459-75.

42. The phrase, "science falsely so called," from 1 Tim. 6:20, was widely used by fundamentalists in the 1920s as a label for evolution. For further comments on fundamentalist views
of science that give priority to "facts" over speculative "theories" or "hypotheses," see Edward B.
Davis, "Fundamentalism and Folk Science Between the Wars," *Religion and American Culture* 5
(1995): 217-48; and idem, "A Whale of a Tale: Fundamentalist Fish Stories," *Perspectives on Science and Christian Faith* 43 (1991): 224-37.

strung together,"[43] an idea illustrated perfectly by the cartoon shown in figure 3, taken from an antievolution pamphlet published by an English journalist in the mid-1930s.[44]

What led fundamentalists to reject modern science so strongly? The example of George Frederick Wright (1838-1921), theologian and amateur geologist, is instructive here.[45] As pastor of the Free Church in Andover, Massachusetts, in the 1870s, Wright had joined his friend Asa Gray in arguing vigorously for the acceptance of theistic evolution, especially in a series of five articles that appeared in *Bibliotheca Sacra*. But in the years following his move to Oberlin Theological Seminary in 1881, other friends, especially Dana and Edward Hitchcock's son Charles — not to mention his own encounter with the heterodox Presbyterian theologian Charles A. Briggs, who very nearly induced a spiritual crisis in Wright — convinced him that the advent of higher biblical criticism and the proliferation of materialistic interpretations of evolution made it necessary to come out against evolution. At the same time, he found that his own traditional views on early biblical history were increasingly out of step with those of professional scientists. Thus when A. C. Dixon (1838-1921) invited Wright to contribute a chapter on evolution to *The Fundamentals* (1910-15), the set of booklets from which "fundamentalism" got its name, he did not hesitate to accept. His essay, "The Passing of Evolution," noted how in recent years evolution "has come into much deserved disrepute by the injection into it of erroneous and harmful theological and philosophical implications." The current view "is one which practically eliminates God from the whole creative process and relegates mankind to the tender mercies of a mechanical universe the wheels of whose machinery are left to move on without any immediate Divine direction." This he contrasted with "Darwinism" as its author had defined it, namely as no more than a theory of the origin of species by common descent. Wright noted how Darwin himself had regarded the origin of life as "an insoluble problem" and that he had "rested on the supposition that the Creator had in the beginning breathed the forces of life into several forms of plants and ani-

43. William Jennings Bryan, *The Menace of Darwinism* (New York: Fleming H. Revell, 1922), pp. 21-23.

44. [Newman Watts,] *Why Be an Ape — ? Observations on Evolution* (London: Marshall, Morgan & Scott, 1936). For very brief comments on this pamphlet, see David N. Livingstone, *Darwin's Forgotten Defenders: The Encounter Between Evangelical Theology and Evolutionary Thought* (Grand Rapids: Eerdmans, 1987), pp. 163-64.

45. For an excellent account of Wright's change of heart, see Ronald L. Numbers, "George Frederick Wright: From Christian Darwinist to Fundamentalist," *Isis* 79 (1988): 624-45; for a shorter version, see idem, *The Creationists: The Evolution of Scientific Creationism* (New York: Knopf, 1992), pp. 30-36.

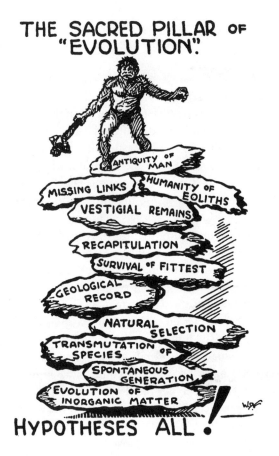

Figure 3
Newman Watts, *Why Be an Ape? Observations on Evolution*
(London: Marshall, Morgan & Scott, 1936), p. 10.

mals, and at the same time endowed them with the marvelous capacity for variation which they now possess." Thus, "by no stretch of legitimate reasoning can Darwinism be made to exclude design." Furthermore, "the proof of Darwinism even is by no means altogether convincing," especially when problems with the earth's limited age and the small steps possible through beneficial variations are considered. "It is therefore, impossible," Wright concluded, "to get any such proof of evolution as shall seriously modify our conception of Christianity."[46]

46. George F. Wright, "The Passing of Evolution," in *The Fundamentals*, 12 vols. (Chicago: Testimony Publishing Company, n.d.), 7:5-20, quoting pp. 5, 8-9, 10, and 19.

This contrasts sharply with the conclusions of Princeton embryologist Edwin Grant Conklin (1863-1952). Once as much of a traditional Christian as Wright, Gray, or Dana, by the early years of the 20th century Conklin had given up his faith in a transcendent creator, mainly the result of his slow acceptance of scientific naturalism, the belief that there is no "supernatural" realm apart from nature. He saw his own spiritual journey as one that "orthodox friends" might interpret as "descending steps," leading him further from the traditional Methodist faith of his youth. "My gradual loss of faith in many orthodox beliefs," he recalled near the end of his life, "came inevitably with increasing knowledge of nature and growth of a critical sense." Especially important in this regard was his reading of Andrew Dickson White's *History of the Warfare of Science with Theology in Christendom* (first version published in 1876, though Conklin cites the much longer 1905 edition) and John William Draper's *History of the Conflict between Religion and Science* (1874). These books "showed the impossibility of harmonizing many traditional doctrines of theology with the demonstrations of modern science." Thus it was no longer possible for Conklin to be religious in a traditional sense,[47] and when he lectured a Philadelphia audience on "The Religion of Science" in the mid-1920s, he identified the essential contents of his faith by denying a personal God, miracles, supernatural revelation, personal immortality, and the efficacy of prayer.[48]

For an intermediate case, consider another Christian biologist, Samuel Christian Schmucker (1860-1943), now virtually unknown but in the early 20th century a nationally prominent popularizer of evolution and eugenics. Though he wrote six books and numerous magazine articles, perhaps his most interesting publication is his contribution to a series of nine pamphlets on "Science and Religion," printed between 1922 and 1931 with funds provided partly by John D. Rockefeller, Jr. under the auspices of The American Institute of Sacred Literature, an extension of the Divinity School at the University of Chicago.[49] Schmucker's tract, called "Through Science to God,"[50] used humming birds to

47. See Conklin's chapter in *Thirteen Americans: Their Spiritual Autobiographies*, ed. Louis Finkelstein (New York: Institute for Religious and Social Studies, 1953), pp. 56-59 and 72-73.

48. Manuscript entitled "Religion of Science very different from religion of tradition & Revelation," Edwin Grant Conklin Papers, carton 14, folder on "Religion and Science," Manuscripts Division, Department of Rare Books and Special Collections, Princeton University Library. Published with permission of the Princeton University Library.

49. For a history of the Institute, see Kenneth N. Beck, "The American Institute of Sacred Literature: A Historical Analysis of an Adult Education Institution," Ph.D. dissertation, University of Chicago, 1968. I intend to write a full history of these pamphlets. Parts of this paragraph are taken from my essay, "Fundamentalism and Folk Science Between the Wars."

50. Samuel C. Schmucker, "Through Science to God: The Humming Bird's Story, An Evolutionary Interpretation," Popular Religion Leaflets, "Science and Religion" Series (Chicago:

illustrate how evolution works by the interplay of natural and sexual selection. Then he derived a moral lesson from the fact that male humming birds have only attractive coloration to draw the mate, not protective coloration to hide from predators: "Here at last, in the bird-world as in the human world at its highest, perfect love has cast out fear." In a concluding section called "GOING DEEPER," Schmucker probed the ultimate questions this suggested to him. Why did beauty, and the care for beauty, seem to increase with time in evolutionary history? Why was the overall trend of evolution "steadily upward, through long, succeeding ages?" His answer was that the laws of nature that had produced this trend were "not the fiat of almighty God," but "the manifestation in nature of the presence of the indwelling God." Thus they were "eternal even as God is eternal." Gravitation, for example, "is inherent in the nature of the bodies. It was not 'put there' by a higher power." Clearly, Schmucker's concept of God was profoundly unorthodox: casting aside all vestiges of a transcendent creator in favor of a wholly immanent God, he constructed an evolutionary theism that made God coeval with the world, indistinguishable from the laws of nature and the evolutionary progress they had produced. Thus he placed his ultimate hope in the process of organic evolution that had created humankind and would, he argued elsewhere, lead inevitably to our moral perfection as we slowly but surely cast off our animal nature. Therefore it is hardly surprising that Schmucker was an advocate of eugenics, which he saw as the means by which humans could carry out God's desire to eliminate sinful behavior.

Evangelicals and Evolution Today

The positions articulated by Gray, Wright, Conklin, and Schmucker correspond closely to the four main patterns that still govern most religious responses to evolution today: *complementarity* in which theological truths exist in a higher realm apart from scientific truths (Gray), *conflict* resulting in the rejection of evolution (Wright), *conflict* resulting in the rejection of Christianity (Conklin), and *doctrinal reformulation* resulting in the rejection of divine transcendence and the wholesale reformulation of traditional Christian doctrine (Schmucker). Many contemporary Christians accept the second pattern in some form, including varieties of old-Earth creationism directly descended from classical concordism. In Ramm's day many still held to the gap theory, but lately this view has become almost extinct, partly owing to strong attacks

---

The American Institute of Sacred Literature, 1926). In the rest of this paragraph I quote from pp. 20-22.

on its exegetical assumptions by those committed to scientific creationism.[51] The day-age theory and other types of what Ramm called "progressive creationism" have also been vilified because, as old-Earth approaches, they require the acceptance of death before the fall, which scientific creationists see as a fatal objection. Indeed modern creationists often follow John C. Whitcomb, Jr., author with Henry Morris of *The Genesis Flood* (1961), in rejecting the whole concordist approach, which he calls "the double-revelation theory," because it "fails to give due recognition to the tremendous limitations which inhibit the scientific method when applied to the study of origins."[52] Since the early 1990s, however, a third type of antievolutionism called "intelligent design theory" has developed a strong following, partly because its adherents typically refuse to discuss divisive issues such as the age of the earth, concentrating instead on the inadequacy of evolution to explain the origin of life, the origin of the "irreducible complexity" exhibited by living things, and (to a lesser extent) the geologically sudden appearance of many new animal forms at certain points in Earth history, such as the Cambrian explosion.

Opponents of creationism and intelligent design theory include a good number of contemporary evangelical scientists and theologians, some of whom have written essays for this volume. Although they often employ the classic notion of two books with one author and agree that the two books do not conflict, they do not believe that the two books tell the same story in different languages. Instead, like Galileo, they view the Bible as a theological text that cannot be brought into scientific discussions at the level of basic facts and theories; and like Gray, they believe that the essential truths of Christian theology — among them the incarnation, the Trinity, and the resurrection — are articles of faith that cannot be proved or disproved by science. They see the role of Scripture, for science, to be that of informing us about foundational assumptions about the world, including assumptions relative to our ability as humans to comprehend the creation placed before us and assumptions about our purpose within the creation as creatures made in the image of God. At the same time, many of these thinkers believe that some traditional doctrines may need to be understood differently in light of modern science — but they reject the excesses of

51. According to Christian Answers (http://christiananswers.net/q-aig/aig-c003.html), the gap theory "undermines the gospel as it allows for death, bloodshed, disease, and suffering before Adam's sin."

52. John C. Whitcomb, Jr., *The Origin of the Solar System* (Phillipsburg, N.J.: Presbyterian and Reformed, 1963), p. 9. The sole purpose of this booklet is to defend the plenary verbal inspiration of the Bible, which Whitcomb believes has been undermined by concordism. Ironically, one of Whitcomb's proof texts is Matt. 22:29, the same passage Bacon used for the opposite purpose. It is not evident that Whitcomb is aware of this.

those who, like Schmucker, would have us deny divine transcendence and all but obliterate the crucial distinction between God and the world, Creator and creatures.[53]

This is not a simple task, either for the writer or for the reader, but it is a task whose time is long overdue. The "noble" tradition of the 19th century has in the two generations since Ramm undergone a revival, and evangelical scholars who accept the authority of Scripture and the truth of modern science are once again thinking creatively and faithfully about the relationship between the two great books of God.

---

53. John Polkinghorne is an outstanding contemporary example of a first-rank Christian scientist who is not afraid to grapple with the hard questions arising out of modern science, yet within a clearly articulated, orthodox understanding of the nature of God and the nature of humanity. See especially *The Faith of a Physicist: Reflections of a Bottom-Up Thinker* (Princeton: Princeton University Press, 1994), in the form of a commentary on the Nicene Creed. I have commented on his views more fully in "Appreciating a Scientist-Theologian: Some Remarks on the Work of John Polkinghorne," *Zygon* 35 (2000): 971-76.

Worshipping the God of Wisdom and Mystery

EDWARD B. DAVIS

Scripture: Job 38

The deep mysteries surrounding the creation of the earth and the creatures that dwell upon it have long captured our imagination. When God demanded Job to answer what no one could answer, when God challenged a creature to tell what only the creator could know, God was effectively pulling rank on all of us. Through the divine gift of reason, applied to the creation, our knowledge of the processes used to create the heavens and the earth has increased remarkably since the time of Job; we have entered into the springs of the sea, seen the treasures of the hail, parted the light, learned the ordinances of the heaven, and numbered the clouds. Yet we are still very much in Job's position: who among us can stay the seas, open the gates of death, or loose the bands of Orion? The more we know, the more we realize how much we do not know.

At the same time, the more we know, the more we see the unfolding of great wisdom, wisdom going back before the foundations of the world. We can proclaim with Edward Hitchcock:

> No one can examine existing nature without being convinced that all its parts and operations belong to one great system. Geology makes other economies of wide extent to pass before us, opening a vista indefinitely backward into the hoary past; and it is gratifying to witness that same unity of design pervading all preceding periods of the world's history, linking the whole into one mighty scheme, worthy its infinite Contriver.
>
> How much, also, does this science enlarge our conceptions of the plans and operations of Jehovah! We had been accustomed to limit our views of the creative agency of God to the few thousand years of man's existence, and to anticipate the destruction of the material universe in a few thousand

years more. But geology makes the period of man's existence on the globe only one short link of a chain of revolutions which preceded his existence, and which reaches forward immeasurably far into the future. We see the same matter in the hands of infinite wisdom, and by means of the great conservative principles of chemical change, passing through a multitude of stupendous revolutions, sustaining countless and varied forms of organic life, and presenting an almost illimitable panorama of the plans of an infinite God.

The Religion of Geology and Its Connected Sciences
(Boston: Phillips, Sampson, and Company, 1851), pp. 482-83

View of the Glacier of Viesh
From Edward Hitchcock, *Elementary Geology*, 3rd ed. (New York, 1842), p. 166.

4 Charles Hodge and B. B. Warfield on Science, the Bible, Evolution, and Darwinism

MARK A. NOLL AND DAVID LIVINGSTONE

Controversies over evolution excite every bit as much passion in the early 21st century as they have ever done. Christian believers who seek humbly to understand the means by which God directs the natural world as well as honest scientists who seek to deal responsibly with what their research reveals are regularly shouted aside by culture warriors heavily invested in the supposed struggle between science and religion. Truth is usually the loser; populist politicking too often drives out patient responsible science.[1]

Two of the great theologians in American Christian history sought a better way. Charles Hodge (1797-1878) and Benjamin Warfield (1851-1921) were the most influential theologians at Princeton Theological Seminary during the first century of that institution's existence. During their tenure, Princeton was widely regarded as the nation's center of Presbyterian intellectual life, and Presbyterians were properly regarded as among the country's leading intellectuals.[2]

---

1. This chapter is adapted and abridged from the Introductions to two books edited by Mark A. Noll and David N. Livingstone: Charles Hodge, *What Is Darwinism? and Other Writings on Science & Religion* (Grand Rapids: Baker, 1994), and *B. B. Warfield's Writings on Evolution, Scripture, and Science* (Grand Rapids: Baker, 2000), both of which contain extensive documentation and bibliography. It draws also on David N. Livingstone and Mark A. Noll, "B. B. Warfield (1851-1921): A Biblical Inerrantist as Evolutionist," *Isis* 91 (2000): 283-304. Mark Noll is solely responsible for the presentation of material here. For wider background on the subject, see David N. Livingstone, *Darwin's Forgotten Defenders: The Encounter Between Evangelical Theology and Evolutionary Thought* (Grand Rapids: Eerdmans; Edinburgh: Scottish Academic Press, 1987); Mark A. Noll, ed., *The Princeton Theology, 1812-1921*, rev. ed. (Grand Rapids: Baker, 2001); and David N. Livingstone, D. G. Hart, and Mark A. Noll, eds., *Evangelical Encounters with Science* (New York: Oxford University Press, 1999). An earlier version of this essay appeared in *Modern Reformation* (May-June 1998): 18-22, 45-46.

2. The best general introduction to the subject of science at the Princeton of Hodge and

61

Hodge was best known in his day as a proponent of classically orthodox Reformed theology. Against several forms of more modern American Christianity, he was a doughty defender of traditional Reformation theology: that all humans were infected by Adam's original sin, that the imputation of Christ's righteousness was the source of salvation, and that redemption came first from God acting upon the believer rather than the reverse. Hodge's widely distributed writings were often surprisingly moderate in their charity to other traditional forms of Christian faith, but there was never any doubting his generally conservative stance.[3] Warfield was regarded by almost all observers, including himself, as carrying on Hodge's legacy. The battles of his day were somewhat different, but the positions he took were very much in line with what Hodge had tried to do in defending the best of the inherited faith. Warfield, thus, argued on behalf of biblical inerrancy, contended for the centrality of God's work (instead of human effort) as the key to salvation, and resisted innovations in thought (like theological modernism) as well as practice (like pentecostal healing), which he regarded as contrary to the Scriptures.[4] Hodge and Warfield, in other words, were resolutely orthodox figures.

Among their many interests, both also wrote learnedly about the most vexing theological issues raised by theories of evolution in their day. The specific assertions that Hodge and Warfield made about science are still worthy of serious consideration today. Even more, however, *the way* in which they wrote about such issues — with patient analysis and unhesitating confidence in both science and Scripture — offers modern believers a better approach than extremist, anti-intellectual, or paranoid combat against the scientific establishment. At the same time, they also offer scientific despisers of traditional biblical faith consequential examples of a responsible respect for science arising directly from Christian belief.

Hodge, Warfield, and most of their colleagues at Princeton shared a common attitude toward science in relation to theology. Their steady goal was to preserve the harmony of truth. Hodge and Warfield refused to countenance any permanent antagonism between the two realms of knowledge: what humans, by God's grace, could discover about the natural world (which owed its origin

Warfield is Bradley John Gundlach, "The Evolution Question at Princeton, 1845-1929," Ph.D. dissertation, University of Rochester, 1995.

3. See, for example, Charles Hodge, *A Commentary on the Epistle to the Romans* (Philadelphia: Griff & Elliot, 1835); idem, *The Way of Life* (Philadelphia: American Sunday School Union, 1841); idem, *Systematic Theology*, 3 vols. (New York: Charles Scribner's Sons, 1871-72).

4. See, for example, B. B. Warfield, *Counterfeit Miracles* (New York: Scribner, 1918); idem, *The Works of B. B. Warfield*, 10 vols. (New York: Oxford University Press, 1932); idem, *The Inspiration and Authority of the Bible* (Philadelphia: Presbyterian and Reformed, 1948).

to God), and what they could learn, again by grace, about the character and acts of God from special revelation in the Bible.

Their common mentality was that of scholars. Hodge and Warfield were alike committed to thorough reasoning. They thought it was a Christian duty to use their minds fully to understand the world. They did not set reasoning about the physical world and interpretations of divine revelation in opposition, but rather held that properly qualified deliverances of the human intellect and properly understood conclusions from Scripture were complementary. As a consequence, they were patient in unpacking detailed arguments in theology as well as in philosophy, and they abhorred merely rhetorical responses to complicated intellectual problems.

Hodge and Warfield also held common intellectual convictions. Theologically, they were Calvinists who maintained traditional Reformed convictions about most subjects, including nature. Specifically, they held that the world owed both its origin and its ongoing operation to the direct activity of God. They believed that God was responsible for the orderliness of natural processes, that the human ability to discern this order in nature was a gift from God, and that investigations of nature testified to the work of a purposeful designer. They also felt that Scripture provided reliable general information about the physical world.

Philosophically, the Princeton theologians were committed to the principles of common-sense reasoning as these principles had been imported to North America in the 18th century by Scotsmen like John Witherspoon (president of Princeton College from 1768 to 1794) and then developed by a host of American commentators. Their common-sense philosophy featured trust in ordinary human intuitions against the skeptical speculations of philosophers like David Hume. Proponents of this philosophy drew on sophisticated arguments by Scots like Thomas Reid and popularizations of those views in works like the *Encyclopaedia Britannica* as edited by Reid's follower, Dugald Stewart. With such support, Americans easily turned aside doubts about the reality of the self and the reality of normal cause-and-effect connections. As testified by the opening discussion of method in Hodge's *Systematic Theology,* the Princeton theologians shared at least some of the American enthusiasm for Sir Isaac Newton, as the doyen of modern science, and Sir Francis Bacon, as the most famous early promoter of an epistemology of induction. The Princetonians' Calvinistic convictions about the debilitating character of sinfulness did not always fit smoothly with their common-sense philosophy. Yet that philosophy was common intellectual coinage in 19th-century America, and they were among the American intellectuals who put it most skillfully to use.

In many ways, the Princetonians' theology of nature and their philosophy of common sense were typical of most American Christians during the 19th and 20th centuries. But unlike at least some other theological conservatives, they also held that Scripture did not need to be interpreted literally when it referred to nature. Perhaps even more untypically, they held that the findings of science should be enlisted to help discover proper interpretations of Scripture.

The Princeton theologians were interested in science for several interrelated reasons. First was confessional. As Calvinists, they believed the physical world was an arena in which God manifested his power and glory. Scientific research, therefore, was a way of finding out more about the world God had made, but also about the God who had made the world. Second was apologetic. The Princeton theologians knew that in the wake of Newton and the Mechanical Philosophy, science was being increasingly used to attack traditional Christian faith. If others used science to discredit Christianity, it was the responsibility of mature believers to show the error of such abuse. Third was social and ideological. They thought that Christian appropriation of science was critical for the health of civilization in America. If science (or any other false source of ultimate value) undercut faith in God, evil would inevitably proliferate, public virtue would retreat, and civilization would be imperiled.

Finally, such views about relationships among science, theology, and civil society also implied much about the Princeton theologians' own role. Hodge, Warfield, and their colleagues were remarkably pious people; personal testimonies abound to their unusual humility. At the same time, they also possessed an extraordinarily lofty conception of their vocation. They were guardians not just of theology, and not only of relationships between science and theology, but of Truth and of Civilization. Part of their concern for the spread of sub- or anti-Christian uses of science was, thus, concern about themselves. If scientists with no concern for the theological traditions they defended succeeded in becoming public arbiters of the culture's most influential questions, it was obvious that the theologians would also be displaced from their positions of cultural authority.

Science in general, therefore, was important to Hodge and Warfield both because of what they believed and because of who they were. Especially as the pace of scientific discovery quickened in the 19th century, and as alternatives to Christian appropriations of scientific knowledge grew more forceful, their concern deepened.

Alike as they were on many matters, Hodge and Warfield did differ — or at least appeared to differ — on whether evolution was acceptable to Christianity. Hodge, who is best known for his short book, *What Is Darwinism?* (1874), but who also wrote much else on science, did not think Darwinism was compatible with the faith. For his part, Warfield over a thirty-year period published

at least forty articles and reviews, some of them substantial, on questions related to evolution. Throughout most of his career, he held that evolution might
be compatible with the Christian faith. Despite this apparent difference, however, to understand the way each theologian approached his work is to see the
substantial continuity of their convictions.

*   *   *

Charles Hodge came to write about Darwin after a lifetime of serious attention
to scientific issues. That interest was partly a familial legacy. Both his father and
his brother were Philadelphia physicians, and Hodge himself attended medical
lectures during several periods of his life, including the trip he took to Europe
as a young theological professor in 1826-28.

Hodge's interests in scientific matters led to a long-time friendship with
Joseph Henry, a professor of science at Princeton College who later was the in-
augural director of the Smithsonian Institution. (Henry, who played a leading
role in developing the physics of electromagnetism, also served several years as
a trustee of Princeton Seminary and was a serious Presbyterian layman.)
Hodge recruited Henry to write for the *Princeton Review*,[5] he included Henry
in the informal meetings where the editorial business of the *Review* was carried out, he worked hard to keep Henry at Princeton when other institutions
tried to lure him away, and he took special delight when Henry was introduced
to the Presbyterian General Assembly in 1843 as a man who carried out scientific duties with a due sense of piety.[6] During the period when Hodge's "rheu-
matic" leg gave him the most difficulty, he even applied electricity to the af-
flicted limb from a machine that Henry had invented. Henry was not
altogether pleased with this experiment, which in fact did not relieve Hodge's
condition, but it does indicate something of the relationship the two enjoyed.[7]
For modern purposes, the Hodge-Henry friendship is significant for its ability
to transcend differences of scientific opinion. Henry, after initially doubting
the compatibility between any form of evolution and traditional Christianity,
eventually came reluctantly to accept a Christianized form of evolution.[8] But

5. For Hodge's appreciation of Henry, see "Joseph Henry," in *Biblical Repertory and Princeton Review: Index Volume from 1825 to 1868* (Philadelphia: Peter Walker, 1870-71), pp. 194-200.

6. A. A. Hodge, *The Life of Charles Hodge* (New York: Charles Scribner's Sons, 1880), p. 239; and *The Papers of Joseph Henry*, ed. Nathan Reingold (Washington: Smithsonian Institution Press, 1985), 2:426; 5:42, 159n.4, 264-65, 353.

7. *Papers of Joseph Henry*, 2:90n., 240-42, 266-67.

8. See Ronald Numbers, *The Creationists* (New York: Knopf, 1992), p. 11.

even though Hodge could not agree, he remained on very cordial terms with his scientific friend.

In addition to his avocational scientific interests, Hodge, at least from the late 1840s, regularly lectured and wrote on issues concerning the relationship of science and Scripture.[9] A letter to the *New York Observer* in March 1863 showed clearly how Hodge felt science and theology should interact.

In this letter, he first affirmed that the Bible could "teach no error" on anything that it touched. But then he hastened to say that the Princeton theologians had always held, "in common with the whole Church, that this infallible Bible must be interpreted by science." True to form, Hodge took pains to spell out what he meant by "science": "ascertained truths concerning the facts and laws of nature." Yet once having made a careful definition, Hodge forcefully affirmed the hermeneutical value of scientific knowledge: "The proposition that the Bible must be interpreted by science is all but self-evident. Nature is as truly a revelation of God as the Bible, and we only interpret the Word of God by the Word of God when we interpret the Bible by science." Hodge then provided an example of what he meant: "For five thousand years the Church understood the Bible to teach that the earth stood still in space, and that the sun and stars revolved around it. Science has demonstrated that this is not true. Shall we go on to interpret the Bible so as to make it teach the falsehood that the sun moves round the earth, or shall we interpret it by science and make the two harmonize?" Hodge closed with a word in the other direction: just as legitimate science must be used to interpret Scripture, so must Scripture be allowed to shape the interpretation of science. In his words, Hodge wanted to avoid both sides of "a two-fold evil." One evil was the overwillingness "to adopt the opinions and theories of scientific men, and to adopt forced and unnatural interpretations of the Bible, to bring it to accord with those opinions." The opposite evil was to "not only refuse to admit the opinions of men, but science itself, to have any voice in the interpretation of Scripture."[10]

The strategy Hodge outlined in 1863 was the strategy he followed eleven years later in *What Is Darwinism?* In the pages of this book Hodge took great pains to define the meaning of "Darwinism" and to distinguish what might possibly be real science from invalid speculation. As he saw it, "Darwinism" entailed three assertions:

---

9. For example, the lecture given in January 1849, with the title, "The Mosaic Account of Creation," Charles Hodge Papers, archives, Speer Library, Princeton Theological Seminary.

10. Hodge to the *New York Observer*, in Noll and Livingstone, eds., Charles Hodge, *What Is Darwinism?* pp. 53-56.

(1) that species undergo evolutionary development over time;

(2) that natural selection (defined as variety, overproduction, and survival of the fittest) explains important aspects of those changes; and

(3) that these changes are ateleological, or entirely the result of random occurrences.

As it happens, Hodge himself had doubts about the compatibility of the first two assertions with biblical Christianity, but he also acknowledged that other orthodox Christians did not. As an example of a scientist who did not, Hodge mentioned several times in his essay Asa Gray, an orthodox Congregationalist who taught at Harvard and who was the most important promoter of Darwin's writings in America. Almost certainly, Hodge also had in mind the president of Princeton College, James McCosh, who was also a reconciler of Christianity and evolution.

It was, however, the third assertion that meant the most to Hodge: "by far the most important and only distinctive element of his theory, that this natural selection is without design, being conducted by unintelligent physical causes." In pursuit of clarity, Hodge repeated that "It is . . . neither evolution nor natural selection which gives Darwinism its peculiar character and importance. It is that Darwin rejects all teleology or the doctrine of final causes." This definition led to Hodge's famous condemnation at the end of the book: "We have thus arrived at the answer to our question, What is Darwinism? It is Atheism. This does not mean, as before said, that Mr. Darwin himself and all who adopt his views are atheists; but it means that his theory is atheistic, that the exclusion of design from nature is, as Dr. Gray says, tantamount to atheism."[11]

*   *   *

Hodge's careful distinction about what he denounced as the atheism of Darwinism paves the way for understanding why B. B. Warfield's more accommodating attitude to evolution was, in fact, largely compatible with that of his revered teacher and predecessor. Warfield's publications on evolution and related subjects included several kinds of writing: major essays devoted to Darwin's biography ("Charles Darwin's Religious Life" in 1888 and "Darwin's Arguments Against Christianity" the next year); several substantial articles directly on evolution or related scientific issues ("The Present Day Conception of Evolution" in 1895, "Creation Versus Evolution" in 1901, "On the Antiquity and Unity of the Human Race" in 1911, and "Calvin's Doctrine of Creation" in 1915); and many

11. Noll and Livingstone, *What Is Darwinism?* pp. 89, 92, 156-57.

reviews, some of them mini-essays in their own right (among the most important of these were reviews of books by James McCosh in 1888, by J. W. Dawson in 1891, by Otto Pfleiderer in 1901, by James Orr in 1906, and by Vernon Kellogg in 1908).

In these writings, Warfield repeatedly insisted on the distinction between Darwin as a person, Darwinism as a cosmological theory, and evolution as a series of explanations about natural development. Of key importance for Warfield was his willingness throughout a long career to accept the possibility (or even the probability) of evolution, yet while also denying Darwinism.

Warfield's strongest assertion of evolution was theological and came in a lengthy paper on Calvin's view of creation from 1915. Warfield ascribed to Calvin what was doubtless his own view as well: "[A]ll that has come into being since [the original creation of the world stuff] — except the souls of men alone — has arisen as a modification of this original world-stuff by means of the interaction of its intrinsic forces. . . . [These modifications] find their account proximately in 'secondary causes'; and this is not only evolutionism but pure evolutionism."[12] To grasp the underlying harmony between this statement and Hodge's earlier equation of Darwinism with atheism, it is necessary to pay strict attention to the distinctions that Hodge cautiously advanced in his 1874 book and that Warfield developed much more boldly in most of his writings on the subject.

As a way of positioning Warfield properly on these subjects it is vital to stress a conjunction of his convictions that has been much less common since his day. Warfield, in short, was both the ablest modern defender of the theologically conservative belief in the inerrancy of the Bible and an evolutionist.

During the late 19th century when critical views of Scripture came to prevail in American universities, Warfield was more responsible than any other American for refurbishing the conviction that the Bible communicates revelation from God entirely without error. Warfield's formulation of biblical inerrancy, in fact, has even been a theological mainstay for recent "creationist" convictions about the origin of the earth.[13] Yet Warfield was also a cautious, discriminating, but entirely candid proponent of the possibility that evolution might offer the best way to understand the natural history of the earth and of humankind. On this score his views place him with more recent thinkers who maintain ancient trust in the Bible while affirming the modern scientific enter-

12. B. B. Warfield, "Calvin's Doctrine of the Creation," in *The Works of Benjamin B. Warfield*, vol. 5: *Calvin and Calvinism* (New York: Oxford University Press, 1931), pp. 304-5.

13. For the direct use of Warfield on the inerrancy of Scripture, see John C. Whitcomb, Jr., and Henry M. Morris, *The Genesis Flood: The Biblical Record and Its Scientific Implications* (Philadelphia: Presbyterian and Reformed, 1961), p. xx.

prise.[14] Warfield did not simply assert these two views randomly; he sustained them learnedly, as coordinate arguments. Accordingly, Warfield's convictions on theology and evolution are as interesting a commentary on our own era's intellectual warfare as they are illuminating for historical conjunctions in his age.

In the course of his career, both Warfield's positions and his vocabulary shifted on the question of evolution. But they shifted only within the constraints of a fairly narrow range. What remained constant was his adherence to a broad Calvinistic conception of the natural world — of a world that, even in its most physical aspects, reflected the wisdom and glory of God — and his commitment to the goal of harmonizing a sophisticated conservative theology and the most securely verified conclusions of modern science. Another way of describing the constancy of his position is to say that while Warfield consistently rejected materialist or ateleological explanations for natural phenomena (explanations that he usually associated with "Darwinism"), Warfield just as consistently entertained the possibility that other kinds of evolutionary explanations, which avoided Darwin's rejection of design, could satisfactorily explain the physical world.

In several of his writings, Warfield worked carefully to distinguish three ways in which God worked in and through the physical world. The most important thing about these three ways is that Warfield felt each of them was compatible with the theology he found in an inerrant Bible, if each was applied properly to natural history and to the history of salvation. "Evolution" meant developments arising out of forces that God had placed inside matter at the original creation of the world stuff, but that God also directed to predetermined ends by his providential superintendence of the world. At least in writ-

---

14. For example, Bernard Ramm, *The Christian View of Science and Scripture* (Grand Rapids: Eerdmans, 1954); Russell L. Mixter, ed., *Evolution and Christian Thought Today* (Grand Rapids: Eerdmans, 1959); D. C. Spanner, *Creation and Evolution: Some Preliminary Considerations* (London: Falcon Books, 1966); Malcolm A. Jeeves, ed., *The Scientific Enterprise and Christian Faith* (Downers Grove, Ill.: InterVarsity Press, 1969); Donald M. MacKay, *The Clockwork Image: A Christian Perspective on Science* (Downers Grove, Ill.: InterVarsity Press, 1974); Thomas F. Torrance, *Christian Theology and Scientific Culture* (New York: Oxford University Press, 1981); Davis A. Young, *Christianity and the Age of the Earth* (Grand Rapids: Zondervan, 1982); Charles E. Hummel, *The Galileo Connection: Resolving Conflicts Between Science and the Bible* (Downers Grove, Ill.: InterVarsity Press, 1986); J. C. Polkinghorne, *One World: The Interaction of Science and Theology* (Princeton: Princeton University Press, 1986); Howard J. Van Till, *The Fourth Day: What the Bible and the Heavens Are Telling Us about the Creation* (Grand Rapids: Eerdmans, 1986); John Houghton, *Does God Play Dice? A Look at the Story of the Universe* (Leicester, England: InterVarsity Press, 1988); Philip Duce, *Reading the Mind of God: Interpretation in Science and Theology* (Leicester, England: Apollos, 1998); and Alister McGrath, *The Foundations of Dialogue in Science and Religion* (Oxford: Blackwell, 1998).

ings toward the end of his life, Warfield held that evolution in this sense was fully compatible with biblical understandings of the production of the human body. "Mediate creation" meant the action of God upon matter to bring something new into existence that could not have been produced by forces or energy latent in matter itself. He does not apply the notion of "mediate creation" directly in his last, most mature writings on evolution, but it may be that he expounded the concept as much to deal with miracles or other biblical events as for developments in the natural world.[15] The last means of God's action was "creation *ex nihilo*," which Warfield consistently maintained was the way that God made the original stuff of the world. It also seems that, in his 1915 article on Calvin, when he considered the soul of every human, Warfield held that God created each soul directly *ex nihilo*.

Throughout Warfield's career, the concept of *concursus* was especially important for both theology and science. By this term he meant the coexistence of two usually contrary conditions or realities. In Warfield's view, just as the authors of Scripture were completely human in writing the Bible, even as they enjoyed the full inspiration of the Holy Spirit, so too could all living creatures develop fully (with the exception of the original creation and the human soul) through "natural" means. The key for Warfield was a doctrine of providence that saw God working in and with, instead of as a replacement for, the processes of nature. Late in his career, this stance also grounded Warfield's opposition to "faith healing." In his eyes, physical healing through medicine and the agency of physicians was as much a result of God's action (if through secondary causes) as the cures claimed as a direct result of divine intervention.[16] For his views on evolution, *concursus* was as important, and as fruitful, as it was for his theology as a whole. It was a principle he felt the Scriptures offered to enable humans both to approach the world fearlessly and to do so for the greater glory of God.

Warfield's writings on evolution, the last of which appeared in the year of his death, 1921, cannot, of course, pronounce definitively on theological-scientific questions at the start of the 21st century. They can, however, show that sophisticated theology, nuanced argument, and careful sifting of scientific research are able to produce a much more satisfactory working relationship between science and theology than the heated strife that has dominated public debate on this subject since the time of Warfield's passing.

15. Warfield deploys a similar vocabulary in a discussion of miracles that he published at about the same time; see "The Question of Miracles," in *The Bible Student* (March-June 1903), as reprinted in *The Shorter Writings of Benjamin B. Warfield*, vol. 2, ed. John E. Meeter (Nutley, N.J.: Presbyterian and Reformed, 1973), pp. 167-204.

16. See Warfield, *Counterfeit Miracles*.

*   *   *

The commitment of Warfield and Hodge to solid empirical science and to the *concursus* of divine and natural action gave them extraordinary balance in sifting the difficult questions of science and faith that beset their era. One of the reasons that many in subsequent decades have failed to retain their equipoise on this subject may be that they have abandoned one or both of these commitments.

5 ## Does Science Exclude God?
Natural Law, Chance, Miracles,
and Scientific Practice

LOREN HAARSMA

S cripture teaches us some theological truths about sparrows, apples, planets, and stars. Jesus taught that a sparrow cannot fall to the ground apart from God's will.[1] God's will also governs apples falling from trees and planets orbiting a star. As the prophet Isaiah wrote, "Lift your eyes and look to the heavens: Who created all these? He who brings out the starry host one by one, and calls them each by name. Because of his great power and mighty strength, not one of them is missing."[2]

We also know some scientific truths about sparrows, apples, planets, and stars. Sir Isaac Newton discovered something astonishing. The motion of falling apples and the motion of orbiting planets — two very different sorts of objects — can be described by the same set of simple equations. Scientifically, we say that falling apples and orbiting planets are "governed" by and "obey" Newton's Laws of Motion and the Law of Universal Gravitational Attraction.

Natural Laws Do Not "Govern" the Universe

The Bible speaks of God's governance. Modern science speaks about "natural laws." Is there a conflict here? Some people would say "yes." Science is so successful at describing the motion of apples, planets, and stars that some people conclude that no further explanation is needed. If science can explain something by natural laws, they believe, then there is no longer a need for God to do anything. Cosmologist Stephen Hawking accurately reports this common belief

---

1. Matt. 10:29.

2. Isa. 40:26, *The Bible, New International Version* (New York: International Bible Society, 1973).

when he writes, "These laws may have originally been decreed by God, but it appears that he has since left the universe to evolve according to them and does not now intervene in it."[3]

This may be a commonly held picture of how God interacts (or doesn't interact) with the universe, but it is not the biblical picture. The Bible proclaims that God is equally sovereign over all events, ordinary or extraordinary, natural or supernatural. God didn't create the universe like a watch to be wound up, started, and then let go, only intervening occasionally. The Bible proclaims that the universe continues to exist and behaves in an orderly fashion only because of God's continual sustaining action. As it says in Psalm 104:

> The moon marks off the seasons,
>   and the sun knows when to go down.
> You bring darkness, it becomes night,
>   and all the beasts of the forest prowl.
> The lions roar for their prey
>   and seek their food from God.
> The sun rises, and they steal away;
>   they return and lie down in their dens.
> Then man goes out to his work,
>   to his labor until evening.
> How many are your works, O Lord!
>   In wisdom you made them all;
>   the earth is full of your creatures.[4]

Note the parallel levels of description in that passage. The sun goes down (a natural event), and God brings night (divine action). The lions hunt prey (a natural event), and they seek their food from God (divine providence). The biblical perspective is clear. If something happens "naturally," God is still in charge. This psalm was written more than two thousand years before modern science existed, and so the psalmist probably wasn't thinking in terms of "natural laws." However, the psalmist certainly knew the difference between ordinary natural events and extraordinary events. The psalms are filled with praise to God for the times in Israel's history when God did something unusual, something miraculous. So the psalmist undoubtedly understood that there is a difference between a supernatural miracle and an ordinary event like the sun going down or a lion hunting. Yet the psalmist insisted that God was in charge of

---

3. Stephen Hawking, *A Brief History of Time* (New York: Bantam Books, 1988), p. 122.
4. Ps. 104:19-24, New International Version

natural events every bit as much as God was in charge of supernatural events. In fact, God is to be praised and worshipped for those natural events.

With a modern scientific understanding of natural laws, neuroscientist Donald MacKay described the biblical view this way: "The continuing existence of our world is not something to be taken for granted. Rather it hangs moment by moment on the continuance of the upholding word of power of its creator."[5]

Scientists talk about natural laws "governing" the universe. Christians who are scientists occasionally use that language as well. From a biblical perspective, however, it is incorrect to say that natural laws "govern." God governs. God created natural laws, and God usually governs creation through the natural laws he designed and created.[6] God can supersede the ordinary functioning of natural laws any time he chooses, but most of the time God chooses to work in consistent ways through those natural laws. As we study God's creation scientifically, we build mathematical models and descriptions of those natural laws which God created and uses. The rationality and regularity of these laws should be seen as a gift without which we would not be able to understand our world.

All too often we forget these basic biblical truths when we talk about the history of stars or species. Science uses natural laws to describe the history of stars and species. New stars form by the gravitational collapse of interstellar clouds. One species can split into two species through mutation and natural se-

---

5. Donald MacKay, *The Open Mind and other essays* (Leicester, England: InterVarsity Press, 1988), p. 23.

6. There are at least two different ways for understanding the status of natural laws, both of which are within the tradition of Christian orthodoxy. One view: God prescriptively determines the activity of all material objects from moment to moment. Natural laws are formulas that merely describe the regularity with which God normally acts. Breaks in "natural laws" are instances where God acts, for particular reasons, in ways which are contrary to, or at least extremely improbable from the standpoint of, the regular patterns of God's governance. Breaks in natural laws are not a fundamentally different type of God's activity, but rather instances where God, because of special circumstances, prescribes activity that is unexpected (from our perspective). A second view: God has gifted his creation and everything in it with certain creaturely capacities. These capacities are designed to interact with each other in regular fashions that we call natural laws. They do not operate independently of God but are dependent upon God for their creation, design, and continued existence. God can interact with his creation through these creaturely capacities within the uncertainty and flexibility of the system (e.g., flexibility evident in quantum and/or "chaotic" systems). God can also interact with his creation through acts of radical reorganization. Some miracles are breaks in natural laws (or very improbable workings through natural laws) that have special personal and/or spiritual significance. Both of these views about the status of natural laws have proponents among Christian scientists. It is worth being aware of both of these views; however, for the purposes of this chapter and this book, it is not worth debating their differences and relative merits.

lection. Does a successful scientific description, in terms of natural laws, mean that God was not involved in these processes — at least not in any significant or creative way? Certainly not. God created those natural laws in the first place. God sustains them and is sovereign over them each and every moment. The biblical view is not that God is absent from events that happen by "natural laws"; rather, natural laws describe how God typically governs his creation.

"Chance" Is Not an Alternative Explanation to God

Some people do use the word "chance" as an alternative explanation to God. When they say that something happened by "chance," they believe that it had no purpose, no significance of any kind, nothing guiding it, nothing that cares about the final results.

This is not the scientific meaning of the word "chance," although some scientists do use the word "chance" this way in their popular writings. Noting the role played by random events in evolutionary theory, George G. Simpson has written, "Man is the result of a purposeless and natural process that did not have him in mind."[7] Similarly, Douglas Futuyma has written, "Some shrink from the conclusion that the human species was not designed, has no purpose, and is the product of mere mechanical mechanisms — but this seems to be the message of evolution."[8] When scientists use the concept of chance in this way, they are adding philosophical overtones that go way beyond the scientific meaning.

When scientists use the concept of chance scientifically, they mean simply this: They could not completely predict the final state of a system based on their knowledge of earlier states. In a scientific theory, the term "chance" is not a statement about causation (or lack of causation); rather, it is a statement about predictability.

One of the surprises of 20th-century physics was the Heisenberg Uncertainty Principle. In classical physics, it is (in principle) possible to know with absolute precision every physical variable (position, velocity, energy, etc.) of any particle. From quantum mechanics we have learned that, in fact, it is impossible to measure every physical variable of a particle with complete accuracy. Even with complete knowledge of the initial conditions of a system, it is

7. George G. Simpson, *The Meaning of Evolution* (New Haven: Yale University Press, 1967).

8. Douglas Futuyma, *Science on Trial: The Case for Evolution* (New York: Pantheon, 1983), pp. 12-13.

impossible to predict the exact outcome of some measurements. Some scientific measurements have results that — not just in practice, but in principle — are randomly determined. Randomness is built into the very mathematical formalism of the theory.

Scientists often use the term "chance" outside of quantum mechanics, but in a different way. In classical mechanics, if a system is sufficiently complicated (a "chaotic" system) it is impossible to have sufficiently complete knowledge of its initial conditions. The final state of the system depends so sensitively upon the initial conditions that, in practice, it is impossible to predict exactly what will happen. In these systems, based upon experience and certain general considerations, various outcomes can be assigned probabilities of occurring, but the particular outcome cannot be predicted. Some common examples of "chaotic" systems include throwing dice and predicting the weather. Biologists and medical professionals use the word "chance" this way. A doctor might tell you the chance that a disease will recur in a patient. In evolutionary biology, a "chance" event is simply an event that affects an organism's survival (e.g., a natural disaster) or genetic information (e.g., a mutation) but that was not caused by the organism itself and could not have been predicted. "Chance" in evolutionary biology or any other branch of science is a semiquantitative statement about our inability to precisely predict final outcomes.

The scientific use of the term "chance" is entirely compatible with a biblical picture of God's governance. Many Bible passages describe God working through apparently random events. "The lot is cast into the lap, but its every decision is from the Lord."[9] Centuries before modern science existed, people understood that some events are unpredictable. Biblical writers proclaimed God as sovereign over random events like casting lots. Biblical writers also proclaimed God's sovereignty over events that we now describe scientifically using probabilities (e.g., the weather). Scientific randomness poses no fundamental problem to a biblical understanding of God's providence. The fact that we cannot scientifically predict the outcome of an event doesn't mean that God cannot be involved in the event, giving it purpose and meaning. Quite the opposite. According to the Bible, chance events are another means by which God can govern.

An analogy or two might be helpful. A scientist has designed a computer simulation of leaves randomly falling off a tree. To anyone observing the simulation, the timing of the falling leaves appears random. However, this scientist can control her computer program to cause any one particular leaf to fall at a particular time and a particular place. The observer would be unable to predict

9. Prov. 16:33, New International Version.

this event or in most cases to observe any difference. In an analogous fashion, God could select the outcome of scientifically unpredictable events in order to achieve particular outcomes.[10] God could do this subtly, interacting with creation in ways that are significant but that we could not detect scientifically. God could also do this dramatically upon occasion, choosing an outcome that is scientifically possible but extremely improbable, something that might even appear miraculous to us.

Another way God might use random processes is to give the created world a bit of freedom. Through the laws of nature, God has given the material creation a range of possibilities to explore, and he gives his creation the freedom to explore that range. For an analogy, consider how some engineers and computer programmers are using "genetic algorithms" in their work. They design a computer program with a goal (e.g., to control a complex manufacturing process). Rather than specify all of the variables in that computer program, the scientists specify for each variable a range of values. The computer randomly selects the variables from the allowed ranges, then measures its own performance on how well it performs its given task. It then randomly alters one or more of the variables, performs the task again, and sees whether it did better or worse. In this way, after enough trials, the computer converges on a set of variables that are ideally suited to performing a particular task. Genetic algorithms in computer programs can also be used for artistic purposes. Some multivariable mathematical functions, when creatively displayed, make very beautiful pictures. An artist can allow the computer program to randomly change one variable, and then another, and another, allowing the computer to explore a wide range of possibilities, generating a whole series of beautiful and unique pictures.

The Bible teaches that God can precisely select the outcome of events that appear random to us. It is also possible that God gives his creation some freedom, through random processes, to explore the wide range of potentials he has given it. Either way, randomness within natural processes is not the absence of God. Rather, it is another vehicle for God's creativity and governance.

Science Is Not Intrinsically Atheistic

Not all scientists share a biblical view of nature. Scientists come from a variety of

---

10. Some Christian writers, such as Donald MacKay, have proposed that God might select the outcome of every apparently random event (e.g., every quantum mechanical measurement).

religious traditions. They can hold very different philosophical and religious views of what these things are that we call "natural laws" and "chance." Nevertheless — and here is something that troubles many people, Christians and non-Christians alike — scientists of many different religious beliefs typically do reach consensus on the same scientific theories and equations. How is it possible that scientists of very different religious worldviews can agree about natural science?

Scholars in the social sciences and humanities know from experience that one's religious beliefs can profoundly affect one's research. Religious beliefs affect how one searches for the truth, and what sorts of evidence and what sorts of answers one is willing to accept. Why is it, then, that in the natural sciences, scholars of many different religious beliefs usually agree about so much? While they might disagree about the philosophical and religious implications of their scientific work, they usually do agree about the scientific results themselves, and they usually agree upon the proper methods for obtaining those results. How is that possible?

One common answer to that question goes roughly as follows: "Science is methodologically naturalistic (or methodologically atheistic).[11] Scientific equations and theories don't refer to God or the supernatural. Therefore, scientific equations and theories are methodologically naturalistic. You don't have to be an atheist to do science. You may still believe that God exists; however, you must act 'as if God doesn't exist' whenever you are doing science."

Many atheists and agnostics do claim that science, by definition, is methodologically naturalistic. In fact, a number of Christians also describe science that way. The stress is on the word "methodological." Philosophical naturalism is a worldview that claims that supernatural entities do not exist. Methodological naturalism, by contrast, is a tool for conducting limited investigations and for discovering limited truths. Methodological naturalism is an acceptable tool for a Christian to use, the argument goes, so long as she remembers that the discoveries made by using this tool are only partial truths.

There is some merit to this answer. It is important to distinguish philosophical naturalism from methodological naturalism. However, this answer is also misleading in some important respects. In order to see how it is misleading, we should ask ourselves, "What must a scientist believe in order to do science? What are the fundamental philosophical beliefs that support scientific investigations of the natural world?"

11. The terms "methodological naturalism" and "methodological atheism" do not always mean the same thing. Sometimes the term "naturalism" simply refers to a systematic study of nature. Other times, the term "naturalism" refers to a philosophical belief that supernatural entities do not exist. In debates about biological evolution, the terms "methodological naturalism" and "methodological atheism" are often used interchangeably, both of them referring to the practice of acting as if supernatural entities do not exist (or at least have no influence on material entities).

Historians and philosophers of science have written entire books in answer to those questions. I will briefly list six points that I believe summarize their answers, acknowledging that this list is, necessarily, a simplification.

Philosophical beliefs that encourage scientific investigation:
1. Events in the natural world typically have (immediate) causes in the natural world. For example: if a tree falls and a sound is heard, then the falling tree in some way caused the sound. The sound was not caused by some "sound spirit" or other metaphysical entity.
2. A linear view of time. The universe is not an endless repeating circle, where every event occurs simply because we happen to be passing that particular point on the wheel of time.
3. These causes and effects in the natural world have some regularity across space and time.
4. These causes and effects can be — at least in part — rationally understood by us.
5. We cannot logically deduce, from first principles, nature's fundamental constituents and behaviors. We must use observations and experiments to augment our logic and intuition.
6. Studying nature in this way is a worthwhile use of time and talent.

Nearly all scientists today hold these beliefs. These beliefs are not scientific. Scientists assume these are true for philosophical and religious reasons. The success of science supports their validity. They are, nevertheless, philosophical statements that lie outside of science.

With the hindsight of science's success, these beliefs may seem obvious to us. Throughout most of human history, however, these beliefs were not widely held. Historically, how did they arise? Many ancient cultures held some of these beliefs, but not others. Most of the brilliant philosophers of ancient Greece, for example, disdained observations and experiments. They held beliefs about the natural world that relied heavily on logical deduction from what they thought were self-evident first principles, but were in fact incorrect.

These particular philosophical beliefs came together at the time of the scientific revolution. Why did the leaders of the scientific revolution hold these beliefs? Several historians of science have argued that they held these beliefs, at least in part, because they held biblical views of the natural world.[12]

12. R. Hooykaas, *Religion and the Rise of Modern Science* (Edinburgh: Scottish Academic Press, and London: Chatto & Windus, 1972).

Some biblical beliefs about God and nature:

1. Creation is not animistic. It is not filled with "gods" or "nature spirits."
2. Time is linear, not circular.
3. God is consistent, not capricious, in his governance of nature. Therefore, there could be regular patterns that we can discover.
4. We are made in God's image and we are made suitable for this world. Therefore, we have hope that we can understand at least some of God's creation through the gifts he has given us.
5. God was free to create as he wished. We are limited and fallen people. Therefore, our preconceptions about how the world should work may not be the same as God's. We must use observations and experiments to learn what God actually did.
6. Nature is God's creation, so it has value and is worth studying.

A biblical view of God and the natural world motivates the six philosophical beliefs listed earlier. A biblical view of God and nature offers us reasons to expect the scientific method to be successful. God can still supersede his ordinary governance via natural laws, but this happens only in exceptional circumstances when God has extraordinary reasons for doing something unexpected. Most of the time, God — the God described, praised, and worshipped in the Bible — works in consistent ways.

We should not claim that biblical beliefs about nature caused the scientific revolution. Historians and philosophers of science are still debating which ideological, social, political, historical, and other factors were most important in bringing about the scientific revolution. Nor should we claim that biblical beliefs compel one to adopt the scientific method. It's not that simple. Scholars are still debating which theological beliefs helped and which hindered the development of modern science. Neither atheists nor Christians should claim to "own" the scientific method.

Clearly, however, the practice of science does not require one to act "as if God does not exist." The claim that science is methodologically naturalistic is misleading. It implies that philosophical naturalism has some sort of ownership of the scientific method, or that the scientific method follows more naturally from philosophical naturalism than from other worldviews. It does not.[13]

13. With the success of modern science, it is tempting to think that atheism naturally and necessarily leads to the philosophical beliefs listed above. Not so. Those beliefs follow naturally from an atheism that is wedded to a mechanistic picture of nature. A mechanistic picture of nature, however, was not a common picture of nature before the rise of modern science. A mechanistic picture of nature is motivated by the success of science. Although some atheists had such

No single philosophical or religious worldview can claim primacy over the scientific method. The philosophical beliefs necessary to do science (such as the six listed above) are fairly limited. They are compatible with many (though not all) religious worldviews. People of different worldviews may disagree about why those philosophical beliefs are true. Atheists and Christians, for example, will give very different answers as to why those philosophical beliefs are true. However, by agreeing that they are, in fact, true, scientists of a wide variety of religious worldviews can work side-by-side and reach consensus on scientific questions.

When a Christian employs the scientific method to investigate nature, a biblical understanding of God and nature motivates her belief that she is using the right method. She is not acting "as if God doesn't exist." She is acting as if there is a God — not a capricious God, but the God of the Bible, who made an orderly world and who still governs it in an orderly fashion.

Overlapping Areas of Science: Theoretical, Experimental, Observational, and Historical

Scientific investigations take many forms. Investigations can be experimental or theoretical, interactive or observational, predictive or retrodictive. It is worth taking a little time to consider how different branches of science, and different styles of scientific investigation, mutually reinforce and correct each other. There are many possible ways to separate science into categories. Since this book is concerned with topics of cosmology, geology, and evolutionary biology, I find it helpful to separate scientific activity into these four overlapping areas: theoretical, experimental, observational, and historical.

"Experimental science" refers to empirical work, typically done in a laboratory, where an object or a system is studied in relative isolation from its environment. Various tools are used to probe the system, to act upon the system and measure how it reacts. These measurements are (ideally) reproducible. Examples of experimental science would include most modern branches of physics, chemistry and molecular biology, plus some other areas of biology.

"Theoretical science" works with experimental science to build empirical models and to postulate the form of natural laws. These theoretical models and laws are descriptions and generalizations of experimental results. They

---

a view of nature before the scientific revolution, it is hardly the case that an atheistic worldview, by itself, necessarily leads to such a view.

help scientists make predictions for the results of new experiments and observations.

"Observational science" is done on systems where we can observe behavior, but these systems cannot be isolated in a laboratory. Few if any tools exist to probe the system and measure how it responds. Experiments are very limited; for the most part we must rely on data that come to us as the system behaves in ways beyond our control. Examples of observational science include astrophysics, ecology, many areas of geology, and many areas of organismal and developmental biology. Observational science attempts to describe and model the observed behavior of the system using known natural mechanisms and laws. Experimental science provides observational science with improved understanding of natural mechanisms and laws, so that improved models can be constructed. Information also flows the other way. Frequently, observational science makes theoretical contributions that are only later supported by experiments in the lab.

"Historical science" is an extension of observational science. It attempts to reconstruct the physical history of a system by assuming, wherever possible, the regular and continuous operation of natural laws over time. Examples include cosmology, some areas of geology, paleontology, and evolutionary biology.

These areas of science overlap. Experimental and observational science blend into each other as the system under study becomes more complex and less controllable. Observational and historical science blend into each other because any study of the present behavior of a system necessarily depends upon inferences about its history, and vice versa. Experimental and historical science are often directly linked. Cosmologists reconstructing the history of stars and galaxies rely on experimental information from particle physics. Geologists perform experiments on rocks to determine their composition. Evolutionary biologists use genetic information gained in the lab. These different styles of scientific investigation reinforce and correct each other. Advances in experimental or observational science allow historical science to make increasingly detailed and predictive models. Historical science often makes theoretical contributions and predictions that are later supported by observation and experiment. By pursuing all of these areas at once, following leads from one branch of science to another, the scientific community makes progress — constructing increasingly accurate scientific explanations of the properties, processes, and developmental history of the natural world.

Miracles

The Bible teaches that God is sovereign over natural events, events that we can now describe scientifically. The Bible also talks about miracles. If we remember that God is equally sovereign over natural and supernatural events, we can stop worrying that science threatens the idea of miracles.

The word "miracle" has a number of meanings.[14] It does not automatically imply a violation of natural cause-and-effect. Many miracles in Scripture are given cause-and-effect explanations, or such explanations are at least plausible. However, when the idea of "miracle" is discussed in a science-and-religion context, usually people are thinking of an event that includes a supernatural break in ordinary chains of natural cause-and-effect.

If natural laws are the way God normally oversees his creation, then God can supersede that ordinary governance in special instances for a good reason. Human beings sometimes behave in unexpected ways for good reasons. You might know a friend very well, know how he typically behaves, know his habits to the point where you can accurately predict how he will act in most situations. Then one day, he does something totally unexpected. But if you investigate why he did something different that day, you'll find out that there were special circumstances — circumstances that you originally didn't understand. Given those special circumstances, you now understand that he actually had good reasons for doing that surprising thing on that particular day — reasons completely consistent with his character. In the Bible, that's often how miracles are depicted. God did something dramatically different, something unexpected based upon how God ordinarily governs creation, but entirely appropriate considering the special circumstances, and accompanied by a verbal explanation of what God was doing and why he was doing it.[15]

Science is an excellent tool for discovering the ordinary patterns of behavior of nature. Science is a poor tool for understanding the spiritual signifi-

---

14. In the Bible, miracles are performed in contexts where the spiritual message should have been clear to the observers. Miracles can be ordinary events with extraordinary timing (e.g., the famine which began and ended with the prophet Elijah's proclamations). Such miracles are not scientifically impossible or even improbable, but the timing was specially arranged by God and accompanied by a spoken revelation explaining the spiritual significance of the event. Miracles can also be highly improbable events with special timing (e.g., some miraculous cures of illnesses). Such miracles were not scientifically impossible, but they were improbable. Miracles can also be events that simply defy explanation on the basis of natural laws (e.g., Jesus' resurrection and postresurrection appearances).

15. This doesn't mean that every event in the Bible described as a miracle was a violation of natural laws; some of them appear to have been scientifically explainable events with extraordinary timing.

cance of an unexpected event. When the unexpected happens, or is reported to happen, the most that science can say is that the unexpected event was highly improbable or impossible given our current understanding of natural laws. But natural laws do not constrain God. It is God the Creator who constrains natural laws, not the other way around.[16]

Science and Supernatural Explanations

Given that God can supersede the ordinary operation of natural laws, how should we do science? Should we do science expecting to find, everywhere we look, evidence of such breaks in the natural chain of cause-and-effect? Or should we utterly exclude the possibility of such breaks when we study creation, always looking for explanations exclusively in terms of natural laws? A biblically informed view of God should warn us against either extreme. Ordinarily, God governs his creation in consistent ways. God's consistency gives us hope and confidence in our search for universal natural laws and applying those laws to most situations. But God is sovereign over those laws. God can also surprise us with unusual, unexpected events.

Is it possible to scientifically prove that God superseded natural laws in a particular event? Or does science rule out any possibility of such things? A practical understanding of what science can and cannot do should warn us against either extreme. Scientists seek to understand puzzling events and puzzling processes. When faced with a particular puzzling event, science can neither prove nor disprove that natural laws were superseded. What can science do? Science tries to build a quantitative, empirical model of the event using its understanding of natural laws plus information about the physical conditions before, during, and after the event.

Attempts to build empirical models meet with varying degrees of success. Scientists studying these puzzling events can reach three general types of conclusions:

16. Other Christian authors writing on the subject of natural laws, chance, and God's governance: Donald MacKay, *Science, Chance and Providence* (Oxford: Oxford University Press, 1978); John Polkinghorne, *Science and Providence* (Boston: Shambhala, 1989); John Polkinghorne, *The Faith of a Physicist* (Princeton, N.J.: Princeton University Press, 1994); Howard Van Till, Davis Young, and Clarence Menninga, *Science Held Hostage* (Downers Grove, Ill.: InterVarsity Press, 1988); Charles E. Hummel, *The Galileo Connection* (Downers Grove, Ill.: InterVarsity Press, 1986); George L. Murphy, *Toward a Christian View of a Scientific World* (Lima, Ohio: CSS, 2001).

1. Explained event. Good empirical models predict that known natural laws can explain the event.[17] (There might still be some puzzling features, but most of the event is well understood.)

2. Partially explained event. Our empirical models are not sufficiently thorough to explain the event entirely. However, on the basis of what we have done so far, we believe that known natural mechanisms are sufficient to account for the event. We believe that future improvements in knowledge, more elegant models, and more computing power will eventually allow us to prove that the event is "explainable."

3. Unexplained event. No known natural laws can explain this event. In fact, there are good empirical reasons for ruling out any model that relies on known natural laws.[18]

---

17. It is worth mentioning again the biblical view that scientifically explained events are just as much dependent upon God's governance as are unexplained events. In addition, even when empirical models successfully explain how an event could happen, that does not necessarily mean that the model correctly describes how the event actually happened. Sometimes, scientifically explained events occur at special times and places, in ways that have special religious significance to a person or a group of people. The argument can be made that such coincidental events must have some unexplained (supernatural) component. Science cannot answer that question positively or negatively. The most that science can do is attempt to determine the relative probability (infrequency) of the event, possibly taking into account known initial conditions. In determining whether or not a coincidental event had a special supernatural component, one must go beyond science to consider historical, philosophical, and religious questions (e.g., Were the event's timing and location predicted beforehand? How soundly does the event fit within an established theological framework? Was there a special revelation accompanying the event?).

18. Some objects or events indicate intelligent crafting. The categories "explained" and "unexplained" become problematic in such cases. For example, a paleontologist might determine that the breakage patterns on the edges of some stones are unexplainable (or highly improbable) in terms of ordinary natural laws. However, if hominid bones are found in the same area, the paleontologist might reasonably conclude that the stones were crafted by hominids to be tools. In this model, the intelligent activity of hominids acts as a special kind of natural mechanism. A similar argument is made in the search for extraterrestrial intelligence. If a sufficiently complex repeating radio signal is discovered, the case can be made that no natural mechanism could produce the complex pattern except for the special type of natural mechanism of intelligent activity. In the debate over biological evolution, some people have pointed to the analogous features between biological life and intelligently crafted objects, thereby arguing that biological life was crafted and assembled by an intelligent agent. This argument is not strictly speaking scientific. It is a philosophical argument. Philosophical arguments have a legitimate role, and sometimes a positive role, in science. They can be used to persuade and as a starting point for marshaling scientific arguments and formulating testable hypotheses. The extent to which this philosophical argument is convincing is, obviously, a point of ongoing debate.

Scientists don't always agree. For any particular event, there may be some debates in the scientific community as to whether it is explained, partially explained, or unexplained. Yet even when there are debates, the great majority of scientists usually do agree. For example, most scientists would agree that supernovas are "explained" events. Most would agree that the development of animals from single-celled zygotes into mature adults falls into the category of "partially explained." A small number of scientists argue that the origin of first life on Earth is unexplained in terms of known natural laws; most scientists argue that it should be considered partially explained. Most agree that the source of the "Big Bang" is unexplained in terms of known natural laws.[19]

How do scientists deal with "unexplained" events? Usually there is no consensus. Individual scientists could reach (at least) five different conclusions about the cause of a scientifically unexplained event:

A. An as yet unknown natural law is responsible for the event.
B. A supernatural event occurred. (The event was caused by an intelligent being of an entirely different reality than our universe.)
C. Superhuman technology brought about the event. (The event was caused by intelligent beings who are contained in and limited by our universe, but with superior technology.)
D. A very improbable event simply happened.
E. A very improbable event simply happened, but this isn't so surprising because there are many universes and we just happen to live in the one where it happened.

A search through popular books and articles written by scientists will turn up examples of each of these five types of conclusions.

Although these five conclusions are very different from each other philosophically and religiously, they play virtually identical roles in scientific studies. Empirical science cannot distinguish between these five possibilities. Each scientist will reach a conclusion based in part upon philosophical, historical, and religious arguments.

Although science cannot decide on the best philosophical/religious conclusion for a scientifically unexplained event, science does play a vital role in deciding whether an event belongs in the category "partially explained" or "unexplained." Philosophical and religious arguments can also properly play

19. There are some speculative theories for "natural" events which could have caused the Big Bang. These theories rely not on known natural laws, but on hypothesized natural laws that have some physical and mathematical analogies with known natural laws.

some role in these debates. In the boundary areas between "partially explained" and "unexplained" events, scientific data, scientific intuition, and philosophical and religious expectations can meet in the same arena. For example, an atheistic scientist might be motivated by her worldview to work hard to push an "unexplained" event into the "explained" or "partially explained" category. This effort might lead her to uncover new natural laws sooner than scientists who don't share her worldview. Alternatively, a scientist might have strong religious reasons for believing that certain events are supernatural, and therefore be motivated to marshal scientific data to show that some events are truly "unexplained." This effort might lead her to uncover flaws in currently accepted empirical models sooner than scientists who don't share her religious beliefs.[20] Scientific conclusions are tentative. Events that today are deemed "explained" or "unexplained" could change their status tomorrow with the discovery of new natural laws or better empirical models. Ultimately, the development of new empirical models plays a decisive role in determining whether a "partially explained" event is "explained" (if the improved empirical models are successful) or "unexplained" (if the improved empirical models argue convincingly against scenarios involving known natural laws). While these new empirical models are still being developed, philosophical and religious arguments can sometimes play a legitimate role in persuasion and inspiring testable hypotheses.

In the following chapters of this book, there are many examples of science attempting, over the years, to construct improved empirical models of partially

---

20. Both of these biases could be pushed to the extreme, to the detriment of science. One could imagine a scientific community so obsessed with finding naturalistic explanations for unexplained events that it wastes vast resources on unproductive pursuits that yield no secondary benefits. One could also imagine a scientific community so complacent about supernatural explanations (or, for that matter, superhuman or many-universes explanations) that it makes virtually no effort to search for new natural explanations for puzzling events. Fortunately, the present-day scientific community does not seem to fit either extreme. Moreover, it should be noted that scientists from every philosophical and religious persuasion spend most of their time trying to push events from the "partially explained" category into the "explained" category.

We should also note that — in addition to disagreeing about whether an event is explained, partially explained, or unexplained — people can also disagree over whether or not a particular event actually happened. For example, if everyone agreed that Jesus' resurrection actually happened, then (almost) everyone would agree that the event was unexplained by known natural laws. Science cannot determine whether or not the disputed event actually happened; historical and philosophical arguments must be used in that decision. Since the event itself is questioned, the debate must often shift to other events that are generally agreed upon (e.g., the written records and the subsequent behavior of Jesus' followers). Scientific intuition and historical and philosophical arguments are then brought forward in the debate over whether these agreed-upon secondary events are also truly unexplained, or merely partially explained.

explained events. In many cases (e.g., supernovas), decades of scientific work have resulted in fairly complete and detailed explanations in terms of known natural laws. Occasionally science has come to the opposite conclusion — that although some event definitely happened, no known natural laws can account for it (e.g., the cause of the "Big Bang"). Most of the time, modern science gives us incomplete answers. Most of the time, scientific investigation tells us that some aspects of an event can be understood in terms of known natural laws, while other aspects are still puzzling — puzzling, but showing great promise for future discoveries.

The Energy Source of the Sun — A Historical Example

By the late 1800s, most geologists had come to a consensus that the earth appeared to be hundreds of millions or billions of years old. This posed a problem for astrophysicists. Astrophysicists could measure the rate at which the Sun was emitting energy. The only natural mechanism known at the time that could produce the Sun's energy was gravitational compression. (As the Sun compresses under its own gravitational attraction, it heats up.) Astrophysicists' calculations showed that gravitational compression could not go on for millions of years. Given the rate at which the Sun was emitting energy, assuming that the source of energy was gravitational compression, the Sun could not be more than a few hundred thousand years old. What was the solution to this scientific puzzle? How could the earth appear thousands of times older than the Sun? Did the astrophysicists get their calculations wrong? Did the geologists get their measurements wrong? Was God miraculously sustaining the Sun's energy output? Or was some as yet unknown natural mechanism providing the Sun's energy?

In this case, that last hypothesis was the correct one. Nuclear fusion — a new natural mechanism — was discovered in the early 1900s. It was shown conclusively to be the source of the Sun's energy. This new natural mechanism brought astrophysicists' calculations of the Sun's age in line with the geologists' calculations of the earth's age. In addition, the discovery of nuclear processes led to the discovery of radioactive dating, which independently confirmed and refined the geologists' earlier calculations.

Newton and Laplace — Another Historical Example

Isaac Newton's discovery of the Law of Universal Gravitation was one of the greatest scientific achievements in history. By combining his theories with the experimental data gathered by other scientists such as Johannes Kepler, Newton showed that the motion of planets going around the Sun, moons orbiting around planets, and objects falling near the earth's surface was described by the same simple universal laws. Newton believed that the Law of Universal Gravitational Attraction was evidence for God's design.

While Newton's equations are simple to write down, their solutions are not always simple. It's easy to solve Newton's equations when there are only two objects (e.g., the Sun and a single planet) gravitationally attracted to each other. They will orbit each other indefinitely in stable and predictable orbits. But as soon as you have three or more mutually interacting objects, it's almost always impossible to exactly solve Newton's equations. You have to approximate. It becomes difficult to calculate whether or not the planets' orbits will be stable indefinitely. When there are three or more objects, it is possible that their mutual interactions will cause one or more of the orbits to become unstable. Our solar system has one Sun, nine planets, plus many moons and smaller objects, all interacting with each other. Are the orbits of all of the planets in our solar system stable over long periods of time, or does their mutual interaction make them unstable?

Newton struggled with this question for some time. He could not come to a definite conclusion, but he eventually came to believe that planetary orbits in our solar system were, in fact, unstable. Each time one planet's orbit brought it close to another planet, they would perturb each other's orbit around the Sun. Newton thought that after a few hundred or thousand years of these perturbations, some of the orbits would become unstable.

How did Newton get around this problem? Newton proposed that God occasionally (every few decades or centuries) sent a comet through the solar system — a comet with just the right mass and just the right trajectory so that its gravitational attraction would "correct" the planetary orbits and keep them stable for another several centuries.

A generation after Newton, Pierre de Laplace built on Newton's work. He found better approximate solutions to Newton's equations. Laplace was able to prove that planetary orbits in our solar system really are stable for much, much longer periods of time — stable without the need for God to perform the occasional correction.

When Laplace presented his book on celestial mechanics to Emperor Napoleon, it is said that Napoleon asked, "Monsieur Laplace, why wasn't the Creator mentioned in your book on celestial mechanics?" To which Laplace is said to have replied, "Sir, I have no need for that hypothesis."

Laplace's cryptic statement has been interpreted in a variety of ways over the centuries. Perhaps he meant, "I don't need God at all." However, Laplace was Roman Catholic, so that's probably not what he meant. Or perhaps he meant, "I'm a better scientist than Newton." He may have been pointing out that, whereas Newton needed God to send comets through the solar system to keep things stable, he had done a better scientific job and proved that such comets weren't necessary. Or perhaps he meant something philosophically provocative, such as, "We don't need God governing planetary motion now that we have a scientific explanation (the law of gravity) for it." If that is what Laplace meant, then he would agree with the modern (but unbiblical) notion that God is uninvolved in events that have scientific explanations. Or perhaps Laplace meant something philosophically very tame, such as, "We don't need to refer explicitly to 'acts of God' when calculating planetary motion."

Whatever Laplace meant, this incident raises some interesting questions. Suppose Laplace's results had come out differently. Suppose Newton's hunch had been correct. Suppose God made the solar system in such a way that planetary orbits really are unstable, requiring a careful "correction" every few centuries. Would Christians consider that a good thing, or a bad thing? Suppose you were alive in the time after Newton's work and before Laplace's. Suppose you were aware that the stability of planetary orbits was an unsolved scientific puzzle. Which way would you hope it would turn out? Would you hope that scientific advances would ultimately prove that planetary orbits are stable, or unstable?

The traditional answer of Christian theology is that God could have created the solar system however he wished. We are in no position to tell God which way is better or worse. Yet if we're honest with ourselves, most of us would have to admit to having a personal preference. Planetary orbits that remain stable indefinitely look like good design. Planetary orbits that become unstable every few centuries seem, to some people, like inferior design. On the other hand, the timely arrival of comets with exactly the right mass and trajectory to correct those orbits would give a powerful argument for God's existence and providential intervention.

The issue of planetary orbits has been settled. Laplace was correct; their orbits are stable over very long periods of time. Many more scientific issues are not yet settled. As we study cosmology, geology, and biology today, we are confronted with new scientific puzzles. How did the solar system form? How rare is the planet Earth as a suitable home for life? How did life begin on Earth? How did modern life forms come into existence? As we examine the scientific data brought to bear on these questions, and as we ponder the theological implications of their answers, we should be honest with ourselves. We come to these questions with our own biases, with our hopes for how the question will ultimately be answered. We don't even all agree on what those biases should be.

Perhaps it is best to minimize the impact of our biases, first, by being aware that we have them, and second, by remembering this biblical teaching: God is just as sovereign over natural laws and natural processes as he is sovereign over miraculous breaks in natural processes.

Scientific Progress

Scientists make progress by building empirical models, looking for natural laws and natural mechanisms to explain as many aspects as possible of the system they are studying. Scientists seek to determine precisely which aspects of a system can be explained in terms of known natural mechanisms and which aspects cannot. By this process, new natural mechanisms are sometimes discovered; old models are refined and sometimes discarded as being inconsistent with the data.

In this way, Newton and Laplace advanced our understanding of planetary motion. They successfully built a model, in terms of known natural mechanisms, that explained and predicted to high accuracy the behavior of orbiting planets. Their success did not diminish God's governance of creation; rather, their success gave us insight into the intelligibility of God's creation and the wisdom of his governance.

In the centuries since Newton and Laplace, a great deal of scientific progress has been made in this way — progress in measurement science, in observational science, and in historical science — progress in understanding the developmental history and the orderly functioning of creation in terms of the natural laws that God created and sustains. As a scientist and as a Christian, I personally see the solution of each new scientific puzzle as a cause for renewed amazement and thankfulness to the Creator.

Scientific Puzzles and Divine Intervention

A great many scientific puzzles remain. There are many scientific questions (e.g., the development of the first life on Earth) for which scientists cannot yet build a model, using known natural mechanisms, which plausibly explains the data. It can be tempting for Christians to see these scientific puzzles as potential evidence for God's existence and nonordinary action in the history of the universe. God is free to supersede his ordinary governance of creation. If God so chose, God could perform events that appear to us as scientifically puzzling or unexplainable. However, a biblical understanding of God's governance should also warn us from too quickly embracing any particular scientific puzzle as evidence of God's unusual intervention.

Consider a hypothetical example in "experimental science." Suppose a scientist claimed that a particular laboratory effect — for example, a 5 percent alteration in the electrical resistance of a sample — was evidence of God superseding natural laws. I doubt if any Christian would rush to embrace this scientist's claim. No matter how thoroughly and convincingly that scientist accounted for all the known natural mechanisms affecting the sample, we would still believe that he had made a mistake, or perhaps we would believe that some as yet undiscovered natural mechanism was at work causing the resistance change. Why? Theologically, we do not expect that God would perform such "miracles" in the lab. Such behavior seems out of character for the God of the Bible. Experientially we note that, in the past, scientific puzzles such as the one just described often have led to new understandings of natural mechanisms.

Even if that scientist could demonstrate to us that the 5 percent alteration in resistance occurred whenever he said a certain prayer, we would still be skeptical that it was evidence of a supernatural break in natural laws. We might believe that an intelligent agent was involved in producing the resistance change, but we would strongly suspect this agent was the scientist herself or else an accomplice. Theologically, we do not expect God to perform miracles on demand in the laboratory. Experientially, we note that charlatans exist both inside and outside the scientific community.

In "observational science" as well, we do not rush to embrace every scientific puzzle as evidence for God's supernatural activity. There is still a great deal we do not understand about how animals grow from single-celled zygotes into adults, or how whales navigate as they migrate (to name just two puzzles among many). We expect that they will become scientifically more and more explainable as we learn more about these systems. We investigate these systems scientifically with an expectation — not an assurance, but an expectation — that God probably governs growing animals and navigating whales, day by day, through the regular and continuous operation of the natural laws he created and sustains. We have this expectation because of God's biblical revelation of his character, and because of our past experiences of learning how God typically governs his creation.

Our experience as scientists and as Christians, combined with God's revelation, leads us to believe that God usually governs his creation through the regular operation of his natural laws — not only within the past few centuries since Newton, but throughout history; not just locally on Earth, but throughout the distant universe. This gives us a good reason for doing "historical science." Using the results of experimental science and observational science, we attempt to reconstruct the history of the universe, the planet Earth, and life on Earth, assuming whenever possible that God used the regular operation of the same natural laws which we see at work in his present-day governance. We do not know for certain how this project will turn out. It might lead us to the discovery that many scientifically "unexplainable" events happened throughout history. Or it might not.

Historical science has greatly advanced since the time of Newton and Laplace. For example, we now have an excellent scientific understanding of how atoms like carbon and iron and uranium have formed and accumulated over billions of years, through nuclear processes in stars and supernovas. When historical science is successful — constructing a model which is internally consistent, theoretically sound, comprehensive in its ability to explain observations, fruitful in guiding research and capable of making detailed predictions — we have a very strong reason for believing that the historical picture given to us by the model is, in fact, an accurate picture of what actually happened. When historical science is successful, we have strong reasons for believing that God chose to govern that part of his creation through the regular operation of natural laws.

Just as with experimental science and observational science, however, many puzzles remain in historical science. God's supernatural activity in the history of a particular system might be detectable, if God so chose. For example, God might have chosen to create the laws of chemistry and biology so that it was impossible for life to arise on Earth without God miraculously superseding those laws. If that is what God did, then scientific research into the origins of life should eventually come to the consensus that the formation of first life on Earth is scientifically "unexplainable" in terms of natural laws. However, that scientists today do not have a detailed scientific model for the formation of first life does not mean that Christians ought to embrace this lack as potential evidence for a miracle. Just as in the hypothetical example of the resistance change in the lab, we ought to consider several scientific, theological, and experiential factors. How much scientific progress has already been made on the question of first life? What are the prospects for future scientific breakthroughs in this area? In this particular instance, do we or do we not have strong theological reasons for expecting that God acted either via natural laws or via superseding them?

Summary

A biblical picture of God and nature assures us that God governs creation in consistent and orderly ways. God gives us the gifts we need to study his creation and partially understand it. Scientists of many religious worldviews can work side-by-side and reach consensus about the natural mechanisms at work in the history and the present functioning of the world. The fact that Christians and non-Christians can work side-by-side in science should give Christians not a sense of fear but a sense of joy and gratitude. As theologian and reformer John Calvin said, "If the Lord has willed that we be helped in physics, dialectic, mathematics, and other like disciplines, by the work and ministry of the ungodly, let us use this assistance. For if we neglect God's gift freely offered in these arts, we ought to suffer just punishment for our sloth."[21]

Scientific progress is made by studying puzzling events and attempting to explain them in terms of known natural laws (or sometimes, in terms of new natural laws which are compatible with older, well-established laws). When science succeeds, its success does not exclude God. Instead, it illuminates God's governance of creation. When science fails to explain an event in terms of known natural laws, it might indicate that God superseded natural laws during that event — but not necessarily. It might also mean that God brought about that event by some unknown natural laws or processes that we might yet discover.

It is tempting to think that we are more faithful to God if we look for evidence of miracles in every scientific puzzle. But hunting for "God's fingerprints" is not necessarily the most faithful approach to study God's creation. Hunting for new scientific explanations, in terms of natural laws that God created and sustains, can be equally God-glorifying — and in many cases may be theologically more defensible. Every time we solve a new scientific puzzle, we are not taking territory away from God's control; rather, we are learning more about how God typically governs his creation. Every time we learn a new scientific truth about God's creation and the gifts that he gave it, it should prompt us all the more to worship the Creator.

21. John Calvin, *Institutes of the Christian Religion,* trans. John T. McNeill (Westminster: John Knox, 1960), 1.16.1.

II SCIENTIFIC EVIDENCE AND THEORY

6 *An Evolving Cosmos*

DEBORAH HAARSMA AND
JENNIFER WISEMAN

Astronomy is perhaps the oldest science. Many ancient cultures recorded the motions of the Sun, Moon, and planets, and sought to explain and predict those motions. Yet astronomy is also one of the most exciting areas of current research. Tremendous discoveries have been made in the last few decades, including planets around other stars, the beautiful processes by which stars form, supermassive black holes in the centers of galaxies, and the accelerating expansion of the universe. Woven throughout these discoveries is the manifold evidence that our universe spans distances in space and time that are nearly incomprehensible in our human experience. These amazing revelations illustrate the power, beauty, and amazing creativity of God.

In this chapter, we can discuss only a few areas of astronomy (but you can pursue the references to learn more). In the first half, we focus on issues of space and time, which are at the core of several perceived conflicts between science and the Bible (see the earlier chapter in this volume by Conrad Hyers). We review the evidence for the tremendous size of the universe, then discuss the evidence that our universe originated about 14 billion years ago (the universe is neither infinitely old, nor only a few thousand years young). In the second half, we will share with you some of the amazing recent discoveries in astronomy, illustrating God's ongoing work in the creation of new stars and the development of galaxies. We mention both astronomical objects that are well understood scientifically and objects that are not, knowing that all are under the sovereign control of God. Our discussion also gives the broad astronomical context for biological evolution — the long time-scales available for life to develop and the production in massive stars of the elements needed for biochemistry.

A Large Universe

Let us start at the beginning of Western science. Like many ancient cultures, the ancient Greeks observed and recorded the motions of stars and planets. In addition, Greek scientists also began to imagine physical models for how the stars and planets move, and to use mathematics in their models. Eratosthenes (276-195 B.C.) not only understood that the Earth was round, but was able to measure the diameter of the Earth (by measuring the angle of sunlight in two Egyptian cities at noon on the same day). He found a result quite close to the modern measurement. Aristarchus (310-230 B.C.) used geometry and measurements of the Moon's position at certain phases to estimate that the Sun is twenty times farther from Earth than the Moon. Combining these data with an estimate of the Moon's diameter, the ancient Greeks made the first estimate of the distance to the Sun, and were off by only a factor of ten or so from the current value of 150 million kilometers (93 million miles). The culmination of ancient Greek astronomy was the work of Ptolemy (ca. A.D. 150). Ptolemy's model placed the Earth at the center of the universe, with all the heavenly bodies moving about it in simple circles or circles with epicycles (an epicycle is a small circular path about a point on the larger circular orbit around the Earth).

Ptolemy's model worked well for over a thousand years, predicting the motions of the planets, Moon, and stars. But by the 1500s, the position of Mars was far off from Ptolemy's prediction, and astronomers began to seek a new model. In 1543, Copernicus published his model of the universe, which placed the Sun at the center with all the planets moving in circular orbits about it. The claim that the Earth was in motion (orbiting the Sun and spinning on its own axis) was revolutionary, and ultimately controversial. Galileo (1564-1642) was a major proponent of the model, but it was shunned by some Church leaders at the time.[1] The Copernican model had important implications for our understanding of the size of the universe — it claimed that the stars were each similar to our own Sun, only so much further away that they appeared very faint. In fact, the stars must be a million or more times further away than the Sun! This sort of calculation was first performed by James Gregory in 1668. In one stroke, the universe became much larger. This distance to the stars, however, relied on the assumption that stars are similar to the Sun. Is there a way to measure the distance without assuming anything?

---

1. For a detailed account of the Galileo controversy from a Christian perspective, we recommend Charles E. Hummel, *The Galileo Connection* (Downers Grove, Ill.: InterVarsity, 1986) and Owen Gingerich, *The Great Copernicus Chase* (Cambridge: Cambridge University Press, 1992). These books expand greatly on the history of astronomy presented here.

Yes. Tycho Brahe (1546-1601) carefully investigated the *parallax* of stars. Parallax is the slight variation in the apparent position of a star (relative to background stars) as the Earth orbits the Sun. In January, the star might appear in one position, but in June when the Earth is on the opposite side of the Sun, the same star will appear to have moved slightly to another position. Brahe knew these position shifts should be happening if Copernicus' model was correct, and so, when he was unable to measure them, he concluded that Copernicus's model was wrong. But actually the problem was that the parallax shifts were much smaller than Brahe thought, and it took over two hundred years for the effect to be measured (by Friedrich Bessel, Wilhelm Struve, and Thomas Henderson in 1838). These distances are all found without any assumptions about the luminosity or properties of the stars.

In modern astronomy, parallax is still our best tool for determining distances to nearby objects. The satellite *Hipparcos* (1989-93) used parallax measurements to find accurate distances to most of the stars within about a thousand light years of Earth. A light year is the distance that light could travel in one year (at its speed of 186,000 miles per second); one light year is nearly 20 million million miles. The *Hipparcos* satellite measured distances to some stars that are over three thousand light years away. Light from these stars has been traveling to us for most of recorded human history. And yet, a thousand light years is actually a small distance compared to the size of our own galaxy.

How can we go about measuring the size of our galaxy? This problem was first tackled by William Herschel in the late 1700s, but later a much more accurate picture emerged when the usefulness of variable stars was discovered. Henrietta Leavitt, working at the Harvard College Observatory, studied a type of variable star called Cepheids. In 1908 she discovered that the variability of a Cepheid (its periodic variations in brightness) was directly related to the average luminosity. In 1915, Harlow Shapley used a similar type of star, called RR Lyrae; all RR Lyrae stars have nearly the same luminosity. Shapley looked at many distant clusters of stars and was able to identify the RR Lyrae stars by their characteristic variations and spectra. Since he knew how bright the nearby stars of this type are, he could use the apparent brightness of the more distant stars to measure their distance (more distant stars are fainter). Through this method, Shapley determined the diameter of our galaxy, the Milky Way, to within a factor of two of the current measurement of about 150,000 light years in diameter. The light from the far side of the Galaxy has been traveling to us for nearly 100,000 years, much longer than recorded human history. We are actually seeing these objects as they were a long time ago, and seeing how God was at work in our galaxy long before human culture was aware of the vastness of his creation.

It was not until well into the 20th century that we learned that the universe is much larger than the Milky Way galaxy. On April 16, 1920, Harlow Shapley and Heber Curtis met at the National Academy of Sciences in Washington, D.C., for what was billed as "The Great Debate." The question was regarding the "spiral nebulae" (see figure 1). Did they reside within the Milky Way? Or were these pinwheels located at great distances, each a great group of stars as large as the Milky Way, galaxies in their own right? The question was not decided that day (although the story of the debate is quite interesting),[2] but the scientific community had to wait only a few years for the answer. In 1923, Edwin Hubble discovered that the Andromeda galaxy was too far away to be part of the Milky Way, and must be its own galaxy (the modern distance is about 2.5 million light years). How did he measure such a great distance? He used the Cepheid variable stars studied by Henrietta Leavitt and was the first to observe individual stars in another galaxy with enough precision to make this sort of measurement. Using Cepheids, the Hubble Space Telescope (named after Edwin Hubble and designed with this project in mind) has directly measured the distances to galaxies over 75 million light years away.[3]

So how big is the universe? Well, you can get an idea of the size by looking at a Hubble photo of a small starless portion of the night sky (see photo with "Worshipping the Creator of the Cosmos" in this volume). Nearly every spot of light in that picture is an entire galaxy! The farther away a galaxy is, the smaller and fainter it will appear. By measuring the size and brightness of many galaxies, astronomers have found that the universe is incredibly large. Some galaxies in this photo are over 5 billion light years away!

Our universe contains over 10 billion galaxies, and our own galaxy, the Milky Way, is just one of them. The Milky Way contains over 10 billion stars, and our own star, the Sun, is just one of them. The astronomical extent of the universe can make our lives on Earth seem not only small but also insignificant. As Christians, however, our significance is not based on our relative size in the universe but rather on the demonstrated love of God for each one of us. The great size of the universe can instead lead us to marvel at the immensity and power of our Creator.

2. Gingerich, *Great Copernicus Chase.*
3. Wendy Freedman, "The Hubble Constant and the Expanding Universe," *American Scientist* 91 (2003): 36-43.

Figure 1: The center of the Whirlpool Galaxy, located 31 million light-years away. The region shown is 30 thousand light-years wide and contains billions of stars. Notice the dark regions along the spiral arms: these are places where newborn stars are lighting up the surrounding hydrogen gas.

Image credit: NASA and The Hubble Heritage Team (STScI/AURA), N. Scoville (Caltech) and T. Rector (NOAO).

An Old Universe

In parts of the North American evangelical community, there has been much controversy about the age of the Earth and the universe. Some Christians believe that the Genesis account declares a young age for the universe (only a few thousand years), while others argue that the Genesis account does not imply any scientific detail about the time frame of creation (see Chapter 2 in this volume). Among scientists, there is a strong consensus that the universe is over 13 billion years old. Is this due to an atheistic bias among scientists? No, many scientists are also people of faith. The consensus among scientists is a result of the strength of the evidence that God has given us in the universe itself.

Our first piece of evidence has already been mentioned in the previous section — the great distances of galaxies. The most distant galaxies are over 10 billion light years away, indicating that the light left those galaxies over 10 billion years ago. The universe must be at least this old. Some counter this by asserting that the speed of light has slowed over the life of the universe, so that light could reach us from these galaxies in a much shorter time. However, the speed of light is a fundamental constant of physics, and a significant change in its value would affect nearly every physical process we know of, from quantum mechanics to electromagnetism to general relativity. Our observations show that the laws of physics in distant galaxies are working in exactly the same way they do on Earth. By observing how physics works there, we have ample evidence that the speed of light had the same value then as it does now.

Another important measure of age in the universe comes from clusters of stars called "globular clusters." Individual stars and star clusters have been studied in detail by astronomers since the 1800s, and the physical processes involved are quite well understood (for instance, nuclear reactions and the behavior of gasses on Earth have been thoroughly studied). Observations of the mass, luminosity, and surface temperatures of stars are found to be in good agreement with our models of how stars change throughout their lives. We have found that high-mass stars burn much brighter and more quickly (a flash in the pan) than low-mass stars (which burn slow but steady).[4] Thus, the proportion of low-mass and high-mass stars in a cluster gives a measure of the cluster's age. Careful studies of globular clusters (like the one shown in figure 2) have revealed their ages to be 10-13 billion years,[5] and thus the universe must be at least

---

4. "Burn" here refers to fusion reactions in the core of the star, not chemical burning. For a detailed explanation of the determination of the ages of star clusters, we recommend Howard Van Till, "The Scientific Investigation of Cosmic History," in *Portraits of Creation,* ed. Howard Van Till (Grand Rapids: Eerdmans, 1990), pp. 82-125.

5. D. H. McNamara, "The Ages of Globular Clusters," *Publications of the Astronomical So-*

this old. This method of finding the age uses observations and calculations completely independent from the measurement of distances to galaxies, yet the two methods result in similar answers. These findings are also consistent with the 13.7 billion year age of the universe as determined by the Cosmic Background Radiation (see next section).

But what about the Earth? Perhaps the solar system is only a few thousand years old, while the rest of the universe is several billion years old. Jeffrey Greenberg, in a later chapter of this volume, reviews the geological evidence for the age of the solar system. Radiometric dating of Earth rocks, Moon rocks, and meteorites indicates that the solar system is about 4.6 billion years old. Again, a completely independent method gives a consistent result.

A counter argument made by some Christians against the great age of the universe is that the universe only appears to be old. They assert that God brought the universe into being only a few thousand years ago, but with the light already on its path toward us, so that the universe appears much older than it is. While God certainly could do this if he wanted, we have to ask whether this is consistent with our theological understanding of his character and how he reveals himself in nature. The light from other stars and galaxies is not just a static background of light reaching Earth, but rather tells the whole life story of those objects, including dramatic changes like the explosion of stars (supernovae), mysterious bursts of gamma rays (see below), and brilliant cores of galaxies changing rapidly in brightness over time. God could have caused the light in route to Earth to show these variations, but that would be creating a whole fictional history of the universe. If we believe that "the heavens declare the glory of God" (Ps. 19:1), then surely we can rely on God to put in the heavens a true and honest record of their existence. To deny this is to deny the many evidences of God's ongoing creativity in the universe.

A Beginning

Could the universe be infinitely old? Or did it begin at a particular moment in time? In the middle of the twentieth century, some scientists were opposed to the "Big Bang" model, in part because that would mean the universe had a beginning at a certain moment in time. A beginning implied the existence of a god to start things off, and smacked of religion. They also had scientific objections to the Big Bang model, such as the large discrepancies between the then-

---

Figure 2: The globular star cluster M15, located 40 thousand light-years away, contains a few hundred thousand stars. Clusters like this one contain some of the first stars to form in our galaxy, about 12 billion years ago. In contrast, the sun is only 4.6 billion years old.
Image Credit: NASA and The Hubble Heritage Team (STScI/AURA)

current age measurements of the universe (these have since been resolved as techniques have improved). They proposed an alternative called the "Steady-State model," in which the universe is infinitely old, with basically the same properties ("steady-state") as far back in time as one can look.[6] Most astronomers now agree that our universe did start off at a particular time — the Big Bang. What evidence do we have for this?

6. G. Burbidge, F. Hoyle, and J. V. Narlikar, "A Different Approach to Cosmology," *Physics Today*, April 1999, pp. 38-44; A. Albrecht, "Reply to 'A Different Approach to Cosmology,'" *Physics Today*, April 1999, pp. 44-46.

There are three major pieces of evidence that the Big Bang occurred. The first is that virtually all the galaxies we see out there are moving away from our own, with the most distant ones moving away at great speed. The entire fabric of space is expanding in all directions. Just as a loaf of raisin bread rises, with all the raisins moving apart from one another, so the universe expands, carrying all the galaxies apart. This expansion of space stretches out every light wave as it travels to us, and thus the light of distant galaxies is shifted to longer, redder wavelengths (thus the effect is called a *redshift*). (The redshift is similar to the Doppler effect, where the motion of the source causes a change in wavelength; the Doppler effect can be heard in the change in pitch of a train whistle as the train approaches and then moves away.) The change in wavelength allows us to measure the velocity of the galaxy moving away from us, and (due to the nature of the expansion) the velocity is directly related to the distance of the galaxy. The exact expansion rate was disputed for a long time, but in the last few years measurements have improved greatly, and many astronomers agree that the expansion rate is about 72 ± 8 kilometers per second per megaparsec.[7] Note that even though galaxies are predominantly moving *away* from us, this is not evidence that we are at the center of the universe. In the analogy to raisin bread, each raisin moves farther from all of its neighbors, and each would see all the other raisins moving away from it. Our galaxy is not unique in the universe, nor does it occupy a special location in it; all observers in the universe see all the other galaxies moving away from themselves.

What happens if we mentally rewind the universe back in time, reversing the expansion? We see that the galaxies, in fact all of space, would have been packed close together at an early moment, the time of the Big Bang. If we assume for a moment that the expansion rate has been constant throughout the life of the universe, the expansion rate implies an age of 14 billion years. This is in reasonable agreement with the age estimates we found above. Scientists have found, however, that the expansion of the universe decelerated initially (due to the matter density resisting the expansion), and that the expansion is currently accelerating (see below).

A second major piece of evidence in support of the Big Bang model is Cosmic Microwave Background Radiation. This radiation gives us a glimpse of the young universe, and a chance to test some detailed predictions of the Big Bang model. In the model, the early universe was extremely hot and dense, but rapidly expanding and cooling. Just as an infrared lamp gives off heat, so the hot, early universe gave off heat radiation. The expansion of the universe, however, caused this radiation to cool and shift to longer and longer wavelengths.

7. Wendy Freedman, "The Hubble Constant and the Expanding Universe."

We now observe this radiation coming to us from all directions in the sky. The WMAP satellite has measured precisely the current temperature of the universe and found it to be 2.725 degrees above absolute zero (-454 degrees Fahrenheit). While that seems extremely cold, the spectrum of the radiation shows that it indeed is a remnant of the early heat of the universe.

The microwave background radiation contains more information about the universe than just its temperature. It actually reveals ripples across the face of the early universe, regions that were slightly warmer or cooler at the time the radiation started traveling to us. The size and clustering of these ripples allow astronomers to make an independent measure of the expansion rate (71 ± 4 kilometers per second per megaparsec), and of how that expansion rate has changed over time. Using this information to mentally rewind the expansion, the best current estimate for the age of the universe is 13.7 ± 0.2 billion years.[8] Just a decade ago, astronomers debated whether the age was closer to 12 billion years or 16 billion years, and now it has been measured to nearly 1% precision!

A third major piece of evidence supporting the Big Bang is the amount of helium we observe. About 24 percent of the ordinary matter in the universe is helium (the rest is mostly hydrogen), which is much more helium than could have been produced by stars or physical processes currently at work in the universe. However, the conditions about three minutes after the Big Bang were just right for the fusion of hydrogen into helium and other light elements like deuterium and lithium. In the past century, we developed a very good understanding of nuclear reactions and can now predict exactly the amount of helium and other elements that would have been produced. The theoretical prediction is in impressive agreement with the measured value.[9] This evidence dates back to the first minutes of the Big Bang, confirming that the universe really did have a hot, dense beginning. To a Christian, the scientific evidence for a beginning to the universe is in beautiful harmony with the picture in Genesis 1 of God bringing forth his creation.

All of these wonders of the cosmos, including its size, origin, and development, are opening up to our investigation through advances in scientific models, observations, and technology. We are privileged to live at a time in history where we can understand some aspects of how God brought the universe into being and can measure how much time has passed since the beginning. In previous centuries, Christians understood the "why" and "who" of creation,

8. C. L. Bennett et al., "First Year Wilkinson Microwave Anisotropy Probe Observations: Maps and Basic Results," submitted to *Astrophysical Journal* (2003), available at http://map.gsfc.nasa.gov/m_mm.html.

9. K. A. Olive, G. Steigman, and T. P. Walker, "Primordial Nucleosynthesis: Theory and Observations," *Physics Reports* 333 (2000): 389-407.

but had no scientific basis for the "how" and "how long." The above results are well-understood areas of cosmology, results that have been tested repeatedly by different scientists using different methods. Natural laws and natural processes have successfully explained the properties and evolution of the cosmos. In other words, we have good scientific descriptions for how God is governing his creation. Although there are also many gaps in our knowledge, processes in the universe that astronomers do not yet understand (such as the origin of gamma-ray bursts or the nature of dark matter), we have no reason to expect that these gaps will be filled by special supernatural action by God. Rather, we expect that, as in other areas of astronomy, we will eventually understand the natural mechanisms God used in these situations. Our lack of understanding is simply an indication of our need for more study.

A Dynamic Universe

Not only does our universe cover vast spans of time and space, but we never seem to exhaust the wonders of its content, its history, and its ongoing activity since the first moment of time. Indeed, our universe is not "static" and unchanging, and neither is our understanding of it! In the remainder of the chapter, we will first describe the formation and changing nature of the material in the universe (like stars and galaxies), and then we will discuss some recent exciting discoveries and intriguing unanswered questions which invite us to further study of the heavens.

Let's start with stars. In the account in Genesis 1:14-19, the stars are mentioned almost parenthetically while most of the description of the fourth day is devoted to the Sun and Moon. Yet the creation of the stars, as revealed by current research and discoveries, is an almost unfathomable act! As mentioned above, there are at least 10 billion stars in galaxies like our own Milky Way. Since each galaxy holds several billion stars, and there are at least 10 billion galaxies in the universe, simple math tells us that our Sun is one of over 100,000,000,000,000,000,000 stars in the universe! Moreover, stars differ from each other in mass, brightness, color, temperature, and chemical makeup. Even the apostle Paul observed that "star differs from star in splendor" (1 Cor. 15:41). Most stars are about the same mass as our Sun, but some are over a thousand times more massive. Some stars are blue and hot, while others have cool outer layers that appear more red. Some have heavier atoms than others in their outer layers, as seen in observations of their detailed light spectra.

Beyond simply counting the stars, modern research has shown us that stars do not stay the same forever but go through a complete life cycle. Stars spend most of their lives steadily fusing hydrogen into helium in their cores, but after they have used up the hydrogen they meet a stormy end. Low-mass stars (like the Sun) will spend some time fusing helium into carbon but will eventually lose their outer layers and become "white dwarfs." Stars with more mass are able to achieve greater temperatures in their cores, allowing heavier elements to undergo fusion, producing not only carbon but also oxygen, silicon, iron, and other elements. Eventually the star dies in a large supernova explosion, which spreads these elements through the nebulous region between the stars. From this material, new stars and planets form (as described below), and so they now contain these heavier elements. Without this dynamic process of fusion in stars and dissipation in supernova explosions, the heavy elements needed for life could not have come together here on Earth. The stars are a "factory" for producing the very carbon and oxygen that we depend upon for life. In fact, there is no other physical process in the universe that can generate these elements in the quantities needed for planets and life; thus, life could not have arisen before the early generations of stars died and spread their atoms throughout the Galaxy.

This life cycle of the stars is one example of God's "continuous creation." God has set up a very dynamic process in the Galaxy that continually brings about new stars. God's creative activity is ongoing, and new stars are forming even now. Creation is not simply a one-time event in the past, but rather a continuing reality. God's creation of new things in the universe cannot be separated from his ongoing governance of the universe.

The physical process of how stars are formed is fascinating, and our understanding has been greatly increased through new telescopes and observation techniques. We are now able to peer into regions of dense gas and dust between stars — "interstellar clouds" — that serve as stellar nurseries.[10] Classic optical telescopes are sensitive to the same optical colors of light that our eyes can detect, but this kind of light is obscured by dust and thick gas, making an interstellar cloud look like nothing more than a dark blotch on the night sky. Many objects in the universe, however, emit most of their light in colors (i.e., other frequencies or wavelengths of light) that are outside of the optical range. Some of these frequencies of light, such as infrared and radio, are not obscured by regions of dense gas and dust. Thus, the sites of star formation are often observed with radio telescopes, which are sensitive to low frequency light from molecules such as carbon monoxide that permeate the cloud. Young stars themselves heat the dust and gas right around them such that they glow in infrared light, and

10. G. D. Bothun, "Beyond the Hubble Sequence: What Physical Processes Shape Galaxies?" *Sky & Telescope*, May 2000, pp. 36-43.

current infrared telescopes have detected "baby" stars, known as "protostars," forming in many dense gas clouds.

Stars form within these interstellar clouds when pockets of dense gas begin to condense under their own gravitational attraction, which tends to pull matter together. Small thermal motions between the molecules in a cloud will keep it from collapsing as a whole, but these dense pockets of calm, cooler gas within the cloud can succumb to gravitational forces and collapse. If there is enough mass, the center of this gas core will become hot enough and dense enough from the compression to incite the fusion of hydrogen atoms in the core into helium, with each such reaction releasing light. Once these light-producing reactions begin, "a star is born." As a core of dense gas collapses, it can fragment into several pieces that may end up as a double star (i.e., a "binary" system) or as a multistar cluster. Unlike our Sun, most stars seem to be in binary pairs, and many are in clusters.

The process of star formation is one of great beauty and drama.[11] As "baby" stars take on more material from the surrounding cloud, they expel as exhaust a small fraction of material from the poles of the star (this is due to processes involving angular momentum conservation and magnetic fields in the system). These "bipolar jets," as they are called, are spectacular fountains of material traveling often at several hundred thousand miles per hour (several hundred kilometers per second) in long collimated beams of brightly emitting gas[12] (see figure 3). Our Sun most likely went through a similar phase during its formation. The beauty continues as these "protostars" develop into regular stars. If the young star is several times more massive than our Sun, its light will have enough energy to ionize the surrounding dense gas cloud out of which it formed. "Ionization" means that electrons in some of the gas atoms are separated for a time from their associated nuclei. These electrons continuously recombine with the nuclei, and as this occurs, light is released from the gas. These ionized gas regions are called "nebulae" and emit bright colors; indeed, regions such as the Orion Nebula (figure 4) are often considered the most beautiful in the sky, though one needs a telescope to see the details of their colors and structure.[13] Outpouring light and particles from the young stars eventually clear away the surrounding gas cloud (as shown in figure 5), leaving the bright shining stars that we see at night.

11. A. A. Goodman, "Recycling in the Universe," *Sky & Telescope,* November 2000, pp. 44-53.

12. T. P. Ray, "Fountains of Youth: Early Days in the Life of a Star," *Scientific American,* August 2000, pp. 42-47.

13. J. Reston, Jr., "Orion: Where Stars Are Born," *National Geographic,* December 1995, pp. 90-101.

Figure 3: The protostellar jet known as HH111. This outflowing gas is emitted from the poles of a young forming star, or "protostar." Such outflows are a regular stage in the process of a star's formation and carry away excess angular momentum, allowing the star to fully condense. This composite image from the Hubble Space Telescope shows the jet in visible light and the dusty disk region around the forming star at the base of the jet in infrared light.

Image credit:
NASA and B. Reipurth
(CASA, University of Colorado)

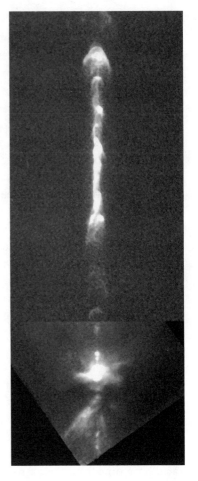

What about planets — how do they form? It has long been theorized that as material falls onto these young forming protostars, a disk of material forms around the equatorial region. Dust particles within the disk gradually clump together and the clumps grow in size. While most of the disk material will eventually be blown away by the star's radiation, thicker clumps of dust in the disk could coagulate and grow and survive as planets. Until recently, these ideas were not testable. But now, equatorial disks have detected observed around several young stars! The Hubble Space Telescope has detected the dark silhouette of a disk across several protostars, and radio telescopes sensitive to millimeter-wavelength light have observed emission coming from these disks around young stars. Will planets form in these disks and survive, like the nine planets

Figure 4. The Orion Nebula as imaged with the Hubble Space Telescope. This bright cloud of colorful gas is actually an active nursery for the formation of new stars. Several massive young, fully formed stars visible near the center of the nebula radiate enough energy to ionize the surrounding gas, which results in the beautiful display. About 700 smaller "baby" stars, buried within the gas cloud, are still in the process of actively forming.
Image credit: NASA, and C. R. O'Dell and S. K. Wong (Rice University)

around our Sun in our own solar system? Time will tell — but many people are studying these disks to understand their properties and likely future.

Not only do stars and planets change over time, but even whole galaxies change in size and composition. God has provided an awesome "time machine" for us to peer back billions of years into the past and watch this process. As mentioned above, the light from distant galaxies takes time to travel to us because it cannot travel infinitely fast. When we observe a distant gal-

Figure 5. The Eagle Nebula, as imaged with the Hubble Space Telescope. This dense cloud of interstellar gas has produced massive young stars (off the top edge of the image) that are now evaporating much of the remaining gas with their powerful ultraviolet radiation. Only the densest regions remain, shielding columns of gas as seen here. Hundreds of young stars are still forming deep within the dense columns, while the exposed tips of the cloud continue to evaporate.
Image credit: Jeff Hester and Paul Scowen (Arizona State University), and NASA.

axy, we are seeing it as it was when it emitted the light, not as it is *now*. By comparing the structure and content of more distant galaxies with those nearby, we can observe how galaxies have changed over the long history of the universe.[14] And indeed they have changed. More of the early galaxies have

14. G. Kauffmann and F. van den Bosch, "The Life Cycle of Galaxies," *Scientific American,* June 2002, pp. 46-58.

irregular shapes, whereas the current galaxy population contains more of the grand spiral design galaxies (as shown in figure 1). In the early universe, whole galaxies often merged together; these mergers would trigger episodes of very vigorous star formation (figure 6 shows a nearby pair of merging galaxies). Studies of the "chemical enrichment" of galaxies over time are under way, comparing the chemical makeup of early, distant galaxies with nearby ones such as our own that have been filled with heavier elements by generations of stars having come and gone within them.

These processes — the development of galaxies, vigorous and ongoing star formation, and the enrichment of current stars and planets with elements produced in the deaths of previous generations of stars — show us that the universe our God has created, and even the creation methods he has chosen, is not "idle" but very dynamic!

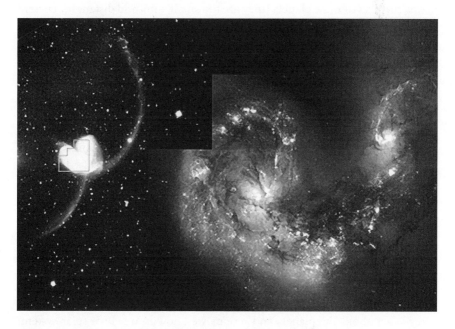

Figure 6. The merging of two galaxies, NGC4038 and NGC4039. The left image, taken from a telescope on the ground, shows the full size of the galaxies, known as the "Antennae," with long tails caused by the mutual tidal forces. The right image, taken with the Hubble Space Telescope, shows the inner core region of the colliding galaxies. The bright clusters of stars have formed during the long collision process. Galaxy mergers such as this appear to have been common in the early universe.

Image credit: Brad Whitmore (Space Telescope Science Institute) and NASA

The Continuation of Discovery

Humankind has learned more about the nature of the universe in this past century than in all the previous ones. Most would agree that advances in technology and broader availability of time and support for such studies have allowed this burst of knowledge. From a perspective of faith, it may be that in fact the Lord has desired us to know a great deal more about his handiwork at this time. In any case, some of the most exciting discoveries in astronomy have been made in only the last few years. We cannot mention them all, but we will discuss a few to share the flavor of excitement in the endless wonders of creation.

To begin with, ever since the acceptance of the Copernican system — a Sun-centered solar system with orbiting planets — and the realization that the Sun is a star, people have wondered if there are planets orbiting other stars. It is only in the past few years that we can now say "yes" to this question through observations rather than speculation. The discoveries have been made not by taking pictures of these planets (they are too small, dim, and distant for current instruments to image), but rather by detecting their effect on the star they orbit. Planets remain in orbit around a star due to the gravitational attraction between the star and the planet. That same attraction causes the star to "wobble" as the planet moves around it. The wobble can be detected as a tiny periodic Doppler shift in the frequency of the light received from the star as it moves back and forth from the person observing it (see discussion above on the Doppler effect). The nature of the frequency shift reveals the mass and distance of the orbiting planet or planets. In this way, more than sixty planets orbiting other stars have been discovered (as of April 2001). All of the planets discovered so far are more massive than Earth, and many are more massive than Jupiter (Earth-like planets would be very difficult to detect this way, currently). Future instruments are being planned that will be able to detect Earth-sized planets and even make images of them, if any are found.[15] Imagine the excitement of finding a planet similar to Earth that is orbiting another star! Or, equally intriguing, imagine how we will feel if we discover that Earth is a very, very unique kind of planet! The possibility of making these discoveries is now at hand.

What about the planets and moons we know in our own solar system? The images returned from the Voyager space probes from a couple of decades ago are still tantalizing to our imaginations. More recently, very intriguing discoveries have been made, including the realization that there is indeed water ice

---

15. L. R. Doyle, H.-J. Deeg, and T. M. Brown, "Searching for Shadows of Other Earths," *Scientific American*, September 2000, pp. 58-65.

on the poles of Mars, and evidence that water may have once filled what are now dry lakebeds on the surface, creating layers of sedimentation imaged with the Mars Global Surveyor. Mars has not always been the barren land it now seems to be. And water may exist even now, possibly harboring conditions acceptable for life, under the frozen surface of Jupiter's moon Europa.[16]

Moving outward from our local solar system to the center of our galaxy, it now appears likely that there is a massive black hole at the center of the Milky Way. Black holes are objects of such high density that the resulting strong gravitational field will not allow even light to escape from them, thus making them invisible. As mentioned above, high-mass stars end their lives in supernova explosions and sometimes leave behind a compact black hole. The black hole at the center of the Milky Way, however, is over one million times as massive as the Sun and did not form this way. Such supermassive black holes may form when a very large amount of mass from, say, a star cluster combines into one unstoppable collapse, creating a black hole with enormous mass and gravitational energy. While objects coming close to the black hole cannot escape, objects moving outside this distance can orbit the black hole, and the orbital speeds of these objects reveal the mass of the central black hole. This is how we know there is probably a supermassive black hole in the center of the Milky Way: stars near the center of the Galaxy are moving very rapidly around an unseen central compact region.[17] The velocities and motions of the stars indicate that the central region is so massive and compact that it can only be a black hole.

It has been found that black holes lie at the center of other galaxies, too.[18] As material falls in toward the central black hole, there is an "exhaust" mechanism, much like that during the formation of individual stars, in which some matter is shot out away from the black hole in collimated jets that move at speeds very near that of light. These jets escape the Galaxy and interact with gas outside, creating huge lobes of emitted light that are many times larger than the whole Galaxy from which the jets formed!

Finally, one of the most astounding and unexpected discoveries of the last few years concerns the expansion of the universe. It was amazing enough when, within the last century, the observations of Edwin Hubble led to the discovery that the galaxies are moving away from each other, and in fact that the very fabric of space itself is expanding. But it had been generally assumed that the mass

16. R. T. Pappalardo, J. W. Head, and R. Greeley, "Hidden Ocean of Europa," *Scientific American,* October 1999, pp. 54-63.

17. A. M. Ghez, M. Morris, E. E. Becklin, A. Tanner, and T. Kremenek, "The Accelerations of Stars Orbiting the Milky Way's Central Black Hole," *Nature* 407 (2000): 349.

18. J. Kormendy and D. Richstone, "Inward Bound: The Search for Supermassive Black Holes in Galactic Nuclei," *Annual Reviews of Astronomy and Astrophysics* 33 (1995): 581-624.

within the universe, exerting its gravitational pull, would eventually pull the galaxies back together, or at least slow down this process of expansion. The latest discovery suggests that the expansion is not slowing down, as was originally thought, but rather speeding up![19] This discovery was first made using observations of supernova explosions in other galaxies, and was recently confirmed by the WMAP observations of the microwave background. The acceleration of the expansion indicates that the universe will not recollapse on itself, but will instead expand forever.

If the universe will expand forever, what does this mean for us and for the future of humanity? Using only our scientific models, we can project the long-term future of the universe. It can seem like a sad projection: the galaxies will continue to move apart, stars within them (including the Sun) will eventually use up all the available fuel and die, and thus trillions upon trillions of years into the future, all will grow dark and cold.

But this is not the complete picture, because the physical world is only part of the revelation God has given us. He has revealed himself to us not only in the heavens (Ps. 19:1-4) but throughout human history, through his word and in the person of Jesus Christ. Indeed, Christ has died, he has risen from the dead, and he has promised that he will come again. At the end of time, the creation itself will become undone as God makes a new heaven and a new earth (Rev. 21:1). Our physical predictions for the future of the universe are meaningful only as long as God continues to sustain the current creation; they will have no meaning after God makes all things new. Scientific models for the universe are the wrong place to find hope for the future, but rather we look to God's faithfulness both in sustaining the current creation and in keeping his promises for the future.

A Universe of Wonder, a Creation to Explore

There are many questions yet unanswered about the awesome universe the Lord has created. In fact, it seems the more we learn, the more questions arise to inspire more study! Perhaps the most wonderful characteristic of the cosmos is that it does obey laws of physics that we can begin to understand, and that God seems to delight in our study and in our sharing of discovery with others.

---

19. C. J. Hogan, R. P. Kirshner, and N. B. Suntzeff, "Surveying Spacetime with Supernovae," *Scientific American,* January 1999, pp. 46-51; L. M. Krauss, "Cosmological Anti-Gravity," *Scientific American,* January 1999, pp. 52-59; and D. Branch, "Type Ia Supernovae and the Hubble Constant," *Annual Reviews of Astronomy and Astrophysics* 36 (1998): 17-55.

So, what are some of the unanswered questions to explore? Perhaps we'd all like to know if life exists only on Earth, or if life is common in the universe. And if there is life elsewhere, could there be intelligent life, and even beings capable of sin and redemption in Christ as we are? Scripture does not confine the possibilities, except for the fact that if there is life elsewhere, it is part of God's creation. And in fact, given that we find all kinds of animal and plant life and tiny one-celled organisms in the most extreme conditions on Earth (such as in deep, high-pressure ocean vents and in high layers of the atmosphere), it does not seem impossible that life may exist on other planets and moons. The first step is to find habitable conditions on other planets and moons (Saturn's moon Titan, with its thick atmosphere, seems like a possible location for cellular life forms to survive, for example) and elements necessary for life (carbon chain molecules, for example, have now been discovered in interstellar space; thus such elements may be plentiful on other planets in other solar systems). As discussed earlier, it seems likely that more and more planets will be discovered orbiting other stars, and that it is possible that some of these may be Earth-like planets that could harbor some form of life. However, there is also evidence that the special conditions that have allowed life to flourish on this planet may be very unlikely to exist anywhere else (such as, for example, protection from harmful cosmic rays and UV radiation by our atmosphere and surrounding magnetic field, and protection from devastating asteroid bombardments because of the gravitational effects of our neighbor Jupiter).[20] Our search for the extent of life in the universe will continue.[21]

Another mystery is the nature of gamma-ray bursts.[22] These flashes of light are the most energetic features of the universe, though many of them last only a few minutes. The light is not visible light that we can see with our eyes, but very energetic photons called gamma-rays. The flashes were seen as early as the 1960s, but the instruments then did not allow astronomers to pinpoint the location of the source. Only through recent studies using new detectors has it become certain that gamma-ray bursts are coming from other galaxies located all over the sky. The brightness of these bursts is even more amazing when you consider that the sources are so distant from us; an individual burst radiates in

20. Hugh Ross, *The Fingerprint of God* (Pittsburgh: Whitaker House, 2000); P. D. Ward and D. Brownlee, *Rare Earth: Why Complex Life Is Uncommon in the Universe* (New York: Copernicus, 2000).

21. A. J. LePage, "Where They Could Hide," *Scientific American*, July 2000, p. 40; J. Tartar and C. F. Chyba, "Is There Life Elsewhere in the Universe?" *Scientific American*, December 1999, pp. 118-23.

22. J. van Paradijs, C. Kouveliotou, R. A. M. J. Wijers, "Gamma-Ray Burst Afterglows," *Annual Reviews of Astronomy and Astrophysics* 38 (2000): 379-425.

a few seconds as much energy as the entire Milky Way galaxy radiates over a few thousand years! These fantastic flashes of energy may originate when the compact remains of old stars, that is, black holes or neutron stars, merge together, and in so doing incite an explosion beyond our imagination. Scientists will continue to study these in coming years.

Where is the dark matter and dark energy? "Dark matter" is the term used to describe matter that we know is there (we see its gravitational effects in galaxies) but that has not been detected through conventional means like telescopes. In fact something like 23% of the content of the universe may be in the form of "dark matter," as determined from recent WMAP observations, while only 4% is composed of ordinary matter. What is it? Some speculate that there may be many small planets and brown dwarfs that are unseen but that compose much of the dark matter. But current discoveries of such objects do not seem to project that there will be enough of them to account for all the dark matter. Our best guess is that there is another kind of tiny exotic particle that we have yet to discover but that fills the universe. An even more perplexing question is the nature of "dark energy," which makes up over 70% of the universe.[23] This term refers to the mysterious stuff that is causing the universe to accelerate in its expansion. This will be a hot topic of research in years to come!

And what about the very beginning of the universe? We have discussed earlier the evidence that indeed time and space as we know it are finite, and that there was a beginning to the cosmos that we call the Big Bang. We understand much of the Big Bang *after* the first fraction of a second: modern astrophysical theory can describe amazingly well how the incredible energy and radiation transformed over time into the material all around us, becoming galaxies, stars, planets, and elements that make up our bodies. The first instant, however, is still beyond the reach of our theories. The universe is governed by four major forces (electromagnetism, gravity, and the "strong" and "weak" forces within atoms) that we understand well at low energies. The first instant of the Big Bang, however, was so incredibly hot, dense, and energetic, that our current theories are inadequate to understand it. Current quantum theories unite all of the forces except gravity, but what is missing in these theories is an understanding of how the force of gravity can also be unified with the other forces at the very beginning of time.[24] Cosmologists and particle physicists are working hard to develop an understanding of "quantum gravity," an idea that will allow

23. C. L. Bennett et al., "First Year Wilkinson Microwave Anisotropy Probe Observations: Maps and Basic Results."

24. M. Rees, "Exploring Our Universe and Others," *Scientific American*, December 1999, pp. 78-83.

us to understand how the universe and all its forces developed from the first moment in time. We could ultimately gain a scientific understanding of God's creation back to the very instant that God created time itself.

Sharing the Wonder

These are just a few examples of the questions we humans can ask about the universe in which we live. But you might wonder, "Should we care about the details of the universe when there are so much trouble and suffering among our fellow humans to which we could devote our time and energy?" The answer is, the Lord cares about both, and thus so should we (Amos 5:4-15)! It is hard for us to conceive that the same God who willed the universe into being 14 billion years ago and has upheld its progression ever since is also interested in the life and happiness and suffering of the tiniest child on this small planet. But he is. When we begin to acknowledge the awesome creativity of our God and the beauty of the universe he has created, we give God glory. And seeing him better makes us turn away from petty strifes and hatred and selfishness. Sharing what we learn about the wonders of the universe with "the least of these" — to give people cause to give God praise — is important, just as is sharing material goods.

When our study of the universe is done in love for God and in service to others, the excitement and blessing overflow! Praise God for his amazing handiwork, and for letting us be a part of it.

O Lord, our Sovereign,
    how majestic is your name in all the earth!
You have set your glory
    above the heaven. . . .
When I look at your heavens,
    the work of your fingers,
the moon and the stars
    that you have established,
what are human beings that you are mindful of them,
    mortals that you care for them?
Yet you have made them a little lower than God,
    and crowned them with glory and honor.   (Ps. 8:1, 3-5, NRSV)

Worshipping the Creator of the Cosmos

DEBORAH HAARSMA

Scripture: Psalm 8

The Hubble Deep Field is one of the most beautiful results of astronomy in recent years. In October 1998, the Hubble Space Telescope spent ten days viewing a tiny portion of the sky that contained no bright stars or galaxies. The result is the accompanying image. Thousands of tiny, colorful galaxies are strewn across the field, in a "God's-eye view" of the universe. One almost expects to see a tiny sign poking out of one of the spiral arms saying "You are here." An image such as this dramatically reminds us of how small our galaxy is in relation to the whole universe, just one of about 10 billion galaxies. And we are vastly smaller than our home galaxy, where the Sun is just one of about 10 billion stars.

How should Christians respond to this century's discovery of the vast size of the universe? Does this prove (as some would claim) that God is only a concept we invented to make ourselves feel more significant? If God really was in charge of this vast universe, how could he possibly be interested in us? This is not a new question. A poet 3,000 years ago asked the same thing: "When I look at your heavens, the work of your fingers . . . what are human beings that you are mindful of them?" (Ps. 8:3-4). The psalmist goes on to offer an answer: "You crowned them with glory and honor. You made them ruler over the works of your hands" (Ps. 8:5-6). This refers back to Genesis, where God established our significance by creating men and women in his own image and commissioning the human race to care for the earth. The psalmist does not intend here to boast of the greatness of humans, but rather foreshadows the ultimate glorification of Christ himself (Heb. 2:5-9). Seen through the lens of the New Testament, the tending of creation is not just humanity's work but Christ's work, to be accomplished through his body, the Church.

Photo: Hubble Deep Field North
Credit: R. Williams (STScI), the HDF-S Team, and NASA

But this is not the only Christian answer to the question of human significance in the cosmos. In the person of Christ we see God himself becoming fully
human. What else could give so much significance to humanity? Our immense
God, who makes the galaxies dance and spin across the Hubble Deep Field, became a tiny baby. How much more approachable could God become? When astronomy shows us the vastness of the universe, we learn anew how large God is,
and how great his grace.

O Lord my God, when I in awesome wonder,
Consider all the worlds Thy hands have made,
I see the stars, I hear the rolling thunder,
Thy pow'r throughout the universe displayed.

And when I think that God, his Son not sparing,
Sent Him to die, I scarce can take it in,
That on the cross, my burden gladly bearing,
He bled and died to take away my sin.

Then sings my soul, my Savior God, to Thee;
How great Thou art, how great Thou art!

Carl Boberg, 1885
(trans. Stuart Hine, 1949)

7 Geological Framework of an Evolving Creation

JEFFREY GREENBERG

People who read both testaments of the Bible as sacred, authoritative witness, God's Word, continue to disagree over the literal meaning (hermeneutical translation) and the intended message (theological exegesis) of scriptural passages. This problem has of course been with us since the early days of the Church. It seems to grow in controversy as we get further from the writers and deeper into a scientific and Western philosophical world. Most evangelical Christians would agree that scriptural errors of interpretation come as a result of our imperfect understanding and not from the text itself. Interpreting geology from the evidence of creation (the other "book" of revelation) is certainly not an infallible practice. However, with care, experience, and the application of minds created by God to oversee his creation, we should be able to interpret nature as biblical exegetes do Scripture. The rocks and fossils of the Earth form patterns we are to "read" in this other version of God's creation story.

The following discussion of geology in natural history provides data as a context for evolution. Examples are not presented to refute "young-earth creationism," "flood geology," or "creation science." Comprehensive publications by authors such as D. A. Young, D. E. Wonderly, G. R. Morton, and H. Ross,[1] and many articles in the journal of the American Scientific Affilia-

---

1. D. A. Young, *Creation and the Flood* (Grand Rapids: Baker, 1977); D. A. Young, *Christianity and the Age of the Earth* (Grand Rapids: Zondervan, 1982); D. E. Wonderly, *God's Time-Records in Ancient Sediments* (Flint, Mich.: Crystal, 1977); D. E. Wonderly, *Neglect of Geological Data: Sedimentary Strata Compared with Young-Earth Creationist Writings* (Hatfield, Pa.: Interdisciplinary Biblical Research Institute, 1987); G. R. Morton, *Foundation, Fall and Flood — A Harmonization of Genesis and Science,* 2nd ed. (Dallas: DMD, 1995); H. Ross, *The Fingerprint of God* (Orange, Calif.: Promise, 1989); and H. Ross, *Creation and Time* (Colorado Springs: Navpress, 1994).

tion, *Perspectives on Science and Christian Faith,* offer vast amounts of evidence to firmly establish the scientific basis for an ancient Earth. These publications are all particularly effective because they are authored by theologically conservative Christians.

A Most Habitable Home Planet

Behold the amazing array of life on Earth! Here is a true staging of a Divine Drama (with apologies to Dante). New and innovative organisms come on the scene. Some remain only a short while; others play longer roles. From the record of their existence, it is apparent that the drama has grown more interesting through time as increasing diversity and complexity characterize life and its interaction.

The stage for life on Earth is provided by the whole range of habitat settings. Investigators continue to find organisms or their traces inhabiting some of the most hostile environments on the planet, including deeply fractured Antarctic ice, hot springs in Yellowstone Park, and along mid-ocean spreading ridges. In spite of some disputed evidence to the contrary, Earth remains the only place in the universe that we know can sustain life. We have long been suspicious of nearby locations, and Mars in particular displays promising signs from the past. Martian fragments as meteorites are thought by some to contain the chemical signature of microbial life.[2] Flowing water was apparently abundant enough on the surface of our neighbor to produce spectacular "marscapes" of stream erosion and deposition. There is also the sparse frost surviving to account for the polar "ice caps" on Mars. Other satellites, Venus, Jupiter's moon Io, and our own Moon exhibit some important geologic properties similar to the nurturing environment of Earth, but in comparison they are all rather monotonous fossils themselves.

Proponents of the Anthropic Principle (AP)[3] conclude that the vitality of Earth is the result of intentional design and not just fortuitous coincidence. Life is possible or inevitable because of the essential set of natural laws and constants. Much has been written in evaluation of the concept. Some works, such as *The Fingerprint of God* and *Creation and Time* by astrophysicist Hugh Ross, are penned in support of biblical Christianity. Other Christians are engaged in defending a theistic creation through the advocacy of "Intelligent Design," which is

---

2. I. Fry, *The Emergence of Life on Earth* (New Brunswick, N.J.: Rutgers University Press, 2000).

3. Anthropic Principle: The concept that the universe and particularly Earth in its setting have all the attributes to make human life and continued existence possible.

similar to Ross's enterprise except that they are gathered under a different sponsoring organization. Not all those who propose evidence for a life-friendly Earth and universe do so with stated religious conviction. In 1982, Paul Davies wrote *The Accidental Universe*[4] to explain the importance of initial conditions and their later consequences in the establishment of an evolved universe leading to Earth, life, and humans. A symposium volume, *Origin and Evolution of the Universe: Evidence for Design?* published in 1987,[5] elaborated on many different aspects touched on by Davies. Among the articles in the 1987 volume is "Anthropocentric View of the Universe: Evidence from Geology" by D. J. McLaren.[6] McLaren and various other volume authors agree that the evidence for design is substantial but does not necessarily lead one to a spiritual explanation. Most recently, *Rare Earth: Why Complex Life Is Uncommon in the Universe*[7] adds more current examples from scientific investigation to the arsenal supporting an AP perspective. All together, hundreds of examples of these fine-tuning phenomena have been cited. Regardless of whether the AP as argument for a creator is persuasive, the unique character of geologic processes and materials constrains the path of natural history. McLaren writes in the conclusion of his paper:

> Life appears to have originated very early in Earth's history, certainly by 3.5 Ga, probably some time before that, and possibly not long after the formation of the crust at 4.2 Ga. Since then Gaia has preserved a stable environment for life within narrow limits, although several major forces, internal and external, have sporadically disturbed the environmental norms. Two complementary evolutionary mechanisms developed: slow evolutionary changes, in equilibrium with the environment, and large changes caused by major environmental disruptions. Evolution appears to be an intricate accelerating system of general processes with chance the driving force, but not the determinant. Over the long time life has existed on Earth, it is difficult to indicate any particular crisis point as more improbable than any other. The timing of major environmental shocks may be largely stochastic, but within the overall time scale they are a normal component of the total environmental flux.

4. P. C. W. Davies, *The Accidental Universe* (Cambridge and New York: Cambridge University Press, 1982).

5. J. M. Robson, ed., *Origin and Evolution of the Universe: Evidence for Design?* (Kingston, Ont.: McGill-Queens University, 1987).

6. D. J. McLaren, "An Anthropocentric View of the Universe: Evidence from Geology," in *Origin and Evolution of the Universe: Evidence for Design?* ed. J. M. Robson (Kingston, Ont.: McGill-Queens University, 1987), pp. 195-209.

7. P. D. Ward and D. Brownlee, *Rare Earth: Why Complex Life Is Uncommon in the Universe* (New York: Copernicus Books, 1999).

Is this appearance of design merely the result of looking back at entirely chance happenings, the effects of *ex post facto* observation? If so, we must embrace the alternative that out of the large (infinite?) number of universes, ours happens to be the one where all this took place. . . . Is postulating infinite universes, all governed by chance, any different from [a] universe with evidence created only in God's mind? Both suggestions are metaphysical, in that each contains a denial of the possibility of their being tested. The terminology differs, but can it seriously be claimed that one is more acceptable than the other? I shall close, not with an answer, but with a plea that man should act, in the absence of any evidence to the contrary, as though he were unique, the sole observer of the universe. Such a moral imperative might finally provide us with the necessary stimulus to ensure our survival.[8]

Earth Systems and Tectonic Development

Earth comprises an extremely complex network of interdependent systems. The term "system" here is defined as the movement of material components from one place to another through the application of energy. In the processes of movement, material and energy are transformed, and all conversions obey the laws of thermodynamics. A closed system without external manipulation (particularly the addition of energy) must run down, that is, tend toward destructive disorder and not produce increasing order. However, Earth's surficial processes do not operate in a closed-system environment. To the best of our knowledge, Earth has the unique planetary attributes of both internal (heat convection) and external (solar radiation) sources of consistent energy.[9] These supply the main driving forces of systemic change. Internal driving energy occurs from primordial heat trapped within and from heat continuously generated by the decay of radioactive elements (mostly ^{40}K). Heat convection cells from the deep Earth serve as conveyor systems, providing new oceanic lithosphere[10] to the surface and recycling old, denser oceanic material back into the lower realms at subduction zones (figure 1). This cycle of crust formation and destruction is the heart of plate tectonic theory and offers an excellent modern explanation for geologic phenomena throughout most of the planet's history.

8. McLaren, "Anthropocentric View," pp. 207, 208.

9. F. Press and R. Siever, *Understanding Earth*, 3rd ed. (New York: Freeman, 2000).

10. Lithosphere: This is essentially the equivalent of a tectonic plate, the upper 100 or so km. of Earth's solid surface. It has the physical property of brittle rigidity in comparison to the hotter, more plastic underlying asthenosphere.

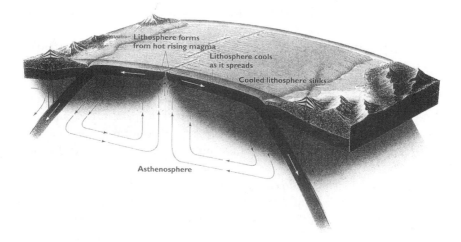

Figure 1. Generalized block section through the Earth depicting the convection flow of heat and magma up from the asthenosphere and across the base of the lithosphere. Rising magma forms new oceanic lithosphere at mid-ocean ridge spreading centers. The older, cooler, denser oceanic lithosphere is shown subducting down beneath the continental edge of one plate on the right and beneath a plate bearing volcanic islands on the left.
From *Understanding Earth* by Frank Press and Raymond Siever, © 1994, 1998, 2001 by Freeman and Company. Used by permission.

The mega theory of plate tectonics is a partner of biological evolution. The concept of continental masses moving about the globe and interacting in the formation of oceans, mountains, and so forth had been around for at least three hundred years before comprehensive elaboration in the early to mid 1900s.[11] The myriad changes in and variety of Earth's surface features are primarily understood as a result of tectonic activity.

There is significant evidence that our planet progressed to the current condition through its own developmental evolution.[12] The earliest time of Earth's existence may likely have been as a poorly defined mixture of solidified compounds, molten liquid and gases swirling about our star ("formless and void," Gen. 1:2). At this early stage of the solar system, Earth cooling had not progressed to the extent of solid, outer crust formation. The oldest known terrestrial rocks (ca. 4 billion years old) are more than half a billion years younger

11. Press and Siever, *Understanding Earth*.
12. S. Drury, *Stepping Stones — The Making of Our Home World* (Oxford and New York: Oxford University Press, 1999).

than some extraterrestrial materials from the solar system (Moon rocks and meteorites).[13]

Before formation of a shielding atmosphere, bombardment by asteroids and planetary and comet debris was relatively frequent. Much of the chemical variety here, including abundant water, may have come from such collisions.[14] It probably took many hundreds of millions of years for Earth to shrink (condense) and consolidate, allowing near-surface rock to persist. It would take even longer for density segregation and degassing[15] to form major compositional layers outward from core to crust and finally out to oceans and atmosphere.

A convenient analogy to envision the early state of plate development is a cooking pot of tomato soup. A transparent pot enables us to watch cycling convection cells rising from the stove's burner up to the soup top (added rice or Worcestershire sauce help!), where cooled soup develops a fragile surface crust. If the pot is boiling, the new crust may fracture and, being denser than the liquid, descend back down the convection current into hotter depths. Earth's earliest masses of crust, especially of continental crust, probably suffered similar fates on a hot, very dynamic unstable surface. The earliest span of Earth time has been appropriately referred to as the "Hadean."

At some point in the first billion years, tectonic activity as we perceive it must have begun. This would involve more stable continental material such as parts of the cooling, thicker lithospheric plates. Since that inception, episodic grand cycles rifted continents to form new oceans, expanded the ocean floors with additions of upwelling magma, shrunk ocean basins by subducting older oceanic lithosphere, and finally collided continental edges of plates to completely close ocean basins. Because these episodes begin and end with masses of different continents assembled by their collision, they are known as "supercontinent cycles."[16] Because they involve the life history of ocean basins, they have also been known as "Wilson cycles," after the noted tectonician, J. Tuzo Wilson of the University of Toronto. The most recent of these cycles began with the global rifting of the supercontinent, Pangea, about 240 million years ago.

---

13. G. B. Dalrymple, *The Age of the Earth* (Stanford: Stanford University Press, 1991).

14. Drury, *Stepping Stones.*

15. Degassing: Processes including volcanism that continue to move lighter, more volatile elements out of the Earth and onto its surface.

16. R. D. Nance, T. R. Worsley, and J. B. Moody, "The Supercontinent Cycle," in *Shaping the Earth — Tectonics of Continents and Oceans*, ed. E. M. Moores (New York: Freeman, 1990), pp. 177-87.

Deciphering Geologic Evidence

Every stage of plate tectonism leaves behind evidence of its existence. Geological studies disclose critical clues for geological detectives who reconstruct natural history, like the events at a crime scene. Popular author John McPhee, in researching his natural history travelogues (many originally published in *The New Yorker*), interviews and accompanies distinguished geologists in the field. In McPhee's *Basin and Range,* the author is so impressed with geologists' analytical ability that he uses the following fable to make his point.

> I once dreamed about a great fire that broke out at night at Nasser Aftab's House of Carpets. In Aftab's showroom under the queen-post trusses were layer upon layer and pile after pile of shags and broadlooms, hooks and throws, para-Persians and polyesters. The intense and shriveling heat consumed or melted most of what was there. The roof gave way. It was a night of cyclonic winds, stabs of unseasonal lightning. Flaming debris fell on the carpets. Layers of ash descended, alighted, swirled in the wind, and drifted. Molten polyester hardened on the cellar stairs. Almost simultaneously there occurred a major accident in the ice-cream factory next door. As yet no people had arrived. Dead of night. Distant city. And before long the west wall of the House of Carpets fell in under the pressure and weight of a broad, braided ooze of six admixing flavors, which slowly entered Nasser Aftab's showroom and folded and double-folded and covered what was left of his carpets, moving them, as well, some distance across the room. Snow began to fall. It turned to sleet, and soon to freezing rain. In heavy winds under clearing skies, the temperature fell to six below zero Celsius. Representatives of two warring insurance companies showed up just in front of the fire engines. The insurance companies needed to know precisely what had happened, and in what order, and to what extent it was Aftab's fault. If not a hundred percent, then to what extent was it the ice-cream factory's fault? And how much fault must be — regrettably — assigned to God? The problem was obviously too tough for the Chicken Valley Police Department, or, for that matter, for any ordinary detective. It was a problem, naturally, for a field geologist. One shuffled in eventually. Scratched-up boots. A puzzled look. He picked up bits of wall and ceiling, looked under the carpets, tasted the ice cream. He felt the risers of the cellar stairs. Looking up, he told Hartford everything it wanted to know. For him this was so simple it was a five-minute job.[17]

17. J. McPhee, *Basin and Range* (New York: Farrar, Straus and Giroux, 1981), pp. 82-83.

Some actual examples help to demonstrate how natural history is interpreted from geologic field evidence.

A. In northern Wisconsin, there are eroded and metamorphosed volcanic rocks nearly 2 billion years in age.[18] In one area these rocks contain metallic ore deposits with geochemical compositions indicating derivation at a mid-ocean-ridge spreading center (figure 1). What used to be near the center of an ancient, extinct ocean is now old, stable North American continent.

B. Undersea volcanic rocks with "pillow" structures make up a prominent layer near the base of the Matterhorn in Switzerland. This layer represents a vestige of an earlier, larger Mediterranean Sea. This also marks the separation between European continental rocks at the base of the mountain from African sedimentary rock units (limestones and sandstones) at the top of the Matterhorn.[19]

C. The occurrences of precious jade in Korea, Japan, and Guatemala are clues to the location of past subduction zones. This is the only tectonic environment on Earth capable of producing the very high pressures and coexisting low crustal temperatures to form the mineral jadeite. Its crystal structure is stable within a very restricted range of suitable conditions.

D. Large blocks of ultramafic rock[20] containing the high-temperature mineral olivine have been tectonically injected up into the cores of many mountain ranges. A most spectacular example of this geology is observed in the Ural Mountains of east-central Russia. The ultramafic material is interpreted to represent uplifted rock from the base of the lithosphere (upper mantle). This now forms the "suture" or zone that welds the formerly separate continents of Europe and Asia. There was once an ocean between the two plates that converged and collided. We find rocks on either side of the Ural suture zone to be very different in age and origin.[21] A more modern case of continent-continent plate collision continues to occur in the Himalayas, a suture between India and Asia.

---

18. J. K. Greenberg and B. A. Brown, "Lower Proterozoic Volcanic Rocks and Their Setting in the Southern Lake Superior District," in *Early Proterozoic Geology of the Great Lakes Region,* ed. L. G. Medaris, Jr., Geological Society of America Memoir 160 (Boulder, Colo.: Geological Society of America, 1983), pp. 67-84.

19. M. G. Rutten, *The Geology of Western Europe* (Amsterdam: Elsevier, 1969).

20. Ultramafic Rocks: This is an aggregation of igneous minerals (mostly silicates) containing relatively high proportions of magnesium and iron and low proportions of silicon. These rocks usually crystallize from very high temperature magmas and characterize the Earth's mantle.

21. V. Nalivkin, *Geology of the U.S.S.R.* (Edinburgh: Oliver and Boyd, 1973).

E. There are numerous features in sedimentary rock, both subtle and not so
    subtle, that provide telltale clues to past geological environments.
    Dinosaur-track expert Martin Lockley can read a great deal of dramatic
    history from the shape, pattern, and coincidence of animal footprints.[22]
    Likewise, a wide range of environmental processes and conditions can be
    concluded from the physical structures and textures in rocks of sedimen-
    tary origin. Highly oxidized sandstones, their cross-bed size and orienta-
    tion, and fossil salt pans indicate that what is now Scotland hosted hot
    desert conditions over 200 million years ago. Rounded, scratched (stri-
    ated) cobbles and boulders of many rock types, surrounded by a clay-rich
    matrix, are some of the distinctive features that suggest the Sahara Desert
    was more like today's Scotland 240 million years ago, that is, it was glaci-
    ated.

Geologists as historians approach existing evidence of the past as clues to
be reconstructed in the right order. This can only be done following the assumption of "actualism" as a guiding principle. Actualism is a modification of
"uniformitarianism," which is usually attributed among geologists to the 18th-
century Scottish churchman, physician, and wealthy farmer James Hutton. The
uniformity principle expresses that "the present is the key to the past." In other
words, modern Earth processes produce observed products, and, if similar
products are preserved in the geologic record, then we can infer the past action
of those modern processes. For example, streams cause stream erosion and produce characteristic stream sediment deposits. Ancient sedimentary rocks that
show all the attributes of stream activity likely resulted from ancient streams.
This of course seems thoroughly logical and has proven to be a reliable general
operating philosophy.

Actualism goes one step further to apply that "what looks like, sounds
like, smells like a goat, etc., is probably a goat." As with Occam's Razor, the most
obvious, consistent explanation is probably the best in practice. We need not
resort to more fanciful hypotheses unless there is a compelling reason to do so.
For Christians, the actualism/uniformity principle corresponds with our belief
that God is the author of order, consistency, and stability in the universe. This
neither supports nor opposes the possibility of miracles.

A last important consideration of uniformity is that it does not mean the
same as gradualism. Actualism/uniformity acknowledges that geological events
then as now occur over a wide range of time scales. Asteroid impact, volcanic
eruptions, floods, earthquakes, mass wasting (landslides, mudflows, etc.), and

22. M. Lockley, *The Eternal Trail* (Reading, Pa.: Perseus, 1999).

other catastrophic events are all instantaneous punctuations in the geologic record. These are dispersed among many longer-lived, slow processes such as
chemical erosion, sea-level fluctuation, cooling of igneous intrusions, uplift of
mountains, burial of sedimentary deposits, and the formation of petroleum.[23]

A Geologic Time Scale

Our modern conception of a geological time scale (figure 2) has itself evolved
from a simple four-part division into a comprehensive and dynamic scheme in
which subdivisions continue to undergo refinement. Good references describing
the development of the time scale and its significance are works by M. J. S.
Rudwick and H. L. Levin.[24] Many geologists have contributed to the establishment and revision of time boundaries. From the early 1800s, regional studies
proposed names for particular sections of documented strata. These were then
placed in chronological order, at first according to superposition (oldest on bottom; see discussion of relative age determination below), and then by successive
changes in fossil organisms. The direct observation of biological remains was
and is powerful evidence for evolution. Widespread documentation of fossil
successions across Europe provided a means of correlating the age of strata, even
if the specific time in question was unknown. The utility of fossil evidence in
correlation has been extended today across oceans to all landmasses.

Generally speaking, the hierarchy of geological time divisions corresponds to the scale of evolutionary variation. For example, the divisions of
greatest duration, **eons**, separate biota into simpler single-celled bacteria and
algae in the Archean, more complex single-celled life and a relative abundance
of multicellular organisms without hard skeletal structures in the Proterozoic,
and finally the maximum diversity of life forms over the last 13 percent of
Earth's history in the Phanerozoic. The next major subdivision of time, the **era**,
has greatest evolutionary significance during the Phanerozoic. The end of the
first two Phanerozoic eras, the Paleozoic and Mesozoic, coincide with tremendous extinction events. The next subdivision into **periods** has its primary derivation from the European studies of the 19th century. Each period is tied to biological evolution such that famous labels have been applied: Cambrian, the "age
of trilobites"; Devonian, the "age of fishes"; Pennsylvanian, the "age of coal"

23. A. N. Strahler, *Science and Earth History — the Evolution/Creation Controversy* (Buf-
falo, N.Y.: Prometheus, 1987).

24. M. J. S. Rudwick, *The Meaning of Fossils: Episodes in the History of Paleontology*, 2nd
ed. (Chicago: University of Chicago Press, 1985). H. L. Levin, *The Earth Through Time*, 6th ed.
(Fort Worth: Saunders, 1999).

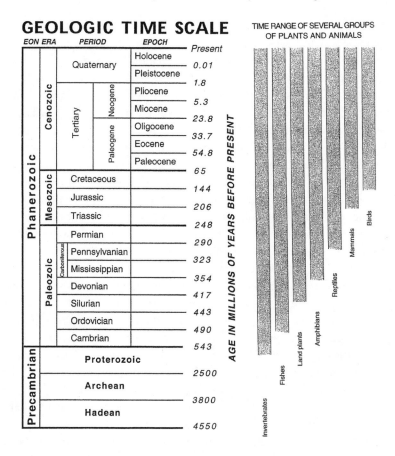

Figure 2. Geologic time scale with subdivisions from eons through epochs.
Geologic dates taken from the 1999 Geologic Time Scale © 1999 Geological Society of America, and time ranges from Levin, *The Earth Through Time*.

(and terrestrial plants). Further refinement of periods by evolutionary distinctiveness has led to further division into **epochs** and even **ages** of geologically brief duration.

Geology and Evolution

It is most appropriate to consider natural history as the progression of changes in living things with corresponding changes in their environments. Texts in historical geology emphasize the geographic variety of past geological conditions and the more distinctive assemblages of fossils.[25] Descriptions are typically done eon by eon and period by period through time from the beginning. Unfortunately, biological evolution and major geologic changes are not usually discussed together in the same chapters of these books. This artificially separates evolution from its context. The advent of major biological innovations often took place concurrently or just after significant geological events. The rates of respective change were not exactly synchronized because the velocity of plate motion (and thus large, gradual change on the order of a few centimeters per year) is not the same as estimated genetic mutation rates or those of other evolutionary selection mechanisms. Some taxa of organisms appear to have recovered relatively quickly from catastrophic events, such as the hypothesized bolide impact disaster at the end of the Mesozoic era.[26] Other groups including the dinosaurs and ammonite cephalopods[27] became extinct. Between extremes, there are groups, perhaps including mammals, that slowly diversified and became more widely distributed than ever before.

To the practice of geology, the mechanisms of biological modification are irrelevant. I tell my students and curious friends that it is not difficult for a Christian geologist to think of biological evolution as the most reasonable explanation available for observed geological facts. The facts are that preserved biota and their traces do change significantly throughout the sequences of rocks on Earth. The change in biological form and function occurs in an observed succession from older ("lower") up through younger ("higher") geologic units. Changes are generally consistent with the modification of what appear to be ancestral forms. How genetic change occurs is not a geological concern. Why organisms change may best be seen as adaptation to variations in geologic environments. With respect to geology, the rates of biological change can only be estimated by comparing fossils with their dated (see discussion below) host rocks. If the enclosing rocks are undated or the dates are not precise enough (especially from fossil layer to fossil layer), then rate correlation may not be resolvable. As Keith Miller states in chapter 8 of this volume, fossil preservation is a selective process itself and does not allow anything like the uninterrupted reconstruction of natural history. However, there are near-contemporaneous sequences of sedimentary deposits that do indicate both

25. Rudwick, *Meaning of Fossils.*

26. Bolide: An asteroid or meteorite that explodes on contact with the Earth's surface. For a discussion of the impact hypothesis see C. Frankel, *The End of the Dinosaurs* (Cambridge and New York: Cambridge University Press, 1999).

27. Cephalopods: Marine mollusks of the class Cephalopoda with tentacles surrounding the mouth. These include squid and octopus and are represented in the past by many varieties with straight or coiled shells.

gradual progression from earlier forms to later (i.e., transitional forms) and times when forms came (sudden first appearance), went (extinction without derived forms), or changed rather abruptly (punctuated change).[28]

"Benefits" of Geological Change

Before a brief description of geological "clocks" that provides the context of time for evolution, a reference back to the Anthropic Principle completes the ecological context. Science fiction writers have mused about the prospect of colonizing other planets or the Moon. Much that they imagine, including cities, gardens, and mines, is likely to remain fictitious because of the relative sterility of other worlds. They are without the dynamic systems to enrich local regions in essential components to support the intricate web of life on Earth. Through the progressive development mentioned above, Earth episodically gained its unique nurturing qualities. Until the level of atmospheric oxygen reached a necessary threshold, important organic structures and functions were impossible.[29] The chemistry of seawater and equilibrium dynamics of carbon dioxide, sulfur compounds, and general nutrient cycling were certainly also critical developments in fostering biological diversity (development of skeletal material, for example).

Modern human culture has come to depend on a great variety of mineral resource deposits. These commodities are available only through the natural processes of terrestrial change. In the case of gold, as an example, several different types of processing are essential to generate an ore-quality deposit, that is, one that is exploitable. Gold probably exists as much less than one part per million (ppm) in the entire planet (if homogeneous). A profitable gold deposit requires approximately 4,000 or more parts per million.[30] The desired ore must be concentrated from the whole-earth abundance through a series of processes. The initial step was the segregation of continental crust from the hotter, denser mantle. This enriched gold by about 100% (.5 up to 1.0 ppm). Next, the continental rocks are further enriched in low-temperature components (and gold) by the intrusion of granite magmas higher into the crust. This consistently occurs along continental-plate margins where subduction zones generate magma (figure 1). A third step of ore concentration can take place around the upper edges of granite bodies, where they host zones of metamorphism and fractures

28. To learn more about the nature of the fossil record, see Keith Miller's paper herein and Rudwick, *Meaning of Fossils.*

29. Drury, *Stepping Stones.*

30. B. J. Skinner and S. C. Porter, *The Dynamic Earth* (New York: Wiley, 1989).

that fill with cooler fluids (veins). Some of the veins themselves may contain enough gold to constitute ore deposits (from 1.0 up to thousands of ppm). However, the veins may be too small or dispersed to offer profitable volumes of gold. Finally, through the process of tectonic uplift and accompanying erosion, the gold-bearing material is preferentially concentrated into streams. Here, gravel-bar accumulations, known as placer deposits, may contain gold at levels well above 10,000 ppm. The 1849 California gold rush began through the discovery of placer deposits that likely were the result of the processing chain described above. Gold is only one example of the multitude of ores that depend upon geologic processing to concentrate and become support for our lifestyles.

Reference to Geological Clocks: Relative and Absolute Age

Geological "clocks" are indicators from natural processes of their duration or specific time of occurrence. The ability to measure absolute geological time is particularly useful within the framework of knowing relative age relationships. In the 1600s, Danish physician Nicholas Steno specified a basic set of common-sense principles to describe the position of rock strata. "Original horizontality," "super-position," and "lateral continuity" refer to the way sediment is deposited. It is typically laid down in horizontal layers, in decreasing age from bottom layers to top and in consistent bodies distributed over an area. Steno's principles were greatly supported by geologists in the early 1800s. William Smith and Charles Lyell respectively contributed the "principle of biological succession" and the "principle of cross-cutting relationships" to our repertoire of interpretive tools.

There are many more natural clocks described in publication than are referred to in this paper. They can be considered in different categories, but only three, Physical Properties, Sedimentary Processes, and Absolute Age Determination, are discussed here.

Physical Properties

Plate dynamics depend on the physical properties of the lithosphere. Direct modern observation of plate motion vectors can be recorded by laser ranging and satellite triangulation (GPS technology). There is no question that plates move and have moved slowly in their interaction. There is no viable evidence that paleovelocities greatly exceeded those of today. Dated samples of ocean-floor volcanic rock are located at distances from their spreading-center origin that indicate relative consistency of plate velocity, at least over the last 160 million years or so (figure 3). Computer models that suggest the possibility of very high plate velocities[31] are not consistent with geological reality. These models are constructed by the manipulation of physical variables. A major problem with this "fast tectonics" operating at any time is that it exceeds natural physical properties of geological materials. For example, rocks of the lithosphere (upper 100 km. or so of the solid Earth) are relatively cool and brittle in comparison with those of deeper regions. Under deforming stresses, rock will behave in a brittle manner unless the strain (effect of stress forces) occurs very slowly.[32] Brittle rock shatters; it does not perform as a coherent unit. This is easily demonstrated in laboratory experiments with different rocks, stress magnitudes, and strain rates. In order to form the more plastic/ductile structural features observed from plate interactions (folded rocks, metamorphic textures, elongated pebbles, or fossils, etc.), slow tectonic convergence, on the order of that currently observed, is necessary.

Davis Young discussed another phenomenon of geologic time related to physical properties.[33] The solidification of magma bodies involves the dissipation of tremendous amounts of heat through poorly conductive rock. For particularly large volumes of magma, such as those that make up sections of the Sierra Nevada range, the Duluth Complex in Minnesota, the Wolf River batholith[34] in Wisconsin, or the Palisades Sill[35] in New Jersey, the calculated times of crystallization cooling are on the order of hundreds of thousands to a few millions of years. The cooling-rate equation is a relatively simple relationship.[36] The time needed to effectively convert many cubic kilometers of sedimentary rocks into high-grade[37] metamorphic mineral assemblages is an even stronger argument for the duration of geologic time.[38]

31. J. Baumgardiner, "Computer Modeling of Large-Scale Tectonics Associated with the Genesis Flood," article prepared for the Third International Conference on Creation, Pittsburgh, 1994 and available on line from the Institute for Creation Research or from the author.

32. G. H. Davis and S. J. Reynolds, *Structural Geology of Rocks and Regions* (New York: Wiley, 1996).

33. Young, *Creation and the Flood*.

34. Batholith: A large body or mass of intrusive igneous rock with more than 100 km. of surface exposure.

35. Sill: An igneous intrusion that is parallel to the planar structure of surrounding rock. These are commonly observed as tabular bodies concordant with sedimentary layering, whereas a "dike" is seen to discordantly cut across layering or other features.

36. J. C. Jaeger, "Cooling and Solidification of Igneous Rocks," in *Basalts: The Poldervaart Treatise on Rocks of Basaltic Composition*, vol. 2, ed. H. H. Hess and A. Poldervaart (New York: Wiley-Interscience, 1968), pp. 503-36.

37. High grade: In metamorphic terms, this applies to rocks that have been converted by relatively extreme temperature and pressure conditions.

38. Young *(Creation and the Flood)* and Strahler *(Science and Earth History)* discuss metamorphism as a refutation of young-Earth creationism and flood geology.

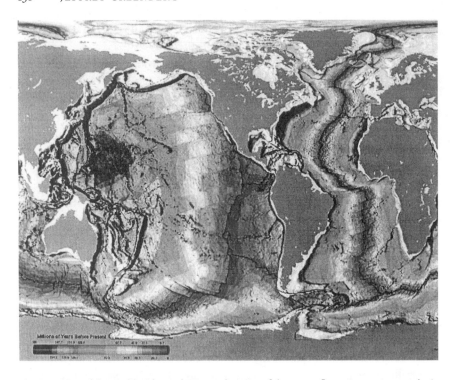

Figure 3. Map of the world with emphasis on the ages of the ocean floor. Ocean topography is depicted with water removed. Areas of seafloor with the same relative intensity of gray tones indicate bands of equivalent age. Note that the age patterns are nearly symmetrical on either side of the mid-ocean ridges (seafloor spreading centers). The ocean floor increases in age away from the ridges, with the oldest known ocean floor volcanic rocks located adjacent to eastern North America, western Africa, and southeast of Japan. The oldest dates have a maximum at about 200 million years ago.
Taken from a National Oceanographic and Atmospheric Agency (NOAA) poster in the public domain.

Sedimentary Processes

There are many types of processes, all related to the erosion, deposition, or maturation of sediment, that indicate the necessity of time spans into the millions of years. Again, the reader is referred to some of the publications mentioned above for details. Two by Daniel Wonderly specifically focus on sedimentary geology, *God's Time-Records in Ancient Sediments* and *Neglect of Geological Data: Sedimentary Strata Compared with Young-Earth Creationist Writings*. Among the more significant examples are glaciation and varved deposits, carbonate reef buildup, abyssal plain deposits, turbidites, evaporites, cave formations, and paleosols. Each of these will be discussed in brief below.

Continental glaciation has left its mark in many places throughout the globe. The most recent "Great Ice Ages" of glacial advances (from about 2,000,000 to about 8,000 years ago) are well preserved in North America and Europe.[39] The areas affected and rates of glacial movement indicate many thousands of years of activity; this impression is multiplied when we realize that some of the glaciated areas were repeatedly covered by ice sheets during sequences of advance and retreat. Further evidence of duration is exhibited by glacial lake deposits. Some of these include "varves," paired layers indicating a year's deposition. Typically, a thinner, darker organic-rich layer develops during the winter when the lake is covered by ice. The frozen condition precludes much sediment from entering the lake. During spring and summer, thawing contributes new sediment runoff into the now-open lake. This produces a thicker, lighter-colored layer. Each season repeats the two-layer deposit. Geologists note various locations where there are thousands to hundreds of thousands of these varve pairs.[40]

Carbonate "coral" reefs exist today in warm water coastal areas of the world. The very precise conditions of warm, clear water and growth within twenty meters or so of the surface help geologists interpret the paleo-environment where ancient, fossil reefs are found (the south side of Chicago, for example). Huge buildups of carbonate reefs may form accumulations thousands of feet in depth.[41] The facts are that these reef communities of organisms grow slowly and are susceptible to erosion by storms and the boring/abrasion action of organisms. The presence of miles of fossil reefs beneath living ones must point to a very long history of relatively stable development.

Abyssal plain sedimentation exists in stark contrast to reef deposition. The plains are truly the flattest large areas on Earth.[42] They are not the deepest parts of oceans; subduction trenches in the southwestern Pacific, off the Aleutian Islands, off western South America, off the West Indies, and so forth are the deepest. However, the plains are generally the most remote from major landmasses. This means that they receive very little sediment volume compared to areas near the continents (source of erosion and sediment). Researchers have placed collectors on the plains to measure the influx of sediment. As expected,

39. D. I. Benn and D. J. A. Evans, *Glaciers and Glaciation* (London: Arnold, 1990).

40. Strahler, *Science and Earth History*.

41. R. E. Sheridan, H. T. Mullins, J. A. Austin, Jr., M. M. Ball, and J. W. Ladd, "Geology and Geophysics of the Bahamas," in *The Atlantic Continental Margin: U.S.*, vol. 1-2: *The Geology of North America*, ed. R. E. Sheridan and J. A. Grow (Boulder, Colo.: Geological Society of America, 1988), pp. 329-64. See also discussion in Chapter 17 of this volume.

42. M. McLane, *Sedimentology* (New York: Oxford University Press, 1995).

the rates of deposition are miniscule; millimeters per thousand years is not an unusual estimate. The sediment itself is composed of wind-blown dust, some volcanic ash, and the tests (skeletons) of microorganisms. The fact that we observe very significant accumulations of ancient abyssal deposits now on land (from sea-level change and tectonism mostly, such as the white chalk cliffs of Dover) strongly suggests long periods of sedimentation.[43]

Turbidite sequences are fascinating clues to Earth processes occurring off the continental shelves. To the geologist interpreter, what is read "in between the lines" is of more temporal importance than the rocks themselves. In the 1920s, the trans-Atlantic cable laid for communications was suddenly broken in several places. Not until later did scientists realize that the damage was caused by underwater avalanches of dense, sediment-laden water. Today these avalanches or "turbidity currents" can be directly observed from submersible craft with cameras. Geologists were already familiar with sedimentary rock sequences of distinctive, "fining upward" character. Experiments in the 1930s recreating turbidity current deposition reproduced the sequences observed in nature. Each sequence of various layers, beginning with coarser-grained sands and gravels and ending on top with very fine-grained silts and clays, could be deposited over a period of months on the ocean floor off continents. However, the amazing realization was that the time between each sequence was of much greater duration, because a huge pile of sediment must first develop on the continental-shelf edge before becoming unstable and spilling over the edge. Estimated sedimentation rates on the shelves indicate that times on the order of thousands of years are necessary to produce some of these accumulations prior to their rapid movement off shelf. Thus single exposures of multiple turbidite sequences in the Alps tell a story many thousands of years long. Multiply one such exposure with many others above and below, and the correct impression is of a truly ancient episode.

Evaporite deposits are minerals precipitated as water is converted to water vapor, especially in warm climates. Rock salt (halite) and calcium sulfate (gypsum) are common evaporitic minerals. These exist in layers of great thickness in certain areas of the Earth. Notable examples are the margins of the Gulf of Mexico, and the Persian Gulf and its margins, and beneath the floor of the Mediterranean Sea. The primary environment of evaporation occurs very near the interface of water and air, that is, evaporites do not develop at depth beneath other sediments. Along the Texas gulf coast, there are great thicknesses of salt buried below miles of silts, sands and gravels.[44] The chronological impor-

---

43. Wonderly, *God's Time-Records*.

44. A. Salvador, "Triassic-Jurassic," in *The Gulf of Mexico Basin*, vol. J: *The Geology of North America*, ed. A. Salvador (Boulder, Colo.: Geological Society of America, 1988), pp. 131-80.

tance here is that (a) the salt itself could be deposited in great thickness only over great time, and (b) the tremendous sequence of sedimentary layers above the salt also represent the great time necessary for the floor of the gulf to slowly subside as a depositional basin. Reconstructed history interprets the salt as a continual deposit from great volumes of seawater invading the newly opened rift between North and South America a bit less than 200 million years ago. Evaporites commonly occur just above volcanic rocks at the base of rift basins.

Caves, particularly those that develop within chemically eroded carbonate rocks (limestones and dolostones), show many features of temporal significance. The formation of "dripstone" stalagmites and stalactites occurs as water slowly seeps through rock and precipitates calcite as carbon dioxide is lost to the air. D. Gillieson[45] lists the rates of observed precipitation from various fast-growing formations, ranging from .01 to 7.66 mm. per year. Many dripstone columns contain annular layers of calcite growth, much like the growth rings in trees. The calcite rings form distinct zones related to changes in drip rate and chemical composition. These factors are mostly from seasonal variations in climate. Examples of thick deposits with many thousands of rings are known from New Mexico and elsewhere. The very existence of major carbonate-cave networks suggests great time and geologic change. Most cave networks are interpreted to have formed initially when sea level and local groundwater tables were relatively high. The rate of chemical dissolution to form passageways along fractures and major cavern "rooms" at the intersection of fractures is again quite small in comparison to the volume of rock removed. Depositional features like dripstone formations can develop only after the caves are raised significantly above prevailing water tables. This could of course also occur if the sea level dropped significantly (as during the Great Ice Ages).

Paleosols are soils buried at some point by later deposition. Geologists find paleosols in many places, both in the subsurface (through drilling) and exposed by erosion. The environmental indication of ancient soil development may be subtle or more obvious.[46] An obvious example would be a zone, perhaps tens of centimeters to meters in thickness, between two beds of marine limestone. The zone contains a red and green horizontally banded clayey interval with aluminum- and iron-oxide nodules, preserved soil structures at the macroscopic and microscopic scale, and the root casts of fossil plants. This interval might be overlain by preserved mud cracks and the tracks of reptiles or insects. All of

45. D. Gillieson, *Caves — Processes, Development and Management* (Oxford, U.K.: Blackwell, 1996).

46. G. J. Retallack, "The Fossil Record of Soils," in *Paleosols — Their Recognition and Interpretation*, ed. V. P. Wright (Princeton: Princeton University Press, 1986), pp. 1-57.

these represent an emergent, terrestrial environment. The surrounding lime-stones contain marine fossils, perhaps corals in growth position, clams, sponges, snails, and so forth. The most reasonable interpretation is of relatively long periods necessary to establish a terrestrial ecosystem before and after established seafloor environments. Absolute times for development can be estimated from modern examples. Depending on climatic conditions and sediment or rock composition, a single soil profile may take hundreds to tens of thousands of years to form. In regions where many paleosols occur in a sequence of geological strata, the impression is of very long periods of environmental change.

Absolute Age Determination

All the preceding "clocks" offer a good sense of duration in the development of geologic features. Alone or combined, these are incapable of specifying any particular time in the past. With the discovery of radioactivity in the late 1800s came the mathematical relationship capable of calculating exact (within limits of accuracy) dates in the past. Scientific methodology for radiometric age determination has become very sophisticated and greatly refined over the last century. There are currently about 40 separate techniques utilizing different radioactive isotopes.[47] Geochronologists, the geologic "daters" in the laboratory, are extremely careful analysts. They employ many safeguards to ensure that the age data obtained are reliable. Because absolute-age determination is a very technical subject, it is difficult for those with little science background to comprehend it. This may lead to skepticism, especially among those suspicious of ancient dates. Explaining the key details of theory and practice needs the skill of an excellent communicator. Therefore, few geology texts containing sections on geochronology are helpful to the layman. Clear and relatively simple discussions have been produced to overcome confusion. Young's treatment[48] is a good starting point, but the information is a bit behind more recent developments. Roger Wiens has written a summary paper specifically for Christians concerned with issues of time. He includes a section on common misunderstandings.[49] Another good treatment for the general public that covers various aspects of geologic time is published by the Arizona Geological Survey.[50]

47. A. P. Dickin, *Radiogenic Isotope Geology* (Cambridge and New York: Cambridge University Press, 1995).

48. Young, *Creation and the Flood* and *Christianity and the Age of the Earth*.

49. American Scientific Affiliation website: http://asa.calvin.edu

50. E. M. Van Dolder, *How Geologists Tell Time*, Down-To-Earth Series 4 (Tucson, Ariz.: Arizona Geological Survey, 1995).

The basic principle applied in calculating radiometric ages is simple: a particular amount of isotope spontaneously "decays" through the emission of energy (plus or minus mass) during regular nuclear fission events. The rates of decay are theoretically (from physical theory) and empirically (from laboratory measurement) constant. To the best of our understanding, they have not, do not, and will not vary under any conceivable condition on Earth. Extreme application of heat, cold, pressure (even explosion), and chemical reaction has caused no change in measured decay rates. Only focused bombardment by high-energy particles (gamma radiation) is capable of penetrating the protective orbits of electrons around atomic nuclei. This is precisely how some nuclear reactions are intentionally propagated in "splitting atoms."

Two basic schemes of radiometric determination are most commonly employed in age investigations. These are the carbon-14 and "parent-daughter" techniques. Carbon-14 or radiocarbon dating has distinctive qualities that make it useful where other methods are of no utility. Carbon-14 is a radioactive isotope of carbon; carbon-12 is the most common and nonradioactive isotope. After one half-life[51] of about 5,730 years, half of any amount of carbon-14 will decay to form nitrogen. Geochronologists will measure the amount of carbon-14 in a sample, measure the amount of carbon-12, and compare this ratio with the current atmospheric C-14/C-12 ratio. The current atmospheric ratio is quite constant. After the ratio is obtained and corrections are made to compensate for established variation (rather minor) in the ratio over the last several thousand years,[52] a date is determined.

The above description oversimplifies the fact that radiocarbon methods are based on critical principles. First of all, anything analyzed needs to have been in atmospheric equilibrium with respect to carbon. This means a constant exchange of carbon-14 and carbon-12 through respiration, photosynthesis, nutrient consumption, or gas trapping (as in ice). As long as the exchange continues, the ratio remains a constant. If the previously open system is closed, say through death, then the carbon-14 will decay and diminish in relation to the carbon-12. The new ratio measured at any time in the history of the closed system is translatable by way of decay rate into time in the past. Examples might include bones from a sacrificed animal found in conjunction with charcoal from the fire of offering. If both materials are found to possess C-14/C-12 ratios about half of the atmospheric ratio (say 1:2000 instead of 1:1000), then approximately one half-life of time has passed since

---

51. Half-life: The time necessary for half of any amount of a radioactive isotope to decay and convert to another element. Each specific isotope has its own half-life determined by a characteristic decay rate.

52. Press and Siever, *Understanding Earth.*

the animal and tree were alive. After two half-lives, the new ratio would be close to 1:4000; three half-lives, 1:8000, and so on. The change is obviously exponential and not linear. Another crucial consideration for any particular technique is the time limit of resolution. For methods involving very long half-lives (slow decay and daughter accumulation, such as Rb-Sr with 48.8 billion-year half-life), younger materials are impossible or at least more problematical. For C-14 with a short half-life, anything older than about 50,000 years before the present is a problem. At the younger end, samples less than a few hundred years old are difficult to impossible to date with radiocarbon. Fortunately, most things of archaeological interest fall within the more optimal brackets of carbon-14 dating.

In "parent-daughter" dating techniques, the amount of decaying parent isotope is measured along with the amount of accumulating daughter product. The ratio of these two elements (such as uranium parent producing lead daughter) at any time is a function of the decay rate and the time since the original amount of parent began to decay. Knowing the measured ratio of elements and knowing the decay rate (in terms of half-life), we can calculate the time of interest. With respect to igneous rocks, the age calculated indicates the time that the magma cooled to solid and the parental isotope then captured in the rock began to convert to its daughter. As mentioned above, there are many screens and safeguards used to be sure that the age data calculated are of real geologic significance. Some concerns that are correctable include (a) the amount of daughter elements trapped in cooled magma (not to be counted as products of the measured parent), (b) the possibility of losing or gaining key elements after solidification (as through chemical erosion or metamorphism), and (c) possible contamination of samples or instrumentation. There is strength in numbers. This principle is applied to eliminate errors in geochronology. For example, several samples are commonly analyzed from the same rock, exposure, or area, so that any one aberrant sample will be suspect. For very important materials, samples may also be analyzed at multiple laboratories, for the same reason. Multiple analyses apply the filtering concept that the "signal" (correct result) will be enhanced and the "noise" (random error) will be eliminated.

I am frequently asked why I think radiometric ages are generally reliable. Even if someone stumbles over the simpler aspects of the dating methods, one can grasp the importance of agreement. The vast majority of published absolute-age data agree with the constraints of the local geology. This is to say, for example, that the average 550 million-year ages calculated for a large group of granite bodies in eastern Egypt[53] confirm their position after older igneous

---

53. J. K. Greenberg, "Characteristics and Origin of Egyptian Younger Granites," *Bulletin of the Geological Society of America* 92 (1981): 749-840.

and metamorphic rocks in the area (about 900 million years old), which the granites intrude (cut across), and before small intrusions of magma (dikes), dated near 140 million years old, which in turn cut the granite. The same granite ages demonstrate agreement in a most convincing manner. Due to their chemical composition, the granites were amenable to analysis by three different parent-daughter radiometric techniques: Uranium-Lead (U-Pb), Potassium-Argon (K-Ar), and Rubidium-Strontium (Rb-Sr). Each method involves unique isotopes with unique half-lives (decay rates). Any problem with one method has no bearing on any other. The Egyptian granites all yielded the same ages within a small margin of error. This degree of agreement is very common.

Siccar Point and the Grand Canyon as Classic and Comprehensive Cases in Reconstructing the Past

James Hutton's fame was earned in large part from his interpretation of time in rock. At Siccar Point along the Scottish coast, he noticed that three generations of sand beaches coexisted (figure 4). One was of course contemporary; the other two offered him compelling testimony of a dynamic Earth in the past. At ocean level, layers (beds) of reddish sandstone jut up nearly vertical from the water. Directly above the steeply inclined beds are very similar sandstone strata but with a more gently tilted orientation. The presence of an irregular surface on the underlying beds and fragments of sandstone cobbles in the basal beds of the upper sandstone helped confirm the following sequence of events in Hutton's mind: (1) deposition of sand along beach #1, (2) burial and subsequent uplift by mountain building, (3) erosion to sea level, (4) deposition of sand along beach #2 on the eroded surface of deformed beach #1, (5) uplift, tilting, and erosion of the entire package, producing sand on the modern beach #3.

In further observation of exposures near his home, Hutton described inclined beds of sandstone underlain by highly contorted metamorphic rocks (schist and gneiss). He recognized that major episodes of geological development and long time spans were necessary to explain what was seen. Without the benefit of modern technology he perceived Earth history in terms of hundreds of thousands to millions of years.

In 1869, one hundred years after Hutton stalked across Scotland, adventurer-geologist John Wesley Powell rafted through the Grand Canyon on the Colorado River. He was early witness to over a vertical mile of complex geological relationships. Tools of interpretation developed over the years since

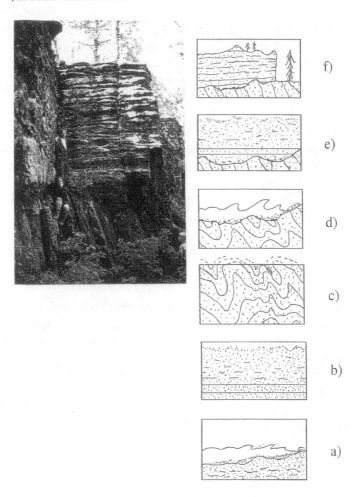

Figure 4. Photo of an angular unconformity exposed in the Black Hills of South Dakota (analogous to Hutton's Scottish exposure). The person below (Laura) is sitting on Precambrian quartzite. The person above (Dave) is standing on the unconformity overlain by lowermost Cambrian sandstone. Note the steeply inclined to vertical layers in the quartzite, and the nearly horizontal bedding in the overlying sandstone. (Photo by J. T. Bean)

The sequence of geological events required to finally produce the angular unconformity is illustrated in the sketches from earliest to most recent (a-f).

a. Original beach sand is deposited;

b. The area is buried deeply, causing the formation of dense sandstone;

c. Uplift, tilting, and metamorphism then occur during a tectonic (mountain building) event;

d. Beach #2 forms on the surface of eroded quartzite;

e. A new stage of burial produces a younger Cambrian sandstone upon the Precambrian surface;

f. A new stage of uplift causes the current outcrop to be exposed.

Powell's wild ride allow us to break down the story of the Grand Canyon into many fascinating episodes.[54]

For the sake of telling its story, Grand Canyon history ("Book of Revelation in the rock-leaved Bible of geology" according to Powell) can be divided into three main "chapters": (1) the early history of continental growth; (2) the transition to a more stable continent; and (3) the repeated history of climatic and relative sea-level change. The essential field relationships are shown in figure 5.

1. The lower elevations of the canyon reveal the basement rock of southwestern North America. These are the products of igneous and metamorphic processes, somewhat analogous to the older rocks Hutton described. The canyon's oldest units are in the Vishnu Metamorphic Complex. It is composed of material originally deposited as sediment and lava flows between about 2,000 million and 1,800 million years ago. The material was subsequently deformed and metamorphosed, perhaps twice by tectonic events between 1,720 and 1,650 million years ago. Even these ancient dates are long after the first consolidation of continental crust exposed to the north, two billion years earlier. Geochemical and structural features in the canyon suggest that the early Proterozoic tectonic episodes included the rifting apart of continental masses followed by collision of diverse geological provinces as plates converged. Volcanic island arcs, such as the modern West Indies or the Aleutians, were swept together and welded on to the growing mass of North America. The first chapter of development ended with the intrusion of mostly granitic magmas up into the metamorphosed rock. Researchers believe that this intrusive episode may signal the end of lateral growth of the continental core in the region. It should be noted that age relationships in the older units are established by absolute methods as well as by cross-cutting relationships. For example, dikes or veins of igneous rock are younger than the fractured host rock. This is in full agreement with available radiometric age data.

2. A conspicuous sequence of tilted sedimentary and minor igneous rocks is exposed in the canyon upon the eroded surface of the older units described above. The entire package of rock units, known as the Grand Canyon Supergroup, can be placed between 1,500 million and 550 million years ago by its position above the dated basement and immediately below fossil-dated strata. Especially in the younger (upper) members of the

54. S. S. Beus and M. Morales, eds., *Grand Canyon Geology* (New York: Oxford University Press; Flagstaff, Ariz.: Museum of Northern Arizona Press, 1990).

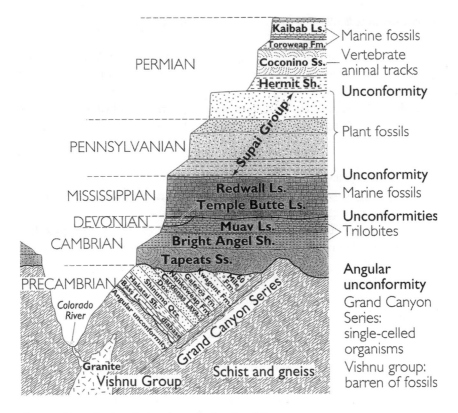

Figure 5. Generalized geologic column for the Grand Canyon.
From *Understanding Earth* by Frank Press and Raymond Siever, © 1994, 1998, 2001 by Freeman and Company. Used by permission.

supergroup, there are fossils of algal structures (stromatolites) and algaelike microfossils. This correlates well with some other areas on Earth where later Precambrian sedimentary rock is exposed. Absolute time markers include an age of 1,100 million years on lava flows from near the center of the supergroup and a paleomagnetic[55] "pole position" in agreement, somewhere between 1,250 and 1,070 million years ago. Together, the

55. Paleomagnetic: This refers to the property of some iron-bearing minerals to retain directional "memory" of Earth's magnetic poles when incorporated in their host rock. This occurs in igneous rock as magnetic minerals crystallize and become locked into position. As Earth's plates move across the globe, paleomagnetic directions (determined in the laboratory) trace a distinctive path. Rocks of the same age on the same moving plate should yield the same paleomagnetic direction. For more detail, see Press and Siever, *Understanding Earth.*

sedimentary and mostly volcanic igneous rocks of the Grand Canyon Supergroup reveal a series of geological events. These include the erosion of an uplifted continental block and development of a continental margin similar to that along the Atlantic edge of North America today. The sea level made several substantial changes during this interval, as indicated by the wide variety in sedimentary materials deposited. The interlayered volcanic units are distinctive evidence of a time when crustal extension and rifting occurred in several regions of Earth.

3. The prominent upper sedimentary beds in the Grand Canyon are horizontal to slightly inclined and span the Paleozoic era of geologic time (ca. 550 to 270 million years ago). Nearby, in exposures outside the canyon, the sequence continues upward into progressively younger strata of the Mesozoic and Cenozoic eras. Careful analysis of sedimentary environments reveals an extensive chronicle of western North American history.

There is a record of rising seas with the evolutionary comings and goings of trilobites, beginning in the Cambrian. An extended time of nondeposition and erosion occurred over the Ordovician and Silurian periods. This gap in the record is represented by the surface between the Cambrian and overlying Devonian fossilized strata, which marked the return of a warm tropical sea. A different trilobite fauna had arrived in the Devonian along with diverse groups of fish. Thick marine deposits of carbonate rocks (represented in part by the famous Redwall Limestone) indicate the persistence of a tropical seaway throughout most of the lower Carboniferous (Mississippian period). The upper surface of Mississippian exposures is deeply incised by stream channels, features signaling the transition to terrestrial environments. This is interpreted as a time of orogeny (mountain building) in the southwestern U.S., contemporaneous with the aggregation of tectonic plates into the Pangea supercontinent. The final series of sedimentary units in the Grand Canyon were deposited at the end of the Paleozoic, during the upper Carboniferous (Pennsylvanian) and Permian periods. Distinctive sedimentary features suggest a variety of nonmarine environments. Reddish and orange sands, silts, and mud were eroded from the mountainous highlands. The characteristic coloration is an indicator of terrestrial oxidation of iron minerals. Other telltale features indicate an eolian (wind blown) deposition of sand dunes, evaporite deposits of gypsum, and tracks of both vertebrate (reptilian) and invertebrate (arthropod) animals. The reconstructed scene is of an arid coastal plain akin to the margin of the modern Persian Gulf.

At the end of the Paleozoic, conditions changed again to become more similar to the early Paleozoic. A new seaway developed with an influx of marine deposits fluctuating between carbonate and quartz-rich sources. Later events recorded in geology nearby and extending into the canyon include the Laramide (Rocky Mountain) Orogeny and volcanism related to regional extension of the crust. Faults and minor igneous invasions form the post-Paleozoic episodes that crosscut all the rocks exposed in the Grand Canyon. Davis Young[56] provides a detailed geological account of the Colorado Plateau and the canyon to demonstrate the overwhelming logic of extended history.

One Final Geological Picture of Life in the Past

The detective work of geologists has shown the ability to re-create scenes in four dimensions. An excellent reconstruction of ancient life and its habitat is presented in the volume *Mazon Creek Fossils*, edited by M. H. Nitecki.[57] Coal strip-mining in north-central Illinois revealed an incredibly rich biota existing there during the Pennsylvanian period of geologic time. Mine trenches, drill-hole samples, and distinctive nodules within soft shale provided the clues to the variable habitats and the inhabitants. A glimpse from one time frozen in our minds shows a coastline with dense vegetation (including tree ferns over 40 feet tall) and a sandy shoreline with stream deltas protruding into shallow water. Offshore there are sand bars and mud flats occurring between them and the shore. In environmental significance, this is similar to what we might observe along the Florida Gulf Coast today. The materials and land/sea features of the ancient environment become apparent from the distribution of their preserved evidence over a wide area. The fourth dimension of time is provided by taking different slices of the geology through the region, from lower to higher in the subsurface section. We see that the coastline of one time does not remain static, but it migrates out into the sea for a geologic while and back again, eventually moving further inland. This indicates the phenomenon of multiple sea-level changes, which were quite characteristic of the Pennsylvanian and coal deposition. In some places, the vertical distribution of materials exhibits a bed of coarse sandstone (coastline) overlain by finer sands and clay-rich shale (more marine), and then in turn overlain by coarser sands again.

A well-defined ecological zonation is presented by the distribution of preserved flora and fauna in the Mazon Creek area. This area is known world-

---

56. D. A. Young, "The Discovery of Terrestrial History," in *Portraits of Creation — Biblical and Scientific Perspectives on the World's Formation*, ed. H. J. Van Till, R. E. Snow, J. H. Stek, and D. A. Young (Grand Rapids: Eerdmans, 1990), pp. 26-81.

57. M. H. Nitecki, ed., *Mazon Creek Fossils* (New York: Academic, 1979).

wide as a classic fossil locality of the highest caliber. Fossils are primarily found as imprints and partially carbonized material within hard nodules of chemically precipitated iron oxide, iron carbonate, and silica. When split open, the nodules expose organisms as diverse as snails, cephalopods, clams, jellyfish, fish, horseshoe crabs, insects, plant stems, leaves, and fruit, and at least one beast of uncertain classification. Some extraordinary samples display plant bark with preserved insect burrowers. The zonation of the organisms found in place beautifully outlines the interpretation of geological environments. One could almost re-create the geology from the fossils without the surrounding rocks. The plant remains are primarily associated with the terrestrial areas. Coals are found where maximum plant debris buildups would occur. The marine fossils are found in the offshore areas and away from the influx of sediment represented by the deltaic environment. The types of marine animals even indicate areas of deeper versus shallower water and contrasts in water chemistry (more versus less saline). Deeper beneath the coal-bearing strata in Illinois there are older geologic units representing very different environments (both marine and terrestrial) and possessing very different fossil assemblages.

Each continent on Earth is rich with detailed historical records available to be seen. There is great diversity preserved horizontally and vertically (through time). Each small area represents only a piece of overall place and overall time. As James Hutton traveled across Scotland and observed now famous exposures of geology, he noted that even the evidence of "great ages" contained no hint of a beginning, just as the contemporary processes of Earth offer no sign of an end.

8 Common Descent, Transitional Forms, and the Fossil Record

KEITH B. MILLER

Introduction

When objections are raised about "evolution," the object of concern is nearly always the concept of common descent. Common descent is the proposal that all organisms, living and extinct, are connected by an unbroken series of ancestor-descendant relationships to a single ancestral life form by a process of descent with modification. All life is genetically related such that it can be pictured as a branching tree or bush. The term "macroevolution" has been coined to refer to this large-scale pattern, and to the various mechanisms that have been proposed to generate the observed patterns of branching and extinction recorded in the fossil record.[1]

There is much confusion in the popular literature about the evidence for macroevolutionary change in the fossil record. Unfortunately, the discussion of evolution within part of the Christian community has been greatly influenced by inaccurate presentations of the fossil data and of the methods of classification. The view of much of the evangelical Christian commentary on macroevolution is that the major taxonomic groups of living things remain clearly distinct entities throughout their history and were as morphologically distinct

---

1. An excellent technical review of current research issues in macroevolution is presented in D. Jablonski, "Micro- and Macroevolution: Scale and Hierarchy in Evolutionary Biology and Paleobiology," in *Deep Time: Paleobiology's Perspective*, ed. D. H. Erwin and S. L. Wing, Paleobiology Supplement to vol. 26, no. 4 (Lawrence, Kans.: Paleontological Society, 2000), pp. 15-52.

In addition to interactions with the other volume contributors, this essay greatly benefited from the critical reviews of Kevin Padian, Peter Dodson, and James Hopson. Of course, any remaining errors are mine alone.

from each other at their first appearance as they are today. There is a clear interest in showing the history of life as discontinuous, and any suggestion of transition in the fossil record is met with great skepticism.

The fossil record provides persuasive evidence for macroevolutionary change and common descent. Fossils provide windows into the anatomy and ecology of long-extinct species. These preserved remains of ancient life forms enable us to reconstruct the evolutionary pathways that led to our diverse living biota. The pattern of appearance of fossil species through geologic time is critical for understanding the timing and environmental context of evolutionary change. In addition, the fossil record also contributes to our understanding of the tempo and mode of evolution, and helps select among competing macroevolutionary theories to explain particular events.

However, before the fossil record can be applied to these issues, two critically important topics need to be addressed. The first concerns the completeness and resolution of the fossil record, and the second concerns classification and taxonomic procedures. As defined by R. M. Schoch, classification refers to the "actual ordering of organisms, either formally or informally, into groups and subgroups based on some particular criteria." Taxonomy is the "theoretical study of the ordering of the diversity of organisms, including the criteria and bases used in a classification of the organisms."[2]

Completeness of the Fossil Record

There are two opposite errors that need to be countered about the fossil record: (1) that it is so incomplete as to be of no value in interpreting patterns and trends in the history of life, and (2) that it is so good that we should expect a relatively complete record of the details of evolutionary transitions within all or most lineages.

How complete then is the fossil record? It can be confidently stated that only a very small fraction of the species that once lived on Earth have been preserved in the rock record and subsequently discovered and described. Our knowledge of the history of life can be put into perspective by a comparison with our knowledge of living organisms. About 1.5 million living species have been described by biologists, while paleontologists have catalogued only about 250,000 fossil species representing a period of Earth history of over 540 million years![3] Why such a poor record?

2. R. M. Schoch, *Phylogeny Reconstruction in Paleontology* (New York: Van Nostrand Reinhold, 1986), pp. 334, 338.

3. D. H. Erwin, *The Great Paleozoic Crisis: Life and Death in the Permian* (New York: Columbia University Press, 1993).

Limits of the Fossil Record

There is an entire field of scientific research referred to as "taphonomy" — literally, "the study of death."[4] Taphonomic research includes investigating those processes active from the time of the death of an organism until its final burial by sediment. These processes include decomposition, scavenging, mechanical destruction, transportation, and chemical dissolution and alteration. The ways in which the remains of organisms are subsequently mechanically and chemically altered after burial are also examined — including the various processes of fossilization (carbonization, pyritization, phosphatization, silicification, recrystalization, permineralization, replacement, etc.). Burial and "fossilization" of an organism's remains in no way guarantees its ultimate preservation as a fossil. Processes such as dissolution and recrystalization can remove all record of fossils from the rock. What we collect as fossils are thus the "lucky" organisms that have avoided the wide spectrum of destructive pre- and postdepositional processes arrayed against them.

Soft-bodied or thin-shelled organisms have little or no chance of preservation, and the majority of species in living marine communities are soft-bodied. Consider that there are living today about fourteen phyla of "worms" comprising nearly half of all animal phyla, yet only a few (e.g., annelids and priapulids) have even a rudimentary fossil record. The inadequacy of the fossil record to preserve with any completeness the evolutionary history of soft-bodied organisms can be illustrated by the conodonts. Originally assigned to their own phylum, they are now linked to the chordates. These soft-bodied animals are represented by tiny toothlike phosphatic fossils that are very abundant in sedimentary rocks extending over about 300 million years of Earth history, and have a worldwide distribution. Conodonts are a very important group of marine fossils for paleontologists, yet until only very recently the kind of organism to which they belonged was completely unknown. Specimens of the worm-like conodont animal have now been discovered in Carboniferous, Ordovician, and Silurian rocks.[5] Thus, only a handful of specimens are known of a very large and diverse group of marine animals known to be extremely abundant and widespread over a tremendous length of time!

The discovery of new soft-bodied fossil localities is always met with great enthusiasm. These localities typically turn up new species with unusual

4. P. A. Allison and D. E. G. Briggs, *Taphonomy: Releasing the Data Locked in the Fossil Record* (New York: Plenum, 1991).

5. R. J. Aldridge and M. A. Purnell, "The Conodont Controversies," *Trends in Ecology and Evolution* 11 (1996): 463-68.

morphologies, and new higher taxa can be erected on the basis of a few specimens! Such localities are also erratically and widely spaced in geologic time, between which essentially no soft-bodied fossil record exists.

Even those organisms with preservable hard parts are unlikely to be preserved under "normal" conditions. Studies of the fate of clamshells in shallow coastal waters reveal that shells are rapidly destroyed by scavenging, boring, chemical dissolution, and breakage. Occasional burial during major storm events is one process that favors the incorporation of shells into the sedimentary record, and their ultimate preservation as fossils. Getting terrestrial vertebrate material into the fossil record is even more difficult. The terrestrial environment is a very destructive one: with decomposition and scavenging together with physical and chemical destruction by weathering.

The limitations of the vertebrate fossil record can be easily illustrated. The famous fossil *Archaeopteryx*, occurring in a rock unit renowned for its fossil preservation, is represented by only seven known specimens, of which only two are essentially complete. Considering how many individuals of this genus probably lived and died over the thousands or millions of years of its existence, these few known specimens give some feeling for how few individuals are actually preserved as fossils and subsequently discovered. Yet this example actually represents an unusual wealth of material. The great majority of fossil vertebrate species are represented by only very fragmentary remains, and many are described on the basis of single specimens or from single localities. Complete skeletons are exceptionally rare. For many fossil taxa, particularly small mammals, the only fossils are teeth and jaw fragments. If so many fossil vertebrate species are represented by single specimens, the number of completely unknown species must be greater still!

The potential for fossil preservation varies dramatically from environment to environment. Preservation is enhanced under conditions that limit destructive physical and biological processes. Thus, marine and fresh water environments with low oxygen levels, high salinities, or relatively high rates of sediment deposition favor preservation. Similarly, in some environments biochemical conditions can favor the early mineralization of skeletons and even soft tissues by a variety of compounds (e.g., carbonate, silica, pyrite, and phosphate). The likelihood of preservation is thus highly variable. As a result, the fossil record is biased toward sampling the biota of certain types of environments and against sampling the biota of others.

In addition to these preservational biases, the erosion, deformation, and metamorphism of originally fossiliferous sedimentary rocks have eliminated significant portions of the fossil record over geologic time. Furthermore, much of the fossil-bearing sedimentary record is hidden in the subsurface or located in poorly accessible or little-studied geographic areas. For these reasons, only a small portion of those once-living species actually preserved in the fossil record have been discovered and described.

Potential of Fossil Record for Recording Evolutionary Change

Given the limitations and biases discussed above, what should be expected from the fossil record? The situation is not as bleak as it may appear from my previous comments. Exceptional deposits such as the Burgess Shale, Hunsrück Slate, Solnhofen Limestone, and Green River Shale do provide surprisingly detailed glimpses of once-living communities. These rare cases of exceptional preservation (fossil Lagerstätten) are essentially snapshots in the history of life and are invaluable in gaining a more comprehensive picture of ancient communities. They also provide some of the most detailed anatomical data.

More commonly, thick sequences of fossiliferous rocks can enable selected skeleton or shell-bearing taxa to be examined at closely spaced intervals. These localities provide opportunities to study patterns of evolutionary change within isolated lines of descent on a time scale of tens of thousands to millions of years. From such fossil sequences important information can be gained on anatomical changes within species populations, and transitions between species and even genera can be examined. However, the time interval recorded by continuous series of closely spaced fossil populations is limited because of changing environmental, depositional, and preservational conditions.

Because of the biases of the fossil record, the most abundant and geographically widespread species of hardpart-bearing organisms would tend to be best represented. Also, short-lived species that belonged to rapidly evolving lines of descent are less likely to be preserved than long-lived stable species. Because evolutionary change is probably most rapid within small isolated populations, a detailed species-by-species record of such evolutionary transitions is unlikely to be preserved. Furthermore, capturing such evolutionary events in the fossil record requires the fortuitous sampling of the particular geographic locality where the changes occurred. Though not common, such fossil records have been discovered, and examples will be discussed below.

Using the model of a branching tree of life, the expectation is for the preservation of isolated branches on an originally very bushy evolutionary tree (figure 1). A few of these branches (lines of descent) would be fairly complete, while most are reconstructed with only very fragmentary evidence. As a result, the large-scale patterns of evolutionary history can generally be better discerned than the population-by-population or species-by-species transitions.

Evolutionary trends over longer periods of time and across greater anatomical transitions can be followed by reconstructing the sequences in which anatomical features were acquired within an evolving branch of the tree of life. Such sequences can be recognized in the fossil record that crosses all levels of the taxonomic hierarchy (species, genera, families, orders, classes, etc.).

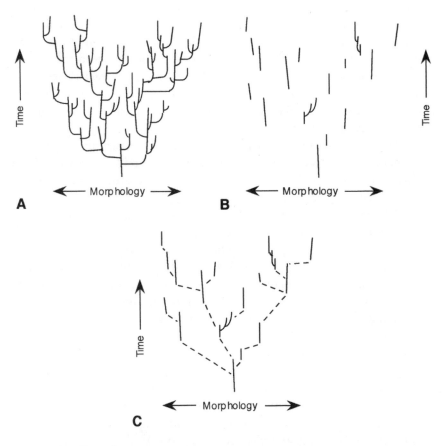

Figure 1. The effects of an incomplete fossil record on the reconstruction of evolutionary relationships. (A) This branching tree (phylogeny) represents how an actual pattern of evolutionary relationships might appear if our knowledge of the fossil record were complete. (B) The actual preserved record of species in the fossil record might look something like this. (C) This branching tree represents a possible reconstruction of the evolutionary tree based on the fossil evidence. Note that the general pattern of relationships is preserved, but that errors have been made with regard to specific ancestor-descendant relationships.

Classification and Transitional Forms

The recognition of transitional forms is as much a reflection of the system of classification being used as it is a statement about the content of the fossil record. The process of classifying living and fossil organisms produces its own patterns that order the diversity of life. It is thus important to recognize that the grouping of organisms in a classification scheme does much more than describe nature: it also interprets it. There has been considerable ferment within the field of paleontology because of conflicting philosophies of classification, and different perceptions of which patterns in the history of life should be reflected in the classification hierarchy.[6] Higher taxa can be either "artificial" groupings of species with similar overall morphologies (Linnean and "evolutionary" taxonomy), or "natural" groups sharing derived characteristics inherited from a common ancestor (cladistic system). In recent years the cladistic system has come to be the dominant method of classification within the paleontological community.

The Linnean classification system was originally based on a typological concept of species. All individuals were compared to an ideal "archetype" that defined the species, and all observed variation was understood as variation from that type. Typology thus excluded transitions *by definition*. Typology imposes its own order on the natural variation of the biological world and is not objectively descriptive of it. To use a geometric illustration, triangles and quadrilaterals have clear typological definitions and are easily separated into two classes of geometric shapes. Now, if one side of the quadrilateral were reduced in length by infinitesimal amounts until it was only two geometric points wide, it would still be a quadrilateral by definition although absolutely indistinguishable from a triangle. The most conceivably gradual transition has been made, yet typologically there were no intermediates! To apply this typology to living organisms and the fossil record and then claim the absence of intermediates is without meaning. Such arguments hinge on our human constructions and categories, not on the reality of variation in the biological world.

The Linnean classification system is hierarchical, with species grouped into genera, genera into families, families into orders, and so forth. This system reflects the discontinuity and hierarchy that is observed among living organisms. However, "this system leads to the impression that species in different cat-

---

6. Extensive discussions of the history and philosophy of various theories of classification can be found in: Schoch, *Phylogeny Reconstruction in Paleontology;* N. Eldredge and J. Cracraft, *Phylogenetic Patterns and the Evolutionary Process* (New York: Columbia University Press, 1980); and D. L. Hull, *Science as a Process* (Chicago: University of Chicago Press, 1988).

egories differ from one another in proportion to differences in taxonomic rank."[7] This impression is false. For example, two species belonging to different classes are *not necessarily* more different from each other than are two species belonging to different genera. When looking backward through time using the fossil record, it is found that representatives of different higher-level taxa become more "primitive," that is, have fewer derived characters, and appear more like the primitive members of other closely related taxa. Higher taxa are distinct and easily recognizable groups only when we ignore the time dimension of the history of life. When the fossil record is included, the boundaries between higher taxa become blurred during the major radiations associated with the appearance of new higher taxa. Even in the modern world, discontinuity is not as great as it may appear superficially. In practice, species are often not easily recognized, and accepted species definitions cannot always be applied.

"Evolutionary" classification came into prominence with the development of the modern evolutionary synthesis in the 1930s and 1940s. This synthesis emphasized gradual intraspecific evolution and the central role of natural selection. The Linnean taxonomic system is used but the underlying concept of typology is rejected. Furthermore, variation within species and the indefinite and often overlapping boundaries of defined groups are recognized. Probably the most important aspect of "evolutionary" classification is that it attempts to group organisms both on the basis of shared ancestry and on the basis of general levels or "grades" of anatomical organization. That is, the groupings are defined to reflect similar adaptations evolved in response to similar environmental contexts.

By contrast with the "evolutionary" system, cladistic classification focuses only on reconstructing the order in which new anatomical features were added in an evolving line of descent. It was developed based on the conviction that biological classification should directly and unambiguously reflect the relative degree of evolutionary relatedness among species (i.e., the branching patterns of the tree of life).[8] The classic expression of this is that under a cladistic system, cows and lungfish would be placed into the same higher taxonomic group, but salmon would be excluded. This is because cows and lungfish share a more recent common ancestor (their lines of descent branch higher in the tree) than do lungfish and salmon. Importantly, cladism does not consider the geological age of fossil specimens, or even distinguish between fossil and living organisms. Thus, it avoids using known species as representatives of ancestors, and instead defines branching points based on the appearance of unique derived anatomical characters. Cladism also rigorously demands that taxonomic names apply to

7. R. L. Carroll, *Vertebrate Paleontology and Evolution* (New York: Freeman, 1988), p. 578.
8. Schoch, *Phylogeny Reconstruction in Paleontology,* p. 13.

all descendants of a single common ancestor (a clade). This results in a groups-within-groups classification (figure 2).

To return to our original question, a transitional form is simply a fossil species that possesses anatomical features intermediate between those of two others within the same branch of the tree of life. That is, they lie in an intermediate position between a more primitive species and a more derived species. It also is informative to realize what transitional forms are not. They are not anatomically intermediate between equally derived forms. We need not look further than Darwin for a clear statement of what transitional forms are.

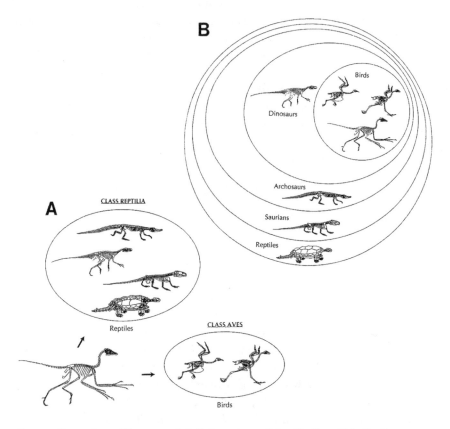

Figure 2. Comparison of Linnean and cladistic systems of classification. (A) In the Linnean system, birds and reptiles are classes of equal rank, and transitional taxa such as *Archaeopteryx* would be forced into one or another group. (B) In the cladistic system, *Archaeopteryx* is a bird, and a dinosaur, and an archosaur, and a saurian, and a reptile, etc.
Reprinted from L. Dingus and T. Rowe, *The Mistaken Extinction: Dinosaur Evolution and the Origin of Birds* (New York: Freeman, 1998), pp. 201-2. Used by permission of Timothy Rowe and the Texas Memorial Museum.

> I have found it difficult, when looking at any two species, to avoid picturing to myself forms *directly* intermediate between them. But this is a wholly false view; we should always look for forms intermediate between each species and a common but unknown progenitor; and the progenitor will generally have differed in some respects from all its modified descendants.[9]

For example, transitional forms are not to be found between living whales and their closest living relatives the hippos, but between whales and their common ancestors with the hippos. Such forms will be unlike anything living today. Transitional forms are found by moving down the tree of life into the past, not by trying to jump from limb to limb.

During the time of origin of a new higher taxon, there are often many described species with transitional morphologies representing many independent lineages. Such transitional forms commonly possess an incomplete suite of traits considered characteristic of the new higher taxon. They may also possess particular features that are themselves in an intermediate state between the ancestral and derived condition. It is usually very difficult if not impossible to determine which, if any, of the known transitional forms actually lay on the lineage directly ancestral to the new taxon. For this reason, taxonomists commonly have difficulty defining higher taxa, and assigning transitional fossil species to one or the other taxon. But, although the detailed ancestral-descendant relationships of specific fossil species may remain unresolvable, the patterns of evolutionary change are in many cases clear and well recorded in the fossil record.

Climbing Down the Tree of Life

As stated above, the diversity of life appears much more discontinuous when viewed at any given point in time than it does when viewed through time. For a given time slice through the tree of life, transitions between taxa are seen only where the slice intersects the branching points of lineages. Once a lineage is split, its branches continue to evolve and diverge such that their anatomical (and genetic) distance increases and they become more readily distinguished taxonomic entities. When we look backward through time using the fossil record, representatives of different higher level taxa are observed to become more "primitive," that is, they have fewer derived characters and appear more like the

---

9. C. Darwin, *The Origin of Species*, 6th ed. (1872) [multimedia CD: *Darwin*, 2nd ed. (San Francisco: Lightbinders, 1997)], pp. 234-55.

primitive members of other closely related taxa. As a result, for lineages with a good fossil record, the appearance of a new higher taxon is associated with the occurrence of species whose taxonomic identities are uncertain or whose anatomies converge closely on those of the new higher taxon. Such patterns are found repeatedly by paleontologists. These patterns provide strong support for the paradigm of common descent and for the origin of higher taxa through evolutionary processes at the population and species level.

The character states used to define higher taxa are determined retrospectively. That is, they are chosen based on the knowledge of the subsequent history of the lineages possessing those traits. They do not reflect the attainment of some objective higher level of morphologic innovation at the time of their appearance. Also, all the features subsequently identified with a particular higher taxon do not appear in a coordinated and simultaneous manner but piecemeal within numerous closely related species lineages, many of which are not included in the new higher taxon. In addition, as discussed above, the species associated with the origin and initial radiation of a new taxon are usually not very divergent in morphology. Were it not for the subsequent evolutionary history of the lineages, species spanning the transitions between families, orders, classes, and phyla would be placed in the same lower taxonomic group.

A long-standing misperception of the fossil record of evolution is that fossil species form single lines of descent with unidirectional trends. Such a simple linear view of evolution is called orthogenesis ("straight origin") and has been rejected by paleontologists as a model of evolutionary change (figure 3). The reality is much more complex than that, with numerous branching lines of descent and multiple anatomical trends. The fossil record reveals that the history of life can be understood as a densely branching bush with many short branches (short-lived lineages). The well-known fossil horse series, for example, does not represent a single continuous evolving lineage. Rather it records more or less isolated twigs of an adapting and diversifying limb of the tree of life. While incomplete, this record provides important insights into the patterns of morphological divergence and the modes of evolutionary change.[10]

Curiously, some critics of evolution view the record of fossil horses from *Hyracotherium* ("Eohippus"), the earliest known representative of this group, to the modern *Equus* as trivial. However, that is only because the intermediate forms are known. Without them, the anatomical gap would be very great.

10. The rejection of orthogenesis, particularly in regard to horse evolution, is discussed by B. J. MacFadden in *Fossil Horses: Systematics, Paleobiology, and Evolution of the Family Equidae* (Cambridge and New York: Cambridge University Press, 1992).

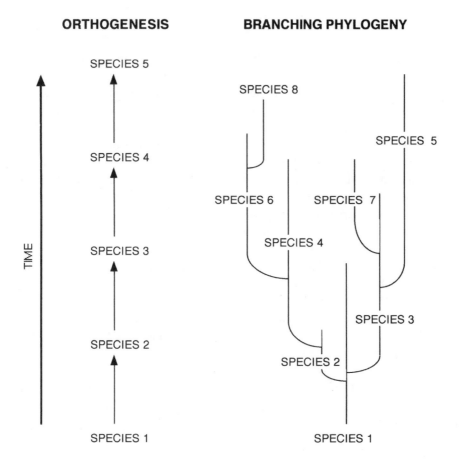

Figure 3. Comparison of a single direct line of descent (orthogenesis) with a branching phylogeny. Diversification (the multiplication of species) is such a pervasive pattern that orthogenesis is likely rare. Fossils from a chronological sequence thus are unlikely to represent direct ancestor-descendant relationships, but rather individual branches on a diversifying tree.

Hyracotherium was a very small (some species only 18 inches long) and generalized herbivore (probably a browser). In addition to the well-known difference in toe number (4 toes in front, 3 in back), *Hyracotherium* had a narrow, elongate skull with a relatively small brain and eyes placed well forward in the skull. It possessed small canine teeth, simple tricuspid premolars, and low-crowned simple molars. Over geologic time and within several lines of descent, the skull became much deeper, the eyes moved back, and the brain became larger. The incisors were widened, premolars took the form of molars, and both premolars and molars became very high-crowned with a highly complex folding of the enamel.[11]

The significance of the fossil record of horses becomes clearer when it is compared with that of the other members of the odd-toed ungulates (hoofed mammals). The fossil record of the extinct brontotheres is quite good, and the earliest representatives of this group are very similar to *Hyracotherium*.[12] Likewise, the earliest members of the tapirs and rhinos were also very much like the earliest horses (figure 4). All these very distinct groups of terrestrial vertebrates can be traced back through a sequence of forms to a group of very similar small generalized ungulates in the early Eocene.[13] The fossil record thus supports the derivation of horses, rhinos, tapirs, and brontotheres from a common ancestor resembling *Hyracotherium*. Furthermore, moving farther back in time to the late Paleocene, the earliest representatives of the odd-toed ungulates, even-toed ungulates (deer, antelope, cattle, pigs, sheep, camels, etc.), and the proboscideans (elephants and their relatives) were also very similar to each other.[14]

Similar patterns are seen when looking at the fossil record of the carnivores.[15] One group of particular interest is the pinnipeds (seals, sea lions, and walruses). These aquatic carnivores have been found to be closely related to the bears, and transitional forms are known from the early and middle Miocene. More broadly, the living groups of carnivores are divided into two main branches, the Feliformia (cats, hyenas, civets, and mongooses) and the Caniformia (dogs, raccoons, bears, pinnipeds, and weasels). The earliest representatives of these two carnivore branches are very similar to each other and

11. The details of horse evolution are discussed in: B. J. MacFadden, "Horses, the Fossil Record, and Evolution," *Evolutionary Biology* 22 (1988): 131-58; and in R. L. Evander, "Phylogeny of the Family Equidae," in *The Evolution of the Perissodactyls*, ed. D. R. Prothero and R. M. Schoch (New York: Oxford University Press, 1989), pp. 109-27.

12. The fossil record of brontotheres is reviewed in B. J. Mader, "The Brontotheriidae: A Systematic Revision and Preliminary Phylogeny of North American Genera," in *The Evolution of the Perissodactyls*, ed. D. R. Prothero and R. M. Schoch (New York: Oxford University Press, 1989), pp. 109-27.

13. Numerous scientific publications discuss the fossil records of the various odd-toed ungulates, or perissodactyls. See L. B. Radinsky, "The Early Evolution of the Perissodactyla," *Evolution* 23 (1979): 308-28; D. R. Prothero and R. M. Schoch, "Origin and Evolution of the Perissodactyla: Summary and Synthesis," in *The Evolution of the Perissodactyls*, ed. D. R. Prothero and R. M. Schoch (New York: Oxford University Press, 1989), pp. 504-29.

14. D. R. Prothero, "Mammalian Evolution," in *Major Features of Vertebrate Evolution*, ed. D. R. Prothero and R. M. Schoch, Short Courses in Paleontology no. 7 (Knoxville, Tenn.: Paleontological Society, 1994), pp. 238-70.

15. Prothero, "Mammalian Evolution."

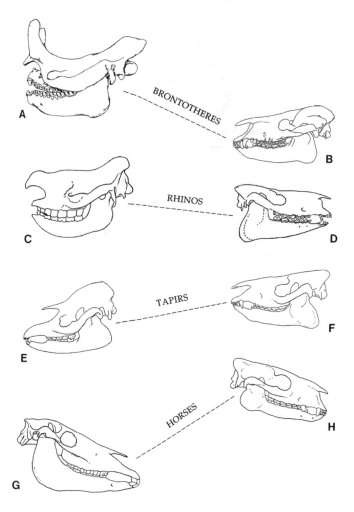

Figure 4. The earliest representatives of the odd-toed ungulates in the Eocene (at right) compared with their highly distinct modern or terminal members (at left). This illustrates well the convergence in appearance of distinct taxonomic groups as you move back in time toward their common ancestor. (A) *Megacerops*, (B) *Eotitanops*, (C) *Rhinoceras*, (D) *Hyrachyus*, (E) *Tapirus*, (F) *Heptodon*, (G) *Equus*, and (H) *Hyracotherium*.

(A), (B), (C), and (E) from H. F. Osborn, *The Titanotheres of Ancient Wyoming, Dakota, and Nebraska*, U.S. Geological Survey Monograph 55 (Washington, D.C.: U.S. Geological Survey, 1929), pp. 30, 37, 290. (D) redrawn from A. S. Romer, *Vertebrate Paleontology* (Chicago: University of Chicago Press, 1966). (F) from L. B. Radinsky, "The Early Evolution of the Perissodactyla," *Evolution* 28 (1979): 308-28, and reprinted by permission of the editorial office of *Evolution*. (G) and (H) from B. J. MacFadden, *Fossil Horses: Systematics, Paleobiology, and Evolution of the Family Equidae* (Cambridge and New York: Cambridge University Press, 1992), p. 199, and reprinted with the permission of Cambridge University Press.

likely derived from a primitive Eocene group called the miacids. Of the early carnivores, an eminent vertebrate paleontologist has stated: "Were we living at the beginning of the Oligocene, we should probably consider all these small carnivores as members of a single family."[16] This statement also illustrates the point that the erection of a higher taxon is done in retrospect, after sufficient divergence has occurred to give particular traits significance.

The taxonomic uncertainty associated with early "stem groups" such as the primitive ungulates and carnivores is a consequence of their position in time at the initial diversification of these groups. The specific suites of anatomical features that came to distinguish the later more derived groups were not acquired simultaneously in a single line of descent but appeared piecemeal over a period of time. Thus, the closer you come to the common ancestors of now distinct and easily recognized groups, the more difficult it is to apply the taxonomic definitions of these derived groups.

Moving farther down the tree of life, the origin of mammals is particularly well documented. Near the appearance of unquestioned mammals in the fossil record, a group of synapsids ("mammal-like reptiles") called cynodonts included species that were exceptionally mammal-like in appearance (figure 5). In skeletal features the approach to the mammalian condition was almost complete.[17] The following mammalian characteristics were possessed by advanced cynodonts: (1) enlarged temporal skull openings for the attachment of jaw muscles, (2) absence of the pineal eye, (3) differentiation of teeth, with front nipping teeth, canines, and molarlike back teeth, (4) a secondary palate permitting respiration while chewing, (5) an enlarged hole for the spinal cord at the base of the skull, and a specialized joint with the neck vertebrae, (6) absence of lumbar ribs (possibly related to the presence of a diaphragm), (7) a nearly erect stance, and (8) an enlarged dentary bone in the lower jaw with an extremely close approach to the mammalian jaw articulation. Furthermore, some workers argue persuasively that some cynodonts had high metabolic rates typical of mammals, or were even endothermic. Their bone microstructure also shows that they grew very quickly, like mammals and unlike typical reptiles and amphibians.[18]

16. A. S. Romer, *Vertebrate Paleontology* (Chicago: University of Chicago Press, 1966), p. 232.

17. An excellent survey of the origin of mammals is J. A. Hopson, "Synapsid Evolution and the Radiation of Non-Eutherian Mammals," in *Major Features of Vertebrate Evolution*, ed. D. R. Prothero and R. M. Schoch, Short Courses in Paleontology no. 7 (Knoxville, Tenn.: Paleontological Society, 1994), pp. 190-219.

18. Two older and more popularized works that argue for endothermy in cynodonts are: R. T. Bakker, "Dinosaur Renaissance," *Scientific American* 232 (1975): 58-78; and B. K. McNab,

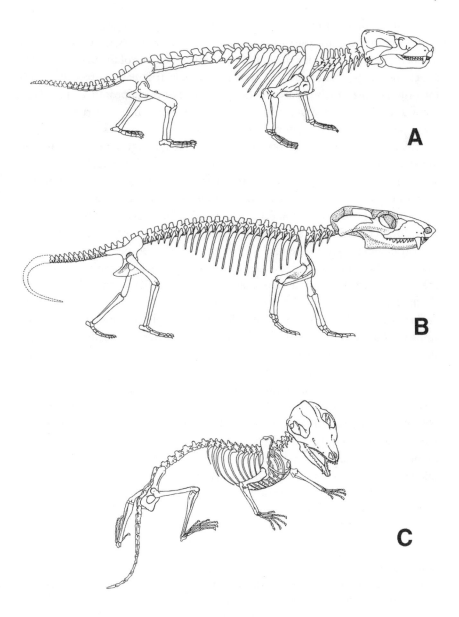

Figure 5. Reconstructed skeletons of cynodonts (advanced "mammal-like reptiles") and an early mammal. **(A)** The early Triassic cynodont *Thrinaxodon* and **(B)** the advanced cynodont *Probelesodon* from the middle Triassic. Note the very mammal-like erect posture of these skeletons. **(C)** The early mammal *Megazostrodon* from the early Jurassic.

All figures reprinted from R. L. Carroll, *Vertebrate Paleontology and Evolution* (New York: Freeman, 1988). (A) and (C) used by permission of F. A. Jenkins, Jr., and (B) used by permission of A. D. Lewis.

The complex of transitional fossil forms has created significant problems for the definition of the class Mammalia.[19] For most workers, the establishment of a dentary-squamosal jaw articulation is considered one of the primary defining characters for mammals. The transition in jaw articulation associated with the origin of mammals is particularly illustrative of the appearance of a "class-level" morphologic character (figure 6). In nonmammalian vertebrates, the lower jaw contains several bones, and a small bone at the back of the jaw (the articular) articulates with a bone of the skull (the quadrate). In mammals, the lower jaw consists of only a single bone, the dentary, and it articulates with the squamosal bone of the skull. Within the cynodont lineage, the dentary bone becomes progressively larger and the other bones are reduced to nubs at the back. In one group of advanced cynodonts, the dentary bone has been brought nearly into contact with the squamosal.[20] The earliest known mammals, the morganucodonts, retain the vestigial lower jaw bones of the earlier cynodonts. These small bones still formed a reduced, but functional, jaw joint adjacent to the new dentary-squamosal mammalian articulation. These animals possessed simultaneously both "reptilian" and mammalian jaw articulations! The "reptilian" jaw elements were subsequently detached completely from the jaw to become the bones of the mammalian middle ear.[21] Better intermediate character states could hardly be imagined!

As with most transitions between higher taxonomic categories, there is more than one line of descent that possesses intermediate morphologies. Again, this is consistent with both the expectations of evolutionary theory and the nature of the fossil record. The prediction would be for a bush of many lineages, most of which would be dead ends. Because of their objective to erect only monophyletic taxa (an ancestor is grouped with all of its descendants), paleontologists now group mammals with the advanced cynodonts, and more broadly with the whole group of synapsids, in a single higher taxon.[22]

"The Evolution of Endothermy in the Phylogeny of Mammals," *American Naturalist* 112 (1978): 1-21. A recent discussion of bone microstructure and growth rates in cynodonts can be found in J. Botha and A. Chinsamy, "Growth Patterns Deduced from the Bone Histology of the Cynodonts *Diamdemodon* and *Cynognathus*," *Journal of Vertebrate Paleontology* 20 (2000): 705-11.

19. The taxonomic problems associated with the definition of mammals are discussed in D. Miao, "On the Origins of Mammals," in *Origins of the Higher Groups of Tetrapods: Controversy and Consensus,* ed. H.-P. Schultze and L. Trueb (Ithaca, N.Y.: Comstock, 1991), pp. 570-97.

20. J. A. Hopson, "Systematics of the Nonmammalian Synapsida and Implications for Patterns of Evolution in Synapsids," in *Origins of the Higher Groups of Tetrapods: Controversy and Consensus,* ed. H.-P. Schultze and L. Trueb (Ithaca, N.Y.: Comstock, 1991), pp. 635-93.

21. A. W. Crompton and P. Parker, "Evolution of the Mammalian Masticatory Apparatus," *American Scientist* 66 (1978): 192-201.

22. Miao, "On the Origins of Mammals."

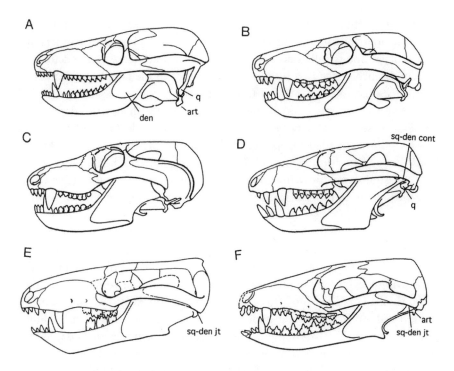

Figure 6. Comparison of the skulls of the cynodonts and early mammals. The cynodont skulls are: (A) the late Permian *Procynosuchus*; (B) the early Triassic *Thrinaxodon*; (C) the middle Triassic *Probainognathus*; and (D) the early Jurassic *Pachygenelus*. The early mammal skulls are: (E) the early Jurassic *Sinoconodon*; and (F) the early Jurassic *Morganucodon*. Note the differentiation of the teeth and the reduction in the bones at the back of the lower jaw (den = dentary, q = quadrate, art = articular, sq-den jt = squamosal-dentary joint).
From J. A. Hopson, "Synapsid Evolution and the Radiation of Non-Eutherian Mammals," in *Major Features of Vertebrate Evolution*, ed. D. R. Prothero and R. M. Schoch, Short Courses in Paleontology No. 7 (Knoxville, Tenn.: Paleontological Society, 1994), pp. 190-219; reprinted with permission of J. A. Hopson.

As in the case of the origin of mammals, the boundaries between higher taxonomic groups become uncertain during the transition from early tetrapods (limb-bearing vertebrates) with amphibianlike reproduction to the first amniotes (tetrapods capable of reproducing on land).[23] The amniotes include

23. An excellent summary of the various early amniote groups and their relationships is by J. A. Gauthier, "The Diversification of the Amniotes," in *Major Features of Vertebrate Evolution*, ed. D. R. Prothero and R. M. Schoch, Short Courses in Paleontology no. 7 (Knoxville, Tenn.: Paleontological Society, 1994), pp. 129-59.

the synapsids (the evolutionary branch including the mammals) and the reptiles (the branch including turtles, lizards, dinosaurs and birds). Members of a
group of tetrapods called anthracosaurs ("reptilelike" tetrapods) occur near
the appearance of the first unquestioned reptiles in the late Pennsylvanian.[24]
The anthracosaurs show a trend toward acquiring features associated with a
fully terrestrial existence and losing those associated with aquatic adaptations.
Some of these animals (the seymouriamorphs and diadectomorphs) were in
fact previously regarded as reptiles.[25] Furthermore, there are older fossil tetrapods that possess features of both the anthracosaurs and the temnospondyls
(the ancestral group for living amphibians) representing the early stages of divergence of the lines of descent that led to the true amphibians and to the
amniotes.[26]

The transition from water to land was one of the most significant events
in animal evolution. Accumulating paleontological and systematic work has
shed new light on the origin of the first tetrapods.[27] Until the mid-1980s, the
most primitive tetrapod known was the late Devonian *Ichthyostega*, with a flattened skull and tail fin. More fossil material for *Ichthyostega* has since come to
light. Based on this new fossil evidence, it has become apparent that the limbs
had a limited range of movement, and the animal was not as well adapted for
terrestrial locomotion as previously thought. It also turns out that this early
tetrapod had eight digits on its fore limbs and seven on its hind limbs rather
than the expected five.[28]

But this is not the end of the story. Several new taxa of early tetrapods are
now known. Many new specimens have been described of an early tetrapod
called *Acanthostega* that had diverged even less from its aquatic ancestry than
Ichthyostega. *Acanthostega* has a more feeble and fishlike fore limb, and both
fore and hind limbs have eight digits.[29] Of special significance is that this
tetrapod had fishlike internal gills and an opercular chamber for aquatic respi-

24. R. L. Carroll, "The Origin of Reptiles," in *Origins of the Higher Groups of Tetrapods: Controversy and Consensus,* ed. H.-P. Schultze and L. Trueb (Ithaca, N.Y.: Comstock, 1991), pp. 331-53.

25. R. L. Carroll, *Vertebrate Paleontology and Evolution* (New York: Freeman, 1988); M. J.
Benton, "Amniote phylogeny," in *Origins of the Higher Groups of Tetrapods: Controversy and
Consensus,* ed. H.-P. Schultze and L. Trueb (Ithaca, N.Y.: Comstock, 1991), pp. 317-30.

26. J. A. Clack, "A New Early Carboniferous Tetrapod with a Melange of Crown-Group
Characters," *Nature* 394 (1998): 66-69.

27. The fossil record of the origin of tetrapods is nicely summarized by R. L. Carroll in
Patterns and Processes of Vertebrate Evolution (Cambridge and New York: Cambridge University
Press, 1997), pp. 300-306.

28. P. E. Ahlberg and A. R. Milner, "The Origin and Early Diversification of Tetrapods,"
Nature 368 (1994): 507-14.

29. Ahlberg and Milner, "The Origin and Early Diversification of Tetrapods," pp. 507-14.

ration.[30] This was an aquatic, not a terrestrial animal! This strongly suggests that limbs evolved not for moving on land but as an adaptation for underwater walking in a shallow-water environment. A less well-known form *(Tulerpeton)* appears to be more advanced than *Ichthyostega,* with more flexible limbs and a reduction in the number of digits to six.

The rhipidistian lobefins are widely considered to have given rise to the first tetrapods. One small group of late Devonian rhipidistians, the panderichthyids, lived near the time of the appearance of the first tetrapods and appear to be closely related to them.[31] These fishes have flattened skulls very similar to those of the early tetrapods. The first known skull of a panderichthyid was in fact initially considered to be a tetrapod. In addition, the anal and dorsal fins are absent, and the tail is very similar to that of *Acanthostega* and *Ichthyostega.* The lobed pectoral and pelvic fins have bones that compare with the limb bones of the tetrapods. Whether part of a single direct lineage or not, panderichthyid fishes and the earliest fossil tetrapods are clearly transitional forms between "class-level" taxa (figure 7).

Recent discoveries have even shed light on the origin of the vertebrates themselves. Until 1999, the earliest known fossil vertebrates were of jawless fishes with a bony armor (called ostracoderms) from the Ordovician.[32] These primitive fishes not only lacked jaws but also an internal bony skeleton and paired fins. However, they were still far advanced from the expected anatomy of the earliest vertebrates and their immediate ancestors. The expectation was that the ancestor of vertebrates would resemble something like the modern lancelet ("Amphioxus"), an animal possessing a stiff notocord, "V"-shaped muscle bundles and a gill pouch. Incredibly, fossils that appear to closely match this description have now been discovered in the early Cambrian of China.[33] Furthermore, fossils likely representing very primitive vertebrates have also just been discovered from China in early Cambrian deposits.[34] These fossils lack any

30. M. I. Coates and J. A. Clack, "Fish-like Gills and Breathing in the Earliest Known Tetrapod," *Nature* 352 (1991): 234-36.

31. See: H.-P. Schultze, "A Comparison of Controversial Hypotheses on the Origin of Tetrapods," pp. 29-67, and E. Vorobyeva and H.-P. Schultze, "Description and Systematics of Panderichthyid Fishes with Comments on Their Relationship to Tetrapods," pp. 68-109, both in *Origins of the Higher Groups of Tetrapods: Controversy and Consensus,* ed. H.-P. Schultze and L. Trueb (Ithaca, N.Y.: Comstock, 1991).

32. P. Forey and P. Janvier, "Agnathans and the Origin of Jawed Vertebrates," *Nature* 361 (1993): 129-34.

33. J-Y. Chen, J. Dzik, G. D. Edgecombe, L. Ramsköld, and G-Q. Zhou, "A Possible Early Cambrian Chordate," *Nature* 377 (1995): 720-22. J-Y. Chen, D-Y. Huang, and C-W. Li, "An Early Cambrian Craniate-like Chordate," *Nature* 402 (1999): 518-22.

34. D-G. Shu, H-L. Luo, S. Conway Morris, X-L. Zhang, S-X. Hu, L. Chan, J. Han,

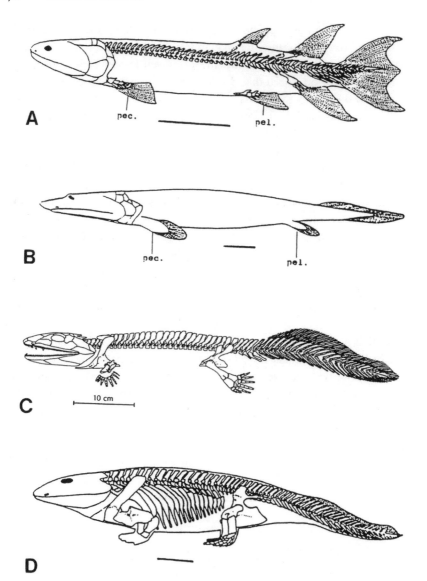

Figure 7. Origin of the tetrapods. (A) The osteolepiform lobefin *Eusthenopteron* (early late Devonian), (B) panderichthyid lobefin *Panderichthys* (early late Devonian), (C) early tetrapod *Acanthostega* (latest Devonian), (D) early tetrapod *Ichthyostega* (latest Devonian).
(A) and (C) from R. L. Carroll, *Patterns and Processes of Vertebrate Evolution* (Cambridge and New York: Cambridge University Press, 1997), p. 300, and reprinted with the permission of Cambridge University Press. (B) and (D) from P. E. Ahlberg and A. R. Milner, "The Origin and Early Diversification of Tetrapods," *Nature* 368 (1994): 507-14. Reprinted with permission from *Nature*, copyright 1994, Macmillan Magazines Limited, and from P. E. Ahlberg.

bony elements but have critical vertebrate features such as zig-zag muscle bundles, branchial (gill) pouches, a pericardial cavity, and a cartilaginous cranium.

Using the fossil record, I have now traced the broad patterns of vertebrate evolution from the modern horse down the tree of life to the earliest preserved vertebrates. In a very real sense, all fossil species within a line of descent are transitional forms in that they are anatomically intermediate in many features between earlier and later forms. Stepping back and looking at the big picture, one can clearly see the many branches of the tree of life (lines of descent) converging toward the point where their branches join (their common ancestors). This pattern continues until all living and fossil vertebrate groups have converged on their single vertebrate progenitor. The fossil record overwhelmingly confirms the evolutionary expectation!

Other Transitions Associated with Major Adaptive Shifts

Of special interest in the history of life are the morphological transitions associated with the major adaptive shifts from water to land, land to water, and land to air. I have already discussed one such transition — the origin of the first tetrapods. These major changes in mode of life opened up tremendous new adaptive opportunities for animal life and were followed by the rapid diversification of these new groups. While the fossil evidence for some of these transitions is minimal, for others exciting parts of the puzzle are being uncovered.

Probably one of the most celebrated and mysterious transitions has been that of the origin of whales from a primitive terrestrial ungulate ancestor. Until 1993 the earliest fossil whales were known only from partial skulls with no postcranial material. However, several very important transitional fossils from Pakistan have been described over the last several years.[35] In fact, there are now twenty-six fossil species of primitive whales known that have been assigned to four families: the Pakicetidae, Ambuloceticae, Remingtonocetidae, and Protocetidae. These together provide an impressive fossil sequence of transitional forms — the "walking whales" (figure 8).

Until very recently, the geologically oldest whales, the pakicetids, were

---

M. Zhu, Y. Li, and L-Z. Chen, "Lower Cambrian Vertebrates from South China," *Nature* 402 (1999): 42-46.

35. J. G. M. Thewissen, "Cetacean Origins: Evolutionary Turmoil during the Invasion of the Oceans," in *The Emergence of Whales,* ed. J. G. M. Thewissen (New York: Plenum, 1998), pp. 451-64. This is an excellent volume with papers devoted exclusively to the new fossil and molecular evidence for whale evolution. For a good popularized account of the discovery of the walking whales see Carl Zimmer, *At the Water's Edge* (New York: The Free Press, 1998).

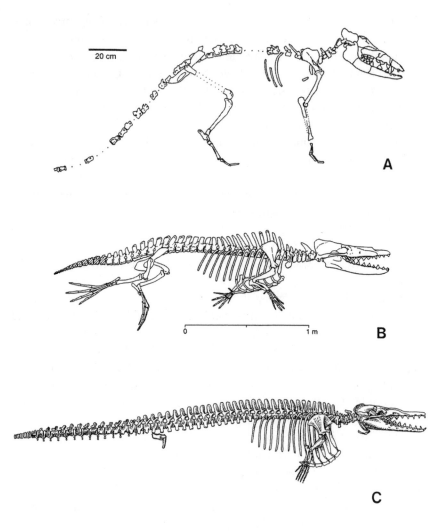

Figure 8. Origin of the whales. (A) Recently discovered skeleton of the terrestrial whale *Pakicetus* (early Eocene), (B) reconstructed skeleton of primitive amphibious whale *Rodhocetus* (middle Eocene), (C) archaeocete whale *Zygorhiza* with very reduced hind limbs (late Eocene).
(A) from J. G. M. Thewissen, E. M. Williams, L. J. Roe, and S. T. Hussain, "Skeletons of Terrestrial Cetaceans and the Relationship of Whales to Artiodactyls," *Nature* 413 (2001): 277-81. Reprinted with permission from *Nature*, copyright 2001, Macmillan Magazines Limited, and from J. G. M. Thewissen. (B) reprinted with permission from P. D. Gingerich, M. ul Haq, I. S. Zalmout, I. H. Khan, and M. S. Malkani, "Origin of Whales from Early Artiodactyls: Hands and Feet of Eocene Protocetidae from Pakistan," *Science* 293 (2001): 2239-42. Copyright 2001, American Association for the Advancement of Science. (C) taken from website of J. G. M. Thewissen and used by permission.

known only from teeth and skulls. However, new spectacular discoveries of substantial parts of the postcranial skeleton have shown these animals to be fully terrestrial and members of the even-toed ungulates (artiodactyls). These discoveries are also consistent with the DNA data that indicate that the hippos, a member of the artiodactyls, are the closest living relatives of the whales.[36] Occurring somewhat later, ambulocetids have also been discovered with preserved postcranial skeletons. Specimens of *Ambulocetus* include enough of the skeleton to reveal that this otter-sized whale had short front limbs and longer hind legs with large feet apparently used in swimming.[37] The remingtonocetids were a group of limbed whales similar to the ambulocetids that may not have left descendants. Occurring yet later in the fossil record were the protocetids. An early appearing member of this group *(Rodhocetus)* possessed somewhat shorter hind limbs than the ambulocetids, indicating a trend toward reduction in limb size.[38] This animal was probably predominantly aquatic and moved on land like modern sea lions. The pelvis of these whales was connected to the vertebral column by only a single vertebra. Later protocetids such as *Georgiacetus* had reduced hind limbs in which the pelvis was completely separated from the vertebral column. These are also the first whales with evidence of a tail fluke.

This progression of fossil forms shows a clear trend from more terrestrial to fully marine adaptations.[39] In early forms body weight was supported by limbs through connections to the vertebral column. These connections were progressively lost in later more marine-adapted forms. Associated with this was a progressive change in swimming from limb propulsion to tail undulation.

The fossil record of early whales is even more impressive because of its paleoenvironmental and geographic aspects. Not only do the fossils occur in the correct chronological order, but they are found in progressively more marine

36. J. G. M. Thewissen, E. M. Williams, L. J. Roe, and S. T. Hussain, "Skeletons of Terrestrial Cetaceans and the Relationship of Whales to Artiodactyls," *Nature* 413 (2001): 277-81; J. Gatesy and M. A. O'Leary, "Deciphering Whale Origins with Molecules and Fossils," *Trends in Ecology and Evolution* 16 (2001): 562-70.

37. A. Berta, "What Is a Whale?" *Science* 263 (1994): 180-81; J. G. M. Thewissen, S. T. Hussain, and M. Arif, "Fossil Evidence for the Origin of Aquatic Locomotion in Archaeocete Whales," *Science* 263 (1994): 210-12.

38. P. D. Gingerich, M. ul Haq, I. S. Zalmout, I. H. Khan, and M. S. Malkani, "Origin of Whales from Early Artiodactyls: Hands and Feet of Eocene Protocetidae from Pakistan," *Science* 293 (2001): 2239-42; P. D. Gingerich, S. M. Raza, M. Arif, M. Anwar, and X. Zhou, "New Whale from the Eocene of Pakistan and the Origin of Cetacean Swimming," *Nature* 368 (1994): 844-47.

39. E. A. Buchholtz, "Implications of Vertebral Morphology for Locomotor Evolution in Early Cetacea," in *The Emergence of Whales*, ed. J. G. M. Thewissen (New York: Plenum, 1998), pp. 325-51.

settings.[40] The most primitive group, the pakicetids, occur exclusively in river channel deposits. The ambulocetids and remingtonocetids are found in coastal and tidal deposits with freshwater influence. Early protocetids also are associated with shallow near-shore environments. Not until the later appearance of fully marine-adapted protocetids are fossils found in clearly open-ocean deposits. These are also the first whales that would have been capable of worldwide dispersal, and they are indeed the first to be found outside Indo-Pakistan! What had been one of the most obscure evolutionary transitions is now one of the best documented. The discovery of the fossil record of such transitions was simply dependent on the serendipitous sampling of the right locality.

The most famous of transitional fossils is the earliest known bird, the late Jurassic *Archaeopteryx.* It is now widely accepted that birds evolved from a group of small theropod dinosaurs, called maniraptorans. *Archaeopteryx* shares numerous features with the maniraptoran theropods. Among these are: a theropodlike pelvis, close similarities of the bones of the forelimbs, including a swivel wrist joint, and the similarity of the hind limbs and feet.[41] A comparison of *Archaeopteryx* to theropod dinosaurs such as *Velociraptor* and *Deinonychus* displays these similarities well (figure 9). Furthermore, many of the features that have been considered characteristic of birds can be found in the various maniraptoran dinosaurs.[42] That is, those features that we associate with "birdness" did not arise simultaneously with *Archaeopteryx,* but were widespread within maniraptoran theropods. These include: thin-walled bones, a calcified breastbone, a wishbone, and a shoulder with a straplike scapula. Some maniraptorans were even capable of a flight-stroke-like movement of the arms. In fact, birds are now recognized as simply a specialized group of feathered dinosaurs!

Spectacular new fossil finds in China have further revolutionized our un-

40. E. M. Williams, "Synopsis of the Earliest Cetaceans: Pakicetidae, Ambulocetidae, Remingtonocetidae, and Protocetidae," in *The Emergence of Whales,* ed. J. G. M. Thewissen (New York: Plenum, 1998), pp. 1-28. This paper discusses the environmental context of the fossil discoveries.

41. J. H. Ostrom, "Bird Flight: How Did It Begin?" *American Scientist* 67 (1979): 46-56; M. K. Hecht, J. H. Ostrom, G. Viohl, and P. Wellnhofer, eds., *The Beginnings of Birds: Proceeding of the International Archaeopteryx Conference, Eichstatt, 1984* (Eichstatt: Bronner & Daentler, 1985).

42. L. Dingus and T. Rowe, *The Mistaken Extinction: Dinosaur Extinction and the Origin of Birds* (New York: Freeman, 1998); K. Padian and L. M. Chiappe, "The Origin and Early Evolution of Birds," *Biological Reviews* 73 (1998): 1-42; P. C. Sereno, "The Evolution of Dinosaurs," *Science* 284 (1999): 2137-47; K. Padian and K. D. Angielczyk, "Are There Transitional Forms in the Fossil Record?" in *The Evolution-Creation Controversy II: Perspectives on Science, Religion, and Geological Education,* ed. P. H. Kelley, J. R. Bryan, and T. A. Hansen, Paleontological Society Paper no. 5 (Boulder, Colo.: Paleontological Society, 1999), pp. 47-82.

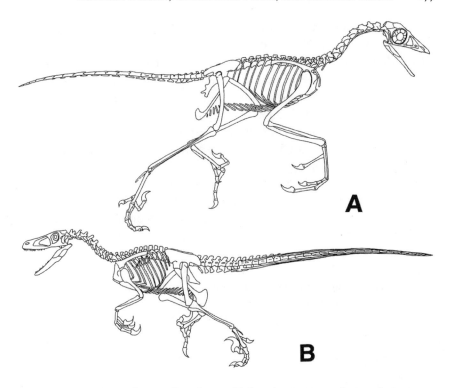

Figure 9. Comparison of **(A)** earliest known bird *Archaeopteryx* and **(B)** *Velociraptor,* a maniraptoran theropod dinosaur. Note the numerous similarities of the legs, arms, and pelvis. Reprinted from D. Norman, *Prehistoric Life: The Rise of the Vertebrates* (New York: Prentice Hall, 1994), p. 178. Used by permission of the artist, Denise Blagden.

derstanding of bird origins. The discovery of the beautifully preserved fossil of the coelurosaur dinosaur *Sinosauropteryx* first indicated the presence of downylike filamentous body coverings on some dinosaurs![43] Subsequently, at least three other dinosaurs, two dromaeosaurids and a therizinosaurid, have been found with similar filamentous coverings.[44] Of great significance are two dromaeosaur specimens that show featherlike structures, some of which show

43. P-J. Chen, Z-M. Dong, and S-N. Zhen, "An Exceptionally Well-Preserved Theropod Dinosaur from the Yixian Formation of China," *Nature* 391 (1998): 147-52.

44. X. Xu, Z-L. Tang, and X-L. Wang, "A Therizinosauroid Dinosaur with Integumentary Structures from China," *Nature* 399 (1999): 350-54; X. Xu, X-L. Wang, and X-C. Wu, "A Dromaeosaurid Dinosaur with a Filamentous Integument from the Yixian Formation of China," *Nature* 401 (1999): 262-66; X. Xu, Z. Zhou, and X. Wang, "The Smallest Known Non-Avian Theropod Dinosaur," *Nature* 408 (2000): 705-8.

divergent branching filaments and others that show a herringbone pattern around a central stem. These structures are very similar to those predicted for intermediate stages in the evolution of feathers.[45] In addition, the extraordinary fossils of two new maniraptoran dinosaurs, *Protarchaeopteryx* and the short-armed *Caudipteryx,* were found to have true feathers.[46] These feathers, however, were symmetrical rather than asymmetrical, and their bearers would have been flightless. It seems increasingly clear that feathers were not the exclusive characteristic of birds! These specimens further blur the boundaries between dinosaur and bird.

Archaeopteryx, while able to fly, differed from modern birds in a number of significant ways: it had a long bony tail, a sternum was absent, its vertebrae were not fused together over the pelvis to form a synsacrum, the bones of its hands and feet were not fused, and air ducts were absent in its long bones. There was thus a substantial anatomical gap between this, the first known bird, and modern birds. However, in the last several years the discovery of new fossil birds has led to the erection of a whole new subclass of primitive birds called the enantiornithes.[47] These early birds display features transitional between *Archaeopteryx* and more modern birds.

Another case of an evolutionary transition involving a major adaptive shift is the origin of the large marine predatory lizards of the Cretaceous — the mosasaurs.[48] Preceding the mosasaurs was a group of middle Cretaceous semi-aquatic lizards called aigialosaurs. Transitions within the aigialosaur lineage include the transformation of terrestrial limbs to fishlike paddles. In turn, the most primitive aigialosaurs closely resembled the fully terrestrial anguimorph lizards, represented today by the varanid or "monitor" lizards (figure 10).

Some enigmatic evolutionary relationships have also been brought into more focus in the last few years. Intriguingly, it has recently been suggested that the origin of snakes may be tied to the evolution of mosasaurs discussed above. A late Cretaceous "snake with legs" *(Pachyrhachis)* has been interpreted by

---

45. X. Xu, Z. Zhou, and R. O. Prum, "Branched Integumental Structures in *Sinornithosaurus* and the Origin of Feathers," *Nature* 410 (2001): 200-203; Q. Ji, M. A. Norell, K-Q. Gao, S-A. Ji, and D. Ren, "The Distribution of Integumentary Structures in a Feathered Dinosaur," *Nature* 410 (2001): 1084-88.

46. Q. Ji, P. J. Currie, M. A. Norell, and S-A. Ji, "Two Feathered Dinosaurs from Northeastern China," *Nature* 393 (1998): 753-61.

47. L. M. Chiappe, "The First 85 Million Years of Avian Evolution," *Nature* 378 (1995): 349-55.

48. M. DeBraga and R. L. Carroll, "The Origin of Mosasaurs as a Model of Macroevolutionary Patterns and Processes," *Evolutionary Biology* 27 (1993): 245-322; see also Carroll, *Patterns and Processes,* pp. 324-29.

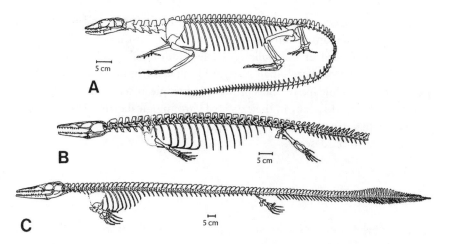

Figure 10. Evolution of mosasaurs from terrestrial lizards. (A) A terrestrial anguimorph lizard, (B) an aigialosaur from the mid-Cretaceous, and (C) an upper Cretaceous mosasaur, *Clidastes*. Reprinted from Carroll, *Patterns and Processes*, p. 325, with the permission of Cambridge University Press.

some workers to be the most primitive known snake. This snake shares many derived features with *Adriosaurus* and the dolichosaurs — long-bodied, short-limbed aquatic lizards. These aquatic lizards appear to be closely related to the mosasaurs.[49] If these relationships hold up to further examination, the ancestry of snakes will have been traced back to terrestrial lizards by way of the extinct marine mosasaurs!

A final example of of how recent discoveries are closing gaps in our understanding of major evolutionary transitions can be found in another group of aquatic mammals — the sirenians. Modern sirenians (manatees and dugongs) are fully aquatic with flipper-like forelimbs, no hindlimbs, and a paddle-like tail. In a parallel to the discovery of the walking whales, fossils of a fully terrestrial sirenian with well-developed fore and hind legs have been discovered in Jamaica.[50] This animal has been named *Pezosiren,* meaning "walking sirenian." While able to support its body out of water, this animal also had several aquatic specializations that clearly placed it within the sirenian group.

49. M. W. Caldwell and M. S. Y. Lee, "A Snake with Legs from the Marine Cretaceous of the Middle East," *Nature* 386 (1997): 705-9. M. S. Y. Lee and M. W. Caldwell, "*Adriosaurus* and the Affinities of Mosasaurs, Dolichosaurs, and Snakes," *Journal of Paleontology* 74 (2000): 915-37.

50. D. P. Domning, "The Earliest Known Fully Quadrupedal Sirenian," *Nature* 413 (2001): 625-27.

Its skeleton indicates swimming by undulation of the spine and paddling by the hind legs in a manner similar to that interpreted for the early whales. Also, like the fossil record of the walking whales, additional fossil sirenians have been found that record each major stage of limb loss from Pezosiren to the living manatee.[51] While likely not representing a single ancestor-descendant lineage, these fossils do occur in the expected chronological order. The fossil record has again substantiated in a most spectacular way the expectations of the model of common descent.

Conclusions

From this brief survey of fossil vertebrates it is clear that transitional fossil sequences between higher taxonomic groups are a common feature of the fossil record. Furthermore, the pace of recent discovery of new fossil forms that bear directly on these important transitions is nothing short of astounding. It is truly an exciting time to be a paleontologist! Probably at no time since the intense fossil hunting expeditions of the late 1800s have so many critical discoveries been made in such a short period of time. The surprising number of spectacular "gap-filling" fossil discoveries made just in the last decade shows the wealth of fossil data that remain to be discovered and interpreted. Such discoveries are critical for clarifying, and sometimes overturning, currently understood patterns of descent.[52] They can also disclose the presence of previously unseen past biological diversity.

The large-scale patterns of the fossil record show that the anatomies of species within a branch of the tree of life (a higher taxonomic group) become less divergent toward the point of origin of that branch. That is, species representing different lines of descent become more similar to each other as they approach their common ancestors. Those species representing the period of origin of a new branch of the tree of life possess both mixtures of anatomical features characteristic of later groups, and structures that are themselves intermediate in character. As a result, when the fossil record is good, the taxonomic assignment of such species is commonly uncertain. The boundaries between previously erected taxonomic groups become blurred. This is why taxonomists are moving from typological Linnean categories such as "fish," "amphibian," or

51. D. P. Domning, "New 'Intermediate Form' Ties Seacows Firmly to Land," *Reports of the National Center for Science Education* 21, nos. 5/6 (2001): 38-42.

52. D. B. Weishampel, "Fossils, Phylogeny, and Discovery: A Cladistic Study of the History of Tree Topologies and Ghost Lineage Durations," *Journal of Vertebrate Paleontology* 16 (1996): 191-97.

"reptile" to a groups-within-groups system that reveals patterns of evolutionary origin and emergence.

The fossil record thus provides good evidence for the patterns and trends in evolutionary history. Though it has its limitations, the fossil record is completely consistent with common descent and with the wide range of evolutionary mechanisms already proposed. Many critical gaps in our knowledge remain, but as is evident from this review, important discoveries are continually being made that intrigue, surprise, and enrich our understanding of the evolutionary history of life.[53]

53. Powerfully confirming this statement, a spectacular discovery of a small feathered dromaeosaurid dinosaur was made while this volume was in press. This dinosaur possessed flight feathers on both its forelimbs and hindlimbs that may have been used for gliding! These new specimens may result in a major revision of current hypotheses on the origin of flight. X. Xu et al., "Four Winged Dinosaurs from China," *Nature* 421 (2003): 335-40.

9   # The "Cambrian Explosion": A Challenge to Evolutionary Theory?

DAVID CAMPBELL AND KEITH B. MILLER

What Is the "Cambrian Explosion"?

Invertebrates like worms, arthropods, or slugs are not particularly glamorous organisms in most people's minds. Yet the Cambrian explosion, a time of rapid diversification of invertebrates, has received extensive popular attention, even gaining some prominence in the media. It often receives impressive billing. The statement in a widely used introductory biology text is typical: "In a span of only 5 to 10 million years at the beginning of the Cambrian . . . all the major animal body plans we see today evolved."[1] The discussion later explicitly equates body plans with phyla. The Cambrian explosion has also received considerable recent attention by evolution critics as posing challenges to evolutionary continuity. But is the attention warranted? To what extent is the Cambrian explosion a real event, and is it really problematic for evolutionary theories?

The words of Darwin are also often cited as evidence of the seriousness of the problem for evolution.

> There is another and allied difficulty, which is much more serious. I allude to the manner in which species belonging to several of the main divisions of the animal kingdom suddenly appear in the lowest known fossiliferous rocks. Most of the arguments which have convinced me that all the existing species of the same group are descended from a single progenitor, apply with equal force to the earliest known species.[2]

1. N. A. Campbell, *Biology,* 4th ed. (Menlo Park, Calif.: Benjamin/Cummings, 1996), p. 623.
2. C. Darwin, *Origin of Species,* 6th ed. (1872 [*Darwin,* 2nd ed., multimedia CD: San Francisco: Lightbinders, 1997], pp. 234-55.

We thank Simon Conway Morris for critically evaluating an earlier version of this manuscript. Any remaining errors of fact or interpretation are ours alone.

When Darwin published his model of descent with modification by means of natural selection, knowledge of the fossil record was in its infancy. There were few fossil candidates for transitions among higher taxa, and the Precambrian and early Cambrian fossil record was virtually unknown. Even the fossils of the now famous Burgess Shale and similar units were as yet undiscovered. After more than a century of paleontological work, the situation has changed dramatically. In keeping with evolutionary expectations, fossils are now known that record several dramatic transitions in the history of life.

Although some young-Earth sources continue to claim that there are no fossils from before the Cambrian,[3] the presence of late Precambrian animals was recognized in the 1950s and became widely publicized by the early 1970s. These are the famous Ediacaran fossils named for fossil-rich beds in the Ediacaran Hills of South Australia and now recognized at sites throughout the world.[4] These organisms are typically preserved as impressions in sandstones and siltstones. Associated with these fossils are trails and simple burrows of organisms that show a limited increase in complexity and diversity toward the Cambrian.[5]

The fossil record of life actually extends far beyond the Ediacaran (ca. 565-545 million years ago) into the deep geologic past. Fossils of algae, protists, and bacteria are present throughout much of the Precambrian.[6] The earliest convincing fossils of bacteria are recognized in rocks 3.5 billion years old, and chemical signatures point to the presence of life even earlier. Finely layered mounds (called stromatolites) produced by the activity of mat-building bacteria and algae appear at about this time and become relatively abundant by around 3 billion years ago. Evidence of eukaryotic algae, possessing membrane-bounded nuclei and internal organelles, dates to about 1,800-1,900 million years ago, or earlier if chemical evidence is accepted. Multicellularity had ap-

---

3. S. M. Huse, *The Collapse of Evolution*, 2nd ed. (Grand Rapids: Baker, 1993).

4. R. J. F. Jenkins, "Functional and Ecological Aspects of Ediacaran Assemblages," in *Origin and Early Evolution of the Metazoa*, ed. J. H. Lipps and P. W. Signor (New York: Plenum, 1992), pp. 131-76.

5. T. P. Crimes, "Changes in the Trace Fossil Biota across the Proterozoic-Phanerozoic Boundary," *Journal of the Geological Society, London* 149 (1992): 637-46.

6. There is extensive literature on the Precambrian record of life. Some important references are listed below. J. W. Schopf, *Earth's Earliest Biosphere: Its Origin and Evolution* (Princeton: Princeton University Press, 1983); J. Lipps, *Fossil Prokaryotes and Protists* (Cambridge, Mass.: Blackwell Scientific, 1993); A. H. Knoll, "The Early Evolution of Eukaryotes: A Geological Perspective," *Science* 256 (1992): 622-27; A. H. Knoll, "Proterozoic and Early Cambrian Protists: Evidence for Accelerating Evolutionary Tempo," in *Tempo and Mode in Evolution: Genetics and Paleontology 50 Years after Simpson*, ed. W. M. Fitch and F. J. Ayala (Washington, D.C.: National Academy Press, 1995), pp. 63-83.

peared by 1,000 million years ago in the form of diverse and relatively advanced seaweeds. The earliest fossils of metazoans (multicelled animals) may be represented by simple disk-shaped fossils found in rocks 600-610 million years old.

Despite the grand claims for the Cambrian explosion, the first appearance of animal phyla in the fossil record actually ranges from the late Precambrian through the Recent.[7] Figure 1 gives a summary of the first known appearances of many animal phyla. The animal phyla known from before the base of the Cambrian (over 545 million years ago) include the most primitive animals along with a few recognizable representatives of more advanced phyla and numerous animals of uncertain affinity. Fossil sponges have been recently recognized from rocks as old as 570 million years and have also been identified in Ediacaran age rocks.[8] Some of the late Precambrian Ediacaran fossils bear resemblances to colonial cnidarians called sea pens or to ctenophores (figure 2), and others appear to represent other cnidarian classes.[9] In addition, the Ediacaran fossil *Kimberella* has recently been interpreted as a mollusk-like organism (figure 3).[10] The occurrence of a primitive member of the echinoderms has also been suggested.[11] Furthermore, the simple burrows of the late Precambrian indicate the presence of bilaterally symmetric wormlike organisms. The presence of "bilateria" is also supported by the spectacular discovery of about 570-million-year-old fossilized animal embryos in China.[12] Thus, these various phyla evolved before the Cambrian radiation, although they rapidly diversified at lower taxonomic levels during the Cambrian.

It is also important to realize that many soft-bodied living phyla (i.e., those lacking preservable hard parts) first appear in the geologic record long af-

7. M. J. Benton, *The Fossil Record 2* (London: Chapman & Hall, 1993); S. Conway Morris, "The Fossil Record and the Early Evolution of the Metazoa," *Nature* 361 (1993): 219-25.

8. M. Brasier, O. Green, and G. Shields, "Ediacaran Sponge Spicule Clusters from Mongolia and the Origins of the Cambrian Fauna," *Geology* 25 (1997): 303-6; C-W. Li, J-Y. Chen, and T-E. Hua, "Precambrian Sponges with Cellular Structures," *Science* 279 (1998): 879-82.

9. The presence of sea anemonelike organisms is reported in J. G. Gehling, "A Cnidarian of Actinian-Grade from the Ediacaran Pound Subgroup, South Australia," *Alcheringa* 12 (1988): 299-314. Furthermore, recently discovered phosphatized embryos dating back to about 570 million years include possible cnidarians. See J-Y Chen, et al., "Precambrian Animal Diversity: Putative Phosphatized Embryos from the Doushantuo Formation of China," *Proceedings of the National Academy of Science* 97 (2000): 4457-62.

10. M. A. Fedonkin and B. M. Waggoner, "The Late Precambrian Fossil *Kimberella* Is a Mollusc-like Bilaterian Organism," *Nature* 388 (1997): 868-71.

11. J. G. Gehling, "Earliest Known Echinoderm — a New Ediacaran Fossil from the Pound Subgroup of South Australia," *Alcheringa* 11 (1987): 337-45.

12. S. Xiao and A. H. Knoll, "Phosphatized Animal Embryos from the Neoproterozoic Doushantuo Formation at Weng'an, Guizhou, South China," *Journal of Paleontology* 74 (2000): 767-88.

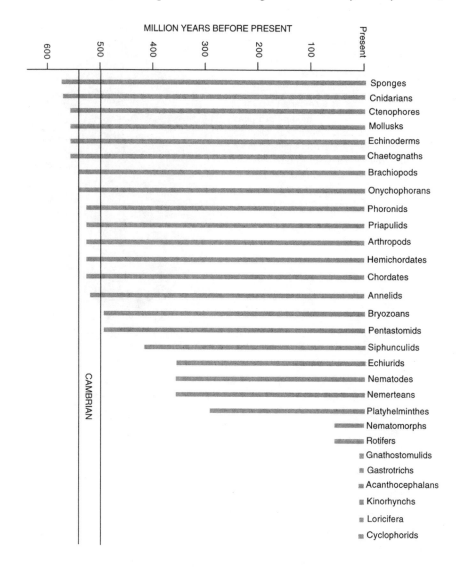

Figure 1. A bar graph showing the first appearances and ranges of living animal phyla and their stem groups in the fossil record.

First appearance data is taken from S. Conway Morris, "The Fossil Record and the Early Evolution of the Metazoa," *Nature* 361 (1993): 219-25, and M. J. Benton, *The Fossil Record 2* (London: Chapman & Hall, 1993), and updated with more recent discoveries discussed in the text.

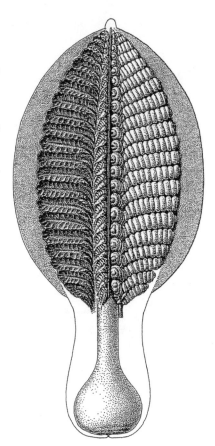

Figure 2. Reconstruction of the late Precambrian Ediacaran fossil *Rangea* by Jerzy Dzik. The fossil impressions of this organism have been interpreted by Dzik as a ctenophore and by other workers as a cnidarian similar to modern sea pens.
Reprinted from J. Dzik, "Evolutionary Origin of Asymmetry in Early Metazoan Animals," in *Advances in Biochirality*, ed. G. Pályi, C. Zucchi, and L. Caglioti (Amsterdam and New York: Elsevier Science, 1999), p. 158, with permission from Elsevier Science and Jerzy Dzik.

ter the Cambrian (see figure 1). As many as six recognized modern phyla have no known fossil record at all! This is not, of course, to claim that the absence of these groups from the fossil record indicates their late evolution. However, their time of appearance must be inferred using criteria other than a strict literal interpretation of the fossil record. This highlights the need to distinguish between the fossil data and our interpretations of them.

The above discussion is not to deny the significance of the Cambrian radiation but to place it in its proper context. It is true that almost all animal phyla with good fossil records (except Bryozoa, also called Ectoprocta) are known from the Cambrian. One of the most important features of the Cambrian "explosion" was the very rapid diversification of organisms with shells, plates, and various other types of hard parts. Some with very poor fossil records are also known from the Cambrian, along with some animals that are difficult to assign to a living phylum.

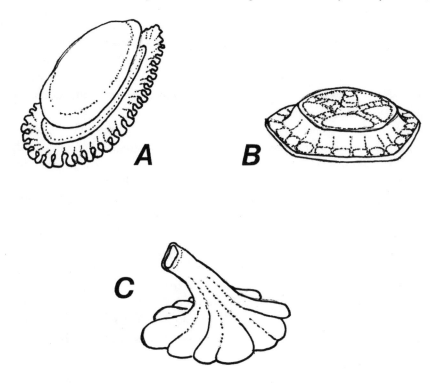

Figure 3. Reconstructions of Late Precambrian Ediacaran fossils interpreted as stem groups to modern phyla. **(A) The mollusk-like organism *Kimberella*, (B) the possible echinoderm *Arkarua*, and (C) *Inaria* interpreted as a sack-like anemone.**

(A) is modified from M. A. Fedonkin and B. M. Waggoner, "The Late Precambrian fossil *Kimberella* is a mollusc-like bilaterian organism," *Nature* 388 (1997): 868-71. (B) modified from J. G. Gehling, "A cnidarian of actinian-grade from the Ediacaran Pound Subgroup, South Australia," *Alcheringa* 12 (1988): 299-314. (C) modified from J. G. Gehling, "Earliest known echinoderm — a new Ediacaran fossil from the Pound Subgroup of South Australia," *Alcheringa* 11 (1987): 337-45.

These latter include intermediates between modern phyla, possible new phyla, and problematic forms. Representatives of several living classes and other lower taxonomic categories also appear in the Cambrian. A few deposits with exceptionally good preservation of fossils, such as the Burgess Shale in Canada,[13] contribute to the wide range of taxa known from the Cambrian. Such deposits with

13. D. E. G. Briggs, D. H. Erwin, and F. J. Collier, *The Fossils of the Burgess Shale* (Washington, D.C.: Smithsonian Institution, 1994); S. Conway Morris, *The Crucible of Creation: The Burgess Shale and the Rise of Animals* (New York: Oxford University Press, 1998). The highly varied Burgess fauna was popularized by S. J. Gould in his book *Wonderful Life: The Burgess Shale and the Nature of History* (New York: Norton, 1989).

exceptional preservation are known as Konservat-Lagerstätten (from the German "conservation deposits"). Similar deposits have since been found around the world in the early to middle Cambrian, notably the early Cambrian Chengjiang fauna of China.[14] Additionally, ichnofossils (trace fossils, such as trails, burrows, and feeding traces) become much more varied and abundant in the Cambrian, suggesting a newly widened range of animal activity.[15]

In the early 1990s, new radiometric dates from close to the Precambrian-Cambrian boundary revealed that it was much younger than previously thought — about 545 million years rather than the 575 million or so years that had been estimated by interpolating between more widely spaced dates.[16] This means that the time interval between the base of the Cambrian and the diverse animal communities of the Chengjiang was only about 20 million years. Even with the earlier dates, the Cambrian diversification had seemed somewhat abrupt. Although several million years sounds like a long time in everyday situations, it is very rapid in geologic terms. The subsequent discovery or recognition of various phyla in the Precambrian has expanded the time interval again, but much evolutionary change clearly occurred within a relatively short interval of the early Cambrian. Why did diversification happen so rapidly in the latest Precambrian to early Cambrian? As we will discuss later, several explanations have been proposed.

Doesn't the Cambrian Explosion Favor Special Creation Rather Than Evolutionary Continuity?

The Cambrian explosion has recently gained popularity as purported evidence against evolutionary continuity. The attention that the Cambrian faunas have received since S. J. Gould's popularization and the high profile obtained by the recent scientific debate on the meaning and significance of the "Cambrian explosion" have helped elevate this particular antievolutionary argument.

There are several problems with antievolutionary use of this event. First, some claims reflect a misunderstanding of the expected evolutionary pattern. Second, it is argued that there are no known intermediates between phylum-

14. J-Y. Chen and G. Zhou, "Biology of the Chengjiang Fauna," in *The Cambrian Explosion and the Fossil Record,* ed. J-Y. Chen, Y-N. Cheng, and H. V. Iten (Taichung, Taiwan, China: National Museum of Natural Science, 1997), pp. 11-105.

15. D. J. Bottjer, J. W. Hagadorn, and S. Q. Dornbos, "The Cambrian Substrate Revolution," *GSA Today* 10, no. 9 (2000): 1-7.

16. S. A. Bowring, J. P. Grotzinger, C. E. Isachsen, A. H. Knoll, S. M. Pelechaty, and P. Kolosov, "Calibrating Rates of Early Cambrian Evolution," *Science* 261 (1993): 1293-98.

level groups, and that these appear in the fossil record with their full complement of characteristic features. We will show that this misrepresents the current state of paleontological data. Finally, many claims rest on the purported inadequacy of conventional evolutionary explanations for the rapid diversification in the early Cambrian. There are in fact a number of hypotheses for this diversification, over which there is currently a lively debate within the scientific community.

Are Patterns in the Fossil Record in Conflict with Evolutionary Expectations?

Some critics of evolution make much of the "top-down" versus the "bottom-up" pattern of appearance of higher taxa. That is, phylum-level diversity reaches its peak in the fossil record before class-level diversity, and the class-level diversity before that of orders, and so forth. These critics interpret this apparent "top-down" pattern as contrary to expectations from evolutionary theory. However, this pattern is an artefact, being generated by the way in which species are assigned to higher taxa. The classification system is hierarchical with species being grouped into ever larger and more inclusive categories. When this classification hierarchy is applied to a diversifying evolutionary tree, a "top down" pattern will automatically result. Consider species belonging to a single evolving line of descent given genus-level status. This genus is then grouped with other closely related lines of descent into a family. The common ancestors of these genera are by definition included within that family. Those ancestors must logically be older than any of the other species within the family. Thus the family level taxon would appear in the fossil record before most of the genera included within it. Another way of looking at this is that the first appearance of any higher taxon will be the same as the first appearance of the oldest lower taxon within the group. For example, a phylum must be as old as the oldest class it contains. Most phyla contain multiple classes, which in turn include multiple orders, and so forth. Thus, each higher taxon will appear as early as the first of the included lower taxa.

Additionally, higher taxonomic levels typically reflect more general aspects of the body plan. Thus, a poorly preserved specimen may be confidently assigned to a particular phylum, but not to any one class. Similarly, a primitive fossil might have the distinctive features of a particular phylum, but not be clearly assignable to any particular class because it is a transitional form. Both of these factors would promote the earlier recognition of higher taxonomic categories than lower ones. An actual example comes from the phylum Mollusca.

The earliest known Precambrian mollusk-like organism is *Kimberella*. It is a primitive organism that lacks several features characteristic of modern mollusks and cannot be assigned to a particular class. In the Cambrian, the first definite representatives of several modern classes appear. For example, a series of fossil forms link certain monoplacophorans (mollusks with a single cap-shaped shell) with the earliest bivalves.[17] However, these early bivalves cannot be confidently assigned to a subclass and probably represent primitive "transitional" forms. In the early Ordovician, definite examples of modern subclasses occur.[18] Finally, higher taxa are generally recognized as reflecting major differences between organisms. Taxa that split from each other over half a billion years ago have had more time to develop major differences than have those that split a few million years ago, and so are more likely to merit recognition as distinct higher categories. The "top-down" pattern of taxa appearance is therefore entirely consistent with a branching tree of life.

Several advocates of special creation or intelligent design claim that the rapid radiation of taxa in the Cambrian is more compatible with supernatural or at least intelligent intervention rather than ordinary natural processes. Ironically, claims that the Cambrian explosion was excessively rapid in part reflect an overemphasis on Cambrian variability and novelty by workers such as Gould, who see the Cambrian explosion as evidence for evolution being highly random. Such opposite conclusions, purportedly founded on the same data, suggest that all these interpretations are based more on the interpreter's presuppositions than on the data. Some of Gould's early claims also reflect an incomplete preliminary knowledge of the organisms. For example, the bizarre *Hallucigenia* has since (in light of fossils from Chengjiang and the restudy of Burgess Shale specimens) been shown to belong to a diverse group called lobopodians that figure prominently in the origin of the arthropods (see discussion below). The new studies show that the original reconstruction of *Hallucigenia* was upside down, part of why it had seemed so strange. The recognition of *Hallucigenia* and other oddities as novel representatives of known groups, rather than as new phyla, decreases the apparent magnitude of the explosion.

17. J. Pojeta, Jr., B. Runnegar, J. S. Peel, and M. Gordon, Jr., "Phylum Mollusca," in *Fossil Invertebrates*, ed. R. S. Boardman, A. H. Cheetham, and A. J. Rowell (Cambridge, Mass.: Blackwell Scientific, 1987), pp. 270-435; A. P. Gubanov, A. V. Kouchinsky, and J. S. Peel, "The First Evolutionary-Adaptive Lineage within Fossil Molluscs," *Lethaia* 32 (1999): 155-57.

18. J. G. Carter, D. C. Campbell, and M. R. Campbell, "Cladistic Perspectives on Early Bivalve Evolution," in *Evolutionary Biology of the Bivalvia*, ed. L. Harper, J. D. Taylor, and J. A. Crame, Geological Society of London Special Publications 177 (London: Geological Society, 2000).

Is There Evidence for the Common Descent of the Phyla?

Significantly, the first question that needs to be addressed is, What is a phylum? As we have seen, a phylum is often identified as a group of organisms sharing a basic "body plan," a group united by a common organization of the body. However, phyla can be understood fundamentally, like all other taxonomic categories, as groupings of taxa that are more closely related to each other than to any other groups. This is the current taxonomic usage.[19] As with all taxonomic categories, organisms within a given phylum may bear close similarities to those from another closely related phylum. In fact, the assignment of a given organism or fossil specimen to a phylum can be just as problematic as assignments to other lower taxonomic ranks.

What we actually see in the fossil record is that the anatomical characteristics that are used to define living phyla did not appear simultaneously but were added over time. This has resulted in the distinction between "crown groups" and "stem groups" in the scientific literature. A crown group is composed of all the living organisms assigned to that phylum, plus all the extinct organisms that were descended from the common ancestor of those living organisms. The stem group is composed of organisms more closely related to one living phylum than to another, but that do not possess all of the distinguishing characters of the crown group. It turns out that the organisms appearing in the early Cambrian are, with few exceptions, not crown groups but stem groups. That is, the complete suite of characters defining the living phyla had not yet appeared. Many crown groups actually do not appear in the fossil record until well after the Cambrian.[20] Many first appearances shown in figure 1 are thus not appearances of living crown groups but of stem groups.

The same historical pattern that we see in the post-Cambrian fossil record we find in the late Precambrian and early Cambrian record. That is, as we approach the roots of the main branches of the tree of life it is increasingly difficult to place fossil organisms in living groups, and fossils are found with affinities to more than one taxonomic group. Excellent examples of the latter are the halkieriids and wiwaxiids.[21] Animals in both these groups were sluglike organisms covered with a variety of overlapping scale and platelike structures, and they are found in earliest Cambrian deposits. The halkieriids bear conical

---

19. See discussion of cladistics in the chapter "Common Descent, Transitional Forms, and the Fossil Record" by Keith B. Miller.

20. G. E. Budd and S. Jensen, "A Critical Reappraisal of the Fossil Record of the Bilaterian Phyla," *Biological Reviews* 75 (2000): 253-95.

21. J. Dzik, "Early Metazoan Evolution and the Meaning of Its Fossil Record," *Evolutionary Biology* 27 (1993): 339-86. See also Conway Morris, "Fossil Record" and *Crucible of Creation*.

mollusklike shells as well as calcareous structures similar to the chitinous bristles typical of polychaete worms. The slightly younger *Wiwaxia* has structures even closer to those of the polychaetes. These various unusual organisms bear resemblances to mollusks, polychaete annelid worms, and possibly brachiopods (figure 4). That is, they are transitional between living phyla.

The mollusks also provide illustrations of the origin of invertebrate classes. As mentioned above, there is good fossil evidence of the transition from primitive cap-shaped monoplacophorans to the first bivalves. There are also likely fossil transitions from monoplacophorans to the first gastropods.[22] Furthermore, a very recent and exciting fossil discovery provides a possible link between polyplacophorans (chitons) and the wormlike aplacophoran mollusks that were previously unknown from the fossil record.[23]

Another example of special interest is the recent work being done on the origin of the arthropods. The armored lobopodians, until very recently an enigmatic group of strange fossils, have become the critical link in reconstructing the assembly of the arthropod body plan. Armored lobopodians were "caterpillarlike" organisms with fleshy lobed limbs and mineralized plates or spines running along their backs.[24] They are similar to the living Onychophora, or velvet worms.

The Cambrian lobopodians occupy a transitional position between several living phyla (figure 5). The oldest known lobopodian bears certain similarities to a distinctive group of worms from the early Cambrian called priapulids. Other lobopodians have anatomical features in common with the arthropods, particularly with peculiar Cambrian stem arthropods such as *Opabinia* and *Anomalocaris*.[25] These latter organisms possessed lobopod limbs but also had gill flaps along their bodies and jointed feeding appendages. Intermediates between lobopodians and the early stem-group arthropods have also been discovered that possessed gills. Of even greater interest is the evidence available from the extraordinary preservation of muscle tissue in a few of these transitional or-

22. Pojeta, Runnegar, Peel, and Gordon, "Phylum Mollusca."

23. M. D. Sutton, D. E. G. Briggs, and D. J. Siveter, "An Exceptionally Preserved Vermiform Mollusc from the Silurian of England," *Nature* 410 (2001): 461-63.

24. There are numerous papers on this recently recognized fossil group. Among them are: L. Ramsköld, "Homologies in Cambrian Onychophora," *Lethaia* 25 (1992): 443-60; L. Ramsköld and H. Xianguang, "New Early Cambrian Animal and Onychophoran Affinities of Enigmatic Metazoans," *Nature* 351 (1991): 225-28.

25. J-Y. Chen, L. Ramsköld, and G-G. Zhou, "Evidence for Monophyly and Arthropod Affinity of Cambrian Giant Predators," *Nature* 264 (1994): 1304-8; G. E. Budd, "The Morphology of *Opabinia regalis* and the Reconstruction of the Arthropod Stem Group," *Lethaia* 29 (1996): 1-14.

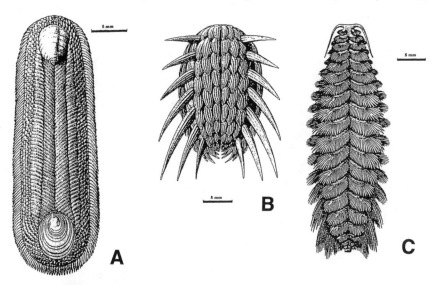

Figure 4. Illustrations of Cambrian organisms possessing features that suggest a close evolutionary relationship between mollusks, annelids, and brachiopods. (A) *Halkieria* from the early Cambrian of Greenland, a mollusk-like organism with annelid, and possibly brachiopod, features; (B) *Wiwaxia* from the middle Cambrian Burgess Shale with both molluskan and annelid features; and (C) *Canadia,* a primitive polychaete annelid also from the Burgess Shale.
Reprinted from J. Dzik, "Early Metazoan Evolution and the Meaning of Its Fossil Record," *Evolutionary Biology* 27 (1993): 361, 367, with permission of Kluwer Academic/Plenum Publishers and Jerzy Dzik.

ganisms.[26] These specimens suggest a progression of steps in the transformation of internal anatomy from lobopodians to true arthropods.

Both the mollusk/annelid/brachiopod and the priapulid/onychophoran/ arthropod groupings indicated by the current fossil data are supported by the genetic data.[27] The genetic data, particularly the gene clusters that control body-plan formation during embryogenesis (the homeobox or *Hox* genes), also help resolve even deeper relationships among the living phyla. The recent sequencing of the genomes of representative organisms from a variety of phyla has revealed that the number of sets of *Hox* genes and their order in the genome

26. G. E. Budd, "Arthopod Body-Plan Evolution in the Cambrian with an Example from Anomalocaridid Muscle," *Lethaia* 31 (1998): 197-210.

27. A. H. Knoll and S. B. Carroll, "Early Animal Evolution: Emerging Views from Comparative Biology and Geology," *Science* 284 (1999): 2129-37; R. de Rosa, J. K. Grenier, T. Andreevas, C. E. Cook, A. Adoutte, M. Akami, S. B. Carroll, and G. Balavoine, "Hox Genes in Brachiopods and Priapulids and Protostome Evolution," *Nature* 399 (1999): 772-76.

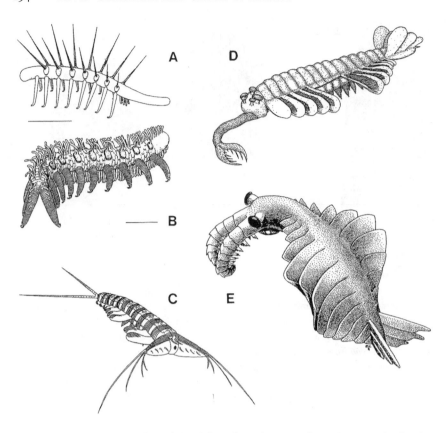

Figure 5. Reconstructions of Cambrian lobopods and stem arthropods. (A) Spine-bearing lobopod *Hallucigenia* from the Burgess Shale; (B) armored lobopod from the early Cambrian Chengjiang locality of Yunnan, China; (C) gill-bearing lobopod *Kerygmachela* from the early Cambrian of Greenland; (D) peculiar stem arthropod *Opabinia* with lobopod limbs also from the Burgess Shale; and (E) stem arthropod *Anomalocaris* from the Burgess Shale.

(A) and (B) reprinted from L. Ramsköld and H. Xianguang, "New Early Cambrian Animal and Onychophoran Affinities of Enigmatic Metazoans," *Nature* 351 (1991): 225-27, with permission from *Nature*, copyright 1991, Macmillan Magazines Limited, and L. Ramsköld. (C) is reproduced by permission of the Royal Society of Edinburgh from G. E. Budd, "*Kerygmachela kierkegaardi* Budd (Buen Formation, Lower Cambrian, N. Greenland)," *Transactions of the Royal Society of Edinburgh: Earth Sciences* 89 (1999, for 1998): 249-90. (D) is reprinted from G. E. Budd, "The Morphology of *Opabinia regalis* and the Reconstruction of the Arthropod Stem-Group," *Lethaia* 29 (1996): 1-14, by permission of Taylor & Francis AS (www.tandf.no/leth) and Graham Budd. (E) is reprinted from D. Collins, "The 'Evolution' of Anomalocaris and Its Classification in the Arthropod Class Dinocarida (nov.) and Order Radiodonta (nov.)," *Journal of Paleontology* 70 (1996): 280-93, with permission of The Paleontological Society.

are surprisingly consistent among bilaterally symmetric organisms. Organisms as different as insects and vertebrates use the same sets of *Hox* genes to determine body axes and limb development.[28] These deep genetic similarities strongly point to a common ancestor. When we move to even simpler grades of organization, the number of *Hox* genes is progressively reduced, with the sponges having only a single *Hox* gene.[29] These observed patterns of *Hox* gene occurrence suggest the repeated duplication of *Hox* genes by mutation during the very early history of the metazoans. Similar patterns are found for other highly conserved genes. The genetic evidence thus serves to extend and reinforce conclusions from the fossil record.

Are Evolutionary Explanations of the Cambrian Explosion Inadequate?

Despite the claimed inexplicability, natural explanations do exist for the Cambrian explosion. (Note: by natural we mean "continuous operation of natural processes," not "devoid of supernatural agency"). However, it is still difficult to assess the relative viability of these various options and to determine which if any of the current proposals will ultimately prove to be upheld by further research and discovery. In part, this reflects our currently limited knowledge. Detailed study of the Precambrian-Cambrian transition has developed only in the past couple of decades. Charles Doolittle Walcott discovered the Burgess Shale fauna in 1909, but he did not recognize the peculiarity of many forms. Extensive restudy began in the 1960s.[30] Recognition of the paleontological significance of this fauna and description of some of the species helped inspire the search for, and recognition of, other similar faunas. The subsequent discovery of the early Cambrian Chengjiang deposits and the recent discovery of phosphatized embryos in the late Precambrian have dramatically expanded the available fossil evidence. Furthermore, genetic sequencing data for a wide range of organisms are only now becoming available. Thus, with only a few decades of intensive

28. S. B. Carroll, "Homeotic Genes and the Evolution of Arthropods and Chordates," *Nature* 376 (1995): 479-85; E. M. De Roberts and Y. Sasai, "A Common Plan for Dorsoventral Patterning in Bilateria," *Nature* 380 (1996): 37-40; N. Shubin, C. Tabin, and S. Carroll, "Fossils, Genes and the Evolution of Animal Limbs," *Nature* 388 (1997): 639-48.

29. J. W. Valentine, D. H. Erwin, and D. Jablonski, "Developmental Evolution of Metazoan Bodyplans: The Fossil Evidence," *Developmental Biology* 173 (1996): 373-81; K. J. Peterson and E. H. Davidson, "Regulatory Evolution and the Origin of the Bilaterians," *Proceedings of the National Academy of Science* 97, no. 9 (2000): 4430-33.

30. Briggs, Erwin, and Collier, *Fossils of the Burgess Shale*.

study, much remains to be learned, and many of the ideas remain poorly tested. Nevertheless, it is at least clear that plausible natural explanations exist.

There are three broad categories of natural explanations for the Cambrian explosion. First, it is possible that some components of the Cambrian's apparent explosiveness reflect our limited knowledge rather than an actual phenomenon. Second, various evolutionary innovations or environmental events may have provided the impetus for rapid evolutionary change. Finally, perhaps what needs to be explained is the post-Cambrian slowdown, not the Cambrian diversification.

The explosiveness of the Cambrian diversification may partly reflect our limited knowledge of the actual evolutionary pattern. In general, the fossil record of soft-bodied animals is very poor.[31] The exceptional preservation of certain Cambrian deposits has greatly augmented our knowledge of the diversity of organisms present at particular times and in particular environmental settings. This preservation seems to reflect unique conditions of the time. Interestingly, the preservational conditions of the Cambrian Lagerstätten are quite different from those of the late Precambrian and record quite different environments.[32] Furthermore, both burrowing and scavenging greatly increased after the Cambrian, which would have destroyed most soft-bodied organisms after their death. Thus, the apparently exceptional diversity of the Cambrian may simply reflect the relatively large sample of soft-bodied organisms that we have for that time. Later Lagerstätten often provide the oldest known fossils for post-Cambrian phyla, classes, and other taxa. The Recent, where we have direct observation of soft-bodied organisms, has many more forms not definitely known from the fossil record. Many deposits have not yet been thoroughly studied, and so our knowledge of the fossil record remains incomplete, and new important discoveries will most certainly be made in the future.

Misinterpreting the fossils that we currently have could also incorrectly produce the appearance of a discontinuity and explosive radiation. The earliest ancestors of most living bilaterian phyla would be expected to be rather generic and wormlike. Such a fossil could not be recognized as the ancestor of a modern phylum until it evolved some distinctive feature of the phylum. One of these ancestral forms must then be fossilized so as to preserve the distinctive feature, and this fossil must be discovered and studied. Only then can we recognize that the phylum has appeared. Thus, many of the mysterious Precambrian

31. See the discussion of fossil preservation in the chapter "Common Descent, Transitional Forms, and the Fossil Record" by Keith B. Miller.

32. Bottjer, Hagadorn, and Dornbos, "Cambrian Substrate Revolution."

and Cambrian fossils may actually represent ancestors of later phyla, but we cannot recognize them as such. Restudy of several such forms (such as the lobopodians and halkierids) has in fact moved their positions from that of bizarre side branches to central roles in the origin of major living groups.

Additionally, measuring "explosiveness" remains contentious. In particular, quantifying morphological disparity has generated a lively scientific debate.[33] From our perspective, many Cambrian animals appear novel and bizarre. However, several living organisms would be just as unfamiliar to a Cambrian time traveler. It remains unclear whether the range of forms in the Cambrian was exceptional or fairly normal. Although some aspects of the variability have been measured,[34] the debate focuses on the relative significance of different kinds of variation. For example, post-Cambrian arthropods include such varied forms as butterflies, barnacles, centipedes, crabs, spiders, and scorpions. However, all of them fall into about five broad categories. Within each category, there is little variation in features such as the number, type, and position of appendages (legs, jaws, gills, antennae, etc.). The early and middle Cambrian arthropods have a wide range of appendage patterns not found in later arthropods (in addition to early representatives of the post-Cambrian groups), but to a casual observer many would appear superficially shrimplike in body form.

Despite these qualifications, few investigators deny that some real event occurred around the beginning of the Cambrian. Numerous hypotheses exist, proposing various key evolutionary innovations or environmental triggers. A particular problem here lies in separating cause and effect. Once rapid diversification is under way, several novel features may quickly appear, and determining what came first is very difficult. Hence, myriad ideas exist, with limited testing. At the molecular level, organisms may have reached a key threshold of genetic organization or evolved a key gene. Exactly what this genetic event may have been remains unclear, at least with our currently limited knowledge of complex molecular processes. One possibility is an increase in the amount of DNA. Large increases in the number of genes appear associated with certain points of significant diversification, such as the origin of animals or of vertebrates. However, other organisms, such as amoebas, have huge amounts of DNA without noticeable increases in complexity. Vertebrates have distinctive ways of regulating gene expression, so they may be better able to make use of additional

33. S. J. Gould, "The Disparity of the Burgess Shale Arthropod Fauna and the Limits of Cladistic Analysis: Why We Must Strive to Quantify Morphospace," *Paleobiology* 17 (1991): 411-23; D. E. G. Briggs, R. A. Fortey, and M. A. Wills, "Morphologic Disparity in the Cambrian," *Science* 256 (1992): 1670-73.

34. R. D. K. Thomas and W. E. Reif, "The Skeleton Space: A Finite Set of Organic Designs," *Evolution* 47 (1993): 341-60.

DNA.[35] A genetic change could underlie morphological or behavioral changes, and so this explanation is compatible with most others.

Several behavioral innovations have been proposed that might have played a role in the Cambrian explosion. Most of these would also have effects on the environment and on other organisms, creating escalating feedback. These include the development of predation, a major increase in active burrowing, and the development of grazing on plankton. Prior to the early Cambrian, there is no evidence for swimming organisms more advanced than jellyfish. However, in the Cambrian several actively swimming, plankton-feeding animals appeared. At the same time, many kinds of planktonic algae became extinct, and the surviving forms were much smaller.[36] Evolution of swimming and plankton-feeding ability leads to the diversification of plankton feeders, but it also affects the bottom-dwelling organisms. Both the fecal material and the carcasses of these animals would have fallen to the bottom, moving large quantities of nutrients from the water column, where they were previously inaccessible to animals, to the seafloor. Even today, most of the nutrients in the deep sea come from these sources.

Similarly, with the early Cambrian came increased complexity and intensity of bioturbation (burrowing, digging, or other moving and mixing of the sediment by organisms). This again represented a new habitat, allowing burrowing forms to diversify, which also disrupted the existing seafloor habitat. For much of the Precambrian and into the early Cambrian, microbial and algal mats largely covered the seafloor. These mats provided a stable base for sessile animals and kept mud out of the water, making it easy for filter feeders to obtain relatively high amounts of food and low amounts of sediment. The advent of algal grazers, extensive burrowing, and other bioturbation disrupted these mats. This created problems for animals adapted to the old seafloor pattern but provided a new habitat of muddy seafloors.[37] Additionally, the constant burrowing unearthed buried nutrients, making them accessible to animals at the surface of the sediment.

Finally, predation and scavenging first appeared in the latest Precambrian and became common in the Cambrian. This development may have produced extinctions in some prey animals while selecting for rapid change in the survivors. Predator-prey interactions seem particularly effective at producing an

35. E. Szathmáry and J. Maynard Smith, "The Major Evolutionary Transitions," *Nature* 374 (1995): 227-32.

36. N. J. Butterfield, "Ecology and Evolution of Cambrian Plankton," in *The Ecology of the Cambrian Radiation,* ed. A. Y. Zhuralev and R. Riding (New York: Columbia University Press, 2001), pp. 200-216.

37. Bottjer, Hagadorn, and Dornbos, "Cambrian Substrate Revolution."

evolutionary escalation, with the prey evolving defenses and the predator evolving ways to overcome them.[38] Again, these factors could complement each other. For example, swimming or burrowing may enable escape from a predator or capture of prey.

Another key innovation occurring around this time was the development of hard parts. This could in part produce a spurious impression of an evolutionary explosion if many different soft-bodied forms, previously unfossilized, simultaneously evolved hard skeletons and thus appeared in the fossil record. Nevertheless, at least the appearance of hard parts must be explained.

A change in ocean chemistry could have favored the formation of hard parts. With the right concentrations of certain ions, normal physiological processes, such as respiration or photosynthesis, may cause precipitation of minerals from seawater or biological fluids. Such "accidental" skeleton production could then be modified through natural selection. In addition, hard parts represent a handy way to store useful ions. For example, carbonate and phosphate ions, present in most skeletons, are good buffers against pH changes.

Hard parts also tie into behavioral changes. A hard skeleton provides a firm attachment for muscles, enabling various activities and motions not otherwise possible. Hard parts also provide a protective armor against predators, and evidence for predation is found almost as early as the first skeletal elements appear in the fossil record. Animals with mineralized armor in turn would provide selection for harder jaws and claws in the predators, and thus an evolutionary escalation in skeletal development. Hard parts may also help support a more complex, large body.

Modification of the nervous system is another possibly important physical innovation. Improved sense organs could also have provided novel evolutionary opportunities. Greater sensitivity to the environment allows greater specialization as well as improved detection of food or danger.

Around this time, continental rearrangement and glaciation also produced environmental changes. The production of new environments, such as colder habitats, could provide open niches for new organisms. Disruption of existing habitats would put pressure on the earlier forms. Some may have become extinct as a result. Even those that survived would have difficulty maintaining their dominance in shifting environments. Temperature also affects water chemistry, with more oxygen and other gases dissolved at lower temperatures. Glaciation on a global scale also occurred just preceding the time of the earliest known Precambrian body fossils, so perhaps climatic change was an important stimulus to Precambrian animal evolution as well. Similar dis-

38. G. J. Vermeij, "The Origin of Skeletons," *Palaios* 4 (1989): 585-89.

ruption of old species and appearance of new ones have occurred in association with other glaciation events in geologic history.

On the other hand, perhaps the real event is the post-Cambrian evolutionary slowdown. At the genetic level, organisms may have had greater flexibility in the Cambrian than they do now. With low levels of competition (as would have been the case before the appearance of many kinds of organisms), flexibility may have been very successful. Also, selective pressure for uniformity would have been low, as even rather suboptimal individuals could have survived and reproduced. However, as more kinds of organisms appear, the competition becomes more severe, and rigid specialization becomes a better strategy. Perhaps the cost of genetic flexibility began to outweigh its advantages as more and more new kinds of organisms appeared. On a small scale, experiments with bacteria produced this pattern, but testing genetics for Cambrian animals remains hypothetical.

Another possibility is that most major body plans and ecological niches were filled in the Cambrian, leaving no room for anything radically new. R. D. K. Thomas and others approached this question by modeling the theoretical range of possible body forms.[39] They then compared the extent to which these forms correspond to Cambrian animals and to modern ones. Most of the options had already been tried by the end of the Cambrian, and relatively few additional forms have appeared since then. Similarly, study of fossil burrows and other traces of activity shows that, even after the largest extinctions known (the Permo-Triassic), the major types and patterns of traces persisted. Thus, no major niches appear to have opened up after they were filled in the Cambrian. At lower taxonomic levels, however, substantial change has occurred. For example, since the Permian mammal-like reptiles, assorted archosaurs, dinosaurs, and mammals have taken their turns as the dominant large terrestrial animals. These are all vertebrates and thus have the same basic body plan and lifestyle, but belong to different classes and orders.

Study of DNA and protein sequences provides a possible source of data on the Cambrian events largely independent of the fossil evidence. Three main types of analyses have been proposed to give insights into early animal evolution. First, some studies have looked for genes that are present in many living animals. Presumably these genes also occurred in their common ancestor. Thus, this research is thought to provide insight into what the early organisms should have looked like, telling paleontologists what sort of fossils to look for. For example, many animals use the same genes in forming the eyes, and so the

---

39. R. D. K. Thomas, R. M. Shearman, and G. W. Stewart, "Evolutionary Exploitation of Design Options by the First Animals with Hard Skeletons," *Science* 288 (2000): 1239-42.

ancestral form may have had eyes. However, they also use some of the same genes for other purposes, and we do not know just what genes the ancestor used for what purpose. Many closely related genes have very different functions. Thus, this approach seems generally problematic. Only a few gene functions are sufficiently fundamental to be confidently extrapolated. For example, no one doubts that the Cambrian animals had the same DNA translation mechanism as modern animals, but this tells us nothing about what they looked like.

Second, some studies have used purported molecular clocks to calculate the time of origin for the major animal groups. These are based on the assumption that the rate of mutation is roughly constant over time. Most of these studies suggest that the animal phyla diverged from each other long before the Cambrian, which suggests that the fossil record as we know it is very incomplete. However, the calibration is often quite poor, with little testing of the assumption of constant rates.[40] Thus, acceptance of these dates requires much caution. On the other hand, fossil and molecular data may be partly reconciled because they do not measure the same thing. As soon as two populations become separate from each other to the point of limiting interbreeding, the accumulation of mutations will lead to the start of molecular differentiation. However, both populations may remain physically similar for millions of years until one or both evolve distinctive physical features. Only when this happens can we recognize the split in the fossil record, and even then the odds are low that the very first individual will be fossilized and discovered.

A third molecular approach comes from the construction of evolutionary trees. (The same can be done with morphological data or a combination of the two.) By analyzing the relative similarity between organisms, we can generate an evolutionary tree showing the most plausible relationships between them. Groups of organisms produced by such analysis are called clades; hence, this type of study is called cladistics. Cladistic analyses of both morphological and molecular data have found that in many cases there are relatively few features to indicate groups among the bilaterian phyla and classes. (Bilaterians are animals with a front, back, left, and right, such as vertebrates, arthropods, worms, or mollusks, as opposed to primitive forms like corals and sponges. Bilaterians have several other morphological and molecular features in common besides symmetry.) This pattern has been suggested to reflect the rapidity of the Cambrian explosion.[41] If new kinds evolved very rapidly, then each group would

40. S. Conway Morris, "Molecular Clocks: Defusing the Cambrian Explosion?" *Current Biology* 7 (1997): 71-74.

41. B. Winnepenninckx, T. Backeljau, and R. De Wachter, "Investigation of Molluscan Phylogeny on the Basis of 18S rRNA Sequences," *Molecular Biology and Evolution* 13 (1996): 1306-17.

have had time to evolve only a few distinguishing characteristics or distinctive mutations before it split into smaller groups. As a result, the smaller groups would have few distinctive features in common with their close relatives, making cladistic analysis difficult. However, limited data could also create this poor resolution. Thus, the evidence from molecular data on the Cambrian explosion remains ambiguous.

What Are the Theological Implications?

This discussion focuses only on the issues of randomness that are particularly associated with the Cambrian explosion. Chapter 4 and Part 3 give more detailed examination of the theological implications. As a whole, theological implications of paleontology are quite limited. We can appreciate God's wisdom and creativity in making and sustaining such a diverse and dynamic creation and in bringing about his purposes through it. However, critical information about what we are to believe concerning God and what duty God requires of man is obtainable only through the revelation of the Scriptures[42] and more fully in the person of Christ. Our understanding of God as Creator, and of our role as God's image bearers must be built on the foundation of Christ.

Many people, both theists and nontheists, see the apparent randomness of evolution as evidence against God's involvement in it. However, "random" and "chance" refer to at least three things. First, there is the mathematical concept of events that can only be predicted by the laws of probability, such as the outcome of flipping a coin. Second, there is the colloquial meaning of "humanly unpredictable." This includes mathematically chaotic events. In this technical usage, chaotic refers to things that follow well-defined laws, but precise prediction of the long-term outcome requires (humanly) impossibly precise knowledge of the initial conditions. A familiar chaotic phenomenon is the weather. Colloquially, chance includes things not mathematically analyzable, such as the course of history. Finally, random can be used in a metaphysical sense to imply a lack of purpose. Exactly where the lack of purpose lies must be identified. For example, if I flip a coin to make a decision, I have a purpose for the event, but neither the coin nor the laws of physics governing its motion have any goal.

Biblically, both mathematically random events (such as casting lots) and colloquially random events (including the weather or the course of history) are under God's control. Most religions and even superstitions (such as a gambler

---

42. Westminster Confession of Faith, sec. 1.1.

trusting in luck) also affirm supernatural influence on mathematical and colloquial random events, and so the attempt to use them as evidence for atheism is unjustified. Conversely, believers should not automatically argue against the existence of random events, in these two senses. The biblical view of metaphysical randomness depends on the level examined. Nothing is outside of God's plan, and so nothing is ultimately metaphysically random. However, physical creation lacks inherent purpose. God made it for his purposes and uses it to bring them about, but it does not have goals of its own. Romans 8:19 describes Creation as longing for the fulfillment of God's purposes, but this is not a physically discernible purpose.

Biological evolution includes both random and nonrandom components. Mathematical randomness may accurately describe the probability of a given mutation occurring and the probability of its becoming established in a population. Some physical patterns of evolution also appear mathematically random. For example, starting with a given ancestor, many groups diversify in all directions — bigger, smaller, longer, shorter, and so forth. This can give a misleading appearance of direction if the ancestor was not in the middle of the possible range. For example, in muricid snails (the source of Phoenician purple dye in biblical times), the ancestral forms had no spines. Today, they range from zero to numerous spines. Thus, the average number of spines has increased greatly. However, this could be mathematically random variation in spine number, as a snail cannot have fewer than zero spines.[43]

On the other hand, natural selection provides a moderate to strong directionality to evolution. In the most extreme cases, a particular mutation is fatal and never spreads within a population. More frequently, mutations have only a slight effect, if any, upon the fitness of the organism, and selection provides only a gradual tendency in certain directions. Evolutionary trends, however, are generated because the environments in which organisms live are not infinitely variable. There are certain basic types of environments that have characterized the Earth for vast periods of time. These environments pose certain consistent selective pressures on the organisms that occupy them. In addition, there are mechanical and functional constraints on the anatomy of organisms. There are a limited number of ways that certain adaptive problems can be solved. One consequence of these constraints is the common occurrence of convergence in the history of life. "Convergence" refers to unrelated organisms that superficially resemble each other because they are adapted to similar life styles. Convergence is a ubiquitous pattern in the history of life.

43. This diversification from a minimum limit is also discussed in S. J. Gould, *Full House* (New York: Harmony, 1996).

Thus, the evolutionary process seems to repeatedly find similar solutions to the same problems.[44]

Many aspects of biological evolution are random in the colloquial sense. While the available possible directions of anatomical change are constrained, the particular course of evolution does not seem predictable. Paleontologists cannot confidently predict which of the Cambrian forms would succeed, which would soon die out, and which would survive a while but then disappear. They can make some guesses, based on the apparent level of success in the Cambrian or whether the preferred habitat is stable, but the only way to be sure is to study later rocks or the present and see what forms survive. This aspect of the Cambrian explosion is probably the one most often cited as evidence for metaphysical randomness.[45] However, this is exactly the contingent pattern of history, which the Bible clearly affirms to be under God's control. Furthermore, God's inclination to confound the wisdom of the wise and choose the weak and despised for honor makes predicting his plan in history not only quite difficult but a recurring surprise. 1 Peter 1:12 notes that even angels cannot predict history's course. What historian would bother noting that an elderly infertile couple moved away from their home country of Babylon? Yet this is how God founded Israel. Given his pattern of action in history, surely we can envision him declaring, "But you, Chordata, though you are small among the phyla of animals, out of you will come for me rulers of the earth." Our failure to discern patterns, except in hindsight, reflects our limitations rather than God's. Catastrophes provide another unpredictable component to evolution. Even the fittest organism may be killed by a meteorite or volcano. However, such events do not take God by surprise.

Metaphysically, biological evolution has no goal or purpose of its own — it is just a pattern of creation. Likewise, organisms are not trying to evolve in any particular way. Again, we should expect this from a biblical viewpoint. All of physical creation is just that, creation, and not independent agents like the pagan gods. At the ultimate level, science provides little help. However, Christians should affirm that nothing is purposeless or undirected since all things are subject to God and work according to his purposes. Only with a theological knowledge of God can we attribute to him the wisdom and creativity shown in creation.

---

44. At the end of his book *The Crucible of Creation*, Conway Morris discusses the implications of convergence for the relative predictability of the course of evolution.

45. The contingent nature of evolutionary history is used in this way in Gould's 1989 book *Wonderful Life*.

Worshipping the Creator of the History of Life

KEITH B. MILLER

Scripture: Psalm 104

S eeing the history of life unfolding with each new discovery is exciting to me. How incredible to be able to look back through the eons of time and see the panorama of God's evolving creation! God has given us the ability to see into the past and watch his creative work unfold. To do so is for me a very worshipful experience, and it has greatly broadened my perception of God's power and unfathomable wisdom. God has chosen to accomplish his creative will through a process that has been ongoing for billions of years. Clearly God cares for the path as well as the destination.

God is the creator not only of the bursting diversity of life that fills this Earth with its intricate web of interrelationships, but also of the astounding array of past life that has passed into extinction. Just as God cares for the sparrow and the lily of the field today, he cared for creatures who have long since vanished from the earth. The vast majority of species that have lived on Earth no longer exist. These creatures, whom we can now only glimpse dimly through the efforts of paleontology, existed for their own sake at God's pleasure. There is so much of creation that declares its glory to God that will be forever beyond human knowledge — separated from us either by a gulf of time or by the vastness of space.

In the passage from Psalm 104 below, God's care for his creatures is portrayed. But significantly, God is also shown as involved in the continual process of death and renewal. This process, involving pain and suffering, is vital for sustaining life on Earth. Why God chose to create using such a process I do not fully understand. However, God is there in the midst of it, and we with the psalmist are drawn in awe to worship.

Baby *Hypacrosaurus* duckbill dinosaurs emerge from their mound nests in a colony of nesting adults.
Artwork by Gregory S. Paul reproduced with permission from his edited book *The Scientific American Book of Dinosaurs* (New York: St. Martin's, 2000).

These all look to you
    to give them their food at the proper time.
When you give it to them,
    they gather it up;
when you open your hand,
    they are satisfied with good things.
When you hide your face,
    they are terrified;
when you take away their breath,
    they die and return to the dust.
When you send your Spirit,
    they are created,
    and you renew the face of the earth.

Psalm 104:27-30 (NIV)

10 *Hominids in the Garden?*

JAMES P. HURD

The **hominid** fossil record reveals how humanity has developed since the time of the earliest hominids. It reads like a great mystery story, a puzzle with most of the pieces missing. Like a mystery story, each newfound piece of the puzzle may force a reinterpretation of all the pieces.

What is the fossil evidence? How has this evidence been interpreted? How do these findings relate to the biblical record and to Christian beliefs about humankind? The answers to these questions will indicate that, if properly interpreted, the fossil record gives a fragmentary but true story of the history of our **species**, a story that can be harmonized with Christian belief and with the biblical account.

The first part of this chapter summarizes some of the techniques and strategies of **paleoanthropology**, the science of human origins. A summary of the hominid fossil record follows, starting from the earliest known hominids up through *Homo sapiens*. The final part suggests how the fossil record might be interpreted, with a special emphasis on a Christian view of **human** origins.

Technical vocabulary (in **boldface**) is defined in the glossary at the end of this chapter.

Foundations of Paleoanthropology

A **fact** is an observation about the natural world. No fact exists without theory, and no sharp division exists between fact and theory. Theories do not arise au-

I owe a great debt to many colleagues, too numerous to mention, who read several drafts of this paper and suggested many revisions and additions. Of course, they should not be blamed for any of the paper's shortcomings.

tomatically from fossil finds. As Margaret Helder says, "A pattern in the [fossil record] is not a theory, it is only a datum to be explained."[1] Facts are analogous to 35 mm. slides lying on a table, items that are meaningless in themselves. A theory is analogous to the whole slide show: the selection and ordering of the slides and the narration of the show. It is the ordering and narration that give context, meaning, and significance to each of the individual slides.[2] Similarly, theory gives context, meaning, and significance to each individual fact. For example, as the paleoanthropologist tells her story, she may refer to a hominid fossil pelvis — a fact. But this simple fact takes its meaning only within the context of a comprehensive theory that, among other things, allows her to recognize the fossil as hominid.

Dating **hominid fossils** is crucial to interpreting their meaning. Dating methods can be divided into *relative* and *chronometric* methods. Relative dating dates in relation to something else. **Stratigraphy** is an example of relative dating. Geologists have developed a standard geological column that illustrates the order in which different geological strata of the earth were laid down. Thus, if a fossil is found in a lower stratum on the standard geological column, paleontologists infer that the fossil is relatively older than one found in a higher stratum. **Biostratigraphic dating** rests on the fact that certain extinct ancestors of the modern horse, cow, or elephant always appear in specific locations in the standard geological column. Hominid fossils found associated with any of these forms can be assigned to the same location in the column.

Chronometric dating techniques determine the specific number of years since the fossil was deposited. The Carbon-14 (^{14}C) method was developed in the late 1940s, and, like the majority of **radioactive dating** methods, is based on the regularity of radioactive decay (see Jeffrey Greenberg's "Geological Framework of an Evolving Creation" in this volume). The **half-life** of the ^{14}C isotope is 5,730 ± 40 years. The chronometric dates rendered by this method have been independently verified by tree-ring dating back to more than 10,000 years.[3] Because of its short half-life, ^{14}C dating is valid only to about 50,000 years ago, and thus is not useful for earlier hominid materials.

Other radioactive isotopes allow dating of more ancient hominid fossil materials. A radioactive isotope of potassium (^{40}K) is trapped in molten rock at the time of a volcanic eruption and creates a kind of time clock that can be read thousands of years later. ^{40}K slowly decays into Argon gas (^{40}Ar) and has a half-

1. Margaret Helder, "No Bridge-building Here," *Origins & Design* 20, no. 1 (2000): 34.
2. An analogy suggested by Prof. Alex Bolyanatz.
3. The width and pattern of tree rings reflect seasonal and climatic variations. Through matching these distinctive patterns in older and older trees, dendrochronology can extend dating techniques back into the distant past.

life of 1.3 billion years. A more recent method (^{39}Ar/^{40}Ar) allows calculating a chronometric date by measuring only the argon in the crystalline volcanic material. In this newer process, ^{40}K atoms are bombarded with neutrons to create an isotope of argon that does not occur in nature (^{39}Ar). The ratio of ^{39}Ar to ^{40}Ar determines the age of the sample. Fission-track dating relies on the periodic, regular fission of ^{238}U atoms in zircon rock. These mini-explosions leave microscopic tracks or fissions in the rock. By using an electron microscope to measure the number of such tracks per given unit area, paleoanthropologists calibrate the chronometric date of the volcanic material — the more tracks, the older the material. Other chronometric dating methods do *not* depend on radioactive decay, for example, amino acid racemization (AAR). AAR measures systematic changes in the amino acids over time.[4]

All of these types of dating have their problems, such as the possibility of contamination of the dated samples, spurious association of the dated samples with the fossils, and many other problems. However, women do not refuse pregnancy tests because they occasionally yield false results. Similarly, paleontologists do not abandon these dating methods merely because they are not perfect. The most credible dates for fossils are established using more than one of these methods, and, when used conservatively and carefully, they give us an increasingly clear record of the time periods of ancient hominid forms.

Just as paleontology is based on multiple dating methods, it is also based on the cooperative work of multiple scientists. In this case, many cooks do *not* spoil the broth; they improve it. The complete investigation of a fossil site demands specialists in the physical sciences (physicists, geologists, chemists), the biological sciences (botanists, palynologists, biologists, ecologists), and the human sciences (anthropologists, archaeologists, ethnographers). These individuals work together to reconstruct the physical and behavioral characteristics of disappeared species.

The fossil record is partial and biased. All the hominid fossils ever found could be stacked up in the average-sized living room, and researchers must work with these fragmentary samples of disappeared populations. Fossils are left only by those populations that happened to live in environments conducive to mineralization, preservation, and later discovery — all other populations leave no evidence. However, collected fossils are like the multitude of clues in a good mystery plot. Properly interpreted, they fit together to tell a coherent story that becomes clearer with each new discovery. Some hominid species such as **Homo erectus**[5] or *Australopithecus afarensis* are represented by dozens of dis-

---

4. Philip L. Stein and Bruce M. Rowe, *Physical Anthropology* (Boston: McGraw-Hill, 2000), p. 262.

5. Formal biological names are in two parts. The first indicates genus, the second, species.

tinct individuals, and by bones from most parts of the skeleton. Recent finds have greatly increased the representation of certain extinct species. For example, the fossils assigned to *Australopithecus robustus* have more than tripled since 1988. Thus the fossil record, though incomplete, offers substantial evidence for extinct hominid forms.[6]

It is exceedingly difficult to classify fossil forms. A species (as opposed to a genus) is a fairly objective classification for living animals because it identifies a category of individuals that freely interbreed with each other but cannot successfully interbreed with another species. However, fossilized skeletons do not breed well. Therefore, paleoanthropologists must make shrewd guesses about whether two fossil forms could have interbred, trying to make analogies based on similarities and differences exhibited by living animals whose species status is known. In these judgments, researchers tend to "lump" or "split." The lumpers allow much variation within a species category but the splitters allow little. For example, the Australopithecine fossils from the Hadar region of Ethiopia vary greatly in characteristics such as adult size, and in the nature of the tibia/talus joint at the ankle. Consequently, lumpers see one variable species here (perhaps males and females); splitters see two or more species.

New discoveries provoke reclassification of previous fossil finds. For example, the fossil assemblages formerly classified together as *Homo habilis* are now considered to represent two or more species.[7] Until recently, paleoanthropologists classified various **Neandertal** forms as subspecies of *Homo sapiens*. Today, DNA evidence has persuaded many to reclassify Neandertal as a separate species, *Homo Neandertal*.[8] (See David Wilcox's chapter in this volume on the evidence for Neandertal's separate species status.) Classification and reclassification have profound implications for the emerging story of human ancestry, and, as new evidence comes in, the human family tree continues to "evolve."[9]

For the last 140 years, the guiding theory for fossil interpretation has been **evolution** through **natural selection**. As defined today, evolution refers to a change in gene frequency over the generations in populations that are subjected to pressures from their environment. These pressures can be a cooling or warming climate, increasing predation, or a change in food resources. Through natural selection, individuals possessing traits that allow them to adapt to these

6. Henry M. McHenry, "How Big Were Early Hominids?" *Evolutionary Anthropology* 1, no. 1 (1992): 8-18.

7. Ian Tattersall, "The Many Faces of *Homo habilis*," *Evolutionary Anthropology* 1, no. 1 (1992): 33-37.

8. An alternative spelling is *Neanderthal*.

9. Elwyn L. Simons, "Human Origins," *Science* (September 1989): 1346.

environmental changes will leave more offspring than those who do not possess these traits. Over long periods of time these adaptive changes accumulate and spread throughout the population. This, by definition, is evolution.

Fossil Evidence before the Genus *Homo*

In this chapter we will somewhat arbitrarily select a few representative hominid fossils for discussion, starting from earlier examples and moving to more recent ones. Figure 1 illustrates reconstructions of skulls of five different species from two hominid genera: **Australopithecus** and **Homo**. The oldest *(A. afarensis)* is about 3.8 million years old. The next *(A. africanus)* is about 3.5 million years old.[10] *Homo habilis,* one of the first species in our own genus, is about 2.4 million years old; *Homo erectus* is about 1.8 million years old; and early *Homo sapiens* is about 100,000 years old. Note that the later skulls have larger, higher braincases and less protruding faces.

First, we will discuss genera that *preceded* the genus *Homo.* Recently, paleoanthropologists gave the name *Ardipithecus ramidus* to a collection of eleven hominid fossils found in 1997 in the Middle Awash area of Ethiopia. These remains, representing the oldest hominid genus yet found, date from 5.2 to 5.8 mya (million years ago) based on the $^{39}Ar/^{40}Ar$ method.[11] The name *ramidus* means root, suggesting that this species lived very close to the time when hominids and **pongids** (apes) diverged.

Australopithecus (literally "southern ape," named after Raymond Dart's early find in Taung, South Africa) is a genus represented by dozens of individuals and hundreds of fossils found exclusively in eastern and southern Africa. The Hadar (Ethiopia) Australopithecine finds have reliable $^{40}K/Ar$ dates of about 3.5 mya based on two datable volcanic layers, one below and one above the finds. A famous example of these is "Lucy," a 40 percent complete adult female skeleton, 1 m. in height and weighing about 30 kg. Lucy has several distinctly hominid characteristics: her canine teeth are reduced and she is definitely bipedal, as evidenced by the architecture of her pelvis, knee, and the tibia/talus region (ankle joint). She also has several apelike characteristics such as curved finger and toe bones. The ratio of her arm length to leg length is greater than later hominids, but less than pongids. The whole assemblage of Hadar fos-

10. These estimates come from William A. Turnbaugh et al., *Understanding Physical Anthropology and Archaeology* (Boston: Wadsworth, 1999), p. 260.

11. Yohannes Haile-Selassie, "Late Miocene Hominids from the Middle Awash, Ethiopia," *Nature* 412 (July 2001): 178-81.

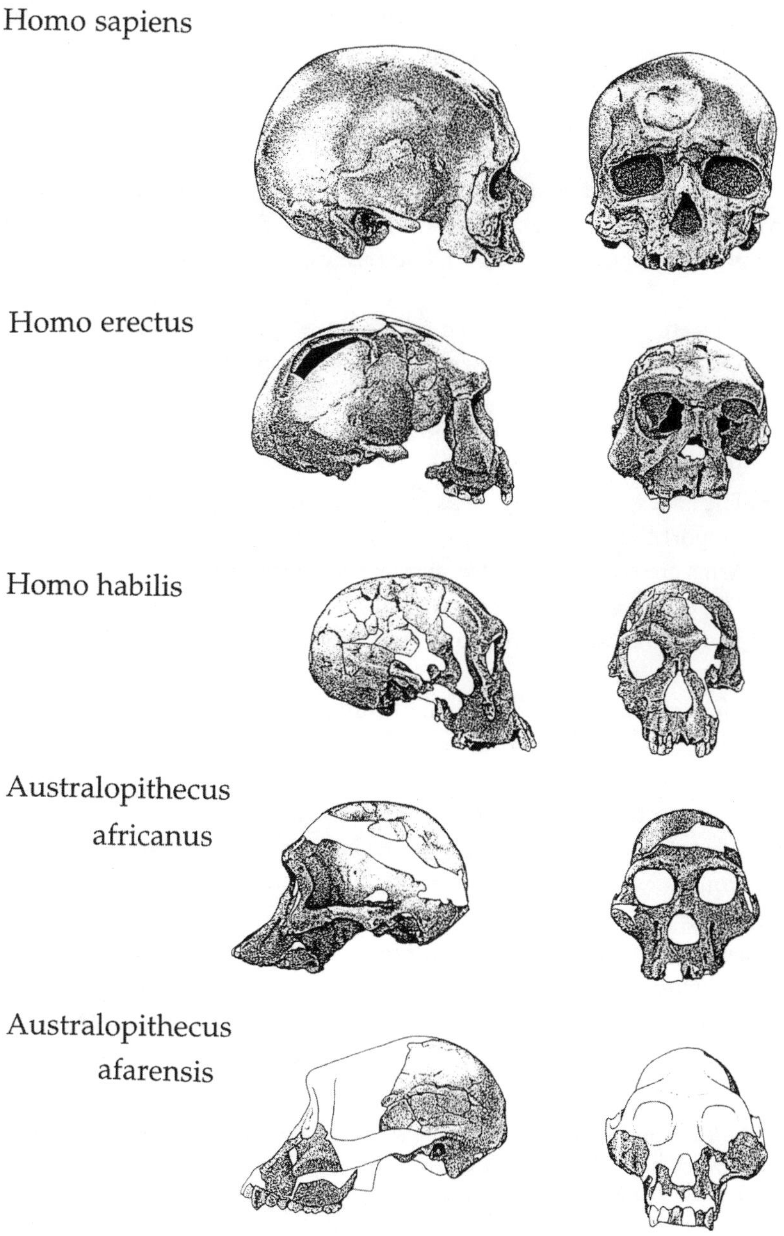

Homo sapiens

Homo erectus

Homo habilis

Australopithecus
africanus

Australopithecus
afarensis

Figure 1. Front and side views of five hominid species.
These illustrations are reprinted from Ian Tattersall, *The Fossil Trail: How We Know What We Think We Know about Human Evolution* (New York: Oxford University Press, 1995) with permission from the Department of Anthropology, American Museum of Natural History.

sils probably represents both sexes, with the males being significantly larger than the females, but both much smaller than later hominids.[12] (This great difference in size between the sexes moderates in later hominid genera.) Australopithecines in general have braincases that range from 400 to 530 cm.[3], compared with the modern human average of 1,350 cm.[3].[13]

No undisputed evidence exists for Australopithecine tool use, and they almost certainly lacked language and the use of fire.[14] All these forms differ from pongids (apes) on several characteristics, including the following:

- All were bipedal and walked fully erect.
- The foot is more a platform and less a grasping tool, in contrast to the pongids.
- The pelvis is more bowled, shorter and broader, with the thighbone sockets modified for bipedalism.
- The knee joint is angled to place the knee more directly under the body to support the full body weight for bipedal walking.
- Arms are relatively shorter, and legs relatively longer, than pongids.
- The dental arcade is more parabolic, rather than parallel.
- The canines are reduced to nearer the size of the adjoining teeth and do not greatly protrude.
- The foramen magnum (spinal opening in the skull) is closer to the front of the skull.

In addition to these two genera, Meave Leakey and her colleagues have published evidence for a new hominid genus based on a 3.5 million-year-old fossil skull found west of Lake Turkana in Kenya which they christened *Kenyanthropus*.[15] Thus, paleoanthropologists have proposed at least three pre-*Homo* genera: *Ardipithecus, Kenyanthropus,* and *Australopithecus*. The earliest two *(Ardipithecus* and *Kenyanthropus)* are based on very recent finds and following further analysis could well be reclassified. All these indicate the great diversity of hominid forms before the appearance of our own genus.

12. The humerus is 85.1 percent of the length of the femur, a proportion intermediate between apes and humans (Simons, "Human Origins," pp. 1345-46).

13. Stein and Rowe, *Physical Anthropology,* p. 331.

14. Stein and Rowe, *Physical Anthropology,* p. 160. The earliest hominid stone tools are associated with a somewhat questionable, fragmentary find in Ethiopia dating to 2.33 mya (Noel T. Boaz and Alan J. Almquist, *Biological Anthropology: A Synthetic Approach to Human Evolution* [Upper Saddle River, N.J.: Prentice Hall, 1997], p. 369).

15. Meave G. Leakey et al., "New Hominin Genus from Eastern Africa Shows Diverse Middle Pliocene Lineages," *Nature* 410 (2001): 433-40.

Fossils of the Genus *Homo*

Homo is the genus designation for all more recent hominid forms, and includes *Homo sapiens,* the species to which all living humans belong. At the beginning of the twentieth century, when the continent, time, and circumstances of human origins were unknown, early paleontologists such as H. F. Osborn and R. C. Andrews began a search for the earliest evidence of humanity in Central Asia. But as Elwyn L. Simons notes, they were ". . . looking in the wrong place, for the wrong ancestors, with the wrong anatomy, at the wrong time."[16]

In 1913, a big-brained hominid skull was uncovered in a quarry in Piltdown, England. The discoverers noted that Piltdown had a strikingly modern skull but an apelike jaw, characteristics that fit neatly into theories of the day that assumed that the enlargement of the brain preceded other skeletal features in evolutionary development. The notion that individuals with apelike bodies and big brains were early ancestors to modern humans (and the fact that England needed an early hominid of her very own) helped explain Piltdown's immediate, enthusiastic acceptance. However, fifty years later, suspicious researchers discovered that the fluoride concentration in Piltdown's skull was much greater than that in the jaw, and concluded that the skull was old but the jaw recent. Indeed, when they drilled into the jaw they found fresh bone, indicating that someone had apparently planted a recent orangutan jaw alongside a truly ancient skull![17] Piltdown was exposed as one of the most clever and notorious frauds in the history of science. This exposure cleared the way for a more accurate view of human origins based on the idea that increasing brain size and complexity was one of the *last* features of our species to develop, not one of the first. The succession of *Homo* forms bears testimony to this fact.

A *Homo* fossil, including skull fragments plus right arm and leg fragments, was found in the Olduvai Gorge in eastern Africa. This form, christened *Homo habilis* ("handyman"), has a skull like later *Homo* individuals, but the stature and limb proportions seem more Australopithecine-like.[18] In comparison with the Australopithecines, *Homo habilis* had a larger braincase — for example, the KNM-ER 1470 habilis cranium measures 775 cm.[3][19] Habilis forms

16. Simons, "Human Origins," p. 1343.

17. The jaw was probably an orangutan's, with the teeth filed down and stained to look old.

18. This individual, designated as OH (Olduvai hominid) 62, was small in height, measuring between 1.0 and 1.25 m. (Stein and Rowe, *Physical Anthropology,* p. 288). Partly because of the large braincase, Ian Tattersall later assigned this skull to a different species, *Homo rudolfensis.*

19. Robert Boyd and Joan B. Silk, *How Humans Evolved* (New York: Norton, 1997), p. 374. Meave Leakey's recent find near Lake Turkana (christened *Kenyanthropus platyops*) shares some features in common with this skull. Other *habilis* craniums measure as little as 509 cm.[3]

tend to have a larger body size than do the Australopithecines, and the females are closer in height to males than is the case with the Australopithecines. Other changes in *Homo habilis* include smaller premolars and molars and lack of a pronounced constriction of the skull behind the eye sockets.[20]

Homo erectus fossils are more recent, and date from about 1.8 mya (or older) to 200,000 years ago. They approach the body size of modern humans and average a cranial capacity of about 1,000 cm.[3]. Specimens discovered in Java, China, Europe, and East Africa tend to have thick cranial bones, large brow ridges over the eyes, and a somewhat constricted skull width behind the eye sockets.[21] The greatest width of *H. erectus*'s skull is toward the bottom, contrasting with modern humans where the greatest skull width is toward the top. An almost complete *H. erectus* skeleton of a twelve-year-old boy was found near Lake Turkana in Africa, who, had he grown to be an adult, would have stood more than six feet tall.[22] *Homo erectus* groups butchered large animals as early as 800,000 years ago, although possibly they did not hunt these animals but only scavenged their carcasses.[23] With regard to environment, *H. erectus* individuals were able to live in more northerly, colder climates where they built crude shelters. They formerly were thought to have controlled fire, but more recent interpretations of the evidence have questioned this. Paleoanthropologists point out that some of the Asian *H. erectus* finds have "shoveled" incisors (a scoop or indentation on the inside of the incisors). This characteristic, they observe, persists in many modern Asian and Inuit (Eskimo) populations. Others note that living Australian Aborigines evidence traces of some characteristics of ancient *H. erectus* forms found in nearby Java.[24]

Homo Neandertal forms, appearing about 200,000 years ago, have been found in Europe, with a few in Africa and western Asia. The last Neandertal (and the last nonmodern hominid species) disappeared from the earth about 25,000 years ago. Where did the Neandertals come from? Many researchers assume that they were descendants of the *Homo erectus* forms that were so widespread and successful until 200,000 years ago in Africa and Eurasia. Neandertals share some characteristics with *H. erectus,* such as a rugged skele-

---

20. Stein and Rowe, *Physical Anthropology,* pp. 334-36.

21. Stein and Rowe, *Physical Anthropology,* pp. 341-42.

22. Stein and Rowe, *Physical Anthropology,* p. 343. The find was designated as KNM-WT 15000.

23. Tools associated with *Homo erectus* are classified as *Acheulian*-type tools. Some archaeologists suggest that *Erectus* did not kill but merely scavenged dead animals (Turnbaugh et al., *Understanding Physical Anthropology and Archaeology,* pp. 288-89).

24. James Shreeve, "Erectus Rising," *Discover* (September 1994): 80-89. These observations favor the Regional Continuity Hypothesis.

ton and large browridges over the eyes. They differ in that they have an occipital bun on the rear of the skull, and the widest part of the skull is higher than it is in *H. erectus.* Rather than the "barn roof" skull that many *H. erectus* forms have, Neandertals have a long, rounded braincase with a volume equal to or slightly larger than that of modern humans (up to 1,625 cm.³).

Initially, researchers believed that Neandertals controlled fire and buried their dead.[25] They created antler assemblages and skeletal bear head assemblages that were interpreted as religious structures, and they used the improved Mousterian hunting and butchering toolkit, with tools greatly advanced over *H. erectus*'s Acheulian toolkits.[26]

Were the Neandertals human? Formerly, paleoanthropologists considered Neandertal as an extinct race of the same species as modern *Homo sapiens.* They pointed to the large braincase and the cultural achievements of Neandertal, and argued that if Neandertal were seen today dressed in a three-piece suit and boarding a subway train in New York, he would not have attracted undue attention. There is strong evidence in Europe that Neandertals coexisted for a long period of time with more modern populations. Since it seemed unlikely that two distinct species could have coexisted indefinitely without one out-competing the other, they must have interbred, and thus by definition were a single species.

In this volume, Wilcox presents evidence contrary to this view, emphasizing the uniqueness of Neandertals. Even though Neandertals are genetically eight times closer to humans than are chimpanzees, no Neandertal-specific gene sequences have been found in modern humans. He reports on research where three samples of ancient mitochondrial DNA (mtDNA) were extracted from three separate Neandertal finds. The genetic distance between these Neandertal mtDNA samples and modern human samples is 3.5 times greater than the diversity that exists among all living human populations. Furthermore, none of these three Neandertal samples is more closely related to modern Europeans than are the other two. Wilcox concludes that the Neandertals are a separate species and did not interbreed with early modern humans in Europe or elsewhere.

---

25. Evidence for deliberate Neandertal burials comes from La Chapelle, La Ferrassie (eight graves), Tabun, Amud, Kebera, Shanidar, and Teshik-Tash (Turnbaugh et al., *Understanding Physical Anthropology and Archaeology,* pp. 317-18).

26. To complicate the picture, Klein observes that the period 150,000 to 40,000 years ago contained *several* species, some quite different from Neandertal, but all of which are extinct today (Richard G. Klein, "The Archeology of Modern Human Origins," *Evolutionary Anthropology* 1, no. 1 [1992]: 5-14).

Fossil Evidence for the Origin of *Homo sapiens*

The earliest anatomically modern hominids date from about 100,000 years ago. By "anatomically modern humans" we mean, at least, creatures that could be classified as *Homo sapiens* and thus, by definition, could interbreed with living human populations. These had a skeletal structure similar to modern humans with many features not present in the Neandertals — a smaller face with a protruding chin, a higher skull with a more pronounced forehead, and a less-robust **postcranial** skeleton.

Where and when did these modern humans originate? Presently, there are two possible answers. Researchers embracing the **Multiregional Evolution Model** (MRE) argue that humans appeared separately in Africa, Asia, and Europe, suggesting that modern *Homo sapiens* arose (perhaps via Neandertal) from *Homo erectus* in all those areas where *H. erectus* forms were widespread. Proponents of this model point to, for example, certain physical similarities between *H. erectus* found in China and modern Chinese. MRE implies, first, that sustained, continuous mating took place over vast distances to maintain the unity of the species. Second, it suggests the somewhat politically incorrect idea that human "races" around the globe reflect deep differences that have existed for thousands of years, all the way back to *H. erectus.*

The **Recent Africa Origin Model** (RAO) envisions *Homo sapiens* first appearing in Africa (or the eastern Mediterranean area), spreading out fairly recently to Europe and Asia, and quickly growing to a large population that eventually replaces the Neandertals and all other preexisting hominids. Under RAO, modern humans would not carry genes that are specific to Neandertal or *H. erectus,* since they did not interbreed with them. Proponents of this model point to mitochondrial DNA studies that indicate a relatively recent African origin for all humans. They emphasize the similarities among all early modern humans everywhere, especially just after they first appear in the fossil record. The RAO model seems to fit better both evolutionary theory and the growing genetic evidence for African origins.

The evidence for the rise of *H. sapiens* does not lie merely in the bones, but also in the archaeological record of tools and other artifacts. The shift to humanlike tools and behaviors came a long time after the modernization of the skeleton. Neandertals in Europe probably manipulated fire, made simple stone tools, and built open-air shelters. However, most paleoanthropologists argue that their toolkits found in various areas of Europe showed little evidence of creativity, complex art, or sophisticated tool design, and were not sufficiently distinct from one another so as to constitute separate tool traditions.[27]

Starting from 40,000 years ago something changed. Richard G. Klein describes this change as "the most dramatic behavioral shift that archaeologists will ever detect."[28] This **Upper Paleolithic** (UP) archaeological period signals a time when novel artifacts appeared in broad areas of Europe, Asia, and Africa. Distinct, identifiable tool-making traditions emerged as people began making extensive use not only of stone, but also of carved bone, antler, and ivory. Large numbers of stone blades[29] appeared, along with smaller, more delicately crafted stone tools (scrapers, burins) and ornamental objects such as pendants and beads. Burials grew much more complex and included rituals or ceremonies. For example, one triple burial at Sungir, Russia that dates to at least 28,000 years ago included an adult male, an adolescent male, and an adolescent female, each of them wearing more than 3,000 beads. The man had 25 ivory bracelets on his arms, the youth had a belt made of 250 polar fox teeth, and the girl had many art objects of ivory and bone.[30] All these novel developments suggest that for the first time people were able to manipulate and develop cultural traditions, including religious traditions.[31]

The most economical interpretation of these archaeological finds is that truly modern peoples migrated to Europe bearing UP toolkits, and eventually replaced the Neandertals and other premodern types who were using the old Mousterian toolkits. This evidence for rapid toolkit replacement supports the RAO.[32]

Interpretation of the Fossil Evidence

All the fossil evidence is useless unless it is interpreted. No one denies that species change their physical characteristics somewhat over time, due to long-term changes in climate, for example. Rather, the debate both inside and outside the

---

27. Klein, "Archeology of Modern Human Origins."

28. Klein, "Archeology of Modern Human Origins," p. 5.

29. A blade is defined as a flake that is at least twice as long as it is wide.

30. P. B. Pettitt and N. O. Bader, "Direct AMS Radiocarbon Dates for the Sungir Mid Upper Palaeolithic Burials," *Antiquity* 74, no. 284 supp. (2000): 269.

31. Pettitt and Bader, "Direct AMS Radiocarbon Dates," p. 269.

32. For a review of the MRE vs. the RAO controversy, see Shelly L. Smith and Francis B. Harrold, "A Paradigm's Worth of Difference? Understanding the Impasse Over Modern Human Origins," *Yearbook of Physical Anthropology* 40 (1997): 113-38.

scientific community is about how powerful natural selection is, and whether it can produce profound changes, such as the creation of new species.

Figure 2 represents a timeline of some of the fossil forms discussed in this paper. This timeline is reliably confirmed by various dating methods including $^{40}K/Ar$, $^{39}Ar/^{40}Ar$, ^{238}U dating, and other methods. Less certain are the *relationships* between these forms. The most economical interpretation is that the later forms are descended from some of the earlier forms, but all the pathways are not known, and all of the forms are now extinct except *Homo sapiens*.

If a "missing link" is seen as a form intermediate between other forms, the hominid fossil record documents dozens of missing links. It is more useful, however, to look for *trends* in the fossil record rather than missing links. The following general trends are observed in the chronology of the hominid fossil record: (1) reduction in the size of canine teeth, (2) development of a larger braincase and a more complexly organized brain, (3) reduction in the maxilla (facial area), (4) increase in body size, and (5) *decrease* in size difference between males and females. In regard to body size, hominids were small until about 2 mya, when they began to approach modern stature. For example, the young *Homo erectus* male KNM-WT 15000 recently found in Kenya had a projected adult weight of 68 kg. and a projected stature of about 185 cm.[33]

The physical transitions from *Australopithecus* to *H. erectus* to *H. sapiens* would have occurred gradually. Early Australopithecines had heads, teeth, and hands like apes, but they walked erect. Later, *H. erectus* forms had more modern heads, teeth, and hands and had stockier bodies to live in a cold, more northerly climate where they fashioned crude shelters, but their average brain size was less than 1,000 cm.[3], with a poorly developed neocortex area. They had no chin, and their bones were more ruggedly built than are those of modern humans. Larger brains, developed chins, and a less rugged skeleton came later with *Homo sapiens*. These trends indicate change over time.

We seek two kinds of markers to document the appearance of modern humanity: morphological changes and cultural changes. Morphologically we ask, could this fossil form fit into the range of modern human physical variation? Culturally we ask, do the artifacts associated with this fossil suggest that these individuals were thinking and acting as modern humans might? The appearance of anatomically modern humans (about 100,000 years ago) greatly precedes the appearance of humanlike cultures. Only at 40,000 years ago do we begin to see evidence of artistic expression, distinct tool traditions, and artifacts that suggest that people were utilizing a mental template in their manufacture such as modern humans might. At this same time we also begin to find un-

33. McHenry, "How Big Were Early Hominids?"

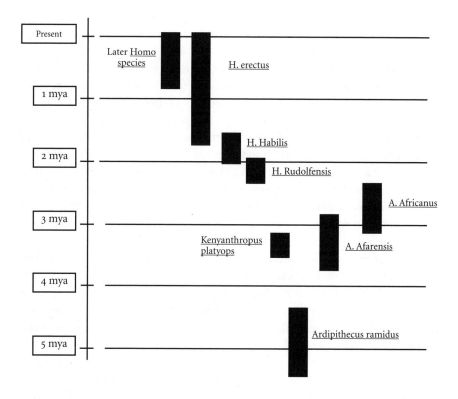

Figure 2. Timelines for various hominid species
Modified from Robert Foley, "In the Shadow of the Modern Synthesis? Alternative Perspectives on the Last Fifty Years of Paleoanthropology," *Evolutionary Anthropology* 10 (2001): 5.

deniable religious artifacts. Some paleoanthropologists believe that this revolution in human culture in the UP was due to a fundamental reorganization of the brain that perhaps made possible the first use of language. As a colleague expressed it, you need new "hardware" to run new "software."

A Christian View of the Fossil Record

God speaks to us in two main ways: through the Bible and through God's natural, created order. Each of these "words" of God must be interpreted. Theologians, hermeneuticians, and exegetes interpret the Bible. Scientists interpret God's workings in nature. Both theologians and scientists make mistakes, change their minds, and even occasionally perpetrate falsehoods for the sake of their own reputations. We now turn to the question of how the paleo-anthropological findings discussed above relate to the biblical account of human origins.

It will be easier to relate the Bible to the fossil record if we consider that the Bible was written before the modern age, before the rise of modern science, and thus is not a science textbook. The great Christian astronomer Galileo affirmed that the Bible teaches us how to go to heaven, not how the heavens go.[34] He did not believe that the Bible was written to teach us science lessons about the stars or plants (or, one might add, paleontology). Rather, the Bible is God's story, a record of God's dealings with a chosen people (the Hebrews), and how Jesus Christ arose from those people to accomplish God's purposes in the world. Thus we should read Genesis not as a natural history or science lesson but as God's sacred story of how he wishes to relate to us, how we should relate to each other, and to the rest of creation.

Rather than set the Bible against science and paleontology, it is more biblical to seek to harmonize these two ways of knowing, since the same God of the Bible is also the God of nature. We need to embrace a worldview that remains true, both to responsible interpretations of the Bible and also to our present scientific knowledge of the world.[35] For instance, instantaneous creation implies an event, but evolution implies a gradual process. We can note that the Bible does not specify whether creation was an event or a process. Each created animal was to reproduce after its "kind." Some biblical scholars have suggested that the kinds in Genesis refer to species, immutable and unchangeable. However, reproducing after their kinds would not rule out the transformation of these kinds over a long period of time. These types of explanations illustrate how we might seek to harmonize our current knowledge of the Bible with our current knowledge of the fossil record.

Adam and Eve and Human Origins

How might we explain theologically the fact that some early fossil populations do not resemble modern apes *or* modern humans? We should not call these

---

34. Stillman Drake, trans., *Discoveries and Opinions of Galileo* (Garden City, N.Y.: Doubleday, 1957).

35. Just as there is no single biblical culture, there is no single biblical cosmology. The Old Testament Hebrew view of the cosmos differed from that of the New Testament writers, and certainly differs from our view of the cosmos today. Thus, in order to properly understand Genesis, one must struggle to discover the concordances or discordances between one's own cosmology and that which is taken for granted in Genesis.

prehuman since most were not human ancestors. Like modern humans, these hominids used stone tools, walked bipedally, and had a humanlike tooth structure.[36] *Unlike* modern humans, they had small braincases, greater arm/leg length ratios, and relatively simple cultural practices. It may be a bit egotistical to imagine that all God's activities in the world have been for the exclusive benefit of humans. Did these forms perhaps represent creations for God's own delight, forms that went extinct for unknown reasons, terminal branches on God's complex tree of life?

Genesis tells us that the eternal, transcendent, and immanent God is *other* than the creation, not identical with it. Humans share a createdness with stars, giraffes, fungi, and granite rocks, yet they are given a special status in this creation. They have a "godness" and the capacity to enjoy, love, and communicate with God. When did this humanness, this godness, appear?

The fossil record gives no indication that humans appeared suddenly. Rather, it suggests continuity between prehuman and human physical forms. Most paleoanthropologists would probably say that humans *became* human through a process of growing intelligence and cultural development. The fossil and genetic records suggest that *Homo sapiens* originated about 100,000 years ago with a modern skeleton. In contrast, Genesis sets Adam and his immediate descendants in a much more recent farming culture. This farming family already possessed a relatively advanced culture including animal and plant domestication. Cain worked the soil and offered to God his fruits of the field. Abel offered the fat parts of the firstborn of his flock of sheep.[37] Archaeologists trace the beginnings of plant cultivation to 7,500-7,000 B.C.,[38] with domestication of cattle and sheep appearing soon after. When Cain left home, he built a "city."[39] However, no cities or even villages appear in the archaeological record until about 9,000 B.C.[40] All these cultural activities correspond to the **Neolithic** cultural period, a period when these features did not appear suddenly or magically but through a long process of what anthropologists call cultural evolution. Davis Young summarizes the implications of this: "If . . . plant and animal domestication was first established around 7500 B.C. and if Cain and Abel were a farmer and a shepherd respectively, then Cain and

36. Pongids generally have tooth rows more in parallel, while hominids have parabolic tooth rows.

37. Gen. 4:2-4. All scriptural references and quotes come from the New International Version of the Bible.

38. D. Zohari, "The Origin and Early Spread of Agriculture in the Old World," in *The Origin and Domestication of Cultivated Plants*, ed. C. Barigozzi (Amsterdam: Elsevier, 1986).

39. Gen. 4:17.

40. Found in the Natufian culture in the Levant.

Abel lived around 7500 B.C."[41] Adam himself seems to have been a Neolithic man, since his task was to work and take care of the garden, and to name the livestock.[42] From the fossil record, however, it is clear that humans originated long before the Neolithic. What, then, is the paleoanthropology of Adam and Eve? Were Adam and Eve not the first humans? Were they not historical persons?

We can sketch out three possible scenarios that seek to harmonize the paleontological record with the biblical account. Each scenario carries with it certain strengths and certain weaknesses (see figure 3).

First, the *Ex nihilo* scenario paints Adam and Eve as recent historical persons, created *ex nihilo* (out of nothing) with no ancestors, human or otherwise. All present-day humans would have descended from this Near Eastern pair in the space of 9,500 years.

A major objection to this scenario is that recent mitochondrial DNA evidence suggests that all humans have descended from an ancestral population living in Africa (or the Levant) 100,000 years ago. *Ex nihilo*, then, would imply that some humans did not descend from Adam. Furthermore, *Ex nihilo* suggests an abrupt change, a lack of continuity with what has gone before, a change we cannot observe in the fossil line of hominids. We do see a transition to anatomically modern humans (about 100,000 years ago) but it does not seem abrupt.[43] If Adam lived at the time of the Neolithic, how should we classify these pre-Adamic forms so abundant in the fossil record? If they walked like humans, worked like humans, and worshipped like humans, were they not human? Did they not have godness?

Ironically, if we attempt to preserve the literal *Ex nihilo* scenario that all modern humans descend from a recent, historical Adam, we are forced to abandon a literal interpretation of large portions of Genesis 4.[44] This is because a literal reading of Genesis 4 informs us that Adam and Eve's family lived in the Neolithic period, 30,000 years *after* the archaeological appearance of religion and human culture! A relatively recent *ex nihilo* creation for Adam seems to discount all the archaeological evidence for human form, human culture, and human spirituality *before* the relatively recent beginnings of plant and animal domestication.

In the *Like Father Like Son* scenario, Genesis 1 and 2 are not two different

41. Davis Young, "The Antiquity and the Unity of the Human Race Revisited," *Christian Scholars Review* 24, no. 4 (May 1995): 380-96.

42. Gen. 2:15-19.

43. This does not necessarily mean, however, that they were fully human in a cognitive or spiritual sense.

44. Young, "Antiquity and Unity."

Figure 3. Implications and problems in the three scenarios of human origins

Scenario:	Ex nihilo	Like Father Like Son	Early Origin
Summary:	Creation of a historical Adam and Eve out of nothing	Humanity fallen from their inception Adam and Eve failed God's trial	Adam and Eve at 40,000 years ago Garden of Eden is modeled on the writer's environment
Scientific Implications	Intervention in the evolutionary process	Adam is descended from premoderns	Hominids before 40,000 years ago were not "human"
Scientific Problems	Violation of observed continuity in the fossil record Ignores abundant evidence of spirituality and immorality before 7500 B.C.	*Homo sapiens* appears about 100,000 years ago	
Theological Implications	Genesis 1–4 are part of human history	Adam had human ancestors Creation of humans in Genesis 1 does *not* overlap with events in Genesis 2 (see figure 4)	Human sin entered the world 40,000 years ago The Garden of Eden is a writer's picture
Theological Problems	If Genesis is read historically, it describes a time too recent for Adam, or, alternatively, humans must have existed before Adam	Genesis 2 implies that Adam was the first human, and Eve proceeded from him Spiritual status of pre-Adamic humans?	How explain pain and suffering *before* Adam and Eve?

versions of the same event, but one continuous story. (See figure 4, illustrating the nonoverlapping features in the first two chapters of Genesis.) Armin Held and Peter Rüst argue that just as soon as God began his creative work in the world, Satan began his corrupting work.[45] Because of Satan's activity in the world, humans chose from the very beginning to depart from God's way. In this scenario, biblical history chronicles God's continuing attempt to redeem a Satan-blighted world. By this account, God brought order out of chaos[46] and created all things, including the first humans (described in Genesis 1 only as *male* and *female*). Humans were unique because they bore God's image. They possessed "language, free will, responsibility, abstract thinking, logic, creativity, deliberate planning, . . . tools, dominion over other creatures, and . . . the ability to enter into a personal faith relationship with God."[47]

Genesis 2 and 3 continue the story, relating the account of a later, *specific* pair of humans: Adam and Eve. Here begins one of God's many initiatives to redeem the fallen world. Adam and Eve were historical persons, but not the first sinners and not the first humans. They were earthy, created of the dust of the earth (that is, they came from the earthy line of fallen humanity). But they received a new spirit because God wished to counteract the Satan-blighted creation. They were unique in that God took them out from sinful humanity, placed them in a perfect environment, and commanded them to care for the garden and to avoid the tree of the knowledge of good and evil. But, like their fathers and mothers before them, they willfully chose disobedience instead of righteousness and eternal life. They had no one to blame for their choice but themselves since they lived in a perfect environment. They were *representatives* of the whole human race in sinning, in the same sense that Christ was representative for the whole human race in redeeming. It is not necessary for us all to be biological descendants of Christ for Christ to redeem us. Why is it necessary for us all to be biologically descended from Adam for him to represent us? If this scenario seems a bit *ad hoc* on the part of God, consider other surprising initiatives of God: providing animal sacrifice for sin, calling out the Hebrew nation, and ultimately, sending the Hebrew God-child who would redeem humanity.

Although *Like Father Like Son* can be harmonized with current scientific evidence, and although Genesis 2 certainly seems to be much more than a mere retelling of Genesis 1, there is a problem with it. The text seems to be referring to the time when humans were *first* created, since "the man became a living be-

---

45. Armin Held and Peter Rüst, "Genesis Reconsidered," *Perspectives on Science and Christian Faith* 51, no. 4 (1999): 231-43.

46. Gen. 1:2ff.

47. Held and Rüst, "Genesis Reconsidered," p. 236.

Figure 4. Comparison of features in the Genesis 1 and Genesis 2–4 accounts

	Genesis 1	Genesis 2–4
Spiritual nature	Man and woman created in image of God	Moral responsibility
		God breathed life into the man, and man became a living being
		Humans communed with God
Materials of creation	None mentioned	Man formed of dust of ground; woman created later from man's rib
Sin	Not mentioned	Temptation by serpent and Fall
Human activities and authority	Told to subdue the earth, rule over it	More "culture" mentioned: Tended garden, cared for it, named animals. Farming way of life.

ing."[48] If this was a first human creation, we are left with the anomaly that the paleontological record demonstrates that other "humans" existed long before Adam and Eve's Neolithic time period. If humans existed before Adam and Eve, however, it is odd that Genesis does not discuss how these earlier humans fell into sin.

A third scenario, *Early Origin*, envisions Adam and Eve living about 40,000 years ago, in the time of the great UP cultural explosion when culture "took off," the time when *Homo sapiens* began to fashion much more sophisticated stone tools and began to practice ritual burial of the dead.[49] The writer of Genesis is describing an actual historical event — the creation of the first creatures who were fully human. Adam and Eve were the first to have fully human brains. They enjoyed a diverse cultural repertoire, built up over millennia of cultural evolution. Thus, they were the first *Homo sapiens* to have the "hardware" and the cultural "software" to be God-conscious, to receive God's spirit and relate to God. They were given the opportunity to be in full fellowship with God, but they chose to disobey and live apart from God. They "fell," and they suffered as a result. Of course, pain, suffering, and death existed in the world long before Adam and Eve since Satan was active from the beginning of cre-

48. Gen. 2:7.
49. Turnbaugh et al., *Understanding Physical Anthropology and Archaeology*, pp. 317ff.

ation. Animals were carnivorous.[50] Natural disasters occurred. Hominids suffered pain also, although perhaps they did not reflect on it, were not fully self-conscious of it. But there was no human *sin* in the world until Adam and Eve since they were the first to consciously go against God's commands.

In this scenario, the ecological and cultural environment described in Genesis 1-4 represents not the historical environment of Adam and Eve but rather that of the *writer*. It is an environment that his readers would have understood perfectly since it pictures a familiar culture with its kinship relationships, plant and animal husbandry, and small towns. Yet the writer paints the garden as a perfect world, emphasizing that Adam and Eve had no excuse for their disobedience of God. This *Early Origin* scenario preserves the historicity of Adam and Eve and sets them at a point in time that harmonizes better with the archaeological data.

A weakness of *Early Origin* may be that it does not adequately explain the curse that God pronounced on the ground because of Adam (but neither do the other two scenarios since it seems the ground was cursed long before humans came along). Perhaps the meaning is that the food quest would become more difficult, and Adam would have to sweat harder against the reluctant soil, outside of the beautiful garden.[51] Second, *Early Origin* may not fully explain the origin of human pain and suffering. However, note that Genesis 3:16 indicates not that Eve would be the first woman to suffer pain in childbearing but that her pain would be *increased*. In short, Adam and Eve would have to live as humans must live today.

When Did Hominids First Get Spirit?

In any scenario, the question still remains: When did hominids first receive spirit, or God-consciousness? God "forms the spirit of man within him."[52] Since spirits do not fossilize, we must examine indirect archaeological evidence that might indicate "spiritness" in hominids.

Paleontologists formerly argued that Neandertals behaved in "spiritual" ways since their burials occur in various sites as early as 90,000 years ago (Tabun, Israel).[53] They argued that Neandertals buried their dead in groups,

50. Ps. 104:21.

51. Gen. 3:17-19.

52. Zech. 12:1.

53. Tabun is a puzzling site. The burials were found in the lower stratum and were part of a Middle Paleolithic Neandertal assemblage. Above this is a UP stratum, sandwiched between the Middle Paleolithic stratum below and another MP stratum above. There are no fossils in the

often in a flexed, sleeping position. The analysis of fossil pollen associated with these burials suggested that the bodies were covered with shrubs and sprinkled with bachelor buttons and hollyhock flowers (the Shanindar site). They practiced toolmaking and hunting and left assemblages of artifacts, such as burials of cave bear skulls, that seemed to indicate the practice of religious ritual. At least this was the traditional interpretation. Why would Neandertals bury their dead rather than abandon them as animals do? Why were adults and children apparently buried close together — were these family groups? Did these acts indicate some idea of the survival of the person, or part of the person, after death? Did these pre-*sapiens* hominids have a spirit with the capacity to relate to God? Their actions certainly seem to indicate spirituality or a religious sense.

However, reanalysis of the data has raised some doubts about whether these burials indicate religion, and even whether they are *burials!* For instance, the fossil pollen was not confined to the area of the burials; it was found all around the site.[54] In general, eliminating religious interpretations of Neandertal culture clears the way for a more recent origin of human spirituality, making it more likely that humans received spirit at the dawn of the Upper Paleolithic. Klein argues that with the coming of the UP, true art appeared, along with religious ritual and distinct tool traditions.[55] Does this explosion of technology and cultural sensitivity in the UP indicate a beginning of God-consciousness? Certainly, these individuals seem to be acting in ways that modern humans might act. On the basis of present archaeological and paleontological evidence, perhaps humans got spirit in the Upper Paleolithic.

UP stratum and no hints of bone tools or of art. The UP stratum has been interpreted as an incursion of a foreign people with more sophisticated lithic technology, followed later by a return and replacement by local people using MP technology (Tim Ingold, *Companion Encyclopedia of Anthropology: Humanity, Culture, and Social Life* [London: Routledge, 1994], p. 94).

54. Recently, anthropologists have questioned the scientific interpretation of these burials. For instance, at Shanindar not only was the fossil pollen found in the graves; it was found throughout the cave where the burials were found. Perhaps the flowers were *not* intentionally put in the graves. This reinterpretation of the Neandertal burials is partly due to the RAO model. This model sees modern humans as a different species from Neandertal; thus the need to "dehumanize" Neandertal and question interpretations that suggest that Neandertals practiced religious behavior. This is an interesting case of theory driving interpretation of the data!

55. Klein, "Archeology of Modern Human Origins."

Conclusion

We have discussed the evidence for fossil hominid evolution and related it to the biblical account of human origins. This evidence suggests a strong, unbroken sequence of forms from *Ardipithecus* to *Australopithecus* to *Homo sapiens*. Although it cannot be proven, the simplest conclusion is that the later forms were descended from the earlier ones. We see a similar continuity in the artifacts that hominids made. The simple Acheulian toolmaking cultures of one million years ago give way to the complex cultures of the UP, where distinct toolmaking traditions emerge, and where symbolic representation, art, and ritualistic burials become ever more sophisticated and more frequent. These developments suggest that certainly by the time of the UP, humans had a God-consciousness; they had spirit.

Whichever scenario of origins Christians embrace, we can agree that God is the creator of all and that humans are unique because they partake of God's spirit. Adam and Eve demonstrated complementary roles and both had a moral responsibility to God. We learn from them that we must take responsibility for our own actions. Adam and Eve's tragic story explains how humans transgress God's commands, become conscious of their own sin, and despair of measuring up to God's standards. Their failure reminds us that we all fall short of God's purpose and will for us.[56] Just as a cuddly lion cub inevitably grows up to be a ferocious hunter, precious little human babies grow up to express their inherent sinful human nature. God's loving response to Adam and Eve (clothing them, protecting them, giving them a promise) gives us confidence that God will also respond to our own condition with love and forgiveness. In this view, Genesis 1–3 helps us understand human godliness, human uniqueness, human moral responsibility, human failure, and God's loving response to that failure. We see ourselves in Adam and Eve, not only in their fall, but also in their great potential in God. This is the meaning of Genesis.

It is illogical and unbiblical to create a false dichotomy between what the fossil record tells us and what the Bible tells us. In the end, there is only one story, God's story, written in his Word and in his Works. Through paleoanthropology, humans can trace the finger of God's works in the world. The God who conceived the universe and spoke it into being is the same God who sustains all its laws and guides all its transformative and emerging processes, including the process of hominid evolution.

---

56. Rom. 3:23 expresses this same idea.

Glossary

Australopithecus. An early genus of hominid.

Biostratigraphic dating. Dating a stratigraphic layer on the basis of fossil organisms found in that layer.

Evolution. Descent with modification. A change in population gene frequencies over the generations.

Fact. A scientific fact is an observation about the natural world. Facts make no sense without their theoretical context.

Fossil. The mineralized remains or traces of an ancient organism.

Half-life. The number of years required for half the atoms of a radioactive isotope to decay.

Hominid. The category humans belong to, as opposed to the pongids (apes). All humans are hominid, but not all hominids are human. Hominids are distinguished from pongids by: (1) customary and continuous bipedal locomotion (walking on two feet), (2) reduced canine teeth, (3) larger brains, and (4) smaller arm/leg ratios.

Homo. The only surviving genus of hominid. Modern humans belong to this genus.

Homo erectus. An early, extinct member of the genus *Homo,* whose fossil remains date from 1.8 mya to 200,000 years ago.

Homo sapiens. Modern humans. Members of the genus *Homo,* of the hominid family, of the order Primate.

Human. A folk category, not a scientific classification. The roughly equivalent scientific term is *Homo sapiens.*

Multiregional Evolution Model. Modern humans evolved from earlier hominids in many areas of the world. This model implies long-distance migrations and interbreeding over long periods of time. (Cf. *Recent African Origin Model.*)

Natural selection. A process whereby the "hostile forces of nature" prejudice certain physical characteristics and favor others. Individuals possessing favorable characteristics will tend to pass them on more successfully than will individuals possessing unfavorable characteristics.

Neandertal. A category of fossil hominid that existed in Europe until as recently as 25,000 years ago. A variant spelling is *Neanderthal.*

Neolithic. "New Stone Age." Defined archaeologically as beginning when plant domestication is first perceived in the archaeological record, about 9,500 years ago.

Paleoanthropology. The study of the origin and early development of hominids, including *Homo sapiens.*

Pongid. The scientific term for an ape.

Postcranial. The part of the skeleton from the neck down.

Radioactive dating. Chronological dating methods based on the regular decay of radioactive isotopes. These isotopes have a fixed half-life since they steadily decay into another form. For example, ^{40}K decays steadily into Argon gas (^{40}Ar) and has a half-life of 1.3 billion years.

Recent African Origin Model. Modern humans originated in Africa or the Levant, spread to Europe and Asia, and eventually replaced all other hominids. (Cf. *Multiregional Evolution Model.*)

Species. A collection of individuals that can interbreed and produce viable offspring. For instance, in the term *Homo sapiens, Homo* refers to the genus and *sapiens* to the species. In the fossil record, species identity cannot be determined directly. Thus, paleoanthropologists classify species on the basis of analogies to living organisms.

Stratigraphic dating. Dating of fossils based on the geologic layer they are found in.

Upper Paleolithic. A cultural period near the end of the last Ice Age where early modern humans produced many cultural innovations.

Bibliography

Boaz, Noel T., and Alan J. Almquist. *Biological Anthropology: A Synthetic Approach to Human Evolution.* Upper Saddle River, N.J.: Prentice Hall, 1997.

Boyd, Robert, and Joan B. Silk. *How Humans Evolved.* New York: Norton, 1997.

Drake, Stillman, trans. *Discoveries and Opinions of Galileo.* Garden City, N.Y.: Doubleday, 1957.

Foley, Robert. "In the Shadow of the Modern Synthesis? Alternative Perspectives on the Last Fifty Years of Paleoanthropology." *Evolutionary Anthropology* 10 (2001): 5-14.

Haile-Selassie, Yohannes. "Late Miocene Hominids from the Middle Awash, Ethiopia." *Nature* 412 (July 2001): 178-81.

Held, Armin, and Peter Rüst. "Genesis Reconsidered." *Perspectives on Science and Christian Faith* 51, no. 4 (1999): 231-43.

Helder, Margaret. "No Bridge-building Here." *Origins & Design* 20, no. 1 (2000): 34-35.

Ingold, Tim. *Companion Encyclopedia of Anthropology: Humanity, Culture, and Social Life.* London: Routledge, 1994.

Klein, Richard G. "The Archeology of Modern Human Origins." *Evolutionary Anthropology* 1, no. 1 (1992): 5-14.

Leakey, Meave G., et al. "New Hominin Genus from Eastern Africa Shows Diverse Middle Pliocene Lineages." *Nature* 410 (2001): 433-40.

McHenry, Henry M. "How Big Were Early Hominids?" *Evolutionary Anthropology* 1, no. 1 (1992): 15-20.

Pettitt, P. B., and N. O. Bader. "Direct AMS Radiocarbon Dates for the Sungir Mid Upper Palaeolithic Burials." *Antiquity* 74, no. 284 supp. (2000): 269.

Shreeve, James. "Erectus Rising." *Discover* (September 1994): 80-89.

Simons, Elwyn L. "Human Origins." *Science* 245 (September 1989): 1343-50.

Smith, Shelly L., and Francis B. Harrold. "A Paradigm's Worth of Difference? Understanding the Impasse over Modern Human Origins." *Yearbook of Physical Anthropology* 40 (1997): 113-38.

Stein, Philip L., and Bruce M. Rowe. *Physical Anthropology.* Boston: McGraw-Hill, 2000.

Tattersall, Ian. "The Many Faces of Homo habilis." Essay review of Philip V. Tobias, *Olduvai Gorge,* vol. 4: *The Skulls, Endocasts and Teeth of Homo habilis* (Cambridge: Cambridge University Press, 1991), and Bernard Wood, *Koobi Fora Research Project,* vol. 4: *Hominid Cranial Remains* (Oxford: Clarendon, 1991). *Evolutionary Anthropology* 1, no. 1 (1992): 33-37.

————. *The Fossil Trail: How We Know What We Think We Know About Human Evolution.* New York: Oxford University Press, 1995.

Turnbaugh, William A., et al. *Understanding Physical Anthropology and Archaeology.* Boston: Wadsworth, 1999.

Young, Davis. "The Antiquity and the Unity of the Human Race Revisited." *Christian Scholars Review* 24, no. 4 (May 1995): 380-96.

Zohari, D. "The Origin and Early Spread of Agriculture in the Old World." In *The Origin and Domestication of Cultivated Plants.* Ed. C. Barigozzi. Amsterdam: Elsevier, 1986.

Finding Adam: The Genetics of Human Origins

DAVID WILCOX

The most difficult issue related to origins is undoubtedly human origins. The question of who we are strikes at the center of the faith. Answers to that question have been a central flash point (at least) since the Enlightenment. How good is the evidence? What must we accept? What must we not? What are the limits within which we must search?

Over ninety years ago, in 1911, Princeton theologian B. B. Warfield began his discussion of the question of human origins by laying out answers to those questions.

> The fundamental assertion of the Biblical doctrine of the origin of man is that he owes his being to a creative act of God. Subsidiary questions growing out of this fundamental assertion, however, have been thrown from time to time into great prominence, as the changing forms of current anthropological speculation have seemed to press on this or that element in, or corollary from, the Biblical teaching. The most important of these subsidiary questions has concerned the method of the divine procedure in creating man. Discussion of this question became acute on the publication of Charles Darwin's treatise on the "Origin of Species" in 1859, and can never sink again into rest until it is thoroughly understood in all quarters that 'evolution' can not act as a substitute for creation, but at best can supply only a theory of the method of divine providence. . . . The question of the antiquity of man has of itself no theological significance. It is to theology, as such, a matter of entire indifference how long man has existed on the earth.[1]

1. Benjamin Warfield, "On the Antiquity and Unity of the Human Race," in *Studies in Theology* (New York: Oxford University Press, 1932), pp. 235-58.

My purpose is to explore the evidence and theories related to God's "method of divine providence" in creating man. Obviously, the more familiar scientific evidence related to human origins consists of the dates and shapes of bones and stones (of skulls and hand axes). We have been studying these "since Darwin." However, the nature and shape of the evidence has been changing in recent years due to the inclusion of genetic data. This genetic data will be my focus, although the "bones and stones" may come into the discussion here and there. (After all, the question of human origins is a question of species formation, but the only *direct* evidence of speciation that can be related to the "biological species concept" comes from genetic data. You can't watch the mating activities of bones.)

An Overview

Let us begin with a very brief overview of those bones and stones. Do we have hard evidence for the books, television specials, magazine articles, and so forth about the "cave man"? It should be obvious that we can't go back and watch our ancestors. Evidence of the past comes from things we see in the present by which we interpret the records of the past. The most obvious living keys are those animals that are most humanlike (hominoid), that is, those species we call the great apes. If they and we were descended from common ancestors, we would expect to find fossil bones of creatures somewhat intermediate between us. And indeed, such bones exist, lots of them, especially skulls.

Roughly speaking, most of these old bones fall into two groups. One group, found in Africa at sites that have been dated as early as 4.5 million years ago, is composed of several species of extinct creatures typically called the Australopithecines. The best-known Australopithecine find (in Ethiopia) was dubbed "Lucy" and has a fairly complete skeleton. There seem to have been several species of different sizes (termed gracile and robust). The Australopithecines can (more or less) be considered modified (bipedal) apes. They had slightly larger brains than chimpanzees, shorter canine teeth, and a shorter pelvis, better for walking upright. The ape most like them today is the pigmy chimp or bonobo, but they definitely were more humanoid than the bonobo.[2]

The second group of old bones are more humanlike and represent species

2. Henry M. McHenry and Kathrine Coffing, "*Australopithecus to Homo:* Transformations in Body and Mind," *Annual Reviews of Anthropology* 29 (2000): 125-46; Bernard Wood and Mark Collard, "The Human Genus," *Science* 284 (1999): 65-71; Mark Collard and Bernard Wood, "How Reliable Are Human Phylogenetic Hypotheses?" *Proceedings of the National Academy of Sciences* 97 (2000): 5003-6.

placed with us in genus *Homo*. The general consensus is that the early *Homo* species such as *habilis* and *ergaster* developed from one of the Australopithecine species, probably *africanus,* and then rather quickly stabilized as *Homo erectus.*

The earliest of these *Homo* fossils has been dated at around 2 million years ago in Africa, and they have also been found at early dates in Asia and Europe. The most complete early skeleton is that of a young boy found at Nariokotome in Kenya. Neck down, these creatures had pretty much a human body. Their bones were thicker than ours (they were much stronger) and their pelvis was a little narrower than ours (smaller heads on their babies). Neck up, however, their skulls were rather different. Their brains were smaller, their faces were bigger and projecting, and their cranium was long and low. Also, unlike the Australopithecines, they are typically associated with chipped stone tools, particularly a pointed, flat, oval tool dubbed the hand axe (what has been termed the "Acheulian tradition"), a tool that is found from Africa to Asia starting 1.5 million years ago.[3]

By 250,000 years ago, some of the archaic hominid populations had brains as large as do modern people, especially those in Europe (the early Neanderthals). Still, their tools had made only a little progress (the "Mousterian tradition" involved more careful edging techniques, etc.). When people with skulls and pelvises like ours first showed up (apparently around 150,000-100,000 years ago, and especially across North Africa), their tools were also basically in the Mousterian tradition. And then, around 40,000 years ago (or possibly earlier in Africa), culture seems to take off.[4]

So, it would seem that they really did live — these creatures that are "in the middle" between the apes and ourselves. Who or what were they? It's not easy to say. We could probably call the various Australopithecine species bipedal apes, but what shall we call the archaic *Homo* groups? They certainly did not seem to act like us. There is no evidence of art; stone tool "cultures" remained the same for mind-boggling periods of time; there is little evidence for burials; and so forth. However, even if we don't know just what they were, they certainly existed.

Now, what is a Christian to make of this data? Certainly people who want to threaten the faith use this information — as they use all information — to attack. A great deal that you have heard has undoubtedly organized that data

3. McHenry and Coffing, "*Australopithecus to Homo,*" pp. 125-46; Wood and Collard, "The Human Genus," pp. 65-71; and Collard and Wood, "Human Phylogenetic Hypotheses," pp. 5003-6.

4. Marta Mirazon Lahr and Robert A. Foley, "Towards a Theory of Modern Human Origins: Geography, Demography, and Diversity in Recent Human Evolution," *Yearbook of Physical Anthropology* 41 (1998): 137-76.

into such an attack. But the data, and even the theories, have no necessary threat in them. It's true that they don't sound much like the description of human creation with which we are familiar. But then, fossils show us the outward appearance of the creation, whereas the Scriptures give us the inside story. Before we can evaluate or integrate these stories, we need to take into account the full picture(s) — the data and the theories — of modern paleoanthropology. And all is not at peace in Mudville.

The Controversy

It is at the point of modern human appearance that paleoanthropology becomes controversial. The burning question is, How did modern humanity arise? Archaic hominids of the *Homo erectus* type apparently spread over Africa and Eurasia considerably more than a million years ago. Likewise, some changes did occur in local regions, producing distinct populations such as the Neanderthals. But then, what happened?

There are two competing disciplinary paradigms for modern human origins, with a considerable spectrum of opinion between them. "Out of Africa" or "Garden of Eden" advocates postulate that modern humans developed from archaic types in Africa around 150,000 years ago. This population then spread out of Africa, displacing all the archaic hominid populations without interbreeding. The "Regional Continuity" or "trellis" advocates postulate that the local archaic populations in various regions of the world simultaneously developed into modern types of humans, with enough isolation to retain regional characteristics — but with enough gene flow to prevent speciation. The level of acrimony is intense, and the partisan commitment is evident.[5]

Most anthropologists held the latter view until a series of dramatic technical developments and new discoveries led to a reevaluation around 1990. These included evidence of "bones and stones" — the electron spin resonance-based date change for the Quazef hominids, for instance, or the ancient fish spears of the upper Semliki River in Congo. However, what really set the ball in play was the first of what was to be — literally — hundreds of studies in comparative genetics. The focus of the rest of this essay will be on this genetic evidence.

---

5. Henry Harpending and Alan Rogers, "Genetic Perspectives on Human Origins and Differentiation," *Annual Reviews of Genomics and Human Genetics* 1 (2001): 361-85.

Are Humans Simply Apes?

We will begin by comparing the human genome sequences with those of the apes. It has been clear for some time that the human genome — however you evaluate it, groups statistically with the genomes of the anthropoid apes.[6] In fact, the chimpanzee and human genomes have about a 98 percent sequence matchup. More precisely, the human genome groups with the genomes of the two chimpanzee species as a monophyletic clade. The term monophyletic clade implies (1) that the organisms in question all have a common ancestor, and (2) that all the descendants of that ancestor are included. Using this technique for taxonomy is termed cladistic analysis. This monophyletic concept is the meaning behind the title of Jared Diamond's book, which calls the human race *The Third Chimpanzee*.

He used the title because the biologically easiest explanation of the data is that chimps are our first cousins — that "we three" are sibling species. Further, all three species are equidistant from the gorilla (the first out-group), with orangutans further out, and with gibbons as most divergent.[7] That certainly puts us humans right in there with the rest of them! And according to a recent careful cladistic analysis of genetic and morphological data sets, molecular data is far more reliable than morphological data for determining taxonomic relationships.[8] Apparently then, God seems to have intended chimps to have genomes closest to humans. Whether this pattern of genetic similarity was mediately realized through a history of common descent, or immediately realized (from dust) through miracles, it clearly shows God's free choice for the nature of humans, a choice made outside of history in eternity.

6. M. Ruvolo, "Genetic Diversity in Hominoid Primates," *Annual Review of Anthropology* 26 (1997): 515-40; P. Gagneux, C. Wills, U. Gerloff, D. Tautz, P. A. Morin, C. Boesch, B. Fruth, G. Hohmann, O. A. Ryder, and D. S. Woodruff, "Mitochondrial Sequences Show Diverse Evolutionary Histories of African Hominoids," *Proceedings of the National Academy of Sciences U.S.A.* 96 (1999): 5077-82; Ann Gibbons, "Which of Our Genes Make Us Human?" *Science* 281 (1998): 1432-34; L. B. Jorde, W. S. Watkins, M. J. Bamshad, M. E. Dixon, C. E. Ricker, M. T. Seielstad, and M. A. Batzer, "The Distribution of Human Genetic Diversity: A Comparison of Mitochondrial Autosomal and Y Chromosome Data," *American Journal of Human Genetics* 66 (2000): 979-88.

7. Ruvolo, "Genetic Diversity," pp. 515-40; Gagneux et al., "Mitochrondrial Sequences," pp. 5077-82; Gibbons, "Which of Our Genes Make Us Human?" pp. 1432-34; and Jorde et al., "Distribution of Human Genetic Diversity," pp. 979-88.

8. Collard and Wood, "Human Phylogenetic Hypotheses," pp. 5003-6.

Human Uniqueness

However, this does not mean that the genome of the human species is indistinguishable from those of the various ape species. It is, in fact, unique and different from any of the anthropoid species in both the *amount* of gene diversity and the *distribution* of gene diversity.

Humans have far less *overall* genetic disparity (sequence differences between genetic sequences) than do any of the ape species — even the rare pigmy chimp or bonobo, *Pan paniscus*. The bonobo has a species' range under 600 km. in diameter, yet a single troop of bonobos usually has more genetic diversity than does the entire human race.[9] The same high disparity is true for the common chimp *(Pan troglodytes)*, which has at least five times greater mitochondrial DNA (mtDNA) diversity than does the entire human race. In fact, there is almost as much (63.4 percent) mtDNA disparity *within P. troglodytes* as *between P. troglodytes* and the bonobo, *P. paniscus*. And subspecies of gorillas, orangutans, and gibbons show even greater genetic disparity than do the chimps.[10] But the range of humans is worldwide, and that worldwide distribution would lead to exactly the opposite prediction.

This low human genetic diversity has been measured in a whole series of genetic systems (mtDNA being the best known). The easiest explanation is that not so long ago (100,000 years, according to "Out of Africa" theory) the human race was much smaller (had a smaller effective population size — fewer breeding individuals) than even local populations of any of the ape species.[11]

A second sort of diversity measure is how a species' total genetic variation is distributed between local populations. Here too, humans are truly unique, different than any of the ape species. *Any* local human population has about 86 percent of the (greatly reduced) genetic diversity of the whole human race (species). That is less local differentiation than shown between the populations of *any* ape subspecies, or even of individual primate social groups. It is, in fact, about the percentage of genetic diversity that individual chimp populations share with their local *sub*species — and significantly more than the same measure in gorilla and orangutan populations (with levels around 65 percent).[12] In

9. Ruvolo, "Genetic Diversity," pp. 515-40; Gagneux et al., "Mitochrondrial Sequences," pp. 5077-82; and Jorde et al., "Distribution of Human Genetic Diversity," pp. 979-88.

10. Ruvolo, "Genetic Diversity," pp. 515-40; Gagneux et al., "Mitochrondrial Sequences," pp. 5077-82; and Jorde et al., "Distribution of Human Genetic Diversity," pp. 979-88.

11. Ruvolo, "Genetic Diversity," pp. 515-40; Gagneux et al., "Mitochrondrial Sequences," pp. 5077-82; and Jorde et al., "Distribution of Human Genetic Diversity," pp. 979-88.

12. Ruvolo, "Genetic Diversity," pp. 515-40; Gagneux et al., "Mitochrondrial Sequences," pp. 5077-82; and Jorde et al., "Distribution of Human Genetic Diversity," pp. 979-88.

other words, local human populations share far more of the total human gene pool than does any local ape population the total ape gene pool.

Certainly one implication is the biological unity of the human race. There are no human "subspecies." Rather, compared to the apes, all of humanity *is* a single subspecies. Those "unique" characteristics that we think of as "racial" differences genetically are completely superficial. The amount of human diversity in the populations of Oslo, Beijing, or Nairobi is in each case around 86 percent of the total diversity of the human race, worldwide. Humans are indeed "of one flesh."

Such differences in genetic population structure imply significant differences in population histories. Simply put, it looks as if the long-term effective population size (breeding number) of the human race has been far smaller than the population size of any of the ape species, including the tiny bonobo population. But the human species is distributed worldwide! Even the archaic hominid populations had ranges far larger than those of any species of ape.

The second implication is that the level of human gene flow (due to migration and intermarriage) among local populations must have been far greater than the rate of gene flow in anthropoid populations. Differences in allelic distribution primarily reflect differences in the rate of gene flow among populations of a species — either at the present, or in the fairly recent past. (Alleles refer to different forms of the same gene.) Populations that are widely separated have less migration (i.e., less "gene flow") and thus show less genetic overlap in genetic frequencies.

So then, the data suggest that humans have had far higher relative rates of gene flow *despite* having spread over a many-fold greater range, with more geographical barriers, more diversity of habitat, and more variation in selection pressures. The *worldwide* effective population size to allow this level of recombination has been calculated under 1,777 individuals.[13] Two models would explain this: either individual humans have been more likely to travel from Java to Botswana for a bride than chimps are to travel 600 km., or the human population has until recently (geologically speaking) lived in a very small area — less than the range of the pigmy chimps.

The facts remain that humans *are* less genetically diverse, and that ape species have retained millions of years worth of genetic diversity. But if true humanity includes archaic forms like *H. erectus,* then "humans" have been spread from Java to South Africa for close to 2 million years. In that case, unless *H. erectus* had a truly remarkable instinct for cross-continental marital mara-

13. E. J. Manderscheid and A. R. Rogers, "Genetic Admixture in the Late Pleistocene," *American Journal of Physical Anthropology* 100 (1996): 1-5.

thons, the human race would have retained far more genetic diversity than have the various ape species, not less. Thus, the evidence from genetic comparison is strong support for the "Out of Africa" paradigm.

Reading the Clock

The genetic argument depends on the concept of the genetic clock, the idea of the slow accumulation of neutral random changes in DNA sequences. The time since two sequences shared a common ancestral sequence can be estimated from how many differences they show. One of the most frequently used genetic clocks is the DNA of the mitochondria, organelles within our cells. The mitochondrial clock is of particular value due to the speed with which it mutates, its existence in multiple copies, and its inheritance entirely from the mother.

However, the argument for human uniqueness depends on comparative gene disparity, not the absolute time shown by the genetic clocks. E. Hagelburg recently suggested that mtDNA may occasionally be inherited from the male, allowing recombination and speeding the clock.[14] But if so, it would speed both ape and human clocks, and thus not change the comparison. Calibration is usually based on the total amount of diversity that has accumulated *between* related species since their estimated divergence; thus, a faster common rate will not change the estimated dates. If recombination is more frequent in genetically diverse populations, as Hagelburg suggests, ape genealogies would be shortened even more than those of humans. And of course, the argument for a unique human history is based not just on mtDNA but also on comparisons with a wide variety of nuclear loci.[15] It is a rather robust hypothesis.

14. E. Hagelburg, N. Goldman, P. Lio, S. Whelan, W. Schiefenhovel, J. B. Clegg, and D. K. Bowden, "Evidence for Mitochondrial DNA Recombination in a Human Population of Island Melanesia," *Proceedings of the Royal Society of London, Series B: Biological Sciences* 266 (1999): 485-92.

15. In a wide variety of different genetic studies such as blood groups and serum proteins (L. B. Jorde, M. Bamshad, and A. R. Rogers, "Using Mitochondrial and Nuclear DNA Markers to Reconstruct Human Evolution," *Bioessays* 20 [1998]: 126-36; J. L. Mountain and L. L. Cavalli-Sforza, "Multilocus Genotypes, a Tree of Individuals, and Human Evolutionary History," *American Journal of Human Genetics* 61 [1997]: 705-18), microsatellite loci (Jorde et al., "Distribution of Human Genetic Diversity," pp. 979-88); Alu repeats (M. Stoneking, J. J. Fontius, S. L. Clifford, H. Soodyall, S. S. Arcot, N. Saha, T. Jenkins, M. A. Tahir, P. L. Deininger, and M. A. Batzer, "Alu Insertion Polymorphisms and Human Evolution: Evidence for a Larger Population Size in Africa," *Genome Research* 7 [1997]: 1061-71), Y chromosome haplotypes (Michael F. Hammer, T. Karafet, A. Rasanayagam, E. T. Wood, T. K. Altheide, T. Jenkins, R. C. Griffiths, A. R.

Far more can be deduced from these studies than simply that all modern humans share a more recent ancestor than do all chimpanzees or all gorillas. Recent genetic studies are unearthing (so to speak) the individual histories of specific populations in the various parts of the earth. For instance, modern people seem to have migrated to Southeast Asia by 70,000 years ago.[16] Or, the source populations of the Polynesians, Indian castes, Native Americans, and Native Australians have been investigated. Prehistoric population waves and settlement patterns can be traced in Europe or Ethiopia or China.[17] The most controversial of these "local" issues is probably whether the Neanderthals died out without descendants, leaving Europe to immigrant Africans. But the bottom line seems to be that the earliest people (everybody's ancestors) apparently started out in Africa more than 100,000 years ago.[18]

How is data of this sort analyzed for evidence of human population history? There are various ways that one can analyze the disparities of genetic systems: for instance, by looking for their pattern of divergence from a common originating sequence based on total branch length. The general technique is termed coalescence theory.

Coalescence theory is based on the concept of the genetic clock. As time passes, mutation produces more and more divergent lineages, and drift randomly removes lineages. The result is an ancient spreading "tree" of diverging genetic sequences that can be estimated from the tips of its branches — people alive today. As time passes, some ancient lineages disappeared and others diversified. The branches are thus said to "coalesce" back to a single postulated ancestral sequence that is the earliest that can be detected — the coalescence

---

Templeton, and S. L. Zegura, "Out of Africa and Back Again: Nested Cladistic Analysis of Human Y Chromosome Variation," *Molecular Biological Evolution* 15 [1998]: 427-41), RFLP data, and so forth.

16. L. Quintana-Murci, Ornella Semino, Hans-Jurgen Bandelt, Giuseppe Passarino, K. McElreavey, and A. Silvana Santachiara-Benerecetti, "Genetic Evidence of an Early Exit of Homo sapiens sapiens from Africa through Eastern Africa," *Nature Genetics* 23 (1999): 437-41.

17. Hammer et al., "Out of Africa," pp. 427-41; Ornella Semino, Giuseppe Passarino, Peter J. Oefner, Alice A. Lin, Svetlana Arbuzova, Lars E. Beckman, Giovanna De Benedictis, Paolo Francalacci, Anastasis Kouvatsi, Svetlana Limborska, Mladen Marcikiae, Anna Mika, Barbara Mika, Dragan Primorac, A. Silvana Santachiara-Benerecetti, L. Luca Cavalli-Sforza, and Peter A. Underhill, "The Genetic Legacy of Paleolithic Homo sapiens sapiens in Extant Europeans: A Y Chromosome Perspective," *Science* 290 (2000): 1155-59; Y. Ke, B. Su, X. Song, D. Lu, L. Chen, H. Li, C. Qi, S. Marzuki, R. Deka, P. Underhill, C. Xiao, M. Shriver, J. Lell, D. Wallace, R. S. Wells, M. Seielstad, P. Oefner, D. Zhu, J. Jin, W. Huang, R. Chakraborty, Z. Chen, and L. Jin, "African Origin of Modern Humans in East Asia: A Tale of 12,000 Y Chromosomes," *Science* 292 (2001): 1151-53.

18. Max Ingman, Henrik Kaessmann, Svante Paabo, and Ulf Gyllensten, "Mitochondrial Genome Variation and the Origin of Modern Humans," *Nature* 408 (2000): 708-13.

point. Assuming that mutation occurs at roughly a constant rate, the pattern of similarity (the tree) can be interpreted as a genealogy. This does not mean, however, that the population originated at the coalescence point. The loss of variability as a probability function means that the genes of even an eternal, stable population would show such an "origin" point.

On the other hand, the pattern of branching and the depth of the tree can indicate much about the history of the population. Populations grow and shrink, remain in one place or move away. When a population is small, diversity is lost rapidly. When it is large, diversity is retained. Larger and expanding populations retain more of the branches that originate at the time of expansion, producing a "bushy" pattern. Stable or shrinking populations will "prune" the tree, leaving a few deep roots. Thus one can estimate the size of the population at different points in its history.[19]

The estimated coalescence point for almost all of the genetic systems studied in humans is between 100,000 and 200,000 years. This does not necessarily mean that we have located Adam and Eve at 150,000 B.C., but it may suggest a bottleneck (a small population) at that point. In fact, fast and slow mutating systems can have different coalescence points giving information about different points in history. Thus, one might be able to look back beyond "mitochondrial Eve" using a "slower" genetic system. The fact that most of the "clocks" correspond is good evidence for the bottleneck.

A second method, mismatch analysis, compares the distribution of the genetic distance between the gene sequences of all pairs of individuals in a sample with that expected under various growth patterns. The overall human "bell" curve of paired mtDNA data is that expected in a population that grew rapidly around 50,000 years ago.[20] Individual populations show signs of expansion at various other dates. For example, in E. Watson's analysis of African tribal populations, she found that most African populations had expanded earlier than populations in other parts of the world.[21]

A third method, the cladistic analysis of one-time genetic events (mutations), is particularly powerful. Cladistic analysis depends on unique and unduplicated events. Genetics is particularly good at providing such events. For

19. Harpending and Rogers, "Genetic Perspectives," pp. 361-85; S. H. Ambrose, "Late Pleistocene Human Population Bottlenecks, Volcanic Winter, and Differentiation of Modern Humans," *Journal of Human Evolution* 34 (1998): 623-51.

20. Harpending and Rogers, "Genetic Perspectives," pp. 361-85; S. T. Sherry, M. A. Batzer, and H. C. Harpending, "Modeling the Genetic Architecture of Modern Populations," *Annual Review of Anthropology* 27 (1998): 153-69.

21. E. Watson, P. Forster, M. Richards, and H. J. Bandelt, "Mitochondrial Footprints of Human Expansions in Africa," *American Journal of Human Genetics* 61 (1997): 691-704.

instance, certain "jumping genes" called LINEs and SINEs (retrotransposons) get inserted at random into the genome. The chances that this would happen twice at the same point is astronomically small. Thus, all individuals holding a particular "haplotype" (presence of such an insert) must share a common ancestor in whom the insertion occurred. This technique has been applied to several large Y chromosome studies that provide a powerful support for "Out of Africa."

For instance, in one study, Michael F. Hammer analyzed haplotypes in the Y chromosomes of 1,522 individuals worldwide. The results supported the general consensus for both the recent coalescence date and population replacement. This study, interestingly, indicated that certain populations likely migrated out of Africa, acquired a mutated form of the "yap" haplotype in the East, and then migrated back into Africa. (Also interesting was that regional continuity advocate Alan Templeton was one of the authors.)[22]

The power of such techniques to reveal forgotten "history" was shown in a similar study by Ornella Semino and others, who used a cladistic analysis of Y chromosome data to analyze the genetic structure of Europe.[23] They concluded that Europe was settled in three waves. The first, 40,000 years ago, was by people from central Asia (bringing in what is usually termed the "Aurignacian" culture). The second wave, 22,000 years ago, just before the last glaciation, came from the Balkans and brought a culture usually termed "Gravettian." The third wave were the Neolithic farmers from the Middle East, moving along the Mediterranean about 10,000 years ago. Half the Y chromosomes in Europe arrived with the first wave, another 30% or so came in with the second wave, and the last 20% traced back to the Neolithic farmers. Similar percentages in European female lineages are reflected in the European mtDNA records.[24] In much the same way, Li Jin and Bing Su have demonstrated through a study of Y chromosome haplotypes that the population of East Asia is a product of a series of immigrations from Africa rather than due to regional continuity.[25] Literally hun-

22. Hammer et al., "Out of Africa," pp. 427-41.

23. Semino et al., "Genetic Legacy," pp. 1155-59.

24. Guido Barbujani and Giorgio Bertorelle, "Genetics and the Population History of Europe," *Proceedings of the National Academy of Sciences* 98 (2001): 22-25; M. Richards, V. Macaulay, E. Hickey, E. Vega, B. Sykes, V. Guida, C. Rengo, D. Sellitto, F. Cruciani, T. Kivisild, R. Villems, M. Thomas, S. Rychkov, O. Rychkov, Y. Rychkov, M. Golge, D. Dimitrov, E. Hill, D. Bradley, V. Romano, F. Cali, G. Vona, A. Demaine, S. Papiha, C. Triantaphyllidis, and G. Stefanescu, "Tracing European Founder Lineages in the Near Eastern mtDNA Pool," *American Journal of Human Genetics* 67 (2000): 1251-76.

25. Li Jin and Bing Su, "Natives or Immigrants: Modern Human Origin in East Asia," *Nature Reviews Genetics* 1 (2000): 126-33; Ke et al., "African Origin of Modern Humans," pp. 1151-53.

dreds of papers like this have been published during the last decade, probing the origins of both local populations and the global human population.

A Consensus on History

From these genetic studies a general consensus about the history of modern humans *(Homo sapiens sapiens)* has emerged, although not without provoking dispute.[26] The ancestors of the human race seems to have existed as a small, homogenous population of about 10,000 breeding individuals in Africa for most of the Pleistocene (perhaps for the last million years or so?). The evidence for this is that the amount of human genetic diversity in a slow mutating system is quite low, is about the same in all human populations, and shows almost complete overlap among all local populations.[27]

Around 80,000 to 100,000 years ago, modern humans are thought to have spread out of Africa into several locations (notably, Southeast Asia) in low numbers. For instance, the "modern" skeleton at Lake Mungo (Australia) has been dated at 62,000 years ago.[28] Either prior to that range expansion, or just after it, some population differentiation probably took place (although nothing like that seen in the chimps). At that time there were not yet modern people in Europe.[29]

Around 50,000 years ago (perhaps 80,000 in Africa), some factor apparently led to a rapid population expansion, "fixing" variation that arose at that

26. John Hawks, Keith Hunley, Sang-Hee Lee, and Milford Wolpoff, "Population Bottlenecks and Pleistocene Human Evolution," *Molecular Biology and Evolution* 17 (2000): 2-22; J. H. Relethford, "Mitochondrial DNA and Ancient Population Growth," *American Journal of Physical Anthropology* 105 (1998): 1-7; Alan R. Templeton, "Out of Africa? What Do Genes Tell Us?" *Current Opinions in Genetics and Development* 7 (1997): 841-47.

27. H. C. Harpending, M. A. Batzer, M. Gurven, L. B. Jorde, A. R. Rogers, and S. T. Sherry, "Genetic Traces of Ancient Demography," *Proceedings of the National Academy of Science U.S.A.* 95 (1998): 1961-67; Ambrose, "Late Pleistocene Human Population Bottlenecks," pp. 623-51; Sherry et al., "Modeling the Genetic Architecture," pp. 153-69; Relethford, "Mitochondrial DNA and Ancient Population Growth," pp. 1-7.

28. C. Zimmer, "New Date for the Dawn of Dream Time," *Science* 284 (1999): 1243-45; A. Thorne, R. Grun, G. Mortimer, N. A. Spooner, J. J. Simpson, M. McCulloch, L. Taylor, and D. Curnoe, "Australia's Oldest Human Remains: Age of the Lake Mungo 3 Skeleton," *Journal of Human Evolution* 36 (1999): 591-612.

29. R. C. Walter, R. T. Buffler, J. H. Bruggemann, M. M. Guillaume, S. M. Berhe, B. Negassi, Y. Libsekal, H. Cheng, R. L. Edwards, R. von Cosel, D. Neraudeau, and M. Gagnon, "Early Human Occupation of the Red Sea Coast of Eritrea during the Last Interglacial," *Nature* 405 (2000): 65-69; Lahr and Foley, "Towards a Theory of Modern Human Origins," pp. 137-76; Ambrose, "Late Pleistocene Human Population Bottlenecks," pp. 623-51.

point. The evidence for rapid expansions is the "star"-shaped or "bushy" gene trees seen in fast mutating systems that are shown by most human populations. Such trees indicate that most of the retained genetic variation arose at a very early point in the history of those populations. They have retained this early pattern of diversity by rapid population expansion. Certain African populations — notably the !Kung, Mbuti and Biaka — show a "bumpy" pairwise distribution. These groups apparently have remained stable since before the expansion point, and they tend to be food gatherers rather than food producers.[30]

Due to the higher African diversity (in several genetic systems), the original human population seems most likely to have been in Africa. However, the "Out of Africa" data could also be explained as due to greater retention of genes in a larger African population, an earlier African population expansion, a less severe African bottleneck, or even the return to Africa of an Asian population.[31]

Obviously, this tentative history begins with a small population source for modern humans, a small population with ancient roots, that is, "Out of Africa." But the controversy between the "Out of Africa" model (replacement) and the "Multiregional Continuity" model (with homogenization) takes new turns. Most researchers have given up on the idea that modern humans show significant gene flows from the regional archaic populations. Rather, the proposed "weak out of Africa" model would have the invading African populations interbreeding to some variable extent with the local archaic populations. Even Milford Wolpoff has conceded that the African genetic contribution was far bigger (that is, contributed the lion's share of the genes in the rest of the world).[32] Either admixture is thought to be too rare to be seen, or the "regional" populations are the geographically separated parts of the later date radiation of modern types.

A large number of rather complex "alternative" scenarios have been proposed. For instance, perhaps the large ancestral population was divided into

30. Yu-Sheng Chen, Antonel Olckers, Theodore G. Schurr, Andreas M. Kogelnik, Kirsi Huoponen, and Douglas C. Wallace, "mtDNA Variation in the South African Kung and Khwe- and Their Genetic Relationships to Other African Populations," *American Journal of Human Genetics* 66 (2000): 1362-83; Watson et al., "Mitochondrial Footprints," pp. 691-704.

31. Relethford, "Mitochondrial DNA and Ancient Population Growth," pp. 1-7; Ambrose, "Late Pleistocene Human Population Bottlenecks," pp. 623-51; Harpending and Rogers, "Genetic Perspectives," pp. 361-85; Hammer et al., "Out of Africa," pp. 427-41; Jorde et al., "Distribution of Human Genetic Diversity," pp. 979-88; Quintana-Murci et al., "Genetic Evidence of an Early Exit," pp. 437-41.

32. Hawks et al., "Population Bottlenecks," pp. 2-22; Gregory J. Adcock, Elizabeth S. Dennis, Simon Easteal, Gavin A. Huttley, Lars S. Jermiin, W. James Peacock, and Alan Thorne, "Mitochondrial DNA Sequences in Ancient Australians: Implication for Modern Human Origins," *Proceedings of the National Academy of Sciences U.S.A.* 98 (2001): 537-42.

very small semi-isolated demes (distinct local populations) that frequently went extinct, being replaced by migration from other populations.[33] Thus all modern humans might be descended from one small portion of a much larger population. In such a model, drift would be high due to small local populations (small effective population size). But that is essentially a variation of the single-source model. A bottleneck (or a series thereof) in a small population would also be compatible with this pattern of data, or perhaps the populations separated and then went through bottlenecks. An alternative model is the "hour-glass" — a large worldwide population shrinks to a tiny remnant, and then re-bounds, thus going through a sharp bottleneck. But a large population before the bottleneck should show a lot more deep variation in allelic lineages.[34]

The Neanderthal Problem

The flash point has been the Neanderthal question. Are we in part descended from the archaic population of Europe, or did the Neanderthals die out without issue? The argument revolves around Neanderthal cultural motifs and their "archaic" anatomical features. For instance, there is a possibility that a child buried 24,500 years ago in the Abrigo do Lagar Velho (Portugal) rock shelter was a Neanderthal/modern hybrid. The debate concerning this has practically descended to the level of character assassination.[35] Frankly, despite all the passion, molecular genetics has made this a moot point.

Three separate Neanderthal mtDNA samples have been extracted from ancient bones and sequenced.[36] The three individuals lived 2,500 km. apart and

33. M. C. Whitlock and N. H. Barton, "The Effective Size of a Subdivided Population," *Genetics* 69 (1997): 427-41; N. Takahata, S. H. Lee, and Y. N. Satta, "Testing Multiregionality of Modern Human Origins," *Molecular and Biological Evolution* 18 (2001): 172-83.

34. Lahr and Foley, "Towards a Theory of Modern Human Origins," pp. 137-76; Ambrose, "Late Pleistocene Human Population Bottlenecks," pp. 623-51.

35. Kate Wong, "Who Were the Neanderthals?" *Scientific American* (2000): 99-107; C. Duarte, J. Mauricio, P. B. Pettitt, P. Souto, E. Trinkaus, H. van der Plicht, and J. Zilhao, "The Early Upper Paleolithic Human Skeleton from the Abrigo do Lagar Velho (Portugal) and Modern Human Emergence in Iberia," *Proceedings of the National Academy of Science U.S.A.* 96 (1999): 7604-9; Ian Tattersall and Jeffrey H. Schwartz, "Hominids and Hybrids: The Place of Neanderthals in Human Evolution," *Proceedings of the National Academy of Science U.S.A.* 96 (1999): 7117-19.

36. Igor V. Ovchinnikov, Anders Gotherstrom, Galina P. Romanova, Vitally M. Kharitonov, Kerstin Liden, and William Goodwin, "Molecular Analysis of Neanderthal DNA from the Northern Caucasus," *Nature* 404 (2000): 490-93; Mattias Krings, Helga Geisert, R. W. Schmitz, H. Krainitzki, and Svante Paabo, "DNA Sequence of the Mitochondrial Hypervariable

perhaps 20,000 years apart in time. The Neanderthal gene sequences all group together, being definitively separated from a reference group of 6,000 modern human sequences. If modern humans evolved from Neanderthals, it would be expected that they would fall within the bounds of the modern distribution.

However, the separation between the three Neanderthals and modern humans is about 3.5-fold greater than the diversity in the whole (modern) human race. Statistically, the common ancestor of the three Neanderthals likely lived 252,000 years ago. The same data would put the modern human ancestor at 176,000 years ago. The common root for both populations would be around 609,000 years ago (365,000 to 863,000). Further, the Neanderthal samples are equidistant from *all* modern groups, not closer to modern Europeans. Also, the Neanderthal separation from modern DNA is backed up by another study using southern blot hybridization of Neanderthal genomic DNA on three Neanderthal samples and one ancient modern specimen.[37]

In addition, Mattias Krings estimates the likely diversity within the Neanderthal population as almost as limited as the diversity of modern humans. If the Neanderthal population had diversity levels like any of the ape species, one could argue that the clump of modern sequences was a component of the Neanderthal gene distribution. Yet the two populations clearly are distinct and separated. Thus, the Neanderthals are a genetic out-group. Given their long centuries of contact with modern humans in Europe and the Levant and the lack of genetic admixture in modern humans, Neanderthals were almost certainly a separate species.

Note that even with only three samples tested, the common root for the three Neanderthals is slightly deeper than the root for the entire (modern) human race. These three Neanderthal specimens had a bit more genetic diversity than that found in modern African populations, and this genetic disparity might possibly increase as other Neanderthal samples are extracted. However, it seems likely that both species grew rapidly from an initial small population, although the modern human source was likely either smaller or later in time than the population leading to the Neanderthals.

Region II from the Neandertal Type Specimen," *Proceedings of the National Academy of Science U.S.A.* 96 (1999): 5581-85; Matthias Krings, Cristian Capelli, Frank Tschentscher, Helga Geisert, Sonja Meyer, Arndt von Haeseler, Karl Grossschmidt, Goran Possnert, Maja Paunovic, and Svante Paabo, "A View of Neandertal Genetic Diversity," *Nature Genetics* 26 (2000): 144-46.

37. Micheal Scholz, Lutz Bachmann, Graeme J. Nicholson, Jutta Bachmann, Ian Giddings, Barbara Ruschoff-Thale, Alfred Czarnetzki, and Carsten M. Pusch, "Genomic Differentiation of Neanderthals and Anatomically Modern Man Allows a Fossil DNA Based Classification of Morphologically Indistinguishable Hominid Bones," *American Journal of Human Genetics* 66 (2000): 1927-32.

On the other hand, Neanderthals are eightfold closer to modern humans than are chimpanzees. They are, in fact, easily as close to us as two local chimpanzee neighbors might be. Therefore, one would expect two such hominid populations to simply fuse — if they were subspecies. But if they had interbred, their genes should be in modern people even if we no longer can see their distinctive features. Coyote mtDNA from past cross-species mating has been extracted from gray wolf populations that show no coyote features.

This is exactly the prediction of the "Out of Africa" model. There is no evidence in Krings's paper — or in the many papers looking at the modern European population — that Neanderthal sequences are present in modern populations. Any level of admixture would have been expected to leave some genetic trace. It is possible that one will yet show up, but given the thousands of individuals who have been sequenced, it is not likely. Therefore, even if the Neanderthal were shown to be our cultural and moral superiors, they still perished without issue. We are not related. Further, modern humans seem to show reduced genetic variation, reduced even when compared with these close hominid "cousins" of ours. Modern Europeans must therefore be descended from a population that displaced and replaced the Neanderthals. Their genes are gone. And we are unique.[38]

So, have we found Adam and Eve back there somewhere? Well, maybe. We have a small population traced back for several hundred thousand years. The coalescence points for most lines of evidence indicate 100,000 to 200,000 years ago. That would suggest a bottleneck — although perhaps extended — during this period. And, this is the time period that seems to show the appearance of modern morphology.[39]

---

38. Recently, an mtDNA analysis has been made of the early modern (62,000 years ago) Murgo Lake skull from Australia (Adcock et al., "Mitochondrial DNA Sequences in Ancient Australians," pp. 537-42). The study reported the presence of an ancient sequence related to the "NUMT" sequence, a nuclear inclusion of mtDNA origin. They concluded that this specimen showed a far deeper ancestral root than even the Neanderthals. This is true, but the root is far more likely to be the common root of the nuclear gene and the mitochondrial gene, due to contamination with modern DNA that reacted to mitochondrial primers. Current understanding would limit effective DNA extraction to around half that time, and only in very cold environments (Colin I. Smith, Andrew T. Chamberlain, Michael S. Riley, Alan Cooper, Chris B. Stringer, and Matthew J. Collins, "Not Just Old, but Old and Cold?" *Nature* 410 [2001]: 771-72). Further, the multiregional party still insists that gene flow among archaic populations would have completely mixed the human species despite the fact that modern population show regional characteristics (J. H. Relethford, "Absence of Regional Affinities of Neandertal DNA with Living Humans Does Not Reject Multiregional Evolution," *American Journal of Physical Anthropology* 115 [2001]: 95-98).

39. For instance the skulls from Guomde (Kenya), Ngaloba (Tanzania), Singa (Sudan), Omo Kibish (Ethiopia), and Jebel Irhoud (Morocco) are all dated to this time range (or slightly

But there is not a clear consensus. For instance, several recent studies with large Y chromosome data bases and new analytical techniques have reported a coalescence point of around 50,000 years ago, a far more recent root than previous studies.[40] Other studies — of beta hemoglobin, PDHA1, a noncoding sequence in chromosome 22, and the HLA antigen presenting series — indicate the presence of much older polymorphisms, perhaps dating back as far as 1.5 million years ago.[41] This would be far older than the mtDNA coalescence.

The Histocompatibility Enigma

Perhaps the most difficult genetic data for an integrative approach are the histocompatibility loci (HLA) found in all vertebrates. These genes encode peptide presentation proteins, proteins that have the task of presenting possible

---

earlier) and seem to have borderline modern morphology (C. Stringer and R. McKie, *African Exodus* [New York: Henry Holt, 1996]; Ian Tattersall, *The Last Neanderthal* [New York: Macmillan, 1995]; Lahr and Foley, "Towards a Theory of Modern Human Origins," pp. 137-76). These fossils typically have a lot of morphological diversity — "modern" faces and brows with ancient occiputs, or vice versa. Perhaps this population was the source population for a speciation bottleneck, and there was a rapid "transilience" event that nailed down modern morphology. Maybe Adam was a chip off their block.

40. Peter A. Underhill, Peidong Shen, Alice A. Lin, Li Jin, Giuseppe Passarino, Wei H. Yang, Erin Kauffman, Batsheva Bonne-Tamir, Jaume Bertranpetit, Paolo Francalacci, Muntaser Ibrahim, Trefor Jenkins, Judith R. Kidd, S. Qasim Mehdi, Mark T. Seielstad, R. Spencer Wells, Alberto Piazza, Ronald W. Davis, Marcus W. Feldman, L. Luca Cavalli-Sforza, and Peter J. Oefner, "Y Chromosome Sequence Variation and the History of Human Populations," *Nature Genetics* 26 (2000): 358-61; Russell Thomson, Jonathan K. Pritchard, Peidong Shen, Peter J. Oefner and Marcus W. Feldman, "Recent Common Ancestry of Human Y Chromosomes: Evidence from DNA Sequence Data," *Proceedings of the National Academy of Sciences U.S.A.* 97 (2000): 7360-65; Peidong Shen, Frank Wang, Peter A. Underhill, Claudia Franco, Wei-Hsien Yang, Adriane Roxas, Raphael Sung, Alice A. Lin, Richard W. Hyman, Douglas Vollrath, Ronald W. Davis, L. Luca Cavalli-Sforza, and Peter J. Oefner, "Population Genetic Implications from Sequence Variation in Four Y Chromosome Genes," *Proceedings of the National Academy of Sciences U.S.A.* 97 (2000): 7354-59.

41. Li Jin, Peter A. Underhill, Vishal Doctor, Ronald W. Davis, Peidong Shen, L. Luca Cavali-Sforza, and Peter J. Oefner, "Distribution of Haplotypes from a Chromosome 21 Region Distinguishes Multiple Prehistoric Human Migrations," *Proceedings of the National Academy of Sciences U.S.A.* 96 (1999): 3796-3800; Eugene E. Harris and Jody Hey, "X Chromosome Evidence for Ancient Human Histories," *Proceedings of the National Academy of Sciences U.S.A.* 96 (1999): 3320-24; Zhongming Zhao, Li Jin, Yun-Xin Fu, Michele Jenkins, Elina Leskinen, Pekka Pamilo, Maira Trexler, Laszlo Patthy, Lynn B. Jorde, Sebastian Ramos-Onsins, Ning Yu, and Wen-Hsiung Li, "Worldwide DNA Sequence Variation in a 10-kinobase Noncoding Region on Human Chromosome 22," *Proceedings of the National Academy of Sciences U.S.A.* 97 (2000): 11354-58.

foreign proteins (called antigens) to the immune system for inspection. They are among the most diverse loci (genes) in the genome, loci with more than 150 very diverse alleles (different versions of the gene).[42] It is thought that heterozygous individuals (with two different versions of the gene) are better protected against disease (fitter) than homozygotes (with two identical versions of the gene). This higher fitness for heterozygotes is termed "over dominance" and is considered to be the cause that maintains the very high levels of diversity in these loci.[43]

The evolutionary question raised by this diversity is (a) whether this diversity has been maintained over millions of years and thus passed on from parent species to daughter species; or (b) whether this diversity was generated rapidly — by point mutation, recombination, and gene conversion — after a species' origin.[44] As usual, there are two schools of thought. One thinks the data show that scores of human alleles are most close to matching chimpanzee alleles. The other school thinks there are only ten to fifteen such truly ancient lineages. The former postulate an effective Pleistocene population size of ancestral humans of over 100,000; the latter, under 10,000.[45] The logic is this: only a *few* ancient lineages are likely to exist in a population with a recent bottleneck. In fact, if the population was much larger prior to the bottleneck, a few very divergent alleles could come through.

However, if the issue is a single couple as source for the human species,

---

42. Austin L. Hughes and Meredith Yeager, "Natural Selection at Major Histocompatibility Complex Loci of Vertebrates," *Annual Review of Genetics* 32 (1998): 415-35.

43. Dustin J. Penn and Wayne K. Potts. "The Evolution of Mating Preferences and Major Histocompatibility Complex Genes," *The American Naturalist* 153 (1999): 145-64; E. Gomez-Casado, G. Vargas-Alarcon, J. Martinez-Laso, J. Granados, P. Varela, R. Alegre, J. Longas, M. Gonzalez-Hevilla, J. M. Martin-Villa, A. Arnaiz-Villena, "Evolutionary Relationships between HLA-B Alleles as Indicated by an Analysis of Intron Sequences," *Tissue Antigens* 53 (1999): 153-60.

44. Luis F. Cadavid, Clare Shufflebotham, Francisco J. Ruiz, Meredith Yeager, Austin L. Hughes, and David I. Watkins, "Evolutionary Instability of the Major Histocompatibility Complex Class I Loci in New World Primates," *Proceedings of the National Academy of Sciences U.S.A.* 94 (1997): 14536-41; Jan Klein, Akie Sato, Saundra Nagl, and Colm O'hUigin, "Molecular Trans-Species Polymorphism," *Annual Review of Ecology and Systematics* 29 (1998): 1-21.

45. Y. Satta, H. Kupfermann, Y. J. Li, and N. Takahata, "Molecular Clock and Recombination in Primate Mhc Genes," *Immunological Review* 167 (1999): 367-79; Tomas F. Bergstrom, Agnetha Josefsson, Henry A. Erlich, and Ulf Gyllensten, "Recent Origin of HLA-DRB1 Alleles and Implications for Human Evolution," *Nature Genetics* 18 (1998): 237-42; Tomas F. Bergstrom, R. Erlandsson, Agnetha Josefsson, S. J. Mack, Henry A. Erlich, and Ulf Gyllensten, "Tracing the Origin of HLA-DRB1 Alleles by Microsatellite Polymorphism," *American Journal of Human Genetics* 64 (1999): 1709-18; Francisco J. Ayala and Ananias A. Escalante, "The Evolution of Human Populations: A Molecular Perspective," *Molecular Phylogentics and Evolution* 5 (1996): 188-201.

both positions pose serious difficulties for Adam's identity. For example, consider the specific histocompatability gene "HLA-DRB1." Even the "few alleles" school of thought holds that there are fifteen or so very *old* alternative allelic lineages, lineages with a coalescence point of 5-10 million years. Whether Adam and Eve were created by providence through descent from a hominid lineage or are an original pair created without ancestors, they can have only 4 DRB1 alleles between them. If one human pair is the sole ancestor of all living people, all the human HLA alleles must be descended from those four "adamic" alleles. All the diversity must have been produced by modifying those four versions of the HLA-DRB1 gene since Adam and Eve were created. Yet a 5-10 million year coalescence would apparently make Adam a "monkey's uncle" (ancestral to at least chimps, gorillas, and humans).

Can Adam be saved? Well, the research is ongoing and hotly debated, and so it is worth waiting to see how the evidence will stack up. It may be that four original alleles might interact in a way that could generate more of the deep lineages in the human group (gene conversion), but that has not yet been demonstrated. One can also postulate "attending miracles" — God improving on the race after the original creation — if one wants to propose that. He could do it, of course, but that can also not be demonstrated.

Conclusion

This is not to deny that God could have made the first modern people from river mud by the direct matter transformation. Perhaps he did, but if he did so, the genetic evidence suggests that he "hid his hand" by giving Adam and Eve characteristics that pegged them into the hominoid tree and indicated a population history. It would be nice to know why.

This is also not to deny that a great deal of the paleoanthropological research may have been conducted in an effort to attribute the origin of humanity to undirected material causes. And it does seem clear that at least some of the researchers get quite emotional in their debate. The level of acrimony in the discussion can be amazing. And indeed, the results have not been those that the passionate end of the "materialist camp" expected. Humanity still sticks out from "nature" like a sore thumb. Let all God's people say amen. . . . With caution.

It is God who is molding the stuff of earth on his potter's wheel to make human beings. We are dust, the Scriptures tell us, made of the stuff of earth. So are the flesh and the genes of apes. So is the mud in a creek bed. How long the wheel spun, and how much time God took to mold us, only gives evidence of how careful he was. Certainly, God breathing spiritual life into Adam is not an event that we can expect to see in the fossil record.

Does this *biological* theory preclude accepting the description in Genesis? As usual, that depends on the interpretation given to those passages. It does suggest the sudden appearance of modern humanity, but questions the idea of a single pair. The likely place of origin — northeast Africa (Ethiopia or Kenya) — does not preclude the Levant. Certainly this theory does not resolve the spiritual status of the archaic hominids.

I want to close by pointing out that it is in this sort of situation where the "rubber really meets the road" in questions of faith and science. The question is the matter of data. Good theology cannot call James "an epistle of straw" when the verses don't fit its theological model. Likewise, good science cannot neglect data that do not fit its theoretical model. It must include and explain everything, or it must leave room for mystery. So, in this case, should I cobble together an "integrative" solution to resolve the tension, or should I wait on the Lord to resolve the issue in his own time through more data? Clearly the Lord knows the answer to these questions. I don't. If I have the faith to walk in obedience, should I be willing to wait with unresolved questions? Or should I insist on an immediate answer? What do you think?

God's Power and Faithfulness:
A Lesson from Nature

LOREN HAARSMA

Isaiah 40:12-31

M any psalms look at the beauty of nature and respond with praise to the Creator. In Isaiah 40, the prophet directs his listeners' attention to nature, but for a different reason. He wants to give them a message that will address their current needs. As verse 27 explains, his listeners are in despair. God seems distant to them. They feel that God is no longer watching over them, no longer caring for them.

The prophet reminds his listeners of God's great power: look at his creation! Creation is vast; the Creator's power is even greater (vv. 12, 15, 22-26). The prophet points to the biggest, most awe-inspiring parts of creation that were believed to exist at the time: the primeval waters (v. 12) and the firmament that encircles the earth (v. 22). Today, we know that creation is even more vast than the prophet's listeners envisioned — our whole solar system (not to mention the nations) is like a drop in the bucket when compared to the size of the universe. And God's power reigns over it all!

The prophet illustrates other divine attributes using examples from creation. Just as the Creator's power is beyond our comprehension, so also his understanding and wisdom are far beyond us (vv. 13-14, 28) — we may not understand what God is doing, but his wisdom is greater than ours. God's faithfulness is displayed every night the stars come out (v. 26) and every morning the Sun rises, reminding us that God does not grow weary of watching over us (v. 28).

The Creator, who is always faithful, whose wisdom is beyond us, whose power overwhelms our own — what does he do for us when we are in despair? "He gives strength to the weary and increases the power of the weak" (v. 29). "Those who hope in the LORD will renew their strength. They will soar on wings like eagles; they will run and not grow weary, they will walk and not be faint" (v. 31).

The Earth from space, from the Apollo 11 mission

Credit: "All photographs on this website are courtesy of the National Aeronautics and Space Administration, specifically the NASA History Office and the NASA JSC Media Services Center."

12 Biochemistry and Evolution

TERRY M. GRAY

Introduction

One hundred years ago biology was largely natural history. Many today still bemoan the fact that natural history has lost center stage in the discipline to cell biology, molecular biology, molecular genetics, molecular physiology, and biochemistry. This shift not only represents the explosion of knowledge in these areas and their stunning success in answering real questions in biology, but it also represents a trend, for better or for worse, towards reductionistic thinking in biology. Molecular biology and biochemistry are the topics of this chapter, but it should be noted that these are relatively new sciences. The 1950s saw the publication of the first protein amino acid sequence. That decade also saw the final pieces of the puzzle fall into place for the hypothesis that DNA is the genetic material, culminating in the Watson-Crick structural model for DNA. The late 1950s to the early 1960s saw the first three-dimensional structure of a protein, but it wasn't until the 1980s and 1990s that hundreds of structures were determined. Recombinant DNA techniques began to be routinely used in the 1980s. Only as recently as the 1980s were DNA sequencing methods commonplace. Of course, now we know the sequence of the human genome, but only as of the year 2000.

The point of this brief historical review is simply to note that the theory of evolution as formulated by Charles Darwin was around for nearly a hundred years before any of the biochemical data existed. Those traditional arguments for evolution are largely based on natural history: taxonomy (the classification of organisms), biogeography (the study of geographical distribution of organisms), comparative anatomy and physiology, and paleontology (the study of the fossil record). These are the sciences that convinced Darwin and other 19th-century biologists that organisms had descended from a common ancestor.[1] Natural historian and evolutionist Niles Eldredge goes so far as to say:

> The nested pattern of resemblance ought to be at the very top of the list of the "proofs" Darwin enumerated in the *Origin* — a list required in all decent high school biology curricula. Oddly enough, though, it is seldom stressed, even by professional biologists. . . . In terms of pure genealogy, the living world carries the marks of its history around with it.[2]

Classical genetics and population biology later joined these disciplines to establish much of the modern-day expression of evolutionary theory. These arguments are addressed in other parts of this volume.

Thus, the evidences for biological evolution from the molecular disciplines presented in this chapter are latecomers to the scene of evidences for biological evolution. Indeed, if one takes a history of science perspective here, there is possible in the new science an extraordinary test of the Darwinian theory, especially of its notion of common ancestry. The molecular data could either confirm or radically disconfirm the historical picture previously assembled.

There is no *a priori* reason to think that the molecular basis of life must reflect an evolutionary history (if there is one). For example, no one believes that the chemistry found in living systems reflects an evolutionary history. The chemical properties of carbon, hydrogen, oxygen, nitrogen and other elements found in living systems are the same as the chemical properties in minerals and synthetic polymers. Water in the cell is chemically the same as water in the oceans, in rivers, or in the clouds. Through our knowledge of large-scale chemical cycles we know that these elements and compounds move back and forth from the biological world to the inorganic world. One could imagine the same to be true in the biochemical world. Perhaps there is only one way to make a cytochrome c molecule that does what cytochrome c does in the cell just as there is only one way to make a water molecule. So just as the absence of an evolutionary pattern in the case of elements and compounds does not disconfirm

---

1. Modern evolutionary theory generally espouses a monophyletic perspective — that all modern organisms have descended from a single ancestral original life form. Interestingly, Darwin wrote in the closing sentence of *The Origin of Species:* "There is grandeur in this view of life, with its several powers, having been originally breathed by the Creator into a few forms or into one; and that, whilst this planet has gone cycling on according to the fixed law of gravity, from so simple a beginning endless forms most beautiful and most wonderful have been, and are being evolved" (The Mentor Edition [New York: New American Library, 1958], p. 450).

2. Niles Eldredge, *Reinventing Darwin: The Great Debate at the High Table of Evolutionary Theory* (New York: John Wiley & Sons, 1995), p. 51.

evolution, neither would the absence of an evolutionary pattern in comparative biochemistry necessarily disconfirm evolution. But the early biochemists noted that there was variation in the chemical structure of biological molecules, that there were variations in the amino acid sequence from organism to organism. Because of the genetic basis of the information contained in those sequences, one might imagine that the history proposed by evolutionary theory might be reflected in those sequences; that is, sequences in organisms believed to be more closely related in evolutionary history would be more similar. Along the same lines, if the genetically based sequences did not reflect the putative evolutionary history, one might suspect the theory as a whole.

Following this line of thinking, biochemistry has spectacularly confirmed the picture from natural history and classical genetics that was already in place. In many ways, one could not have asked for a more striking test and confirmation of a theory. In the eyes of many, although admittedly speaking from the biases of a molecular biologist and biochemist, the biochemical evidences provide the most compelling of all the evidences for evolution.

We have been careful in this volume to define our terms. So, let me make it clear from the outset which of the many possible meanings of evolution that I am talking about. The molecular data primarily address the question of common ancestry and suggest that all organisms do indeed descend from a common ancestor. Observation in real-time of mutations and other genetic changes that occur in biological systems confirms what many refer to as microevolution. The inferences drawn from the molecular data also confirm what many refer to as macroevolution, that is, a common evolutionary history that even unites the larger taxonomic categories of class and phylum and even kingdom. The biochemical data also address questions concerning the origin of novel biological functions, although with much less certainty. The question of the origin of life *is not* addressed by this examination of the biochemical data. This is not to say that this question could not be addressed. But we are concerned here with showing that the biochemical data suggest that dogs, cats, and mice all share a common ancestor, that mammals, birds, and reptiles all share a common ancestor, that plants, animals, and fungi (eukaryotic organisms) all share a common ancestor, and even that bacteria and eukaryotic organisms share a common ancestor (although here things are a bit fuzzier due to phenomena known as lateral or horizontal gene transfer). That is, all organisms on Earth are branches of the same tree of life.

While we are on the subject of definitions and perspectives, it should also be noted that I write as a theist. What I write here appears to have much in common with those who argue that these evolutionary arguments result in an atheistic naturalism. Such a conclusion is not a necessary conclusion and in re-

ality is an unwarranted conclusion. I believe that the world around us is a creation of God and is lawfully governed by his providential hand. Evolutionary
explanations of natural history are no more necessarily atheistic than are physical explanations of planetary motions or physical-chemical explanations of
atomic and molecular structure.

Finally, by way of introduction it is worth noting that the above very positive assessment of the evidences from biochemistry has been challenged recently by biochemist Michael J. Behe in a popular book entitled *Darwin's Black
Box: The Biochemical Challenge to Evolution.*[3] Behe does not challenge the spectacular evidence for common ancestry provided by protein and nucleic acid sequence comparisons; in fact, he seems to admit to it.[4] He argues at a significantly different level that the machinelike complexity of many biochemical
systems cannot arise by evolutionary mechanisms. He concludes that there
must be an intelligence behind the origin of those systems. Without necessarily
denying Behe's theistic claims, we will attempt to show that evolutionary mechanisms indeed are able to give rise to the sort of complexity that we observe in
living systems and that Christians should not be so quick to jump on the band-
wagon of irreducible complexity to support a belief in the so-called collapse of
evolution.

In this chapter we will review the evidences that support evolutionary
theory from the disciplines of biochemistry, molecular biology, and molecular
developmental biology. The major headings are (1) the unity of biochemistry;
(2) sequence comparisons of cytochrome c; (3) the evolution of hemoglobin;
(4) molecular developmental biology and evolution; and (5) the evolution of
molecular machines and other "irreducibly complex" systems.

The Unity of Biochemistry

All living things on Earth share a common biochemistry.[5] This is nowhere
more clearly demonstrated than in an example from the modern pharmaceuti-

---

3. Michael J. Behe, *Darwin's Black Box: The Biochemical Challenge to Evolution* (New
York: The Free Press, 1996).

4. Behe writes: "For the record, I have no reason to doubt that the universe is the billions
of years old that physicists say it is. Further, I find the idea of common descent (that all organisms share a common ancestor) fairly convincing, and have no particular reason to doubt it"
(Behe, *Darwin's Black Box,* p. 5).

5. I will not provide references for all of the biochemistry discussed in this chapter. Most
of what is discussed can be found in any college-level biochemistry textbook. My favorite is
D. Voet and J. G. Voet, *Biochemistry,* 2nd ed. (New York: John Wiley & Sons, 1995).

cal industry's use of recombinant DNA technology. Human insulin (produced by Eli Lilly with the trade name Humulin®) used to treat human diabetes is produced by bacteria into which has been inserted the genetic material coding for human insulin. The DNA molecules containing the genetic information are chemically the same in both bacteria and humans. The process of transcription by which the information contained in DNA is converted to RNA is fundamentally the same in both bacteria and humans. The RNA molecules containing this transcribed information are chemically the same in both bacteria and humans. The process of translation, by which the RNA-containing information is converted to a specific sequence of amino acids that folds up spontaneously into a functional protein, is basically the same in both bacteria and humans: the protein synthesis machinery, the ribosome, the translation molecules themselves, transfer RNA's or tRNA's, and even the proteins that attach certain amino acids to certain tRNA's, aminoacyl-tRNA synthetases. The genetic code, that correspondence between three units of the RNA sequence (a triplet or codon) and one unit of the protein sequence, an amino acid, is identical among virtually all organisms from bacteria to humans. (We will discuss the exceptions below.) The protein can be synthesized in bacteria, purified and processed in the laboratory or manufacturing plant, and then injected into a human body. There it is indistinguishable, structurally and functionally, from the molecule that should have been synthesized in the human body in the first place.

Let me clearly say that these processes are not identical in all of the details and that there is much interesting biochemistry in the differences. But the unity is there for all to see: across the biological spectrum we see the same DNA and RNA structures made from the same chemical building blocks (ribonucleotides and deoxyribonucleotides) and proteins made from the same twenty amino acids. In animals some of these twenty amino acids are not even synthesized by the organism itself but must be obtained from the diet, but nonetheless the same twenty amino acids are used in the proteins synthesized.

Most biochemists come away from their undergraduate and even graduate training with a rather flat view of the organism. In many respects this is unfortunate because biology really is about the organism, and for the biochemist the organism sets the chemical agenda. But the fact of the matter is that our knowledge of biochemistry comes from a hodgepodge of sources — whatever happens to be the easiest to purify for detailed study — so that much of what we know comes from bacteria *(E. coli)* and "domesticated" animals that are butchered or easily grown for such study such as cows, pigs, sheep, rats, and mice. When new organisms are studied in detail, the fundamental process is nearly always found to be the same with a few interesting twists unique to the biology of that particular organism.

Not only is this true for the biochemical processes dealing with genetic information such as replication, transcription, translation, and the genetic code, but it is also true for much of the fundamental metabolism in an organism. Metabolism is the sum of all the processes by which molecules are broken down to produce energy and molecular building blocks (catabolism) and all the processes by which biochemicals are synthesized (anabolism). Glycolysis, the ten-step process of converting the six carbon sugar glucose into two smaller three carbon units in order to produce energy (in the form of ATP, one of the ribonucleotides found in RNA), is virtually the same in every organism. When a high school or undergraduate biology student learns this process, it is rarely not presented as biologically universal. Again, there are differences in the details, especially in the ways the process is regulated in different organisms, but the unity is obvious. The same is true for the Kreb's cycle, the process by which the three carbon units that are the end product of glycolysis are converted to carbon dioxide and more ATP. It is also true for oxidative phosphorylation, the process by which the energy from the molecules produced in the Kreb's cycle is converted to ATP, using up oxygen and producing water in the process. We could go on to include photosynthesis, fat metabolism, amino acid synthesis and degradation, and nearly every metabolic pathway.

So what is the source of this unity? Let's first reflect on the answer to this question without invoking special creation. The simplest explanation is that organisms share a common biochemistry because they originate from a common ancestor. (This is referred to as monophyletic origins.) When I grow a bacterial culture, why do the billions or trillions of cells at the end of the experiment have a common biochemistry? It is because they derive from a common ancestral single colony that originally derived from a single ancestral cell. When the original cell divided, it passed its biochemistry on to the daughter cells, which in turn passed their biochemistry on to their daughter cells, and so forth. We could say the same thing about the biochemistry of my children compared to my own or my parents' or my grandparents'. In some ways, this is to state the obvious. We *know* that the progeny organisms in these observed cases share a common biochemistry because of the reproductive processes that give rise to them. It is a fairly simple inference to say that a common biochemistry among all organisms is a consequence of a similar reproductive process. This is just another way of saying that all organisms on Earth today share a common ancestor. This conclusion is not that controversial unless you have an *a priori* reason for thinking that it is not possible.

Some have proposed that there are independent origins for each of life's major groupings. (This is referred to as polyphyletic origins. See note 1.) The common biochemistry would be common because there is only one way (or at best a few ways) to accomplish the biological function that is needed. While this possibility cannot be ruled out completely, it does seem somewhat unlikely. For example, there does not seem to be any particular physical-chemical or biological reason why the UUU codon should be associated with the amino acid phenylalanine and not the amino acid leucine. On the basis of what we know today, the codes for those particular amino acids could be switched as long as the information specifying them in the genetic material is also switched. Yet it is not. The UUU codon always specifies for phenylalanine in each major kingdom and phylum. It would appear to be a huge coincidence for the same biochemistry to occur in these major branches without some common source. A common biochemistry with polyphyletic origins (apart from special creation) is highly implausible. There is a possibility of sharing biochemistry through what is known as lateral or horizontal gene transfer. This will be discussed later. In one sense, however, this is another form of common ancestry, although it becomes independent of normal reproductive biology.

If we invoke special creation there are few rules. God can do whatever he pleases. Thus, we could argue that common biochemistry is the result of God's sovereign choice. Organisms have a common biochemistry not because they have some common ancestry but because they have a common Creator and Designer who chose to give them a common biochemistry. (It must be said here from a theistic perspective that even the common ancestry conclusion is not necessarily contrary to saying that a common biochemistry is the result of God's sovereign choice.) It must be noted that there is little reason that one would come to this conclusion on the basis of observation without some *a priori* belief that this was the way that God created. It is a commitment to a special creationist perspective (whether it is of the six twenty-four-hour-day variety or of the progressive creationist variety) that prejudices one against the conclusion that common biochemistry is a consequence of a common ancestry.

When we look at the patterns of variation in the biochemistry and in the genetic information, the special creationist arguments become even more convoluted. As we will see when we look at some specific examples in detail, it is not that we simply have a common biochemistry but that we have variation in that biochemistry that reflects the kinds of nested hierarchies that one would expect if it arose as a consequence of common descent. For example, mammalian biochemistry is more similar among the mammals than it is to other groups. Vertebrate biochemistry has more similarity within the group of vertebrates than to arthropods. These variations do not compromise the observation of a common biochemistry, that is, it is still obvious that the biochemistry is basically the same. But, there is no biological reason why the Special Creator and Designer should create with those patterns. One is led to the conclusion, if one is operating from a special creationist perspective, that God made it look as if common descent had occurred when it fact it had not.[6] Since I do not believe that the biblical accounts require me to accept a special creationist perspective, I can make the simpler conclusion from these patterns of variation that common descent has taken place.

Example 1: The Genetic Code

With a handful of exceptions all organisms share the same genetic code. The genetic code is that relationship between a specific sequence of three (a triplet of) RNA subunits (nucleotide bases) and a particular amino acid. The so-called standard genetic code is shown in figure 1. Notice, for example, that UUU codes for the amino acid phenylalanine. When the protein synthesis machinery reads along the RNA molecule, it synthesizes an amino acid chain (a protein) that is specified by that information. Notice that there are three triplets that do not specify for an amino acid but are indicators that the protein synthesis machinery should stop, that is, they convey the information that this is the end of the chain. These are the codons UAA, UAG, and UGA. As noted in our very first example in this discussion, organisms as diverse as the bacterium *E. coli* and the vertebrate *H. sapiens* share the same genetic code so that information derived from humans can specify the exact same protein in a bacterium.

The early molecular biologists observed that this code was the same among diverse organisms and argued that it must be universal. Once life had originated and the genetic code developed, it would be nearly impossible to change the code. For example, if a mutation resulted in CUU coding for the amino acid threonine instead of the amino acid leucine, then in every protein synthesized by that cell threonines would be substituted for leucines when CUU appeared in the RNA message. This would be such a drastic consequence that the organism could not survive. Some biologists went so far as to say that if the code were not universal this would be a blow against evolutionary claims.

As the genetic systems from more organisms were determined, it was found that, indeed, there were a few exceptions. These exceptions are in mitochondria and in ciliated protozoa. In ciliated protozoans UAA and UAG code for the amino acid glutamine rather than stop. Other than that, the code is

---

6. We might call this "apparent common descent" analogous to the "apparent age" solution that young-Earth creationists have for the evidence for an old Earth and an old universe. While I do think that there are theological problems with such solutions, at least in them is the admission that the scientific evidence points to the conclusion of common descent or great antiquity.

Figure 1. The Standard Genetic Code

First Position	Second Position				Third Position
	U	C	A	G	
U	UUU Phe	UCU Ser	UAU Tyr	UGU Cys	U
	UUC Phe	UCC Ser	UAC Tyr	UGC Cys	C
	UUA Leu	UCA Ser	UAA Stop	UGA Stop	A
	UUG Leu	UCG Ser	UAG Stop	UGG Trp	G
C	CUU Leu	CCU Pro	CAU His	CGU Arg	U
	CUC Leu	CCC Pro	CAC His	CGC Arg	C
	CUA Leu	CCA Pro	CAA Gin	CGA Arg	A
	CUG Leu	CCG Pro	CAG Gin	CGG Arg	G
A	AUU Ile	ACU Thr	AAU Asn	AGU Ser	U
	AUC Ile	ACC Thr	AAC Asn	AGC Ser	C
	AUA Ile	ACA Thr	AAA Lys	AGA Arg	A
	AUG Met	ACG Thr	AAG Lys	AGG Arg	G
G	GUU Val	GCU Ala	GAU Asp	GGU Gly	U
	GUC Val	GCC Ala	GAC Asp	GGC Gly	C
	GUA Val	GCA Alal	GAA Glu	GGA Gly	A
	GUG Val	GCG Ala	GAG Glu	GGG Gly	G

identical to the standard code. It is not difficult to imagine a scenario whereby such a change could get fixed into an isolated branch of the tree of life. For example, there are well-known bacterial mutations where the stop codon codes for an amino acid. These mutations are known as suppressor mutations because they suppress other mutations where a triplet coding for an amino acid in the middle of an essential protein was mutated to a stop codon. Since the protein synthesis was stopped in the middle of the protein, the essential protein was not made. The mutation where the stop codon was changed to a codon that coded for an amino acid suppressed the otherwise deleterious mutation because it allowed the protein to be synthesized.

The exceptions in mitochondria are similarly small deviations from the standard code. Some involve a stop codon being used to code for some amino acid. Others involve the opposite where a coding triplet in the standard code codes for a stop codon. In no cases are all of the triplets used in the standard code to code for a given amino acid changed. Again, the changes involve only slight changes from the standard code. Most biologists today believe that mitochondria were once free-living bacteria-like organisms that developed a symbiotic relationship with other cells. Mitochondria genomes are smaller than normal bacteria and they synthesize only a few proteins. This reduction in the size of the genome and the number of proteins synthesized by that genome made it easier to make small changes in the code without the widespread deleterious effect that one would observe otherwise.

In both cases, these exceptions are rooted very deeply in the tree of life. See figure 2. The variations are on branches that separated from the main branch early in evolutionary history. Such a pattern is what one would expect if there were to be deviations from universality: minor deviations on isolated branches. Thus, despite the overstated claims of some of the early molecular biologists, the deviations in the near-universal code are easily explained with common descent. However, one might wonder, given the near universality of the code, why, in a special creationist scenario, the Creator would produce exceptions. Of course, it's hard to ask such questions in that scenario since the Creator can do whatever he pleases. But, again, if he created in such a way, he made it look as if evolution had occurred.

Example 2: Sequence Comparisons of Cytochrome C

As soon as the protein-sequencing techniques developed by Sanger were available, Emanuel Margoliash, Emil Smith, and other investigators set out to study evolution using these methods. Cytochrome c was regarded as an excellent candidate for study since it is part of the oxidative phosphorylation pathway of all eukaryotic organisms. Comparisons of sequences of cytochrome c from different organisms produced an evolutionary tree that was nearly identical to what had been ascertained from comparative biology and the fossil record.

In the common biochemistry among organisms it is fairly straightforward to identify corresponding components. (However, this is not always

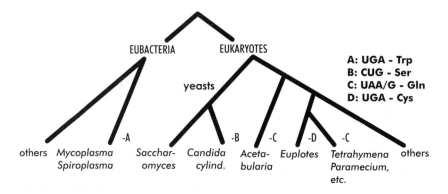

Figure 2. A phylogenetic tree based on the exceptions to the standard genetic code found in bacteria and the nuclei of eukaryotes. Notice that the branches marked "others" represent the standard genetic code found in most organisms.

From John Gerhart and Marc Kirschner, *Cells, Embryos, and Evolution: Toward a Cellular and Developmental Understanding of Phenotypic Variation and Evolutionary Adaptability* (Malden, Mass.: Blackwell Science, 1997). Reprinted by permission of Blackwell Science, Inc.

straightforward, as we will see when we look at the globin gene family.) Molecular evolutionists distinguish between orthologous proteins, proteins that are structurally similar and functionally identical (related to one another by speciation events), and paralogous proteins, proteins that are structurally similar but not functionally identical (related to one another by gene duplication events). One particular easy example is cytochrome c. Cytochrome c is a small protein of around 100 amino acids that transfers electrons from one complex of the electron transport chain to another complex of the electron transport chain. (These complexes themselves are easy to identify as being orthologous, so the case for cytochrome c being orthologous in these systems is also easily determined.)

The function of a protein is determined by its three-dimensional structure, which in turn is determined by its amino acid sequence, which is determined by its genetic information. One might imagine that there is a unique relationship between the amino acid sequence of a protein and its three-dimensional structure, but there is not. A variety of similar amino acid sequences give rise to a three-dimensional structure that is able to perform the cytochrome c function. In fact, in vitro the cytochrome c from one organism is able to interact properly with electron transport chain components from other organisms. In cytochrome c only about 40 of the 100 amino acids are identical when one compares cytochrome c of two organisms. Apparently, there are amino acids at certain places in the sequence that are essential for proper structure and function. These are known as invariant amino acids in the sequence. In comparing sequences between organisms it is also apparent that there are conservative substitutions. For example, whereas isoleucine and leucine are not identical amino acids, they are similar chemically — fairly bulky, hydrophobic (oil-like) amino acids. There would be little structural or functional change in cytochrome c if an isoleucine were substituted for a leucine in the sequence. Finally, there are what are known as hypervariable amino acids. These are positions in the protein that seem to serve merely as spacers. It does not seem to matter what amino acids are in those positions; the protein still folds up into the correct three-dimensional structure and functions correctly biochemically.

As a result of the conservative and hypervariable amino acids there will be some variation among organisms in the details of the common biochemistry. These variations can be examined to see if any interesting patterns emerge. This is exactly what the protein chemists of the 1960s did. Figure 3 shows a small portion of the amino acid sequence of cytochrome c from a variety of organisms lined up so that the maximum number of amino acids align.[7] The amino sequence of chimpanzees and humans is identical. The rhesus monkey sequence matches exactly with the human sequence except at position 102, where an alanine has been substituted for a threonine. Cow, pig, and sheep cytochrome c's are identical and differ from dog cytochrome c by three amino acids: positions 88, 92, 103. Figure 4 is a matrix giving the pairwise comparison of the known sequences. From this data it is apparent that sequences cluster into families of sequences. For example, the birds in the table are more similar to each other than to the mammals or insects. Using this data it is possible to construct a tree showing the logical relatedness of these sequences (see figure 5). The sum of each branch on the tree between two organisms gives the total number of differences between those two organisms, as shown in figure 4.

The tree that is generated using this methodology is virtually identical to the evolutionary tree established by taxonomy (the classification of organisms) or by paleontology (the fossil record with the appearance of organisms over the course of time). As was noted earlier, there is no obvious chemical or biochemical reason to expect this result. Thus, common ancestry, as hypothesized by the early evolutionists on the basis of taxonomy and paleontology, was a testable hypothesis using this research program involving sequence comparisons. The

7. The optimal alignment is not always obvious and is a challenging computational problem. Consequently, there are minor ambiguities in both alignments and the data derived from those alignments. While such ambiguities may reduce the certainty of the result, they do not undermine the general result.

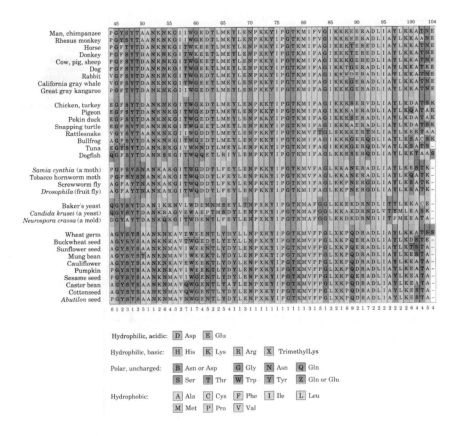

Figure 3. Alignment of cytochrome c sequences from several eukaryotic organisms. Only residues 45 to the C-terminus are shown. The letters represent the one letter code for the amino acids, and the shade represents the chemical character of the amino acid.

After R. E. Dickerson, *Scientific American* 226, no. 4 (1972): 58-72, with corrections from R. E. Dickerson and R. Timkovich, in P. D. Boyer, ed., *The Enzymes*, 3rd ed., vol. 11 (Academic Press, 1975), pp. 421-22. Used by permission of the Irving Geis Foundation.

results could have been a startling disconfirmation of the common ancestry hypothesis. Or, at best, the results could have been a nonconfirmation showing that evolutionary relatedness is not reflected in biochemistry (much the way that it is not reflected in the periodic table). But, instead, the results provide a striking confirmation of common ancestry: exactly what one would expect if common ancestry together with the imperfect transmission of genetic information had occurred. From a long-range history-of-science perspective, this is a dramatic independent test using a completely novel methodology of a hypothesis that had originated from a very different set of observations.

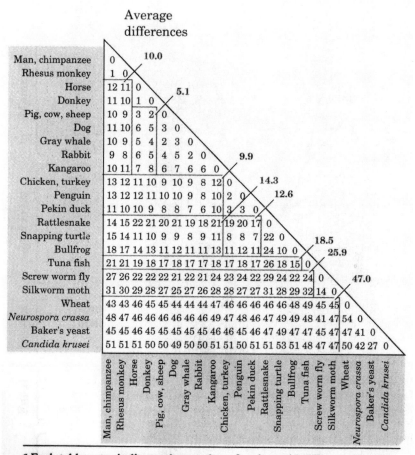

a Each table entry indicates the number of amino acid differences between the cytochromes *c* of the species noted to the left of and above that entry.

[Table copyrighted © by Irving Geis.]

Figure 4. Comparison matrix using the cytochrome c alignments from figure 3.

Taken from D. Voet and J. G. Voet, *Biochemistry*, 2nd ed. (New York: John Wiley & Sons, 1995). Used by permission of the Irving Geis Foundation.

The field of molecular evolution largely involves the comparisons of sequences and the construction of these family trees. By and large the results are the same over and over again no matter what protein is studied. The cytochrome c and many other protein families are largely confined to the eukaryotic branch of the tree of life. As nucleic-acid-sequencing techniques

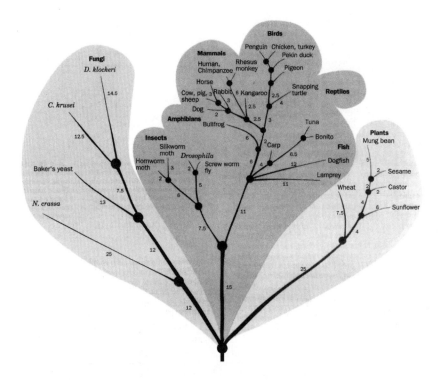

Figure 5. Phylogenetic tree from cytochrome c comparisons shown in figures 3 and 4.
Taken from D. Voet and J. G. Voet, *Biochemistry*, 2nd ed. (New York: John Wiley & Sons, 1995); after M. O. Dayhoff, C. M. Park, and P. J. McLaughlin, in M. O. Dayhoff, ed., *Atlas of Protein Sequence and Structure* (National Biomedical Research Foundation, 1972), p. 8. Reprinted by permission of John Wiley & Sons and the National Biomedical Research Foundation.

were applied to the study of RNA and DNA sequences, similar results were produced. The study of ribosomal RNA performed by Carl Woese has allowed the evolutionary interpretations to be extended beyond eukaryotes to include all forms of life on Earth.[8] Today, sequence comparisons so dominate the field that many evolutionists believe that the most authoritative trees are those that result from molecular data. This is not to say that there are not active debates or disagreements among molecular evolutionists or between molecular evolutionists and paleontologists. Some of these issues will be discussed below. But the broad, overarching conclusion is virtually indisputable: the tree of life is one of the best-supported models in science.

8. C. R. Woese, "Archaebacteria," *Scientific American* 244 (1981): 98-122.

A criticism of the molecular evidences for evolution cited frequently by Christian critics of evolution is found in *Of Pandas and People*.[9] This criticism largely echoes Michael Denton's criticisms in *Evolution: A Theory in Crisis*.[10] First, it should be pointed out that Denton does not dispute the primary result, that is, that sequence comparisons give nested hierarchies that match nearly exactly those produced by taxonomy and paleontology. In fact, Denton's diagrams which group organisms on the basis of sequence comparisons can be thought of as evolutionary trees viewed from the top rather than the side (see figure 6). As we have said before, this alone provides a striking confirmation to the common ancestry hypothesis, especially in the context of our knowledge of how this information is transmitted from generation to generation and how it is altered by mutation. However, the criticisms go a bit deeper surrounding the concept of equidistance. For example, a close inspection of figure 4 reveals that the sequence of cytochrome c for the silkworm moth is equidistant from the sequences of the horse (27), pigeon (25), turtle (26), carp (25), and lamprey (30). Denton mistakenly believes that evolutionary theory predicts that since lampreys and fish are ancestral groups to mammals, birds, and reptiles, their sequences should be more similar to the sequences of insects. This is a common error of critics of evolution. It is a failure to distinguish between a common ancestor and an extant descendant of the common ancestor. While a fish may have been a common ancestor to modern mammals, birds, and reptiles, a fish is also the common ancestor to modern fish. The extant descendants of fish are not the same as the ancestral fish — they have continued to evolve (especially at the molecular level, if not at the morphological level) just as much as their cousin mammals, birds, and reptiles. Thus, equidistance is what we expect if we compare sequences from modern day organisms. It is true that if we could obtain the sequence of the common ancestor, it would have fewer differences from the out-group (insects in the example we have been discussing), but each extant organism — horse, pigeon, turtle, carp, and lamprey — would be equidistant from the common ancestor. These ancestral sequences and the number of differences are represented at each of the branch points in figure 5.

Denton himself presents this solution to the equidistance problem but criticizes it because it requires that the rate of incorporation of a mutation into the lineage is a function of real time rather than generation, that is, it is the same for each organism whether the generation time is many years or a few days or weeks. For some reason he finds this implausible. If mutations accumu-

9. Percival Davis and Dean H. Kenyon, *Of Pandas and People: The Central Question of Biological Origins*, 2nd ed. (Dallas: Haughton, 1993).

10. Michael Denton, *Evolution: A Theory in Crisis* (Bethesda: Adler & Adler, 1986).

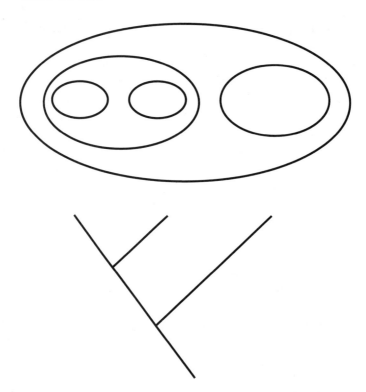

Figure 6. Denton (see note 10) used diagrams such as the top diagram to group organisms according to shared characters. For example, the two smaller ovals might represent two different bird species, whereas the two medium ovals would represent two classes of vertebrates, say, birds and mammals. The large oval would represent the common phylum of these two classes. The bottom diagram shows the same information as a phylogenetic tree.

late through random chemical changes, rather than through replication errors, one would expect a real time dependence rather than a generation time dependence. Denton argues that a real time dependence would give the same rate for each different protein, but that is not what is observed, that is, different protein or nucleic acid families show different rates of change. The most common explanation for this is that there are different functional constraints on different proteins and that these functional constraints slow down the rate of mutation incorporation. A protein like cytochrome c not only must fold correctly and preserve a functional heme binding-site, but also must interact with other cell components such as cytochrome c oxidase and cytochrome c reductase. It is more functionally constrained than a protein such as myoglobin, which must only fold correctly and preserve a functional heme and oxygen binding-site.

(Of course, there may be other unknown interactions involving myoglobin.) Understanding differences in mutation rates requires knowledge of the details of how biochemical systems work.

A more recent critique of the molecular data is given in *Icons of Evolution* by Jonathan Wells.[11] In discussing the evolutionary tree of life and the Cambrian explosion, he discusses how many evolutionists appeal to the molecular data to solve the problems that seem to be unsolvable using normal taxonomic and paleontological methods. The careful reader will note in this discussion that Wells addresses only the recent debate in the literature over the timing of early rise and diversification of the metazoa based on fossil and molecular data — he does not discuss the fact that there is widespread agreement over the tree branching topology, that is, how the different groups are connected on the tree. The unsuspecting reader might be led to believe that the discipline is in chaos, that there is no agreement on the fundamental questions, and that the special creationist position is an equally valid option given the lack of consensus. In this particular instance the main area of disagreement is in the dating of the origin of the first metazoans based on the agreed upon phylogeny. The dates based on molecular data range from 670 mya to 1,200 mya. The evidence from the fossil record places the earliest metazoans at around 570 mya. Of course, we may be comparing apples and oranges here. It is well known that morphological evolution is not necessarily reflected in the molecular data, especially if we are looking at sequences such as cytochrome c or ribosomal RNA whose biological roles have little to do with morphology.[12]

11. Jonathan Wells, *Icons of Evolution: Science or Myth? Why Much of What We Teach about Evolution Is Wrong* (Washington, D.C.: Regnery, 2000).

12. J. W. Valentine, D. Jablonski, and D. H. Ervin, in a review article entitled "Fossils, Molecules and Embryos: New Perspectives on the Cambrian Explosion" (*Development* 126 [1999]: 851-59), write: "While the time of origin of the Metazoa is not known, an age of 700 Ma or less would not conflict with the evidence now at hand, though it may have been significantly earlier. Is 170 million years long enough for the evolution of the Cambrian fauna from the earliest animals? Clearly, much of the body-plan evolution was accomplished by changes in patterns of gene expression. Many genes that mediate the development of disparate phyla are conserved after over half a billion years of independent evolution in lineages that have evolved independent architectures. Gene regulatory elements were probably the most important actors in this process. The rapidity of this sort of evolution has not been formally evaluated, but the use and reuse of established signaling pathways and other regulatory cascades seem likely to provide evolutionary shortcuts in the production of novel morphologies. We have every reason to believe that the pace of evolution as suggested by plausible interpretations of the fossil record could easily be achieved." Wells cites this paper to demonstrate the disagreement between the fossil evidence and the molecular evidence. It is more accurate to say that this paper suggests that changes in sequences reflected by amino acid and nucleotide sequence comparisons are not necessarily synchronized with morphological changes reflected in the fossil record.

The final critique in Wells's book points to the recent finding that, depending on what gene or sequence you are looking at, the branching at the very root of the tree (i.e., where the "universal" common ancestor is) is different. This is especially true among bacteria and archaea. Many molecular evolutionists today cite this as evidence of horizontal or lateral gene transfer, that is, mechanisms for the transmission of genetic information that are unrelated to the normal mechanism of reproduction.[13] Mechanisms of this sort are well known in bacteria and provide much of the methodological basis of modern-day genetic engineering. Genetic information from foreign sources — plasmids, viruses, and pieces of DNA — can be picked up by the bacteria, expressed, and in some cases even incorporated into the organism's genome. Biologists are finding that this mixing up of genomes is much more common than originally thought. A nearly universally accepted example of this is the endosymbiosis theory where eukaryotic mitochondria and plasmids are believed to be derived from bacteria and blue-green algae that entered into symbiotic relationships with an ancient eukaryotic host organism. Genetic information has been transferred between host and symbiont such that some of the genetic information used in modern-day mitochondria, for example, comes in part from the mitochondrial genome and in part from the host genome. Again, we have examples of known mechanisms that would produce an interconnected "thicket of life" rather than a tree of life.

Wells uses this difficulty to undermine the whole molecular evolutionary enterprise. Again, the careful reader should notice that the evolutionary tree of eukaryotes (those derived from cytochrome c as discussed above, or hemoglobin, or the eukaryotic branch of the ribosomal RNA data, etc.) is largely untouched by these interesting findings. If horizontal gene transfer is a real phenomenon, then, of course, it will complicate the determination of evolutionary relationships using sequence comparisons. But this does not undermine the whole enterprise — it just means that things are more complicated than we originally believed. But that's the way science always works! As we accumulate more data we find exceptions to our earlier more simplistic conceptions and make our models more complex to accommodate the new data. Horizontal gene transfer may indeed make it impossible to find the "universal" common ancestor, but the phenomenon itself may be telling us that our search for the "universal" common ancestor is misguided. Does this mean that evolution didn't occur? Does this now become evidence for special creation? This is the way that Wells and others use these new results. To me, these results simply make the puzzle more fascinating and more interesting to study.

13. W. F. Doolittle, "Phylogenetic Classification and the Universal Tree," *Science* 284 (1999): 2124-28.

The Evolution of Hemoglobin

Hemoglobin is another well-studied system where sequence comparisons have resulted in significant evolutionary insights. There are hemoglobin and myoglobin in most animals. Each of these proteins could be used to establish an evolutionary tree similar to the one determined for cytochrome c. However, the hemoglobin subunits and myoglobin are similar to each other and appear to have been produced as a result of gene duplication events which resulted in different proteins, each of which went its separate way in evolution. We will discuss the details of this gene duplication process, its consequences in globin biochemistry, and the evolutionary implications of this process, especially how this phenomenon is an explanation of how new information can arise.[14]

Hemoglobin is a complex molecular machine. The elucidation of the detailed molecular mechanism of reversible oxygen binding and its relationship with respiratory physiology is one of the few triumphs of reductionistic biochemistry. Hemoglobin is made of four protein subunits, each one having a heme group and an oxygen-binding site. Two of the four subunits are identical and are denoted alpha, and the other two are identical and are denoted beta. Alpha subunits and beta subunits are very similar in three-dimensional structure and also similar in amino acid sequence. An alpha subunit and a beta subunit assemble together to form an alpha/beta dimer. Two alpha/beta dimers make up the intact hemoglobin tetramer. There are two forms of hemoglobin: the deoxy form with no oxygen bound and the oxy form with oxygen bound. A key difference between the deoxy form and the oxy form appears to be a rotation of about 15° of one alpha/beta dimer relative to the other alpha/beta dimer. In the detailed structure it is as if there were two interlocking gears and in going from one form to the other they slipped a cog. The physiological observations are explained very nicely by this model. Oxygen does not bind very readily to the deoxy form of hemoglobin, so at low oxygen concentrations the fraction of possible oxygen molecules bound is very low. This corresponds to the condition of the blood in the tissues away from the lungs. However, when two of the four possible oxygen-binding sites have oxygen bound, the oxy form becomes the more stable energetically and the whole tetramer switches over to the oxy form. Now the remaining two sites have a high oxygen affinity and bind oxygen very readily. So, at the critical oxygen concentration there is a cooperative oxy-

14. Again, I will not cite individual references for this section. This is a summary of material found in Voet and Voet, *Biochemistry,* and R. E. Dickerson and I. Geis, *Hemoglobin: Structure, Function, Evolution, and Pathology* (Menlo Park, Calif.: Benjamin/Cummings, 1983). A more recent discussion is in R. Hardison, "The Evolution of Hemoglobin," *American Scientist* 87.2 (1999): 126-37.

gen binding. This is the condition of the blood in the lungs. As the blood returns to the tissues, the oxygen concentration drops, the release of the first two molecules of oxygen results in a switch back to the deoxy form, which then makes the release of the remaining oxygen molecules easier, resulting in the dumping of oxygen to the tissues.

Hemoglobin is a complex molecular machine.[15] Do we have any hints as to how such a complex molecular machine arose by evolutionary means? As a result of protein sequence comparisons in several organisms and as a result of the analysis of the structure of the globin coding regions of the genome, it is possible to construct a very plausible picture of the origin of this system.

Another structural detail must be noted before we proceed with the evolutionary story. The alpha/beta dimer self-assembles as a consequence of greasy patches on the surface of each protein. This principle of assembly is due to the same principle that causes oil drops in water to spontaneously coalesce (and what causes the proteins to fold up into a three-dimensional structure in the first place). Interestingly, myoglobin, the oxygen storage protein found in muscle, has a very similar structure to the hemoglobin monomers, but it does not have the surface greasy patches, and so it does not form multiple subunit assemblies. The two alpha/beta dimers self-assemble by the same principles to form the tetramer.

While no doubt wrong in some details, here is a plausible evolutionary scenario that describes the origin of this molecular machine. We will start with a monomeric oxygen-binding globin such as those found in some insects, annelids, and mollusks and even in plants. The origin of the first globinlike structure will not concern us, although there is some speculation that it may have arisen from cytochrome a which binds to the same kind of heme group.[16] These groups do not have globins that have differentiated oxygen-storage functions (myoglobinlike) and oxygen transport functions (hemoglobinlike). These globins do not have the complex oxygen-binding behavior that hemoglobin has but are similar in their oxygen-binding properties to myoglobin.

15. Behe (*Darwin's Black Box,* pp. 206-7) discusses briefly the myoglobin/hemoglobin system and concludes that one cannot infer design from it. I agree with Behe in that conclusion, but I disagree that the hemoglobin example does not illustrate irreducible complexity. Hemoglobin is a "whole" that will not function as a cooperative oxygen-carrier molecule without all the parts interacting in a specific way. As such it is irreducible (as are all "wholes"). But Behe does not want to consider hemoglobin to be irreducibly complex because he can imagine an evolutionary pathway to construct it. This illustrates the tautologous nature of Behe's claim that Darwinian evolution cannot produce irreducible complexity. See the discussion in chapter 13 of this volume.

16. See also, D. Minning et al., "Ascaris Haemoglobin Is a Nitric Oxide-Activated 'Deoxygenase,'" *Nature* 401 (1999): 497-502.

A key first step is a gene duplication event that allows the preservation of the original functional protein but provides a second copy of the gene that can be altered by mutation, providing a source of new material on which selection can operate. There are multiple versions of globin genes that differ by only a few amino acids in insects and mollusks. In humans alpha and beta hemoglobin exist in gene clusters containing multiple copies of each type of gene. In the alpha cluster there are two identical copies of the alpha gene, two copies of the alphalike zeta globin (found in fetal hemoglobin), and one alphalike pseudogene that appears not to be expressed. In the beta cluster there are five different betalike genes and one betalike pseudogene. It appears from various lines of argument that these have arisen by gene duplication followed by mutations. Some of the mutated copies appear to be functionless, whereas some of them appear to have new functions (for example, in fetal hemoglobin with altered oxygen binding). These gene duplications are preadaptations, that is, changes that occur for other reasons, but once they have occurred they provide the necessary conditions for some selectable function.

Sea lamprey globin evidences what might be the next intermediate stage. Sea lampreys have a separate myoglobin for oxygen storage and a hemoglobin-like molecule for oxygen transport. Lamprey hemoglobin is dimeric rather than tetrameric. It does display cooperative oxygen binding, though. Lamprey deoxyhemoglobin forms dimers that dissociate upon oxygen binding. The dimer contacts are in exactly the region of the molecule where one alpha-beta dimer interacts with the other alpha-beta dimer. This is the region that modulates the 15° rotation and the cog-slipping effect that were described above. Murray Goodman and coworkers cite evidence from their sequence comparisons that suggest that mutations accumulated in this region of the molecule at four times the rate for the molecule as a whole during the evolution of this new function.[17] Clearly, the cooperativity of oxygen binding is a consequence of dimerization. But dimer formation is the result of greasy patches on the surface of the protein, which could well have arisen by a few amino acid substitutions (or even one as is the case in deoxyhemoglobin S fibers in sickle-cell anemia). Dimer formation would have been a Darwinian preadaptation to the evolution of cooperative oxygen binding.

The next step in hemoglobin evolution is the result of a gene duplication of the ancestral hemoglobinlike gene into the modern alpha and beta globin genes. Again, the original oxygen-transporting function could be preserved, while mutations acted upon the second copy of the gene. The very similar but

17. M. Goodman, G. W. Moore, and G. Matsuda, "Darwinian Evolution in the Genealogy of Haemoglobin," *Nature* 253 (1975): 603-8.

slightly different version of the globin allowed for the formation of the alpha-beta dimer that upon interaction with another alpha-beta dimer allowed the preservation of the tetramer structure even upon oxygenation. Again, Goodman's group believes that their sequence comparison data suggest that the alpha-beta dimer interface accumulated mutations at nearly twice the rate as that for the whole molecule during the evolution of this new function. Again, the gene duplication event and the alpha-beta dimer formation are pre-adaptations to the formation of the complex tetramer.

In the 450 million years since the origin of the hemoglobin tetramer there has been ample time to finely tune the primitive transport function. There does appear to be additional evolution, especially related to the rise of warm-blooded creatures and (as already mentioned in my discussion of the gene structure of the human alpha and beta gene clusters) the rise of placental mammals and their special adaptations utilized in oxygen transport.

Molecular Developmental Biology and Evolution

Comparative studies of developmental biology at the molecular level are now suggesting that gene duplication events such as those described for hemoglobin may explain major morphological changes that have been observed over the course of evolution. Advances in the study of gene regulation in the past decade have been applied to the discipline of developmental biology. While in many ways this field is still in its infancy, these studies are yielding incredible insights into the process by which a single, undifferentiated cell becomes a complex organism. The genes responsible are being discovered and sequenced, the timing of gene expression is being determined, and the distribution of gene product molecules in the developing organism is being understood. This explosion of knowledge of developmental biology at the cellular and molecular level is occurring in a variety of organisms representing a good cross-section of the animal kingdom: human, mouse, and zebrafish among the vertebrates; Drosophila among the arthropods; and nematodes. Consequently, there has been a resurgence in comparative developmental biology that has spawned a renewed interest in evolutionary questions among developmental biologists. (This interest area is referred to as "evo-devo" studies.) Prominent developmental biology textbook writer Scott Gilbert even refers to a new evolutionary synthesis that brings together neo-Darwinism, molecular biology, developmental biology, paleontology, and complexity theory.[18]

18. Scott F. Gilbert, *Developmental Biology*, 5th ed. (Sunderland, Mass.: Sinauer Associates, 1997).

It will not be possible to review this entire field, and I refer the reader to fuller discussions of modern developmental biology found in books such as Gilbert's *Developmental Biology,* John Gerhart and Marc Kirschner's *Cells, Embryos, and Evolution,*[19] or Rudolf A. Raff's *The Shape of Life.*[20] Additionally, recent years have seen the sequencing of the whole genomes of many of these organisms. Studies of these whole genomes in isolation and in comparison are sure to shed great light on these (and other heretofore unasked) questions.[21] The amount of data here is vast, and we are just beginning to scratch the surface. In this overview I will look at three studies from the past decade that provide evidence for a macroevolutionary picture and even yield insights into how major morphological change might have occurred.

Hox *Genes*

Homeotic genes (*Hox* genes) were first discovered in Drosophila and specify fly body parts. One example is the *Antennapedia* gene.[22] In the dominant *Antennapedia* mutation fly legs grow out of the head instead of normal antennae. In the recessive *Antennapedia* mutation antennae grow in place of legs. The proper expression of this gene is believed to control the development of the second segment in the fly thorax. Another example is the bithorax homeotic gene complex (BX-C). A combination of three mutations, BX-C results in the third segment in the fly thorax being identical to the second segment, giving the fly four wings instead of two (flies are members of the insect order Diptera, meaning two wings). It seems very likely that changes in BX-C are some of the evolutionary changes that occurred in going from ancestral four-winged insects to the Diptera. Further, molecular genetic analysis of this family of genes revealed that they regulate the expression of other genes, that is, these genes code for transcription factors (DNA binding proteins that turn genes off and on) or they are regulatory sites (binding sites on the DNA where the transcription factors

19. John Gerhart and Marc Kirschner, *Cells, Embryos, and Evolution: Toward a Cellular and Developmental Understanding of Phenotypic Variation and Evolutionary Adaptability* (Malden, Mass.: Blackwell Science, 1997).

20. Rudolf A. Raff, *The Shape of Life: Genes, Development, and the Evolution of Animal Form* (Chicago: University of Chicago Press, 1996).

21. For example, see G. M. Rubin, "Comparing Species," *Nature* 409 (2001): 820-21, and W.-H. Li, Z. Gu, H. Wang, and A. Nekrutenko, "Evolutionary Analyses of the Human Genome," *Nature* 409 (2001): 847-49.

22. Yet again, I will not cite individual references for this section on *Hox* genes. This is a summary of material found in Gilbert, *Developmental Biology,* and Voet and Voet, *Biochemistry.*

bind). The evolutionary implications of this class of genes are striking. Small changes in regulatory genes involved in an organism's developmental pathway can have large-scale effects on the morphology of the organism.

In Drosophila, *Hox* genes (HOM-C for homeotic complex) are organized in two distinct clusters: the *Antennapedia* homeotic gene complex (ANT-C), consisting of *labial (lab)*, *probiscidia (pb)*, *Deformed (Dfd)*, *Sex comb reduced (Scr)*, and *Antennapedia (Antp)*; and BX-C, consisting of *Ultrabithorax (Ubx)*, *abdominal A (abdA)*, and *abdominal B (abdB)*. The linear order of these genes on the chromosome (the same order as listed above) corresponds to their regulation of segmentation in the fruit fly from head to tail: *lab*, *pb*, and *Dfd* regulate head segments; *Scr*, *Antp*, and *Ubx* regulate thoracic segments; *abdA* and *abdB* regulate abdominal segments. Mice and humans have similar head- to tail-regulating *Hox* genes. Mice and humans have four *Hox* clusters: *Hox*-A, *Hox*-B, *Hox*-C, and *Hox*-D. The genes in these clusters are orthologous to the genes in Drosophila HOM-C. For example, mouse *Hox-a1*, *Hox-b1*, *Hox-d1* are all more similar to Drosophila *lab* than to other *Hox* genes in the mouse cluster (there is no *Hox-c1* gene — apparently it has been deleted from the cluster). Similarly, the vertebrate *Hox* 2, 4, 5, 6, 7, 8, and 9-13 genes are orthologous to the Drosophila *pb*, *Dfd*, *Scr*, *Antp*, *Ubx*, *abdA*, and *abdB*, respectively. In transgenic flies, the human *Hox-b4* gene can restore the function from a mutant *Dfd* gene in Drosophila. If we use the same sort of arguments advanced previously for cytochrome c and the globins, these similarities in sequence, genetic structure, and function suggest that these clusters in Drosophila and vertebrates are derived from a common ancestral cluster. Somewhere early in the vertebrate lineage a series of gene duplication events occurred that gave rise to four separate clusters. Interestingly, amphioxus, a nonvertebrate chordate, has only a single *Hox* complex, suggesting that the gene duplication events occurred after the origin of the chordate lineage but before the origin of the vertebrate lineage. Nematodes have only a single *Hox* cluster.

All of the *Hox* genes themselves are similar in sequence. They show the same paralogous relationship to one another as do myoglobin, alpha hemoglobin, and beta hemoglobin. It is not unreasonable to infer that the entire complex arose through a series of gene duplications. Some have even speculated that the evolution of complex animal body plans is a consequence of this series of gene duplication events giving rise to the *Hox* cluster.[23] More complex body plans are "simply" variations on the segmentation regulated by these *Hox* complexes. In comparing the vertebrate *Hox* complexes with insect *Hox* complexes,

23. P. W. H. Holland, "Major Transitions in Animal Evolution: A Developmental Genetic Perspective," *American Zoologist* 38 (1998): 829-42, and Valentine, Jablonski, and Ervin, "Fossils, Molecules and Embryos."

it is apparent that other gene duplication events have taken place. For example, there is no insect *Hox* gene that corresponds to the vertebrate *Hox* 3 genes. It is present in amphioxus and appears to be the result of a *Hox* 2 gene duplication. This duplication event must have occurred before the duplication events that gave rise to the four different vertebrate *Hox* clusters since three of the four clusters have this gene. Similarly *Hox* 10-13, present in vertebrates but not in insects, would have arisen due to a gene duplication event in *Hox* 9. Amphioxus has *Hox* 9 and *Hox* 10, so again, a history of these duplication events can be postulated by theses sorts of comparisons — in this case, a gene duplication event of the *Hox* 9 *(abdB)* occurring after the insect-chordate divergence, but prior to the amphioxus-vertebrate divergence.

It is worth noting again at this point that these are macroevolutionary relationships. On the basis of these deep homologies, we are able to establish relationships between animal phyla. We do not need to know the mechanism of evolutionary change in order to establish the relationship. While no doubt there is much theory (and inference) involved in establishing evolutionary relationships on the basis of these sorts of sequence comparisons (see the discussion above), these macroevolutionary relationships signify in part "the fact of evolution" versus theories about its mechanism(s).[24] I continue to be amazed at skeptics who point to the Cambrian explosion and the "sudden" appearance of animal phyla who seem to ignore the relationships indicated by the molecular and genetic data.

The Pax 6 Gene

The *Pax 6* gene is a master control gene that orchestrates a cascade of around 2,500 genes involved in eye morphogenesis.[25] This gene was first found in mice and humans and was called *Small eye* in mice. Heterozygotes have eye defects including the absence of an iris. The homozygous mutation is lethal, and embryos lack eyes altogether and have other brain and sensory organ defects. Furthermore, functional eyes can be caused to form on fly legs, wings, halteres, and antennae by expressing *Pax 6* in other parts of the developing fly. The molecular developmental details of this system are in the process of being worked out and, while fascinating, will not be discussed in detail here. It is the comparative molecular genetics story that will occupy us. The *Pax 6* gene is also found in

24. S. J. Gould, "Evolution as Fact and Theory," *Hen's Teeth and Horse's Toes: Further Reflections in Natural History* (New York: Norton, 1983), pp. 253-62.

25. Gilbert, *Developmental Biology,* and W. J. Gehring and K. Ikeo, "Pax 6: Mastering Eye Morphogenesis and Eye Evolution," *Trends in Genetics* 15 (1999): 371-77.

Drosophila and corresponds to the *eyeless* (ey) gene that has been known since the early days of Drosophila genetics. The *Pax 6* gene is over 90 percent identical in Drosophila and mice (mouse and human *Pax 6* are identical).

What is most amazing about *Pax 6* being present in both vertebrates and insects and having a similar role in eye development is that vertebrate and insect eyes are so different. Vertebrates have a camera-type eye whereas insects have compound eyes — very different eye morphologies (and technologies). On the basis of eye morphology and developmental pathways evolutionists have long argued that the different kinds of eyes are the result of convergent evolution, that is, similar structures and functions not descending from common ancestors but resulting from different evolutionary pathways. It was estimated that eyes evolved *independently* over forty times in different animal lineages. The existence of a common master control gene involved in eye formation is a complete surprise and suggests that eye evolution is divergent from a common ancestor (at least at the molecular level). The *Pax 6* gene then is yet another molecular marker on which a phylogenetic tree for animals can be constructed. While there are sequence differences, presumably as a consequence of the evolutionary distance between vertebrates and insects, the vertebrate *Pax 6* gene can function in Drosophila.

Pax 6 genes with similar functions have now also been found in birds, frogs, fish, amphioxus, sea urchins, squids, ribbon worms, nematodes, planaria, and sea squirts. These organisms represent the major animal groups and a diversity of eye morphologies. Again, these genetic similarities that control such a fundamental aspect of the organism, that is, eye formation and other central nervous system development, suggest descent from a common ancestor. However, the differences in body morphology, in this case in eye and brain morphology, also suggest that some of the interesting questions in evolution relate to the details of the cascade controlled by master control genes such as *Hox* and *Pax*. How regulatory linkage occurs and is played out in different lineages continues to be an area of active research.[26]

Comparative Chromosome Maps among Mammals

The genome map of the 1999 genome issue of *Science* was entitled "Comparative Genomics — Mammalian Radiation."[27] Chromosome maps of several dif-

26. Gerhart and Kirschner *(Cells, Embryos, and Evolution)* have a lot of discussion on this topic.

27. S. J. O'Brien, M. Menotti-Raymond, W. J. Murphy, W. G. Nash, J. Wienberg,

ferent mammalian orders were examined to find chromosomal rearrangements that then can be viewed as evolutionary events (much like amino acid sequence substitutions) from which phylogenetic trees can be derived. This is significant on two counts. First, the evolution of mammalian orders is referred to as a "radiation." In the fossil record the great diversity of mammals appears in a geologically short time interval around 65 million years ago. Such radiations make it very difficult to generate a phylogenetic tree. Second, because mammals are all so closely related, it is hard to construct a tree from amino acid sequence data. For cytochrome c only twelve amino acid substitutions separate the most divergent mammals (figure 4). For the globins the number of substitutions vary between thirty and fifty for the different orders of mammals. However, the number and type of chromosome rearrangements produce a set of characters that results in a very well defined phylogenetic tree. One of the intriguing claims is that it may in fact be major chromosomal rearrangements that produce isolated (not interbreeding) populations or subpopulations.

The point I wish to stress is very basic. All the mammalian orders have similar chromosome maps. It is possible to identify which chromosomes (or chromosome segments) correspond to chromosomes (or chromosome segments) in other mammals. The genome map in the issue of *Science* mentioned above has all of the mammalian orders shown compared to the human chromosomes. The genetic similarity, as discussed before, suggests common ancestry, although special creationists will appeal to common design. But, why the differences if there is common design? The differences in light of the unity are what make the evolutionary argument so compelling. The rearrangements are readily understood as historical events superimposed upon the functional genome. Due to the nature of sexual reproduction at the cellular level, rearrangements will wreak havoc on chromosome alignment and recombination events, so such historical events are not without significance. The evolution envisioned here is macroevolutionary in nature. We are determining relationships between major orders of mammals via this mode of analysis.

The Evolution of Molecular Machines and Other "Irreducibly Complex" Biochemical Systems

The general pattern that emerges from the study of many systems in many different organisms is that gene duplication and lateral gene transfer have oc-

---

R. Stanyon, N. G. Copeland, N. A. Jenkins, J. E. Wornack, and J. A. M. Graves, "The Promise of Comparative Genomics in Mammals," *Science* 286 (1999): 458-81.

curred throughout the history of life. These processes themselves provide some data by which evolutionary relationships can be determined, but they also provide the raw materials for the generation of novelty. The idea of preadaptation or exaptation is important here.[28] Duplicated genes (with their expressed proteins) result from "normal" biological processes. As we saw in the proposal for hemoglobin evolution, the existence of these additional genes is preadaptation for "unintended" but possibly useful incipient novel functions. However, once a novel incipient function exists, no matter how poor it is, it can be improved by natural selection. This becomes the general answer to Michael J. Behe's irreducible complexity problem.[29] The initial function does not arise as a result of Darwinian natural selection. Of course, Behe is quite correct in saying that natural selection cannot act on a system unless it is already present. But no one disagrees with that. The question is, "Are there other mechanisms that could produce the initial function?" The answer is yes: gene duplication, random mutation, and self-assembly of protein subunits. Novel genes that come from other organisms via lateral gene transfer also occur via "normal" biological processes. Some of these genes (or gene complexes) may function intact in the new organism and bring that structure and function to the organism. But also, the expression of these laterally transferred genes in the context of a different organism with different biological macromolecules present could produce novel interactions that result in useful incipient functions. Once they are formed, no matter how poorly, selection can operate to improve them.

Most of the evolutionary explanations for the origins of complex biological systems follow this line with good cause. For example, the blood-clotting system consists of many proteins encoded by genes in the same gene family. A gene duplication scenario is a reasonable inference.[30] Similar examples are found in the literature concerning other systems.[31] In chapter 13 of this volume

28. A commonly used example of preadaptation or exaptation at the organismic level is used to explain the origin of wings. Clearly, a part of a wing does no good for flying. But, suppose winglike structures and feathers arose for other purposes, say, for thermal protection or for balancing. Such a structure might be useful for fall protection or gliding, and natural selection would operate to improve it. In this example, we are moving into the commonly criticized "just so story" mode. I recognize that danger, especially in this example, and do not necessarily endorse this particular speculation. It is presented here simply as an example.

29. Behe, *Darwin's Black Box.*

30. R. F. Doolittle and D. F. Feng, "Reconstruction of the Evolution of Vertebrate Blood Coagulation from a Consideration of the Amino Acid Sequences of Clotting Proteins," *Cold Spring Harbor Symposium of Quantitative Biology* 52 (1987): 869-74.

31. G. W. Litman, "Sharks and the Origins of Vertebrate Immunity," *Scientific American,* November 1996, pp. 61-71; A. L. Hughes and M. Yeager, "Molecular Evolution of the Vertebrate Immune System," *Bioessays* 19 (1997): 777-86; E. Melendez-Hevia, T. G. Waddell, and

we speculate concerning the origin of cilia, flagella, and the vision system. Clearly, more data is needed, especially comparative data. As whole genome research continues, and organisms beside mice and men have their genome sequences determined, our ability to test current ideas and develop more robust evolutionary explanations will certainly grow.

Theological Musings

The defense of evolutionary theory presented in this chapter is more or less the standard account put forward by mainstream evolutionists regardless of their theological orientation. In fact some readers might hear this defense and wonder what it is doing in a volume devoted to a Christian perspective on this subject. Isn't this just the same molecular evolutionary theory that atheists use to claim that God is unnecessary? The authors of this volume all share the belief that there is nothing inconsistent about our Christian faith, which declares that God is the Creator of heaven and earth, and our acceptance of the theory of evolution as described variously in this volume. However, as noted in the introduction, there is a wide range of theological perspectives found among the contributors. It will be illustrative to give some of my theological perspectives to see how one might bring together a "creationist" position and an evolutionist position.

I come from a fairly conservative Calvinistic theological perspective. I believe that Scripture teaches that God is absolutely sovereign over all his creation. Whatever comes to pass was ordained by him. This extends to the smallest creaturely action. The Westminster Shorter Catechism speaks of God governing all his creatures and all their actions. Natural processes are controlled absolutely by God. There is no such thing as chance from God's point of view — he knows the outcome and he determines the outcome. Even the actions of free agents are known by God and controlled by God. Many will object at this point and say that there is no such thing as free agency in a world absolutely controlled by God in the way I have described. Others will object that there is no such thing as authentic creaturely action and that God acts coercively over his creation if what I say is true. Still others will object on the basis of the problem of evil. But I reject all of those objections and agree that there is real

M. Cascante, "The Puzzle of the Krebs Citric Acid Cycle: Assembly of the Pieces of Chemically Feasible Reactions, and Opportunism in the Design of Metabolic Pathways during Evolution," *Journal of Molecular Evolution* 43 (1996): 293-303. A long and continually updated list of evolutionary explanations for complex biological systems is found on the worldwide web at http://www.world-of-dawkins.com/Catalano/box/published.htm.

free agency, that there is authentic uncoerced creaturely action, and that God is not the author of sin. However, I join the ranks of many who have gone before me and say that Scripture reveals that absolute divine sovereignty and genuine creaturely freedom and responsibility both exist. And so, while we may not be able to understand how to resolve the apparent contradiction using human reason, we readily affirm both truths. As for the problem of evil — I am not convinced that the Scriptures would have us sacrifice the sovereignty of God in order to preserve his reputation. It simply remains a mystery that we may not be able to solve as creatures. There has been much discussion into the manner of God's interaction with creation — some in this very volume. Interestingly, in Charles Hodge's *Systematic Theology* he concluded a long discussion of the doctrines of providence, concursus, and, in general, God's interaction with creation with the following line: "All we know, and all we need to know, is; (1) that God does govern all his creatures; and (2) that his control over them is consistent with their nature, and with his own infinite purity and excellence."[32]

Thus all of the events envisioned by an evolutionist are under God's oversight (as are all events). This includes random events such as mutations, chance encounters of particular genomes, recombination events, mating events in populations, which sperm actually fertilizes a given egg, and so forth. From a human and scientific perspective these are all random events. From God's perspective, exactly what he ordained to occur occurs. We can list all of the mechanisms that we have cited earlier, gene duplication, lateral gene transfer, novel interactions that produce novel functions, existence in an environment where a particular function will be useful. These too occur according to God's plan and purpose. So, in one sense there is no such thing as a natural occurrence, if by natural we mean occurring autonomously of its own accord without being empowered to exist and being governed by God. In this view, Stephen Jay Gould's question in *Wonderful Life*, "What would happen if we played the tape of life all over again?" gets answered in a very different way.[33] Gould has to answer that it most likely comes out very differently because of all the contingencies in the course of natural history. My view says that it comes out exactly the same way without denying any of the contingencies because of God's sovereign control. The upshot is that God is as much in control of the outcome of the process as he is if he had zapped things into existence without any process. Obviously, this is not the random, undirected evolution of atheistic naturalists (or of Darwin). However, I will be quick to add that

32. C. Hodge, *Systematic Theology* (Grand Rapids: Eerdmans, 1977), p. 605.
33. S. J. Gould, *Wonderful Life* (New York: Norton, 1989).

from our perspective as scientists (or from the perspective of the evolving creature) things are random and undirected.[34]

Finally, some words are in order concerning the origin of man. The arguments for evolution given above fully include human beings in the macroevolutionary picture. There is nothing in the biology or biochemistry of *Homo sapiens* that would suggest that our origin is not explained by this same evolutionary explanation. However, the biblical account of man's origin seems to suggest a rather unique origin of humanity, both physically and spiritually, that would put man outside this process.[35] Personally, I have to admit that I have not settled this question in my own mind. As I have argued, I think the evolutionary conclusion is the best explanation of the evidence from an examination of the creation itself. On the other hand, I feel the exegetical force of the argument from Scripture that says otherwise. I am content to remain in a state of cognitive dissonance on this issue until further clarity comes my way.

34. The word "purpose" (or "purposeless") is often found in this context. Philosophers of biology distinguish between several levels of purpose and have invented several terms accordingly such as teleology and teleonomy (see E. Mayr, *Toward a New Philosophy of Biology: Observations of an Evolutionist* [Cambridge, Mass.: Belknap Press of Harvard University Press, 1988]). Clearly, the phrase "structure-function," which is a common notion in biology, can be taken to mean structure-purpose. When evolutionists say that evolution is purposeless, they are simply saying that structures do not evolve to anticipate future needs. Ultimate purpose or God's purpose for a given evolutionary event is not in view and cannot be in view in this context. I do not think that science addresses such questions.

35. Theologians in my tradition, such as B. B. Warfield, have been open to the possibility that man's body could have evolutionary origins but that his soul was specially created in the creation of Adam and Eve. Others have not been open to that possibility. For example, in commenting on the creation of Adam in Gen. 2:7, John Murray wrote, "That which constituted man as man also constituted him as living creature." He argued that this precluded any sort of animal ancestry of man, even if you restricted it to his body.

13 Complexity, Self-Organization, and Design

LOREN HAARSMA AND TERRY M. GRAY

I magine a square dance with 30,000 dancers. Each dancer has a personal style and a unique way of interacting with other dancers. In addition to the dancers, several hundred dance callers try to organize the dance, each one yelling instructions to the dancers and to other callers. Their goal is not merely to keep the dance organized but also to help the dancers respond appropriately to the ever-changing music. This imaginary scene gives a picture of the organized complexity of a single living cell. Human cells have approximately 30,000 genes encoded in their DNA. These genes control the formation of proteins and other chemicals that the cells need. These proteins and other chemicals interact with each other — and with their environment — in complicated, multistep, interlocking chemical reactions.

Another way to get a sense of the complexity of a living cell is to look at the *information* encoded in its DNA. Modern, complex life forms require a great deal of information encoded in their DNA in order to survive. The human genome, for example, contains approximately three billion base pairs, which would require six billion "bits" of information to specify.[1] By contrast, the bacterium Mycoplasma has the smallest currently known genome — about half a million base pairs. The earliest life forms are believed to have had much smaller genomes than that.

Modern life's complexity and information content pose an interesting challenge for the theory of evolution. It is easy to understand how evolution,

---

1. This number overestimates the actual information content of human DNA because many of those base pairs can be substituted for each other, or in many cases simply deleted, without adverse effects. At present, we can only roughly estimate the amount of information which is actually important for constructing and regulating the cell's proteins and other molecules. Estimates range from tens of millions to a few hundred million "bits." These are still impressively large numbers.

using just the natural mechanisms of mutation and natural selection, can produce small changes in species over time. But is it possible for simple life forms, over time, to evolve into much more complex life forms — life forms with novel capabilities far beyond those of simpler forms? Charles Darwin believed that complexity and novelty could evolve over time. In *The Origin of Species,* Darwin developed some hypotheses for how this might happen. Since Darwin's time, scientists have tested and improved upon his hypotheses and invented new ones. Most scientists today are convinced that biological evolution can, under the right conditions, lead to increased complexity and novelty. Not everyone agrees.

Using theological language, we could ask the questions this way: Did God design the laws of nature so that biological evolution is limited to making small-scale changes in species? If so, then God, at various points throughout biological history, must also have miraculously superseded ordinary evolution to form newer, more complex life forms. Alternatively, did God design the laws of nature so that biological evolution could, through its ordinary operation, bring about gradual increases in biological complexity and novelty? If so, God could have created modern life forms (and the entire history of life seen in the fossil record) using biological evolution under his ordinary providential governance, without the need for extraordinary miracles.[2]

Using language that is more religiously neutral, we might ask the questions this way: Are the natural mechanisms of biological evolution limited to only small-scale tinkering with a species' existing capabilities? Or can we scientifically explain how biological evolution could produce the complexity we see in modern life forms?

For the present, we cannot definitively answer to those questions. Scientists still have much to learn about how living cells work. Scientists have sequenced the entire genomes of only a few species. Once a species' genome is sequenced, there is still a great deal to be learned about how those genes function

2. It is important to use the term "design" carefully. In recent years, some people have appropriated the name "Intelligent Design" for a particular theory — the theory that biological evolution is limited to making small changes so that biological complexity could have been produced only if God (or someone) superseded evolution during biological history. See, for example, Phillip Johnson, *Darwin on Trial* (Downers Grove, Ill.: InterVarsity, 1991); and William Dembski, *The Design Inference* (New York: Cambridge University Press, 1998). Whatever might be said, good or bad, about the scientific and theological arguments of Intelligent Design theory, we are troubled by the appropriation of the word "design" to exclude evolution. Intelligent Design theory, the way it is typically presented, seems to offer the following choice: *either* modern life forms evolved *or* they were designed. That is a false choice. Christian theology says that modern life forms were definitely designed by God, whether God used ordinary evolution or superseded it.

in a living cell, and a great deal more to be learned about how much those genes can evolve biochemically from generation to generation. We need to study the evolution of complexity for many more decades before the "limits" of evolution are well understood. While we do not yet have definitive answers, we do have some hints — hints both from biology and from computer science.

Under certain conditions, complexity can self-organize. "Self-organized complexity" is a small but growing field of research in computer science and mathematics. Many of its research topics[3] are inspired by biology. In the next sections of this chapter, we will look at some examples of self-organized complexity taken from computer science and from physics. These examples will demonstrate not only that self-organized complexity is possible but also that there are multiple strategies for achieving it.

In the second half of this chapter, we will turn our attention back to evolutionary biology. It turns out that biological life does have the properties necessary for complexity to evolve and self-organize.

Multiple Strategies for Self-Organized Complexity

If you wanted to create an example of self-organized complexity, what strategy would you use? It turns out that there is more than one strategy, and the one you choose would depend upon your goals. I will give examples of just three such strategies in the next sections of the chapter.

1. *Preprogrammed self-assembly.* Component pieces are designed so that random interactions between them eventually lead to assembly of the desired complex object or objects.
2. *Information transfer from the environment.* A relatively simple object can become more complex by incorporating information about its environment into itself, via a process of random exploration and feedback.
3. *Interaction among agents.* A collection of simple objects or agents can, via random interactions and feedback, produce a complex web of interactions that lead to increased productivity or survivability.

Although these three strategies differ from each other, they share some common features. All three have an element of *randomness* built into the algorithm. The randomness allows them, over time, to try many different combinations. In addition to the randomness, there are *rules* that govern how strong or

3. E.g., neural networks, cellular automata, artificial life, genetic algorithms, and others.

successful each particular combination is. The entire process is *iterative;* the output from one round or one generation is used as input for the next.

A Rotating Clock "Molecule" — One Example of Preprogrammed Self-Assembly

One particular computer program that demonstrates self-assembly is a sort of screen-saver program. Its rules are loosely modeled on the behavior of atoms and molecules.[4] The screen is divided into "cells" arranged in rows and columns. Each screen cell can either be blank or can have one artificial "atom" in it. There are eight types of atoms (designated 1-8). The screen is updated once per second. Each time the screen is updated, atoms can move, appear, and disappear. Neighboring atoms can join to form molecular chains of 2, 3, 4 or more atoms in length. Molecules can move and rotate, and molecular bonds can break. All of these processes are governed by five equations (rules) and eight preselected numbers that determine probabilities.

If you observe this program running for a few minutes, you will see atoms appear, move, and disappear from the screen. Simple molecules form, move, rotate and break apart. All of these events happen randomly, although some of them happen with higher probabilities than others. Given enough time and careful observation, the laws (equations and probabilities) that govern their behavior could be inferred from their behavior.

If you start with a blank screen and leave the program running for a few days, something interesting will happen. In several places on the screen you will see this circular 8-atom molecule:

$$
\begin{array}{cc}
1 & 2 \\
8 \qquad\quad 3 \\
7 \qquad\quad 4 \\
6 & 5
\end{array}
$$

This molecule (and its rotational and reflection counterparts) is absolutely stable. Unlike any other atom or molecule, no matter how long you watch this particular molecule, it will never break apart. Moreover, it has another unique property. Without fail, this molecule rotates exactly one notch per screen cycle. It functions as a clock.

4. The rules and the source code for the program are available from the author upon request.

The rules that govern the behavior of this particular molecule are exactly the same rules that govern every other atom and molecule. If you studied the five equations and eight probabilities that govern atomic and molecular behavior, it would not be obvious (at first glance) that such a stable, functional molecule should exist at all. Its stability and its regularity are *emergent novel properties*. None of the individual atoms are stable. None of them exhibit regular motion. The stability and regularity of this molecule emerge from the equations that govern its motion only when all of its component pieces are properly assembled.

In addition, this molecule exhibits *interlocking complexity*.[5] Each of the eight atoms acts according to slightly different probabilities from the others. Each one of the eight atoms is required, in exactly its proper (relative) position, for the molecule to be stable and to reliably function as a clock. If any one atom is missing, or if any two are transposed, it will not function properly and it will not be stable.

This clock molecule can *self-assemble*. You could also assemble these clock molecules "by hand." You could interrupt the program while it was running, rewrite the memory locations specifying the screen cells of various atoms and their neighboring bonds, and then restart the program with one or more newly created clock molecules in place. It is possible to do this, but it is not necessary. If the five equations are written correctly, and if each of the eight probabilities is set within a fairly narrow range, the molecule self-assembles. Starting from a blank screen, clock molecules self-organize out of simpler elements (atoms) in about 100,000 screen cycles. This self-organization happens only when the equations and probabilities are designed and *fine-tuned* to encourage self-organization.

When this program is run, in addition to producing one or more clock molecules, it produces a complex environment with hundreds of other types of molecules on the screen. As the program is currently written, these other molecules are not stable. By slightly rewriting the rules, however, these other molecules could become stable. When the program starts, the environment is simple — a blank screen requiring almost no information to describe. The longer the

---

5. In his book *Darwin's Black Box: The Biochemical Challenge to Evolution* (New York: The Free Press, 1996), Michael Behe uses the term "irreducible complexity." He uses the term in at least two different ways. (1) For systems that must have all of their component pieces to function properly; if any piece is missing, the system does not function. (2) For systems that cannot be produced by a step-wise evolutionary process. Although there is some overlap between these two classes of systems, they are not equivalent, nor is one a subset of the other. They need to be distinguished. For this chapter, I will use the term *interlocking complexity* for the first type, and *nonevolvable complexity* for the second type.

program is run, the more complex the environment becomes and the more information it would take to describe it. *With the right sort of rules, a random, iterative process can start with a simple environment and self-assemble a complex environment.*

A Maze-Navigating Program —
Information Transfer from the Environment

Nearly all of us have played with mazes printed on paper, drawing a path through the maze that doesn't get stuck in any dead ends. Computer programs have been written to draw such mazes, and computer programs have been written that can learn how to navigate these mazes. Some of these programs use evolutionary algorithms and feedback from the environment to "learn."

Imagine a maze-navigating computer program begins at the maze's entry point and reads an instruction string to tell it whether to move left, right, up or down. The program starts with a randomly generated instruction string (say, ten bits long) and tries to follow it. (The instruction string can be thought of as the "genome" of the program. It provides the program with information it needs to survive in the maze.) If the program hits a wall in the maze, or if it traces over a position where it has already been, before it gets to the end of its instruction string, it stops and generates an error signal. If the program gets an error signal, it randomly flips one bit in its instruction string and tries again from the entry point. Eventually, by this random process, the program will find a ten-bit instruction string that it can follow to the end of the string without getting an error signal. When this happens, the program increases the length of the instruction string by duplication, creating a twenty-bit string. It then continues to navigate the maze (always starting at the entry point). Now when it generates an error signal, it randomly flips not just any bit, but only one of the last ten bits of its instruction string. After repeated trials, it will once again hit upon an instruction string that it can follow to the end of the twenty-bit string without error. Once again it will lengthen its instruction string by duplicating the last ten bits. It will again run the maze with a thirty-bit string, generating error signals and randomly flipping one of the last ten bits, until it successfully follows a thirty-bit string. This procedure continues until the program finally finds the "exit" of the maze.

If the maze is large, the final instruction string for the maze-navigating program can be quite large. In fact, the size of the instruction string is limited only by the complexity of the maze and the resources of the computer. The instruction string is packed with information on how to successfully navigate the maze. If the instruction string is N bits long, there are 2^N possible instruction strings, but only a tiny handful of them (or possibly just one) could successfully navigate the maze.

By this random iterative process, using feedback from the environment, a very simple computer algorithm can generate a string of information that is arbitrarily large. The information content of the instruction string can easily become much larger than the size of the rest of the program. Where does the information come from? The information comes from the maze itself, the "environment" of the program. This example demonstrates that evolutionary processes can transfer information from a complex environment into an instruction string, a string that is used by an entity to survive in its environment. The more complicated the environment, the more information can be transferred.

Although the maze-navigating program increases its complexity and information content, it never displays *novel* behavior. It becomes better and better at navigating the maze, but that's all it does. In order for novel behavior to arise from self-organization, you need a modified strategy.

The Economy — an Example of Interaction among Agents

Our modern industrial economy is very complex.[6] There are thousands of different industries and occupations. Occupations range across agriculture, health care, education, manufacturing, transportation, energy, and many others. Within a given industry, there are many specialties. In the food industry, people specialize in cultivating plants, raising livestock, and processing, transporting, and retailing food. In the energy industry, people specialize in exploration, extraction, refining, transportation, and distribution. The economy displays interlocking complexity. If one industry or subindustry (e.g., oil refining, or manufacturing equipment for oil refining) were to stop working altogether, the entire economy would suffer greatly unless a substitute industry were available.

Industrial economies do not achieve their complexity all at once. Their complexity is built up slowly, over time, from much simpler economies. As new technologies or techniques are invented, a few people specialize in providing that particular good or service. Others specialize in providing the raw materials for the new good or service, while others use the good or service to produce other things. The entire economy adjusts and becomes more efficient and productive. The interlocking complexity builds up slowly, over time, as individuals

---

6. Thanks to Glenn Morton for pointing out this example.

interact with each other in new ways, finding combinations of interactions that increase their productivity.

An important feature of the economy — necessary for the self-organization of complexity and novelty — is the presence of *redundancy* and *multitasking*. As an example of redundancy: one factory produces racing bicycles, while different factories produce mountain bikes, children's bikes, scooters, or unicycles. If the racing bike factory reduces or stops production, some people who rely on those bikes will be inconvenienced, but most could adapt to using the alternatives. As an example of multitasking: the racing bike factory might spend only half of its time making racing bikes and the other half making related products, such as exercise bikes. Another example of multitasking: the factory supplies racing bikes to not one but several different industries (e.g., professional bicycle racers, amateur biking clubs, bicycle messenger services, people who use bikes to commute to work, etc.). This sort of multitasking increases the likelihood that the bicycle manufacturer will interact with another industry (e.g., an electric motor manufacturer) to combine resources. The combination of resources could produce totally new products (e.g., electric mopeds, or perhaps electric gear-and-chain winches). *The presence of redundancy and multitasking allows, under the right circumstances, for the self-organization of novelty as well as complexity.*

Artificial Life

The economy is not a perfect example of self-organized complexity because the agents who interact are human beings, not automatons. Humans are intelligent and (sometimes) make intelligent decisions about how to interact with each other. However, automaton agent-interaction can be implemented or simulated with computer programs.[7] This leads to a new area of research known as artificial life.

Most research on artificial life is done on computers.[8] Computer program "agents" exist in a virtual environment. They interact randomly with the environment and, in some cases, with each other. Interactions that increase productivity or survivability are retained for the next iteration, while random

---

7. A simple model for such interactions, along with mathematical analysis, is given by Barbara Drossel, "Simple Model for the Formation of a Complex Organism," *Physical Review Letters* 82 (21 June 1999): 5144-47.

8. A good source for web links on artificial life research is http://www.alcyone.com/max/links/alife.html. See also Steven Levy, *Artificial Life* (New York: Pantheon Books, 1992).

new ones are tried. In many artificial life programs, evolutionary algorithms are used that allow the agents themselves to evolve from generation to generation.

Some artificial life programs, like the maze-navigator, increase in complexity but not novelty. In the maze-navigator, each instruction in the "genome" has a one-to-one correspondence with behavior (move up, down, right, or left). There is no redundancy or multitasking. Other artificial life programs do show the evolution of novelty. In some programs, the novelty arises from interaction among the agents. If the rules are structured properly, a complex interlocking web of agent interactions will eventually self-organize. In other artificial life programs, a *single* program can evolve novelty. This happens when the instructions in the "genome" of the program use redundancy and multitasking. Redundancy: certain behaviors (e.g., reproduction) can be achieved by many different combinations of instructions. Multitasking: any particular instruction of the genome can be incorporated into several different behaviors (e.g., exploration, digestion, reproduction) depending upon the context. In these sorts of programs, novel behaviors can evolve.[9]

As we've already noted, there are multiple strategies for self-organizing complexity. No single artificial life program demonstrates all of them. No artificial life program perfectly mimics biological life. Artificial life programs are, however, useful tools for increasing our insight into the capabilities and limitations of self-organization.

Self-Organization and the History of Life

Scientific evidence suggests that self-organized complexity — in one form or another — is a regular feature of the history of the universe.

Shortly after the Big Bang, the universe was a fairly uniform place. One portion of it looked much like every other portion of it. Over the next 10 billion years, through the operation of natural laws and random events, the universe became a much more complicated place. Now it contains white-hot stars and cold interstellar nebulas, dense neutron stars and sparse intergalactic voids. Out of all the different kinds of atoms that exist today, only hydrogen and helium were present in any appreciable quantities during the first few minutes after the Big Bang. All the rest — including carbon, oxygen, and other atoms necessary for life — self-organized over the subsequent billions of years through fusion in stellar cores and supernovas. One particularly interesting part of the universe,

9. One example is Tom S. Ray's "Tierra" artificial life program, which can be found at http://dlife.annexia.org and http://www.santafe.edu/~smfr/tierra/intro.html.

for us, is the self-organization out of interstellar dust of a yellow star and a planet with a rocky crust, liquid water, an atmosphere, and a wide variety of atoms and simple organic molecules on its surface. The young planet earth was a complex environment compared to the early universe. It seems remarkable to us that the laws of nature are so finely tuned as to cause the self-assembly of all these things — stars and planets and atoms and liquid water and simple organic molecules — self-assembly of the perfect environment for biological life to begin. Yet the scientific evidence indicates that this is exactly what happened.

The next step in the history of life is the least understood — the formation of first life. In the complex environment of the young planet earth, with its liquid water and atmosphere and rocky surfaces and steady influx of energy, is it possible that simple organic molecules could self-organize into a living, reproducing organism? Given our current scientific understanding, it is far too premature to definitely answer either yes or no. There are many hypotheses for how first life might self-assemble on the early earth. All of these hypotheses are still speculative. The most widely accepted hypothesis is a multistep process something like this: First, in the right environment (hypotheses include underwater thermal vents, shallow surface ponds, sandy beaches, volcanic craters, clay deposits, and weathered feldspar), simple organic molecules concentrated and self-assembled into strings of nucleic and amino acids (RNA and proteins). Second, when enough of these molecules were concentrated together, they formed an interacting auto-catalytic system that jointly catalyzed their mutual reproduction.[10] Third, these RNA-and-protein catalytic systems evolved, with RNA and eventually DNA taking on the role of information storage, which we see in all living cells today.

---

10. Stuart A. Kauffman (*The Origins of Order: Self-Organization and Selection in Evolution* [New York: Oxford University Press, 1993], p. 285), writes, ". . . this new view, which is based on the discovery of an expected phase transition from a collection of polymers which do not reproduce themselves to a slightly more complex collection of polymers which do jointly catalyze their own reproduction. In this theory of the origin of life, it is not necessary that any molecule reproduce itself. Rather, a collection of molecules has the property that the last step in the formation of each molecule is catalyzed by some molecule in the system. The phase transition occurs when some critical complexity level of molecular diversity is surpassed. At that critical level, the ratio of reactions among the polymers to the number of polymers in the system passes a critical value, and a connected web of catalyzed reactions linking the polymers arises and spans the molecular species in the system. This web constitutes the crystallization of catalytic closure such that the system of polymers becomes collectively self reproducing . . . [this new body of theory] is also robust in leading to a fundamental new conclusion: Molecular systems, in principle, can both reproduce and evolve without having a genome in the familiar sense of a template-replicating molecular species." See also Stuart A. Kauffman, *At Home in the Universe: The Search for Laws of Self-Organization and Complexity* (New York: Oxford University Press, 1995), and idem, *Investigations* (New York: Oxford University Press, 2000).

Once first life is in place, the role of self-organized complexity is much better understood — although far from completely understood — in biological evolution. We know of several evolutionary mechanisms that increase the size of a cell's genome (e.g., gene duplication, horizontal transfer, polyploidy, endosymbiont capture). Combined with natural selection, this allows information transfer from the environment to the cell's genome. In addition, the genomes of living organisms display redundancy and multitasking, allowing for the evolution of novelty and interlocking complexity.

Known Evolutionary Mechanisms

Gene Duplication

One of the remarkable results of modern biochemistry, molecular biology, and molecular genetics is the finding that there are large gene families and superfamilies. Examples are: the globins (oxygen binding and transport), the serine proteases (digestion and blood clotting), the immunoglobulins (immune response), protein kinases (cell signaling), the myosins, dyneins, and kinesins (cell motility), the G-protein family (cell signaling), cell surface receptors (cell signaling), various classes of DNA binding proteins, and the nucleotide binding domain of many glycolytic and citric acid cycle enzymes. Many more could be listed. The simplest explanation for the existence of these gene families is the phenomenon known as gene duplication.

Gene duplication is caused by a replication error where a segment of DNA is replicated again when a recently synthesized segment of DNA is separated from the template, loops out, and binds again to the template at the beginning of the duplicated segment (see figure 1). Duplication events can also be caused by the insertion of mRNAs into the DNA, or by the action of transposable elements or viruses that replicate the DNA and insert it into other places in the genome. If a functional gene is duplicated, then mutation events can occur on the duplicated (nonfunctional) copy and differences can be produced. These mutated duplicated genes, if expressed, may result in slightly different and more specialized functions than the original gene. Perhaps, a single gene coded for a protein that had a general multipurpose function. Once a gene duplication event occurred, each copy of the gene would be subject to a mutation/selection process that would result in both genes producing proteins with more specialized functions.

A detailed proposal for the evolution of the globin family is found in the chapter "Biochemistry and Evolution." In that example, the myoglobin gene ap-

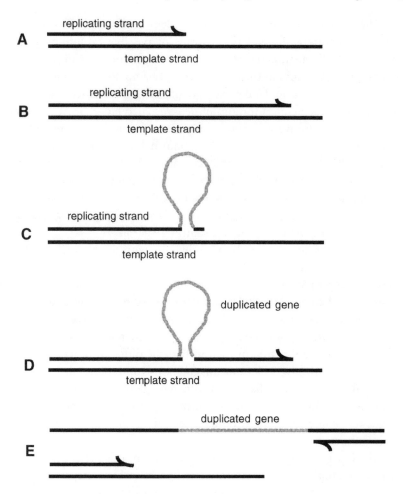

Figure 1. A possible mechanism for gene duplication. (A) Normal replication of DNA where a replicating strand is coded for by a template strand. (B) A segment of DNA is synthesized. (C) The recently synthesized segment loops off the template and rebinds to the template at the end of the loop. (D) The region already replicated in the loop is resynthesized. (E) In the next generation, the duplicated region of DNA is fully replicated on both strands. The original template strand and its next generation replicated strand will not contain the duplicated region.

pears to be the most ancient. Gene duplications appear to have produced the more specialized hemoglobin subunits that result in a new function (oxygen transport) and increased complexity (allosteric effects and cooperative binding). The existence of fetal globins and other variants with slightly different oxygen-binding properties of functional importance is further evidence of this process.

The globin story can be pressed a bit further (and a bit more speculatively) to illustrate additional mechanisms of possible evolutionary significance. Sickle-cell anemia is caused by a single amino acid substitution (glutamic acid to valine) in the beta subunit of hemoglobin. Valine is a hydrophobic (oily) amino acid. Under the high globin concentrations of red blood cells and low oxygen concentrations of deoxygenated blood, the beta subunits stick together and form a new macromolecular structure (the hemoglobin S fiber) that causes red blood cells to adopt abnormal shapes. These oddly shaped red blood cells block blood flow and cause the anemia. The mutant hemoglobin appears to be advantageous in malaria-affected populations. A possible explanation is that the oddly shaped red blood cells have a shorter lifespan, preventing the microorganism that causes malaria from going through its full life cycle, thus making the individual resistant to malaria.

Now for the speculation. In an individual with the hemoglobin S gene, the hemoglobin produced has two functions — one is the normal cooperative oxygen-binding function in the hemoglobin heterodimer; the other is as the subunit of the hemoglobin S fiber that deforms red blood cells and causes the shorter cell lifespan. If a gene duplication event resulted in two copies of this gene, then the two functions could be separated with mutation/selection subsequently refining the function of each so that the different functions could be regulated appropriately. To let our imaginations run even further afield, suppose that the existence of cells packed with hemoglobin S fibers provided some interesting new function for the organism — perhaps some novel structural cell type that conferred some advantage upon the organism with that new cell type.

The last paragraph is simply my imagination. But the process is highly plausible. A simple mutation (in this case known to have occurred) confers a new structure (and perhaps a new function) on the organism. Gene duplication followed by further mutation/selection results in a new structure and function. This scenario is a key answer to the conundrum expressed in Michael Behe's book *Darwin's Black Box* when he lays out the difficulty of evolving molecular machines. Preadaptations or exaptations are preexisting structures or behaviors that are put to a novel use in a new context, either in a new environment or in the presence of other previously absent structures. Gene duplication removes the constraint of the original function and allows for the novel use to be improved upon by normal Darwinian mutation and selection mechanisms. The existence of gene families as described above suggests that this process has been at work in generating much of the diverse functionality of modern organisms.

The globin family evolution described above produced novelty through the process of gene duplication alone. Simple oxygen binding was converted to cooperative oxygen transport and malarial resistance through gene duplication with mutation and selection. But what if the duplicated gene has an interaction with other already existing cell components (perhaps themselves also being produced by duplicated genes)? Possibly because of the way biology and biochemistry textbooks are organized, we tend to think of cell components as being as compartmentalized as the chapters in this book. Granted, there is significant compartmentalization in cells, especially in eukaryotic cells. However, we must recognize that all of these parts are in a complex mixture of proteins, nucleic acids, metabolites, metabolic precursors, and so forth. Thus there are all sorts of opportunities for proteins to come into contact with other proteins in novel arrangements. With some incipient function and gene duplication they can proceed via Darwinian mechanisms to produce highly specialized interactions. Here are a couple of examples. These are examples based solely on the notion of gene duplication (the existence of gene families) and of components combining in new ways to give new functions. Apart from more detailed comparative biochemistry and genetics, I cannot tell which structures and functions are the original and more primitive structures and functions, and which are the novel and derived structures and functions. Perhaps the vast amount of genome data from the major biological groups will shed some light on that in the near future.

Cilia are cell surface organelles that either create cellular movement or move fluids over the cell surface. Are there any components of the cilia that function in other parts of the cell in ways that could have been preadapted? The answer is an obvious yes. Tubulin and its assembled macrostructure, microtubules, function in many other ways than in cilia. Microtubules are involved in cell structure and in mediating vesicle movement and chromosome movements during mitosis. In addition, there is the microtubule-associated motor protein dynein. There are cytoplasmic dyneins and kinesins that function as motors moving chromosomes, vesicles, and organelles along microtubule tracks. It seems to me that a cytoplasmic microtubule with a cytoplasmic motor protein is an incipient cilia. We don't even have to use much evolutionary imagination to come up with that. It seems very plausible that the various ciliar components could have arisen independently, selected for other purposes, and that a primitive cilia function could have arisen from a novel assembly of those already existing components. Gene duplication of some of the component genes would have produced versions of the components that could be improved by mutation and selection. All of the motor proteins described above are part of the same gene family.

The biochemistry of vision provides us with another example. Behe has argued that the vision system is also an irreducibly complex system (nonevolvable complexity using the distinctions previously discussed). Does preadaptation get us anywhere in the discussion of the origin of vision? Again, the answer is an obvious yes. First, if we restrict ourselves to light reception, then I think that it's fair to say that a nerve cell is a preadaptation to vision. Given a nerve cell, I don't have to explain where all those components come from (at least when explaining vision). Second, transducin, one of the key proteins involved in the light signal transduction from rhodopsin to nerve cell, is a member of the G protein family, a large family involved in all sorts of signal transduction events, including hormone signaling. The main novel feature of transducin is its specificity for rhodopsin. The generic G protein is a preadaptation for transducin. Finally, rhodopsin, the main light reception protein, is a membrane protein similar in structure to other sensory receptors and to hormone receptors. These other receptors whose physiological effects are also mediated by G proteins may have been preadaptations for rhodopsin. Since all of these components are members of large gene families, it seems plausible that gene duplication was involved here too. Gene duplication plus mutation and selection in the context of the incipient function produced by an interaction of all these components already present could account for the novel function.

Production of Novel Combinations

Novel combinations of cellular components can be produced in several ways. Sexual reproduction involving chromosome shuffling and recombination generates novel combinations of components that can result in novel structures and selectable functions. Some biologists think that this ability to produce novelty by recombination is one of the reasons for which sexual reproduction was selected. Artificial life experiments have suggested that large jumps in fitness can occur when novel combinations of several characters exist in the same "organism" due to normal genetic exchange mechanisms. These characteristics were useful in their own right but in combination with others, perhaps several others, produced a novel combination that was even more valuable. Once the novel combination exists and a selectable function exists, then normal mutation and selection mechanisms can operate. Perhaps the original vision systems arose in this way as described previously. Each component was a functional member of a previously existing system, but never existed in the same system together. Through various exchanges of genetic information, recombination or otherwise, these components all function together to form the primordial vision system. Darwinian mechanisms can now operate to "perfect" that system.

Notice that the original selectable system arose by a non-Darwinian mechanism. In my opinion, this is the simple and decisive blow against Behe's nonevolvable irreducible complexity.

Novelty is produced in other ways as well. These can be grouped together under the headings of horizontal or lateral gene transfer. Normal exchange of genetic information in sexually reproducing organisms occurs from parent to progeny through mechanisms that occur during meiosis involving shuffling of the chromosomes and genetic recombination. In bacterial conjugation genetic material is replicated and transmitted from one bacterial cell to another, and then through genetic recombination it forms novel combinations. Such exchanges are intraspecies, that is, the genetic information is exchanged between members of the same species. Horizontal or lateral gene transfer involves the exchange of genetic information between different species. This has been observed to occur via mobile genetic elements such as plasmids, transposons, viruses, Drosophila P elements, and so forth. Even naked DNA is known to be taken up by cells. Novel functional genes or even novel biochemical machines or systems coded for by one of these mobile genetic elements can be introduced into a new biological context. While the incorporation of a novel function all at once via this mechanism is important and a possible way that novelty was propagated once it occurred, there are also the unpredictable consequences of such novelty encountering the new context in the cell or organism incorporating that new genetic information. Such new combinations of structures and functions could generate new assemblies with new, although perhaps very primitive, functions that could be subsequently improved upon by Darwinian mechanisms.

The bacterial flagellum is a complex, biochemical machine that somewhat defies the imagination when trying to imagine an evolutionary pathway for its origin. Yet recent studies of certain pathogenic bacteria by Jorge E. Galan and Alan Colmer have uncovered a possible pathway.[11] The type III secretion system delivers bacterial proteins into "host" cells that have been infected by the bacterium. These bacterial proteins modulate host cellular processes and consequently regulate the nature of the bacterial-host cell interaction. While the biochemistry of this system is fascinating in its own right, the main relevance for our present discussion is that several components of this system are similar and belong to the same gene family as components of the bacterial flagellar system. Galan and Colmer note:

11. Jorge E. Galan and Alan Colmer, "Type III Secretion Machines: Bacterial Devices for Protein Delivery into Host Cells," *Science* 284 (21 May 1999): 1322-28.

Gram-negative pathogenic bacteria most likely acquired their type III secretion systems through some mechanism of horizontal gene transfer. This is supported by the observation that these systems are often encoded in extra chromosomal elements or within pathogenicity islands, which are segments of chromosomal DNA that are absent from related nonpathogenic bacteria. These islands often have a GC content that deviates from that of the chromosome of the host organism, and they are usually bounded by remnants of insertion sequences, bacteriophage genes, or transposable elements.[12]

The authors speculate that these systems evolved as an evolutionary adaptation of the flagellar export apparatus. But it is also conceivable that the flagellar system is an evolutionary adaptation of this secretion system. If the latter is the case, then a plausible scenario is that a horizontal gene transfer event resulted in the type III secretion system components being placed in a biochemical context where additional components already present for other functions could be utilized in novel ways such as a flagellum. Even if the type III secretion system is a modification of the flagellar system, it still illustrates the main point that via horizontal gene transfer and/or gene duplication novel functions can be generated from already existing components.

As more and more DNA sequences of bacterial genomes are determined, the assumption that there is a simple phylogenetic tree connecting the organisms is clearly wrong. Molecular evolutionists studying bacterial phylogenies no longer talk about a single common ancestor, a single trunk from which the whole tree branches.[13] Different phylogenies are produced depending on the proteins or genes whose sequences are being compared. It appears that there has been a lot more interspecies transfer of genetic information than heretofore expected. We are now talking about a tangled web of life rather than a simple bush or tree. This perhaps is the single best evidence for the existence and importance of horizontal or lateral gene transfer. When coupled with the known biological processes previously mentioned, this explanation becomes extremely plausible. Perhaps early in the evolution of life such mechanisms of genetic information transfer were easier and the genome was much more fluid. The comparative genetics done so far seems to suggest that this is the case.

An extreme version of horizontal or lateral gene transfer is found in the endosymbiont capture theory that explains in part the origin of the complex

12. Galan and Colmer, "Type III Secretion Machines," p. 1323.
13. W. Ford Doolittle, "Phylogenetic Classification and the Universal Tree," *Science* 284 (25 June 1999): 2124-28; idem, "Lateral Genomics," *Trends in Biochemical Science* 24 (December 1999): M5-M8.

eukaryotic cell. The proposal is that the primitive eukaryote became a host to various prokaryotic organisms and that this symbiotic relationship stabilized in subsequent evolution. The symbiotic origin of mitochondria and chloroplasts from primitive bacteria and blue-green algae has nearly universal acceptance. Mitochondria and chloroplasts have their own DNA and reproduce themselves autonomously from the "host" cell. Their genomes and some of their biochemical structures and processes (e.g., the ribosome) are more similar to bacteria and blue-green algae, respectively, than to the cells in which they are contained. An excellent discussion of this idea is found in *Tracing the History of Eukaryotic Cells: The Enigmatic Smile* by Betsey D. Dyer and Robert Alan Obar, two students of Lynn Margulis, who originally proposed the theory.[14] Attempts to account for the origin of other features of eukaryotes, such as motility systems, in terms of symbiosis have met with less success. Again, the incorporation of oxidative phosphorylation and photosynthesis into the primitive eukaryote is the major consequence of this landmark evolutionary event. But, as the host and symbiont interact with each other in new ways, even more novelty can be generated. Additional mechanisms for the generation of novelty include changes in the level and location of the expression of certain genes, "old" proteins taking on new functions, exon shuffling (which is a permutation of the gene duplication idea), and new macromolecular assemblies being formed from "old" proteins. These and other mechanisms and patterns for the generation of novelty are discussed in John Gerhart and Marc Kirschner, *Cells, Embryos, and Evolution.*[15]

The concept of emergence is central to this discussion and is illustrated by several of the examples that have been discussed. Much attention has been given to this concept in the philosophy of biology arena.[16] A simple phrase that summarizes the idea is that the whole is more than the sum of the parts. The complex system has properties that are not predictable from the component parts, and those properties are dependent on the presences of all of the component parts. Several of the examples that we have discussed illustrate this idea. The cooperative oxygen binding of hemoglobin is an emergent property. An alpha subunit or a beta subunit in isolation binds oxygen much like myoglobin — tight binding that is released only at very low oxygen concentrations. When

14. Betsey D. Dyer and Robert Alan Obar, *Tracing the History of Eukaryotic Cells: The Enigmatic Smile* (New York: Columbia University Press, 1994).

15. John Gerhart and Marc Kirschner, *Cells, Embryos, and Evolution: Toward a Cellular and Developmental Understanding of Phenotypic Variation and Evolutionary Adaptability* (Malden, Mass.: Blackwell Science, 1997).

16. Francisco Jose Ayala and Theodosius Dobzhansky, eds., *Studies in the Philosophy of Biology: Reduction and Related Problems* (Berkeley: University of California Press, 1974).

alpha/beta dimerization and dimerization of alpha/beta dimers to form tetramers occur, cooperativity of oxygen binding emerges. The oxygen binding of the hemoglobin tetramer also becomes subject to regulation by a variety of effector molecules: carbon dioxide, 2, 3-bisphosphoglycerate, and hydrogen ion. This biochemical example is a simple illustration of the idea. Several crucial points are illustrated, however. First, hemoglobin functions as a whole, and its function can be discussed without reference to the component parts. We speak of the hemoglobin molecule with its oxygen-binding behavior and the way various effectors interact with it. Second, there is nothing mystical or mysterious about this idea of emergence. The physical-chemical basis for the macromolecular assembly is reasonably well understood, as are the specifics of the interactions that lead to the emergent properties. Nonetheless, these properties are properties of the whole and can be utilized in higher order systems and discussed with little or no reference to the components.

One of the simplest examples of emergent properties involves phospholipid molecules in aqueous medium. Given the physical-chemical properties of the phospholipid molecules and of water, these molecules will spontaneously form bilayers with the oily phospholipid tails pointing toward the inside of the bilayer and the polar phosphoglyceryl head pointing toward the outside of the bilayer toward the water. These bilayers will circle around upon themselves to form vesicles — a spherical bilayer with an aqueous interior and an aqueous exterior. What has emerged? There are now an *inside,* an *outside,* and a membrane separating the two. None of this makes sense in terms of phospholipids or water molecules. It is only with the assembly that we can speak of the emergent properties of inside and outside. Again, we can speak of the whole vesicle with these properties with no concern for the component parts. And again, we see nothing mystical or mysterious. The existence of the whole is readily explained by the component parts, but, nonetheless, there are novel properties at the higher level of organization.

The idea of emergent phenomenon extends much beyond biomolecular assemblies. Cells themselves can be viewed as complex assemblies with emergent properties. While much (although not everything) is known about the constituent parts of cells and how they operate at a physical-chemical level, cells function as foundational wholes in biological contexts. There is a level of organization and complexity that is oblivious to the underlying composition of the whole. The patterns and behaviors that exist at that higher level of organization and complexity are unique. As such they demand theories and explanation that are appropriate for that level. This is why biologists spend very little time talking about quarks. Such relationships among parts and wholes are common throughout biology. For example, organisms are wholes made of component parts, but they behave as wholes and interact with other things as wholes. The same could be said of populations and ecosystems. These sorts of relationships are not unique to biology and exist in the physical sciences, psychology, economics, politics, and so forth. In every case, interacting components or agents give rise to novel structures, functions, or behaviors that are structures, functions, or behaviors of the whole.

One of the consequences of this relationship between parts and wholes is that emergent phenomena look as if each component was specifically positioned to play its particular role, that is, as if it was designed to interact with other components in specified ways. But the whole is always irreducible. In biological assemblies, where mutation and selection have acted to optimize the interactions, the design inference may even be stronger. Here is a crude analogy. Imagine a pile of rocks of lots of different sizes formed by some avalanche. Then through wind, water, or other kinds of weathering, all the loose rocks are removed. What is left standing is the tightly knit complex structure where every piece is essential to the structural integrity of the whole. It might even appear as if all the rocks were carefully placed to give the final sturdy structure, that is, that the whole structure was designed. In the analogy, the parts are the individual rocks; the whole is the intact final structure. Interestingly, all of the original rock pile was essential for the original structure to form, but in the final structure some of the parts necessary for its formation are missing. There is a sense, given this scenario, that one cannot determine how the rock structure formed in detail.

The application to the origin of novel molecular structure might be as follows. Molecules present in the cell for other functions assemble in a fashion determined by simple physical-chemical interactions such as those described in the hemoglobin dimerization or the phospholipid bilayer. You might imagine this to be our pile of rocks. Given enough different interacting molecules and the right interacting molecules, a new primitive function might emerge from this assembly. Once the new function has emerged, mutation and selection operate to remove the loose and unnecessary pieces and to fine-tune the interactions. In the end each component plays an essential role, and each component is structurally and functionally interconnected with all the others; in other words, the system has become irreducibly complex. As with the rock formation, there is a sense that one cannot determine in detail how the molecular assembly formed.

The single most perplexing feature of modern organisms pertaining to the origin of life may be the best evidence for the proposal outlined above that life originated as an interacting auto-catalytic system. Life is a complex web of interactions where proteins are required for nucleic acid synthesis and nucleic acids are required for protein synthesis. Similarly, the metabolites that fuel it are the synthetic precursors for protein and nucleic acid synthesis, yet they require proteins for their own synthesis. Origin of life investigators have had a difficult time envisioning a proteins-only solution. The RNA world scenario has fared somewhat better, but it is not clear how proteins get integrated. The replicating closed auto-catalytic system described by Stuart A. Kaufmann has the advantage that the complex web of interactions is built in from the outset. In essence, this view acknowledges irreducible complexity, that is, the system has to be sufficiently complex in order for auto-catalytic behavior to emerge. There is no stepwise evolution of this emergent property; it suddenly appears (as with all emergent properties) once the polymer complexity has achieved the threshold level. Thus, the system is complex and whole from the start. Indeed this is what living systems appear to be.

Self-Organization, Design, and Miracles

We started this chapter by asking these questions: Did God design the laws of nature so that biological evolution is limited to making small-scale changes in species? Or did God design the laws of nature so that biological evolution could, through its ordinary operation, bring about gradual increases in biological complexity and novelty?

We have seen that complexity can self-organize by a variety of strategies. Computer programs allow us to investigate what sorts of properties are necessary for complexity to self-organize. Living organisms and biological evolution seem to have those properties. We also have seen some specific biological examples where there is good genetic evidence that complexity did, in fact, evolve.

Human beings are clever enough to devise systems in which complexity self-organizes, and the scientific evidence suggests that God has chosen to use self-organized complexity for at least *some* of cosmological and biological history. But does this prove that God used natural mechanisms to create *all* forms of biological complexity? Does this mean that God *never* miraculously superseded evolution during biological history? Of course not. The jury is still out on that question.

Only within the last few years have biologists mapped out the entire genetic sequence of a handful of species. Within a few more decades, we will probably map the genetic sequences of many species. Even then, we will have only begun the work of understanding the capabilities and limits of evolution. In order to know whether or not some complex piece of biological machinery could have evolved, we must not only know each species' genetic sequences, but also understand in great detail how gene products interact with each other in living cells. As biologists learn more, they might eventually discover that there are some, or even many, complex biological systems for which there are no plausible evolutionary scenarios. As biologists learn more, they might eventually discover that there is no plausible scenario for natural mechanisms to self-assemble even the simplest of living cells. As biologists learn more, they might also come to the opposite conclusions. In the meantime, it is premature to say for certain whether God used evolution to produce all known biological complexity, or if God superseded evolution in a few or many cases. We still have much to learn about the wonders of God's creation and God's creativity.

Some Christians study the complexity of modern life and hope to find there, in that complexity, proof that the natural mechanisms of evolution are not enough. They hope to use this as evidence for God's existence and miraculous intervention in biological history. Other Christians study the complexity of modern life and have a very different reaction. They are excited by the fact that God has created a universe where, under the right conditions, complexity can self-organize via the natural mechanisms that God designed and governs.

For us, as we consider the evidence from cosmological history that God used natural processes to form galaxies, stars, planets, and the atoms necessary for life; as we consider the evidence that God used natural processes in geological history to form the earth's atmosphere, ocean, dry land, and simple organic molecules; as we consider the evidence from biological history and consider the incredible array of evolutionary mechanisms which we already know that God has created and uses; it seems most promising — both scientifically and theologically — to study biological complexity expecting to find more evidence that God designed into it the ability to self-organize.

III THEOLOGICAL IMPLICATIONS AND INSIGHT

14 Is the Universe Capable of Evolving?

HOWARD J. VAN TILL

One Doctrine, Many Portraits

Let's be candid. We Christians disagree about a lot of things. We disagree about matters of doctrine, about issues of gender and sexuality, about political agendas and social programs, and, yes, even about our styles of worship. We have split the "church universal" into thousands of denominational fragments — each tempted to see itself as the one with the clearest vision of *true* Christianity.

One particular disagreement provides the occasion for this book. Christians have not been able to agree on their evaluation of the scientific concept of evolution. Some see this concept as one that is clearly and forcefully forbidden by scriptural teaching. Others see it as something on which the Bible is silent, an idea that will have to be evaluated on its scientific merits alone. Some see the evolutionary paradigm as an unwelcome threat to cherished Christian doctrines, while others welcome it as a stimulus to rearticulate historic Christian theology in light of what the sciences have learned about the Creation.[1]

But these differences in judgment regarding a scientific concept need to be seen in the larger context of agreement on one of the fundamentals of the Christian faith. In spite of the great diversity of their perspectives on numerous other issues, Christians generally agree in seeing the universe as a *Creation* — that is, as something that has being only because *God gives it being.* Furthermore, the universe is a Creation not merely because God acted as its Creator at some first moment of time, but because the universe is equally dependent on God's functioning as its Creator *at all times.* I have often suggested that the historic Judeo-Christian doctrine of creation is better summarized by saying that

---

1. I choose to capitalize the word "Creation" whenever it is used as the proper name of the universe to which God has given being.

the universe is God's Creation than by saying that *the universe was created by God*. The Creator/Creation relationship is equally important at every moment of time.

Disagreements among Christians do arise, however, when we reflect on the particular character of the Creation and the details of its formational history. We may agree on the theologically rich *doctrine* of creation, but we disagree on what constitutes an acceptable *portrait* of the universe's formational history — a what-happened-and-when account of the particular way in which the diversity of physical structures and life forms in the Creation became actualized in the course of time. All Christians are *theological* creationists, but the Christian community has long entertained an interesting diversity of portraits of the Creation's formational history. One of the purposes of this book is to offer the reader a portrait that has been informed by the *scientific* study of the universe — a systematic investigation that has been enriched by ideas contributed by numerous scientists, including a large number of scientists who are committed to seeing the universe as the manifestation of divine creativity and generosity.

If the Universe Is a Creation, Then . . .

For the remainder of this chapter I will direct my comments primarily to Christians who are, for one reason or another, uncomfortable with the word *evolution* or with the scientific concept that it represents. In North America a fairly large number of people fall into this category. A strident shouting match known as the creation/evolution debate has raged here for decades. Christians have been told by parents, friends, teachers, and preachers that evolution is the enemy of the Christian faith. Evolution has been blamed for nearly every evil found in human culture. Antievolution sentiment is as prevalent today as it ever was.

So, let's drop the focus on evolution for a moment and direct our attention instead to the concept of the world as a Creation. If the universe is a Creation, as Christians hold, then what might it be like? What might be the fundamental character of a Creation, and what kind of formational history might follow from that character? My concern to pay attention to the Creation's *formational history* is obviously occasioned by the creation/evolution debate and the religious and educational turmoil that it has spawned.

I suggest that step one in our quest for a faith-enriching concept of the Creation's character should be a simple reminder that if the universe is a Creation, then every aspect of its *being* — every contribution to what the universe *is* — must be seen as something that was intentionally given to it by its Creator. Whatever qualities the universe now possesses were, we theological creationists believe, given to it by God. Furthermore, by the same reasoning, whatever qualities the universe does *not* possess were intentionally withheld from it. The particular character of the universe is, from this perspective, the product of *conceptual design* — that is, of the Creator's *intentional and purposeful choice* to give it precisely the kind of character (or being) that it now has.

Can we fully apprehend the Creator's intentions and purposes? Surely it would be the height of human arrogance to claim that we could. So, let's focus for now on another matter that is highly relevant to current discussion regarding "design" — the need to distinguish between the *designing* (purposeful planning) of something and the *actualizing* (forming, constructing, or assembling) of what was first designed.[2]

In today's language, to *design* something is to *thoughtfully conceptualize* something — a piece of furniture, an automobile, a computer, a house, a painting — *for the purpose of accomplishing some objective.* Design, here considered as an action, is *an act of the creative and purposeful mind.* The action of designing involves many stages of thinking — formulating an objective, conceptualizing various means of achieving that objective, evaluating the relative merits of possible means, and selecting one particular plan and strategy, to name just a few of those thought processes.

Some of that design action will necessarily be concerned with the manner in which the designed entity will eventually become actualized (that is, transformed from a mental concept into an actual object). For instance, the design team for a new truck will be keen to consider just what parts must be crafted and how those component parts will then be assembled into a complete vehicle. Nonetheless, the process of *designing* the truck — an action of minds — is wholly distinct from the process of *assembling* it — an action of "hands." And the fact that the assembly line employs both human hands and the mechanical "hands" of computer-controlled robots does not alter or diminish the distinction of mind action (designing) from hand action (forming and assembling parts into a completed vehicle).

From here on, therefore, if we refer in this chapter to the universe as having been *designed*, we will be referring specifically to its having been *thought-*

---

2. I draw attention to the need for this distinction for a particular reason. The activity of the modern Intelligent Design movement has led to a resurgence in questioning whether or not there is empirical evidence for the idea that the universe, or some particular feature of living organisms, was "intelligently designed." It is my judgment that reflection on this question has the potential to be fruitful, but only if the distinction between *planning* and *assembling* is studiously maintained.

fully conceptualized by the Creator for the accomplishment of the Creator's objectives. And when we talk about the manner in which the various physical structures and life forms became *actualized* in the course of time, we will be addressing a *distinctly different concern.* Questions about the details of the Creation's formational history are questions about the actualization of forms within a designed universe. To be as explicit as we are able, when we as Christians entertain the possibility that the formational history of the universe is evolutionary in character, we are *not* questioning the fact that the Creation was conceptually designed. Rather, we are simply evaluating one way in which the various physical structures and life forms may have been actualized in time. Any discussion of design and actualization that fails to make this distinction between planning and assembling is sure to generate time-wasting confusion. More seriously, it could lead to unnecessary division within the Christian family and to a weakening of its witness to the scientific community.

To summarize the discussion so far: If the universe is a Creation, then every aspect of its *being* — every contribution to what the universe *is* — must be seen as something intentionally given to it by its Creator. If we are interested in reflecting on the Creation's formational history we will be eager to grow in our knowledge of the formational processes that may have contributed to the actualization of the Creator's intention for the appearance of new forms in the course of time. With what "formational gifts" did the Creator equip the Creation? Specifically, is the Creation gifted with the requisite formational resources to make evolutionary development possible? *Is this Creation, by divine intention, capable of evolving?*

Taking Inventory of the Creation's Formational Resources

To get to the heart of questions regarding the possibility of an evolving Creation I find it helpful to introduce and employ some new terminology. One such term is the *formational economy* of the universe. Before defining it, however, let me suggest that the reader prepare by setting aside all associations of the word "economy" with thrift or frugality. Think instead of such concepts as the global *economy* or the European *economy* — vast systems of resources and capabilities that contribute to the activities of production, commerce, and exchange.

> Definition: The *formational economy* of the universe is the set of all of the resources, potentialities, and capabilities of the universe that have contributed to its formational history.

Let me provide a bit of clarification for three particular terms used in this definition. (1) By *resources* I mean such entities as the interactive fundamental particles of matter that occupy the universe and the dynamic space-time context in which they function. (2) By *potentialities* I mean the possibilities for functional physical structures (such as atoms, molecules, stars, or planets) and for viable living organisms. (3) By *capabilities* I mean to call attention especially to the universe's abilities for organizing or transforming its resources in such a way as to actualize some of its structural and formal potentialities.

This may still seem like a rather abstract concept. So, to give the reader a better idea of what this new term — the universe's *formational economy* — means and to see how it might be useful, let me offer a few examples of the resources, potentialities, and capabilities that I have in mind. In each case I will also provide illustrations of the manner in which they are thought to have contributed to the formational history of the physical universe. Physicists tend to see the world of matter as a hierarchy of structures that are made up of more elementary units or subassemblies. An iceberg, for instance, is a massive structure made mostly of water *molecules*. Water molecules, in turn, are tiny structures made of *atoms* — two of hydrogen and one of oxygen. But atoms are themselves structures composed of *atomic nuclei* surrounded by *electrons* in patterned motion around them. Atomic nuclei are also structures, made up of "nucleons" of two kinds — *protons* and *neutrons*. Even protons and neutrons are now known to be structures built of elementary particles called *quarks*. The scientific investigation of the universe's formational history is concerned to find out how these various structural systems came to be assembled.

As envisioned within the scientific portrait of the universe's early formational history, there was a very brief period of time during which no particles of any form of matter were able to exist. The temperature was simply too high and only *photons* — elementary units of lightlike energy — could survive. But photons have the remarkable capability to transform their energy into pairs of material particles. As the expanding early universe cooled, this process of *pair production* led to the formation of several species of particles, including quarks and the three-quark structures that we call protons and neutrons. Expressing this in our new formational economy vocabulary, here is what took place: photons of lightlike energy (playing the role of *resources* within the universe's formational economy) exercised their capacity for pair production (an example of a *formational capability*) to materialize particles like quarks and nucleons (thereby actualizing for the first time what had earlier been only *potential structures*). As participants in the *formational economy* of the universe, *resources* employed their formational *capabilities* to actualize *potentialities*.

Following this brief era (a small fraction of a second) during which protons and neutrons were formed by pair production, there was a longer period (about a minute, according to calculation) during which smaller particles like electrons were actualized in a similar manner. (Many more varieties of particles were also produced, but we need focus only on protons, neutrons, and electrons for now.) During the next several minutes protons and neutrons engaged in another remarkably constructive process. These nucleons — themselves the products of pair production — have capabilities for interacting and combining to assemble larger atomic nuclei by a process called *thermonuclear fusion*. Protons are the nuclei of hydrogen atoms. The interaction of hydrogen nuclei and neutrons can, in the right circumstances, lead to the formation of helium nuclei composed of two protons and two neutrons. During a ten to fifteen minute period following the pair production era, conditions throughout the young universe were correct for the occurrence of a thermonuclear fusion process in which about one-fourth of the hydrogen present was transformed into helium. Once again, *resources* (protons and neutrons) exercised their *formational capabilities* (in the thermonuclear fusion process) so that *potential structures* (mostly helium nuclei) became actualized for the first time.

The self-organizational and transformational themes should be coming clear by now, but let's consider a couple of additional examples in slightly more familiar territory. The material product of the pair production and fusion processes noted above was a relatively hot mixture of mostly protons (hydrogen nuclei), helium nuclei, and electrons. Initially this mixture was far too hot for further constructive action, but after about a million years of expansion the universe cooled down to the temperature at which a new and more complex structure — the atom — was able to survive without being "cooked to death." In this cooler environment electrons and nuclei were able to interact and assemble themselves into stable atomic structures with the electrons settling into their patterned motion around individual nuclei of hydrogen and helium. Note once again that a constructive process has spontaneously taken place. Nuclei and electrons *(resources)* interacted (exercised their *formational capabilities*) to form whole atoms (to actualize *potentialities*).

At this stage of its formational history the universe becomes a transparent mixture of hydrogen and helium atoms in the more familiar gaseous form. One byproduct — called the *cosmic background radiation* — of this atom formation era is still detectable today and has been the object of intense scientific scrutiny. In fact, the observed character of this remnant of the "primeval fireball" provides strong affirmation of the whole Big Bang scenario for the universe's early history.

After the atom formation era, constructive processes continued at both large and small scales. On the largest scale slight irregularities in the distribution of the hydrogen-helium mixture were subject to gravitational amplification that eventually led to the formation of gargantuan galaxies during the first billion years of the universe's formational history. Within galaxies gravity collected gas into smaller globules and compressed them still further into ordinary stars. The central regions of stars became hot enough to ignite once again the thermonuclear fusion process.

Returning to the microscopic scale, the product of fusion in the interiors of stars is a progression of heavier atomic nuclei, including those of familiar elements like carbon, oxygen, nitrogen, and silicon. Aging massive stars are known to expel some of these elements back into interstellar clouds from which second and third generation stars can form.

One of the interesting byproducts of star formation is the formation of planets in orbit around the central star. Where does the material of earthlike planets come from? From the pressure-cooker cores of first generation stars. What are our bodies made of? The "dust of the earth," we say, but Earth-dust is really stardust — the product of formational processes that took place earlier in the "element factories" deep in the interiors of stars. Our bodies are made of stardust! The matter of which our bodies are made has a formational history that links us to the stars of the nighttime sky. The Creation is an astoundingly integrated system of resources, capabilities, and potentialities.

But our bodies need more than atoms, of course. They need the atoms to be assembled into numerous multiatom structures called molecules. To reflect on the assembly process that takes us from atoms to molecules we must move from cosmology and astronomy to the realm of chemistry. Or do we? Astronomers long considered the stark and harsh environment of space to be so inhospitable to molecules that there was little or no effort expended to search for them. A few relatively simple molecules like hydrogen (H_2), carbon monoxide (CO) and water (H_2O) were known to exist in gaseous interstellar clouds, but surely there was no chance for larger and more complex molecules to form in these cold, low density clouds, right? Organic molecules assembled in frigid, dark interstellar nebulae? No way! And complex biomolecules like the amino acids needed for living organisms? Not a chance!

Wrong, wrong, and wrong again! Astronomers had vastly underestimated the formational capabilities of atoms and molecules. In the last three decades astronomers have discovered approximately a thousand large molecular cloud complexes within the Milky Way galaxy. These molecular clouds typically contain numerous species of molecules, some of them astoundingly complex, far more complex than had been expected. The actual formational economy of atoms and molecules is far more robust than astronomers and chemists had first imagined. Molecular clouds, cold and rarified by earthly standards, evidently provide all the resources and environmental conditions needed to make possible the formation of more than a hundred known molecules. Among these are several organic molecules relevant to life, including formic acid ($HCOOH$), acetic acid (CH_3COOH), ethyl alcohol (CH_2CH_2OH), and glycolaldehyde ($HOCH_2COH$), an eight-atom sugar molecule. Furthermore, given the observation of a number of closely related biomolecules, there is warranted optimism for the eventual observation of the amino acid glycine (NH_2CH_2COOH), one of the building blocks of protein molecules essential to life on Earth.[3]

Because this organic material is borne by interplanetary dust, by comets, and by meteors that enter our own atmosphere, it is reasonable to ask whether it might have been a major contributor to the mix of ingredients that participated in the formation of early life forms on planet Earth. We don't know the answer with certainty, and perhaps we never will. Neither are we able to demonstrate beyond all shadow of doubt that these materials, given the right environmental circumstances, actually possess the requisite formational capabilities to actualize the potentialities for primitive living structures.

What we do know, however, is enough to bring us to utter amazement at the richness of the universe's formational economy. At every step of the remarkable series of constructive processes that we have just considered the pattern is essentially the same: *resources* employ their formational *capabilities* to actualize new structures that represent *potentialities* that were part of the very being of the universe from the outset. And as we go from simple to more complex structures we encounter progressively more diverse capabilities. New capabilities, ones that we could scarcely have imagined before seeing them in action, emerge as more complex configurations become actualized in the course of time. The universe appears to be richly equipped to actualize increasingly complex structures that make possible the emergence of new and more wondrous capabilities for further action.

The sciences are continually expanding our knowledge of the resources, potentialities, and formational capabilities that contributed to the universe's ability to actualize the structures and forms that we now see. Perhaps what we know today, amazing as it is, will someday seem like only the tip of the iceberg. The question is, How much yet remains to be discovered? How robust (well equipped) is the Creation's formational economy?

---

3. A news report on the glycolaldehyde observation can be found at the website for the National Radio Astronomy Observatory www.aoc.nrao.edu/pr/sugar.html. A list of 110 observed molecules and information regarding glycine can be found in the review essay, Lewis E. Snyder, "The Search for Interstellar Glycine," *Origins of Life and Evolution of the Biosphere* 27 (1997): 115-33 (published by Kluwer Academic).

A Brief Interlude on Potentialities

Before we return to the main question, let me comment briefly on the importance of *potentialities* to our evaluation of the evolving Creation concept. Given the character of the universe, triple-quark structures like protons and neutrons were always possible in principle but could not become formed or assembled until the circumstances were suitable. These structural potentialities were present from the beginning but could not be actualized until some time later. Similarly, the heavier atomic nuclei were structural potentialities from "time zero" but could not be actualized until the environmental conditions for thermonuclear fusion could be maintained. The formation of atoms and molecules falls into exactly the same pattern. Atoms and molecules were potential structures from the beginning but could not become actualized (self-assembled from the resources at hand) until the environmental conditions allowed certain formational capabilities to be exercised fruitfully.

If we chose to go beyond this discussion of inanimate physical structures and to consider the formation of living organisms, we would find it useful to introduce the idea of a *potentiality space* in which each potentially viable organism is represented by a point in an imaginary, multidimensional "space." Each viable species (with some degree of variation among its membership) would be represented by a cluster of nearby points in potentiality space. Closely related species would appear as clusters of clusters in this hypothetical space of potential organisms. In the spirit of our discussion so far, this potentiality space would have to be recognized as an essential part of the Creation's being that was present, by divine intention, from the very beginning. In the course of time different portions of it would become occupied as new life forms become actualized. What happens in the course of time is not so much the *creation* of new species but rather the *actualization of certain potentialities for the first time*.[4] What is new is the fact that some portion of the potentiality space of life forms becomes occupied for the first time. Atoms and molecules do not have the capacity to create anything (in the fundamental sense of giving being to something from nothing), but they may well have the formational capabilities to actualize one of the Creation's God-given potentialities for the first time.

---

4. There has been a lot of confusing talk by atheists and Christians alike about atoms, molecules, and cells having the ability to "create" new species of living organisms. I find it far more accurate, however, to speak about the appearance of new species as the *first actualization* of a potentiality that was an integral part of the universe's being from the beginning of time. Using the verb "create" in this context invites confusion with its more theologically profound meaning of "to give being" to *something* in place of an authentic *nothing* that excludes even potentiality.

As I see it, the unimaginably vast array of potentialities for both physical structures and living forms is an immensely important aspect of the Creation's being that needs to be appreciated far more than it has been. These potentialities were part of the Creation's being from "time zero." Actualized structures and forms came later. Potentialities are a part of the Creation's *being*. Actualization is part of the Creation's *formational history*.

The Question That Often Divides Us

Earlier in this chapter we asked the question, Is this Creation capable of evolving? Given the concept of the "formational economy" of the universe, we are now in a position to state that question in a new and very precise way. *Is the formational economy of the universe sufficiently robust (amply equipped) to make possible — without need for occasional episodes of form-imposing divine intervention — the actualization of both (a) all types of physical structures (atoms, molecules, planets, stars, galaxies, etc.) and (b) all of the forms of life that have appeared in the course of time?*

The possibility of evolution hinges on the answer to this question. If the answer is yes, *and if the particular features of the universe's formational economy are suitable,* then an evolutionary development of both physical structures and life forms becomes possible.[5] A no answer, on the other hand, would rule out the possibility of evolutionary development and would require some form of *episodic creation* scenario, in which occasional episodes of form-imposing divine intervention would be needed in order to bring about the actualization of particular life forms.[6]

If one were to take popular literature and the most common journalistic mindset as representative, the contemporary creation/evolution debate is built on the premise that yes and no answers to the question above are determined by reli-

---

5. The concept of evolutionary development in the formational history of life entails the idea of a sequence of life forms related as parent and offspring. One could also envision differing forms of life developing independently from raw materials, as in the now discredited idea of spontaneous generation. But in the judgment of the scientific community the formational economy of the universe does not support that manner of actualizing the succession of life forms that have appeared throughout Earth's history.

6. Episodic creationism, more commonly known as *special creationism,* comes in a variety of versions: young-Earth special creationism, old-Earth special creationism, progressive creationism and most forms of intelligent design theory. The common theme in all of these versions is the emphasis on the need for occasional episodes of divine form-conferring intervention to actualize certain new structures or life forms.

gious commitments alone. Those persons who answer yes are commonly presumed to be committed to (or blindly duped by) a God-denying naturalistic worldview built on the premise that "Nature is all there is and it needs no Creator to give it being."[7] In a similar fashion all persons who are committed to the Judeo-Christian doctrine of creation are usually expected to answer no, and to defend some sort of episodic creationist portrait of the Creation's formational history.

To say it as plainly as I can, I find this simplistic either/or approach to questions regarding the relationship of the theological concept of creation and the scientific concept of evolution to be both intellectually shoddy and religiously offensive. To be a theological creationist does *not* in any way commit a person to holding an episodic creationist portrait of the Creation's formational history. And to find substantial merit in the scientific concept of evolution does *not* in any way commit a person to holding a naturalistic worldview.

In order to develop this point of view more fully, let me begin by stating a principle on which nearly all contemporary scientific theorizing about the universe's formational history is based. Because it is so commonly held, it is seldom stated explicitly. However, given the important role it plays, I shall both name it and state it in the vocabulary we have just developed.

> The Robust Formational Economy Principle (RFE Principle): The formational economy of the universe is sufficiently robust to make possible the actualization of all of the types of physical structures (atoms, molecules, stars, planets, and the like) and all of the forms of living organisms that have appeared in the course of the universe's formational history.

The two basic questions I want to address now are these: (1) Is the RFE Principle true; that is, does the universe actually possess such a robust formational economy? and (2) If the universe actually conformed to the RFE Principle, would that state of affairs favor an evolving Creation perspective or the worldview of naturalism?

---

7. In this chapter I will use the terms *naturalistic worldview* and *naturalism* interchangeably to represent a worldview that excludes not only the idea of *supernatural intervention* (coercive divine action in which God occasionally exercises overpowering control over creatures) but also the idea that there exists any divine being that acts on or interacts with the universe in any way. This type of worldview could, with more precision, be called *maximal naturalism,* in distinction from a *minimal naturalism* that rejects only the idea of supernatural intervention and remains agnostic in regard to the reality of non-coercive divine action. In his book *Religion and Scientific Naturalism: Overcoming the Conflicts* (Albany: SUNY Press, 2000), theologian David Ray Griffin articulates a form of naturalistic theism that envisions God and God's effective action in a way that rejects maximal naturalism but incorporates minimal naturalism.

Is the RFE Principle True?

Is the Robust Formational Economy Principle true? That is a difficult question. Neither a yes nor a no answer can be conclusively demonstrated. If, for instance, I wanted to demonstrate that the RFE Principle were false, I would have to know which particular formational resources, potentialities, or capabilities were both *essential* to the truth of the RFE Principle and *absent* from the universe's actual formational economy. No biochemist, mathematician, philosopher, or professor of law has that knowledge. And if I wished to demonstrate that the RFE Principle were true, I would have to know all of the resources, potentialities, and capabilities that contribute to the universe's formational economy, and I would have to demonstrate that these are sufficient to make possible the actualization of every type of physical structure and every form of living organism that has appeared in the course of the universe's formational history. No physicist, biologist, theologian, or philosopher knows that much.

Given this lack of complete knowledge, we are left with no choice but to use our best judgment in coming to a position on the truth of the RFE Principle. One can arrive at a tentative answer by many differing routes, or one can choose to take a stand on the basis of many differing considerations. I will speak briefly about my own choice later in this chapter, but I want first to identify one common approach that I find wholly unacceptable: choosing to reject the RFE Principle simply because the preachers of naturalism have staked a claim of ownership for this important concept. Numerous vocal proponents of naturalism have said — in effect, if not in these exact words — "If the universe conforms to the Robust Formational Economy Principle, then naturalism is more likely than theism to be true." I find this claim to be both unwarranted and annoying. Far more disturbing to me, however, is the fact that many Christians have echoed the same sentiment. I find no warrant whatsoever for this sentiment, whether it is expressed by an atheist or by a Christian. I can easily see why a proponent of naturalism would find it advantageous to make this claim, but I do not see why a Christian would let it stand unchallenged or would attempt to build a case against evolution on the basis of this groundless assertion.

Does Naturalism Own the RFE Principle?

Let us suppose for now that the Robust Formational Economy Principle is true. I have just stated my judgment that naturalism has no legitimate claim to ownership of the RFE Principle. But how would a person decide which worldview, if any, might rightly claim ownership? My standard suggestion is to grant ownership to whichever worldview provides the most satisfying answers to questions of the following type:

1. Why is there any universe at all, rather than nothing? What (or Who) is the source of its being?
2. How does the universe that exists come to have such a robust formational economy?
3. Why is the outcome of the exercise of this formational economy so fruitful as to include rational and morally aware creatures like us?

There are a number of apologists for naturalism who write popular works built on the premise that the natural sciences provide the warrant for naturalism's answers to questions of this sort. One of the more colorful and strident examples of this can be found in the works of Oxford chemist Peter Atkins. A few samples of Atkins' rhetoric will, I believe, demonstrate the character of his answers to the three questions above and the strength (or weakness) of his claim for naturalism's ownership of the RFE Principle.

In a brief book peculiarly titled *The Creation,* Atkins tells us about the state of affairs at the beginning. His employment of some familiar biblical terminology is quite obvious.

> In the beginning there was nothing. Absolute void, not merely empty space. There was no space; nor was there time, for this was before time. The universe was without form and void.[8]

What did that initial state of nothingness lead to?

> By chance there was a fluctuation, and a set of points, emerging from nothing and taking their existence from the pattern they formed, defined a time. . . . From absolute nothing, absolutely without intervention, there came into being rudimentary existence. The emergence of the dust of points and their chance organization into time was the haphazard, unmotivated action that brought them into being.[9]

Eventually, of course, one must account not only for the existence of points of space and moments of time, but of an entire economy of formational resources sufficiently robust to make possible the actualization of things, from quarks to quasars and from protozoa to human beings. While most of us might

8. Peter Atkins, *The Creation* (San Francisco: Freeman, 1981), p. 119.
9. Peter Atkins, *Creation Revisited* (San Francisco: Freeman, 1992), p. 149.

be inclined to see this as a formidable assignment, Atkins writes as if this entailed no difficulty whatsoever. In a chapter titled "Obvious Things," Atkins says,

> A great deal of the universe does not need any explanation. Elephants, for instance. Once molecules have learnt to compete and to create other molecules in their own image, elephants, and things resembling elephants, will in due course be found roaming through the countryside. . . .
>
> Some of the things resembling elephants will be men. They are equally unimportant. . . . Their special but not significant function is that they are able to act as commentators on the nature, content, structure and source of the universe and that, as a sideline, they can devise and take pleasure from communicable fantasies.[10]

If we were to take Atkins' rhetoric seriously, then we should express no amazement whatsoever at the robustness of the universe's formational economy. Its panoply of resources, potentialities, and formational capabilities seems to inspire no awe or wonder at all in Atkins. It would appear that he finds such things entirely expectable. How would Atkins reply if I were to ask him the three questions posed at the beginning of this section? I don't know for certain, but I could well imagine the conversation going something like this:

Question: Mr. Atkins, why is there something (like a universe) rather than nothing? What is its source of being?

Answer: Universes just happen. Absolute nothing is the source of their being.

Question: Mr. Atkins, how does the something that exists come to have such a robust formational economy?

Answer: No explanation needed. This is just one of those "obvious things" about universes that happen to exist.

Question: Mr. Atkins, why is the outcome of the exercise of this formational economy so fruitful as to include rational and morally aware creatures like us?

Answer: It just is. And any suggestion that the presence of these potentialities is indicative of meaning or purpose is nothing more than a "communicable fantasy."

Sorry, Mr. Atkins, but I do not find this rhetoric to be intellectually fulfilling. Neither do I find it to contribute anything constructive to the human at-

10. Atkins, *The Creation*, p. 3.

tempt to make sense out of the totality of our experience as rational and morally aware beings within the universe as we know it. If this is the best that naturalism can offer, then your claim that this worldview has any right to declare ownership of the Robust Formational Economy Principle rings exceedingly hollow. If the RFE Principle is true, naturalism of this variety can offer no warrant for the astounding richness of the universe's formational economy beyond a facile appeal to happenstance.

It has often been pointed out to me by Christian critics of evolution that from the standpoint of naturalism, it appears to be *necessary* for the RFE Principle to be true. Furthermore, I am told, the "scientific establishment" (whatever that means) wants it to be true so that its (alleged) commitment to naturalism will appear to be scientifically warranted. So, it would seem to follow that, since naturalism is the enemy of Christian theism, we should reject all of its assumptions, including the assumption that the universe conforms to the RFE Principle.

However, as we all know well, the fact that some proposition must be true in order for an opposing worldview to be warranted does not automatically make that proposition false. To illustrate this, suppose we turn the tables and look at Christianity from the standpoint of naturalism. Clearly the credibility of historic Christian theology depends on the truth of the proposition that Jesus of Nazareth lived and died two millennia ago. Would a proponent of naturalism be warranted, therefore, in rejecting the truth of that proposition merely because it was essential to Christianity? Surely not. The truth or falsity of the proposition that Jesus lived and died some two thousand years ago will have to be evaluated on other grounds.

So also with the truth or falsity of the RFE Principle. It cannot be rejected by Christians simply because naturalism requires it to be true or claims ownership of it. The truth or falsity of this principle must be evaluated on other grounds.

Could Any Worldview Claim the RFE Principle as Its Own?

If the preachers of naturalism have no right to claim ownership of the Robust Formational Economy Principle, and if they can provide no basis for the remarkable state of affairs that it represents, then are proponents of any other worldview in a better position to do so? The reader will by now have a good idea regarding how I am inclined to answer this question, but let me first go back to some unfinished business.

I said earlier that I am inclined to accept the RFE Principle as a valid statement regarding the character of the universe. I have also candidly acknowledged that the truth of the RFE Principle is *assumed* by the natural sciences and *required* by naturalism. The question is, then, why do I favor the acceptance of the RFE Principle and the idea that the formational economy of the universe has the requisite resources to make its evolutionary development possible?

Some vocal critics of this position have a ready answer. Christian scientists who favor an evolutionary portrait of the Creation's formational history, say the critics, (1) were effectively brainwashed into this frame of mind by their education in secular graduate schools; (2) are overcome by eagerness to maintain the approval of their secular colleagues in the sciences; and (3) are afraid that criticizing the judgment of the "scientific establishment" might lead to a loss of research grant support. The clear implication of these accusations is that Christian scholars who favor the concept of evolution are either not sufficiently keen of mind to see that they have been duped by the secular establishment or not sufficiently honest in spirit to speak truthfully.[11]

My personal experience, however, leads me to an entirely different conclusion. The vast majority of the biologists that I know personally are Christians. Nearly all of them accept the RFE Principle without hesitation and find considerable merit in the scientific concept of biotic evolution. Their articulation of the basis for their judgment makes abundantly clear to me that they are neither dull of mind nor duplicitous in the expression of their beliefs. Read the other chapters in this book and you will have ample evidence in support of this thesis.

I acknowledged above that the truth of the RFE Principle is assumed by the natural sciences, but the choice of the word *assumed* must be clarified to avoid a serious misunderstanding, one that is commonly exploited by skeptics of scientific theorizing. In this context, "is assumed" means "is taken to be warranted on the basis of evidence, even if it is not strictly provable." By the nature of the scientific enterprise, theories can be falsified by empirical observation, but they cannot be *proved,* in the narrow logical sense of the term. Holding to any scientific theory — whether it be a theory about the motion of the planets around the Sun or a theory about some aspect of biological evolution — is the outcome of judgment exercised by a person or by a professional community. Assuming the soundness of the RFE Principle is just such a judgment. And calling it an assumption rather than a self-evident truth is an admirable display of candor on the part of the scientific community. Having been engaged for a couple of centuries in the work of formulating and evaluating theories that ac-

---

11. I see no need to cite specific examples of this rhetoric here. I would, however, suggest that the reader be alert to these sentiments in the literature of the antievolution movement.

count for the empirical data relevant to the formational history of life, professional biologists have found that theorizing based on the RFE Principle has been abundantly more fruitful than theorizing based on the rejection of that principle. It's as simple as that. It's a matter of honestly acknowledging the actual track record of the principle in question.

Since I am not a biologist, I find it appropriate for me to seek out the judgment of the professional community of biologists for their evaluation of theories in their own domain of competence. What I hear the biologists say, however, rings true to my personal experience in other natural sciences such as physics, astronomy, and cosmology. Recall our earlier examples of the particular resources, capabilities, and potentialities that contributed to the formational history of nucleons, atomic nuclei, atoms, and molecules. In the physical sciences it is abundantly clear that proceeding on the assumption of the truth of the RFE Principle has brought about remarkable progress in our understanding of the formational history of the elements, of stars, and of the overall structure of the physical universe. We can make sense of numerous features of today's physical universe as the outcome of its formational history, assumed to be consistent with the RFE Principle.

From a scientific standpoint, understanding the formational history of living organisms might represent a considerably more complex challenge, but I see no warrant for the expectation that a foundational assumption that was fruitful in the physical sciences would need to be scrapped by the biological sciences. Each day, our knowledge of the formational resources for systems of living organisms increases. And each day we have opportunity to grow in our amazement at the robustness of the universe's formational economy. To expect, therefore, that it nonetheless has gaps of the sort that would make a few steps in the evolutionary development of life impossible strikes me as wholly unwarranted. In the context of the widespread success of the RFE Principle, those who claim the presence of gaps (formed by missing capabilities) in the universe's formational economy bear the burden of proof.

We may not know with certainty whether or not the universe satisfies the RFE Principle, but we must, I believe, remain open to the distinct possibility that it does. Recall our earlier reference to the experience of astronomers with molecules in space. One lesson that we might glean from that experience is this: never underestimate the formational capabilities of the universe. Atoms and molecules turned out to have far more capabilities than they were first thought to have. The spontaneous formation of progressively more complex molecular systems proved to have a far higher probability than astronomers and chemists had first thought. Probabilities can be computed only on the basis of what we know at the time. What we do not yet know about the formational economy of the universe, however, might well make possible (or even inevitable) what we compute today to be unlikely. Arguments of the form, "Since we do not know of any natural process to accomplish the formation of X, then X must have been assembled by direct divine action," must, I believe, be viewed as unlikely to be fruitful in the long run. It certainly would have been fruitless as an explanation for the presence of organic molecules in interstellar clouds. My personal expectation is that it will be equally unfruitful as an explanation for the appearance of specific forms of life on Earth.

But my inclination to expect the RFE Principle to be true is rooted not in my reflection on these scientific matters alone but on the way in which these scientific judgments and my theological commitments reinforce one another. In fact, I would venture to say that for the vast majority of persons who are not scientists, their attitude toward the truth or falsity of the RFE Principle is based more on religious commitments than on scientific argumentation. I appreciate the effort put forth by Christian scientists to look carefully at the empirical data and to demonstrate its bearing on the credibility of an evolving Creation scenario, but I suspect that many readers do not feel adequately prepared to evaluate the actual scientific merit of the claims and counterclaims presented in the literature. That being the case, I will continue to direct my attention to a number of foundational theological considerations.

The Generously Gifted Creation Perspective

Does the universe satisfy the RFE Principle? That is, is the formational economy of the universe sufficiently robust to make possible — *without need for occasional episodes of form-imposing divine intervention* — the actualization of *both* (a) all of the types of physical structures *and* (b) all of the life forms that have appeared in the course of time? It is now time to indicate the theological basis for my own positive answer to this question. I shall do so in the context of a candid acknowledgment of personal worldview commitments that have necessarily played a role in my crafting of this perspective.

I have consciously sought to construct a *portrait* of the universe's formational history that: (a) begins with and builds upon the historic Judeo-Christian *doctrine* of creation, (b) is well informed by the natural sciences, and (c) is not simply a reaction to the rhetorical excesses of naturalism (of the sort noted above, for example). Note that I have here used the distinction between *doctrine* and *portrait* that I introduced earlier. I take the Judeo-Christian *doctrine* of creation, in its most basic form, to be the *ontological proposition* that the being of the universe is radically dependent on the Creator's action of giving it being. *Portraits* of the universe's formational history, on the other hand, are *what-happened-and-when accounts* of the manner in which the vast spectrum of physical structures and life forms came to be actualized in the course of time.

The approach that I am here advocating as the *Generously Gifted Creation Perspective* is built upon the premise that the universe is a Creation. That is, I believe that the universe exists now only because its Creator has *given it being* and continues to *sustain it in being* from moment to moment. In this context *to create* something is *to give being to something in place of nonbeing, whether initially or in continuation. I see nothing in the character of matter that would support the idea that it is self-creating or self-existent. Hence the need for a Creator who is transcendent to, or at least more than, the physical universe.*[12]

I take the *being* of the Creation to include: (a) all that it *is* at any moment (its resources, properties, constituents, etc.); (b) all that it is *capable of sustaining* (a "potentiality space" representing all sustainable structures, configurations, life forms, etc.); and (c) all that it is *capable of actualizing* (all of its formational capabilities for reaching particular sites in potentiality space).

Given the premise that the universe is a Creation, then each of its resources, potentialities, and capabilities can be celebrated as a *gift of being* that is indicative of the character and intentions of the Creator. The robustness of the Creation's economy of resources, potentialities, and capabilities would, in that case, be indicative of both the Creator's *creativity* (in the action of conceptualizing something that would accomplish the Creator's intentions) and the Creator's *generosity* (in the act of giving such integrity and fullness of being as this robustly gifted universe appears to possess).

If this attitude is applied to the universe's capabilities for forming new structures and organisms (that is, its capabilities for reaching previously unoccupied sites in its potentiality space), then each capability that contributes to the Creation's *formational economy* is a gift of being that we may celebrate as a manifestation of the Creator's creativity and generosity. Contrary to the usual rhetoric (coming from both parties engaged in the tiresome creation/evolution debate), the *more* robust the universe's formational economy is, the *more* the universe owes to its Creator for the richness of its being. In the context of this consideration I find it especially ironic when Christian opponents to evolution appear to argue the contrary position: the *less* robust the universe's formational economy, the *more* it needs a Creator or Designer. In other words, their claim is that the chief evidence of a Creator or Designer is the presence of gaps in the

---

12. See Lother Schäfer's book, *In Search of Divine Reality: Science as a Source of Inspiration* (Fayetteville: University of Arkansas Press, 1997), for a stimulating review of empirical evidence for "the mind-like background of physical reality."

universe's formational economy. Elsewhere I have characterized this strategy as "the celebration of gifts withheld."[13]

In the spirit of the perspective just outlined, I am inclined to have high expectations regarding the wealth of formational capabilities that comprise the universe's formational economy. To be specific, I expect it to be complete — gapless — lacking no resources or capabilities that would be needed in order to bring about the formation of any cosmic structure or life form in the course of time. Why should the RFE Principle be true? Because the robustness of the universe's formational economy is indicative of the Creator's creativity and generosity.

An evolving Creation must be a Creation gifted with all of the formational capabilities to make something as remarkable as evolutionary development possible. In such a universe, occasional form-imposing divine interventions are not needed in order to actualize new creaturely forms. Does that mean that God's creative action is not needed in order for evolution to proceed? No, it surely does not. To propose that God *need not intervene* is not to say that *God need not act in any way whatsoever.* God is, we presume, wholly free to act in any way that is consistent with God's character and God's will. The question is whether or not *form-imposing interventions* are characteristic of God's creative action.

I see two problems with the idea of God actualizing new forms by occasional intervention. First, by placing emphasis on the need for occasional interventions, it might appear that God's creative action is needed only occasionally. The doctrine of God's occasional action too easily degenerates into a doctrine of God's usual inaction. As I noted earlier, God's acting as Creator is equally important at all times. A second problem with the idea of occasional form-imposing interventions is that they not only would represent breaks in the creaturely cause/effect relationship but would also constitute occasions on which God coercively overpowers creaturely action. But coercive overpowering sounds very much like a violation of the very being once given to the Creation.

If God is to be equally active as Creator at all times, and if God would not choose to coercively overpower the members of the Creation or violate the being of the Creation, then what is the nature of the divine creative action that is equally necessary at all times? In other words, *if the Creator need not intervene, then what does the Creator do?* My first response to this question is familiar: God must act at all times to *sustain the universe in being.* If God is at all times the

13. Howard J. Van Till, "Intelligent Design: The Celebration of Gifts Withheld?" in *Darwinism Defeated? The Johnson-Lamoureux Debate on Biological Origins*, ed. Denis O. Lamoureux (Vancouver: Regent College, 1999), pp. 81-89.

Source of the Creation's being, then God must act at all times to sustain the universe in its being. That theological point has long been made.

My second response is less familiar (and, I must candidly acknowledge, a bit more conjectural). Recall one of our earlier questions: Why is the outcome of the exercise of the universe's formational economy so fruitful? What is it that leads the exercise of creaturely capabilities to be so remarkably successful in actualizing things from thoughtless atoms to thinking animals? From a purely scientific standpoint, there is no obvious answer. But perhaps we should not be looking to science for an answer to this sort of question. Perhaps we get a more insightful suggestion from biblical language like that found in Genesis 1:22, referring to the fish and birds that were called to join the ranks of creatures. "God blessed them and said, 'Be fruitful and increase in number and fill the water in the seas, and let the birds increase on the earth.'" We have no way to capture the *essence* of God's action of blessing in our limited conceptual vocabulary, but this text does offer a suggestion on how to recognize the *outcome* of divine blessing: take note of the fruitfulness of creaturely action. Creaturely fruitfulness is evidence of divine blessing. God need not coercively overpower creaturely action, nor substitute for what creatures lack, because the divine blessing — active at all times — ensures a fruitful outcome. Is there empirical evidence for divine creative action today? Yes, we're surrounded by it.

The *Generously Gifted Creation Perspective* outlined above stands in contrast to naturalism because it deals with questions of the universe's ultimate origin (that is, questions regarding its Source of being) in the manner of the Judeo-Christian doctrine of creation. At the same time this perspective also stands in contrast to the several versions of episodic creationism (including the Intelligent Design version) in its acceptance of the RFE Principle and its positive attitude toward an evolutionary portrait of the Creation's formational history.

As I see it, the case for ownership of the RFE Principle does not at all go to naturalism, which simply takes it as an unexplained given. On the contrary, I would argue that ownership of this principle regarding the universe's formational capabilities belongs to theism, which attributes the robust character of the universe to the Creator as the creative and generous Source of its being. The remarkable state of affairs represented by the RFE Principle is a tribute to the Creator's unfathomable creativity and unlimited generosity in conceptualizing and conferring to the Creation the astounding wealth of being to which the RFE Principle attests. I believe that the case for theism is not at all weakened by such a wealth of formational resources; in fact, I would argue that theism is instead strengthened by it.

Some people are inclined to look for evidence that the universe's "natural" formational capabilities were inadequate to the task of assembling some new biotic structure or life form in the past. If such "capability gaps" could be found, then (as the familiar argument goes) these gaps must have been bridged by occasional episodes of form-conferring divine intervention (often called acts of "intelligent design" these days). But if the universe is a Creation, as we Christians profess, then its *natural* capabilities are part of its *God-given* nature. That being the case, I am more inclined to look for the Creator's signature in the generosity with which the Creation's formational gifts have been conferred. In other words, I think the Creator is better known by what the Creation *can* do rather than by what it *cannot*. That's the *Generously Gifted Creation Perspective*.

Recommended Reading

Given the deep concern that many readers have regarding what the early chapters of Genesis can contribute to this discussion, I would recommend Nahum Sarna's book, *Understanding Genesis* (New York: Schocken, 1970). Written by a biblical scholar from the Jewish community, this book assists the reader in hearing the text of Genesis as it was heard in its original ancient Near Eastern context. For a fresh theological and pastoral approach to Christian reflection on God's creative activity I recommend W. H. Vanstone's brief book, *The Risk of Love* (New York: Oxford University Press, 1978), first published in Great Britain (1977) as *Love's Endeavour, Love's Expense*. This work was especially influential in stimulating me to portray God's creative activity, not primarily in the language of form-imposing power, but rather in terms of God's infinite creativity and loving generosity in the giving of being to a Creation richly gifted with dynamic capabilities.

Is it possible that modern evolutionary biology could stimulate an enrichment of Christian theology? I believe that this is not only possible, but that the partnership of biology and theology is essential if Christianity is to regain its relevance to the modern university. Kenneth R. Miller's book, *Finding Darwin's God: A Scientist's Search for Common Ground Between God and Evolution* (New York: HarperCollins, 1999), presents this case from the perspective of a Christian biologist. For readers interested in being stimulated to awe and wonder at the Creation's remarkable capabilities for actualizing complex structures and organisms I heartily recommend both Stuart Kaufmann's book, *At Home in the Universe: The Search for the Laws of Self-Organization and Complexity* (New York: Oxford University Press, 1996), and Brian Goodwin's book, *How the Leopard Changed Its Spots: The Evolution of Complexity* (New York: Simon & Schuster, 1994).

15

Special Providence and Genetic Mutation: A New Defense of Theistic Evolution

ROBERT JOHN RUSSELL

> The phenomenon of *gene mutation* is the only one so far known in these sciences which produces gross macroscopic effects but seems to depend directly on changes in individual molecules which in turn are governed by the Heisenberg indeterminacy principle.[1]
>
> WILLIAM POLLARD

> γενηθήτω τὸ θέλημά σου
> "Let it come about the will of thee."
>
> MATTHEW 6:10B

Introduction

For over a century, Christians have found ways to accommodate or to integrate the Darwinian theory of biological evolution into systematic and philosophical theology. Antagonism to evolution has also characterized this period, particu-

---

1. William G. Pollard, *Chance and Providence: God's Action in a World Governed by Scientific Law* (London: Faber and Faber, 1958), p. 56.

This paper is a shortened and revised version of a longer and more detailed paper previously published as Robert John Russell, "Special Providence and Genetic Mutation: A New Defense of Theistic Evolution," in *Evolutionary and Molecular Biology: Scientific Perspectives on Divine Action*, ed. Robert John Russell, William R. Stoeger, S.J., and Francisco J. Ayala (Vatican City State: Vatican Observatory; Berkeley: Center for Theology and the Natural Sciences, 1998). I am grateful to Keith B. Miller and George Murphy for very helpful editorial comments on this version of my paper.

larly among Protestant fundamentalists, in part as a response to atheists who used Darwinian evolution to attack Christianity. Today the majority of scholars who take seriously the mutually constructive interaction between theology and science support the core conviction that evolution is God's way of creating life. God is both the absolute, transcendent source of the universe and the continuing, immanent creator of biological complexity. God gives the universe its existence at every moment *ex nihilo* and is the ultimate source of nature's causal efficacy, faithfully maintaining its regularities which we describe as the laws of nature. God provides the world with rich potentialities built into nature from the beginning, including the combination of law and chance that characterize physical and biological processes. God also acts in, with, under, and through these processes as immanent creator, bringing about the order, beauty, complexity, and wonder of life in what can be called either God's general providence (appropriate to a more traditional, static conception of nature) or continuous creation (*creatio continua*, emphasizing the dynamic character of the universe).[2] This broad set of views is frequently called "theistic evolution"; it has representatives on all sides of the conservative/liberal spectrum, including Roman Catholics, Anglicans, Protestants, and Anabaptists.

In this paper I will start with theistic evolution and attempt to press the case for divine action further. Along with creation and general providence (or continuous creation), can we also think of God as acting with specific intentions in particular events, that is, can we think in terms of special providence when the scene is nature and not just God's special action, or "mighty works," in personal life and history? And can we do so without being forced to argue that God's special action constitutes an intervention into these processes and a violation of the laws of nature that God has established and that he maintains? To many, the connection between special providence and intervention has seemed unavoidable, resulting in a forced option. (1) Liberals focus on our subjective response to what is really only God's uniform, general action. This strategy avoids interventionism but reduces God's action to a uniform, single act

2. General providence is roughly equivalent to the traditional set of terms: preservation, concurrence, and governance. God preserves or sustains the existence of the world; God governs the processes of the world, giving them their regular and intelligible structure; and God concurs with these structures, granting the world its creaturely integrity and limiting God's special acts of providence to extraordinary occasions. For an interesting discussion of the relation between these traditional terms and God's action at the quantum level, see Nancey Murphy, "Divine Action in the Natural Sciences," in *Chaos and Complexity: Scientific Perspectives on Divine Action,* ed. Robert John Russell, Nancey Murphy, and Arthur R. Peacocke (Vatican City State: Vatican Observatory; Berkeley: Center for Theology and the Natural Sciences, 1995), pp. 324-57.

and drifts towards deism. (2) Conservatives argue for special providence as the particular and objective acts of God, but at the price of interventionism. Moreover both options must face the challenge of theodicy: Why does God not act in the face of the pain, disease, suffering, and death that pervade the history of life on earth?

Meanwhile, critics of Christianity, such as Richard Dawkins, Carl Sagan, Daniel Dennet, and Jacques Monod, have claimed that since chance pervades biological evolution, any claim about God's action in evolution is unintelligible. In response, fundamentalists attack Darwinian science and seek to replace it with "creation science." Unfortunately, by doing so they play directly into the hands of the atheist, since they implicitly agree that it is Darwinism, and not its atheistic interpretation, which must be attacked. This ignores the fact that theistic evolution offers the real attack on atheism by successfully giving a Christian interpretation to science — thus undermining the very assumption that fundamentalists and atheists share, namely, that a Darwinian account of biological evolution in terms of variation and natural selection is inherently atheistic.[3]

The purpose of this paper is to move us beyond these options to a new approach: a noninterventionist understanding of special providence. This approach is possible theologically only if nature, at least on some level, can be interpreted philosophically as ontologically indeterministic in light of contemporary science. This would mean that nature, according to science, is not an entirely closed causal system. Instead, the laws that science discovers at least at one level would suggest that nature at that level is open: there are what could be called "natural gaps" in the causal regularities of nature that are simply part of the way nature is constituted. In particular, my claim is that chance at the level of quantum mechanics underlying genetic mutation is a sign not of epistemic ignorance but of such genuine openness. At the microscopic and subatomic level, nature is ontological indeterministic. If this claim is sustained, we can view nature theologically as genuinely open to objective special providence without being forced into interventionism. I will refer to this as a "noninterventionist view of objective special providence."[4]

---

3. This has the added liability of implicitly undercutting the integrity of those Christians who faithfully pursue research in mainstream biology, as well as the vast number of Christians who, while not being biologists as such, accept it and give it a Christian interpretation. How much better it would be if those promoting "creation science" and "intelligent design" would attack atheism instead of evolutionary biology and its Christian interpretation!

4. This term was first introduced in *Chaos and Complexity* together with a working typology on divine action. Both emerged through numerous conversations with Nancey Murphy and Tom Tracy, in which we sought to express a growing consensus at previous CTNS/

With this approach, God can be understood theologically as acting purposefully within the ongoing processes of biological evolution without disrupting them or violating the laws of nature. Indeed, as its transcendent Creator, God has made a world that is open to divine action, and as its immanent and ongoing Creator, God acts in nature! God's special action results in specific, objective consequences in nature, consequences that would *not* have resulted without God's special action. Yet, because of the irreducibly statistical character of quantum physics, these results are entirely consistent with the laws of science, and because of the *(ex hypothesi)* indeterminism of these processes, God's special action does not entail a disruption of these processes. Essentially what science describes as variation at the genetic level without reference to God is precisely what God is purposefully accomplishing, working invisibly in, with, and through the process of nature. Moreover, though these results may originate directly at the quantum level underlying genetics, they lead eventually to indirect effects on populations and species by genotype-phenotype expression and natural selection. Finally, regarding theodicy, my suggestion will be that we place the topic of biological evolution within a broader theology of both creation and redemption instead of focusing narrowly on creation alone, for God is not the source of pain and death but its redeemer.

I want to emphasize the importance of this approach. It offers a synthesis of the strengths of both liberal and conservative approaches by combining special providence and noninterventionism. It undercuts the atheistic claim that evolution makes divine action impossible as well as the fundamentalist response that to defend divine action we must attack evolution. It may thereby lead to a new period of creative discussions of evolution and Christian faith.

The paper is divided into four sections. In section 2, the claim is elaborated as a hypothesis expressed in five steps, a section on methodology in "theology and science" is offered, and arguments in support of the hypothesis are given. Section 3 reviews the history of the hypothesis, including early sources, critical voices, and recent constructive developments, and the challenge posed by theodicy in light of evolution. The paper ends with a short concluding paragraph.

VO conferences about how to characterize types of views regarding divine action. See the introduction in Russell, Murphy, and Peacocke, *Chaos and Complexity*, pp. 9-13. For a recent response, see Owen Thomas, "Chaos, Complexity and God: A Review Essay," in *Theology Today* 54, no. 1 (April 1997): 66-76. See specifically pp. 74-75.

The Hypothesis and Its Warrants

Special Providence and Genetic Mutation: A Theological Hypothesis

The theological hypothesis to be explored in this paper can be expressed in five steps:

1. The basic perspective of the hypothesis is theistic evolution: *Grounded in Christian faith and life, systematic theology speaks of the Triune God as Creator: the absolute source and sustainer of an intelligible and contingent universe (i.e., creatio ex nihilo), and the continuing actor who, together with nature, brings about what science describes in a neo-Darwinian framework as the biological evolution of life on earth (i.e., creatio continua). Thus the 3.8 billion years of biological evolution on earth is God's way of creating life (i.e., theistic evolution).*

2. Theistic evolution is explicitly expanded to include providential divine action: *God is not only the ultimate cause of all existence but also the source of its meaning and ultimate purpose. Thus, God not only creates but guides and directs the evolution of life toward the fulfilling of God's overall purposes.*

3. Providence includes both general and special providence, and both are taken here to be objective. *Not only is God's action here to be understood in terms of general providence, God's providing evolution as a whole with an overall goal and purpose, but it is also understood in terms of special providence, God's special action having specific and objective consequences for evolution. These consequences would not otherwise have occurred within God's general providence alone, and they can be recognized as due to God's action only through faith. Note: here I am assuming that God's special action, though special and objective, is mediated through the natural processes with which God works. Thus God's action is neither unilateral, unmediated, nor reducible to a natural process. Finally I am assuming that God acts directly in particular ways in the context of the genome, though this action may have indirect consequences at the level of the phenotype and its eventual and occasional expression in populations by natural selection, which we may also identify as acts of divine objective special providence.*[5]

---

5. I am drawing the distinction between direct and indirect acts from the context of the philosophy of action as it has developed around the problem of human agency. By a "direct act" I mean an act that an agent accomplishes without having to perform any prior act to bring it about. By an "indirect act" I mean an act that an agent accomplishes by setting into motion a sequence of events stemming from a direct act that the agent performs. In this paper, I am considering the possibility that when we consider events at the level of the phenotype as acts of God, they are actually the indirect acts of God. According to the idea being explored here, God acts directly at the level of the genotype, and the sequence of events so initiated results in an effect in

4. Now in a crucial move responding to the problem of rendering our theological program intelligible in light of science, we require that objective special providence be understood as noninterventionist: *God does not act by violating or suspending the stream of natural processes or the laws of nature but by acting within them, though without a theological perspective we cannot recognize the effects of God's actions as, in fact, the effects of God's action. Indeed these laws and processes are open to God's action because God made them that way. Our account of divine action does not rely on a gap in our current scientific knowledge but on the positive content of that knowledge. Because of that knowledge, our account of divine action does not require God to create gaps in an otherwise closed causal order but relies on the intrinsically open character of natural processes as the creation of God.*

5. With these requirements in mind, we present the core hypothesis: *The noninterventionist effects of God's special action occur directly at the level of, and are mediated by, those genetic variations in which quantum processes play a significant role in biological evolution. The current hypothesis is that if divine action within evolution is to be both direct and noninterventionist, the most likely locus of these effects, and perhaps the only such locus, is the level of genetic mutation. It is specifically at this level that I claim such direct effects may arise in a noninterventionist way, that is, in a way entirely consistent with the known laws of physics, chemistry, and molecular biology. Moreover, if the effects of God's action do indeed occur directly at the level of genetic variation as we claim they do, they may have bottom-up consequences that indirectly affect the course of evolution.*[6]

---

the phenotype. From this it follows that all indirect divine acts are mediated. A direct divine act may be mediated, but it is possible to conceive of a direct divine act that is "immediate" or "unmediated." In this case, God performs such an act unilaterally without taking up the existing material or natural processes.

God's acts of creation *ex nihilo* should be considered as direct or basic acts: each event in the universe, and not just the first (if there were one, such as at t = 0), depends on God's direct act as its Creator. This also means that each direct act of creation is an immediate divine act: God creates each event *ex nihilo*, not in, with, and through the events that precede it. So, whereas in the context of providence one can refer to a mediated direct act, in the context of creation one can not. Note: I am indebted to the discussion of divine action found in Thomas Tracy, "Particular Providence and the God of the Gaps," in *Chaos and Complexity: Scientific Perspectives on Divine Action*, ed. Robert John Russell, Nancey Murphy, and Arthur R. Peacocke (Vatican City State: Vatican Observatory; Berkeley: Center for Theology and the Natural Sciences, 1995), particularly pp. 294-96, and in private conversations. I am using the term "direct act" as roughly equivalent to the term "basic act" as it is frequently found in Tracy and elsewhere.

6. "Bottom-up causality" usually refers to effects occurring at a higher level due to processes at a lower level, such as temperature and pressure of a gas arising from the kinetic energy of its atoms and their exchange of momentum with the container. Compare this with "top-

However, for this claim to hold, we must show that quantum processes may be interpreted philosophically in terms of ontological indeterminism and that quantum processes are relevant scientifically to genetic variation.

In short, God created a world open to God's action, a world in which God acts both to maintain its regularities and to bring about the evolution of life and humanity. Quantum processes, created by God, provide the ontological openness for God's action. Their fundamental role in evolution is a crucial means by which God provides the wondrous gift of life.

Arguments in support of these claims will be given in the following sections of this paper. First, however, a number of important methodological issues and criticisms must be addressed.

Methodology in "Theology and Science"

How does theology as "faith seeking understanding" relate to science?

This is a project in constructive theology, with special attention to a theology of nature. This hypothesis should be taken not as a form of natural theology, nor one of physico-theology, and most certainly not an argument from design. Instead it is part of a general constructive Trinitarian theology pursued in the tradition of "faith seeking understanding" *(fides quaerens intellectum)*. Its sources lie in Scripture, tradition, worship, reason, and experience, as these are brought into correlation with contemporary culture, *including here the results of science and the concerns for nature.* Although I believe God's special action is intelligible in the context of, and coherent with, our scientific view of the world because of the indeterministic character of the natural processes as suggested by a plausible philosophical interpretation of quantum physics, such special action cannot be discovered by the natural sciences as such, nor can it be based on them. Science will see only random events described, as far as they can be by science, by the theories of science. The positive grounds for an alleged divine action are theological, not scientific.

I wish to emphasize, then, that this hypothesis is not drawn from science even though it aims to be consistent with science. Science would not be expected to include anything explicitly about God's action in nature as part of its scientific explanation of the world. Theology, however, in *its* explanation of the

---

down causality" that refers to relations between a higher and a lower level, as in mind-brain, or organ-cell, and to "whole-part causality" or constraint, which refers to relations between boundary conditions and internal states at the same level, vortices produced in a liquid when heated in a pot, or quantum eigenstates in a square potential well.

world, can and should include both. This is as it should be for the mutual integrity of, and distinction between, the two fields of inquiry and for the recent views of epistemology that require that theology include and be constrained by, while transcending, science in its mode of explanation.

Is this an explanation of how God acts?

Similarly, my proposal should not be read as an explanation of *how* God acts,[7] or even as an argument *that* God acts. It is only a claim that *if* one believes for theological reasons that God acts in nature, as I do, then quantum physics provides a clue as to one possible location or domain of action. More precisely, it locates the domain in which that action — however mysterious it truly is in itself — may have an *effect* on the course of nature, namely, in the domain of the gene.

Isn't this a kind of "gaps" argument?[8]

There are two kinds of arguments regarding gaps, which I do not believe correctly describe this proposal.

Type I: Epistemic gaps in science as a token of our ignorance: Many gaps in our current understanding of nature will eventually be filled by new discoveries or changing paradigms in science. The argument is that we ought not stake our theological ground on transitory scientific puzzles.

I agree with this concern. Epistemic gaps as such in science *will* be filled by science, and theology should *not* be evoked as offering the type of explanation that science could eventually provide. My proposal, however, is *not* about epistemic gaps. Instead it is a claim that depends on the contents of what is *known* by one branch of science, namely, quantum mechanics, and on a reasonable interpretation of quantum mechanics, namely, ontological indeterminism. According to this view of quantum mechanics, what we *know* is that we cannot explain why a specific quantum mechanical outcome occurs, only its probability of occurring.

Type II: Ontological gaps in nature *caused by occasional divine intervention:* The concern here is that God occasionally intervenes in nature, causing gaps in the *otherwise seamless* natural processes by violating, or at least suspending, these processes in an act that breaks the very laws of nature that God previously created and constantly maintains. Such a claim depicts God as, in ef-

---

7. For example, it is not meant as a solution to the problem of "double agency" or to what Austin Farrer referred to, when addressing the God-world relation, as the "causal joint."

8. I am using terms in a slightly different way than Tracy does. See Tracy, "Particular Providence and the God of the Gaps," pp. 290-92.

fect, against God! It also tends to suggest that God is normally absent from the web of natural processes, acting only in the gaps God causes.

Again, I agree with these concerns; we *should* avoid an interventionist argument as far as possible; obvious exceptions arise in the incarnation and resurrection of Christ.[9] *This* proposal in fact does so because it does not view the gaps in nature as disruptions of what would otherwise have been a closed, causal process. Instead it assumes that (1) the laws and processes of nature are neither violated nor suspended by God's action but maintained by God; (2) it is precisely the laws that God maintains that tell us that there already are *ontological* or *causal* gaps throughout nature. Moreover, (3) since these gaps occur through the quantum world, the God who acts through them is the God who is universally present in and through that action, not an occasional and normally absent actor.[10]

What about historical relativism and philosophical underdetermination?

Why should we work with quantum physics when it will eventually be replaced, and when it can be given competing philosophical implications? Actually these are very general issues: How should the historical relativity that inevitably surrounds *any* scientific theory affect the philosophical and theological discussions of that theory? It is, in fact, a crucial methodological issue lying at the heart of *any* conversation about "theology and science." A decision regarding it is required of every scholar in the field. I will try to describe mine here, though all too briefly.

One option would be to disregard theories that are at the frontier of science; instead, we should stick with proven theories. I don't agree with such an overly cautious approach for two reasons: (1) The theories that we know are "proven" are the ones that have been the most clearly falsified! We know pre-

---

9. In the same review essay, Thomas makes the important point — with which I agree — that many authors who turn to a noninterventionist approach in theology and science treat interventionism pejoratively. This is unfortunate since it confuses the issue and undercuts a potentially useful concept. My concern here for a noninterventionist approach is not meant to disparage interventionism per se but to avoid its *unnecessary* application in the context of evolution. For key issues such as the incarnation, the resurrection of Christ, and Pentecost, an interventionist approach might be justifiable and necessary, after suitable nuancing, since when the domain of God's action is eschatological (i.e., the "new heavens and new earth") the "laws of nature" (i.e., God's faithful action) themselves will be different, and "intervention" may cease to be a useful concept.

10. Indeed, regardless of the issue of quantum mechanics, God is already present and acting ubiquitously in nature in and through all the laws of nature and as the source of nature and the laws of nature.

cisely in which domains classical physics applies for all practical purposes, namely, when we can ignore quantum physics (i.e., in the limit that Planck's constant h → o) and relativity (i.e., in the limit that the speed of light c → infinity). But classical physics is in principle false; as a fundamental perspective, its view of nature and its explanations of the world are wrong. (2) Unfortunately, however, it is with this classical view of nature that the theology of previous centuries, and much of contemporary theology, have in general operated. It has contributed to the divisions between conservatives and liberals over issues such as divine agency and special providence, and it was a major fact underlying what Gilkey called the "travail" of neo-Orthodoxy and biblical theology. In addition, both the atheistic challenge to theistic evolution and the fundamentalist attack on evolution have almost without exception ignored the quantum mechanical aspects of genetic variation and presupposed classical science and a mechanistic, deterministic metaphysics. Thus their arguments, too, are fundamentally flawed. So, sticking only with proven theories is out.

Another option is to "pick and choose" among frontier issues but omit quantum physics. After all, along with the possibility of historical relativism is that of *metaphysical underdeterminism:* quantum physics can, after all, be given a deterministic interpretation as Bohm did, and this fact, combined with its historical relativity, makes its appropriation seem doubly risky. My response is that the determinism suggested by Bohm's approach is definitely not classical determinism but a highly nonlocal view in which the whole of nature determines each part to be as it is.[11] Even if we were convinced of his approach, we would not fall back into classical metaphysics.

My response here is to press the charge even further. Why stop with quantum mechanics? *Any* scientific theory is open to competing metaphysical interpretations; indeed, metaphysics is *always* undetermined by science. So this concern about quantum mechanics applies, in principle, to *any* metaphysical interpretation of *any* scientific theory. Indeed, it is an issue not only for a theistic but even for a naturalist or an atheistic interpretation of science!

My approach, instead, is to engage in the conversation with quantum mechanics, as with any scientific theory, in full realization of the tentativeness of the project — but engage, nevertheless. This is warranted for three reasons: (1) We are doing constructive theology, *not natural theology let alone physico-theology.* Hence a change in science or in its philosophical interpretation would at most challenge the constructive proposal at hand, but not the overall viabil-

---

11. Technically, Bohm first introduced the quantum potential that "guides" elementary particles in terms of their overall environment. He later reformulated the underlying ontology in terms of what he calls the "implicate order."

ity of a theology of divine action in nature, whose warrant and sources lie elsewhere in Scripture, tradition, reason, and experience. (2) As the experimental violation of Bell's Theorem shows us, any future theory will have to deal with some aspects of current quantum phenomena, and it is these general features and their metaphysical implications that are our focus here. (3) We should welcome the specificity of this approach and the vulnerability it produces to problems like these, for by illuminating the actual implications of a concrete example of a noninterventionist approach to objective special divine action, we enhance the strengths as well as reveal the limitations of that approach, and this in turn leads to further insight and research.

Is a "bottom-up" approach to divine action warranted and does it exclude other approaches?

Does our focus on God's action in the domain of quantum mechanics and genetic mutations limit or restrict our understanding of God's action to a "bottom-up" approach to divine action?

My response is that we should *not* see the present focus as a *general* limitation or restriction of divine action to "bottom-up" causality alone. Instead, I see the present argument as located within a much broader context, namely, the theology of divine action in personal experience and human history, because that is primarily where we, as persons of faith, encounter the living God as God reveals Godself to us. Here we clearly need to consider a variety of models, including both "top-down," "whole-part," and "bottom-up" causes and constraints, and their roles within both embodiment and nonembodiment models of agency. Moreover, we will eventually need to work out the relations between these models in detail by integrating them into a consistent and coherent, adequate, and applicable metaphysical framework.

The question here, though, is why and how God might be thought of as acting within the evolutionary processes via a form of bottom-up causality. Granted that God is the creator of the universe per se; without God there would be no universe, nor would the universe exist moment by moment. Granted that God maintains the efficacy of nature, whose regularities, which we call the laws of nature, manifest God's faithfulness and rational intelligibility as Creator. Granted that these laws have just the right statistical ingredients to allow for the production of "order out of chaos" as part of God's creative actions. Granted that in some situations, such as our personal encounter through faith with God, we might introduce top-down language about God's action. But can we adequately understand God's action within the evolutionary processes out of which we arose as expressing God's intention in ways that go beyond that of maintaining the existence of these processes and allowing their built-in "potentialities" to work themselves out over time? And can such an understanding of God's action be rendered in an intelligible way if we restrict ourselves to top-down causality and whole-part constraint *alone?*

I believe it cannot. Top-down causality is helpful when considering the action of conscious and self-conscious creatures with some capacity to respond to God's self-communication as gracious love.[12] But it is hard to see what constitutes the "top" through which God acts in a top-down way when conscious, let alone self-conscious, creatures capable of mind/brain interactions have not yet evolved. Remember, we are trying to understand the evolution of organisms over a period of nearly four billion years, ranging from the simplest primitive forms to the present vastly rich profusion of life.

In fact, a top-down approach would be incompatible with our choice of a noninterventionist strategy for divine action. If God acts at the "top" level of complexity at a given stage in evolutionary history, that level of complexity must be ontologically open, that is, it must be described by laws that can be interpreted in terms of metaphysical indeterminism.[13] Yet, until the evolution of organisms capable of even primitive mentality, the "top" levels would presumably have been within the domain of the "classical" sciences reflecting the ontological determinism of Newtonian physics. Hence special divine action would be unintelligible *without* intervention during those early stages of evolutionary biology prior to and leading to the development of a central nervous system. But if we do not include this early period within the scope of our discussion of special providence, then we once again risk circularity: God's special action can occur only after a sufficient degree of biological complexity has been achieved, but it cannot be effective within the processes by which that degree of complexity is achieved. For both these reasons, then, the top-down strategy seems stymied.

Perhaps we should try whole-part constraint arguments instead. The challenge here is to find phenomena in preanimate biology that display *genuinely* holistic characteristics. The ecological web is often cited as a candidate, due to its inherent complexity and its seemingly endless openness to external factors, but in my opinion it fails to be genuinely holistic in principle because of the underlying determinism of the processes involved, no matter how complex or distant. Unless one returns to the quantum level, where holism and indeterminism are displayed ubiquitously, I see little hope that God's action

---

12. Process theology may claim to respond to this question nicely since all actual occasions are capable of responding to God's subjective lure.

13. George Ellis makes a related claim in "Ordinary and Extraordinary Divine Action: The Nexus of Interaction," in *Chaos and Complexity: Scientific Perspectives on Divine Action,* ed. Robert John Russell, Nancey Murphy, and Arthur R. Peacocke (Vatican City State: Vatican Observatory; Berkeley: Center for Theology and the Natural Sciences, 1995), pp. 359-95.

within the early stages of evolution can be described in noninterventionist ways using whole-part constraint arguments.[14]

Thus on critical reflection, and contrary to the hopes of most previous attempts at theistic evolution, it seems unlikely that top-down or whole-part approaches are of much value when we are seeking to interpret evolution at the precognitive and even preanimate era in terms of special divine action.

Arguments in Support of the Hypothesis

Point 1 is the standard move in theistic evolution that is presupposed here without further discussion. Points 2 and 3, the importance of a theology of objective special providence, and point 4, the problem of interventionism and the possibility of a noninterventionist approach, are discussed on the next few pages. To address point 5 I will then offer support for an indeterministic interpretation of quantum mechanics, for the importance of genetic mutations in biological evolution, and for the role of quantum mechanics in these mutations.

Why is a "noninterventionist view of objective special providence" important theologically?

(i) Background to the Problem of Divine Action: Historical Perspectives

The notion of God's acting in the world is central to the biblical witness. From the call of Abraham and the Exodus from Egypt to the birth, ministry, death, and raising of Jesus and the founding of the Church at Pentecost, God is represented as making new things happen.[15] Through these "mighty acts," God creates and saves the world. From the Patristic period through the Protestant Reformation, faith in God the creator was articulated through two distinct but interwoven doctrines: creation and providence. The doctrine of creation asserts

---

14. The universe has other important holistic characteristics, but its status as a unitive object of scientific study — the meaning of speaking of the universe "as a whole" — is problematic. Moreover, in both cases (the ecological web, the universe) we are again at the "classical" level where divine action would be limited, presumably, to intervention. Quantum gravity/quantum cosmology may be an important exception. Cf. Robert John Russell, Nancey Murphy, and C. J. Isham, eds., *Quantum Cosmology and the Laws of Nature: Scientific Perspectives on Divine Action* (Vatican City State: Vatican Observatory; Berkeley: Center for Theology and the Natural Sciences, 1993).

15. See, e.g., Gen. 45:5; Job 38:22–39:30; Ps. 148:8-10; Isa. 26:12; Phil. 2:12-13; 1 Cor. 12:6; 2 Cor. 3:5.

that the ultimate source and absolute ground of the universe is God. Without God, the universe would not exist, nor would it exist as "universe."

The doctrine of providence[16] presupposes a doctrine of creation but adds significantly to it. While creation stresses that God is the cause of all existence, providence stresses that God is the cause of the meaning and purpose of all that is. God not only creates but guides and directs the universe toward the fulfilling of God's purposes. These purposes are mostly hidden to us, though they may be partially seen (i.e., revealed) after the fact in the course of natural and historical events. The way God achieves them is hidden, too. Only in the eschatological future will God's action throughout the history of the universe be fully revealed and our faith in it confirmed. General providence refers to God's universal action in guiding all events; special providence refers to God's particular acts in specific moments, whether they be found in personal life or in history.

The rise of modern science in the 17th century and Enlightenment philosophy in the 18th, however, led many to reject the traditional view of providence. Newtonian mechanics depicted a causally closed universe with little, if any, room for God's *special* action in specific events. A century later, Pierre-Simon Laplace combined the determinism of Newton's equations with epistemological reductionism (that the properties and behavior of the whole are reducible to those of the parts) and metaphysical reductionism (that the whole is simply composed of its parts), thus portraying nature as a closed, impersonal mechanism. This in turn led to the concept of interventionism: if God were really to act in specific events in nature, God would have to break the remorseless lock-step of natural cause and effect by intervening in the sequence, and thus violating the laws of nature.

Catholic and Protestant theology in the 19th century produced a variety of responses to science and modern philosophy. We may very roughly group these into the "liberal" response, which involved a fundamental questioning not only of theological content and structure but even of its method, and the "conservative" response, which upheld traditional formulations and tended to reject "modernity." With the advent of Darwin's theory of evolution, the reaction of both liberals and conservatives was particularly complex. Some Anglo-Catholic liberals tended to accommodate or even integrate Darwinism into Christianity without interventionism since they viewed God as immanent in nature. Others reacted more positively to evolutionary theories that were ratio-

---

16. For helpful introductions to the doctrine of providence, see Michael J. Langford, *Providence* (London: SCM, 1981); Julian N. Hartt, "Creation and Providence," in *Christian Theology: An Introduction to Its Traditions and Tasks,* 2nd ed., rev. and enlarged, ed. Peter C. Hodgson and Robert H. King (Philadelphia: Fortress, 1985).

nalist and immechanical. Conservative reactions were equally mixed. Some, particularly Calvinists such as Asa Gray, accepted Darwin's theory of evolution; other conservatives, including Protestants such as Charles Hodge and Roman Catholics such as Edward Cardinal Manning, rejected it.[17]

(ii) Aspects of the Situation in the 20th Century

During the first half of the 20th century, Protestant theology was largely shaped by the "neo-orthodoxy" of Karl Barth, who returned theology to its biblical roots, thematized God as the "wholly other," and affirmed the objective action of God in creating and redeeming the world. In the 1940s and 1950s, the "God who acts" became a hallmark of the ensuing "biblical theology" movement.[18] These approaches seemed to offer a *tertium quid* between liberal and conservative theologies, but to many, by the 1960s, their internal problems seemed overwhelming. According to Langdon Gilkey neo-orthodoxy equivocates between conservative language, with its objectivist, interventionist view of divine action, and the liberal interpretation of nature as a closed causal system, with its subjectivist view of God's action.[19]

And so we find ourselves back once again to a key theological problem: Should special providence be understood entirely as our subjective response to God's uniform and undifferentiated action, or can it include an objective dimension of divine agency that grounds our response to special events? Rudolf Bultmann,[20] Gordon Kaufman,[21] and Maurice Wiles[22] represent the subjectiv-

---

17. For a detailed analysis see Claude Welch, "Evolution and Theology: Détente or Evasion?" in his *Protestant Thought in the Nineteenth Century,* vol. 2: *1870-1914* (New Haven: Yale University Press, 1985). James R. Moore offers an excellent account in his *The Post-Darwinian Controversies* (Cambridge and New York: Cambridge University Press, 1979), pp. 280-298. I am grateful to Keith Miller for emphasizing Moore's analysis to me. (See Welch, *Protestant Thought,* p. 207, n. 35.)

18. See, for example, G. Ernest Wright, *God Who Acts: Biblical Theology as Recital* (London: SCM, 1952); Bernard Anderson, *Understanding the Old Testament* (Englewood Cliffs, N.J.: Prentice-Hall, 1957).

19. Langdon B. Gilkey, "Cosmology, Ontology, and the Travail of Biblical Language," *The Journal of Religion* 41 (1961): 194-205, esp. p. 198.

20. Rudolf Bultmann, *Theology of the New Testament,* Complete in One Volume, trans. Kendrick Grobel (New York: Charles Scribner's Sons, 1951/1955); idem, *Kerygma and Myth,* vol. 1, ed. H. W. Bartsch (London: SPCK, 1964), pp. 197-99; idem, *Jesus Christ and Mythology* (New York: Charles Scribner's Sons, 1958), particularly ch. 5.

21. Gordon D. Kaufman, *Systematic Theology: A Historicist Perspective* (New York: Charles Scribner's Sons, 1968).

22. Maurice Wiles, *God's Action in the World: The Bampton Lectures for 1986* (London: SCM, 1986); idem, "Religious Authority and Divine Action," *Religious Studies* 7 (1971): 1-12, reprinted in Owen Thomas, "Chaos, Complexity and God," pp. 181-94.

ist interpretation, Charles Hodge,[23] Donald Bloesch,[24] and Millard Erickson,[25] the objectivist view.

(iii) A Key to the Problem: The Presumed Link between Objective Special Providence and Intervention

Since the Enlightenment, the idea of objective special providence seemed to entail divine intervention. As Nancey Murphy has argued,[26] the cause of this linkage was the combination of mechanistic physics and reductionistic philosophy. If the physical world is a causally closed, deterministic system, and if the behavior of the world as a whole is ultimately reducible to that of its physical parts, the action of a free agent — whether human or divine — must entail a violation of natural processes. Thus, though disagreeing on practically everything else, most liberal, neo-Orthodox, and conservative theologians took for granted the link between objective special providence and intervention. Thus by and large the choice has been either to affirm objective special providence at the cost of an interventionist and, in some cases, an anti-Darwinian theology, or to abandon objective special providence at the cost of a scientifically irrelevant and, in many cases, a privatized theology. In this light, a third option is crucial.

(iv) Breaking the Link: A Noninterventionist View of Objective Special Divine Action

It seems clear that any purported "third option" will require a concept of objectively special providence that does *not* entail divine intervention. Such a concept could serve as a genuine *tertium quid* to conservative and liberal notions of special providence, combining strengths borrowed from each. In specific, we will seek to speak about special divine acts in which God acts objectively in an unusual and particularly meaningful way in, with, and through the processes of nature without intervening in, or suspending, the laws of nature (which are themselves the result of God's general providence/continuous creation). I refer

23. Charles Hodge, *Systematic Theology,* 3 vols. (New York: Scribner's Sons, 1891).

24. Donald G. Bloesch, *Holy Scripture: Revelation, Inspiration and Interpretation* (Downers Grove, Ill.: InterVarsity, 1994).

25. Millard Erickson, *Christian Theology,* One-volume ed. (Grand Rapids: Baker, 1983).

26. Nancey Murphy, *Beyond Liberalism and Fundamentalism* (Valley Forge, Pa.: Trinity, 1996), ch. 3. I am indebted to her analysis here, and to her references to the conservative sources cited above. See also A. R. Peacocke, *Theology for a Scientific Age* (Oxford and Cambridge, Mass.: Blackwell, 1990), pp. 139-40.

to this type of divine action as a "noninterventionist view of objective special providence."

Quantum Physics and Ontological Indeterminism

In classical physics, nature is a closed causal system described by deterministic equations, and when we say that things happen "by chance," we really mean that, for all practical purposes, we can simply ignore the underlying, complex, deterministic processes.[27] Chance actually carries two meanings. (1) It can refer to variations in a single trajectory or in a repeated process: tossing a football and flipping a coin are simple examples. (2) It can refer to the juxtaposition of two unrelated causal trajectories. A simple example would be two cars crashing at an intersection; a more subtle example is the random relation between a given genetic mutation and the adaptivity of its phenotype.[28]

Quantum physics gives us a very different understanding of chance in several ways.[29] First of all, the myriad of chance events at the atomic and sub-atomic level actually give rise to the basic features of the classical world: for example, the impenetrability of matter, chemical properties such as valency and color, and the fundamental forces of nature such as electromagnetism and gravity.[30]

---

27. Chaos theory is not an exception. Recent studies show that chaotic systems, though often unpredictable in principle, are nevertheless describable by deterministic equations, and thus they support a deterministic view of nature philosophically. Their theological importance is discussed in Russell, Murphy, and Peacocke, *Chaos and Complexity*. In general, classical chance is represented mathematically by Boltzmann statistics (the familiar "bell-curve") and pervades not only physics but equally biology, from Mendel's laws to the Hardy-Weinberg theorem.

28. This is of course the famous example of chance that led Jacques Monod to argue against belief in God's action in the world. See Jacques Monod, *Chance and Necessity* (New York: Knopf, 1971). I will offer a response to Monod below.

29. For an introduction aimed at science undergraduates, see P. C. W. Davies, *Quantum Mechanics* (London: Routledge & Kegan Paul, 1984). The classic work is P. A. M. Dirac, *The Principles of Quantum Mechanics*, rev. 4th ed. (Oxford: Clarendon, 1958). Recent works for the general reader include J. C. Polkinghorne, *The Quantum World* (Princeton: Princeton Scientific Library, 1989).

30. The statistics employed by quantum mechanics actually come in two varieties, and both are strikingly different from classical statistics. Particles such as protons and electrons obey Fermi-Dirac statistics and thus the Pauli exclusion principle. These lead to the impenetrability of matter and its "space-filling" character. They also produce chemical properties such as valency and color. Particles such as photons and gravitons obey Bose-Einstein statistics and carry the fundamental forces in nature, such as electromagnetism and gravity. In this sense quantum

Second, quantum physics points not so much to underlying but ignorable causal processes as to processes and events that seem not to be completely caused but "just happen": that is, to ontological indeterminism in nature. To see this we must note that elementary particles, such as electrons and photons, are described by a "wave function" that develops deterministically in time according to the Schrödinger wave equation.[31] However, when an irreversible interaction occurs between, say, a photon and a complex molecule, the wave function "instantly" changes from representing many possible states of the photon to a single state.[32] The key point here is that the "collapse of the wave function" is *not* described by the Schrödinger equation, and thus the final state of the photon cannot be predicted beforehand. Note: This situation is often called "the measurement problem"[33] since interactions such as these obviously characterize what we call "measurements" in the laboratory. The point I wish to stress is that they also can occur anywhere particles interact with sufficiently complex objects to make the interaction irreversible. We will follow custom here and call such irreversible interactions "measurements" regardless of the "size" of the complex object.

The "collapse of the wave function" suggests that "chance" in quantum physics is much more subtle than mere epistemic ignorance. From the beginnings of quantum physics in 1900 up to the present, physicists and philosophers of science have wrestled with the philosophical implications of quantum mechanics, exploring a variety of interpretations that represent both deterministic and indeterministic alternatives.[34] To complicate matters even further, during

---

statistics, with its two distinct forms and their differences from everyday chance, underlies and accounts for the fundamental properties of our everyday world See the discussion in R. J. Russell, "Quantum Physics in Philosophical and Theological Perspective," in *Physics, Philosophy and Theology: A Common Quest for Understanding,* ed. Robert J. Russell, William R. Stoeger, and George V. Coyne (Vatican City State: Vatican Observatory, 1988).

31. I am restricting this discussion to nonrelativistic quantum mechanics.

32. To be more precise, the wave function represents a product of the states of the photon and of the complex molecule.

33. The theoretical issues lying behind "the measurement problem" form one of the most subtle and most controverted topics in the philosophy of quantum physics. A fuller treatment would take far more space than is possible here. See for example, Robert John Russell, "Divine Action and Quantum Physics: A Fresh Assessment," in *Quantum Physics: Scientific Perspectives on Divine Action,* ed. Robert John Russell, Philip Clayton, Kirk Wegter-McNelly, and John Polkinghorne (Vatican City State: Vatican Observatory; Berkeley: Center for Theology and the Natural Sciences, 2001).

34. Quantum physics can be interpreted *philosophically* as posing fundamental limitations on epistemology (Bohr's "Copenhagen" interpretation), or as indicative of ontological determinism (Einstein, Bohm), or of ontological indeterminism (Heisenberg). Other interpretations include many worlds (Everett), idealism/the role of consciousness (Von Neumann,

the past three decades reflections on Bell's theorem have underscored the nonlocal and nonseparable character of quantum phenomena, making each of these earlier interpretations even more problematic.[35]

While the debate is far from settled, there are strong arguments supporting Heisenberg's view that the measurement problem points to *ontological indeterminacy* in nature.[36] From this perspective, the use of statistics in quantum mechanics is not a mere convenience to avoid a more detailed causal description. Instead, quantum statistics is all we can have, for *there is no underlying, fully deterministic natural process.* According to this interpretation of quantum physics, the total set of natural conditions affecting the process and, thus, the total possible set of conditions that science can discover and describe through its equations are *necessary but insufficient* to determine the precise outcome of the process. The future is ontologically open, influenced but *under*determined by the factors of nature acting in the present. Following Heisenberg's suggestion,[37] we can view the wave function as representing a superposition of "coexistent potentialities": a variety of distinct states are simultaneously possible but none fully actual. These potentialities evolve continuously and deterministically according to the Schrödinger equation until an irreversible interaction occurs with a larger system. The result is that one state is actualized, but *which* one is actualized is not determined by physics. Thus Heisenberg pointed to ontological indeterminism in nature.

Returning to our theme of divine action, we can see the importance of

---

Wigner, Wheeler), nonstandard logic (Gribb), observer-free formulations such as the decoherent histories approach (Griffiths, Omnès, Gell-Mann and Hartle), and so on. See Max Jammer, *The Philosophy of Quantum Mechanics: The Interpretations of Quantum Mechanics in Historical Perspective* (New York: John Wiley & Sons, 1974); Russell, "Quantum Physics in Philosophical and Theological Perspective"; Sheldon Goldstein, "Quantum Theory without Observers," *Physics Today* (March and April 1998). For an accessible account, see Nick Herbert, *Quantum Reality: Beyond the New Physics* (Garden City, N.Y.: Anchor, 1987). For a more specific focus on the "measurement problem," see n. 36 below.

35. See, for example, James T. Cushing and Ernan McMullin, eds., *Philosophical Consequences of Quantum Theory: Reflections on Bell's Theorem* (Notre Dame, Ind.: University of Notre Dame Press, 1989); Chris J. Isham, *Lectures on Quantum Theory: Mathematical and Structural Foundations* (London: Imperial College Press, 1995).

36. Heisenberg's ontological interpretation of quantum physics has a number of current supporters. See Isham, *Lectures on Quantum Theory,* pp. 131-32; Davies, *Quantum Mechanics,* p. 4. For earlier sources and references on the ontological interpretation of indeterminacy, see H. Margenau, "Reality in Quantum Mechanics," *Philosophy of Science* 16 (1949): 287-302. See W. Heisenberg, *Philosophic Problems of Nuclear Science* (London: Faber & Faber, 1952); K. Popper, *Quantum Theory and the Schism in Physics* (London: Hutchinson, 1956).

37. Werner Heisenberg, *Physics and Philosophy: The Revolution in Modern Science* (New York: Harper & Row, 1958), p. 185.

Heisenberg's interpretation of quantum mechanics. If his interpretation is correct, we can view nature theologically as genuinely open to God to participate together with nature in the bringing to actuality a specific potentiality in time. Where science employs quantum mechanics and philosophy points to ontological indeterminism, faith sees God acting with nature to create the future. This is neither a disruption of the natural process nor is it a violation of the laws of physics. Instead it is God fulfilling what nature offers, providentially forming creation to be the future that God promises for it.

Third, individual quantum processes can give rise to specific differences in the ordinary world. Granted that quantum processes give rise to the classical world and its ordinary, bulk properties due to the kind of statistics that govern quantum processes. Still this does not mean that the specific effects of *every* quantum event get "averaged out" by the sheer number of such events. Instead, specific quantum processes *can* have an irreversible effect on the classical world, as the now-standard "example" of the infamous "Schrödinger's Cat" thought experiment demonstrates.[38] In fact, any "measurement" (i.e., irreversible interaction between an elementary particle and a more complex object) can result in a "Schrödinger's Cat" effect. I prefer the particularly vivid example of vision, in which a single photon absorbed by one's retina can produce a mental impression![39]

Let me summarize what we have seen so far. Quantum physics can be interpreted philosophically in terms of ontological indeterminism. Quantum processes give rise to the ordinary world of our experience, and they also allow for individual quantum processes to trigger irreversible and significant effects in that world. In doing so they offer us a clue as to how things in general come to be as they are, *as well as* how things in particular happen within the general environment. Together these facts open up the possibility both for noninterventionist general divine action, which indirectly results in creating and sustaining the world, and for noninterventionist special divine action, which can indirectly result in special events in the world. But why is this relevant specifically to divine action in evolution? This leads to our next section.

---

38. Here the life of a cat hangs in the balance over a single radioactive decay event. If the event does not occur, the cat is spared; if it does, it triggers a Geiger counter whose voltage spike causes lethal gas to be released into a chamber holding the cat. For a readable account and a helpful discussion of the underlying philosophical issues, see John Gribbin, *In Search of Schrödinger's Cat* (New York: Bantam, 1984) and *Schrödinger's Kittens and the Search for Reality* (Boston: Little, Brown, 1995). I dislike this story for obvious reasons, but it has become too famous to easily "sanitize." Still the Geiger counter example is sufficient to make the point and perhaps can be used in the future without reference to Schrödinger's cat.

39. See Russell, "Quantum Physics in Philosophical and Theological Perspective," p. 369, n. 2.

What role does genetic mutation play in biological evolution?

According to contemporary biological science, life on earth extends back approximately 3.5–3.9 billion years. All living species have evolved from extremely simple organisms whose origins are barely understood. According to the neo-Darwinian theory of evolution,[40] the vast biological complexity we see in the fossil record and among the 2 million species we now know to exist can be explained in terms of two fundamental principles: variation and natural selection. Variations occur in the hereditary material that alter the chance for survival and procreation of organisms carrying that material. With the discovery of the molecular structure of DNA by Watson and Crick in 1956, we know that hereditary information is carried by the sequence of nucleotides whose groupings as genes form the DNA molecule. Mutations in DNA during replication can involve either a substitution, an insertion, or a deletion of one or a few pairs of nucleotides in the DNA. Those variations that happen to be favorable to the survival of the organism tend to spread throughout the species from generation to generation, while less favorable or harmful variations tend to decrease. This process of natural selection, or "the differential reproduction of alternative hereditary variants," results in the species being increasingly adapted to its environment.[41] During sexual reproduction, these variations are recombined in countless ways (through "crossing over").

Mutations can occur spontaneously in DNA, or they can be induced by ultraviolet light, X rays, or exposure to mutagenic chemicals, often as the result of human activity. Because genetic mutations occur at random with respect to the environment of the organism, their consequences for progeny are more likely to be neutral or harmful. Occasionally, however, they increase the adaptive fit of an organism to its environment, and the mutation is passed on through successive reproduction. Natural selection, writes Francisco J. Ayala, "multiplies beneficial mutations and eliminates harmful ones."[42] Although the

---

40. See Francisco J. Ayala, "The Evolution of Life: An Overview," particularly the section entitled "The Process of Evolution," in *Evolutionary and Molecular Biology: Scientific Perspectives on Divine Action*, ed. Robert John Russell, William R. Stoeger, S.J., and Francisco J. Ayala (Vatican City State: Vatican Observatory; Berkeley: Center for Theology and the Natural Sciences, 1998). Also see Neil A. Campbell, *Biology*, 2nd ed. (Redwood City, Calif.: Benjamin/Cummings, 1987, 1990). Dawkins, Wilson, Gould, Mayr, and others have sought to expand neo-Darwinism, while others such as Kauffman, Wicken, Goodwin, Ho and Saunders suggest we move outside the neo-Darwinian paradigm. For a helpful discussion and references, see the paper by Ian G. Barbour, "Five Models of God and Evolution," in *Evolutionary and Molecular Biology: Scientific Perspectives on Divine Action*, ed. Robert John Russell, William R. Stoeger, S.J., and Francisco J. Ayala (Vatican City State: Vatican Observatory; Berkeley: Center for Theology and the Natural Sciences, 1998).

41. Ayala, "The Evolution of Life," p. 36.

42. Ayala, "The Evolution of Life," p. 40.

rate of variation in a population can occur due to a variety of factors including mutations, genetic drift, gene flow, sexual reproduction, and nonrandom mating, variation itself is ultimately due to genetic mutation. According to W. F. Bodmer and L. L. Cavalli-Sforza, "mutation in its broadest sense is, by definition, the origin of new hereditary types. It is the ultimate origin of all genetic variation; without it there would be no genetic differences, and so no evolution."[43] Masatoshi Nei claims that "mutation is the driving force of evolution at the molecular level."[44] Ayala argues that "gene mutation and duplication [are] the ultimate sources of all genetic variability."[45]

What role does quantum physics play in genetic variation?

In this paper I am adopting the *theological* view that God's special action can be considered as objective and noninterventionist if the quantum events underlying genetic mutations are given an indeterminist interpretation philosophically. If it can be shown scientifically that quantum mechanics plays a role in genetic mutations, then by extension it can be claimed theologically that God's action in genetic mutations is a form of objectively special, noninterventionist divine action. Moreover, since genetics plays a key role in biological evolution, we can argue by inference that God's action plays a key role in biological evolution, and our hypothesis is warranted.

Thus it is of central importance to this paper that we discuss the precise role of quantum mechanics in certain types of genetic mutation. In specific, we must ask: (1) To what extent is variation the result of classical processes such as hydrodynamics, thermodynamics, statistical mechanics, chaotic dynamics, chemistry, geology, ecology, and so on, with their presupposition of classical chance; and (2) to what extent is variation the result of quantum physics acting at the atomic and subatomic levels, principally in genetic mutations? I believe a reasonable answer to these questions is the following:

Classical sources: Sources of variation in organisms that probably have an entirely classical explanation include: chemical mutagens; mechanical/physical mutagens (including physical impacts); and chromosome segregation. Sources of variation in species include genetic drift; gene flow; and nonrandom mating.

Quantum sources: Sources of variation in organisms that may include a

43. W. F. Bodmer and L. L. Cavalli-Sforza, *Genetics, Evolution and Man* (San Francisco: Freeman, 1976), p. 139.

44. Masatoshi Nei, *Molecular Evolutionary Genetics* (New York: Columbia University Press, 1987), p. 431.

45. Francisco J. Ayala, "The Theory of Evolution: Recent Successes and Challenges," in *Evolution and Creation,* ed. Ernan McMullin (Notre Dame, Ind.: University of Notre Dame Press, 1985), pp. 78, 82.

quantum process, or at least involve a semiclassical (classical/quantum) process: point mutations, including base-pair substitutions, insertions, and deletions; spontaneous mutations, including errors during DNA replication, repair, and recombination; radiative physical mutagens (including X rays and ultraviolet light); and crossing over.

There are, however, some very interesting and as yet unsettled questions here. Further scientific research is required for us to gain a clearer understanding of the relative importance of quantum processes and classical processes in variation, including such specific topics as chromosome number mutation, chromosome structure mutation, transposons, and DNA mutagenesis. Some of the outstanding questions yet to be explored include:

- To what extent do point mutations arise from the interaction of a single quantum of radiation and a single proton in a hydrogen bond in a specific base?
- How important are quantum effects in the phenomenon of crossing over?
- To what extent does cooperativity, being a semiclassical effect extending over several base pairs, minimize the quantum aspects of genetic variation?
- Do discrete changes in phenotype, from more interwoven macroscopic changes (e.g., single versus multiple insect wings; gross macroscopic changes, e.g., the proverbial "wings to arms" change) to changes traceable to a point mutation of a single base pair of DNA, result in turn from a single quantum interaction, or from a series of separate base-pair mutations, each the result of a single quantum interaction?
- What is the relative importance of monogenetic effects compared with the polygenetic effects and/or effects of the entire genome in phenotypic expression?
- To what extent are the linkages between genes and expression so nonlinear that the possibility of an analysis of the genetic basis of expression is seriously impaired?
- Which are the most crucial factors leading from a point mutation or a series of point mutations to significant changes in the population? For example, the mutation must occur in the germline, and amplification requires the faithful replication of the DNA mutation, producing billions of copies of the original mutation.[46]
- To what extent do environmental factors, from such quantum factors as

---

46. I am grateful to David Cole for stressing these points to me.

radiation to such classical factors as chemical and physical effects at the subcellular level and ecological factors at the level of populations, contribute to evolution?

Thus it is hoped that further scientific research will clarify the roles of classical and quantum sources of genetic variation and shed further light on the central theological hypothesis of this paper regarding a noninterventionist, objective interpretation of special divine action in the evolution of life.

Chance and the Challenge to Purposeful Divine Action

"Chance" in evolution raises at least two distinct challenges to divine action: (1) to the possibility of divine action as such, and (2) to the possibility of God achieving a *future* purpose by acting *in the present*. The bulk of my paper deals with the first challenge. Here I will turn, briefly, to the second. The challenge arises because "chance" in evolution involves more than genetic variation. In addition we must consider a variety of domains that involve random factors: the multiple paths leading to the expression of genotype in phenotype, processes influencing the survival and reproduction of progeny, and changes in the ecosystem in which natural selection plays out. Finally, we must consider the juxtaposition of these two streams: the stream of (ontological) chance events at the molecular level and the second stream of (epistemic) chance events at the environmental level, where natural selection occurs. Since these streams are uncorrelated, *their* juxtaposition is random. It is in *this* sense in particular that evolution is often called "blind." How, then, can God anticipate the eventual consequences of God's action at the quantum level of genes given all these varying factors?

To respond we must first locate these questions within the perennial issue of the relation of time and eternity. Here I claim that *God can know what are for us the future consequences of God's actions in our present and that God's having such knowledge must not entail a violation or suspension of the laws of nature.* This claim assumes that God does not *foresee* our future from our present or *foreknow* our future by calculating the outcome from our present. Instead, God as eternal *sees* and *knows* the future in its own present time and determinate state. God's knowledge of what is for us the indeterminate future is God's eternal knowledge of an event in what is its own present, determinate state. Thus, theologically, God can have knowledge of the future consequences of God's actions in the present.[47]

47. But the commitment to noninterventionism raises an additional issue here: How are

Theological Sources, Criticisms and Recent Developments

Early Sources

We begin our account of theological sources with the writings of Karl Heim, Eric Mascall, and William Pollard. In 1953 Heim suggested that, since Laplacian determinism had been overturned by quantum indeterminism, God could now be thought of as acting at the quantum level.[48] In a paraphrase of Matthew 10:29, Heim wrote: "No quantum-jump happens without your Father in heaven." In Heim's opinion, this led to the further claim that the world of ordinary experience is entirely determined by God's action at the quantum level. "All events, however great, we now know to be the cumulation of decisions which occur in the infinitesimal realm."[49] In his 1956 Bampton Lectures, Mascall developed a similar view to that of Heim, though he suggested that divine action in this context is that of primary and unmediated causality.[50]

In 1958 Pollard advanced a more complex form of the argument.[51] To the scientist, quantum processes are entirely random; to the Christian, God can be seen as choosing the outcome from among the quantum mechanically allowed options. Pollard then added two key reservations: (1) this view of God's action does not imply that God acts *as* a natural force, and (2) it is not a form of natural theology, since belief in divine action is based on theological, not scientific, grounds. "Science, for all its wonderful achievements, can of itself see nothing of God. . . ."[52] With these reservations in mind, we turn to Pollard's central idea of linking quantum indeterminism with genetic mutation. "[T]he phenomenon of gene mutation is the only one so far known in these sciences which produces gross macroscopic effects but seems to depend directly on

---

we to think about the ontological status of the future that God is to have knowledge of in light of special relativity? For a recent discussion of the meaning of time in relativity, see C. J. Isham and J. C. Polkinghorne, "The Debate over the Block Universe," in *Quantum Cosmology and the Laws of Nature: Scientific Perspectives on Divine Action,* ed. Robert John Russell, Nancey Murphy, and C. J. Isham (Vatican City State: Vatican Observatory; Berkeley: Center for Theology and the Natural Sciences, 1993). My current research project deals directly with these and related issues.

48. Karl Heim, *The Transformation of the Scientific World* (London: SCM, 1953). For a lucid discussion of Heim and others see John Y. Fenton, "Random Events and the Act of God," *Journal of the American Academy of Religion* 25 (March 1967): 50-57.

49. Heim, *Transformation of the Scientific World,* p. 156.

50. E. L. Mascall, *Christian Theology and Natural Science: Some Questions in Their Relations,* The Bampton Lectures, 1956 (London: Longmans, 1956), pp. 200-201. I am grateful to Kirk Wegter-McNelly for calling my attention to Mascall's ideas.

51. Pollard, *Chance and Providence,* p. 27.

52. Pollard, *Chance and Providence,* p. 86.

changes in individual molecules which in turn are governed by the Heisenberg indeterminacy principle."[53]

Next Pollard made the connection between chance in science and divine causality. Since science points to indeterminism in nature, theology can posit that God provides the ultimate cause for particular natural events. Finally, Pollard countered the critics of religion who claimed that chance undermines providence; instead, ". . . those secular writers who feel that they have demolished the Biblical view of creation and evolution as soon as they have established the statistical character of the phenomena involved, have unwittingly done the one thing necessary to sustain that view."[54]

This argument resurfaced two decades later in the writings of Mary Hesse and Donald M. MacKay. Chance, as MacKay put it, ". . . stands for the *absence* of an assignable cause."[55] Thus what appears to us as a random event may be taken as the action of a supremely sovereign God. According to Hesse, "just because chance is necessary to the evolutionary history that Monod accepts, there must be irreducibly random outcomes that scientific theory cannot explain. It follows that this theory cannot refute a theistic hypothesis according to which God is active to direct the course of evolution at points that look random from the purely scientific point of view."[56]

But Hesse went further than Mackay and Pollard, recognizing that, in order to launch a robust response to Monod, this view would have to be housed within a systematic framework, including theology, ethics, and epistemology.[57] Hesse, however, did not cite the possible role of quantum physics in genetics, nor did she refer to Pollard.

Critical Voices

In 1966, Ian G. Barbour, though appreciative of much of Pollard's work, raised questions about the kind of total divine sovereignty Pollard supports.[58] He also

53. Pollard, *Chance and Providence*, p. 56.

54. Pollard, *Chance and Providence*, pp. 92, 97.

55. Donald M. MacKay, *Science, Chance and Providence* (Oxford: Oxford University Press, 1978), p. 33.

56. Mary Hesse, "On the Alleged Incompatibility between Christianity and Science," in *Man and Nature*, ed. Hugh Montefiore (London: Collins, 1975), pp. 121-31; see p. 128 for the quotation.

57. Hesse, "On the Alleged Incompatibility," p. 130.

58. Ian G. Barbour, *Issues in Science and Religion* (Englewood Cliffs, N.J.: Prentice-Hall, 1966), pp. 428-30.

stressed the idea of God as acting through both order and novelty, and the extension of the domain of God's action to all levels of reality.

In his 1979 Bampton Lectures Arthur Peacocke launched a major challenge to Monod's evolutionary atheism with its attendant claim that the universe is purposeless. Instead, evolution provides the matrix of God's continuous and immanent creative action; working in, under, and through it, God brings forth the full potentialities of nature. In passing, Peacocke supported Pollard's claim that quantum phenomena represent the *only* domain of ontological indeterminacy, at least below the level of consciousness in animals.[59] Still, Peacocke dismissed Pollard's view as allowing one to arbitrarily "pick and choose" which chance events are to be credited to providence. In a very recent essay, Peacocke explained why he rejects the relevance of quantum indeterminacy to the problem of divine action. "[The] inherent unpredictability [of quantum events] represents a limitation of the knowledge even an omniscient God could have of the values of these variables and so of the future trajectory . . . of the system."[60] Unfortunately this comment misconstrues the issue as I see it: Before God acts, the quantum system is a superposition of potential states that evolves deterministically via the Schrödinger equation. But during a measurement, God *acts* together with nature to determine which quantum potential becomes actual. Now the system is in a definite state, and it can lead to specific results in the future.

Since 1986, John Polkinghorne has raised several concerns regarding divine action and quantum physics.[61] (1) Quantum physics is subject to competing interpretations, including deterministic ones. This should caution us from drawing metaphysical conclusions too quickly from quantum physics. (2) Finally, there is the quantum measurement problem, whose unsolved and

59. A. R. Peacocke, *Creation and the World of Science* (Oxford: Clarendon; New York: Oxford University Press, 1979), pp. 95-96.

60. Arthur Peacocke, "God's Interaction with the World: The Implications of Deterministic 'Chaos' and of Interconnected and Interdependent Complexity," in *Chaos and Complexity: Scientific Perspectives on Divine Action,* ed. Robert John Russell, Nancey Murphy, and Arthur R. Peacocke (Vatican City State: Vatican Observatory; Berkeley: Center for Theology and the Natural Sciences, 1995), p. 279; see Murphy, "Divine Action in the Natural Sciences," p. 355, for a striking counter-argument to Peacocke.

61. John Polkinghorne, *One World: The Interaction of Science and Theology* (London: SPCK, 1986), p. 72; idem, *Science and Creation: The Search for Understanding* (London: SPCK, 1988), p. 58; idem, "The Quantum World," in *Physics, Philosophy and Theology: A Common Quest for Understanding,* ed. Robert J. Russell, William R. Stoeger, and George V. Coyne (Vatican City State: Vatican Observatory, 1988), pp. 339-40; idem, *Science and Providence: God's Interaction with the World* (Boston: New Science Library, 1989), pp. 27-28; idem, *Reason and Reality: The Relationship between Science and Religion* (Philadelphia: Trinity, 1991), pp. 40-41.

complex status should also caution us from appealing to quantum physics too readily. Polkinghorne returned to these issues in 1995. Here he actually sets to rest his first concern: though other interpretations are possible, ontological indeterminism ". . . is a strategy consciously or unconsciously endorsed by the great majority of physics." But Polkinghorne adds to his second concern the argument that, because measurements occur only occasionally, this approach would limit God's action to "occasions of measurement" and suggest an "episodic account of providential agency."[62] Now it is certainly true that the measurement problem is connected with tremendously complex issues in the philosophical foundations of quantum mechanics, as I suggested above, so that caution is in order here. It is also true that indeterminism arises only during an irreversible interaction with more complex objects. My point, however, is that these interactions are not limited to physical measurements in the lab; instead they occur throughout the universe wherever elementary particles are irreversibly absorbed by objects ranging from complex molecules and interstellar dust to those of the ordinary macroscopic world. To me this suggests a God who acts throughout innumerable occasions in the universe, and thus a much more comprehensive view of divine action than the term "episodic" suggests.

Recent Constructive Developments

Beginning in 1993, several scholars have developed the themes set out here in much more detail. Thomas Tracy[63] rejects an "epistemic gaps" view of divine action in which we use "God" to explain things we simply do not (yet) understand for *theological* reasons, citing Dietrich Bonhoeffer: "[It is wrong] to use God as a stop-gap for the incompleteness of our knowledge. . . . [Instead] we are to find God in what we know, not in what we don't know."[64] But are there "causal gaps"[65] in nature that would then allow for noninterventionist divine

62. John Polkinghorne, "The Metaphysics of Divine Action," in *Chaos and Complexity: Scientific Perspectives on Divine Action,* ed. Robert John Russell, Nancey Murphy, and Arthur R. Peacocke (Vatican City State: Vatican Observatory; Berkeley: Center for Theology and the Natural Sciences, 1995), pp. 152-53.

63. Thomas F. Tracy, "Particular Providence and the God of the Gaps," in *Chaos and Complexity: Scientific Perspectives on Divine Action,* ed. Robert John Russell, Nancey Murphy, and Arthur R. Peacocke (Vatican City State: Vatican Observatory; Berkeley: Center for Theology and the Natural Sciences, 1995), pp. 289-324.

64. Dietrich Bonhoeffer, *Letters and Papers from Prison,* ed. Eberhard Bethge, enlarged ed. (New York: Macmillan, 1979), p. 311.

65. Bonhoeffer, *Letters and Papers from Prison,* p. 290.

action? The message of classical physics is that there are none; nature is a closed causal system. Theologians such as Rudolf Bultmann then concluded that there is no room for divine action short of intervention.[66] Now, however, science has changed, and if we adopt an indeterminist interpretation of quantum mechanics,[67] nature is ontologically open, suffused with causal gaps. Thus quantum mechanics may be relevant to a theology of noninterventionist special providence.

To strengthen the case, Tracy puts conditions on the kind of causal gaps that would be relevant to theology.[68] First, they must be part of the world's regular, ordered structure so that God's action through them will play an "ongoing and pervasive role in contributing to the direction of events." Second, they should lead to differences in that order. According to Tracy, who cites my previous work here, this is precisely what quantum physics provides.[69] On the one hand, the overwhelming majority of quantum events do indeed give rise to the ordinary, ordered structure called the classical world. On the other hand, individual quantum events, though falling within the statistical distributions of quantum theory, occasionally have "significant macroscopic effects over and above contributing to the stable properties and lawful relations of macroscopic entities." Here Tracy cites the "Schrödinger's Cat" thought experiment as well as the connection between quantum events acting as a source of genetic mutation and the effects on evolution.[70]

In sum, quantum mechanics allows us to think of special divine action as the "providential determination of otherwise undetermined events." Moreover, though pervasive in its effects on the world's structure, God's action will remain hidden within that structure. God's action will take the form of realizing one of several potentials in the quantum system, not of manipulating subatomic particles as a quasi-physical force. Meanwhile we are still free to think in terms of divine action at other levels of nature, including God's interaction with humanity and God's primary act of creating and sustaining the world.

66. Bultmann, *Jesus Christ and Mythology*, p. 65. See also Gordon Kaufman, "On the Meaning of 'Act of God,'" in *God the Problem* (Cambridge, Mass.: Harvard University Press, 1972); John Macquarrie, *Principles of Christian Theology*, 2nd ed. (New York: Scribner, 1977).

67. Tracy of course is well aware of the fact that there are competing interpretations of quantum indeterminism, and this fact, he writes, should "keep us cautious" ("Particular Providence and the God of the Gaps," pp. 315ff.).

68. Tracy, "Particular Providence and the God of the Gaps," pp. 316-18.

69. Here Tracy cites an earlier version of this paper that was actually published in the *CTNS Bulletin*. See also Russell, "Quantum Physics in Philosophical and Theological Perspective," esp. p. 345.

70. Tracy, "Particular Providence and the God of the Gaps," p. 318, n. 64.

Tracy closes with a key question. Does God act to determine all quantum events or merely some? Pollard took the first option since it was consistent with his commitment to divine sovereignty, but Tracy is hesitant about this for theological reasons. Instead he finds it helpful to explore the latter view briefly here while keeping both options open for further thought.[71]

Nancey Murphy[72] gives one of the most sustained and balanced arguments to date for divine action in light of quantum mechanics. According to Murphy, a theologically acceptable understanding of divine action must be consistent with the claim that God creates, sustains, cooperates with, and governs all things. It must include special divine action without exacerbating the problem of evil. Though it must be consistent with science, it might offer a new metaphysical view of matter and causality that takes into account the nonreducible hierarchy of complexity through either "bottom-up" or "top-down" causation.[73] Moreover, divine action is mediated: God never acts (apart from creation *ex nihilo*) except through cooperation with created agents.[74] This means that "God's governance at the quantum level consists in activating or actualizing one or another of the quantum entity's innate powers at particular instants." It also means that "these events are not possible without God's action."

Murphy then turns to the relation between God's action at the quantum level and its macroscopic effects via bottom-up causality. She claims that the ordinary macroscopic properties of matter ". . . are consequences of the regularities at the lowest level, and are *indirect* though intended consequences of God's direct acts at the quantum level."[75] Thus God acts as sustainer of the macro-level by means of God's action at the quantum level. But does God act in *every* quantum event to bring it to actualization, or only rarely? Unlike Tracy, who wants to keep the options open, Murphy claims that every quantum event involves a direct divine act. One reason is that "God must not be made a competitor with processes that on other occasions are sufficient in and of themselves to bring about a given effect." Another is to avoid any sense of God's action as intermittent or occasional; instead, God's action is "a necessary but not sufficient condition for every (post-creation) event."[76]

---

71. Tracy, "Particular Providence and the God of the Gaps," pp. 320-22.

72. Murphy, "Divine Action in the Natural Sciences," pp. 324-57.

73. Murphy, "Divine Action in the Natural Sciences," pp. 329-38.

74. "To say that each sub-atomic event is solely an act of God would be a version of occasionalism, with all [its] attendant theological difficulties. . . ." These include: exacerbating the problem of evil, verging on pantheism, and conflicting with the belief that God gives the world an independent existence. Murphy, "Divine Action in the Natural Sciences," pp. 340-42.

75. Murphy, "Divine Action in the Natural Sciences," p. 346. The italics are Murphy's.

76. Murphy, "Divine Action in the Natural Sciences," p. 343.

Murphy sees her proposal as coming closest to, but actually being preferable to, that of Pollard since she believes hers allows for human freedom by insisting on both top-down and bottom-up causality and by stressing God's underdetermination of the outcome of events. Similarly, she believes that her proposal minimizes God's responsibility for evil, thereby softening the problem of theodicy.

In her closing section Murphy turns to several "unanswered questions," including Polkinghorne's concern that such a view leads to an "episodic" account of divine action. In response she cites my claim that "the general character of the entire macroscopic world" is in some sense a result of quantum mechanics, and thus the universe as a whole is the realm of divine action. "I have been assuming Russell's position throughout this paper. Yet even if Russell is correct . . . does the fact that God is affecting the whole of reality . . . *in a general sense* by means of operation in the quantum range allow for the sort of special or extraordinary divine acts that I claim Christians need to account for?"[77] Murphy leaves the matter unsettled.

I would like to close by reflecting briefly on the key issues raised by Tracy and Murphy. I've already responded to Murphy's closing question in my earlier reply to Polkinghorne. I think that indeterminacies related to the measurement problem are much more pervasive than the term "episodic" suggests. Moreover, quantum events can lead to a significant difference in the bulk state of a macroscopic object or process. In particular, the phenotypic expression of a genetic mutation is the biological analog of amplifying a quantum effect into a macroscopic result in physics. God has indeed created a universe in which God's special providence can come about in the long stretches of evolutionary biology without intervention.

Does God act directly in some or in all quantum events? Tracy's option seems to violate the principle of sufficient reason, since some quantum events would occur without sufficient prior conditions, constraints, or causes. On the other hand it underscores the "special" character of "special providence": God's direct acts in key quantum events are special not only because their indirect outcome is special, but also because God normally does not act in other quantum events beyond creating them and sustaining them in being. Moreover, Tracy's approach provides a fruitful basis for thinking of God's occasional, special action in terms of self-limitation: God *could* act together with nature to co-determine all quantum events, but God *abstains* from such action in most cases. Murphy's option is consistent with the principle of sufficient reason, but if God acts in all quantum events, and if I adopt a

77. Murphy, "Divine Action in the Natural Sciences," p. 357.

voluntarist view of free will, it is not clear to me how we can enact our free will *somatically*.

I would suggest one alternative view. We may think of God as acting in all quantum events in the course of biological evolution until the appearance of organisms capable of even primitive levels of consciousness. From then on, God may continue to work in terms of the quantum-genetic domain, but God may then abstain from acting in those quantum events underlying bodily dispositions, thereby allowing the developing levels of consciousness to act out their intentions somatically. This approach combines certain aspects of both Murphy's and Tracy's approaches; it includes the idea of divine self-limitation; and it gives to them all a temporal character. God bequeaths us not only the capacity for mental experience via God's special action in evolution and the resulting rise of the central nervous system, but also the capacity for free will and the capacity to enact our choices by providing at least one domain of genuine indeterminacy in terms of our somatic dispositions.

The True Challenge of Evolution to Christian Faith: Theodicy

Finally, I believe the problem of theodicy is stunningly exacerbated by all the proposals, including my own, that God acts at the level of genetics. If God is intimately at work at the level of the gene, is not God also responsible for the disease, pain, suffering, and death brought about by these genes? Why does God allow the overwhelming majority of genetic mutations to end in failure of the organism? This is, of course, the perennial problem of theodicy — Why does a just, good, and powerful God allow real evil? — but now with the domain extended beyond the human world to include all of life on earth and throughout the universe.

My first response is to stress that pain, suffering, disease, death, and extinction are facts that any theological interpretation of evolution must deal with; they are not unique to this approach. An all-too-frequent response is to remove God from the detailed history of nature. Instead, God created the universe with certain potentialities, and the history of life is the mere unfolding of these potentialities, at least until humanity comes along to respond to God's personal revelation. Disease and death are simply the natural prerequisites for the evolution of life. But restricting God's action in this way does not resolve the problem of theodicy or the question of the origin of sin. It simply raises these problems to the level of cosmology: Why did God choose to create this universe with this particular set of laws of nature and their unfolding consequences? Could not God have produced a universe in which life evolved without death, pleasure existed without pain, joy without sorrow, free will without moral failure?[78] Moreover, a world thus stripped of God's special providence and tender, constant attention seems a much more troubling one to me than a world in which God is genuinely, even if inscrutably, at work, caring for every sparrow that falls. By keeping God at a distance from the suffering of nature, we thereby render that suffering all the more pointless, its outcome all the more hopeless.

A more fruitful response begins with the insight that God created this universe with the evolution of moral agents in mind. In such a universe suffering, disease, and death are in some way coupled with the conditions for genuine freedom and moral development. But can this account for the magnitude of suffering in nature across billions of years and the essential role of death in the evolution of biological complexity and, in at least one species, moral agency?[79] A variety of promising responses to this question are being pursued in the current literature. One approach is to emphasize the (either voluntary or metaphysical) limitation on God's action required by genuine creaturely freedom and the suffering of God with nature. Another approach is to suggest that God's redemptive action may well be hidden in the wake of apparently contradictory evidence, as the history of life on earth so poignantly provides, and awaits eschatological completion. This then means evolution must somehow provide the occasion, albeit hidden, not only for *creatio continua* but even more profoundly for healing, cruciform grace to continuously redeem creation and guide it into the new creation. A key component in this approach is the "crucified God" scenario principally developed by Jürgen Moltmann,[80] with its stress on the God who suffers with us and redeems us by God's suffering. But this approach, in turn, depends critically on a robust version of Christian eschatology, in which the present creation is radically transformed through the resurrection of Jesus into the new creation, the "new heavens and the new earth."

My current thinking is in this direction. I am proposing that the doctrine of creation, and with it providence, offers a necessary but, in the final analysis, inadequate framework for responding to the problem of theodicy. In

78. One could try to answer these questions, of course, by a "many worlds" strategy, a "these laws are the only possible ones" strategy, or a "best of all possible laws" strategy, and so on. My point is simply that removing God from the detailed history of nature does not automatically eliminate the challenge of theodicy.

79. See, for example, Holmes Rolston III, "Does Nature Need to Be Redeemed?" *Zygon* 29, no. 2 (June, 1994): 205-29.

80. Jürgen Moltmann, *The Crucified God: The Cross of Christ as the Foundation and Criticism of Christian Theology* (Minneapolis: Fortress, 1993).

fact, I would venture a further step. The long sweep of evolution may suggest not only an unfinished and continuing divine creation but even more radically a creation whose theological status as "good" may be fully realized only in the eschatological future.[81] But this leads to what I consider as the most fundamental challenge: how to make Christian eschatology intelligible in light of Big Bang cosmology, with its "freeze or fry" scenarios for the future of the universe.

Theodicy, thus, leads to eschatology, and the challenge of relating evolution and creation pales in comparison with that of relating eschatology and cosmology. It is time we faced these challenges.

Conclusions

I have sought in this paper to explore the thesis that God created a world open to God's loving and gracious action, a world in which God acts both to maintain its regularities and to bring about the evolution of life and humanity. Quantum processes, created by God, provide the ontological openness for noninterventionist objective divine action. Their fundamental role in evolution is a crucial means by which God provides the wondrous gift of life. Unlike atheists, who point to "blind chance" in evolution as undercutting Christian theology, and fundamentalists who agree with them and attempt to replace evolution with a pseudoscience, evolution is precisely what Christians can celebrate as the result of God's creating and providential action in the world. The blind chance science uncovers is the hidden action of the living God who creates life.

As always, though, the real challenge to Christianity is the problem of evil, including not only human, moral evil resulting from sin, but "natural evil": pain, suffering, death, and extinction in nature. It is time Christians refrained from attacking evolution or spending energy on useless alternatives and focused their faith and reason on this truly fundamental challenge: If God works through evolution, why does God not act to prevent so much of the suffering in nature; indeed, is there no other way that life and humanity could have "evolved" than through this 3.8 billion year history?

It is to this genuinely fundamental question that I have turned in my own

81. See Wolfhart Pannenberg, *Systematic Theology*, vol. 3 (Grand Rapids: Eerdmans, 1998), ch. 15, esp. pp. 645-46; Karl Barth, *Church Dogmatics* III/1 (Edinburgh: T. & T. Clark, 1958), esp. pp. 385-414; Ted Peters, *God, the World's Future: Systematic Theology for a Postmodern Era* (Minneapolis: Fortress, 1992), pp. 134-39, 307-9; and Ted Peters, ed., *Cosmos as Creation: Theology and Science in Consonance* (Nashville: Abingdon, 1989), pp. 96-97.

writings, and to which I call my fellow Christians, for this is where we face the most stringent challenge to Christian hope. For myself, the way forward will be a version of the "crucified God," developed originally in the context of the human atrocities of the 20th century, and now reformulated in light of the cruciform character of the history of life on Earth, and it will require that we face the "mega-challenge" of rendering eschatology intelligible in light of scientific cosmology.

16 Christology, Evolution, and the Cross

GEORGE L. MURPHY

The Scope of Christology

Jesus Christ is the center of Christian faith, and theological claims should therefore be evaluated by christological criteria. Unfortunately Christ has sometimes been limited to a role in a narrowly conceived process of salvation, so that his significance for an evolutionary understanding of creation has been obscured. The importance of Christ is illustrated, however, precisely by the variety of critical roles that he plays in Christian thought. Limiting ourselves for the moment to the Gospel of John, we see that Christ is indeed "the Savior of the world" (4:42).[1] But he is also the divine self-communication who reveals God to us (1:18). Christ is the agent of creation of all things (1:3) and the source of life for the Christian community (15:1-8). An exploration of each of those themes will help us better to understand evolution as part of the work by which God creates the world, saves it from destruction, and brings it to fulfillment.

Part of the discussion in the following pages will involve making use of ideas that can be found in the Christian theological tradition in order to take evolution into account in a coherent christology. This is of course not an attempt to argue that Irenaeus or Luther, for example, believed anything like a modern scientific theory of evolution. Extracting statements or ideas from a theologian always runs the risk of distorting that person's overall view. Our purpose here, however, is not to study the thought of individual doctors of the Church, but to carry out the constructive task of developing an important part of theology to take new discoveries about the world into account while maintaining continuity with Scripture and the theological tradition.

---

1. Biblical quotations are from the New Revised Standard Version unless otherwise noted.

The Work of the God Revealed in Christ

Questions about the consistency of creation and evolution have been discussed by other authors in this collection who have dealt in different ways with the accounts of creation in Genesis and the relevant scientific data and theories. But there are other ways of getting at this issue, equally important and equally biblical, though somewhat less direct. We need to begin by asking a fundamental question about God.

Ever since the development of modern scientific theories of evolution, some Christians have wanted to say in one way or another that evolution is "God's way of doing things."[2] Statements like that are challenging to other Christians who assume certain concepts of "God" to be given and concentrate their attention on the word "evolution" with all its connotations. Can evolution, and especially some neo-Darwinian version of the theory, really be consistent with our idea of God? Simply to pose the question seems to reveal some discord. How could a God who is all-good and all-powerful make use of randomness and natural selection to bring forth and develop life? It is true that natural selection is not the whole story of evolution, and that "Nature red in tooth and claw" is an exaggerated description of the process, but privation, competition, suffering, death, and extinction do play essential roles in it. Can a loving God be understood to create in such an apparently pitiless fashion?

We should not, however, begin with an unexamined idea of God and then ask whether or not evolution is compatible with it. We need first to ask, "Who is the God to whom we are to look as the creator?" As John 1:1-18 makes clear, it is the God revealed by Jesus Christ, a God who differs in important ways from conventional pictures of deity. This is the God whose "hour" of glorification is his being "lifted up from the earth," the event of cross and resurrection (John 12:20-33).[3] Paul refers to this event in his Letter to the Philippians (2:6-11), speaking of Jesus Christ

> who, though he was in the form of God, did not regard equality with God as something to be exploited, but emptied himself [*heauton ekenōsen*], taking the form of a slave, being born in human likeness. And being found in human form, he humbled himself and became obedient to the point of death — even death on a cross. Therefore God also exalted him and gave him the name that is above every name, so that at the name of Jesus every

2. This is attributed to John Fiske in Lyman Abbott, *The Theology of an Evolutionist* (Boston and New York: Houghton, Mifflin, 1897), p. 3.

3. Raymond E. Brown, *The Gospel According to John (i–xii)* (Garden City, N.Y.: Doubleday, 1966), pp. 465-80.

knee should bend, in heaven and on earth and under the earth, and every tongue should confess that Jesus Christ is Lord, to the glory of God the Father.

In his commentary on Philippians, Gordon Fee points out that there are two parts to the descent of Christ that is described here. "As God he emptied himself" (vv. 6-7) and "as man he humbled himself" (v. 8).[4] Moreover, Fee argues, "in 'pouring himself out' and 'humbling himself to death on the cross' Christ Jesus has revealed the character of God himself."[5]

If this is correct, if the character of the true God is shown to us in the saving work of the cross, then we may expect that all of the divine activity will be consistent with this character. We should not be surprised if this God in his creative and providential work "makes himself nothing" (cf. the NIV rendering of *heauton ekenōsen*) and "humbles himself" rather than overwhelm the world with arbitrarily exercised power. Dietrich Bonhoeffer called attention to this when he pointed out that the accounts of Jesus' healings in Matthew 8:1-17 conclude with a citation from Isaiah 53:4, "He took our infirmities and bore our diseases." Christ "is weak and powerless in the world," Bonhoeffer says, "and that is precisely the way, the only way, in which he is with us and helps us. Matt. 8:17 makes it quite clear that Christ helps us, not by virtue of his omnipotence, but by virtue of his weakness and suffering."[6]

How can these insights be incorporated in a theology of God's ongoing work in the world? Some theologians have explored a kenotic understanding of divine action, the name being taken significantly from the word used of Christ's "emptying" in Philippians 2.[7] The basic idea here is that God voluntarily limits his action in the world, rather as a parent limits what he or she does to allow a child to grow and gain some understanding of its world and control of its environment and its life.

If we were to leave it at that, it would seem that a kenotic theology speaks about only what God does *not* do rather than about any positive divine activity. A complete theology of divine action must emphasize that God actually does do things in the world. A model of a craftsperson who uses tools in order to accomplish a task provides one way of picturing what has been described as di-

---

4. Gordon D. Fee, *Paul's Letter to the Philippians* (Grand Rapids: Eerdmans, 1995), pp. 191-229.

5. Fee, *Paul's Letter to the Philippians,* p. 196.

6. Dietrich Bonhoeffer, *Letters and Papers from Prison,* enlarged ed. (New York: Macmillan, 1972), pp. 360-61.

7. Ian G. Barbour, *Religion and Science* (San Francisco: HarperSanFrancisco, 1997), pp. 315-18.

vine cooperation or concurrence with natural processes in traditional doctrines of providence.[8] Of course all models have limitations, and it must be remembered (as we will discuss in the next section) that, unlike a human worker, God is ultimately the creator of all the tools which God uses.

Kenosis means then that God normally acts only in ways that are consistent with the capabilities of the instruments that God uses. From the standpoint of human beings this means that God limits divine action to what can be accomplished in accord with the rational patterns of the universe which God has ordained, patterns which we approximate by our scientific laws.[9] This idea is similar to the old distinction between God's *absolute* and God's *ordinate* power.[10] God could do anything which does not involve self-contradiction, but chooses to limit the use of this power.

If God acts in this way then it will be possible to describe what goes on in the world in terms of natural processes, without any reference to the God who works through them. These processes are then not only instruments of God but, in Luther's phrase, "masks of God" which hide the creator from our direct observation.[11] This would mean that God's involvement in what happens in the world is to be discerned by faith, and will not be discovered by the methods of the natural sciences.

It is crucial (literally!) to keep in mind the basis for this understanding of divine action, which is God's revelation in the crucified Christ.[12] The concept of kenosis is not simply a device which enables theologians to explain why science can operate without the idea of God, or a way of allowing the world some freedom, though it does do both of those things. The biblical basis for kenosis is the cross and resurrection of Christ, and the view of divine action which it suggests is an expression of Luther's theology of the cross with its claim that "true theology and the recognition of God are in the crucified Christ."[13]

Consistent application of that belief will affect more than our under-

8. Benjamin Wirt Farley, *The Providence of God* (Grand Rapids: Baker, 1988); Heinrich Schmid, *The Doctrinal Theology of the Evangelical Lutheran Church*, 3rd ed. (Minneapolis: Augsburg, 1961), pp. 170-94.

9. George L. Murphy, "The Theology of the Cross and God's Work in the World," *Zygon* 33 (1998): 221-31; idem, "Chiasmic Cosmology and Creation's Functional Integrity," *Perspectives on Science and Christian Faith* 53 (2001): 7-13.

10. Margaret J. Osler, *Divine Will and the Mechanical Philosophy: Gassendi and Descartes on Contingency and Necessity in the Created World* (New York: Cambridge, 1994), ch. 1.

11. Martin Luther, "Psalm 147," in *Luther's Works,* vol. 14 (St. Louis: Concordia, 1958), p. 114.

12. Murphy, "The Theology of the Cross."

13. Martin Luther, "Heidelberg Disputation," in *Luther's Works,* vol. 31 (Philadelphia: Fortress, 1957), p. 53.

standing of God's involvement in evolution. In all our study of the world, the God who is present and active is the God revealed in the cross, the God who is (to use an image which the 2nd-century Christian apologist Justin Martyr took from Plato) "placed crosswise [*echiasen*] in the universe."[14] The present discussion is part of a theological research program termed "chiasmic cosmology" which is based on that idea.[15]

The approach taken here also has a good deal in common with that of Nancey Murphy and George F. R. Ellis. They have given a detailed treatment of the relationships of science, theology, and ethics that is centered on the belief that "kenosis is the underlying law of the cosmos."[16]

At the same time, this concept of divine action is consistent with the picture of the world which modern science has developed, a picture of a universe whose features have come about through natural processes in accord with scientific laws over long periods of time. The existence of a universe and the fact that it can be described in terms of mathematical laws are not things which science itself can explain. But given such a universe, the evolution of quantum fields in the first fractions of a second of the Big Bang, the fusion of nuclei in "the first three minutes,"[17] the later condensation of galaxies, stars, and planets, chemical reactions which led to the development of life on earth, and the further evolution of living things can all be seen as the means through which the triune God has been at work. From a theological standpoint, evolution is an example of the doctrine of providence.

There is, of course, a great deal which we still do not understand about the history of the universe, and some new scientific ideas will probably be needed. In particular, we are still quite uncertain about chemical evolution, the ways in which life first came about from nonliving molecules. But our basic theological approach as well as the previous successes of science both lead us to expect that God did bring about life through natural processes which science can, in principle, discover, and not by some sort of intervention which overrode those processes.

We still have to deal with the question of the processes that actually are involved in biological evolution and, in particular, natural selection. The traditional problem of theodicy, how an all-good and all-powerful God can allow

14. "The First Apology of Justin," in *The Ante-Nicene Fathers*, vol. 1 (Grand Rapids: Eerdmans, 1979 reprint), p. 183.

15. George L. Murphy, "Chiasmic Cosmology: An Approach to the Science-Theology Dialogue," *Trinity Seminary Review* 13 (1991): 83-92.

16. Nancey Murphy and George F. R. Ellis, *On the Moral Nature of the Universe* (Minneapolis: Fortress, 1996), p. 251.

17. Steven Weinberg, *The First Three Minutes*, updated ed. (New York: Basic, 1993).

evil, is sharpened by evolution, for God apparently does not just allow evil but uses it in order to create. It is true that this seems to give evil some purpose, but it also raises questions about the character of a deity who would work in this way. It is hard for many people to understand how a good and loving God, one whose "compassion . . . is for every living thing" (Sir. 18:13), could create by forcing millions of generations of living things through a relentless process of competition, want, struggle, and extinction.[18]

The Bible, however, witnesses to a God whose characteristic work is to bring about good in spite of what, from the standpoint of creatures, negates the very possibility of good. In Romans 4 Paul speaks of God as the one who "justifies the ungodly" (v. 5), "gives life to the dead and calls into existence the things that do not exist" (v. 17) so that it is possible to hope against hope (v. 18).

God does not simply stand above the evolutionary process and make it happen. In the incarnation God becomes a participant in that process, taking a place on the side of the *losers* in the "struggle for survival" — for in the short run Caiaphas and Pontius Pilate are the survivors. And the resurrection of the crucified means that natural selection, important as it is as an evolutionary mechanism, is not God's last word. There is hope for those who do not survive.

The *Logos* as the Agent of Creation

In the previous section we put some emphasis on the fact that the universe that God has created obeys rational laws. The ability of science not only to describe observed phenomena but also to predict quantitatively new ones indicates that there is inherent in the universe a rational order that is not (as some postmodern critics imagine) simply a projection of our own mental patterns. This has led some people, such as physicist Paul Davies, to argue that "the mind of God" can be discovered from science, without appeal to revelation.[19]

The Christian tradition has come at this in a quite different way. The Nicene Creed states that "all things were made" through the preexistent Son of God who would become incarnate in the child born of the virgin Mary, a claim with support from John 1:1-18, 1 Corinthians 8:6, Hebrews 1:3, and Colossians 1:16. The first of these passages is especially important for it speaks of the one through whom all things were made as the divine *logos,* the Word or Reason of God. There is thus a connection with the theme of the world's rationality, a

18. E.g., Henry Morris, "The Wolf and the Lamb," *Back to Genesis* (September 1994): a-c, pp. b-c.
19. Paul Davies, *The Mind of God* (New York: Simon & Schuster, 1992).

connection that was exploited by such early Christian apologists as Justin Martyr. They called attention to what they saw as similarities with the concept of a cosmic *logos* or World Reason in contemporary Stoicism and Middle Platonism.[20] It is important to realize, however, that what lies behind the Johannine use of the word *logos* is the Old Testament ideas of the prophetic "word of the Lord" and God's creative speech in Genesis 1, as well as perhaps the divine "utterance" *(memra)* of the Aramaic translations of the Hebrew scriptures. The use of the *logos* concept in John is not based, at least directly, on Greek philosophical ideas.[21]

The Christian concept of the *logos* cannot simply be identified with a rational pattern which is immanent in the created world, for "all things came into being through him" (John 1:3). Thomas Torrance has emphasized the importance for the Christian doctrine of creation of the *contingent* rationality of the world.[22] God in his freedom has created a rational universe, but it could have been rational in some other way. There are other patterns that could have been realized besides those that the natural sciences discover, some of which are investigated by pure mathematicians. The *logos* must be thought of not only as the source of our world's pattern but as containing all possible patterns for all possible worlds.

This means that the mathematical pattern of the universe that we have been able to approximate more and more closely with our laws of physics is a fundamental aspect of creation. We can hardly help recalling the statement attributed to Plato that God is always doing geometry, though we know now that the mathematics of creation is far more complex and dynamic than the Euclidean geometry of the ancients.[23] P. A. M. Dirac, one of the creators of modern quantum theory, expressed this Platonic theme:

> One could perhaps express the situation by saying that God is a mathematician of a very high order, and He used very advanced mathematics in constructing the universe. Our feeble attempts at mathematics enable us to understand a bit of the universe, and as we proceed to develop higher and higher mathematics, we can hope to understand the universe better.[24]

20. L. W. Barnard, *Justin Martyr* (London: Cambridge, 1967), ch. 7.

21. Brown, *The Gospel According to John (i–xii)*, appendix 2.

22. Thomas F. Torrance, *Divine and Contingent Order* (New York: Oxford, 1981).

23. Plutarch, *Moralia*, The Loeb Classical Library, vol. 9 (Cambridge, Mass.: Harvard University Press, 1969), pp. 118-19. Plutarch says here, "While this statement is not made explicitly in any of Plato's writings, it is well enough attested and is in harmony with his character."

24. P. A. M. Dirac, "The Evolution of the Physicist's Picture of Nature," *Scientific American* 206.5 (1963): 45-53.

Given these laws realized in an actual universe, we may be able to understand how the various features of the world have developed, as we indicated in the last section. It may even be possible to explain how matter and space-time have come into being in terms of a satisfactory marriage of general relativity and quantum theory.[25] But why the laws of physics are as they are, why this particular pattern is "activated" in a real universe, is something which science itself cannot explain. A person can simply stop at that point and refuse to ask any further questions, taking the view of Bertrand Russell: "The world as a whole just is, that's all. We start there."[26] But if we are not content with that, the Christian doctrine of creation through the divine *logos* offers itself as an answer to questions about the existence of a rational world.

This idea of the *logos* as the source of the laws of physics might suggest a rather abstract and uninspiring picture of a mere catalog of designs for possible universes. The Christian claim is that we know *who* the *logos* is, not from philosophical or scientific investigation but from Jesus Christ, the *logos* made flesh (John 1:14). And the Word became flesh in a way shocking to the sophisticated and philosophically knowledgeable of the world, not as a philosopher or an emperor but as a carpenter (Mark 6:3) who would suffer and die on a Roman cross.[27] And it is on the incarnation and the cross-resurrection event that we now concentrate our attention.

The Renewal of Creation

Jesus Christ is, as we have emphasized, the Word of God through whom creation came into being, the Second Person of the Trinity. He is also fully human, the Son of Mary. Jesus was born and grew to maturity (Luke 2:7, 40, 52), was tempted (Matthew 4:1-11), limited in knowledge (Mark 5:30 and 13:32), got tired (John 4:6), and finally suffered and died. The Letter to the Hebrews (2:17) summarizes this by saying, "he had to become like his brothers and sisters in every respect."[28]

Jesus is, moreover, human as part of the whole history of our species: he

---

25. Willem B. Drees, *Beyond the Big Bang* (LaSalle, Ill.: Open Court, 1990), ch. 2.

26. Quoted by W. Norris Clarke, S.J., in *Prospects for Natural Theology*, ed. Eugene Thomas Long (Washington: Catholic University of America, 1992), p. 165.

27. William L. Lane, *The Gospel According to Mark* (Grand Rapids: Eerdmans, 1974), pp. 201-3.

28. NRSV's inclusive rendering "brothers and sisters" of *tois adelphois* is needed to bring out the proper sense in modern English. If women were not included here, then they would not be saved through the incarnation.

did not bring his humanity from heaven. The genealogies of Matthew 1 and Luke 3, while notoriously very different, both make this clear. Luke traces Jesus' ancestry back to the beginning of the human race. Matthew emphasizes his descent from Abraham and David, but the inclusion in Matthew 1:1-17 of not only the foreigner Ruth but also the prostitute Rahab, and of Tamar and "the wife of Uriah" who contributed to the descent of the Messiah through illicit liaisons, highlights the disreputable aspects of family history which most families try to sweep under the rug.

We will soon see how important an emphasis on Christ's full humanity and participation in human history is for an adequate theological treatment of evolution. But first we must take what may seem to be a historical detour.[29]

The theological controversies of the 4th century brought the Christian Church to see the necessity of affirming Christ's full divinity: Only the creator can really be the savior in the fullest sense. The debates of the following century showed the need also to affirm the full humanity of Christ: Only one who shares completely in human nature can save the entire human being. These debates culminated in the classic Definition of Chalcedon of 451, which taught

> one and the same Son, our Lord Jesus Christ, at once complete in Godhead and complete in manhood, truly God and truly man, consisting also of a reasonable soul and body; of one substance with the Father as regards his Godhead, and at the same time of one substance with us as regards his manhood; like us in all respects, apart from sin. . . .[30]

It has been a perennial temptation for Christians to neglect or even deny (most often tacitly) aspects of the humanity of Jesus, sometimes in pursuit of a theological agenda and sometimes with the intention of freeing him from aspects of human life that do not seem sufficiently exalted. The anger of many Christians at the 1988 film *The Last Temptation of Christ* provides an illustration. Certainly some legitimate criticisms can be made of that movie, but much of the reaction stemmed from a refusal to believe that Jesus really could be tempted. Such an attitude is theologically disastrous. Besides ignoring Hebrews 4:15, it would mean that the incarnation did not really touch the aspects of human life which are most deeply enmeshed in the problem of sin and are in need of healing.

One of the axioms of early christological debates, which can be regarded as a paraphrase of Hebrews 2:17, was "That which is not taken [by the *logos* in

29. See, e.g., Aloys Grillmeier, *Christ in Christian Tradition*, vol. 1 (Atlanta: John Knox, 1975). Basic texts are in Henry Scowcroft Bettenson, ed., *Documents of the Christian Church* (London: Oxford University Press, 1943), pp. 29-52.

30. Bettenson, *Documents of the Christian Church*, pp. 51-52.

the incarnation] is not healed."[31] Every aspect of genuine human nature is saved only by being taken up by God in the life, death, and resurrection of Christ. The importance of this is best seen by considering one of the many counterexamples that have been developed in the history of doctrine, the 4th-century heresy of Apollinarius.[32] He taught that the divine *logos* played the role of the rational soul, or mind, of Christ. This provides a model for understanding incarnation but it is an inadequate model, for it would mean that not our minds but only our bodies would be saved, for there would have been no human mind involved in the life of Christ. And it is the human mind, after all, which is a much more serious source of sin than is our physical body.

God's assumption of humanity involves more than simply being united with a static human nature. It means that the *logos* lived a developing and changing human life from conception through death. Beyond that, it means that he became part of the history of Israel and of the whole of humanity, as the genealogies of the Gospels indicate. Irenaeus, in the latter part of the 2nd century, gave attention to this with his concept of *recapitulation:* Christ passed through all the stages of human life in order to sanctify them all, and summed up or recapitulated the previous history of humanity, doing over again — but this time without sin and error — the things in which Adam had failed.[33] While Irenaeus relied on what he saw as the general sense of Scripture rather than specific texts for this concept, it is not difficult to find the theme used in the Bible, perhaps most vividly in the Gospel of Matthew. God's son again comes out of Egypt (Hos. 11:1; Matt. 2:15) and passes the tests in the wilderness which Israel, God's "firstborn son" (Exod. 4:22), had failed (Matt. 4:1-11).

The idea that we are descended from "beasts" is one reason why many people have been repelled by evolutionary theory. And the idea that Christ would share that relationship is especially shocking to many Christians. This sense of revulsion is easily turned into an argument against human evolution. One collection of antievolution material puts it this way:

> [T]heistic evolution . . . makes man a half-evolved, half-created being who is a remodeled ape, so to speak. It also makes the Lord Jesus Christ into a very specially made-over ape. But the Bible says that He is the Creator of the universe. . . .[34]

31. Grillmeier, *Christ in Christian Tradition*, pp. 321, 531.

32. Grillmeier, *Christ in Christian Tradition*, pp. 329-43.

33. Basic texts are in Bettenson, *Documents of the Christian Church*, pp. 29-30. For discussion of the theology of Irenaeus see Gustaf Wingren, *Man and the Incarnation* (London: Oliver and Boyd, 1959).

34. Robert E. Kofahl, *Handy Dandy Evolution Refuter* (San Diego: Beta, 1980), p. 17.

Of course humans as "remodeled apes" is an inaccurate description of the evolutionary account of human origins, but we may let that pass now. It is more important to meet the thrust of this objection head on, and to say that *as* one sharing a common ancestry with the apes, Christ is the Creator of the universe. That certainly may be offensive, but it is really less so (for our prehuman ancestors were under no curse) than the claim that the one who died an accursed death (Gal. 3:13) as a criminal is the Son of God and Creator of the universe.

The divine condescension that accepted the form of a slave and death on a cross accepted also our bestial ancestry. "That which is not taken is not healed," and by his incarnation, cross, and resurrection Christ heals us as members of our evolved species. The "flesh" which the Word became was not some idealized human nature, abstracted from the evolutionary process, but real historical humanity.

But *how* does Christ heal the human condition? It is easy enough to say that salvation comes through the life and work of Christ, but how are these actually effective? Theologians have debated those questions for centuries and have proposed several "theories of the atonement."[35] An adequate theology of salvation requires that we first have some understanding of the problem of sin — that is, of what we are saved *from*. Since sin is a departure from what God intends for humanity, this requires in turn that we be able to say something about that intention. An evolutionary view of humanity poses the questions in a new way, but the theological tradition does provide some resources for dealing with the subject in this new context.

The views of the atonement which have been held widely in the Western Church, and today especially in the evangelical community, are often some variant of the argument given by Anselm: Christ the God-Man is able to make satisfaction for, or pay the penalty for, the violation of divine honor and justice involved in the original sin traceable to Adam and the actual sins which all people commit. On the other hand, Aulén argued in *Christus Victor* that the picture of Christ as victor over the tyrants of sin, death, and the law had a great deal of support from the church fathers and Luther, and deserved to be understood as the "classic" view of the atonement. His analysis of this view, as well as of theologies of the "Latin" type like that of Anselm and the "subjective" view, often associated with Abelard and popular with many liberal Protestants, had considerable influence on 20th-century theology.

35. The literature is extensive. See, e.g., Anselm of Canterbury, "Why God Became Man," in *A Scholastic Miscellany*, ed. Eugene R. Fairweather (New York: Macmillan, 1970); Gustaf Aulén, *Christus Victor* (New York: Macmillan, 1961); Gerhard Forde, "The Work of Christ," in *Christian Dogmatics*, vol. 2, ed. Carl E. Braaten and Robert W. Jenson (Philadelphia: Fortress, 1984), pp. 1-99; Robert P. Lightner, *Evangelical Theology* (Grand Rapids: Baker, 1986), pp. 65-99.

While these models are not necessarily incompatible with evolution, they are usually discussed in the context of an essentially static view of creation. Before the rise of biblical criticism and evolutionary theories, Western Christians normally read the early chapters of Genesis as describing the creation of already perfected human beings in a finished world. Luther's exaggerated description in his lectures on Genesis of the physical and mental endowments of Adam in Paradise is not atypical.[36] The entry of sin into the world, described in Genesis 3, was then seen as a precipitous fall from this perfect situation. If this is the case then salvation will naturally be understood as restoration of the primordial condition, and those who are saved will, in the resurrection, be returned to the "state of integrity" enjoyed by Adam and Eve before the fall.

The fact that scientific knowledge of early human beings and their closest relatives makes the existence of such a state of integrity in actual history quite problematic is only one problem with this approach. A careful look at the Bible and the theological tradition should make us ask whether we should even try to retain that concept of human beings already perfect in their origin.

Genesis does not tell us that the first humans were beautiful, intellectually brilliant, theologically astute, free of any defects, or had physical abilities beyond those of present-day human beings.[37] Descriptions of them like Luther's are pure speculation. Genesis 1–2 (and in fact the whole Bible) tells us very little about the first man and woman. Whether we read these chapters as a historical account of real human beings or as theological statements about humanity and its relationships with God and the world, we can get from them almost no information about an unspoiled human nature unless we bring preconceptions about it with us to the task. This would be very strange if we were intended to understand the biblical portrait of the first human beings in a state of integrity as the pattern of what genuine humanity is to be.

But that is not where we are to look for a model of humanity as God intends it to be. That model is not the "first Adam" but the "last" (1 Cor. 15:45), Jesus Christ. Karl Barth made this clear when he entitled his book on Romans 5 *Christ and Adam* rather than (as mere temporal order would lead us to expect) *Adam and Christ*.[38] It is Christ who shows us humanity as God intends it to be. Thus we are told in Ephesians 4:13 that we are to come "to maturity, to the measure of the full stature of Christ."

36. Martin Luther, "Lectures on Genesis, Chapters 1-5," in *Luther's Works,* vol. 1 (St. Louis: Concordia, 1958), p. 62.

37. There is the tradition of the primordial human as "the signet of perfection, full of wisdom and perfect in beauty . . . in Eden, the garden of God" in Ezek. 28:11-19. This is not presented by Ezekiel as history, however, but as a "broken myth" used to speak of the fate of the king of Tyre.

38. Karl Barth, *Christ and Adam* (New York: Harper & Brothers, 1956).

This being the case, we can say that there is already a significant "evolutionary" theme in Scripture. Of course that does not mean that we find neo-Darwinian biological evolution in the Bible. But there is there a view that humanity is to grow and develop toward the type of humanity that we see in Christ, and that the goal of creation is union with God. The Letter to the Ephesians (1:10) tells us explicitly of God's "plan for the fullness of time, to gather up all things in him [Christ], things in heaven and things on earth."

When we look at tradition of the Eastern Church we find a picture of early humanity rather different from that of the West, and more in line with the developmental picture that we have sketched. The 2nd-century apologist Theophilus of Antioch explained the prohibition of the tree of knowledge by saying, "Adam, being yet an infant in age, was on this account as yet unable to receive knowledge worthily."[39] According to Irenaeus, "The man was a young child, not yet having reached a perfect deliberation," and "it was necessary for him to reach full-development by growing in this way."[40] While for Augustine and the Western Church the perfection of humanity was actually realized in Paradise before the entry of sin, for Irenaeus and much of the Eastern tradition, humanity was created perfect only in a potential sense. God gave humanity the capability to progress, with divine grace, toward full and perfect humanity.[41]

Consider then the first small group of hominids (we need not decide here just how small, or precisely where or when they lived) who had evolved to be capable of self-consciousness and communication. Theologically, we understand the process through which this state had been reached as one example, albeit a very important one, of God's providential action through secondary causes. These humans are able in some way to receive and to some degree comprehend God's Word, to trust God, to know God's will for them and to obey it. They are at the beginning of a road along which God wants to lead them and their descendants to fully mature humanity and complete fellowship with God.

But they are also able to refuse their trust, and can disobey God's will for them. And they do. They take a wrong road, one that leads away from God. They and their descendants are soon alienated from God. The path they are on leads humanity away from the goal that God intends for them. They are lost in the woods, and night is coming on.

The idea of "taking a wrong road" is (like "the Fall") a metaphor for the human condition and should not be pressed too far. It is interesting, however,

39. Theophilus of Antioch, "Theophilus to Autolycus," in *The Ante-Nicene Fathers*, vol. 2 (Grand Rapids: Eerdmans, 1979 reprint), p. 104.

40. St. Irenaeus of Lyons, *On the Apostolic Preaching* (Crestwood, N.Y.: St. Vladimir's Seminary, 1997), p. 47.

41. Timothy Ware, *The Orthodox Church* (Baltimore: Penguin, 1963), pp. 224-25.

that this picture of a gradual departure from the course which God intends is the way that Athanasius seems to have seen the problem of sin.[42] More importantly, it is the picture which the early chapters of Genesis convey. The disobedience in the Garden is followed by Cain's murder of Abel, Lamech's exultation in unbounded vengeance, the wickedness and corruption that lead to the Flood, the hubris of the tower of Babel, and the breakdown of community. It is a process of falling, of moving away from God.

Finally, with the call of Abram, God begins a program of getting humanity back on the right road. Throughout the Old Testament people are called to "turn back" *(shubh)*, the common Old Testament term for "repent": "Return to the LORD your God, for he is gracious and merciful . . ." (Joel 2:13). Finally Jesus appears, inviting people to follow him.

It is very important at this point to realize that it is *not* the condition of being on a journey, of being unfinished or in process, which itself is sinful. Being participants in the evolutionary process means being God's creatures, which is good. The problem of sin is not that we are on a road, but that we're on a *wrong* road, one "that leads to destruction" (Matt. 7:13).

If this is the human problem, then salvation must mean being put back on the right road. It is the renewal of creation, not as a return to a perfect primordial state but as a reorientation of creation to its proper goal. The work of Christ is to be seen as re-creation, and anyone who is in Christ is a new creation (2 Cor. 5:17).

The theme of re-creation is closely connected with Irenaeus's concept of recapitulation, though again we should recognize that we are putting new meaning into that concept when we connect it with modern evolutionary theory. Gustaf Wingren points out the broad scope of Irenaeus's idea.

> The content of the term *recapitulatio* is both rich and diverse. There is, for instance, the idea of a restoration of the original in the word, a purificatory movement pointing backwards to the first Creation. This restoration is accomplished in Jesus's struggle against the Devil in a conflict which repeats the history of Adam, but with the opposite outcome. The idea of a repetition is thus part of the conception of recapitulation, but in a modified form — modified, that is, by the idea of victory. But since man was a growing being before he became enslaved, and since he is not restored until he has begun again to progress towards his destiny, man's restoration in itself is more than a mere reversion to his original position. The word *recapitulatio* also

42. Athanasius, "On the Incarnation of the Word," in *A Select Library of Nicene and Post-Nicene Fathers of the Christian Church*, 2nd series, vol. 4 (Grand Rapids: Eerdmans, 1978 reprint), pp. 37-39. See also p. lxxi of the Prolegomena by Archibald Robertson.

contains the idea of perfection or consummation, for recapitulation means that man's growth is resumed and renewed. That man grows, however, is merely a different aspect of the fact that God creates. Growth is always receptive in character, something derived from the source of life. Man's resumed growth is for this reason identical with the life which streams from Christ, the Head, to all believers. And Christ is the Creator's own creative Word, the "hand" by which God gives life to man.[43]

As the language of "victory" indicates, this idea of re-creation has a good deal in common with the model of atonement in which Christ is seen as the one who defeats the evil powers which hold humanity in bondage. But the idea of the work of Christ as a reorientation of creation also has some similarities with the "subjective" or "moral influence" model, according to which the example of Christ's sacrifice changes people's hearts. This is sometimes seen as a very weak notion of atonement, as indeed it can be, but it is possible to see the cross as having a real power, and not just as a passive example. We might, for example, use the model of a magnet to illustrate Christ's saying "I, when I am lifted up from the earth, will draw all people to myself" (John 12:32).[44] And Anselm, trying to explain the need for the incarnation, does not see it as a matter of satisfying God's honor or justice in the abstract, but of accomplishing God's purpose for creation.[45]

These various ways of speaking about salvation and atonement are, in other words, not mutually exclusive. Different images and models may be useful for different purposes — for preaching, for teaching groups at various levels of maturity, and for interactions with the natural sciences. Finally it is the Christ crucified and risen who saves, not one or another theory about how his death and resurrection are effective.

To this point we have, along with much of the Christian tradition, spoken about Christ as the savior of humanity. The scope of salvation in the Bible, however, is not that narrow. We have already noted the verse in Ephesians (1:10) which speaks about God's plan to bring together "all things" (ta panta) in Christ. That same phrase is used in Colossians 1:20, where we are told that

43. Wingren, *Man and the Incarnation*, pp. 173-74.

44. Kent S. Knutson, *His Only Son Our Lord* (Minneapolis: Augsburg, 1966), pp. 72-75.

45. Anselm expresses this in a way that seems odd to modern thought. God foresaw a definite number of rational beings who were to enter into the celestial city and enjoy the contemplation of God. The number of fallen angels is to be made up from among human beings. See Anselm, "Why God Became Man," pp. 125-34 and 182. The idea goes back to Augustine: See St. Augustine, "The Enchiridion" (ch. 28), in *A Select Library of Nicene and Post-Nicene Fathers of the Christian Church*, vol. 3, 1st series (Grand Rapids: Eerdmans, 1978 reprint), p. 247.

through Christ "God was pleased to reconcile to himself all things, whether on earth or in heaven, by making peace through the blood of his cross." In Romans 8:18-25 it is "the creation" which looks forward to liberation from its bondage to decay. If we realize that we are not fully human as isolated individuals, but only in relationship with the rest of creation, we will see that we cannot really be saved unless the rest of creation is too.

We need not imagine that nonhuman animals have somehow sinned, or enter into speculations about "Dog heaven." What resurrection might mean for extinct species, for the dinosaurs and the dodo, must be quite obscure to us. But if God's purpose is genuinely cosmic, as the language about new heavens and a new earth (Isa. 65:17 and 66:22; 2 Pet. 3:13; Rev. 21:1) indicates, we should give some thought to how that purpose is fulfilled in Christ.[46] And here, perhaps surprisingly, we find that an evolutionary view of creation suggests answers that are not available to theologies which see humanity as a separate creation.

One of the consequences of evolution is that each human being bears within him- or herself some common history and structure with other living things. We share the same genetic code with other organisms, the molecular structure of crucial substances like hemoglobin is very similar to that of other mammals (with differences depending on the degree of relationship in the evolutionary process), and many human anatomical structures are homologous to those of other animals. We have some history in common with insects, somewhat more with fish, and a great deal with other primates. The relationships even extend to the inorganic realm, and beyond the earth. The carbon in our bodies was formed in stellar interiors and dispersed by supernovae, and all the matter in the universe can be traced back to a common origin in the Big Bang.

By assuming our common humanity in the incarnation, God took on these evolutionary relationships and became a participant in this history. Christ, like the rest of us, is a cousin of apes and a distant relative of the dinosaurs. We return to the offense of the bestial ancestry of the Son of God, but see it now in a quite different light. "That which is not taken is not healed," but there is a very real sense in which now "all things" are taken up in the incarnation of the Word. Like the scandal of the cross, this offense is in God's hands the means of salvation.

---

46. C. S. Lewis discussed how the salvation of animals might be understood in *The Problem of Pain* (New York: Macmillan, 1962), ch. 9. A letter of Evelyn Underhill's to Lewis in which she criticized his treatment because it dealt only with tame animals is in *The Letters of Evelyn Underhill* (London: Longmans, Green, 1943), pp. 300-302.

The Evolution of the Body of Christ[47]

The work of Christ is made effective in the world through the Church, as the Holy Spirit inspires proclamation of the gospel, worship of God, making of disciples, and service to the world. We consider now the relationship between evolution and the Church, the Body of Christ.

Uses of this image in the New Testament are vivid. In 1 Corinthians 12:12-31 and Romans 12:4-8 Paul draws out the idea that members with differing gifts and functions are united into a single body. In Ephesians the image has cosmic scope, with Christ the head of the body, which is a "new humanity" (2:15). The Pauline concept has similarities with another biological picture, that of Christ as the vine and disciples as branches (John 15:1-8; cf. Ps. 80:8-19). J. A. T. Robinson traced Paul's idea of the Body of Christ to his experience on the Damascus road and the revelation that Christ was being persecuted in his members.[48]

Since "all things" have been created for Christ, the body of which he is the head is the primary creation (Col. 1:16-18). The formation of a people of God follows the origin of the world in time, but in God's intention "before the foundation of the world" (Eph. 1:4), the old is for the sake of the new.

As the universe begins with God's creation *ex nihilo*, the Church begins with the cross and resurrection of Jesus. The gospel that calls the Church into being is the same Word by which God created and sustains the world. But the creation story that begins with Genesis 1:1 is one of *mediated* creation, God commanding the elements of the world to bring forth life (Gen. 1:11, 20, 24): God acts in the world through natural processes. There is a parallel to this in the means of grace, proclamation of the gospel and the sacraments, through which the Holy Spirit builds up the Church. The connections between the sacraments and the Body of Christ in 1 Corinthians are significant in this regard:

> For in the one Spirit we were all baptized into one body. (1 Cor. 12:13)

> The bread that we break, is it not a sharing in the body of Christ? Because there is one bread, we who are many are one body, for we all partake of the one bread. (1 Cor. 10:16-17)

The unity of the body follows from common incorporation through baptism and communion in one meal. The Spirit's sustenance of the Church through

47. For further discussion see George L. Murphy, "The Church in Evolution," *Seminary Ridge Review* 5.1 (2002): 38-50.

48. John A. T. Robinson, *The Body* (Philadelphia: Westminster, 1977), p. 58.

the means of grace parallels God's sustenance of biological organisms through natural processes.

When we consider the development of the Body of Christ through time, we have something stronger than analogy between creation and new creation. To speak of thoroughly mediated creation of life is to speak of divine activity by means of evolution, and Teilhard de Chardin suggested that the Body of Christ is the next stage of evolution.[49]

The earliest fossils are of single-celled organisms. A few of these came together to form multicellular systems, and evolution led to specialized organs that enabled functions to be carried out efficiently. The stage was thus set for consciousness and human personality. As Teilhard put it, "union creates . . . differentiates . . . [and] personalizes."[50] This is like Paul's picture of the Body of Christ, in which differentiation of members according to their spiritual gifts means unity and strength. Just as multicellular organisms developed from single cells, Teilhard argued that the Body of Christ is a hyper-personal organism. People become most fully themselves as members of this body, without any crushing out of individual personalities: Union differentiates and personalizes.

Faith sees the Church as the Body of Christ, just as it sees the world as God's creation. The natural sciences enable us to understand the world in itself, but it is faith, not science, which sees it as creation (Heb. 11:3). In the same way, the social sciences can understand Christian communities within the world, but it is a statement of faith that they are parts of one body of which Christ is the head. Just as faith is needed to see God's hand in what goes on in the world, it is required if we are to relate developments in churches to the intention and activity of the Holy Spirit.

If the Body of Christ evolves, it will not be identical today with the Church of the 1st century. Some things remain constant, just as the chemical elements and laws of biochemistry provide a stable basis for biological development. The Church must continue to be centered on the gospel proclaimed by the apostles, but belief that today's Church should be the same in all ways as during the apostolic period parallels a "creationism" which denies biological evolution. Various features of the Church, such as forms of worship and ministry and even formulations of doctrine, should not be expected to be the same in the 21st century as in the 1st.

We can learn something about the Church by considering evolutionary

49. Pierre Teilhard de Chardin, *Christianity and Evolution* (New York: Harcourt Brace Jovanovich, 1969), pp. 16, 66-72.

50. Pierre Teilhard de Chardin, *Activation of Energy* (New York: Harcourt Brace Jovanovich, 1970), pp. 115-16.

history from the standpoint of faith. It would not have been possible, at any time in the history of life on Earth, to predict which lines of development would succeed. A hundred million years ago the future seemed to belong to dinosaurs with overwhelming size and power, and not to insignificant mammals. Even if the asteroid impact that ended the dinosaurs' reign had been foreseen, it would have been natural to think that dominant mammals would develop as the dinosaurs did, toward great strength and size. But the cutting edge of evolution was something quite different, intelligence, a feature not apparent in the world before the emergence of humanity.

If asteroid impacts and other cataclysms have played a major role in the history of life on Earth, a picture of slow change and adaptation of species is incomplete.[51] Sudden catastrophes can introduce entirely new situations. The threat of Jeremiah (26:1-19) that the temple would be destroyed sounded blasphemous to those who heard it, for the building of Solomon's temple seemed to be an irreversible development in God's history with his people. It was not: The temple was destroyed, yet God remained faithful to his promises.[52] And centuries later there is another surprising turn when the risen Christ becomes the true temple and dwelling of God with his people (John 1:14; 2:19-21).[53]

Similar things can happen with orderings of ministry, forms of worship, and expressions of theology that have developed during the Church's history. They may represent the Spirit's will for the Church at one time, but are not irreversible. Characteristics that were advantageous in one environment may become useless or detrimental when the environment changes. If the species survives, such features may be lost or become vestigial.

Apparently promising lines of development, both in biological evolution and in the history of God's people, have been cut off, with development taking new directions. We can trace continuities and changes in the past. Scientifically, we can understand their logic in terms of adaptation to the environment. Theologically, we can discern divine faithfulness amid change. But we cannot, in the middle of things, foretell changes in species or in the structures of the Church that the Spirit wills for the next century.

The Church is not, even in its full extension throughout space-time, the totality of God's new creation, the new heavens and earth, but it has a crucial place in the cosmic transformation. Its members are the "first fruits" of God's creatures (James 1:18), and through the Church God's wisdom is to "be made

---

51. Stephen Jay Gould, *Wonderful Life* (New York: Norton, 1989).

52. James A. Sanders, *Torah and Canon* (Philadelphia: Fortress, 1972), pp. 85-87.

53. George L. Murphy, "The Incarnation as a Theanthropic Principle," *Word & World* 13 (1993): 256-62.

known to the rulers and authorities in the heavenly places" (Eph. 3:10). If the Church is, as Luther said, simply "the holy believers and lambs who hear the voice of their Shepherd,"[54] belief in the resurrection and eternal life means that the Church is an eschatological reality. It will not be replaced by the Kingdom of God, for the ultimate realm of God will be larger than the Church.

The final vision of Revelation 21 is of the heavenly city come to earth (v. 10). The Church is part of this vision, for the Lamb and those written in the Lamb's book of life are in the new Jerusalem (v. 27). There is, indeed, no temple there (v. 22) — present ecclesiastical structures, like the Jerusalem temple, are at best of penultimate significance. But all the good that has been accomplished in history is saved and incorporated into this resurrection reality. "People will bring into it the glory and the honor of the nations" (v. 26).

54. Martin Luther, "Smalcald Articles" (3, 12) in *Concordia Triglotta* (St. Louis: Concordia, 1921), p. 499.

The Peaceable Kingdom

LAURIE J. BRAATEN

They will not hurt or destroy on all my holy mountain; for the earth will be full of the knowledge of the LORD as the waters cover the sea.

Isaiah 11:9 (NRSV)

Journal Entry:
Saturday, August 3, 1996, day 15 of the Maine section of the Appalachian Trail. [My wife] Brenda and I have had some hard days behind us — rains, flooded crossings, and knee, calf, ankle, and arch problems. On top of it all we miscalculated on the food and I am tiring easily as my glycogen stores are quickly being depleted. So it is with apprehension that we face crossing the Bigelow and Avery Mountains. We get an early start and are immediately impressed with the beauty of the rolling trail. We see the three peaks of the Bigelows and off in the distance the Averys — are we really going to walk that far today?

I stop to repair my broken gaiter strap on a boulder as Brenda pushes ahead. I hear a nasally squawk. I "spish" it out expecting a nuthatch; to my surprise it is a chickadee. Closer inspection reveals it has a brown cap — a Boreal Chickadee, my first one! Usually shy, this one is obviously used to free handouts from passing hikers. We ascend and descend the Bigelow where we find large boulder caves; ladders assist us in the steeper sections. Above the tree line we sample the Bilberries and Mountain Cranberries — tart but tasty. The views from the mountain are clear and stupendous. We stop at the East summit for a 1:00 lunch. We fellowship with two young college students — united by our common love for the outdoors and backpacking. We push on toward the West Peak; I fill our empty water bottles at a small refreshing spring. The Averys are two horns — between them is a long walk and a nice pond, where we take a quick dip. After descending the South Peak, I fetch some more

Photo: Crossing a beaver dam on the Appalachian Trail.

water at a spring where two unidentified birds hop from branch to branch while they eye me with curiosity.

The terrain is uneven and rolling; descending the mountains is taking longer than we expected. It is early evening and we are anxious to find a campsite. In one flat spot I am suddenly aware of a grouse running beside me, then it trots off into the woods, attempting to distract me from her now adolescent chicks that are well camouflaged and hiding in the ground cover. Rounding a bend ahead of Brenda, I see a large beaver pond with a massive dam, the largest I have seen. There must be a beaver here somewhere. I pause, watching. Brenda catches up, waits a minute, and then starts out. Almost immediately I see ripples below the far end of the dam — "Brenda, there's a beaver over there!" We stand together and eventually see more ripples; a small head occasionally surfaces in the distance. The beaver starts making a circle — no, a series of circles, spiraling closer and closer to our shore. We hold perfectly still as his head emerges out of water. "Shhh, don't scare it away!" I whisper. The beaver is now within twenty feet of us; his head emerges and he is looking right at our spot. I can't believe he doesn't see us — then it dawns on us — he does see us! He has

17 An Evolving Creation and Environmental Issues

JEFFREY GREENBERG

Introduction: Dynamic Systems Binding Life and Nonlife

Biological evolution is necessarily linked to change in landscape, atmosphere, and oceans through time.[1] Diversity in these features constitutes the rich variety of life environments, and by adaptation life conforms to its environment. This close alliance between life and environment has led scientific and philosophical thinkers to see also the compatibility from the opposite perspective. Organisms cause the modification and evolution of environments as well. James Lovelock's Gaia concept goes as far as to interpret the Earth's interaction between living and nonliving components as a type of mega organism itself.[2] Evangelical Christians might be uncomfortable with the New Age associations of Gaia, but there can be no doubt that living things and environmental elements influence change in each other. There is a sort of feedback control of change seen in certain examples. A near-equilibrium stability in populations seems to be the natural ground state of existence. When a particular species expands its population much beyond its usual size in a given area, the impact of resource depletion may temporarily result in habitat loss for that or another species. A die-off may result, or, if possible, the population will migrate out of the area to seek new resource support. In many cases, the decrease in exploitation enables the degraded region to recover. Such episodes of boom or bust are common in most habitats. This is true with regard to predator-prey relationships or during "plagues" of invading locusts.

The Earth seems to be made with resilient systems. Geographer Richard

---

1. See the chapter "Geological Framework of an Evolving Creation" in this volume.

2. J. E. Lovelock, *Gaia: A New Look at Life on Earth* (Oxford and New York: Oxford University Press, 1979); idem, *The Ages of Gaia* (New York: Bantam, 1988).

Huggett has characterized the various realms of material dynamics on Earth as "spheres," including the "ecosphere" which encompasses all the interactive components of life environments.[3] Major enduring shifts in environmental systems are rare over short time scales. Perhaps only an asteroid collision has the potential for near-instantaneous alteration of conditions that could affect global environmental change. This fortunately is not a known occurrence in the recent geological past. Earth systems can recover rather quickly from other brief phenomena like earthquakes, floods, fires, or volcanic eruptions. Ecological recovery quickly followed the disastrous fires of Yellowstone National Park in 1988, the eruption of Mount St. Helens in 1980, and the perennial floods of the Amazon River and the Nile prior to its damming.[4] Major long-term agents of change are considered to occur naturally from lithospheric (plate tectonic) reorganization and the eccentricity of Earth orbit.

It is instructive to consider other cases of natural change in specific localities. Students in my classes are often aghast to realize that northern Wisconsin was a site of ocean-floor volcanism, desert sand dunes swept across northern Scotland, continental glaciers advanced across the Sahara, and dinosaurs lived on a subtropical Antarctica.[5] The Badlands of South Dakota pose another interesting case of change.[6] During 30 million years or so, the sedimentary environment adjacent to and contemporaneous with the uplift of the Black Hills changed from Cretaceous marine (cephalopod-bearing black shales) to Oligocene prairie, woodland, and finally wetlands.[7] The environmental shift was accompanied by an adapted fauna filling new ecological niches as they developed. All of the Oligocene forms, including titanotheres and oreodonts,[8]

---

3. R. J. Huggett, *Geoecology* (London: Routledge, 1995); idem, *The Evolving Ecosphere* (London: Routledge, 1997).

4. H. J. DeBlij, *Nature on the Rampage* (Washington, D.C.: Smithsonian Institution, 1994); A. Scarth, *Vulcan's Fury: Man Against the Volcano* (New Haven: Yale University Press, 1999); N. J. H. Smith, E. A. S. Serrao, P. T. Alvim, and I. C. Falesi, *Amazonia — Resiliency and Dynamism of the Land and Its People* (Tokyo: United Nations University Press, 1995); J. Waterbury, *Hydropolitics of the Nile Valley* (Syracuse, N.Y.: Syracuse University Press, 1979).

5. S. M. Stanley, *The Earth and Life through Time*, 2nd ed. (New York: Freeman, 1989); J. J. W. Rogers, *A History of the Earth* (Cambridge: Cambridge University Press, 1993).

6. J. P. Gries, *Roadside Geology of South Dakota* (Missoula, Mont.: Mountain, 1996).

7. P. R. Bjork and J. R. McDonald, "Geology of the Badlands and Pine Ridge Area, South Dakota," in *Geology of the Black Hills South Dakota and Wyoming*, ed. F. J. Rich (Alexandria, Va.: American Geological Institute, 1985).

8. Titanotheres were a group of mostly large, rhinoceroslike herbivores displaying a wide variety of skull ornamentation (horns, etc.). Oreodonts were smaller, dog- to sheep-sized grazers known only from North America. Some are thought to have possessed defensive poison glands behind their eye sockets.

have since become extinct, replaced by other beasts serving the same ecological function. A contrasting historical record exists in the coral reef carbonate platform of the Bahamas. This region has sustained an essentially consistent environment over the last 100 million years.[9] Exploratory drilling by petroleum companies indicates that reef ecosystems persist there throughout 30,000 feet of strata.[10] Bahamian geologic history is analogous to ancient civilizations built successively upon the ruins of predecessors. Periods of constructive reef growth are interrupted by episodes of storm destruction or die back. The environment remained relatively the same while the evolution of reef organisms (algae, corals, foraminifera, sponges, mollusks, etc.) produced notable variation in species filling the same ecological niches.

As Huggett mentions, the complexities of environmental shifts operate at different time scales, depending on the "sphere" of influence.[11] The mobility of the atmospheric and hydrospheric realms allows relatively rapid alteration of conditions (chemical composition, temperature, current direction and velocity), whereas the more solid stuff of the lithosphere (rocks) is much slower to change through tectonic plate motion, uplift, and erosion. Likewise, vegetation patterns are more fluid than the geometry of most landscapes. Animals and less mobile plant communities do tend to migrate with the geographical shift in their habitat. At our scale of observation, some natural evolutionary shifts appear smooth and gradual because they are relatively slow. The creep of soil down a hill slope, the lateral meandering of a stream, or the migration of sand dunes are noticed only after long periods of observation. Of course the migration of the North American tectonic plate away from Eurasia at approximately 4 cm. per year is even less perceptible.[12] The wide variation in time scales of events can be appreciated from figure 1.

Genetic drift in biological evolution is also a very slow process by the reckoning of direct human observation. We record mutation-based variations in short-lived species like fruit flies but cannot witness the major adaptive shifts as contrasts among distinctive taxonomic groups, say from fish to amphibian to reptile to bird.

The concept of punctuated equilibrium in biological evolution is a useful

9. R. E. Sheridan, H. T. Mullins, J. A. Austin Jr., M. M. Ball, and J. W. Ladd, "Geology and Geophysics of the Bahamas," in *The Atlantic Continental Margin: U.S.,* vol. 1-2: *The Geology of North America,* ed. R. E. Sheridan and J. A. Grow (Washington, D.C.: Geological Society of America, 1988), pp. 329-64.

10. H. G. Mutter, *Field Guide to Some Carbonate Rock Environments, Florida Keys and Western Bahamas* (Dubuque, Ia.: Kendall-Hunt, 1977).

11. Huggett, *Evolving Ecosphere.*

12. F. Press and R. Siever, *Understanding Earth* (New York: Freeman, 2000).

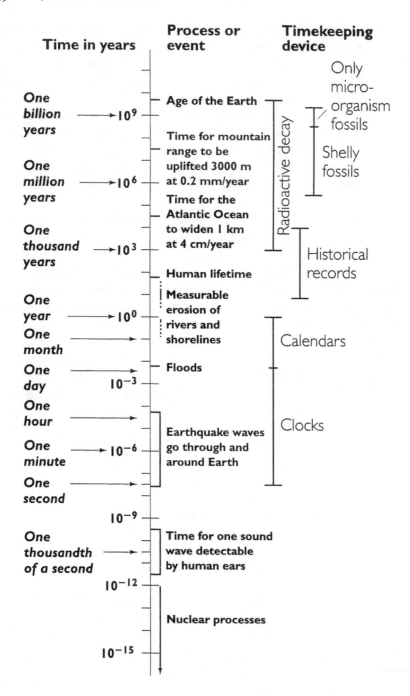

Figure 1. Comparison of various time scales used to describe various Earth processes.

way to perceive dramatic environmental shifts as well.[13] Fossil organisms often seem to exist in a basically unmodified state for long spans of time (stasis) before evolving dramatically over a relatively brief span (punctuation, saltation). It is possible that what we view after the fact is accumulated minor changes that reach a threshold when there occurs a rapid conversion to new forms. Nature does exhibit other threshold phenomena such as earthquakes along fault zones of accumulated elastic strain, chemical equilibrium shifts in supersaturated media, and hill-slope failure. In each case, there is a seemingly gradual buildup prior to catastrophic change.[14] What appears at first to be linear, steady-state change is really the summation of many episodic shifts toward an inevitable end. The nonlinear complexities of the behavior are masked by time.[15] The direction of change is not random in the sense of anything being possible. Natural laws programmed into all of Earth's spheres constrain the results of evolution. Some, including Stephen Gould, conclude that the product of evolution is contingent upon the initial system conditions (à la chaos theory). Christians see the constraints as ordained, for example, as expressed in many of the contributions in this volume.

The one wild card in all the influential components of Earth is humanity. We are capable of affecting local and global systems unlike any other factor. Enlightening research by the University of Maine geologist R. L. Hooke estimates that the activities of people are as effective as all natural Earth processes (geomorphic agents) combined in changing the physical, chemical, and biological state of the world.[16] For example, land-use practices throughout the world greatly accelerate the addition of soil and other sediment into stream systems. The divine image confers great creativity and industry on us, but, because of our fallen nature, the image is distorted. We are to exercise God-given wisdom in caring for the creation placed in our charge.[17] Ample evidence indicates that the responsibility inherent in our role is generally ignored or rejected. This is sadly true of Bible-believing Christians as well as other citizens of the planet.

13. D. H. Erwin and R. L. Anstey, eds., *New Approaches to Speciation in the Fossil Record* (New York: Columbia University Press, 1995).

14. S. J. Gould, "Toward the Vindication of Punctuational Change," in *Catastrophies in Earth History,* ed. W. A. Berggren and J. A. Van Couvering (Princeton: Princeton University Press, 1984), pp. 9-34.

15. Huggett, *Evolving Ecosphere.*

16. R. L. Hooke, "On the Efficacy of Humans as Geomorphic Agents," *GSA Today* 4 (1994): 217, 224-25; R. L. Hooke, "On the History of Humans as Geomorphic Agents," *Geology* 28 (2000): 843-46.

17. F. A. Schaeffer, *Pollution and the Death of Man* (Wheaton, Ill.: Tyndale House, 1970); F. A. Schaeffer, *How Shall We Then Live?* (Old Tappan, N.J.: Revell, 1976); W. A. Dyrness, "Are We Our Planet's Keeper?" *Christianity Today,* April 8, 1991, p. 41.

Our attitudes must be judged by the full testimony of Scripture as special revelation as well as by the testimony of Creation itself, in God's general revelation.[18] There are evangelicals with economic and political commitments that even deny the existence of significant environmental problems.[19] Perhaps with a better understanding of the evolving creation and its function in the economy of its creator, Christians in particular will improve in stewardship.

Who God Is and How the Earth Works

Change is the nature of almost everything. Among all that exists, God alone is unchanging. Even his Word, the Bible, is interpreted with refinements as we learn more from archeology, linguistics, and cultural studies. Two aspects of the character of God may be sufficient to define his reign over all Creation. The Lord God of the Bible is both all-powerful (omnipotent) and all-loving, "good" (omnibenevolent). All his other attributes pertinent to this discussion are established in these two. It therefore follows that everything God does or intends is good. This is true even though fallen human nature cannot see the good, especially over the short term. The ultimate paradox is that the horrific sacrifice of God himself in Jesus was the means of our deliverance from eternal loss.

Given evolution, at least in the general geologic sense, and the character of the creator, it can be argued that this God-ordained way of creating and the Creation itself are good. By studying the natural systems and Earth history, we can gain insight into the way it all is supposed to function. In other words, we seek wisdom in the ways that the Earth is designed[20] to operate so that life is sustainable within the framework of change. Many environmental problems are the negative consequence of human interaction with the rest of Creation. These occur either from getting in the way of natural systems, such as living too close to a destructive volcano (residents of Montserrat in the West Indies, for

18. S. Bouma-Prediger, "Creation Care and Character: The Nature and Necessity of the Ecological Virtues," *Perspectives on Science and Christian Faith* 50 (1998): 6-21. See also the following chapter in this volume by L. Braaten.

19. E. C. Beisner, *Where Garden Meets Wilderness — Evangelical Entry into the Environmental Debate* (Grand Rapids: Eerdmans, 1997). J. Ball, "The Use of Ecology in the Evangelical Protestant Response to the Ecological Crisis," *Perspectives on Science and Christian Faith* 50 (1998): 32-38.

20. The terms "design" and "genius" are primarily in reference to faith-based conclusions by theists. Many Christians, supported by Rom. 1:18-20, believe that the data of nature in Creation should serve as apologetic evidence for a creator. This is particularly true of the fine-tuned harmonious character of Earth's interacting systems.

example), or from our detrimental alteration of a natural system, such as over-withdrawal of groundwater resources (Mexico City or the Ogalala Aquifer as examples). To resist some processes of change or establish unnatural conditions may be to act contrary to God's intended direction of evolution. It is also easy to envision how our activities may greatly speed up the process of natural change and initiate crises beyond the capability of a system to adjust. In the case of the Ogalala Aquifer in the central United States, the natural groundwater system is governed by equilibrium, the balance of discharge with recharge.[21] If exploited wisely (discharged at or below the rate of recharge), the aquifer's resource would be sustainable. It can be argued that as part of an evolving creation, resources are not meant to remain unchanged and available indefinitely. However, today there are few valid excuses for ignoring science and ruining the blessing of natural resources.

Health Metaphor

One ironic aspect of modern life is that we in the developed nations especially are living longer lives but maybe not "naturally." Without the wonders of medical science, human beings may actually be genetically programmed to die earlier on the average than seventy years ago.[22] Modern blessings of emotional stress, poor diet, lack of exercise, and harmful chemicals all contribute to our current state. Our decreased natural health is countered by pharmaceuticals and technology. This may make life longer, but is it better? Are we genetically evolving in the right direction? Earth's physical and chemical systems mirror our own modern changes. In DuPage County, Illinois, little natural environment remains from presettlement times. In populous, developed areas, it is of course very difficult to maintain natural features of the land. Modern human substitutes of landscape, trees, waterways, and atmospheric conditions have typically been poorly conceived. The new landscape, like our modern bodies, must constantly be pampered to keep from failing. The analogy follows that progress has placed many of us on artificial lifestyle support. There is little there to evolve. The future will not inherit much of enduring significance, "good," from our suburban re-creation of Creation.

Notable among DuPage's re-creations are the faulty exploitation of fresh-

21. J. Opie, *Ogalala — Water for a Dry Land,* 2nd ed. (Lincoln: University of Nebraska Press, 2000).

22. M. A. Benarde, *Our Precarious Habitat* (New York: Wiley, 1989); D. M. Kammen and D. M. Hassenzahl, *Should We Risk It? — Exploring Environmental Health and Technological Problem Solving* (Princeton: Princeton University Press, 1999).

water resources and a chaotic ecological imbalance. The county now resorts to the introduction of Lake Michigan water (25 mi. away) by pipeline. This was necessitated by the contamination of a shallow, high-capacity glacial aquifer[23] and the gross depletion of a deeper bedrock aquifer. The loss of these two local water sources was probably not inevitable. It may have been avoided by careful planning, zoning, and development in concert with natural systems.

DuPage County's surface and ground waters are contaminated by several sources including road salt, petroleum, domestic waste, and a myriad of hazardous chemicals (fertilizers, pesticides, herbicides, etc.). An obvious effect of this pollution has been on aquatic organisms. Certain algae, microinvertebrate animals, and plants as key "indicator species"[24] have disappeared from DuPage wetland areas in just the last decade. Loss of indicator species and decreased biodiversity are established signs of ecological illness (see below). Local suburbanites may be amused by deer, coyotes, fox, and even beaver that pass through their neighborhoods. We might even get the impression that nature is invading us. In reality, extensive land conversion has forced some animals out of existence and others to behave in strange ways as they attempt to survive in an alien world. Poodles have become the prey of coyotes.

Science can provide us with knowledge of how natural systems are supposed to function. One definition of health is soundness and the absence of disease. In reference to the human organism, it means a body functioning as intended. A simple-systems analysis of the body indicates a vastly complex interaction of different parts in harmonious interdependence. Injury or germs threaten the continuance of health. Poor maintenance and substance abuse may also cause system failure. As a sign of creative genius, we were fearfully and wonderfully made to exist and prosper in all varieties of potentially hostile environments. We have defense systems that allow us to sustain stress and injury, to harbor dangerous microbes, and even to poison ourselves, and survive. Today, for the most part, we understand the approximate limits of our self-preserving biochemistry. After years of alcohol or tobacco use, a tolerance threshold may be reached. Like a fifty-year-old soccer player's Achilles tendon, resilience is finally lost and failure is imminent. Study of natural laws and Earth systems demonstrates that the health of environments is correctly perceived as analogous to the human body.

23. An aquifer is the permeable body of material (rock, soil, etc.) that serves as the conduit for groundwater flow.

24. An indicator species is an organism sensitive to certain environmental conditions within a given ecosystem. For example, the live canary in a mine indicated enough good air to sustain miners, or some amphibians show sensitivity through their unique skin to air pollution and ultraviolet radiation. The decline of these organisms in an ecosystem may signal problems of air quality or ozone depletion.

Frontier colonists settle along a stream providing them transportation, potable water, good hunting, and protection from invasion on one side of their new village. They also find the stream a convenient receptacle for their waste. After a few generations, a larger town now exists on the site and other settlements are established both up and down stream. The volume of water extracted from the stream and the amount of waste materials introduced reach a threshold where the flow regime no longer maintains good water quality. The stream has become "ill" in terms of its proper function. As a consequence, other components of the local (and perhaps, regional) ecosystem are adversely affected. The consequences of systemic failure might be reversed, or this particular patient might die, having no hope for any ecological recovery. In relation to its effect on evolution, the degraded stream ecology could eliminate significant biodiversity from the area (note the section on biodiversity below).

One actual case of stream degradation occurred when the Army Corps of Engineers channeled the Kissimmee River in central Florida.[25] Channeling transformed the naturally meandering curves into a straight ditch with uniform depth and width. This was completed in the 1960s as one of the many flood control and drainage projects that have nearly eliminated the Everglades as a unique environmental treasure. Within several months of its conversion, the Kissimmee system lost an abundance of its plant and animal species. This project was so obviously wrong that it is being reversed with the restoration of the river's natural geometry. As with heart-bypass surgery or angioplasty, remedial efforts in south Florida may save the region from death and re-create some of the natural flow of its lifeblood.

Soil Evolution and Health

The development of soil in many regions of the world offers another relevant metaphor. In order for the soil to become a functional, thriving ecocommunity, there needs to be the "death" of preexisting rock as well as organisms. *In situ* soil development commonly occurs very slowly as the agents of weathering and erosion decompose bedrock. It is quite likely that thousands of years are necessary for this conversion under conditions of a temperate climate.[26] A mature soil profile typically provides some vital environmental services. A prime capa-

25. A. F. Randazzo and D. S. Jones, *The Geology of Florida* (Gainsville: University Press of Florida, 1997).

26. N. C. Brady and R. R. Weil, *Elements of the Nature and Properties of Soils* (Upper Saddle River, N.J.: Prentice-Hall, 2000).

bility of healthy soil is to supply nutrients to the web of plants, insects, worms, and microorganisms. There is also the seemingly miraculous aspect of soil as a water filtration system. The small particle size (less than .0256 mm.) and geochemistry of clay tend to facilitate the removal of metal ions, organic molecules, and microbes. This is done through a combination of absorption and adsorption, in which the pollutants are attracted to the clay by electrostatic charges. A very small total volume of clay-rich material represents a huge surface area for filtration. Even highly contaminated water can become purified to drinking quality after passing through a few meters of soil. Utilizing this natural system in water treatment (septic system) is far more efficient than the typical urban or suburban sewerage–water treatment design.[27] Some newer designs have cleverly incorporated the natural concept into large-scale systems that serve entire communities.[28]

Mature soils may result from long-duration, slow processes, but they and their utility can be destroyed rapidly by human activity. Modern construction of buildings, roadways, and other structures excavates soil and effectively ruins its evolved architecture. Combining this modification with the loss of rainwater infiltration due to surface covering (roofs, pavement, etc.) creates large areas where groundwater is disrupted and flash flooding can occur. Improper farming practices commonly destroy soil utility through overuse (nutrient loss), erosion, pollution from additives, or combinations of these. The imbalance between natural formation and human-induced soil erosion is on the order of ten times more soil removed as produced each year.[29] The loss of soil vitality sooner or later results in a spiral of ecological ills affecting all manner of life, including human, beyond the immediately rooted plants. Eroded soil commonly ends up in streams or other water bodies, causing additional negative impacts. Coral reefs and coastal fisheries have been badly damaged by soil sediment derived from agriculture, deforestation, mining, and coastal development in many places such as the Philippines and Indonesia.[30]

27. R. D. Woodson, *Builders' Guide to Wells and Septics* (New York: McGraw-Hill, 1996).

28. The organization, Future Water International (FWI), directed by visionary CEO, J. R. Shaeffer, has designed and built many water-recycling systems throughout the United States and in various other areas around the world. The basic concept of water management for FWI is to collect domestic wastewater, treat it aerobically, store it, and finally use it as a nutrient-rich resource when reintroduced upon lawns or agricultural plots.

29. L. Wilkinson, ed., *Earthkeeping in the '90s* (Grand Rapids: Eerdmans, 1991), for example, pp. 28-30.

30. D. H. Chadwick, "Coral in Peril," *National Geographic* 195 (January 1999): 30-37.

Our Legacy from Adam and Noah (Biodiversity)

Life on this planet has a wonderfully rich history of change in accord with the progression of environments through time. The fossil record indicates increasing diversity and brilliant innovations enabling life to colonize every imaginable (and some perhaps unimagined) niche in Creation. Our stories of Adam naming the beasts and birds and Noah's responsibility to preserve each creature convey a sense of holy delight and purpose in the great biological diversity. The fossils also record certain times in the past where the trends toward increased diversity were disrupted by major extinctions.[31]

The extinction that included the dinosaurs at the end of the Mesozoic is probably the most famous episode. However, the so-called "Great Extinction" at the end of the Paleozoic was the most effective in removing organisms in the past. Approximately 90 percent of all species living in the Permian period (290-245 million years ago) did not survive into the Mesozoic. Although these episodes appear sudden from a geologic perspective, they were probably extended over hundreds of thousands to a few millions of years. Their causes may have been as simple and dramatic as the results from asteroid impacts, or perhaps the causes were more complex interactions of geologic phenomena, such as profuse volcanism, climate changes, and variations in ocean currents.[32]

Scientists today realize that plant and animal species are being lost from Earth at an unprecedented rate. Even if it is not true that thousands of species per year are lost,[33] more modest estimations still indicate a tremendous decrease in biodiversity. In terms of rate, the Permian extinction is being dwarfed! There is no debate concerning the cause of this loss; it is from human activity — primarily land conversions and habitat destruction.[34] It can be argued that people are not external influences on the environment but another one of Earth's vital system components.[35] It can also be reasonably argued that we as

31. V. Courtillot, *Evolutionary Catastrophes — The Science of Mass Extinction* (Cambridge: Cambridge University Press, 1999).

32. Courtillot, *Evolutionary Catastrophes;* C. Officer and J. Page, *Tales of the Earth — Paroxysms and Perturbations of the Blue Planet* (New York: Oxford University Press, 1993).

33. V. Morell, "The Variety of Life," "Wilderness Headcount," and "The Sixth Extinction," *National Geographic* 195 (February 1999): 6-59.

34. Morell, "The Variety of Life," "Wilderness Headcount," and "The Sixth Extinction"; J. X. Kasperson, R. E. Kasperson, and B. L. Turner II, eds., *Regions at Risk — Comparisons of Threatened Environments* (Tokyo: United Nations University Press, 1995).

35. J. J. Hidore, *Global Environmental Change* (Upper Saddle River, N.J.: Prentice-Hall, 1996); Lovelock, *Gaia.*

the peak of God's creation (and evolution), by our very nature, make such a significant impact on Earth systems. The scientific and ethical question is whether or not this scale of influence is "good" or necessary.

It is not a difficult scientific task to describe the good of a diverse ecosystem. This can be done with respect to human benefit,[36] from the perspective of ecosystem health[37] or with regard to evolutionary trends.[38] Of course, this good is most strongly impressed on us with regard to the God-given value inherent in living things. The loss of diversity in environments capable of and intended to foster a rich variety of interdependent organisms can eliminate system equilibrium. This point was made above concerning extreme runaway populations that outcompete other species. The victorious homogeneous population is incapable of fulfilling all the functions provided by the various losers of the competition. This leads to further loss of species by spiraling feedback of cause and effect. A homogeneous population is also susceptible to genetic weakness such as diseases. The genetic legacy passed on suggests evolutionary trends that are unhealthy for the entire system, human and otherwise. The human role in the loss of biodiversity derives from intention as well as accident.

There are too many recent examples of our complicity in the loss of ecosystem components (species). Particular losses have instituted a chain reaction of negative consequences on other organisms. One common scenario is the intentional removal of "dangerous" predatory species from the top of the food chain. This is true for wolves over huge regions of the Northern Hemisphere. Direct results include the overpopulation of deer (such as in the United States) or plagues of unchecked varmint species (such as rats or rabbits) that destroy crops.

Deforestation in many places has directly and indirectly led to ecological disasters. Removal of Central and South American trees, among other human activities, has caused the conspicuous absence of many migratory songbirds from their previous North American habitats. Clear-cut logging in Mexico also threatens the migratory patterns of Monarch butterflies that pollinate Milkweed species in the United States and Canada. There are current reports of loggers spraying Monarchs with poison in an effort to devalue trees as crucial, protected habitat. Coastal development has eliminated the natural fringe of mangrove forests from many of Earth's more tropical regions. The mangrove thrives in brackish to saline waters. It is marvelously adapted as the essential

36. G. C. Daily, ed., *Nature's Services — Societal Dependence on Natural Ecosystems* (Washington, D.C.: Island, 1997).

37. M. J. Jeffries, *Biodiversity and Conservation* (London: Routledge, 1997).

38. C. Bright, *Life Out of Bounds — Bioinvasion in a Borderless World* (New York: Norton, 1998).

base of a complex marine ecosystem.[39] Its tangled roots and branches shelter bird rookeries above water. Underlying tidal surfaces provide traps for decaying vegetation and mud. The trapped material in turn serves as the nursery for a food chain beginning with microorganisms and ending with major game and food fish (and humans) at its top. As mangroves are destroyed, so are the dependent rookeries and fisheries.

The Florida Everglades is a thoroughly unique integration of geology and biology. Decades of development and replumbing of the spectacular natural water system have devastated the fragile ecology.[40] The flow of freshwater across south Florida has been diverted and contaminated by federally subsidized agricultural interests. Less than 20 percent of the natural flow continues to the areas needing constant replenishment. Three of the results seen since the flow conversion include impacts on alligators, on the endangered Everglades Kite, and on biological productivity in Florida coastal waters.

Low water levels in the Everglades and a moratorium on hunting have pushed alligators into suburban developments (more poodles on the menu). The Everglades Kite is a rare falconlike raptor that feeds exclusively on the habitat-specific Apple Snail. Low water levels and pollution have made the snail scarcer and thus increase the extinction threat to the kite. An extensive network of flood-control canals in southeastern Florida drains freshwater into saltwater areas unadapted to the sudden chemical contrast. This water shock also occurs in Florida Bay, the Gulf area just west of the Keys. Here there is a tremendous decrease in the flow to an area dependent on dilution by freshwater. In both areas, major communities of organisms are degraded and getting worse. On the Florida east coast, coral reefs are diseased and dying.[41] Their demise is similar to the eco-disaster of the loss of rain forest mentioned below. On the Gulf side of Florida, sensitive Turtlegrass habitat is declining as overall salinity increases.

I was raised in southern Florida in the late 1950s and into the early 1970s. The subtropical climate there is a perfect "hothouse" for the flourishing of all sorts of plants and animals. Up until the early 1970s, it was possible to describe the entire ecosystem in terms of indigenous biota. Now the region is a patchwork of microenvironments inhabited by bizarre organisms.[42] Alien species

39. J. C. George, *Everglades Wildguide,* Handbook 143 (Washington, D.C.: U.S. Dept. of Interior, 1997).

40. N. Duplaix, "South Florida Water — Paying the Price," *National Geographic* 178 (July 1990): 89-113.

41. F. Ward, "Florida's Coral Reefs Are Imperiled," *National Geographic* 178 (July 1990): 114-32.

42. D. Simberloff, D. C. Schmitz, and T. C. Brown, eds., *Strangers in Paradise — Impact and Management of Nonindigenous Species in Florida* (Washington, D.C.: Island, 1997).

have been introduced and many outcompete natives for the available niches. It was a great surprise to return periodically from undergrad and grad school to see the shift in "wildlife" south of Miami. My own backyard seemed to bloom with new plants every year without being planted. One year featured a purple passion vine, and twenty months later it was replaced by a red passion vine, a completely different species not native to North America. Parrots, Mynah birds, iguanas, Cuban Anoles and African tree snails displaced residents that had been established for centuries or millennia. The Everglades system has hosted even stranger replacements. Freshwater sloughs that slowly move from north to south through the Glades (the "River of Grass")[43] are supposed to be home to communities of Largemouth Bass and sunfish varieties, along with garfish. However, in 1977 I first beheld the same waters containing the new neighbors of Peacock Bass, Oscars, and Mayan Cichlids (all from south of the border) and Tilapia (from Africa). The indigenous fish, except for gars, are in the greatly threatened minority.

The alien invasions in south Florida are similar to those of Hawaii that destroy native species in Hawaii. These changes occur because (a) new organisms are intentionally introduced as a resource (food, timber, etc.) or to control other species (in Florida, Australian Pines and Melaleuca trees were planted as windbreaks and to absorb water); (b) new organisms escape from zoos, pet stores, and so forth (Mynah birds, walking catfish, and a now-established community of chimpanzees in the Everglades are examples), and (c) new organisms fill degraded habitats, considered no longer healthy and functional (many insect varieties and rodent pest species).

Destruction or modification of habitat is a more serious threat to biodiversity than are invasive species. I can bear witness to the rapid development of southern Florida in people's hurry to migrate from other places and to profit financially from the land rush. Entire land-class units, pine uplands and coastal hammocks, have been eradicated in less than thirty years. Elsewhere, as in the Amazon Basin, hundreds (if not thousands) of plant species have been removed from Earth's greater community before we have even had a chance to learn from them.[44] We have learned through the concept of co-evolution how fragile and intricate are the interdependencies of some organisms. For example, there are rare flower-bearing plants that are fertilized by only one, equally rare species of insect. This fact has come to knowledge in some cases only after clearing forest. Some biologists are now running ahead of the bulldozers to record new life forms soon before their demise. Many are amazed to realize that

43. M. S. Douglas, *The Everglades: River of Grass* (Atlanta: Mockingbird, 1974).
44. Morell, "The Variety of Life," "Wilderness Headcount," and "The Sixth Extinction."

one ancient forest tree may be an ecosystem in itself with several new species in its boughs.[45] There has to be a strong sense that our lust for wealth is ruining something God intended to be maintained.

Interesting research has documented the detrimental results of natural habitat fragmentation. L. K. Page studied the link between shrinking forest lands in northern Indiana and the distribution of a parasite, the Raccoon Roundworm *(Baylisascaris procyonis),* which is deadly to human beings as well as other mammals.[46] The isolation of small forested tracts has attracted unnaturally high concentrations of raccoons and mice as intermediate hosts of the parasite. The overall rate of infection in other mammals has also increased significantly. The direct result of human land conversion is a literal and figurative loss of health. The rapid conversion of farmlands and forests to suburban housing, strip malls, and industrial parks in northern Illinois has also produced a dramatic increase in populations of raccoons, opossums, skunks, coyotes, deer, and geese.

Unfortunately, these species are adjusting to suburban habitats with behavior far from natural. Canada Geese in particular have become a significant nuisance over the last dozen years or so. Many of them no longer migrate south. Instead they stay all year, overbreed, and prefer to congregate in large numbers on playgrounds, golf courses, and bodies of water. Their feces carrying *cryptospiridia* and *giardia* foul the suburbs, and little can legally be done to prevent it.

The future of degraded ecosystems is a grim prospect. From agricultural practice and historical anthropology we understand that the loss of genetic variability sets the stage for disease epidemics.[47] And yet, because of the same push for maximized, short-term financial gain, monoculture is substituted for natural-system harvesting of resources. Just one of the reasons that rain forests are destroyed is to be replaced by plantations of fast-growing cash trees. In order to protect monoculture species or hybrids from mass susceptibility to pests or disease, they are heavily treated with chemicals and are more recently being genetically modified. As modern "Frankenstein" creations, corn, soybeans, and salmon are among those being redesigned with foreign DNA segments. These are patented life forms possessing human improvements that are not well anticipated in the biosphere. They may prove to be more beneficial than hazardous,

45. Morell, "The Variety of Life," "Wilderness Headcount," and "The Sixth Extinction."

46. L. K. Page, "Ecology and Transmission Dynamics of *Baylisascaris Procyonis,*" Ph.D. dissertation, Purdue University, 1998.

47. A. E. Platt, *Infecting Ourselves — How Environmental and Social Disruptions Trigger Disease,* Worldwatch Paper 129 (Washington, D.C.: Wordwatch Institute, 1996); J. Tuxhill, *Nature's Cornucopia — Our Stake in Plant Diversity,* Worldwatch Paper 148 (Washington, D.C.: Worldwatch Institute, 1999).

but only patient, careful trials would tell. Unfortunately, the rush for fame and fortune has not allowed adequate time for impartial testing. Pollen from genetically modified corn has already proven to be poisonous to beneficial insects.[48] Damage of one part of the system causes breakdowns in other components.

What Are We Becoming?

It is certainly heretical to suggest that people have ever consistently lived as the Lord intended after the Fall. We might romanticize about the goodness of the good old days. However, there is more than just sentiment in desiring a civilization that studies, respects, and lives in appropriate harmony with the rest of Creation. Technology in the modern era has made quantumlike changes, "progress," throughout most of the globe. Only the more primitive societies and ardent technophobes maintain simpler lifestyles, closely dependent upon Earth and each other. This may have been true of small-scale, family farmers in the United States, but that species is approaching extinction.[49] Whether chosen or imposed, simpler living has less negative impact on others, animate or inanimate. Natural Earth systems are generally more sustainable than mankind's highly engineered substitutes. Human physical longevity was mentioned above as one sign of progress with ominous implications. As we re-create the things of God in nature in our own imagination, what becomes of God's image in us? This is really the paramount concern about evolution from this point in time onward.

Many evangelical Christians are troubled by the idea of loving nature. We fear the unorthodox nature worship of pantheism but might miss the proper theological point. When spiritually healthy, we should love the things of God because he does. This is best explained as a created aspect of the divine image in us. Being led beside still waters has the potential to restore our souls. Likewise, significant time spent among many types of landscape, plants, and animals has the common effect of inspiring great affection. The loss of natural places resulting from technological progress can only impoverish our souls. Evangelical social critics and media personalities often accuse other people (politicians, educators, celebrities, etc.) of undermining biblical morality in American culture.

48. J. E. Losey, L. S. Raynor, and M. E. Carter, "Transgenic Pollen Harms Monarch Larvae," *Nature* 399 (May 20, 1999): 214.

49. G. Gardner, "Preserving Global Cropland," in *State of the World* (Washington, D.C.: Worldwatch Institute, 1997), pp. 42-59; S. C. Blank, "The End of the American Farm?" *The Futurist* 33.4 (April 1999): 22-27. Also, see articles in *Creation Care*, Winter 2001, published by the Evangelical Environmental Network in Pennsylvania.

Could it be that our ignorance of God's purpose in Creation is causing all of us, evangelicals as well, to subvert his will? In this respect, the selfish rush toward technological paradise and ever more affluent lifestyles is one of our major evolutionary legacies for future humans. Contrast that with a large road sign I saw in Uganda in 1993, "Please plant trees for the lives of our grandchildren."

Knowledge Requiring a Response

For the Christian believer, this discussion of environmental issues in the context of evolution requires a response. Students in geology and environmental science classes at Wheaton College express frustration with feelings of helplessness when confronted with environmental problems. They are agitated by the litany of ills that exist and want instruction in how to remedy problems. Instructors are rightly accused of often setting a negative stage without providing direction for relief. I can offer the following steps for faith-based action. First, we must know enough about an issue to realize its critical scientific and ethical dimensions. Then we need to consider that natural systems are intended to function properly where possible. If this function is threatened, then protection and preservation may be necessary. If the system is already in bad shape, then remedial action may be needed to reestablish proper function. This progression of analysis leads to a decision and then beyond to some form of action. The type of action depends on a person's capabilities and priorities. Prayer at least is in order for all situations. Political contact may be possible through writing or other communication. Participation in clean-up efforts (along a stream, for example) or fund raising can be quite helpful. Getting one's church involved in Creation stewardship programs is also a wonderful calling. Personal commitment will usually cause us to examine our own lifestyles; this does seem to be at the root of most modern environmental problems. Evangelical organizations, such as Target Earth, the Evangelical Environmental Network, and the Christian Environmental Council, serve to provide information to those looking to contribute. There are many Christian publications that provide a variety of helpful perspectives on our God-mandated role as stewards of Creation.[50]

50. R. G. Stewart, *Environmental Stewardship* (Downers Grove, Ill.: InterVarsity, 1990); D. Larsen and S. Larsen, *While Creation Waits — A Christian Response to the Environmental Challenge* (Wheaton, Ill.: Harold Shaw, 1992); F. Van Dyke, D. C. Mahan, J. K. Sheldon, and R. H. Brand, *Redeeming Creation: The Biblical Basis for Environmental Stewardship* (Downers Grove, Ill.: InterVarsity Press, 1996); S. L. LeQuire, ed., *The Best Preaching on Earth* (Valley Forge, Pa.: Judson, 1996); W. D. Roberts, ed., *Down-to-Earth Christianity — Creation Care in Ministry* (Wynnewood, Pa.: Evangelical Environmental Network, 2000).

There are also publications, including *Fifty Ways You Can Help Save the Planet,* that convey practical action ideas.[51] Even if we are unimpressed by predictions of global environmental disasters (such as sea-level rise from the melting of polar ice), we must consciously decide to choose the way that God has already shown us. Qualified Christians who are scientists offer help to understand the right way.[52]

In a small Tanzanian village south of Lake Victoria, an old Christian man understands. He was a boy there seventy years ago when forest, savanna, and wetlands were home to elephants, hippos, leopards, impalas, giraffes, zebra, and wildebeests. Today, the trees are all gone, removed over thousands of square kilometers to make way for the cattle of pastoralists. With the trees went all the animals but a few species of bird, reptiles, and insects. Streams that used to flow most of the year are completely dry. The only water essential for human life is available in scattered *charkos,* muddy pits, open to all sources of contamination. Women walk long distances each day to bring the fouled water to their families.

The old man of Shinyanga Province has begun a renaissance. The dirt yard of his house has become a tree nursery. With his labor force of great-grandchildren and their friends, he babies seeds from leguminous (nitrogen-fixing) trees under a shaded porch. He fashions seed cups from the shucks of maize, placing a seed and soil with some precious water in each. When just under a meter in height, the saplings are transplanted to the rear of his property where a new forest is slowly retaking its territory. It will take many such efforts to reverse the degradation in Tanzania, but the idea of restoration is spreading. The old man has become an evangelist for Christ and Christ's good creation as he travels to other villages, sharing his dream.

51. T. Campolo and G. Aeschliman, *Fifty Ways You Can Help Save the Planet* (Downers Grove, Ill.: InterVarsity, 1992).

52. B. R. Reichenbach and V. E. Anderson, *On Behalf of God — A Christian Ethic for Biology* (Grand Rapids: Eerdmans, 1995); J. Houghton, *Global Warming — The Complete Briefing,* 2nd ed. (New York: Cambridge University Press, 1997).

Being Stewards of the Creator God

JEFFREY GREENBERG

He turned rivers into a desert,
    flowing springs into thirsty ground,
and fruitful land into a salt waste,
    because of the wickedness of those who lived there.
He turned the desert into pools of water
    and the parched ground into flowing springs;
there he brought the hungry to live,
    and they founded a city where they could settle.
They sowed fields and planted vineyards
    that yielded a fruitful harvest;
He blessed them and their numbers greatly increased.

PSALM 107:33-38

We humans and particularly we Christian believers have much to learn about our proper place in the world. This should come in large part from an understanding of and respect for Earth's natural processes.

What does it mean to have "dominion" or "rule" over creation (Gen. 1:28)? We, as stewards, are given power and authority — but what of godly fear to be sober, cautious, wise, compassionate, and to exhibit the fruits of the Spirit (Gal. 5:22)? The exercise of power without these other attributes is tyranny. We have arrived at a point in time of great technological power. For example, expensive and sophisticated technology is being used to extract, purify, and conserve precious water resources. However, at the same time this life blood is wasted or contaminated by our cultural fixation on technology.

Many think that if something can be accomplished, it will be, regardless of the ethical considerations. This may be true. Every undone deed might be viewed as a challenge to our pioneering spirit of conquest. By contrast, our faith provides constraint by asking whether or not something ought to be done. Of course, technology and industry as expressions of God-given creativity need not be evil in themselves. It just seems that we don't know when to quit. The Lord provides manna and we complain or try to store it up. If he did provide geese laying golden eggs, I would thoroughly expect to see them killed for short-term profit. We seek perfection for our children and yet are unable to stop the intentional brutal neglect, abuse, and slaughter of millions of fellow humans each year. We want to be like God and yet do a rather poor job of just being people.

Francis Schaeffer's famous question, "How shall we then live?" must become a focus for life of the Church. Our creative talents are invested in us for God's purposes — but what are they? How can we balance our bent toward creative production through technology with the need to sustain essential functions in Creation? The Parable of the Talents (Matt. 25:14-30) seems to suggest that simply preserving resources is not the answer. I admit my frequent confusion. If the recent trends in global markets are any indication of our condition, we should conclude that being overly conservative with our "talents" is no threat. Orgies of greed and fantasies of economic welfare are driving us; driving us away from the wealth God has already set before us. Perhaps we should take heart in individual stories of hope — like a family from East Africa slowly and patiently planting trees in a desertified landscape. God is sovereign, and I ultimately doubt that he would allow us to completely subvert the good he has set in operation throughout creation. He always has a faithful remnant. My hope is for Christians to be faithful in practicing godly lifestyles as well as in thinking and saying the right doctrinal things.

A Prayer:
Gracious Jesus;
You were there when it all began,
And welcomed the crafting of the Father's love.
For your pleasure all was made,
And most of all,
You rejoiced at our conception from the stuff of this world.
We were made like you and to be yours.
You gave us everything to love and to tend,
But we are not just like you.
We do not understand the limits of our relationship with you
        and the rest of your great works.
We have taken the bounty you provided without fulfilling
        our responsibility.

Lord, the mistakes of our selfishness have caused all creation
　　　to suffer and groan for relief.
Our selfishness and your love drove you to the Hill of Shame and Death.
Your sacrifice makes hope possible.
May your holy power of redemption be manifest.
May all of creation be reconciled to you.
May we your people be agents of that reconciliation.
AMEN.

18 May the Glory of the Lord Endure Forever!
Biblical Reflections on Creation Care

LAURIE J. BRAATEN

The essays in this volume have been about the "E word" — the word that is one of the most controversial among many confessing Christians today, "evolution." Hot debates and accusations fly when the topic is broached. Essays in this volume have made the plea that this controversy is unfounded, that evolution and the Christian view of creation are not necessarily contradictory. Another "E word," while not quite as controversial, also has the potential to raise many Christians' doctrinal dander; it is the word "ecology," or more correctly, "environmentalism." While there is a growing "green" movement in all quarters of the Church today and environmental issues are being brought to the forefront by many Christians,[1] there are still those who assume either that concern for the environment is not a Christian concern, or that it is at heart against the

---

1. It would not be possible to review all the literature on this subject, and so many important treatments will be overlooked. For a well-written environmental theology from a Wesleyan perspective see James A. Nash, *Loving Nature: Ecological Integrity and Christian Responsibility* (Nashville: Abingdon, 1991). Other helpful works on stewardship of creation, or creation care (terms many Christians now prefer over environmentalism), include Loren Wilkinson, ed., *Earthkeeping in the Nineties: Stewardship of Creation*, rev. ed. (Grand Rapids: Eerdmans, 1991); and Fred Van Dyke et al., *Redeeming Creation: The Biblical Basis for Environmental Stewardship* (Downers Grove, Ill.: InterVarsity, 1996). For a convenient survey of the place of environmentalism in the mid- to late-20th-century Church see Roderick Frazier Nash, "The Greening of Religion," ch. 4 of his *The Rights of Nature: A History of Environmental Ethics* (Madison: University of Wisconsin Press, 1987), pp. 87-120. For a review of several works from the late 1990s from a variety of theological perspectives, see William Greenway and Janet L. Parker, "Greening Theology and Ethics: Five Contemporary Approaches," *Religious Studies Review* 27 (2001): 3-9. A very useful typology of the four major ways that Christians approach the environment has been developed and frequently published by Jim Ball: e.g., his "The Use of Ecology in the Evangelical Protestant Response to the Ecological Crisis," *Perspectives on Science and Christian Faith* 50 (1998): 32-38.

clear teaching of Scripture. So to associate evolution and ecology in one essay is perhaps asking for double trouble.[2]

What the two have in common is another E word — the earth and its inhabitants; or, in other words, *creation* — and that's where God comes in. If we really believe that "in the beginning God created the heavens and the earth," then when we talk about the creation we should begin to reflect on the Creator. The other essays in this volume have asked the reader to do just that. They have argued that when scientists discuss evolutionary processes, they are in fact describing the handiwork of God the Creator. The current essay adds a new twist: If this creation is God's work, how do Christians properly relate to it? More specifically, is there a "Christian environmentalism"? Further, if evolution is God's way of creating, then how does this fact add anything to our understanding of our relationship to creation? These two concerns provide the foci of this essay: a brief account of a Bible-based environmentalism, or creation care,[3] with

2. Another essay in this volume has already broached the subject; see Jeffrey Greenberg, "An Evolving Creation and Environmental Issues."

3. There are problems with each of the terms commonly used to connote stewardship of creation. Many avoid "environmentalism" because it is often used anthropocentrically. Others object that "nature" implies a sphere autonomous from God, governed by "natural law." Further, humans are often seen as separate from nature. Such persons prefer to use "Creation" (e.g., Van Dyke, *Redeeming Creation*, pp. 39-40; see Bernhard W. Anderson, *From Creation to New Creation: Old Testament Perspectives*, Overtures to Biblical Theology [Philadelphia: Fortress, 1994], p. 31). Adopting this terminology, some writers refer to the totality of the members of Creation as "Humans" and "the Rest of Creation" (e.g., Ball, "The Use of Ecology," p. 33). Some defend the term "nature," arguing that "creation" is a much more comprehensive theological term than nature, encompassing "the heavens and the earth" (Gen. 1:1), which is designated in the ancient creeds as "things seen and unseen" (see Michael Welker, "What Is Creation? Rereading Genesis 1 and 2," chap. 1 in his *Creation and Reality* [Philadelphia: Fortress, 1999], pp. 6-20). James Nash argues that "the integrity of the doctrine of creation — indeed, the glory of the Creator — is diminished when we use the word 'creation,' which stands for 'the whole,' to describe only a small 'part,' such as this earth or, worse, nonhuman nature." Nash defines nature as "the biophysical world, of which humans are fully parts and products." Those who use "nature" customarily speak of its living inhabitants as "humankind" and "otherkind" (see James Nash, "Toward the Ecological Reformation of Christianity," *Interpretation* 50 [1996]: 7-8). Even the term "stewardship" has been brought under fire as being too managerial and anthropocentric. The fear is that we humans will manage creation for self-serving enjoyment, or for our personal "eco-challenge," thereby doing harm in the name of good. See Kathleen Braden, "On Saving the Wilderness: Why Christian Stewardship Is Not Sufficient," *Christian Scholar's Review* 27 (1998): 254-69. I am afraid we have run out of terms. I have chosen to use all of the terms from time to time, but in awareness of the inadequacies of each. My favorite term is creation, however, which is the term used by Paul in Rom. 8:19-23 (this passage will be discussed later).

commentary on how evolutionary theory might supplement these biblical observations.

Some General Observations on Interpreting the Creation Accounts

Most discussions on creation care include an investigation of the creation narratives in Genesis 1 and 2.[4] Writers in the current volume have already noted some of the problems associated with trying to read the poetic and theological creation narratives as if they were scientific descriptions of the making of the universe. It is important that we read these creation texts in light of their own historical, social, literary, and theological contexts.

Most importantly, interpreters need to consider the type of literature they are dealing with and its theological intent. The creation narratives of the Bible are not scientific documents composed to satisfy the intellectual curiosity of the reader concerning exactly how the world came into being. Nor is their primary point that we have lost a Golden Age. Rather, they are a special type of narrative that explains *who* the Creator is and how this Creator informs *present* realities.[5] The creation narratives tell of God's assessment of creation *now,* and what God intends as the final outcome for creation. It is no accident that most of the texts that deal with eschatological matters (the end times) describe the consummation of God's work as a renewal of creation.[6]

There is widespread agreement that the creation narratives of Genesis 1–2 convey a sense of God's design for properly ordered relationships in creation. The first and foremost relationship is that of God with all that he has created. Likewise, humans, created in the image of God, are designed to function in loving relationship with God, other humans, the rest of creation, and themselves.

---

4. Biblical scholarship observes that Genesis 1 and 2 contain two separate accounts of creation. For a treatment of this topic, and for general information on interpreting these texts, see the essay in this volume by Conrad Hyers, "Comparing Biblical and Scientific Maps of Origins."

5. Compare the comments in the essay in this volume by Robin Collins, "Evolution and Original Sin."

6. E.g., "Creation is basically an eschatological doctrine in the sense that it has a future horizon. . . . The opening words of Genesis, 'In the beginning God,' correspond to the prophetic expectation, 'In the end God'" (Anderson, *From Creation to New Creation*, p. 34). Influenced by the early Greek Christian tradition, John Wesley worked out his views of salvation of the individual, society, and the cosmos as a renewal of God's creation purposes; see, e.g., Randy Maddox, *Responsible Grace: John Wesley's Practical Theology,* Kingswood Books (Nashville: Abingdon, 1994), pp. 65-93, 252-53 (and throughout, see Index under "Eastern Orthodoxy"); and Theodore Runyon, *The New Creation: John Wesley's Theology Today,* Kingswood Books (Nashville: Abingdon, 1998), p. 13 and passim.

The presence of sin, however, distorts all these relationships.[7] We will now turn to these and other texts to see how they bear on creation care.

The Intrinsic Value of Creation

The most basic reason for Christians to care for creation is out of love for God. We love God and others because God first loved us.[8] Humans often restrict their love to those who benefit them, but Scripture makes it clear that to love like God requires we love everyone, even the unfriendly, the enemy (Matt. 5:43-48) and the ungrateful (Luke 6:35). Although these passages concern love for our human neighbor, it is clear that God's love does not stop there. God's love and concern extends to animals, sparrows (Luke 12:6), and the lilies of the field (Matt. 6:28-30). By extension we ought to show concern for what concerns God, and love what God loves. John Wesley encouraged the Christian to care for God's creatures as God does, to "imitate him whose mercy is over all his works."[9] According to James Nash,

> Our neighbors to be loved are all of God's beloved creatures. The "love of nature" is simply the "love of neighbor" universalized, in recognition of our common origins, mutual dependencies, and shared destiny with the whole creation of the God who is universal love.[10]

Like the law of love toward one's neighbor, love of creation extends to all, irrespective of any utilitarian benefit we may derive from it.

God's love for and inner satisfaction with all of creation is established in

7. According to Maddox (*Responsible Grace*, p. 68), Wesley included all of these relations in his teachings on the subject. For similar views see Colin E. Gunton, *Christ and Creation,* The Didsbury Lectures (Grand Rapids: Eerdmans, 1990), pp. 102-3, 105; Holmes Rolston III, "Does Nature Need to Be Redeemed?" *Horizons in Biblical Theology* 14 (1992): 168. More will be said concerning the image of God in a later section of this paper.

8. See John 13:34; 1 John 4:19; Eph. 5:1-2. For a concise summary of the biblical teaching on love see Laurie J. Braaten, "Love," in *Eerdmans Dictionary of the Bible*, ed. David Noel Freedman (Grand Rapids: Eerdmans, 2000), pp. 85-86.

9. John Wesley, sermon LX on "The General Deliverance," §III.10; in *The Works of John Wesley*, 3rd ed., ed. Thomas Jackson (London: Wesleyan Methodist Book Room, 1872), 6:251. On Wesley's teaching concerning the love of creation see also Runyon, *The New Creation*, p. 204; and Michael E. Lodahl, "The Cosmological Basis for John Wesley's Gradualism," *Wesleyan Theological Journal* 32 (1997): 24-29. Nash (*Loving Nature*, pp. 139-61, passim) argues that since God loves nature, and the heart of the Christian message and ethics is to love as God loves, then we should, like God, love creation.

10. Nash, "Toward the Ecological Reformation of Christianity," p. 9.

the first chapter of Genesis. God's personal evaluation of his handiwork is that it is "good" — Genesis 1 contains the pronouncement six times (Gen. 1:4, 10, 12, 18, 21, 25). "Good" is a comprehensive word; it can mean "beneficial, correct, pleasant, beautiful, or delightful."[11] The text emphasizes God's inner contentment and pleasure with creation when it says that God *saw* that creation was good, and after the sixth day "*very* good" (v. 31). According to Bernhard Anderson,

> . . . God looks upon the finished creation and [sees] that every creature corresponds to the divine intention and fulfills its assigned function. . . . This is an aesthetic judgment in the sense that in the view of the Cosmic Artist all creatures function perfectly in a marvelous whole without fault or blemish. The essential goodness of God's creation is a recurring theme in Israel's praises.[12]

Some think that the goodness of creation relates primarily to humans — "the crown of creation" — for whose benefit, they say, God has made everything. But Genesis bases the goodness of creation on *God's* evaluation, not on human utility: each part of the whole is pronounced "good" for its own sake. God is pleased as he looks on and enjoys his masterpiece. God's enjoyment of his handiwork for its own sake is verified elsewhere in Scripture. The book of Job emphasizes that many aspects of God's creation are beyond human wisdom, control, and benefit (Job 38–41). Nature's terrifying creatures do not serve or obey humans, they are for God's amusement and pleasure alone; God "sports" with monstrous beasts as if they were household pets or sparring partners (Job 40:15–41:11; cf. Ps. 104:26).

In Psalm 104 God's creating and sustaining power gives equal worth to *all* of his handiwork through the Spirit — God plants and waters *his* trees; animals go out to hunt prey at the setting of the sun just as humans go to work with the sun's rising. God assigns humans and animals their own "shifts," and God provides food for each![13] Turning back to Job, God tells him that he is not capable

---

11. For these definitions of the Hebrew טוֹב (*ṭôb*) see Ludwig Koehler, Walter Baumgartner, and Johann Jakob Stamm, *The Hebrew and Aramaic Lexicon of the Old Testament*, trans. M. E. J. Richardson (Leiden: Brill, 1994-2000), 2:370-71 (henceforth cited as KB); and Andrew Bowling, "*ṭôb*," in *Theological Wordbook of the Old Testament*, ed. R. Laird Harris et al. (Chicago: Moody Bible Institute, 1980), 1:345-46.

12. Anderson, *From Creation to New Creation*, p. 31.

13. See esp. vv. 10-23 and 27-30. While the creation stories of Genesis assign humans a special role and responsibility, Anderson observes that "it is striking that Psalm 104, which displays affinities with Genesis 1, puts both humans and animals on a level of equality in God's creation. The poet says 'all of them' . . . depend on the Creator for their livelihood and are animated

of judging whether or not the Creator is fair, because Job does not understand the mysteries of God's provision for creation. God works in the heavens "to bring rain on a land where no one lives, on the desert, which is empty of human life, to satisfy the waste and desolate land, and to make the ground put forth grass" (Job 38:26-27, NRSV).

> God brings rain not only on the just and the unjust, but on the desert as well as the sown land. The wilderness is — quite literally — not Godforsaken. These lines bring a very important voice into the conversation about the environment and respond to what is all too commonly viewed as the main line of the Bible's understanding. The notion that all creation is to serve human interests is rejected.[14]

Not only the grass of the desert but also the entire earth is the Lord's and all that is in it; it is not ours to dispose of at will.[15] Ultimately it is God who gives value to creation according to his proclamation that it is "good." When humans seek after lesser "goods," we do not have the right to rescind God's greater "good" by destroying habitats or obliterating species.

Evolutionary theory adds a new dimension to our understanding of creation as intrinsically valuable. We now know that God took fifteen billion years to create the Universe as it is today, that life on earth began four billion years ago, and that humans *(Homo sapiens)* have only been here a fraction of that time (200,000 years). For the nearly 4 billion years before the arrival of our first

---

by the divine [spirit] . . . , which renews them day by day in a *creatio continua*" (*From Creation to New Creation*, p. 32; cf. pp. 86-87).

14. Gene M. Tucker, "Rain on a Land Where No One Lives: The Hebrew Bible and the Environment," *Journal of Biblical Literature* 116 (1987): 14-15.

15. E.g., Lev. 25:23; Josh. 22:19; Ezek. 36:5; Hos. 9:3; Ps. 85:1; 89:11; 24:1; etc. The Land of Promise was held by Israel like a feudal estate: Israel was granted "fief-right, not ownership." Biblical laws regarding land and its use, including sabbaticals for the land (fallow years), leaving gleanings for the poor, the offering of tithes, etc., were based on God's ownership of the land; for discussion and references see Etan Levine, *Heaven and Earth, Law and Love,* Beihefte zur Zeitschrift für die alttestamentliche Wissenschaft 303 (Berlin: Walter de Gruyter, 2000), pp. 60-63; see also Anne M. Kitz, "Undivided Inheritance and Lot Casting in the Book of Joshua," *Journal of Biblical Literature* 119 (2000): 606-10. Psalm 115:16 seemingly supports the idea that God has surrendered the earth to humans. The context of the verse, however, concerns the limits of the nations' understanding of God and his ways, here signified by the limited dwelling space of humankind; cf. Levine, *Heaven and Earth*, pp. 19, 25 (contrast Deut. 10:14). Nowhere does Scripture imply that humans are not accountable for their use of the earth and its resources. Like the gift of the Promised Land to biblical Israel, human occupation and use of the earth are to be on God's terms. The Bible consistently holds people accountable for land damage, whether caused directly or through violation of God's cosmic laws (e.g., Hos. 4:1-3; Rev. 11:18).

human ancestors God was sustaining and bringing into being new creatures, about *each* of which it could be said "God saw it . . . and God said, 'it is good.'" God was enjoying, reveling in, admiring, and appreciating his handiwork long before humans had arrived. If we were to represent the 4 billion years of terrestrial life by a single year, then humans would have arrived on the scene in the wee hours of the morning of December 30. If humans are the "crown of creation," then why did God wait so long to create us? To assume that all that exists on this earth has been put here for us and that God does not care if we destroy it contradicts our knowledge of God's creation processes and is the height of arrogance.[16]

All this talk about loving and valuing creation may sound strange to those who were taught "Do not love the world, or the things in the world . . . and the world and its desires are passing away."[17] A quick read through the New Testament can be confusing since it seems to contradict what we have said about the goodness of God's creation. The solution lies in the recognition of how the New Testament typically uses the word "world" *(kosmos)*. Occasionally it connotes God's good creation (e.g., Matt. 24:21; John 1:10; Acts 17:24; Rom. 1:20; Eph. 1:4; Rev. 13:8), but usually "world" designates the world system, "this present age," or culture characterized by rebellion against God. This is not the material world *per se*, rather a world of idolatrous culture not submitting to the rule of God.[18]

It is sometimes claimed that environmentalists worship creation. It is true that there are some non-Christian environmentalists on the extremist fringe who worship creation. This is not an intrinsic or necessary part of environmentalism, however, whether secular or Christian. Likewise, it is sometimes asserted that those who teach evolution make the processes of creation, or "natural law" into their god instead of the God of Abraham, Isaac, and Jacob. Other essays in this volume have argued that this is not intrinsic to evolution but rather part of the faith system of some non-Christian scientists.[19] Ironically, those who are in the most danger of making creation their god are not those who find intrinsic value in creation or marvel at the evolutionary processes at work in it; rather, it

16. So Nash, *Loving Nature*, pp. 99, 105-6.

17. 1 John 2:15, 17 (NRSV). The Church has always struggled with the problem of whether to flee from the world to keep from an idolatrous affection toward the things of this life, or whether to embrace the world with a healthy love for God's creation; see H. Paul Santmire, *The Travail of Nature: The Ambiguous Ecological Promise of Christian Theology* (Philadelphia: Fortress, 1985), passim.

18. See the concise summary of the use of "world" in the New Testament in Alan Richardson, *An Introduction to the Theology of the New Testament* (London: SCM, 1958), pp. 207-8.

19. E.g., Loren Haarsma, "Does Science Exclude God? Natural Law, Chance, Miracles, and Scientific Practice," esp. the section: "Science Is Not Intrinsically Atheistic."

is those who objectify creation as human resources and thereby serve "mammon." Living for power, wealth, and accumulation of possessions are some of the most powerful temptations toward idolatry that the Western, European, and Northern nations face today. Putting economic concerns — or any concern — above God's concerns is functional idolatry.[20] This is the inordinate "love of the world" condemned in Scripture. As Colin E. Gunton states, this is ultimately self-worship; it is "human self-divinization" which is "seen in the sometimes conscious attempt to transfer to [humans] the attributes of divinity: omniscience, omnipotence, etc., and in the corresponding treatment of the world as a mere object to which we may behave as we wish." Further, this "worship of human capacity" behind much of today's "mechanisation or technologisation of reality" is manifest in our current "ecological problem."[21]

True Christians who teach evolution or advocate creation care do not worship the creation; rather, they find in creation "the book of nature" that points to God the Father of our Lord Jesus Christ. This leads to our next point:

Creation Glorifies God

The heavens and earth declare the glory of God — this is a grand theme in Scripture. Creation is valuable to God because the earth and all its inhabitants give glory to the Creator. In the grand doxological chorus at the end of the book of Psalms, all creation is exhorted to join God's people in praising their Creator from the heavenly bodies to the great sea creatures in the depths of the ocean (148:3-4, 7). The mountains, fruit trees and cedars, wild and domestic animals — all are called to participate in this song of praise (148:9-10). All creation's entities are capable of glorifying their Creator God (Ps. 19:1-6; 96:11-13; 98:4-9; 145:10) because of God's compassion for *all* his works (Ps. 145:9, 15-16). As the end-time drama unfolds before John, the seer has a vision of all the company of heaven and earth singing praises to the Father and the Lamb, including "every

20. As I was writing this essay the news on the radio reported that President George W. Bush (who claims to worship the God of the Bible) was reversing a campaign pledge regarding the environment. The United States, he said, would be backing out of its commitment to sign the International Kyoto (Global Warming) Treaty. He stated, "The [American] economy is more important than the environment, the economy is more important than everything." I will leave it to the reader to judge whether or not this statement is idolatrous. Regarding his assumption about the economy, it is doubtful that there will be significant economic suffering in this country if we were to adhere to the terms of this treaty. It is clear, however, that many people and the entire creation will surely suffer as global temperatures rise.

21. Gunton, *Christ and Creation*, pp. 105, 106.

creature in heaven and on the earth and under the earth and in the sea, and all that is in them" (Rev. 5:11-13, NRSV). While we usually dismiss such references as being "merely poetic," their poetry contains a profound truth that is missed by those who reduce creation to a machine, matter in motion, goods for human consumption.[22] For centuries there have been those in the Church that have taught that creation is God's other book, the "book of nature" that reveals God's power, wisdom, goodness, and glory.[23] Closer investigation of creation's workings by scientists, naturalists, and poets serve only to bring further glory to the Creator who designed and sustains such intricate, delicate, and powerful systems of life. *Expressing admiration for God's works of creation and redemption is how we praise the Creator.*[24] Far from being a threat to the sovereignty of God, the study of the evolutionary processes of creation may lead the Christian to a further sense of awe for the creation, breaking out in an expression of glorious praise to the Creator.

For those who can see creation glorifying God there is an opportunity to get a glimpse of "his eternal power and divine nature" (Rom. 1:20, NRSV) in the things he has made. Genesis presents the entire creation as a cosmic sanctuary where the Creator is present, glorified, and to be worshipped. This is evident by the literary parallels between the account of the creation of the world and the description of the construction of the desert sanctuary.[25] Both end with a refer-

22. While it is sometimes asserted that the Hebrews "desacralized" nature, and so paved the way for modern science and technology, it has been shown that this "desacralizing" took place at a much later date. Francis Bacon (1561-1626) promoted his aggressive program of exploiting the earth for maximum human use by intentionally countering the widespread notion that the earth is to be respected as a living organism. See Carolyn Merchant, *The Death of Nature* (San Francisco: Harper, 1989), pp. 164-90. For creation as sacramental see Nash, *Loving Nature*, pp. 111-16.

23. For a summary of how the Church has used the "book of nature" in its contemplative spirituality see Diogenes Allen, *Spiritual Theology: The Theology of Yesterday for Spiritual Help Today* (Boston: Cowley, 1997), pp. 105-7, 109-24.

24. True praise of God is completed by recounting the great works of God in creation or redemption, not by repeating the words "Praise the Lord," as in many of today's so-called "Praise Choruses." The phrase "Praise the Lord," a translation of the Hebrew term *hallelujah*, is an *exhortation* to praise appearing at the beginning of many biblical psalms. Its purpose is not to *offer* praise; rather, it *invites* worshippers to enter into praise. The praise follows in the declaration or description of God's deeds, found in the body of the psalm. Similarly, today we would not praise someone by saying, "I just want to praise you!" and leave it at that. Rather, we might say something like, "I would like to praise you for a job well done!"

25. Joseph Blenkinsopp, *Prophecy and Canon: A Contribution to the Study of Jewish Origins* (Notre Dame, Ind.: University of Notre Dame Press, 1977), pp. 59-64. For recent summaries see Thomas W. Mann, *Book of the Torah: The Narrative Integrity of the Pentateuch* (Atlanta: John Knox, 1988), p. 112; and Dianne Bergant, *The Earth Is the Lord's: The Bible, Ecology, and Worship*, American Essays in Liturgy (Collegeville, Minn.: Liturgical, 1998), pp. 23-24.

ence to the Sabbath (Gen. 2:1-3; Exod. 31:12-17). The words declaring that God "finished" the creation and "blessed" and "hallowed" the seventh day (Gen. 2:2-3) correspond to Moses' finishing of the tabernacle and the Lord blessing it and hallowing it (Exod. 39:43; 40:9). Just as the "Spirit of God" (Gen. 1:2, NIV) rested on the pre-creation void, the Spirit of God endowed the workman with skills needed to construct the sanctuary (Exod. 31:3ff.; 35:31ff.). Early Jewish interpreters observed that the word for the "lights" that God placed in the sky in Genesis 1:14-16 is used elsewhere only of the lights in the tabernacle (Exod. 39:37, etc.).[26] The goal of creation is the Sabbath rest that points back to the good finished creation, where God is glorified through his handiwork. Creation, likewise, points to the Sabbath and tabernacle (temple) worship. If creation is God's sanctuary, then when we desecrate creation for our short-term needs, we are desecrating holy ground.

From these considerations it seems that instead of saying the creation is called to join humans in praise of God, it is more accurate to say that humans are called to "enter" the cosmic sanctuary and join the ancient choir of creation that has ever been singing the Creator's praises. John Wesley, generally known as a field preacher and theologian, was also interested in science ("natural philosophy") as a window into the "wisdom of God." Commenting on the usefulness of the study of nature, Wesley said,

> By acquainting ourselves with the subjects in natural philosophy, we enter into a kind of association with nature's works and unite in the general concert of her extensive choir. By thus acquainting ourselves with the works of nature, we become, as it were, a member of her family, a participant in her felicities; but while we remain ignorant, we are like strangers and sojourners in a foreign land, unknowing and unknown.[27]

26. See *Midrash Tanḥuma* on Gen. 1:14.

27. *A Survey of the Wisdom of God in Creation,* cited by Runyon, *The New Creation,* p. 202. Concerning God's presence in creation, in his sermon XXXIII, "Sermon on the Mount III," Wesley said that "we should look upon nothing as separate from God, which indeed is a kind of practical atheism . . . [for God] . . . pervades and activates the whole created frame, and is in a true sense the soul of the universe" (cited in Runyon, *The New Creation,* pp. 206, 207; for the sermon see *Wesley's Works* [Jackson], 5:278-94 [citations are from §I.11, p. 283]). Other references to how Wesley saw the study of creation as enriching the religious life, see Frank W. Collier, *John Wesley among the Scientists* (New York: Abingdon, 1928), especially ch. 12, "Wesley and the Ministry of Physical Science," pp. 289-304. Also of special relevance to the readers of this volume is ch. 7, "Wesley and Evolution," pp. 148-204. It should be noted, however, that Wesley wrote before Darwin and so considered death, pain, and suffering as a result of the Fall, not as part of creation from the beginning (cf. sermon LVI, "God's Approbation of His Works," *Wesley's Works* [Jackson], 5:206-15).

The Human Place in Creation

From what has been said above, it is apparent that there is a strong thread in the Bible designating humans as fellow creatures with the rest of creation. It is also true, however, that humans are distinctive because they are created in the image of God (Gen. 1:26-28). Since at least the time of Francis Bacon people have argued from Genesis that God has given humans unrestrained dominion over nature.[28] Many have pointed to the blessing "to be fruitful, multiply, and fill the earth" as warrant for lack of family planning or population control. When this passage is read in isolation from its literary and historical context, such anthropocentric interpretations seem justified. But when it is seen in context, a much different interpretation emerges.

It is widely recognized that the description of the image of God is grounded in royal language — humans are created to convey God's rule on earth.[29] But what picture do we have of God's rule? It is not the rule of tyranny but the rule of benevolence that serves the interest of all of his created subjects. This is borne out in a number of ways by diverse treatments of this passage. As Nash states, "The image incorporates the God-given assignment to exercise dominion or governance *in accord with God's values*."[30] In a discussion on the image of God in the context of Genesis 1 and beyond, Wesley observed that humans were created to be God's "vicegerent," "through whom the blessings of God" were to flow to other creatures.[31] Michael Welker observes that in the

---

28. See note 22. For a discussion of the widely articulated "ecological complaint against Christianity," see the sources mentioned in this study, especially Nash, *Loving Nature*, pp. 68-92. Much ink has been spilled on the topic of the meaning of the image of God; it is not my intention to rehearse all the issues here.

29. Even the term "image" is probably borrowed from the ancient custom of monarchs setting up images of themselves throughout their realm to remind the peoples of their authority; see Gerhard von Rad, *Genesis*, rev. ed, trans. John H. Marks, Old Testament Library (Philadelphia: Westminster, 1972), p. 60.

30. Nash, *Loving Nature*, p. 105. He gives as an example the just ruler of Psalm 72 (p. 104). William Dyrness ("Stewardship of the Earth in the Old Testament," in *Tending the Garden: Essays on the Gospel and the Earth*, ed. Wesley Granberg-Michaelson [Grand Rapids: Eerdmans, 1987], p. 53) relates the image of God to the picture of the ideal ruler of Deut. 17:14-20. The notion of God's rule over creation is expressed as the well-known topic of the "Kingdom (reign) of God." For two ecological treatments of Scripture based on the Kingdom of God see the articles in *Direction* 21 (1992): Elmer A. Martens, "Forward to the Garden of Eden" (pp. 27-36), and Gordon Zerbe, "Ecology according to the New Testament" (pp. 15-26).

31. John Wesley, "The General Deliverance," §I.3. Wesley uses the term "inferior creatures" to refer to animals since they lack the human ability to be "capable of God" (§I.5). Wesley was careful to point out that God cares for all of creation (§I.1), and decried the unnecessary

context of the image of God, Genesis 1:30 is a "vision of the vegetarian community of solidarity between human beings and animals."[32]

Norbert Lohfink corrects some common misunderstandings of the image of God in Genesis 1:28. First, he observes that the blessing "to be fruitful and multiply and fill the earth" was not meant to be a universal command "to all future generations." Rather, it was primarily directed toward biblical Israel and the nations, enabling them to have the numbers necessary to occupy their respective lands.[33] For the nations this was fulfilled in Genesis 10; for Israel, ironically, this was fulfilled in Egypt (Exod. 1:7). Because the command has already been fulfilled, "The topic is exhausted."[34] Even without this helpful study it should go without saying that the command to fill the earth was not meant for a planet with more than six billion people. Furthermore, humans were not the only creatures to whom God gave such a blessing, and when our numbers eliminate habitats for these *other* creatures, *they* are unable to fulfill their God-given command to occupy *their* space. As Susan P. Bratton states, "The blessing to be fruitful and multiply is a shared blessing."[35]

Second, Lohfink argues that the words "dominion" and "subdue" do not necessarily connote harshness and violence. "Subdue" *(kbš)* probably has a limited sense of taking possession of a land where only beasts currently dwell. It is also sometimes used in the sense of "to take possession" of the land of Canaan, and so in Genesis 1 may simply mean "take possession" of the earth.[36] Likewise, "dominion" *(rdh)* may not mean "tread down" as is commonly argued; rather, it may simply mean to "rule, command, lead, or direct." In Psalm 68:27 it is used

---

cruelty of "the human shark" toward even the animals that render service (§II.6). See *Wesley's Works* [Jackson], 6:241-52. Wesley taught that children should be trained to love all of God's creatures, no matter how frightening (snakes) or ugly (toads), in order to imitate the love of Christ. The pure in heart, he taught, see all things as full of God. For a discussion of these ideas in Wesley, with references, see Runyon, *The New Creation*, pp. 200-207. For a discussion of Wesley's teaching that all things are full of God, see Lodahl, "The Cosmological Basis for John Wesley's Gradualism," esp. pp. 21-29.

32. See Gen. 1:29-30; Welker, *Creation and Reality*, p. 70.

33. Earth and land are translations of the same Hebrew word.

34. Norbert Lohfink, "'Subdue the Earth?' (Gen 1:28)," in his *Theology of the Pentateuch: Themes of the Priestly Narrative and Deuteronomy,* trans. Linda M. Maloney (Minneapolis: Fortress, 1994), pp. 7-8. Scholars have long noted the abundant use of creation fertility language in this Exodus passage.

35. Susan P. Bratton, *Six Billion and More: Human Population Regulation and Christian Ethics* (Louisville: Westminster/John Knox, 1992), p. 107; she continues: "Humans should not 'steal' the blessing from the rest of creation and reproduce to such a great extent that they completely displace other creatures from the earth or greatly inhibit the ability of other species to reproduce" (p. 108). See also pp. 42-43, 106-9.

36. Lohfink, "Subdue the Earth?" pp. 11-12.

of Benjamin "accompanying" his brother tribes in festal procession. It is possible that it has the same connotation as "to shepherd."[37] Furthermore, the first "rule" *(mšl)* that God ordains in creation is not granted to humans, but to the Sun and Moon, for the obvious benefit of creation.[38]

Finally, the ultimate picture of God's ideal ruler is Christ, the Messiah who administers God's rule by serving others (Mark 10:45). Christ is the image of God who transforms the Church and creation into what God has intended from the beginning (2 Cor. 4:4; Col. 1:15). The picture of God that Christ gives is of the servant Messiah, who, though he has the power of God, empties himself in loving service (Phil. 2:6-8; Eph. 5:1-2).[39] As the image of God, Christ is "the paradigm of dominion."

> Thus when interpreted in the context of Christ, the realization of the image and the proper expression of dominion are not manifestations of exploitation, but rather *representations of nurturing and serving love . . .* [which includes expressions of] justice, in an ecological context.[40]

Genesis 2 contains another version of the account of creation that more explicitly highlights the role of humans as fellow creatures and caretakers of the earth. The Lord God forms the man, *'adam,* out of the dust of the ground, *'adamah;* or, as it is often said, he formed the *human* out of *humus* (Gen. 2:7). This is the very stuff that nourishes the plants of the field (v. 8), and from which God forms the animals (v. 19). Animals, plants, and humans share the same basic elements and nutrients. The Bible attests to a kinship between humans and the rest of creation. "This affirmation of relationality is, moreover, enhanced by the theory of evolution. . . . We evolved relationally; we exist symbiotically."[41] Recent genetic research confirms just how closely humans are related to other creatures; we share over half our genes with plants and animals, almost 99 percent is shared with chimpanzees.

Adam's posture before this matrix of life is to be one of respect: he is placed in the garden to "serve" and "watch over" (or "protect") the soil (Gen.

37. Lohfink, "Subdue the Earth?" pp. 11-12. It should be observed again that the primary meaning of this text rests not so much on the meaning of isolated terms as in the general tenor of the passage as a whole.

38. Gen. 1:14-17. "The sun and moon do not govern by force but by oversight" (William P. Brown, *The Ethos of the Cosmos: The Genesis of Moral Imagination in the Bible* [Grand Rapids: Eerdmans, 1999], p. 46).

39. Dyrness, "Stewardship of the Earth in the Old Testament," p. 53; and Wilkinson, *Earthkeeping in the Nineties,* pp. 294-99.

40. Nash, *Loving Nature,* p. 105.

41. Nash, *Loving Nature,* p. 97.

2:15; 3:23).[42] In the agrarian setting of this passage, humans are given the charge to protect the "garden." It is not stated that this care-taking responsibility is *only* for the sake of human life, for all of created life depends upon it. The Bible and science both teach us that we are connected by means of the soil to the rest of creation, which is not only our neighbor but also our distant and not-so-distant family. We are not only all caught up in the same web of life, but also we are all made from the same raw materials. This "ecological kinship" brings with it "moral responsibilities" toward the rest of creation.[43] Care for creation is care for our own distant kin — it is simply the right thing to do.

But isn't evolutionary theory, when applied to humans, actually antihuman and antienvironmental? If humans are part of the evolutionary process, it could be objected, then wars, theft, greed, self-aggrandizement, and environmental destruction can be justified on the grounds of natural selection and evolutionary design. If other species prey on one another and compete for habitat, then why not say that humans are only following their evolutionary instincts when they conquer other species and occupy their habitats? At its worst, evolutionary theory seems to reduce humans to just another animal guided by instinct, at the mercy of the genome. What this should teach us about our place in the environment, it might be argued, is that we should take and exploit as much of it as possible, because "that is what we do." How could this picture of creation possibly glorify God?

The objection is grounded in a real commonality between humans and animals — we are all initially, as Nash says, *"natural predators."* We, like the rest of the animal kingdom, survive by destroying and consuming; something has to die in order for us to live. Unlike other animals, however, we are not limited to an ecological niche, nor by natural selection. Rather we have the ability to adapt almost any environment to our liking through our creative capacities.[44] Herein lies the problem: we are capable of unlimited pursuits to fulfill desires beyond what we actually need, resulting in harm to our neighbors, human and nonhuman alike. Being *"creative predators,"* we have a moral responsibility to choose *not* to reach for unlimited power. We can opt to be either *"profligate predators"* or *"altruistic predators."*[45] We have a choice because our capacity for

42. Gen 2:15; Adam is still supposed to "serve" the soil when he and Eve are cast out of the Garden (Gen. 3:23). This translation of the Hebrew terms '*bd* and *šmr* reflects their more common meanings. In most Bible translations they are translated as "till" and "keep" here. For further discussion see, e.g., Wilkinson, *Earthkeeping in the Nineties*, pp. 287-88.

43. Cf. Nash, *Loving Nature*, pp. 97-98.

44. Rolston, "Does Nature Need to Be Redeemed?" pp. 164-65; Braden, "On Saving the Wilderness," p. 259.

45. For a discussion of love, predation, and moral accountability see Nash, *Loving Nature*, pp. 146-52.

God makes us morally accountable creatures. Some argue that for humans physical evolution has stopped; we are now creatures who live by culture. Choosing the former is what differentiates us from the animals. As Holmes Rolston phrases it, "When animals act 'like beasts,' as nonmoral beings, nothing is amiss, evil, or ungodly. But if humans go no further, something is amiss; indeed, in theological terms, something is ungodly." The irony is that animals are not tempted to possess the whole, while we humans, who have risen to a higher moral state, pursue that very goal. Animals usually limit themselves by nature; we humans must limit ourselves by moral choice.[46]

Humans have a moral responsibility to rise above a mere animal existence and make self-conscious choices for the benefit of all of creation. This is where our study of Genesis might help us avoid our sinful tendency to grasp at unlimited power and possessions. Since we are part and parcel of the rest of creation, we can learn from the rest of creation that as *natural predators* we should limit our desires to inhabit a limited niche, respecting the niche of other creatures and taking only what we actually need. The dominion mandates in Genesis 1 and the service mandate in Genesis 2 not only assure humans a place in creation, but they limit that place to what furthers God's benevolent rule and enhances God's power of blessing to all of creation. In short, when humans do not limit their predatory acts toward the rest of creation then they violate God's creation mandates for all of the creation.

Redemption as Cosmic Event

Does nature need to be redeemed? A colleague thought the idea was ludicrous: "Do atoms and molecules need forgiveness for their sins?" This understanding reflects what the Church has commonly taught about redemption. Redemption is usually narrowly understood as forgiveness for sins or payment for the penalty of sins. While this is certainly an aspect of redemption, it does not provide the fully developed picture of redemption in the Scriptures. The concept of redemption is borrowed from everyday life. To redeem is to physically rescue something (or one) to restore it back to its normal or intended place, enabling

---

46. Rolston, "Does Nature Need to Be Redeemed?" p. 163. Rolston correctly associates this tendency with the Pauline idea of "the natural [human]." He connects moral accountability with our ability to choose the destructive opposite course, the "fruit of the tree of the knowledge of good and evil" in Genesis. "When humans emerge in culture, we emerge into, and at the same time fall into a process that contains the seeds of its own destruction, which was not true before. We rise to, and fall into a moral process. We rise to a vision of the good that has evil as its shadow side" (p. 164). Cf. the discussion in Braden, "On Saving the Wilderness," p. 259.

it to fulfill its intrinsic (God-given) purpose.[47] So redemption has a twofold aspect, rescue *from* some unwanted condition, restoration *to* wholeness. In the Old Testament redemption is not usually from personal sin but from some physical circumstance over which the redeemed person or thing has no control. When redemption is primarily defined as forgiveness *from* sin rather than restoration *to* something, then the meaning of the term loses the richness of its biblical heritage.[48]

This idea of cosmic redemption, or the restoration of creation, is as old as the first pages of the Old Testament. As we have seen, Genesis 1–2 tells of God's design for all of creation, both for now and the future. Humans are on Earth to extend God's care for the earth and its creatures so that God's benevolent intentions for creation might be fulfilled. This is nothing short of redemption. In the rest of Genesis and Exodus (and beyond), we read of God calling a people to begin the process of restoring all nations, peoples, and ultimately all creation back to their intended state. As they were on the verge of entering into covenant with God at Sinai, God, owner of "the whole earth," gave Israel a priestly vocation to fulfill God's creation purposes. Commenting on Exodus 19, Terrence Fretheim says, "The function of the law is to set out Israel's vocation in the world, to bring the created order — human and non-human — into closer conformity with creation as God intended it, characterized in particular by righteousness, mercy, and the fear of God."[49]

47. See the standard Bible dictionaries for a discussion of the terminology and meaning, e.g., R. C. Denton, "Redeem, Redeemer, Redemption," in *Interpreter's Dictionary of the Bible,* ed. George Buttrick (Nashville: Abingdon, 1962), 4:21-22. It is worth noting that most of the traditional terms connoting God's redeeming work, such as salvation, and deliverance, connote a positive restoration to God's intended purposes.

48. Situations occasioning redemption include impoverishment due to debt, war, or famine; loss of property or captivity due to theft or war; etc. The Exodus is often called God's redemption (Exod. 6:6; 15:13; Mic. 6:4) because God rescued Israel from slavery to restore them to the Promised Land. Christ's work is called redemption or ransom (1 Cor. 1:30; 1 Pet. 1:18) sometimes stated as from sin (Col. 1:14; Rom. 3:24). Redemption of the person (the "body") will be complete at the resurrection (Rom. 8:23; Eph. 4:30). With rare exception (e.g., Ps. 130:8) the language of redemption from personal sin is not used until the New Testament. However, it is probably going too far to state that every mention of redemption in the New Testament "always [implies] deliverance from sin and its effects" (Denton, "Redemption," p. 22). This idea of restoring creation to its original intention is a theme of ancient Greek and contemporary Eastern Orthodox Christianity, which emphasizes the positive aspects of redemption; see Wilkinson, *Earthkeeping in the Nineties,* pp. 302-6; Nash, *Loving Nature,* pp. 80-81. It is now widely agreed that Wesley was strongly influenced by the Greek tradition in his understanding of salvation; see note above.

49. Exod. 19:5-6; see Terence Fretheim, "The Reclamation of Creation: Redemption and Law in Exodus," *Interpretation* 45 (1991): 361.

Redemption as restoration provides the background for many of the "cosmic" passages of the Bible. For example, the theme of a "(re)new(ed)[50] heaven and earth" (Isa. 65:17-25; Rev. 21:1-8) concerns the restoration of all creation. Christ, as the image of God (Col. 1:15), fully embodies God's beneficent rule of blessing ordained in Genesis 1. "And through him God was pleased to reconcile to himself all things, whether on earth or in heaven" (Col. 1:20 [NRSV]; cf. Eph. 1:10). Likewise, in his role as Messiah, Christ conveys God's rule by blessing his land and all of creation.[51] Paul speaks of the entire creation groaning in travail as it hopefully awaits the completion of God's work, releasing it from the "bondage to decay" so that it might "obtain the freedom of the glory of the children of God" (Rom. 8:18-24 [NRSV]).[52] This passage clearly intertwines human redemption and the redemption of creation.[53] Christ's cosmic work is literally "grounded" in the incarnation. By assuming human flesh and redeeming it, Christ embodied the evolutionary history that humans share with the rest of creation, and so he redeems the cosmos.[54]

Nature will be finally redeemed; indeed, nature is being redeemed. Just as God's power transforms us and his grace daily sustains us, so God is sustaining all of creation — and this is redemption.[55] As Holmes Rolston observes, the evolutionary process of growth and reproduction, or "regeneration," is the primary way that nature is being and will continue to be redeemed. Redemption of nature includes rescue from the effects of past and present human sin, but more importantly, it is the constant renewal that enables creation to fulfill

50. The Hebrew word for "new" can also mean "renewed"; its verbal form can mean "restore." The same root is used for the Moon, which renews itself every month; KB, s.v. the roots listed under חדשׁ [ḥdš] (1:293-95).

51. E.g., Psalm 72. For a brief discussion see Laurie J. Braaten, "The Voice of Wisdom: A Creation Context for the Emergence of Trinitarian Language," *Wesleyan Theological Journal* 36 (2001): 45. Another title for the king was "son of God" (2 Sam. 7:14; Ps. 2:7; 89:27). As adopted children of God through the Spirit, Christians are joint heirs with Christ (Rom. 8:14-27) and so anticipate and participate in the "messianic" role of conveying God's blessing to creation.

52. The travail of this passage is due to the curse upon creation because of constant human sin (Gen. 3:17). Creation is being redeemed not because it has sinned, but because human sin negatively affects it (see Frank Moore Cross, "The Redemption of Nature," *Princeton Seminary Bulletin* 10 [1989]: 95).

53. Note how suffering, groaning (or travailing), and redemption are applied to both humans and the rest of creation.

54. See Nash, *Loving Nature*, pp. 108-11; and the essay in this volume by George L. Murphy, "Christology, Evolution, and the Cross."

55. We have already considered the creation and/or redemption context of such passages as "In [Christ] all things hold together" (Col. 1:17 [NRSV]) and "When you send forth your spirit, they are created; and you renew the face of the ground" (Ps. 104:30 [NRSV]).

God's ongoing purposes.[56] This redemption of nature is the broader context of human redemption, and not *vice versa*.[57]

If nature is the object of God's redeeming love and reveals the glory of God, then why does it sometimes appear to be out of control? The "dark side" of creation appears in the power of "natural" disasters (sometimes called "acts of God"!). It is also seen in the messy business of animal predation, sickness, plague, and death — all necessary components of evolutionary theory. Other essays in this volume have observed that these problems of God's justice (theodicy) are ancient dilemmas and are not to be blamed on evolutionary theory; nor, we could add, are they reasons not to embrace creation care.[58]

As we search for answers we must be honest and admit that there is no entirely satisfactory solution to the problem of pain and suffering; we can only offer partial explanations. One approach to the problem of "natural evil" is to posit that God's relation with creation is analogous to his relation with humans. "In him we live and breathe and have our being" (Acts 17:28 [NRSV]), and without his sustaining power all life would immediately turn to dust (Ps. 104:29). God in his love has also granted us freedom to respond in loving relationship to him and others. Because we are free, we are capable of using our God-sustained power for ungodly purposes. It seems that God grants creation the same freedom that he grants humans. While God sustains all of creation, he does not appear to micromanage it. Just as God does not normally overrule human actions, even when they cause harm, so God does not normally overrule "natural" processes.[59] And just as God's "strange work" accomplishes his pur-

56. Rolston, "Does Nature Need to Be Redeemed?" pp. 150-51, 170. Rolston characterizes redemption as (1) "rescue from harm," (2) adding "value" to a life that is "rescued" and "restored," and (3) the "transformation" and "renovation" of life (p. 150).

57. For the cosmological setting for human transformation in Wesley's theology see Lodahl, "The Cosmological Basis for John Wesley's Gradualism," pp. 17-32. It is common to note that the doctrine of the resurrection makes sense only in the context of the redemption of nature (see Frank Moore Cross, "The Redemption of Nature," p. 101). See above on Romans 8.

58. See the essays in this volume by Keith B. Miller, "An Evolving Creation: Oxymoron or Fruitful Insight?" and John Munday, Jr., "Animal Pain: Beyond the Threshold?" The problem of the justice of God (theodicy) is intrinsic to a theistic religion with a creator god. Many Christians have just not thought about the implications of their faith when they claim that God is the Creator of the heavens and earth.

59. Denis Edwards, *The God of Evolution: A Trinitarian Theology* (Mahwah, N.J.: Paulist, 1999), pp. 43-44. Creation, however, does not seem to have moral awareness, and so "activities" of its members are not intended for moral good or evil (except, perhaps, in the case of household pets!). The overall creative process, however, is designed for the benefit of all of creation.

poses in spite of and even through intentional human evil, so God can even use cosmic mishaps to accomplish his goals.[60]

Another approach notes that the destructiveness of the storm and other natural displays can serve as a picture of the mysterious power of our awesome God, and as a reminder of how small we humans are before him.[61] They may remind us of our *hubris:* thinking that we are invincible, we build in floodplains and pave over natural drainage areas. Destructive storms may also remind us that we sometimes suffer for the sake of the needs of others: the storm that brings flooding and destruction may supply much-needed moisture and nutrients to other inhabitants of creation.

Scripture seems to acknowledge predation as a necessary part of creation that is allowed and even sustained by God (Gen. 9:3; Ps. 104:21).[62] Evolutionary theory and the fossil record show that predation has been here since the dawn of life. That predation is not God's ultimate intention for creation, however, is evident in the recurring portrait of the peaceable kingdom in the creation narratives and visionary portraits of the end times.[63]

---

60. The phrase "strange work" is taken from Isa. 28:21 where God uses the militaristic intents of pagan nations as agents of discipline against his rebellious people. See also Gen. 50:20 and Rom. 8:28 — notice the context of suffering: the groaning and to-be-redeemed creation and cosmic peril! For a discussion of providence and the freedom of creation see the essay in this volume by Loren Haarsma, "Does Science Exclude God? Natural Law, Chance, Miracles, and Scientific Practice."

61. A common way of describing the theophanic appearances of God in the Old Testament is through the awesome powers of nature; see Theodore Hiebert, "Theophany in the Old Testament," in *Anchor Bible Dictionary*, ed. David N. Freedman (New York: Doubleday, 1992), 6:508-10; and Donald E. Gowan, *Eschatology in the Old Testament* (Philadelphia: Fortress, 1987), pp. 111-12.

62. An essay in this volume discusses the issues of predation; see John C. Munday, Jr., "Animal Pain: Beyond the Threshold?" In the opinion of this reader the good points of this essay would be much stronger if the author resorted less frequently to the sovereignty of God (whose design of creation the reader is not to challenge) on the one hand, and to Satan (who is blamed for some of creation's problems) on the other.

63. See Isa. 11:6. W. Sibley Towner ("The Future of Nature," *Interpretation* 50 [1996]: 28) observes that "apparently the eschatological texts of the Bible view the end of predation as a cipher for a general future rectification of relationships within the created order." See also Gowan, *Eschatology of the Old Testament*, pp. 102-4, 108-9. According to Wesley the Scripture teaches that the new creation would contain animals (i.e., representatives from each species), and that predation would no longer exist there. He also speculated that all life would be elevated, humans becoming like the angels, and animals perhaps becoming like humans with a capacity for God. He argued that this reward in the next life vindicated the justice of God since innocent animals suffered on earth. This destiny of animals encourages humans to have the same mercy for animals that God has. Further, he stated, "Yea, let us habituate ourselves to look forward, beyond this present scene of bondage, to the happy time when they will be delivered therefrom into the liberty of the children of God" ("The General Deliverance," III.1-12, in *Wesley's Works* [Jackson], 6:343-52]).

The problem of predation brings to mind the ultimate evil — death.[64] Death is tied up with life on this earth; it is part of the evolutionary process. How can God endorse such a system? One could look at the evolutionary system of death and decay and see its positive value: they are necessary for the emergence of new life. Death is a necessary evil, and it does not take an acceptance of evolutionary theory to observe this fact in the world around us. We cannot even conceive of life without death. For anything to live it is going to be at the price of the death of others. As such, creation may be viewed as "cruciform," it can serve as a parable or symbol of God's suffering work in Christ. As Holmes Rolston states "The secret of life is that it is a passion play."[65] Out of unjust suffering arises the power of new, resurrection life. But this new life, like the resurrection of Christ, also points us forward in hope that life will someday conquer the final enemy, that death will be defeated (1 Cor. 15:26).

That the Glory of the Lord May Endure Forever

We began this essay asking how evolution, ecology, and God might be brought peaceably together. We have briefly made some points concerning how they are inextricably linked. Ecological concerns challenge the "debaters of this age" to give a contemporary focus to the issues regarding evolution and creation. In the words of Holmes Rolston, "Ecology is a time-slice out of evolution."[66] Evolution asks questions of the past not out of idle curiosity concerning origins but out of an earnest desire to understand what creation is now, and where it is headed. This is also the task of creation care: we look back at the creation narratives to determine what God intends for creation *now,* and what God's *future* for creation might be. As we ponder our place in creation, it is obvious that we have been, in the words of James Nash, "profligate predators." As we look at Scripture we get a vision of what it means to be "altruistic predators."

In closing, let us reflect on Psalm 104, which expresses the comprehensiveness of God's work as a call to worship the Creator. We are summoned to enter the cosmic sanctuary. We marvel at the diversity of life in creation, each

64. Other essays in this volume have already addressed the theological problem of asserting that death has always been a part of the created order.

65. Rolston, "Does Nature Need to Be Redeemed?" p. 160; see his discussion of cruciform creation on pp. 158-62. See also Keith B. Miller, "Theological Implications of an Evolving Creation," *Perspective on Science and Christian Faith* 45 (1993): 150-60, condensed web version at http://mcgraytx.calvin.edu/ASA/PSCF9-93Miller.html, p. 3; and George L. Murphy, "Christology, Evolution, and the Cross."

66. Rolston, "Does Nature Need to Be Redeemed?" p. 160.

part of which invites us to join them in praise of our — their — Creator. The Creator has given us the power to convey his blessing to all creation, a power that we sometimes turn selfishly toward ourselves. But God cannot rejoice forever in the glory from his works (v. 31) if humans destroy them. And so the psalm concludes with the one negative note in this hymn of praise: "Let sinners be consumed from the earth . . ." (v. 35). We might contextually paraphrase: "Those who consume the glory of God will themselves be consumed." Profligate consumption destroys worship. We cannot worship with our sisters and brothers in Christ if we are preoccupied with manipulating and dominating them to satisfy our lust for power. Neither can we worship with our fellow creatures if we are obsessed with turning them into consumables. Let us tend to the creation below as we seek the things that are above, and then we can join with all the company of heaven and earth and sing:

> Praise God from whom all blessings flow
> Praise him all creatures here below,
> Praise him above ye heavenly host,
> Praise Father, Son and Holy Ghost. Amen

19

Animal Pain: Beyond the Threshold?

JOHN C. MUNDAY, JR.

The presence of pain in a morally ordered cosmos has tortured the minds of the reflective of every generation.[1]

Introduction

The common destiny of man and beast is suffering and death. In the present life, before its inevitable end, all creatures face the struggles of illness and pain. Suffering is commonly explained in relation to morality, and for many circumstances we seem to be satisfied with this approach. The moral approach, however, often loses force for people who suffer much from bodily ills through no fault of their own. Consequently, some turn from morality to an existential or naturalistic approach. Others appeal to God's overall purpose in creation. Christians recognize that sin can produce suffering, but are comforted by the Holy Spirit and by the thought of eternal life.

When we explore the suffering of animals, both the moral and theistic justifications are forced to be more complex and indirect. The animal world knows nothing of eternity and appears to lack self-consciousness and appreciation of the ministry of the Comforter. Hence it must face the pains of life and death unprotected. Is there a moral problem concerning the pain experienced by animals?

The 150 years of arguments about biological evolution include frequent reference to the moral question of animal suffering. Young-Earth creationists and even some old-Earth adherents have considered the question to be important, the former finding it a strong reason for rejecting the evolution paradigm, and the latter troubled by its implications for God's character.

1. George Stewart, *God and Pain* (New York: Doran, 1927), p. 11.

435

We will see that drawing from both nature and Scripture is the surest pathway to a satisfactory perspective. To reach that goal, we consider theodicy, the problem of justifying God in relation to the world's evil, including both human and animal suffering. Scripture on sin and death is analyzed. We also consider biological design, necessary for survival in a physical world obeying the laws of nature, and refer as well to the picture of nature in Scripture. The Bible's comments about animals help explain the behavior of man and of God as he deals with his unruly subjects. Those comments provide clues to a biblically harmonious perspective about animal pain.

The fact that some intellectual satisfaction may be realized from this study does not totally erase the discomfort we all feel at the bedside of suffering, whether it is of man or beast. Suffering works in all of us a profound humility before our animate nature and touches our being at its core. It brings us face to face with our Creator. Whether this is true for animals must remain an impenetrable mystery, because only humans are known to communicate with each other about God.

Theism, Suffering, and Morality

Andrew Linzey believes that the moral question about animal pain arises only in a theistic worldview:

> But it is difficult to see how in either naturalistic or Darwinian terms violence within the natural order presents a *moral* problem. If there is no God, no moral source of the universe as we know it, violence is not a problem to be sorted out, it is simply a fact to be accommodated. . . . Violence in the natural world can only be a moral problem for those who believe in God. . . . The difficulty for Christians is how to reconcile a loving, holy Creator with a created world that operates a parasitical system with suffering and pain as an inherent feature. . . .[2]

In Hebrew and Christian religion, the one Creator is always viewed as morally perfect and just. God's work is self-described as "good" four times in Genesis 1, and after creating man, "God saw all that he had made, and lo! It was very good" (Gen. 1:31).

His creations include Satan, other spirits, and man, all of whom have a moral nature. They were created sinless but have the capability for sin, being endowed with free choice of thought and action.

2. Andrew Linzey, *Christianity and the Rights of Animals* (New York: Crossroad, 1989), p. 59.

If animals have no moral nature[3] and therefore cannot be found morally culpable, then their suffering and death must be explained as arising elsewhere. For human beings, sin and other factors bring a circle of closure for the suffering soul. These include our injurious choices, personal and national sin, the struggles to overcome odds or achieve success, and self-imposed disciplines. None of these human factors helps very much to explain animal suffering — they have no referent for the animal in his world of experience. We thus turn to a moral scapegoat. Explaining animal suffering, given that animals are naturally amoral, may first appear to be as simple as finding another guilty party. This approach leads directly to finding God as Creator responsible, or to blaming man, or possibly the fallen angels.

To find God immediately responsible for human and animal suffering is awkward, at best, in any moral conception of God and nature. Even in Job, the premier book concerned with suffering of innocent human beings, God's moral perfection and righteous judgments are never impugned. No defense of God's justice is ever offered.[4] The immediate cause of Job's problems, furthermore, is Satan. Only in the depths of theodicy is God's ultimate responsibility for suffering recognized, in that he made creatures with free will.

Thus, the fundamental question may be framed this way: Is animal suffering a given feature of nature as created by God? Or is it a consequence of human sin or that of fallen spirits? If it is incorporated into God's creation inherently, what are the moral implications for our understanding of God?

However, even if human sin is involved, sometimes it fails as an adequate explanation. For many human beings, the degree, quality and circumstances of suffering call for explanation beyond personal guilt or choice of action. Often the question is asked, "Why do the innocent suffer?" To the extent a suitable answer is found for why innocent humans suffer, perhaps some satisfaction will be gained for why animals also suffer.

Animal Consciousness and Pain

For all except the higher animals, consciousness is obviously limited, and prob-

---

3. So believed by C. S. Lewis, who also believed that animals are incapable of sin and of virtue. Further, he said "'Life' in the biological sense has nothing to do with good and evil until sentience appears." Trees kill other trees, but this is neither good nor evil. See C. S. Lewis, *The Problem of Pain* (New York: Collier/Macmillan, 1962, reprint 1986), pp. 129-30.

4. Edmund E. Sutcliffe, *Providence and Suffering in the Old and New Testaments* (London: Thomas Nelson, 1953), p. 113.

ably absent altogether. Therefore, in pondering animal pain, we may limit our consideration to how pain affects only the higher animals.

The problem of animal consciousness is critical to the question posed by pain and suffering. As noted by Marian S. Dawkins, "there are major obstacles to finding out whether other species are conscious,"[5] although it is "more plausible that they do [have consciousness] than not."[6] There are three degrees to consider — sensation, perception, and self-awareness.[7] Higher animals have sentience, but we may "distinguish sentience from consciousness."[8] Dogs, cats, apes, horses, elephants, whales, and dolphins — all are obviously pain-sensitive and may appear to be conscious. But a succession of sensations or perceptions is merely sentience, not consciousness, which is the awareness of experiencing sensations. We should not read "into the beast a self for which there is no real evidence."[9]

While animals "think" in some sense, this is only one facet of "mind." The other facet is "subjective feelings."[10] Observations show that baboons practice deliberate deceptions.[11] It can be shown that animals "want" things, and that they consider choices and understand purchase costs and penalties, but as to whether they feel as we do, "the answer . . . still eludes us."[12]

Some investigators distinguish between "perceptual consciousness" and "reflective consciousness." The latter is "difficult to detect in animals, if it occurs." And self-awareness goes beyond reflective consciousness.[13] Of greatest interest is whether an animal has conscious awareness of its (possible) conscious awareness. Experiments with mirrors show that apes have awareness but not necessarily self-awareness.[14] Thus, while observations sometimes strongly hint at higher levels of consciousness and cognition, in the end the critical issue of self-aware consciousness must be left as an open question. Not the least of the difficulties is deciding on good definitions for consciousness and associated terms.

One feature of the question is language. As evidence for conscious awareness, language is significant but may not be critical for the issue. Note that hu-

5. Marian S. Dawkins, *Through Our Eyes Only? The Search for Animal Consciousness* (Oxford: Freeman, 1993), p. 3.

6. M. Dawkins, *Through Our Eyes Only?* p. 2.

7. M. Dawkins, *Through Our Eyes Only?* p. 4.

8. Lewis, *Problem of Pain,* p. 131.

9. Lewis, *Problem of Pain,* pp. 132-33.

10. George Page, *Inside the Animal Mind: A Ground-Breaking Exploration of Animal Intelligence* (New York: Doubleday, 1999), p. 127.

11. Page, *Inside the Animal Mind,* p. 134.

12. Page, *Inside the Animal Mind,* pp. 149, 153, 160.

13. Donald R. Griffin, *Animal Minds* (Chicago: University of Chicago Press, 1992), p. 246.

14. Griffin, *Animal Minds,* p. 249.

man babies "talk" by means of actions.[15] While animals have been found to engage in communication, and to have memory, ability to learn, and ability to assess situations, none of these is critically relevant to the self-aware experience of pain or to consciousness.[16] Further, complexity of behavior does not in itself imply consciousness,[17] as our computer age easily demonstrates. Neither does apparent thinking ahead nor transference of appropriate action to new situations.

Few animals give evidence of communications regarding the future or the past. The point here is that some component of human suffering is related to our capacity to reflect on the present and anticipate the future. If animals lack this capacity, or have significantly reduced capacity for it, then their capacity for suffering must be considered as also reduced.

Thus we may question whether an animal experiences pain and suffering, in the course of living and dying, with the same degree of conscious experience as humans. Do we dare argue by analogy from the human being? No matter how clever and complex, to conclude the animal has a soul or self-awareness like that of humans is an argument from analogy.[18]

In the extreme, animal pain, suffering, and death are all linked. Death can come extraordinarily quickly in the animal world, but often it does not. However, large predators often kill their prey by means that inflict, so far as we know, a minimal level of pain. Predation commonly involves attack on the neck and throat, which is significant for minimizing pain. In Judaism, where ritual sacrifice of animals has been developed with a keen sensitivity to minimizing the animal's pain and suffering, killing is accomplished by a clean slicing of the throat with a very sharp knife. Other methods of sacrifice are forbidden. Rabbi Bleich asserts that "*shehitah* is the most humane method of slaughter known to man."[19] The "paucity of sensory cutaneous nerve endings in the skin covering the throat . . . ensures that the incision causes no pain." Because the carotid arteries and the jugular veins are severed, blood loss is swift, pressure drops precipitously, and oxygen tension in the brain plummets. Injuries to human beings, and experiments with animals, confirm that consciousness is lost quickly, as electroencephalograph recordings on sacrificed sheep, calves, and goats document the collapse of brain waves in three to seven

15. M. Dawkins, *Through Our Eyes Only?* p. 12.

16. M. Dawkins, *Through Our Eyes Only?* p. 43.

17. M. Dawkins, *Through Our Eyes Only?* p. 57.

18. Page, *Inside the Animal Mind,* p. 105.

19. J. David Bleich, "Judaism and Animal Experimentation," in *Animal Rights and Human Obligations,* ed. T. Regan and P. Singer (Englewood, N.J.: Prentice Hall, 1977), ch. 3, pp. 61-114, 97.

seconds.[20] Experience of pain during the last seconds of *shehitah* is minimal to nonexistent.

Pain is an experience or a psychophysical perception. It is well known that the perception of pain can be altered significantly. Jules H. Masserman (Northwestern University) showed that cats can be "trained to administer [an electric] shock [to] themselves by walking up to a switch and closing it." Conversely, the "mere anticipation of pain . . ." can make a nonpainful event painful, as evidenced by brain-wave modifications.[21] The phenomenon of phantom-limb pain after amputation is also well known.

Thus, pain has "sensory" and "affective" components. The modifiability of pain indicates the "plasticity and modifiability of events occurring in the central nervous system."[22] In the perception of pain, its quality and intensity are influenced by history, meaning, and the "state of mind," including the creature's "present thoughts and fears as well as his hopes for the future,"[23] if he has any.

We may distinguish therefore between the psychophysical sensation of pain and the psychospiritual and reflective experience of pain. Corey relates African explorer David Livingstone's recount of being attacked by a lion — "The shock produced a stupor. . . . It caused a sort of dreaminess in which there was no sense of pain nor feeling of terror. . . . This peculiar state is probably produced in all animals killed by carnivora; and if so, is a merciful provision by our benevolent Creator for lessening the pain of death."[24] Perhaps animals are always experiencing a similar, somewhat stuporous, level of consciousness, especially self-awareness, in comparison to ours.

Linzey argues, contrary to the above, that animal experience of pain can be great, and that animals may even have some potential for intimacy with the Holy Spirit. Nature is "infused at all levels . . . with the power of the Spirit."[25] While the latter is true in a general sense, only by God's revelation could a claim

20. Bleich ("Judaism and Animal Experimentation," pp. 97-101, n. 17) explores the question of pain in ritual slaughter at some length, with references to medical literature and the Jewish method of slaughter. It may provide a small amount of comfort that the self-slaughter by Jews at Masada in 70 A.D., to avoid capture by the besieging Romans, involved slaughter by incision at the throat.

21. Ronald Melzack, "The Perception of Pain," in *Psychobiology: The Biological Bases of Behavior*, ed. James L. McGaugh, Norman M. Weinberger, and Richard E. Whalen (San Francisco: Freeman, 1966), ch. 37, pp. 299-307, esp. pp. 300-301.

22. Melzack, "Perception of Pain," pp. 305, 307.

23. Melzack, "Perception of Pain," p. 307.

24. David Livingstone, *Livingstone's Africa*, quoted in M. A. Corey, *Back to Darwin: The Scientific Case for Deistic Evolution* (Lanham, Md.: University Press of America, 1994), p. 373.

25. Linzey, *Christianity and the Rights of Animals*, p. 66.

about animals experiencing the Holy Spirit as a Person ever be verified. Scripture provides no warrant for thinking so.

Acknowledging the uncertainties surrounding the capacity of animals to consciously suffer extreme pain, from here on we simply accept that animals do suffer, and that they suffer enough to provoke a meaningful concern about why they should have to.

Paradigms

The direction that a Christian takes toward the question of animal pain turns on the chosen paradigm concerning nature and its creatures. The young-Earth paradigm brings the question of animal pain to the forefront in the most acute way scripturally. In contrasting young-Earth and old-Earth paradigms, the full range of scriptural arguments bearing on animal pain are given their sharpest impact.

Under a young-Earth scenario derived from monolithic biblical literalism, God's creation of the world took six twenty-four-hour days about ten thousand years ago.[26] Adam, the first living person with God-consciousness, originally enjoyed unimpaired communion with God. Before the Fall, his physical body bore no scars of sin, and presumably he experienced no pain and suffering. Both man and beast enjoyed immortality and nonviolence. Disease, injury, aging, and death came to animals and man because Adam sinned, was separated from the Tree of Life, and was banished to the briar patch outside the Garden. Nature was transformed and animal predation began.[27]

This conceptual edifice is completed by noting that fossil residues in geological strata constitute a record of animal death. If such death occurred only after the Fall, then by logic the fossils were deposited within human history. The only historical event that can be plausibly reckoned as the sufficient cause of the fossil record is Noah's Flood. Thus is birthed Flood Geology.[28]

Henry M. Morris, a leading young-Earth creationist, says, "There was no death or suffering of sentient life in the Creation, pronounced by God to be 'very good,' until after man brought sin into the world and God pronounced a Curse upon the earth."[29]

Those who believe this paradigm find the full cause of animal pain and

26. Henry M. Morris, *The Biblical Basis for Modern Science* (Grand Rapids: Baker, 1984).

27. For a typical young-Earth creationist view of the pre-Fall earth, see Morris, *Biblical Basis for Modern Science.*

28. John C. Whitcomb and Henry M. Morris, *The Genesis Flood* (Phillipsburg, N.J.: Presbyterian and Reformed Publ. Co., 1961), pp. 270ff.

29. Henry M. Morris, *Studies in the Bible and Science* (Grand Rapids: Baker, 1966), pp. 91-92.

suffering in human sin. The simplicity of this view is very appealing. By sinning, Adam and Eve initiated a devastating transformation of the cosmos, introducing entropy and death throughout. That Satan also fell at some time is usually ignored. All animal suffering will cease when the new creation comes at the end of the age.

The old-Earth paradigm in contrast adopts the standard geologic timetable and sees the fossil record as a drawn-out sequence of biotic environments. While old-Earth Christians agree that God created the heavens and the earth in all fullness over a long period of time, within that framework variant conceptions exist. They involve differences over whether biological species developed via an unbroken "chain of being," or through abrupt appearances of new forms not derived from previously existing forms.[30] Thus, the sequence and processes of his creative acts are disputed. Theistic evolutionists say that God guided biological evolution as it is commonly understood. Progressive creationists hold that God at times intervened with novel creations, such as the first life, and the several groups of vertebrates (fish, birds, mammals, and man), while evolution produced the finer details.

The old-Earth paradigm allows various degrees of both creative acts and biological evolution to be intermixed. No matter what the mixture, animal suffering and death occurred throughout the geological ages before the appearance of human beings. While Adam and Eve brought suffering and death (both physical and spiritual) upon themselves, and through sin increased the suffering of animals in subsequent generations, the animal suffering that preceded man is not their fault. Adam and Eve were not accountable for conditions prior to their existence, although God may have designed the world to provide for their probationary existence. The other option is that animal suffering is part of the created order, without concern for human beings.

For many people, evolution intensifies the problem of animal suffering. Specifically, accepting biological evolution as God's way of creating animal species means that he deliberately employed long ages of animal living and dying, with natural selection weeding out the unfit.

Views from History

Church fathers and scholastics sometimes commented on animal consciousness and pain's connection to human sin. Augustine held that "Beasts are alive,

---

30. Charles E. Hummel, *The Galileo Connection: Resolving Conflicts between Science & the Bible* (Downers Grove, Ill.: InterVarsity, 1986).

but . . . have no part in reason," as "there is something lacking in their souls which allows them to be subjected by us. . . ."[31] He added that "To seek bodily pleasures and to avoid pain is the whole endeavour of animal life,"[32] and "An animal lives but has not intelligence."[33] The difference between man and animal lies in man's rationality and the fact that "beasts can be tamed by human beings, but human beings cannot be tamed by beasts."[34] Man made in the image of God was made to rule over the irrational.[35] On why sinless animals suffer Augustine had no answer.[36]

Aquinas emphasized the hierarchy of man over animals and saw the killing of animals as permissible.[37] Similarly, Luther regarded animals as subordinate to man by the dominion mandate. Animals, he said, are irrational "brute beasts" meant only for this world. Nevertheless, the Fall impaired man's exercise of dominion, which at the beginning was a harmonious mastery of animals, not the slaying for meat introduced after the Flood.[38]

Theodicy — Justifying God and Acknowledging Evil

The moral question concerning suffering has always been central. It leads to theodicy — an understanding of God in which his justice, righteousness, and loving character can be maintained in the face of both human and animal suffering.

Many would agree that ". . . death stands as the ultimate question mark attached to any defense of God." In addition, theodicy must encompass not

31. Augustine, "On Free Will" *(De Libero Arbitrio)*, book I, vii, 16, in J. H. S. Burleigh, ed., *Augustine: Earlier Writings* (Philadelphia, Pa.: Westminster, 1953), p. 122. On p. 121, "beasts lack reason."

32. Augustine, "On Free Will," book I, vii, 18, in Burleigh, *Augustine,* p. 123.

33. Augustine, "On Free Will," book II, iii, 7, in Burleigh, *Augustine,* p. 138.

34. Augustine, *83 Questions on Various Topics,* 13 (*Corpus Christianorum, series Latina,* 44A:20), in Gillian Clark, "The Fathers and the Animals: The Rule of Reason?" in *Animals on the Agenda,* ed. Andrew Linzey and Dorothy Yamamoto (Urbana, Ill.: University of Illinois Press, 1998), p. 68.

35. See Augustine, *City of God (De civitate dei),* 19.14-15.

36. Augustine, *Literal Commentary on Genesis,* 3:16.

37. St. Thomas Aquinas, *Summa theologiae,* Part I, Q. 64.I. See Dorothy Yamamoto, "Aquinas and Animals: Patrolling the Boundary?" in *Animals on the Agenda,* ed. Andrew Linzey and Dorothy Yamamoto (Urbana, Ill.: University of Illinois Press, 1998), p. 80.

38. Martin Luther, *Luther's Works* 1 and 2 passim (St. Louis, Mo.: American Edition, 1958-86), in Scott Ickert, "Luther and Animals: Subject to Adam's Fall?" in *Animals on the Agenda,* ed. Andrew Linzey and Dorothy Yamamoto (Urbana, Ill.: University of Illinois Press, 1998), pp. 90-99.

death alone but all three of the "disturbances" that upset the cosmic order — "evil, suffering and death. The first of these unwelcome visitors consists of moral evil, natural evil, and religious evil."[39]

For some the existence of evil produces a disinclination to believe in God. Rick Rood puts the common argument like this:

> . . . it is irrational and hence impossible to believe in the existence of a good and powerful God on the basis of the existence of evil in the world. . . . 1. A good God would destroy evil. 2. An all-powerful God could destroy evil. 3. Evil is not destroyed. 4. Therefore, there cannot possibly be such a good and powerful God.[40]

Rejecting this extreme view, we maintain that to require God to justify his actions is arrogant hubris. God does not have to morally defend anything he does. It is the Creator's prerogative to set up creation according to his will and pleasure. We must conform our notion of love and morality to his. Why presume his love and his morality should preclude all sufferings of man and beast, and that it is always wrong for the innocent to suffer? Jesus was made *perfect* (complete) *through suffering* (Heb. 2:10, 18). Our proper pursuit is to comprehend both physically and spiritually what he has done and is doing. Instead of moralizing on the basis of presumed innocence, we should focus on God's freedom. The Apostle Paul noted in Romans 9:14-16: *There is no injustice with God, is there? May it never be! For He says to Moses, "I will have mercy on whom I have mercy, and I will have compassion on whom I have compassion." So then it does not depend on the man who wills or the man who runs, but on God who has mercy.*

Evil in Scripture means calamity, and bad or negative experience, in addition to malevolence and wrongdoing. God is wholly righteous, but Scripture says that he brings calamity — *I am the LORD, and there is no other. I form the light and create darkness, I bring prosperity and create disaster; I, the LORD, do all these things* (Isa. 45:6-7).[41] God here takes ultimate responsibility for at least some calamity. On the ground that he is the Creator, ultimately he is responsible for all calamity. That declaration is not the same, however, as finding him unjust to have originated calamity, or to cause it immediately.

---

39. James L. Crenshaw, "Introduction: The Shift from Theodicy to Anthropodicy," in *Theodicy in the Old Testament*, ed. James L. Crenshaw (Philadelphia, Pa.: Fortress, 1983), p. 1. Crenshaw (p. 4) says that ancient Israel resolved the problem of undeserved suffering in seven ways: "retributive, disciplinary, revelational, probative, illusory, transitory, or mysterious."

40. Rick Rood, "The Problem of Evil (How Can a Good God Allow Evil?)" at http://www.origins.org/articles/rood-problemevil.html, February 2003.

41. NIV. The King James Version uses the word "evil" in place of "disaster."

Moral philosophers distinguish moral evil from natural evil:

Moral evil — ". . . the willfully chosen bad actions of humankind, for which the prime responsibility must lie with the perpetrators."[42] This evil originated with Adam.

Natural evil — "Physical evil, the disease and disaster that make life painful and hazardous."[43] Such evil is from the operation of nature, yielding "(1) animal disease and death; (2) human accidents, birth defects, disease and pain; (3) natural disasters such as earthquakes, hurricanes, and drought; and (4) the death and decay of plants."[44] That plants kill each other is ignored, presumably because no one attributes consciousness to them.

Many point out, in extensive literature, that a world such as ours is the only world that permits free-will human beings. Thus, to accept our status is to accept the world, with its attendant human and animal suffering, as a necessity. This is a common approach for most theodicy.

To explain how God is just in allowing evil, there are "two basic strategies. . . . The first is to deny or diminish the reality of evil." Augustine's classic formulation was that evil is "the privation of the good."[45] As the 20th century has made abundantly clear, malevolence is too real to be explained as the absence of its opposite.

"The second strategy is to claim that bad things happen as the necessary cost of other very good things. The celebrated 'free-will defense' in relation to moral evil is an example. . . . [Allowing evil brings the] greater good of human freedom and moral responsibility."[46] In human society, we permit our growing children more and more freedom, trusting that their developing maturity will eventually overrule impulses for evil. We tolerate the evil that does occur as they mature. Similarly, God uses evil in the form of pain to produce the "complex good."[47]

However, the free-will defense for moral evil explains only so much. "The free will defense is not meant to explain *why* these things occur. The free will

42. John Polkinghorne, *Science and Theology: An Introduction* (Minneapolis: Fortress, 1988), p. 93.

43. Polkinghorne, *Science and Theology*, p. 93.

44. Marvin L. Lubenow, "Pre-Adamites, Sin, Death, and the Human Fossils," *Creation Ex Nihilo Technical Journal* 12, no. 2 (1988): 222-32, see especially 225.

45. Polkinghorne, *Science and Theology*, p. 93.

46. Polkinghorne, *Science and Theology*, p. 93.

47. Lewis, *Problem of Pain*, p. 117.

defense is only meant to show that no logical incompatibility has been demonstrated between God and harm."[48]

For physical evil there is "an analogous 'free-process defense.' . . . [The] evolutionary exploration of . . . potentiality is a better world than one produced ready-made by divine fiat. In such an evolving world there must be malfunctions and blind alleys."[49] Some cells mutate into harmful forms while others mutate into new forms of life.[50] Nature must operate by law (lest it be arbitrary and incomprehensible, and, furthermore, unsuitable for persistent life-forms), and free human and animal behavior resulting in pain is an unavoidable consequence.

To avoid a world that is merely "God's puppet theatre," God lets man and nature develop with both contingency and freedom, accepting "the consequences that will flow from free process and from the exercise of human free will."[51] The general Christian approach, then, to justifying both moral evil and natural evil is a freedom defense — to be free, man and animal must be open to pain, suffering, and even death.

God is not remote from this suffering, because Christ "emptied himself, taking the form of a servant," and suffered and died on the cross (Phil. 2:6-8 [RSV]). In his divine capacity, God has therefore fully suffered along with man and animal. George Murphy has explored how an evolutionary view, with its chain of being, profoundly links the physical suffering of animals to human suffering; thus at the cross all the suffering in creation is incorporated into Christ.[52]

Suffering as Punishment

Hardly anyone objects to suffering that results from wrong behavior. No one besides Christ is sinless. Lest man conclude there is no ultimate penalty for sin in the next world, there must be penalty in this world. Human suffering is necessary if wrongdoing is to be punished.

Our objection is that it is inconsistent for suffering to also occur in the

---

48. William L. Craig, in "A Classic Debate on the Existence of God," University of Colorado at Boulder, November 1994, with Dr. William Lane Craig and Dr. Michael Tooley, http://www.origins.org/offices/billcraig/docs/craig-tooley3.html, October 2000. Emphasis added.

49. Polkinghorne, *Science and Theology,* p. 93.

50. Polkinghorne, *Science and Theology,* p. 94.

51. Polkinghorne, *Science and Theology,* p. 95.

52. See the article "Evolution, Christology, and the Cross" by George Murphy in this volume.

absence of wrong behavior. And animals, which behave by instinct, cannot do wrong. Suffering not linked to wrongdoing becomes arbitrary, without an acceptable cause. Some say therefore that to avoid animal cruelty, God *must* make them less conscious than humans.

But animals have a natural role in this world of man's probation. To be in the same world, man and animal must have similar physical construction, and both must be susceptible to pain and suffering.

Finally, both man and animal suffer natural evil arbitrarily. Note that nature as God's agent is *no respecter of persons* (Acts 10:34), so that at times the sufferer appears to be chosen randomly. If nature had no randomness, we would be compelled to always recognize God in the events that happen, and therefore we would be unable to voluntarily love him. Human freedom and nature's freedom are therefore linked, and the consequences include both arbitrary suffering and suffering as punishment.

Animal Death, Suffering, Struggle, and Waste

The above is a rather antiseptic framework provided by theodicy, resting on the philosophic classification of evil and its usual explanation in the freedom defense. However, is that framework fully satisfying when we personally confront animal pain and suffering? If God is love, as proclaimed in Christianity, then why should man or beast suffer and die at all? Why should animals have to struggle to survive? And why should there be aeons of wastage of animals? Thus there are essentially four issues to consider: death, pain and suffering, struggle, and waste.

From an ecological point of view, all are bound up together in the "balance of nature." The predator-prey relationships of the food web encompass much of this balance, but disease, aging, and accidental injury and death are also involved.

With regard specifically to evolution, the above issues are germane but not crucial. All the issues must be satisfied by a conception of God's justice, whether or not evolution is true. Whether God deliberately employed these attributes of nature to generate biodiversity is the only question specific to evolution. God's intention in evolution is separable from the four issues because all four could operate in a world without evolutionary "progress."

Death

The hominid and human ancestor record includes infant, young, and child death. This fact generates strong responses — "For anyone to claim that God would call this history 'good' is almost to question the nature of God."[53] "The idea that God would create a world where this type of death takes place and call it 'very good' offends our sensibilities."[54]

Given that man is recent and that hominids are a tiny fraction of all the animals that ever lived, the deaths of humans and hominids constitute a physical mole-hill compared to the mountain of animal death in general.

Death *per se* as the cessation of life is what disturbs us, and we seek a rationale justifying it, even for animals by extension. The death event is unique for each creature. To animals themselves, however, it is probably not an issue at all.

Pain and Suffering

Pain and suffering may be considered separable from the question of death. Not all dying is full of suffering (so far as we know). However, pain and suffering appear to be universal. The situation was described by Tennyson as "Nature, red in tooth and claw."[55] Satan could be involved here, because Scripture associates him with disease (see Job, Luke 13:16, 1 Cor. 5:5, 1 Tim. 1:20).[56] How can nature's design be reconciled with a loving God, even if the freedom defense is the justification for evil?

Struggle for Survival

Henry M. Morris focuses on death and pain but also emphasizes the struggle for survival:

> The very nature of Christian morality is squarely opposed to that of evolution. . . . The thesis of struggle and self-interest is completely foreign to

---

53. Lubenow, "Pre-Adamites," 225.

54. Lubenow, "Pre-Adamites," 230.

55. Marjorie H. Nicolson, ed., *Selected Poems of Alfred, Lord Tennyson* (Boston: Houghton Mifflin, 1924), p. 173: "In Memoriam" (publ. 1850), LVI, 7 stanzas on man: "Who trusted God was love indeed/And love Creation's final law — /Tho' Nature, red in tooth and claw/with ravine, shriek'd against his creed — ."

56. See Lewis, *Problem of Pain*, p. 89.

Christianity, the very basis of which is love and selflessness. It is not possible that a God of love and goodness would institute a universal law that demands continual struggle and hunger and suffering and death. . . .[57]

Not only young-Earth creationists see this as a problem. Michael Lloyd noted the contradiction that Christ laid down his life that others might live, while in predation animals take each other's lives.[58]

Waste in Evolution

J. P. Moreland and John Mark Reynolds ask about evolution's wastage: "How could a good God intentionally allow the wasteful and horrific deaths of billions of animals over billions of years before man's sin (much less directly will to employ this struggle as his primary means of creating)?"[59] Paul Nelson and Reynolds add that

> the secular account of natural history is a bloody one . . . full of dead-end species and waste. Evolution . . . consumes life upon life to allow the fittest to survive and adapt. It is wasteful. It is inefficient. It is "red in tooth and claw." . . . What is the justification for all that animal pain?[60]

Old-Earth creationists frequently voice such thoughts. As John Polkinghorne says, "evolution is a costly business."[61] C. S. Lewis said that fecundity and the death rate constitute "a double scheme for securing the maximum amount of torture."[62] The most difficult problem for them to face is that pain, suffering, and death are a necessary part of God's creation prior to Adam's sin. Evolutionists also say the same thing.[63] Stephen J. Gould chal-

57. Morris, *Studies in the Bible and Science,* pp. 92, 93.

58. Michael Lloyd, "Are Animals Fallen?" in *Animals on the Agenda,* ed. Andrew Linzey and Dorothy Yamamoto (Urbana, Ill.: University of Illinois Press, 1998), p. 148.

59. J. P. Moreland and John Mark Reynolds, eds., *Three Views on Creation and Evolution* (Grand Rapids: Zondervan, 1999), pp. 21-22.

60. Paul Nelson and John Mark Reynolds, "Young Earth Creationism," in *Three Views on Creation and Evolution,* ed. J. P. Moreland and John Mark Reynolds (Grand Rapids: Zondervan, 1999), p. 47.

61. Polkinghorne, *Science and Theology,* p. 77.

62. Lewis, *Problem of Pain,* p. 135.

63. See Probe Ministries, "Christian Views of Science and Earth History," at http://www.origins.org/orgs/probe/docs/viewscie.html, October 2000. Rich Milne and Dr. Ray Bohlin.

lenged the notion of God when he said, "The price of perfect design is messy relentless slaughter."[64]

Blaming God and Evolution

Even Charles Darwin wondered why an all-powerful deity would create via evolution, a painful and wasteful process. Darwin reasoned,

> A being so powerful and so full of knowledge as a God who could create the universe, is to our finite minds omnipotent and omniscient, and it revolts our understanding to suppose that his benevolence is not unbounded, for what advantage can there be in the sufferings of millions of the lower animals throughout almost endless time?
>
> Did He [God] cause the frame and mental qualities of the dog to vary in order that a breed might be formed of indomitable ferocity, with jaws fitted to pin down the bull for man's brutal sport?[65]

Thus God is blamed for discard of millions of generations of individual organisms over the geological ages. As M. A. Corey notes, "Implicit in the assertion that a good God has deliberately chosen to create the world through normal evolutionary pathways is the assumption that He has found the sacrifice of millions of animals throughout evolutionary history to be morally defensible."[66]

But evolution is not to be singled out in this regard. Notice that long ages of waste occurred whether or not evolution was responsible for biological development.[67] In fact, evolutionary thinking provides a small degree of solace against wastage and death, as against other old-Earth perspectives. These still

---

64. Stephen Jay Gould, "Darwin and Paley Meet the Invisible Hand," *Natural History* (November 1990): 8. See also Stephen Jay Gould, *Rocks of Ages: Science and Religion in the Fullness of Life* (New York: Ballantine, 1999).

65. Quoted in Ronald W. Clark, *The Survival of Charles Darwin* (New York: Random House, 1984), pp. 77 and 53, as quoted in Corey, *Back to Darwin*, p. 10.

66. Corey, "The Morality of Evolution," ch. 14 in Corey, *Back to Darwin*, pp. 372-84, 372.

67. Such generational "waste" is of a different character than the "waste" of high fecundity such as prodigious seed production in every generational step. And plant fecundity may strike us differently than animal fecundity. Many turtle eggs hatch, but few baby turtles make it to the open ocean. This is more disturbing than the fact that most maple seeds die unused. Some solace is gained from the fact that higher organisms appear to waste fewer offspring. Evolution's generational waste is also different from the "waste" involved in entropy production in the course of carrying on life. In sum, the unqualified use of the word "waste" for all three features of the biotic process lacks specificity, leading to confusion.

must contend with wastage and death, but without evolution's claim to be responsible for the "progress" involved in speciation and phylogeny. Thus, concerning animal pain, steady-state biology can be thought worse than evolution.

Therefore, to speak of evolution's waste is to falsely accuse. The whole history of life irrespective of speciation and phylogeny is the issue. Seeming "waste" has occurred over aeons of time no matter whether evolution is true or not.

Nevertheless, evolution's wastage of organisms remains troublesome from the perspective that God is intentional and purposeful. Christ in resurrection demonstrated his power over death (Rev. 1:18) and his intention to lead his children to the blessed eternal state. As the Apostle Paul said, *The last enemy that shall be abolished is death* (1 Cor. 15:26). Corey notes that ". . . the problem of evil . . . is irreconcilable with the goodness of God only as long as one insists on viewing this world as a would-be hedonistic paradise. . . . But what if the purpose of the world isn't pleasure at any cost, but *instruction?*"[68]

It is striking that very few humans regard their own lives as wasteful because of pain and suffering, terminating in death, and this is quite often true in the midst of enormous pain and suffering. Existence is preferable to nonexistence. In personal circumstances we are partially existential about our own death, and this carries over to animal death occurring all around us continually.

Young-Earth adherents claim biological evolution cannot be true, because it requires that God brought the present creatures into being through countless ages of pain and death, something a loving God would never do. While Morris cannot square "tortuous aeons"[69] with a loving God, he accepts God's loving judgment in Noah's Flood, which by his cataclysmic conception was planet-wide and produced the same amount of death. Thus the young-Earth view does not resolve the issue.

Non-Christians, perhaps taking their cue from young-Earth creationists, use the arguments about evolution's wastage but in converse fashion; they claim that young-Earth creationists are wrong both about evolution and about God. Gould argues that a loving God would never subject animals to millions of years of wasteful death and suffering.[70] He has often concentrated on what he regards as inefficiencies in nature, seeing them as evidence that forecloses an intelligent designer.[71]

68. Corey, *Back to Darwin*, p. 201. See also John Hick, *Evil and the God of Love* (New York: Harper & Row, 1977).

69. Morris, *Biblical Basis for Modern Science*, p. 193.

70. Gould, *Rocks of Ages*.

71. Stephen Jay Gould, *The Panda's Thumb: More Reflections on Natural History* (New York: Norton, 1980).

Ultimately, blaming man, or finding wastage justified by a world created for him, proves insufficient. Blaming man directly cannot suffice, given the preceding history of life on Earth. The freedom defense works better but is still tied to man, linking man's free will to nature's freedom and contingency. But behind the freedom defense lies the need to understand God for having chosen to create a world of freedom.

Scriptural Challenges

Young-Earth creationists do raise Scriptural arguments deserving attention. They attribute animal death to man's sin on the basis of Romans 5:12, which says: *Therefore, just as through one man sin entered into the world, and death through sin, and so death spread to all men, because all sinned.* Morris says that, according to Romans 5:12 and 1 Corinthians 15, "Adam was the first man, and as a result of his rebellion (sin), death and corruption (disease, bloodshed, and suffering) entered the universe. Before Adam sinned there could not have been any . . . animal or human death."[72] Morris and supporters neglect the portion of Romans 5:12 that reads: *to all men, because all sinned.* The verse does not say that death spread to animals. Romans 5:12 speaks only of man, but it commonly is forced to include animals by young-Earth commentators.

John Pye Smith noted in contrast that Romans 5:12 refers "to the access and dominion of death *over man.* . . ." If the first humans had not sinned, they would "have undergone *a physical change different from dying,* which would have translated them into a higher condition of happy existence."[73] Thus the sting of death had particular meaning for them — becoming subject to the same death as befell animals. They knew they would fall from superior creatures to inferior. Not only would they succumb to temporal or corporal death, but they would also cross "the gulf of death in senses infinitely more awful."[74]

Young-Earth creationists point to the absence of any mention of animal death until after the Fall. Thus any conception that puts death, disease, and suffering before the Fall is believed contrary to Scripture. Morris and others hold that "Genesis 1:29-30 teaches us that the animals and man were originally cre-

72. Henry M. Morris, "Why the Gap Theory Won't Work," in *Back to Genesis,* No. 107 (San Diego: Institute for Creation Research, 1997) at http://www.christiananswers.net/q-aig/aig-gaptheory-problems.html, October 2000.

73. John Pye Smith, *The Relation between the Holy Scriptures and Some Parts of Geological Science* (London: Jackson and Walford, 1848), p. 260.

74. Smith, *Holy Scriptures and Some Parts of Geological Science,* p. 260.

ated vegetarian."[75] Further, despite murder and violence, man was not given authority to kill either his own kind or animals until after the Flood. Genesis 9:2-3 records the beginning of dread of man among animals, as meat eating was introduced, a change from the original creation of peace. A response to this line of argument is that the original grant of plants for food was of liberty but not restriction; also, it could hardly apply to marine carnivores.

Animal death from sin is also discerned within Romans 8:20-21: *For the creation was subjected to futility, not of its own will, but because of him who subjected it, in hope that the creation itself also will be set free from its slavery to corruption into the freedom of the glory of the children of God.* The word *corruption* is always taken by biblical literalists to refer to death and dying, although other interpretations concerning corruption are possible;[76] it could be a reference to the earth's moral contamination. Remember that an unprosecuted murder on the land is a stain and a moral corruption, requiring purification (Gen. 4:10; Deut. 21:1-9). Furthermore, animal death is not the point of Romans, which instead focuses on whether or not the believer is living by the Holy Spirit rather than by the flesh.

Concerning creation being *subjected to vanity* (Rom. 8:20),[77] the common claim is that the entire cosmos was affected by the Fall. Smith understood in contrast that the word "creation" denotes that part of creation influenced by man, "and that 'vanity' denotes the frustration of high and holy purposes" caused by wickedness, cruelty, and abuse.[78]

Young-Earth creationists complete their arguments on Romans by quoting 8:22. It says that *we know that the whole creation groans and travails in pain together until now.* Morris says, "Clearly the whole of creation was, and is, subject to decay and corruption because of sin. The fossil record shows disease, decay, and death."[79]

Alan Hayward countered Morris by noting that threatening death to Adam if he sinned (Gen. 2:16-17) required his understanding of what death was, implying that he had already observed death in the animal world.[80] Smith noted, in 1848 before Darwin published the *Origin of Species*, "I have formerly thought that our first parents had never witnessed death, til they beheld with

75. Morris, "Why the Gap Theory Won't Work," at http://www.christiananswers.net/q-aig/aig-gaptheory-problems.html.

76. See John C. Munday, Jr., "Creature Mortality: From Creation or the Fall?" *Journal of the Evangelical Theological Society* 35.1 (March 1992): 51-68.

77. KJV. The New American Standard uses the word "futility."

78. Smith, *Holy Scriptures and Some Parts of Geological Science*, p. 257.

79. Morris, "Why the Gap Theory Won't Work."

80. Alan Hayward, *Creation and Evolution* (London: Triangle, 1985), p. 182.

agony the first sacrifice. . . . Rather, the denunciation in Gen. iii.17, would seem to imply that they understood *what* the penalty was, in consequence of their having witnessed the pangs of death."[81] Smith reprinted observations by an unknown writer from August 1839 in the *Christian Observer*. The writer noted the vast gulf between man and animals before the Fall — to such a man the curse brought "a deep degradation, to be sunk to the level of that creation over which he was made lord."[82]

Another claim is that just as the new earth will involve no death, so did the original earth. While Scripture says the lion shall lie down with the lamb (Isa. 65:25) in the future new earth, and there will no longer be weeping and crying, the focus is not on the whole earth but only on the *holy mountain* of God, and God's people centered on Jerusalem (Isa. 65:19). Furthermore, there will be human death (Isa. 65:20).[83] Only in the next world, sometimes called Paradise, does Scripture say there will be a total absence of pain and tears (Rev. 7:16-17).

Smith argued further that death is necessary, in that "all living organized beings are maintained in life by the assimilation into themselves of portions of dead organized beings. . . . The law of dissolution, that is death, is therefore *necessary* to organic life."[84] This is paralleled in Christ's death for us.

Smith also noted that microscopic life on plants is inevitably destroyed by herbivores; thus, no strict immortality of animal life is possible. "Grasses, leaves, seeds, and fruits, which are the food of the herbivorous races, swarm with insect life."[85] Genesis 1:29-30 does say that the green plants are given as food, omitting mention of animals, but plants when consumed carry a host of animal life.

In summary, claiming animals died only after the Fall is brought into sharp focus by the young-Earth use of Scripture. But deeper analysis leads to a different conclusion. Also, the argument depends on quantity, not quality. Passing from thousands to millions of years somehow crosses the threshold from morally and theistically acceptable to unacceptable amounts of animal pain. In a sense, the young-Earth proponent says that animal pain over aeons is too much for evolution to bear. The amount allowed since man's recent Fall, however, is considered justified.

Old-Earth creationism and theistic evolutionism generally allow more latitude on the animal pain issue but exclude the possibility that man's Fall

---

81. Smith, *Holy Scriptures and Some Parts of Geological Science*, pp. 256-57.
82. Smith, *Holy Scriptures and Some Parts of Geological Science*, pp. 256-57.
83. Munday, "Creature Mortality," p. 60.
84. Smith, *Holy Scriptures and Some Parts of Geological Science*, p. 254. Italics original.
85. Smith, *Holy Scriptures and Some Parts of Geological Science*, p. 256.

caused it. Because man's accountability is denied, the focus shifts to God himself. The options that are allowed are essentially variations on the freedom defense and include the following:

1. God made nature to operate as it does in order to provide a suitable probationary existence for man — man is the reason for, but not the cause of, animal pain.

2. God made nature to operate as it does for its own sake — "God saw that it was good" (Gen. 1:25), and animal pain is not specifically related to man in his probation.

3. Animal death resulted from the fall of angels. This position puts the direct blame for animal pain on Satan and his cohort. The corollary is that only man's physical and spiritual death resulted from the Fall. This position still must justify why God allowed Satan to sin.[86] And it fails to explain animal form and function as depicted in both nature and Scripture (which is discussed later).

The first option, that nature was designed as the stage for man's probation, is essentially the popular freedom defense in theodicy: a suitable probation for man necessitates a world in which animal suffering and death can occur. The difficulty for many is that nature's freedom and an animal's pain must then be seen as the *instrument* used by God to instruct man. As Lloyd says, the instrumentalists "would have us believe . . . that God deliberately created a world including pain, for the good that it would do us."[87] Worse, creation produced a world of competition and struggle, which must be overcome by redemption; thus, God is at war with himself and has allowed that the end justifies the means.[88]

The second option, that nature is simply given as such, provokes an inquiry into why God is just if what he creates involves pain and suffering (irrespective of man).

The third option, blaming Satan, is held by only a few. Eric Mascall thought that "the defection of certain of the angels has had as one of its consequences a disorganization of the material world and the dislocation of its functions."[89] The gap theory for interpreting Genesis 1 and the fossil record takes

---

86. These three options are essentially the same as those presented and discussed by Lloyd, "Are Animals Fallen?"

87. Lloyd, "Are Animals Fallen?" p. 152.

88. Lloyd, "Are Animals Fallen?" pp. 153-54.

89. Eric Mascall, *The Importance of Being Human* (London: Oxford University Press, 1959), p. 83, as quoted by Andrew Linzey, "The Place of Animals in Creation: A Christian View,"

this tack: Satan fell to earth during a claimed interval between Genesis 1:1 and 1:2, and the resulting cataclysm produced the fossil record.

An additional but unpopular view was advanced by Origen, who believed that animal suffering was given "as rewards or punishments for the manner in which they used their free will."[90] Animals are hardly regarded today as having a morally based free will.

God's Love

An objection to all the options is still that animal pain seems contrary to God's love and goodness. In this response, old-Earth believers may agree with young-Earth creationists. However, because a strong argument can be made from both Scripture and science that animals died before the Fall,[91] we have to rethink the notion that pre-Fall animal death and suffering are contrary to God's love. Such a conception of God's love is too narrow and sentimental. As noted earlier, this world appears not intended for a pleasure house of hedonism but as a school of instruction and place of probation.

If extreme human suffering and death are justified in a schoolhouse framework and involve our high level of conscious awareness, then animal suffering and death, given an animal's less intense consciousness, can at least be weakly justified in connection with our probation. If by evolution we are linked to animals physically, then animal suffering is linked to human suffering. Evolution, Thomas E. Hosinski believes, removes the ontological distinction between man and animal, requiring that God's providence for man and animal be consistent.[92]

By such reasoning, some may still find that the most satisfactory answer is the simple first option that animal pain is rooted in man's sin. If that is the case, then logically we must ask why God allowed so much animal pain before the Fall. Wouldn't less pain have accomplished the same purpose? It is easier to justify post-Fall animal pain by man's sin than the vastly greater amount of animal

---

in *Animal Rights and Human Obligations*, ed. T. Regan and P. Singer (Englewood, N.J.: Prentice Hall, 1977), p. 143, n. 10.

90. Linzey, *Christianity and the Rights of Animals*, p. 59.

91. Munday, "Creature Mortality."

92. Thomas E. Hosinski, "How Does God's Providential Care Extend to Animals?" in *Animals on the Agenda*, ed. Andrew Linzey and Dorothy Yamamoto (Urbana, Ill.: University of Illinois Press, 1998), p. 138. He says (p. 139): "the natural world appears to be a large-scale experiment in the pursuit of possibilities, in which the outcomes are largely a result of freedom, contingency, and even chance."

death before the Fall. Is it fair to have set up such a world in anticipation of man's sin and probationary needs?

If God guided evolution and perhaps even intruded immediately with special creations from time to time, certainly he could have speeded up the process so as to minimize animal pain and suffering. Stephen R. L. Clark noted how some believe that long-term evolution was required to produce the human being, and then remarked that such a view necessitates a revision of the concept of divine omnipotence.[93]

From these heavy considerations, some find it convenient to simply retreat. "Some more contemporary Christians have met the problem by simply denying that God is concerned with pain in the animal creation. They take as their starting-point the prevalence of pain within the natural order as revealed by the natural sciences and offer theological justification for it."[94] Linzey charges that "these voices [are] theological retreats from the issue in question," threatening the "doctrine of a loving, holy God" with "a morally outrageous deity. . . ."[95]

Ultimate Redemption?

If animals have no immortal souls, the pain problem may be worse. If they cannot hope in a future life, how can they be comforted for their undeserved suffering? Linzey says that "if animals are not to be recompensed with an eternal life, how much more difficult must it be to justify their temporal sufferings?" Animals "cannot *choose* to sacrifice themselves" and must be coerced.[96]

Ultimately, as Linzey notes, "Why is there any pain at all?"[97] Both animals and human suffer. "Of course there are important differences between men and mice, but there are no morally relevant ones when it comes to pain and suffering. It is for this reason alone that we need to hold fast to . . . the inclusive nature of Christ's sacrifice and redeeming work." Linzey claims that Christ has reconciled "*all* flesh," including that of animals.[98] In some way, Linzey believes

93. Stephen R. L. Clark, "Is Nature God's Will?" in *Animals on the Agenda,* ed. Andrew Linzey and Dorothy Yamamoto (Urbana, Ill.: University of Illinois Press, 1998), p. 128.

94. Linzey, *Christianity and the Rights of Animals,* p. 59. See Peter T. Geach, *Providence and Evil* (Cambridge: Cambridge University Press, 1977), pp. 77, 79, and quote from p. 79.

95. Linzey, *Christianity and the Rights of Animals,* p. 60.

96. Linzey, *Christianity and the Rights of Animals,* p. 57.

97. Linzey, *Christianity and the Rights of Animals,* p. 60.

98. Linzey, *Christianity and the Rights of Animals,* pp. 60, 61. See also Murphy, "A Theological Argument for Evolution," *Journal of the American Scientific Affiliation* (now titled

"God in Christ will restore each and every creature."[99] It is not clear if he means that dead creatures will be given another life in a future state.

One can develop an argument that suffering animals are included in Christ's redemption, and will individually be recompensed, but there is no compelling scriptural evidence in support.

The Dominion Mandate

The differences between man and animal do justify different perspectives on human and animal suffering — the differences have a moral dimension because God granted dominion to man at the beginning and gave animals to man as food (Gen. 9:3). Unless a moral difference is accepted on the basis of man's dominion, man has no right at all to take an animal's life. We would all be obligated to be vegetarians, and Old Testament sacrifice was a mistake.

This is not to say that, by the dominion mandate, man is entitled to inflict animal pain without limit. To the contrary, the dominion mandate is a noble obligation for environmental stewardship, with care to avoid cruelty to animals. What the dominion mandate establishes is that under certain conditions man may legitimately cause animal pain. Dominion could not possibly mean to prevent all animal pain (an impossibility); if no pain and predation were built into nature, then rule over animals would have no force. It is a stretch to argue, as some have, that dominion never was intended to include animal pain.

Thus the existence of animal pain *per se* cannot be found fundamentally immoral. God allowed for animal pain in the pre-Fall world, both in nature and at the hand of man.

Common Ground

There is a small amount of common ground across the major paradigms. In all, animal suffering is ultimately the design of the Creator. Even though the young-Earth paradigm blames man's sin as the proximate cause, which is not true for an old-Earth paradigm, in both paradigms God is the ultimate or primary cause. This common ground carries us back to the root of theodicy,

_____

Perspectives on Science and Christian Faith) 38 (March 1986): 19-26; and Murphy, "Christology, Evolution, and the Cross," in this volume.

99. Linzey, *Christianity and the Rights of Animals*, pp. 61, 62. See also Andrew Linzey, "Introduction" to Part 3: Disputed Questions, in *Animals on the Agenda*, ed. Andrew Linzey and Dorothy Yamamoto (Urbana, Ill.: University of Illinois Press, 1998), p. 119.

where we seek to understand why God would subject amoral and innocent animals to any suffering at all.

We have established, however, that Scripture does not allow us to maintain that animal suffering is inherently wrong.

Evolutionary Considerations

Surprisingly, whether biological evolution is true or not has little consequence at this point. Biological evolution claims that accumulation of characteristics over many generations produced the diversity of species from a monotonic population of original life forms. It appears that God used evolution for at least some speciation and phylogeny. "The fossil record reveals that species typically survive for a hundred thousand generations, or even a million or more, without evolving very much. . . . After their origin, most species undergo little evolution before becoming extinct."[100] During periods of stasis, the pain and suffering continue unabated. Extreme conditions are thought to result in more rapid evolution, when more suffering and dying might have occurred. In either stasis or punctuation, and no matter what evolutionary mechanisms were at work, suffering and dying have been the universal experience of animals for hundreds of millions of years.

If instead phyla arose partly or wholly by direct creative acts at intervals throughout Earth history, the fact remains that the predator-prey relations in nature's food web have persisted since the various organisms first arose. Thus, whether biological evolution is true or not, all higher animals have been suffering and dying since their first appearance.

The theological consequence is twofold. One is to buttress the position that animal pain is not intrinsically immoral. The second is that because evolution has operated via nature's contingent freedom, God has allowed his creation to self-develop in context with his own immediate creative power.[101] Animal pain is therefore partially generative for biodiversity, analogous to pain's instructional role in human life.

---

100. Steven M. Stanley, *The New Evolutionary Timetable* (New York: Basic Books, 1981), p. 11.

101. For some this diminishes God in his transcendence. In the extreme, some but not all theologians are led into process theology. See the review by Jay B. McDaniel, "Can Animal Suffering Be Reconciled with Belief in an All-Loving God?" in *Animals on the Agenda,* ed. Andrew Linzey and Dorothy Yamamoto (Urbana, Ill.: University of Illinois Press, 1998), pp. 161-70. McDaniel resists finding God guilty, holding that nature has a full range of capacities, including suffering; and while not all think existence with suffering is better than nonexistence, God's love eventually triumphs.

The Divine Purpose

Animal pain and suffering can thus be understood apart from man's sin as a cause. But finding it justified entirely in anticipation of man's probation is difficult. In that case it is something like a sacrificial tradeoff. It has a weak scriptural parallel in the fact that God ordained Christ's suffering from the foundation of the cosmos, and justified Old Testament saints in anticipation of it. Animals suffered long before man appeared and sinned, because God had anticipated what he would do concerning man and designed the world with that end in mind. But the parallel is deficient because the animals are innocent while man is not.

The anticipatory sacrifice has a problematic appeal — subjecting animals to pain for aeons before man ever existed seems to violate the notion of fairness, that is, of justifiable cause and effect. It is one thing to sacrifice a few animals for one man but another to sacrifice millions for one man.

Such moral reasoning again leads back to God, not to man. We may ask why God finds it moral to impose animal pain and death. Recognizing that to figure out God is difficult, some Christians in this quandary will resort to a more naturalistic viewpoint. God's mystery in the matter can then be laid up to future revelations here on earth or beyond the grave.

The Naturalistic Facet

The naturalistic view is attractive, in part because it sets aside the question of God and morality. Many people respond through an existential naturalism: Raymond G. Bohlin says that Richard Dawkins's book *River Out of Eden* contains "a discussion of the ubiquitous presence of 'cruelty' in nature, even mentioning Darwin's loss of faith in the face of this reality. Of course, his answer is that nature is neither cruel nor kind, but indifferent. That's just the way nature is."[102]

Existentially, animal pain is part of the way the physical world works. This answer is basically option one but is framed agnostically. It might be termed a natural theodicy: God has made the world the way it is, and man's sin has nothing to do with it, except when his behavior worsens the intensity of animal pain and suffering. Animal pain is nature's given.

---

102. Raymond G. Bohlin, *Up a River Without a Paddle: A Darwinian View of Life,* http://www.origins.org/orgs/probe/docs/dawkins.html, October 2000, reviewing Richard Dawkins, *A River Out of Eden: A Darwinian View of Life* (New York: Basic, 1995), the fourth in a series entitled "The Science Masters Series."

Natural Order

Exploring the natural order enables a study considerably broader than if only the Bible is used. God has expressed himself through two revelations, the general revelation in nature and the special revelation in his Word, Jesus Christ, as recorded in Scripture. A natural order approach permits a study of creature design, behavior, habitat, and ecological setting (including predator-prey relations in the food web) to establish what is "natural" and therefore "moral."

Individual organisms manifest very obviously a biological design suited to survival. This leads even atheistic naturalists to discuss design.[103] Sense organs, nervous systems, and immune systems reveal the intricate way animals are constructed for success in life.

Sense organs give animals the means to detect environmental conditions and particularly to find food and avoid dangers. Nervous systems process sensor outputs and control behavioral responses. The nervous and endocrine systems constitute the master controller of physical sensors, internal organ function and coordination, and active muscular responses. Appropriate corrective actions are provoked by the varying levels of awareness and pain.

Immune systems are particularly designed for resisting tiny invaders — viruses, bacteria, and allergens. The immune system is also able to deal with diseased host cells. Such defenses manifest extreme, delicate, and complex environmental sensitivity.

These physical systems by their very essence indicate that creature design is intended to meet the physical challenges of existence. We may say, almost as a tautology, that physical sensitivity is natural. Some of the physical sensitivity is experienced as pain. Pain is thus a natural component of the natural order. At some level of pain the experience of suffering emerges.

Is animal pain and suffering a necessary component of protective sensitivity? A switching mechanism must operate to change animal behavior when either danger or injury and disease appear. The higher the level of consciousness, and the more complex the behavioral choices subject to perception and cognition, the more this switching mechanism must provoke attention-getting perceptions. Pain is an effective feature of the switching mechanism. High discomfort seems to be an appropriate perception for bringing about the necessary responses to ensure physical survival.

---

103. See, for example, Jacques Monod, *Chance and Necessity* (New York: Random House, 1971). Monod like all atheists sought to avoid the traditional concept of *telos* or God-ordained purpose in biological design; nevertheless, he introduced the term *teleonomy* to indicate the obvious "law of design" in nature.

There appears to be an evolutionary advantage for conscious experience of pain, but "how could natural selection generate consciousness if unconscious animals can do the same tasks?"[104] But if consciousness has already emerged, then pain has biological significance in preventing serious injury. Pain is influenced by previous experience, as animals raised in isolation "feel" none.[105] Note that "there is no simple direct relationship between a wound per se and the pain experienced."[106] Ivan Pavlov showed that dogs came readily to electric shock, burning, and wounding of skin before feeding. Thus, "meaning" is associated with pain.

Organism survival mechanisms involving pain are widely regarded as a product of evolution. We may recognize, however, that they are necessary whether or not evolution is true to any degree. This is so because the mechanisms must be present for any individual organism to be successful in its own life.

Animal Nature in Scripture

Exploring animal design by an appeal to nature alone is inadequate here; the topic requires scriptural input. It provides a context for connecting the various considerations discussed earlier. As Scripture says, *But ask the animals, and they will teach you, or the birds of the air, and they will tell you* (Job 12:7).

Creation

The point relevant to the issue of animal pain is that the creation story concerns the natural order we observe (contrary to the young-Earth paradigm). A plain sense of realism in the creation story indicates that God gave nature its present attributes. Therefore, we may look for animal pain in God's original acts of creating, rather than seeing animal pain as the consequence of man's sin.

---

104. R. Dawkins, *River Out of Eden*, pp. 8-9.

105. Melzack, "Perception of Pain," ch. 37, pp. 299-307, 299.

106. Henry K. Beecher, Harvard Medical School, as quoted in Melzack, "Perception of Pain," p. 300.

Animal Attributes

Scripture emphasizes the relationship between man and God, but there are numerous appeals to animal behavior. From the way it is treated we may draw conclusions regarding God's design of nature.

God says in Job 39:14-15: *For (the ostrich) abandons her eggs to the earth, and warms them in the dust, and she forgets that a foot may crush them, or that a wild beast may trample them.* The losses that naturally occur are implicitly part of God's foreknowledge and plan for nature's processes.

Quite generally, predator-prey relationships are depicted straightforwardly. No mention about their morality or relation to the Fall is given. That wild beasts tear their prey is treated as a matter of fact (Isa. 11:6-9; Mic. 5:8; Nah. 2:12). God implies his own responsibility for animal predation when exalting himself in Job 38:39.

In Psalm 104:20-21, sometimes regarded as a creation hymn, the psalmist addresses God: *Thou dost appoint darkness and it becomes night, in which all the beasts of the forest prowl about. The young lions roar after their prey, and seek their food from God.* God is recognized as having made the lion predatory.

As noted earlier, frequently creationists claim that the original creation involved peace and no carnivores among the animals, because the new earth of Isaiah 11 and 65 will reflect the original condition. However, Isaiah 11 foretells not an Earth totally pacified, but one in which Israel is able to subdue its enemies. Further, creatures in the new earth are not immortal (Isa. 65:20). If these prophecies collate double fulfillments, only complex speculation would enable untangling the two and eliminate creature death from the new earth.

Thus, in a passive way, Scripture treats present animal behavior as a given.

Predatory Animal Nature as Analogue

Zephaniah 3:3 compares sinful rulers to wild beasts: *Her princes within her are roaring lions, her judges are wolves at evening; they leave nothing for the morning.* Similarly, Ezekiel 22:27 likens princes to tearing wolves. In Habbakuk 1:8, leopards, wolves, and eagles are used to describe enemy armies. In Hosea 8:1, an eagle is used to describe the Lord's enemy who rebels against law. The psalmist sees his enemy as a lion in Psalm 7:2 and Psalm 57:4. Even our chief adversary, the devil, is likened to a lion in 1 Peter 5:8.

Creatures as Agents of Judgment

Locusts bring destructive judgments. The plagues in Egypt involved insects and frogs. Scripture plainly asserts that the primary cause of their behavior was God. Jeremiah 4:7 and 5:6 compare agents of the Lord to wild beasts.

Elsewhere, the terrible attributes of predatory animals are used to describe the Lord himself. In Amos 3:8 and Hosea 11:10 and 13:7-8, God is like a lion. Even Job laments that the Lord is a lion in Job 10:16.

The righteous warrior is also likened to a lion in Proverbs 28:1. Significantly, David as a righteous warrior is depicted as a type of Christ, and David overcame lions (1 Sam. 17:34-35). Ultimately, Christ himself is presented as the Lion of Judah (Rev. 5:5).

Christ and Animals

However, Christ is also the friend of animals in their suffering. He told parables focusing on the rescue of lost sheep (Luke 15:3-6) and animals falling into pits (Matt. 12:11-12). He was also at peace with animals in the desert (Mark 1:13) — was this a reminder of peace at creation?[107] However, he also sent demons into swine that then perished (Luke 8:30-37). Richard Bauckham says this was the lesser of two evils: before "his time" he could not send demons to the abyss, so he sent them into swine and let them reveal their destructive nature.[108]

From the above examples, it is seen that predator-prey relationships in nature are used as metaphors for God's punishment of wayward man. However, the human being is *worth many sparrows* (Matt. 10:29-31),[109] and thus animal suffering may be analogous to human suffering, with both types seen as inevitable consequences of man's freedom.

Ecology and Scripture

The biotic world has producers, consumers, and reducers. There is no mention

---

107. See John Muddiman, "A New Testament Doctrine of Creation?" in *Animals on the Agenda*, ed. Andrew Linzey and Dorothy Yamamoto (Urbana, Ill.: University of Illinois Press, 1998), p. 30.

108. Richard Bauckham, "Jesus and Animals I: What Did He Teach?" in *Animals on the Agenda*, ed. Andrew Linzey and Dorothy Yamamoto (Urbana, Ill.: University of Illinois Press, 1998), p. 48.

109. See Corey, *Back to Darwin*, p. 374.

in Scripture of reducers, which convert dead and dying animals and plants to raw materials. They were not known until the scientific revolution birthed the microscope. However, Scripture often mentions scavengers (ravens, vultures) and flesh-eating animals.

How should animal anatomy and behavior suited for hunting and killing be understood? Some Bible students believe changes occurred in animals at the Fall, but they have looked in vain for a direct indication in Scripture. The Fall includes a curse on the land but not on animals (Gen. 3:17-19). It would be a stretch to include animals (especially predatory marine creatures such as sharks). Adam was promised that the land would produce thistles and briers, making his work for sustenance difficult. While the land was cursed, alteration of the entire biosphere or the cosmos, including the introduction of thermodynamic entropy, was not in view. Difficult farming is the natural consequence of man's obstinate disregard of God's direction, rather than a consequence of creative alterations of the way nature operates.

The mention of form and function in Scripture points instead to a biological world that functioned originally the same as it does at present. The early chapters of Genesis indicate a continuity of animal form and function from pre-Fall to post-Fall conditions. First, Genesis 1:24 categorizes land animals into three types: cattle, wild beasts, and creeping things. The category of cattle is most provocative because the emphasis is on domesticated animals. If the cattle were significantly different before the Fall, describing them as domesticated at their creation would have made no sense. Similarly, the category of beasts implies nondomesticated, wild untamed animals. This is entirely consistent with the notion that some of them were carnivores originally.

Second, the land animals, plus the birds and sea creatures of Genesis 1:20-21, are reported matter-of-factly, as if Moses' audience around 1300 b.c. would understand and recognize what Adam himself saw. The report of Adam's naming animals also has matter-of-factness.

Thus, lions are always lions in Scripture. The abundant use of analogies employing predatory animal nature strongly indicates that predation is intrinsic to God's original design of nature.

Animal Reconciliation in Christ — an Animal Heaven?

God declared in Genesis 1 that all his creation is good. In the larger sense, the Son's incarnation confirmed that all of nature is worth the redemption from sin.[110]

---

110. See the extension of this view by Murphy, *Journal of the American Scientific Affilia-*

Romans 8:21 declares that *the creation itself also will be set free from its slavery to corruption into the freedom of the glory of the children of God.* Thus, some commentators find that Christ as Redeemer redeemed all things, including the reconciliation of animals from human sin, and, going further, that all animal pain "will be made good."[111] Theologian Keith Ward claimed even further that a future existence for all animals is necessary: "theism would be falsified if physical death was the end."[112] He also claimed that since God is love, God would not "create any being whose sole destiny was to suffer pain."[113] Linzey asks, "Can God leave to one side what is intrinsically valuable to him?"[114] Animal hope in Christ thus has its supporters.

But much doubt remains. Solomon said, *Who knows if the spirit of man rises upward and if the spirit of the animal goes down into the earth?* (Eccles. 3:21). There is nearly a "complete silence of Scripture and Christian tradition on animal immortality. . . ."[115] Thus, claiming an animal heaven is an argument from silence and consequently weak. Furthermore, "immortality has almost no meaning for a creature which is not 'conscious'" in much more than the sentient sense,[116] and we have seen the difficulty in being certain about that. Therefore, a tight theodicy on animal pain cannot depend on an animal heaven.

Human Responsibility toward Animals

Notwithstanding the perspective that animal pain is natural and therefore moral, Scripture holds man responsible for considerate treatment of animals (Ps. 145:9, 16; Prov. 12:10). Man is obligated to be a good steward (Gen. 1:28; Exod. 23:5, 12; Lev. 22:24; Num. 20:8; 22:32; Deut. 5:14; 20:19; 22:4; 25:4). In sum, cruelty to animals is prohibited, and the lawful use of animals for food (Gen. 9:3) and bearing burdens shall be accomplished in ways to minimize *tza'ar*

---

tion, and "Christology, Evolution, and the Cross," in this volume. Murphy links redemption to all creatures through man's presumed evolutionary origin.

111. Linzey, "Place of Animals in Creation," pp. 115-48, esp. p. 120.

112. Keith Ward, *Rational Theology and the Creativity of God* (Oxford: Basil Blackwell, 1982), pp. 201-2, as quoted in Linzey, "Place of Animals in Creation," p. 121.

113. Keith Ward, *The Concept of God* (Oxford: Basil Blackwell, 1974), p. 223, as quoted by Linzey, "Place of Animals in Creation," p. 144, n. 16.

114. Linzey, "Place of Animals in Creation," p. 145, n. 17.

115. Lewis, *Problem of Pain*, p. 137. Lewis (*Problem of Pain*, p. 138) allows for the possibility of a "rudimentary selfhood" in higher animals. For other views, see Linzey, "Place of Animals in Creation," and Munday, "Creature Mortality."

116. Lewis, *Problem of Pain*, p. 137.

ba'alei hayyim — the "pain of living creatures."[117] However, the divine concern is greater for man, for Christ noted: *Are you not worth much more than [the animals]?* (Matt. 6:26).

God's Plan — the Conclusion

Is God's plan evolution? If the answer is yes, then because evolution involves species competition, and predator-prey relations, the plan of God inherently involves animal pain. If, however, all creature death is the consequence of human sin, then animal pain is man's responsibility. Yet holding man directly responsible for animal pain and death requires accepting the young-Earth paradigm, against both Scripture and science. The scriptural evidence against a young Earth and post-Fall creature death is based on balanced interpretation of Genesis 1, Romans, and elsewhere, and by Eden's geography that precludes Flood Geology. Science is overwhelmingly in favor of an old Earth and cosmos.

Therefore, the question whether the lion's killing of a wildebeest on an African savannah in ages past is a direct consequence of human sin can be answered in the negative. God alone is the cause.

Significantly, Earth age does not affect the argument for the post-Flood world. Genesis 9:3 states that animals were given as food for man after the Flood. Thus God's plan for the post-Flood world deliberately includes animal pain.

We have seen that evolution is not the crux of the animal pain issue. Any old-Earth view, whether evolutionary or not, must encompass aeons of animal pain. Evolution fares better than steady-state biology in addressing animal pain because at least it helped generate biodiversity.

The corollary question was whether God designed nature anticipating man's future need under probation. Man needs to experience a temporal penalty for wrongdoing, including death and dying and encounters with wild beasts, as a lesson for the possibility of an eternal penalty for sin. The possibility of anticipatory design remains open.

Another supportable view is from the freedom defense in theodicy: to enable man's freedom, nature had to be designed with its own freedom including animal pain. God has granted his creation a freedom and contingency based on the law of nature, making it open to not only dynamic behavior and complexity but also novelty.

God's character concerning animal pain then is the last issue we need to

117. See Bleich, "Judaism and Animal Experimentation," pp. 61-114.

resolve, because he made the decision as to nature's design. We must no longer see his character solely through the lens of our own human circumstance, and through our own definitions of morality and justice.

Do we find it acceptable that his creating is responsible for millions of years of animal pain? The choice is before us whether or not to submit to him as Creator and Merciful Judge, as urged in Romans 9. In this regard we will seek to comprehend and construct morality concerning animals according to what he has done and said, not according to our own standard of fairness, equity, and justice. We are bound as responsible stewards of the dominion to treat animals in nature with respect. But our concern need not dwell for long on the natural suffering and dying of animals, whose level of consciousness and therefore living experience of pain and suffering are only dimly revealed to us.

Essentially the same choice was faced by Job with regard to his own suffering, whether to accept God as good, despite his suffering, or to reject that idea and turn away from God. A century ago, James Batley expressed the choice this way:

> In the natural world we may see the workings of providence. Side by side with providence we find mystery. A wise man will not be so oppressed by the unsolved riddles of nature as to lose sight of the workings of God's providence in its course. Now if these are the facts as to the natural world, may we not expect them to hold good also in the spiritual world?
>
> Now, if this view is correct it follows that man is not in a position to call in question the justice of God. In order to judge of the merits of a case it is necessary to know the *whole truth* about it. It is becoming in man to wait humbly and seek to *learn* more of the ways of his Creator.[118]

Whether we are satisfied with this outcome regarding animal pain will depend on personal sensitivities. Most of us will be content to let God maintain the natural world, and concentrate on those dominion activities we find within our circle of influence and responsibility as sons of God. At the end is the cross, by which we know that God fully understands suffering, because he experienced it himself.

---

118. James Y. Batley, *The Problem of Suffering in the Old Testament* (Cambridge: Deighton, Bell, 1916), pp. 174-75.

20 *Evolution and Original Sin*

ROBIN COLLINS

Introduction

Probably the major area of perceived conflict between the theory of evolution and Christian theology centers on the Christian doctrine of original sin. As traditionally formulated, this doctrine has involved three claims: (1) the claim that there was a first human couple, Adam and Eve, who existed in a paradisal state of spiritual, moral, and intellectual rectitude, without corruption or sin, from which they fell by disobeying God; (2) the claim that our nature is fallen as a result of this sin, and thus bound over to evil; and finally, following Augustine, it has often been considered part of this doctrine that (3) all human beings are guilty of the sin of Adam, and hence everyone is deserving of eternal death.[1]

Addressing the question of original sin involves at least five different dimensions, that of Scripture, theology, Church tradition, science, and experience. In this paper, I will attempt to put all these dimensions together into a coherent view of original sin. The view I will suggest is what I call the historical/ideal (HI) view, and I will argue that this view is scripturally, theologically, experientially, and scientifically sound and retains the important theological core of the traditional idea. I will end by briefly indicating how this view fits into a coherent model of how God works within an evolving creation.

---

1. As stated in the new catechism of the Roman Catholic Church (which reflects the traditional teaching), Adam and Eve were created in "an original state of holiness and justice," from which they fell (Article 375). Furthermore, "this sin affected the *human nature* that they would then transmit in a *fallen state*" (Article 404) (from *Catechism of the Catholic Church* [New York: Doubleday, 1995]).

I would like to thank Keith Miller, George Murphy, John Yeatts, John Stanley, Doug Jacobsen, Richard McGough, Sandra Ellis-Killian, Thomas Ryba, and my wife Rebecca Adams for helpful comments on an earlier version of this paper.

The Historical/Ideal View

Although the HI view denies that human beings were ever in a paradisal state, it nonetheless holds that the Garden story in Genesis 2–3 is rich in theological meaning along several dimensions. First, this view claims, the original state described in the Garden story represents an ideal state that was never realized. The idea is that Genesis 2 falls into the category of a "golden age" story. As the prominent anthropologist and historian of religion Mircea Eliade has pointed out, the idea of an ideal golden age was a widespread motif in the ancient world and symbolically represented the ideal for human beings.[2] In light of the way these sorts of golden age stories functioned in many ancient cultures, it is reasonable to suppose that the Genesis story would, among other things, serve as a symbolic story that provides a preliminary and partial sketch of what an ideal relation with God would be like.

Second, according to HI view, Adam and Eve play two further representative roles, that of representing "everyperson" — that is, each one of us — and that of representing the first hominids, or group of hominids, who had the capacity for free choice and self-consciousness. With this capacity for self-consciousness and free choice, the HI view hypothesizes that these hominids also became aware of God and God's requirements, but more often than not rejected them. One could even imagine that this awareness was particularly clear, uncluttered by the spiritual darkness that eventually clouded the minds of the human race because of its turning away from God. (See my discussion of Romans 1:18-32 in the next section for a scriptural justification of this claim.) So, in this sense, these first ancestors were in what could be considered an original state of "justice and holiness," free from bondage to sin. Nonetheless they were subject to various temptations arising both from the desires and instincts they inherited from their evolutionary past and from various new possibilities for self-centeredness, self-idolization, self-denigration, and the like that came with their new self-consciousness. Instead of the "Fall" being thought of as distorting human nature as in the traditional view, however, under the HI view the sinful acts of our first ancestors created a form of spiritual and moral darkness along with an accompanying bondage to sin.[3] The moti-

---

2. Mircea Eliade, *Myth and Reality* (New York: Harper and Row, 1963), pp. 50-51.

3. At least part of this spiritual bondage is bondage to the "principalities and powers" in heavenly realms (e.g., see Col. 1:13; Eph. 6:12). One way of understanding these principalities and powers, which fits well with the HI interpretation, is provided by Walter Wink's extensive and important study of the New Testament's use of these terms. The phrase "principalities and powers," Wink claims, primarily refers to those *spiritual and invisible* forces and patterns that correspond to the internal dimensions of human existence, culture, and institutions, and that in turn

vations for preferring this view over the more traditional view will become clearer below.

Under the HI view, therefore, original sin refers to: (1) the sinful choices of these hominids, (2) the continuing sinful choices of the succeeding generations including ourselves as we come to self-consciousness, and (3) the resulting bondage to sin and spiritual darkness that is inherited from our ancestors and generated by our own choices. This spiritual darkness and bondage is hypothesized to be inherited in analogy to the way in which we inherit the genetics and culture from our ancestors. It should be stressed, however, that just as cultural inheritance operates at its own level, the psychological and social, this inheritance is hypothesized to operate on its own level (namely, the "spiritual") and therefore cannot be reduced to some sort of genetic or cultural inheritance, though it is no doubt deeply intertwined with these other levels. Further, like our cultural inheritance, this spiritual inheritance is not just personal but has a communal dimension. And the hypothesis of such an inheritance makes sense. First, the existence of a spiritual dimension is plausible, being recognized by all major faith traditions throughout the world. Second, given that there is a spiritual dimension to human beings, it makes sense that it would be inherited, just as our physical and cultural characteristics are inherited.[4]

---

exert great influence and control over human behavior. This spiritual or invisible dimension is claimed to be inextricably part of the nature of human culture and institutions, but not reducible to its outer manifestations. In the same way that the free choices of each individual affect our culture, though culture is something that transcends the sum of individuals, Wink claims that human sin has perverted this spiritual dimension from its true calling, as given in Col. 1:16. Wink links this perversion with the Fall, which he sees as referring to the "sedimentation of thousands of years of human choices for evil." According to Wink, the redemption we have in Christ in turn has broken the hold these powers have over our lives, and further enables us to help redeem them to their true purpose (see, e.g., Col. 1:13, 20). For a general account of Wink's idea, see his highly acclaimed *Engaging the Powers: Discernment and Resistance in a World of Domination* (Minneapolis: Fortress, 1992). For a more exegetical treatment of relevant New Testament passages, see his *Naming the Powers: The Language of Power in the New Testament* (Minneapolis: Fortress, 1984).

4. Similar interpretations of original sin have been offered by many others, such as theologian and Christian apologist Bernard Ramm (*Offense to Reason: A Theology of Sin* [San Francisco: Harper and Row, 1985], ch. 5), scientist-theologian Allan Day ("Adam, Anthropology and the Genesis Record — Taking Genesis Seriously in the Light of Contemporary Science," *Science and Christian Belief* 10.2 [1998]: 115-43), scientist-theologian John Polkinghorne (*The Faith of a Physicist: Reflections of a Bottom-Up Thinker* [Minneapolis: Fortress, 1994], p. 15), and Walter Wink (see note 3). None of these authors work this idea out in detail, however. Somewhat related theories of original sin can be found in the contemporary Roman Catholic theologians Piet Schoonenberg, S.J., and Bernard Loergan, S.J. For references to the writings of these thinkers and for an accessible summary of some major Western understandings of the doctrine of original sin, see Tatha Wiley, *Original Sin: Origins, Developments, Contemporary Meanings* (New York: Paulist Press, 2002).

Further, I submit, this understanding of original sin increases the overall plausibility of the doctrine. First, under this understanding, original sin can be seen as a natural consequence of the assumption that human beings are spiritually interconnected and that they have free will: if our ancestors had free will, it makes sense that they might have misused it, and thus that this misuse would have had negative spiritual consequences for us, their descendants. Second, the hypothesized original state of relatively "clear" awareness of God by our first ancestors follows from the assumption that God did not abandon the human race to moral and spiritual darkness from the very beginning. Without this hypothesis, one is left with a picture of God as an "abandoning father."

Finally, it should be noted that although the HI view is in close conformity with many aspects of the traditional doctrine of original sin, with one qualification it disagrees with the idea that the Fall somehow deeply affected human nature, an idea advanced in both the Western and Eastern branches of Christianity. One problem with this idea is that it is not found in Scripture, as we will see when we look more closely at the relevant scriptural passages below. In fact, as I will argue below, Scripture seems to suggest something closer to the HI view — that is, the loss of direct awareness of God and bondage to sin. Another problem with this idea is that it is difficult to make sense of how human nature could have been corrupted or distorted, especially within an evolutionary perspective. There are three major views of the human person: the view that we are merely physical objects, the view that we have a soul that emerges from the brain/body (either as an irreducible aspect of the brain or as a separate "immaterial" [or quasi-material] entity), and the view that we have a soul or spirit that is directly created by God and united with the body at conception or sometime between conception and birth. Under the first view, the Fall would have had to somehow corrupt or deeply distort our physical bodies, which seems particularly implausible from an evolutionary perspective. Under the second view, one would have to postulate that the Fall corrupted or distorted the laws governing the emergence of the soul from the brain in such a way that the soul now emerges in a distorted form. Under the third view, since God creates each soul/spirit individually, it seems that God would have to create each soul/spirit in a corrupt or distorted state in response to the Fall, which implies that the Fall did not directly cause each soul/spirit to be distorted. Finally, one might claim that the Fall disrupted the relation between soul/spirit and body. This would mean that God changed the laws governing the relationship between the soul and body in response to the Fall, which once again implies that the Fall did not directly corrupt human nature.

I'm not claiming that there is no way around these difficulties, only that they present a significant problem. One could, for instance, try to circumvent this problem by holding a view in which original sin is a sort of inherited "virus" that infects the soul as soon as it is created by God; or one could conceive of the soul as an inherited "form" of the body whose distorted nature gets passed on from generation to generation. As explained above, the HI view does not run into these difficulties because it views the spiritual dimension of our existence as analogous to the cultural dimension; and since the latter can clearly be corrupted, it is plausible to think that the former can. Further, as argued in the next section, the HI view has a significant basis in Scripture. Finally, one could understand this communally shared spiritual dimension of human experience as constituting a core part of our nature. Understood in this way, the HI view is compatible with the traditional idea that our nature was distorted or wounded by the Fall.

The Scriptural Dimension

Introduction

In this section, we will develop the scriptural basis for the HI interpretation sketched above. To do this, we first need briefly to discuss the nature of the inspiration of Scripture. We will assume that the inspiration of Scripture takes at least two forms: (1) God's enlightening human beings, both individually and as a community, at a very deep, semiconscious level that involves their entire orientation to the world; and (2) God's enlightening humans, both collectively and individually, at a more explicit conscious and propositional level, thereby enabling human beings explicitly to grasp new truths about the nature of reality and God — for example, that God created everything that exists or that God is Lord of Israel.[5] Further, I assume that this revelation would be expressed

---

5. Of course, there are other possible means of inspiration than these two, but they do not seem to undercut our main point below. Of particular relevance is the widely held theory of inspiration among more conservative Protestants that God inspired Scripture by guiding the hand of the authors, editors, and redactors, at least in limited contexts. One who holds this view must either hold that this guidance was very limited, or that such guidance often preserved the culturally conditioned viewpoint of the author, even for those cases in which the viewpoint is in contradiction to the moral and spiritual truths affirmed in other parts of Scripture. For example, in Ecclesiastes, the author states that "humans have no advantage over the animals; for all is vanity" (3:19); and in Ps. 137:9, a blessing is pronounced on anyone who will smash the babies of the Babylonians against a rock. Each of these passages clearly expresses the viewpoint of the author, not of God. Many other examples could be cited. So, even those who adopt this theory of inspiration must admit that the text often preserves the culturally determined viewpoint of the author. Thus, in general, one cannot dispense with the need to look for the theological truth be-

through the various literary genres produced by the culture at the time, such as psalms, story, history, letters, and the like.

Now, revelation of form (1), which is arguably the deeper and involves the entire human being, is most naturally expressed through symbol, metaphor, stories, and other related forms of literature. Jesus, for instance, extensively used the rhetorical devices of parable and paradox. Given that much of our understanding of the world is subconscious or implicit — that the conscious, explicit understanding that we can express in propositions is only the tip of the iceberg — we would expect much of revelation in Scripture to take this form. This will be particularly important when we address Genesis 1–4.

On the other hand, revelation in the form of (2) would probably most naturally take the form of propositional revelation — that is, specific theological claims such as those found in the Pauline letters — but it could also be conveyed through literary genres. Often, however, the writer through whom propositional revelation is expressed will have an undeveloped grasp of this revelation: for example, Paul and the other New Testament authors appear to have had an undeveloped concept of the trinitarian nature of God, which is one of the main reasons it took three centuries for the Church to resolve the issue by developing the doctrine of the Trinity. Further, as biblical scholars are well aware, in practice it will often be difficult to exactly determine what the author is claiming, and whether the claims are to be taken universally or applied to a particular cultural situation.

Especially in these cases the theologian must try to determine the truth about reality that the author only partially grasped or the truth that underlies what the author says. This is where sources of information external to those normally used in exegesis play a key role: in determining what an author intends to say or what a text meant to the hearers at the time, one must restrict oneself to information such as the author's other writings, the character and background of the author, and the culture at the time. Bringing in modern science, for instance, would be inappropriate. But, in determining a truth that the author only partially grasps, or that underlies what an author is saying, one can appropriately bring in the full resources of information one has available, such as philosophy and science.

Now, this is true of any author we might consider to be inspired, even if he or she was not inspired directly by God. For example, when trying to understand the deep truths of Shakespeare's plays, which certainly went beyond even the in-

---

hind the text, something I claim science can help us find. Further, as I argue below when we discuss Romans 5, even if God explicitly guided the writing of a text, there are good reasons for God to use the culturally conditioned, prescientific ideas of a culture as vehicles for revelation.

tention of Shakespeare, it is fair to bring in all the insights of later authors, and even some areas of science, such as that of psychology. This is even more true for Scripture, of which we believe in some sense that God is the ultimate author. If God is the ultimate author, we would expect Scripture to point to truths beyond the grasp of any individual author, indeed truths that people might not be able to understand nearly as well without the knowledge gained from modern science.

Accordingly, after attempting to determine as best that we can the intention of the author or the meaning of a passage for the hearers at the time, we will use all of our knowledge, including that of science, to try to understand the theological truth to which the text is pointing. This means that we will inevitably go beyond what the text actually claims, while nonetheless trying to remain grounded in a careful exegesis of the text. In other words, we properly use every resource at out disposal to search out the theological truths hidden in the text.

Given these preliminaries, we will now turn to looking at the major Scriptures relevant to the doctrine of original sin.

The Pauline Epistles: Romans 1:18-32

Romans has been commonly recognized as the major scriptural basis for the traditional formulation of the doctrine of original sin, with several passing references elsewhere in the New Testament epistles, such as 1 Corinthians 15:22, 45. Further, it is commonly agreed that the idea of original sin is not in itself found in Genesis 2–3, which is one reason this doctrine is not part of Jewish theology.[6] This, of course, is not to deny that Genesis 2–3 both provides the backdrop for the doctrine and can be interpreted in such a way as to support the doctrine.

Given this situation, I will begin by looking at the relevant Scriptures in Romans. In discussing original sin and evolution, commentators typically focus on the so-called *locus classicus* of original sin, Romans 5, often entirely neglecting Romans 1:18-32. It is my contention, however, that it is primarily in Romans 1, not in Romans 5, that Paul gives his account of the "Fall" of human beings — that is, his account of why we are in a state of bondage to sin. These passages in the first chapter of Romans lay the foundation that is assumed throughout the rest of Romans: that all human beings are unrighteous, in bondage to sin and spiritual darkness, and under the judgment of God. According to Paul,

---

6. See, for example, Rabbi Joseph Telushkin, *Jewish Literacy: The Most Important Things to Know About the Jewish Religion, Its People, and Its History* (New York: William Morrow, 1991), pp. 27-29.

... the wrath of God is revealed from heaven against all ungodliness and wickedness of those who by their wickedness suppress the truth. For what can be known about God is plain to them, because God has shown it to them. Ever since the creation of the world his eternal power and divine nature, invisible though they are, have been understood and seen through the things he has made. So they are without excuse; for though they knew God, they did not honor him as God or give thanks to him, but they became futile in their thinking, and their senseless minds were darkened. . . .

Therefore God gave them up in the lusts of their hearts to impurity, to the degrading of their bodies among themselves, because they exchanged the truth about God for a lie and worshiped and served the creature rather than the Creator. . . . And since they did not see fit to acknowledge God, God gave them up to a debased mind and to things that should not be done. They were filled with every kind of wickedness, evil, covetousness, malice. . . . (vv. 18-32)[7]

Commentators differ concerning who Paul is talking about in this passage. One view, and one that seems to me the most likely, is that Paul is primarily talking about the human race in general, not each individual person. Understood in this way, this passage essentially says that because the human race as a whole has turned away from the knowledge of God and of right and wrong, our minds were darkened and we fell into idolatry. Another possible interpretation is to take this passage as saying that each individual person was once aware of God and God's requirements, but at some point — perhaps as each of us came to self-consciousness — we decided to "suppress the truth in unrighteousness." Standing alone, however, this latter interpretation does not accord well with the empirical fact that some people grow up in situations or cultures in which the existence of God, let alone God's requirements, are only dimly perceived, if at all.

Finally, one could claim that Paul is talking only about the Gentiles in these passages. Even if Paul's immediate concern is the Gentiles, however, the basic claims that Paul makes here are certainly applicable to everyone, both collectively and individually. If one simply were to restrict the applicability of this passage to the Gentiles, then one would be in the implausible position of claiming that this is how the Gentiles came into bondage to sin, but that the Jews came into bondage to sin by some other route.

It seems to me, therefore, that the most plausible understanding of the theological truth of this passage is that the suppression of truth has occurred

---

7. All Scripture quotations in this paper are from the NRSV translation.

both at the level of human beings in general — so that one is to a large extent born into a culture that suppressed the truth — and to varying degrees at the level of each individual person, so that we all participate in this suppression to some extent. That is why we are "without excuse," both collectively and individually. Whichever way one interprets these passages, however, whether as referring to people individually or collectively, or some combination of the two, the important point for our purposes is to note that, according to this passage, the knowing suppression of the truth is the reason why our minds are spiritually darkened and we are in bondage to sin. Romans 1:18-32, therefore, could be understood as presenting Paul's account of original sin.

Now, understood as referring to humanity collectively, this account of original sin is essentially the HI account for which I have been arguing: namely, that our bondage to sin and spiritual darkness is the result of successive acts of "suppressing the truth in unrighteousness" by our ancestors, and that this bondage and darkness is strengthened and continues insofar as each of us freely contributes to this suppression of truth.

Romans 5:15-19

We will now turn to Romans 5:15-19, the *locus classicus* of the doctrine of original sin. In several places in Romans 5 (vv. 15, 17, 18, 19), the Apostle Paul refers to Adam as a single individual. In Romans 5:15, for instance, Paul states that ". . . if the many died through *one man*'s trespass, much more surely have the free gift and the grace of one man, Jesus Christ, abounded to the many." So, doesn't this show that the New Testament teaches that Adam is a single individual and, contrary to the HI view, that such an individual was the source of sin? Here we can invoke a distinction that philosopher Richard Swinburne makes between the *statement or assertion* of a speaker when he or she utters a sentence and the *presuppositions* of the statement.[8] According to Swinburne, "The statement [a speaker makes] is whatever the speaker, by public criteria, is seeking to add to the existing beliefs of the hearers."[9] In contrast, the presuppositions of an utterance can be thought of as the set of assumptions that the speaker and hearer hold in common, and which form the context in which the statement is framed.

This distinction is important for trying to understand what theological truths Scripture "teaches" or points to. Assuming, as briefly discussed above,

8. Richard Swinburne, *Revelation: From Analogy to Metaphor* (Oxford: Clarendon, 1992), pp. 28-33.
9. Swinburne, *Revelation*, p. 33.

that revelation takes the form of God's opening individuals and communities to new and truer understandings of the world, at both a conscious and a subconscious level, we would not expect revelation to extend to the text's presupposition. The reason for this is that God's revelation to communities or individuals did not involve God's showing them the entire truth about reality, such as the scientific nature of the cosmos. Thus, in expressing the revelation given to them by God, they would naturally use many of the prescientific concepts and beliefs of the time as vehicles for this revelation.

Further, even if God explicitly directed the writing of the text, in general we would not expect God to override the widely held cultural beliefs in delivering divine revelation unless those beliefs were particularly harmful. One reason for this is that, as philosopher Peter van Inwagen has pointed out, using a culture's own belief system is often the most effective way of conveying some truth. Van Inwagen presents the analogy of trying to teach Amazonian natives some basic techniques of hygiene necessary for midwives. One method is to teach them modern germ theory. As van Inwagen points out, however, such a method, even if understood, might quickly be forgotten in their culture since it has no model or precedent, and there are no educational institutions to sustain this knowledge. He then suggests that a more effective technique might be to refine and purify the existing medical lore of the natives. So, for instance, if the natives believed that childhood fever was caused by demons, then "why not teach them that the demons must make their way into bodies of new mothers via the hands of midwives, and that this path could be blocked by scrupulous rituals of washing before delivery?"[10] Unless the belief in demons was particularly harmful, it seems that such a method would be preferred since it would likely be much more effective in achieving the immediate goal of preventing childbirth fever. Perhaps, with a further development of their culture, the natives would come to understand that the demons were not to be taken literally, but merely represented germs.

Now, it is often argued that in Romans 5 Paul is not trying to inform his hearers that Adam and Eve are literal individuals; rather, it is claimed, Paul's real interest in this passage is about Christ.[11] Following this line of reasoning, Paul's talk of sin coming into the world through *one* man, Adam, can plausibly be considered a presupposition of the text — it is the common cultural framework of belief that Paul and his hearers share, and which Paul uses to make his

10. Peter van Inwagen, *God, Knowledge, and Mystery: Essays in Philosophical Theology* (Ithaca, N.Y.: Cornell University Press, 1995), pp. 141-42.

11. See, for example, Paul Ricoeur, *The Symbolism of Evil* (New York: Harper and Row, 1967), pp. 238-39.

theological points about Christ. This is particularly suggested by Paul's repeated use of the phrase "just as" (and similar phrases) such as in verse 18: "Therefore just as one man's trespass led to condemnation for all, so one man's act of righteousness leads to justification and life for all."

As an analogy, compare what Paul says with the following fictitious statement that one could imagine being in a contemporary editorial: "Just as Dr. Frankenstein could not see the grave consequences of his action in creating his 'monster,' we must be very careful before undertaking any sort of human genetic engineering." Surely, we would not take the editorialist as *asserting* that Frankenstein really existed, but rather as using the well-known story of Frankenstein as a vehicle to make a point about the dangers of genetic engineering. Or, suppose that in one of the epistles Paul made a statement such as "just as the Prodigal Son had to experience the depths of suffering among the pigs before coming to his senses, we must all. . . ." Surely, we would not take Paul as asserting that there was a real Prodigal Son, but rather we would immediately understand that Paul was using Jesus' parable of the Prodigal Son as a vehicle to make a theological point.

Similarly, one could argue, we should not take Paul to be asserting that Adam really existed, even if Paul himself believed in a literal Adam.[12] As New Testament scholar J. D. Dunn writes in his commentary on Romans 5,

> an act in mythic history can be parallel to an act in living history without the point of comparison being lost. So long as the story of Adam as the initiator of the sad tale of human failure was well known, which we may assume (the brevity of Paul's presentation presupposes such a knowledge), such a comparison was meaningful.[13]

Although I find it plausible that Paul's reference to Adam as a single individual is a presupposition of the text, I nonetheless feel uncomfortable with entirely dismissing Paul's discussion of Adam as theologically superfluous. For, arguably, Paul is also trying to say something about Adam, namely, that there is an analogy between the way Christ's redemption works and the way we got into our state of bondage to sin, though admittedly Paul's discussion of Adam is of secondary theological importance.

So, what theological truth about the source of our bondage to sin, if any,

---

12. As Swinburne notes (*Revelation*, p. 29), since the presupposition of a statement is not itself the information that the speaker intends to convey to his hearers but just a vehicle for something else, its status as a presupposition does not depend on whether the speaker believes it.

13. J. D. Dunn, *Romans 1–8*, Word Bible Commentary 38A (Dallas: Word, 1988), p. 289.

might Paul be expressing here? Since around the time of St. Augustine, Paul has been interpreted in these passages as saying that our nature is fallen, that original sin involves an inherited change in our nature. Is this really what Paul is claiming? As many exegetes have pointed out, if we carefully look at the relevant passages, Paul nowhere claims or presupposes that our natures became distorted through Adam's sin.[14] Rather, Paul presupposes that Adam is responsible for the entrance of sin into the world; it is the continuing sin of the human race, however, that brings death: "Therefore, just as sin came into the world through one man, and death came through sin, and so death spread to all *because* all have sinned" (Rom. 5:12). As for the condemnation of all people resulting from Adam's sin (v. 18), this could have simply resulted from everyone becoming sinners, and as a result being under condemnation, in the same way that (spiritual) death "has spread to all because all have sinned" (v. 12).[15]

Further, it should be noted, the story of the Fall in Genesis 2–3 never says or even suggests that Adam's and Eve's nature was distorted. Rather, the punishment is banishment from Eden and thus banishment from the uninhibited relationship with God that Eden symbolized. Thus in accordance with the HI view, the Fall story seems to be about how we came to lose the state of direct awareness of and fellowship with God.

Our next question is, How can we fit these passages in Romans 5 together with what Paul says in Romans 1 as explicated above? The traditional doctrine of original sin says that our bondage and condemnation are solely or almost entirely the result of Adam's first sin: once Adam sinned, human beings were

14. Neither does any other Scripture in the New Testament state that human nature was distorted. Ephesians 2:3 comes closest, asserting that we are "by nature children of wrath." But even here, many commentators interpret the word "nature" as referring to ingrained habit, not something intrinsic to us (see Ramm, *Offense to Reason*, p. 47). Rather, in accordance with the HI view (see n. 3), Scripture predominately speaks of us being cut off from the life of God, being under spiritual darkness (Eph. 4:17-18), being slaves to sin (Romans 6), and being subject to the powers of darkness (Eph. 2:1-3; Col 2:15). Further, insofar as Paul speaks of the "flesh" (e.g., Rom. 8:6), we need not interpret it as an inherited distortion of our nature stemming from Adam, but as those desires that have been inherited from our evolutionary past and which are one of the prime sources of sinful temptation.

15. Following Augustine, this condemnation has traditionally been interpreted as involving every person being guilty for Adam's sin. At least in part, however, Augustine based this doctrine on a faulty Old Latin translation of Rom. 5:12, which read "death spread to all men *in whom* [i.e., Adam] all men sinned," instead of the correct translation which reads "death spread through all men *because* all men sinned" (see Paul Blowers, "Original Sin," in *Encyclopedia of Early Christianity*, 2nd edition, ed. Everett Ferguson [New York: Garland, 1997], p. 839). Further, as Blowers (p. 839) notes, "there is little evidence among the Greek fathers for a notion of inherited guilt or physically transmitted sinfulness." Thus, Augustine went contrary to the tradition at the time.

from then on in bondage to sin. If we adopt the traditional interpretation, however, there is an immediate tension, if not conflict, with Romans 1. As we discussed above, the account in Romans 1 seems to imply (when extended to all humanity) that our bondage to sin was not simply a result of a single act of Adam but a collective suppressing of the truth by the human race.

One plausible way to avoid this tension, I suggest, is to understand Adam, in light of evolutionary theory, as theologically representing both everyman and the very first members of the evolving group of hominids that had gained moral self-consciousness.[16] This combines the understanding of Adam as representing "everyperson" (see discussion of Genesis below) with one in which Adam has a historical reference. Given this understanding, one of the main theological truths underlying this passage, or to which this passage points, is that sin *entered* the world from the very beginning, as soon as the evolving group of hominids leading up to human beings became morally conscious. Further, this sin of "suppressing the truth" and turning away from God was imitated by other members of the evolving group of hominids, and thus effectively snowballed until we all became deeply in bondage to sin.

Admittedly, this last move in which Adam represents the very first members of self-aware, free-willed hominids instead of a single human being living in some state of spiritual and moral rectitude is not an interpretation that one would come up with apart from modern science. Nonetheless, it certainly seems to be a plausible reading, and a reading that retains the core theological idea that our human condition of spiritual darkness and bondage to sin was largely the result of free choice, not the way humans were created (or made by nature). Moreover, there is some basis in the text itself for thinking that Adam is being used to represent the first acts of disobedience, not merely the first human being. As Paul certainly would have been aware, in the Genesis story the disobedience is a joint act of both Eve and Adam, yet Paul never mentions Eve. This suggests that within the text, Adam's disobedience implicitly represents the disobedience of both of them, not just a singular Adam. The idea of Adam representing the first self-aware hominids, therefore, could plausibly be considered a natural extension of this representative role already implicit in the text.[17]

Finally, this whole passage can be viewed as leading up to Romans 6,

16. Of course, this is not to say that Paul intended for "Adam" to represent these hominids, or that the readers at the time would have understood it in that way. Rather, just as the meaning of a poem can transcend its meaning for the author or the people at the time, what a term such as "Adam" represents or means can transcend that given by its historical context.

17. I should finally note that I deal with the other texts (such as 1 Cor. 15:22) that suggest a singular Adam in the same way as I do the text in Romans 5, though I am not sure what to say about 1 Tim. 2:13-14.

where Paul emphasizes that it is through our unity or connection with Christ, particularly in his death, that we are redeemed. In light of this, the point of Romans 5:12-19 can be thought of as drawing a parallel between the transmission of sin from Adam and the transmission of righteousness from Christ. If Adam is viewed as single individual, however, our connection with him seems very remote, and hence it becomes difficult to see how or why his sin would have such devastating consequences on us. Was there some spiritual "gene" that got mutated with Adam's sin that was then passed on to all succeeding generations? And even if there was, why would an all-good God allow this "gene" to be passed on to the rest of us? Further, God's failing to prevent this corruption from occurring, or spreading, does not fit well in the singular Adam scenario, since within that scenario God is already pursuing an interventionist policy: Why not go all the way and intervene some more to stop the effect of Adam's sin, or give Adam and his children a strong and resilient disposition not to sin?

However, if viewed as representing our ancestors, particularly our remote ancestors, our spiritual connection with Adam suddenly makes sense as part of the interconnectedness of all human beings. As explained above, just as we inherit from our ancestors physical and cultural characteristics, it also makes sense that we would inherit their spiritual characteristics — in this case, the accumulated weight of spiritual darkness and bondage to sin. To eliminate such an inheritance, God would have had to eliminate human spiritual interconnectedness in general, not simply the effects of a single act of sin. Accordingly, this interpretation explains why God would not eliminate the deleterious effects of the sin of "Adam" (as representing our remote ancestors). Further, in the process, it deepens the theological import of the idea of original sin by linking it with the fundamental interconnectedness of all human beings.

Genesis 1–4

Before going into a more detailed discussion of Genesis 1–4, we will first present a cluster of internal textual reasons why it should not be understood as literal history. (For the scientific evidence against a literal reading, see next major subsection below.) To begin with, Genesis 2 and 3 have the literary marks of a symbolic story. First, the serpent is clearly symbolic. The text says, "now the serpent was more crafty than any other wild animal that the Lord God had made. He [the serpent] said to the woman . . ." (Gen. 3:1). Clearly a literal serpent is not more crafty than a dog or a cat. (Just look at its brain size!). And serpents don't talk. Of course, this would have been known by the authors, editors, and redactors responsible for Genesis, and hence they probably did not intend for it to be taken literally. There is no more reason to take the serpent in Genesis as a literal serpent than there is to try to become literally as wise as a serpent. Indeed, it would make sense to use the serpent to represent the poisonous lie, or source of the poisonous lie, that led to Adam and Eve's disobedience: snakes were strange creatures whose venomous bite was often deadly.

Other features of the story are also clearly symbolic: a tree of life, a tree of good and evil, and God, who presumably does not have a physical body, walking around in the Garden. If one does try to take the story literally, one runs into other well-known problems. Genesis 2:19 strongly implies (in the original Hebrew) that God formed the animals after creating Adam;[18] in Genesis 4:15 God puts a mark on Cain so others will not kill him; and in Genesis 4:17 Cain takes a wife, and later his sons take a wife — all indicating that there were groups of people living at the time. To fit this into a literal interpretation of Genesis, one would have to hypothesize that Adam and Eve had other sons and daughters before Cain slew Abel. Further, one would have to hypothesize that these sons and daughters produced enough progeny to populate the surrounding regions before Cain got his mark. This hypothesis of additional sons and daughters, however, seems to go strongly against the so-called "plain" reading of the text, the very thing a literal interpretation is purportedly trying to preserve. For instance, a "plain" reading of Genesis 4:25 suggests both that Seth was the next son in line after Abel and that he was born after Cain got his mark, implying that there were no other living human beings around to murder Cain or for Cain to marry.

How then are we to interpret Genesis 1–3? Much has been written about how to understand Genesis. Let me present what I believe to be a plausible reading. To begin, in interpreting Genesis we must consider the ancient Near Eastern context. Stories about the origin of the world were common in the ancient world. The purpose of these stories was primarily to establish a framework of meaning in which to understand the world and society, along with one's place in them. Academics call stories that serve this function "myths," whether or not those stories are true or false. One of the most common myths in the ancient world was one in which the universe began in a state of chaos, which was identified with evil. This chaos in turn was overcome by the imposition of order through some sort of primeval violence.

The ancient Babylonian epic of *Enuma Elish* is a good and relevant example. In this story, Tiamat the primordial mother and Apsu the primordial father represent the chaotic primordial waters which are commingled and undis-

---

18. The NIV translation implies that God formed the animals before Adam. The Hebrew scholars I have consulted, however, say that such a translation is "a real stretch."

turbed. The younger gods, the offspring of the Tiamat and Apsu, disrupt this primordial peace, and, because of this, Apsu plots revenge against them. But they kill Apsu before he can do anything, making Tiamat inflamed with rage. She therefore gives birth to monsters — a viper, dragon, great lion, mad dog, and scorpion-man — and prepares for battle against the gods. Eventually, Marduk, who is her most able offspring, is able to kill Tiamat; Marduk produces the cosmos out of her divided corpse and creates human beings out of her blood. Thus, in this myth, evil is part of the fabric of creation. The production of the world arises out of a primordial conflict of vengeance.

This myth, along with the recognition that in the ancient world the various heavenly bodies were often considered deities, provides the basis for understanding the new theological framework of meaning that Genesis 1–3 is trying to establish. First, Genesis 1 establishes that the world has its origin in God, and hence is in essence good, not primordially evil or the result of violence as in the myths mentioned above. In fact, Genesis 1 says seven times that creation is good, ending with the words "very good" after the creation of human beings. This goodness, however, does not mean that creation is complete or perfect. As Romans 8:20-22 and other New Testament passages make clear, nature has yet to be redeemed from its "bondage to corruption." Rather, I suggest, from a New Testament perspective, to say that nature is good means that the *essential* nature and calling of creation is to be a full participant in the divine life, in which case nature will become fully itself.

Second, Genesis 1 establishes that the heavenly bodies are not divinities, but creations of God. Just as one might put profound insights into a form of a poem — since, among other things, a poem has more impact than prose and is easier to remember, repeat, and enact — the author or authors of Genesis put these insights into a poetic form structured around the sequential repetition of days.

Genesis 2 and 3 address more fully the origin of human beings and particularly the origin of evil. Contrary to other surrounding myths such as the Babylonian *Enuma Elish* recounted above, evil is not portrayed as being primordial or essential to creation, but as resulting from the contingent free choice of a first human couple, Adam and Eve. Evil is not naturally the way things are supposed to be. Thus, not only is God distanced from evil, but the Genesis narrative involves a colossal shift in point of view from a perspective in which evil and violence are part of the fabric of creation and the primordial nature of things. Practically speaking, the yearly ritual reenactment of the Babylonian myth by the king, in which the king symbolically represents Marduk's slaying of Tiamat, reifies violence as the way to establish order, in both creation and society. On the other hand, in the Genesis story human violence (as represented by the slaying of Abel by Cain) is portrayed as being the result of loss of fellowship with God through disobedience, not something primordial or *essential* to being human.

It is important to point out, however, that there is nothing in the Genesis story that indicates that inclinations toward evil and violence — or at least inclinations that can lead to evil and violence in certain circumstances — were not present from the beginning. Rather, the point of the Genesis story is that it is not part of our *essential* nature (that is, what it is to be human) to be evil or violent toward one another; from a New Testament perspective, we will become fully human only when we become full participants in the life of God.

Indeed, two features of the story indicate such inclinations were already present. First, the fact that Adam and Eve so readily gave in to the temptation to disobey God shows that they already had inclinations to "be like gods"; one cannot be tempted to do what one has absolutely no desire to do. As common experience shows, and as James 1:14 indicates, temptation always plays off some desire one already has.

Second, the figure of the serpent shows that things were not perfect in the Eden. Although traditionally the serpent has been identified with Satan, neither the Genesis story nor any other Scripture actually makes this identification. (The closest that Scripture comes to identifying the serpent as Satan is in Revelation 12:9, where Satan is referred to as "that ancient serpent.") Within the Genesis story, there are positive reasons *not* to identify the serpent with Satan. To begin with, the idea of Satan was a later development and thus was not part of the cultural vocabulary at the time Genesis was written. Moreover, the serpent is a natural creature, a "beast of the field" (Gen. 3:1), not some supernatural agency. Given this, I suggest that *within the Genesis story* the serpent itself can plausibly be thought of as representing those inclinations — such as selfishness, the need for control, and the like — that often tempt us to do evil.[19] As Paul Ricoeur says, the serpent could be interpreted as "a part of ourselves that we do not recognize . . . the seduction of ourselves by ourselves, projected onto the seductive object."[20] This fits in with the book of James, which says that "one is tempted by one's own desire, being lured and enticed by it" (1:14).

The particular inclination in the Genesis story is to be like God, knowing good and evil. Even though these temptations are based in our own desires and hence in some sense internal to ourselves, we often consider them as also in

19. Following Christian tradition, one could also postulate that within Scripture taken as a whole the serpent represents both these inclinations and Satan, since Satan is traditionally thought to tempt us through our own desires.

20. Ricoeur, *Symbolism of Evil*, p. 256.

some sense external to ourselves. As Paul states in Romans 7:14-20, the "sin na-ture" or flesh often seems to be a force inside us pushing us to do that which our inner person does not really want to do, and thus is in a sense external to who we are.

Within an evolutionary framework, these inclinations that tempt us to evil can be seen as partly involving those inclinations toward self-preservation, self-interest, aggression, and kinship interest that result from natural selection. Such inclinations are not themselves evil since they can often lead to beneficial actions, such as keeping oneself alive. But they provide the temptation or basis for evil action. It is our choosing to follow these temptations over the good that often results in actual evil. Our evolutionary history, however, does not provide the whole story here. Despite the popularity in certain circles of biological reductionism, human beings are more than the sum of their genes or instincts. We have self-consciousness, which opens up the possibility of radically new sorts of evils, such as self-idolization, self-centeredness, self-hatred and deni-gration, and the like; human wickedness and perversion, therefore, arises out of more than just our primitive biological instincts.

Finally, it is important to note that the word "Adam" is "the common noun in Hebrew for 'humankind.'"[21] Only in Genesis 1–5 and 1 Chronicles 1:1, when used without the article, does it function as a proper name.[22] Thus, the word "Adam" can represent human beings in general or a particular human be-ing. This has suggested to many people that Adam in Genesis 1 is a figure that is representative of human beings in general, and thus the story is about the "fall" of every human being as we come to self-awareness. To understand this inter-pretation, one could imagine substituting every occurrence of Adam in Genesis 1–4 with the word "everyman."

Although I think this interpretation captures an important representative role of Adam, I would suggest that "Adam" should also be understood as having a historical reference, as also representing what could be called the "stem-father" of the human race. In evolutionary terms, such a "stem-father" would be the first group of evolving hominids who gained moral and spiritual aware-ness. This idea of Adam representing the "stem-father" fits better with Paul's use of "Adam" in Romans 5 than *merely* viewing "Adam" as representing human beings in general. Moreover, it fits better with the fact that there is a continuous saga connecting Genesis 1–4 and the later chapters of Genesis, which recount the call of Abraham and the formation of Israel and clearly purport to be his-

---

21. Bruce Metzger and Michael Coogan, eds., *The Oxford Companion to the Bible* (New York: Oxford University Press, 1993), p. 10.

22. Metzger and Coogan, *Oxford Companion*, p. 10.

torical. Given this, and given the fact that the early chapters of Genesis should not be read as literal history, as I mentioned above, I suggest that a plausible interpretation of the early chapters of Genesis is to regard them as a theological commentary on and partially symbolic reconstruction of *primal* history using the concepts and rerenderings of the various stories around at the time, such as the Babylonian *Gilgamesh* epic. In this way, it is sort of prophecy in reverse: just as prophecy, in the popular sense of prediction, uses images and concepts of the time to theologically comment on the future, Genesis 1–11 does the same for the past.[23]

Indeed, I suggest, chapters 1–11 should be considered an extended theological commentary on the "Fall" of the human race, beginning with the various first humans represented by Adam and Eve, and then continuing with the story of Cain and Abel, the Flood, and the Tower of Babel. Up until the time of Abraham, the initiatives that God takes are all negative and ultimately ineffective, simply means of temporarily slowing down the tide of evil; immediately after the Flood, for instance, sin and evil began all over again. One theological message here is that our bondage to sin is so deep that it cannot be cured simply by wiping out the bad people. Rather, only a positive initiative on God's part can solve the problem of human sin. Thus, just as Paul's account of the Fall in Romans 1:18-32 is a prelude to his discussion of salvation through faith in Christ, Genesis 1–11 becomes a fitting theological prelude to the story of the call of Abraham, in which God makes the first positive initiative to solve the problem of human evil, an initiative that from a Christian perspective foreshadows the work of Christ.

Finally, the following analogy might help those who still feel uncomfortable with reading the early chapters of Genesis symbolically or "mythically," as I have suggested. Imagine God inspiring Hollywood. What would God do? Would God make Hollywood write only true stories? No. God would probably inspire them to write more edifying fiction, not override the kind of writing that they are already doing. So, if, as scholars tell us, writing origin stories was a common practice in the ancient world (much as futuristic science fiction is a common practice today), it makes sense that God would inspire an author or community to write an inspired version of such a story using the concepts and myths around at the time as raw materials. Further, such a story could convey theological truth in a much more powerful, imaginative way than any mere

23. For a fuller development of this view and a discussion of others, such as Karl Barth, who held a similar view of Genesis, see Ramm, *Offense to Reason*, ch. 4. Of course, this interpretation does not exhaust the theological purpose of these texts. For example, these texts also functioned as commentaries on the surrounding nations and as theological alternatives to their myths.

prose could. Indeed, the text itself seems to almost cry out that it is not literally history, being loaded with symbolism.

At least part of the continuing resistance to reading the early chapters of Genesis in a nonliteral, symbolic way, I believe, is motivated by two factors. First, unlike parables or "once upon a time . . ." stories, we are not familiar with the genre of literature to which I am suggesting Genesis 1–11 belongs: namely, a theological commentary on and partially symbolic reconstruction of primal history using the concepts and stories of the time as raw materials. Many readers thus tend to overlook the literary markers — such as the anthropomorphism of God's walking around in the Garden — that indicate it is a symbolic story. Consequently, they are tempted to read it literally, as has been done traditionally. Nonetheless, there do exist some analogies. One analogy to this sort of literature is the historical novel, which attempts to provide a generally accurate, though nonliteral account of some period in history.[24] Another analogy is certain plays of Shakespeare, such as Othello, which reworked older stories in order to provide a profound commentary on human existence. Similarly, Genesis 1–11 can be understood as a reworking of older stories and myths to provide a theological commentary on the origin and nature of human evil.

Second, I suggest, among many contemporary Christians, the desire to read Genesis as literal "scientific" history is often motivated by a latent form of scientism, in which one holds that the most legitimate and informative form of discourse is the type that occurs in science, thereby relegating other more imaginative forms of discourse to an inferior status as far as helping us understand the nature of reality. Thus, in their own way, many advocates of a literal reading of Genesis fall into a similar trap as those who let the purported findings of science drive their theologizing.

Comparison with Other Views

In the following subsections, we will explicate and then evaluate various other competing views of original sin.

---

24. Furthermore, such novels attempt to link their fictional characters with actual historical characters and events. In a similar way, Genesis links its theological reconstruction, such as the genealogies in chs. 1–11, with the historical figures such as Abraham.

Historical/Literal Interpretation

The traditional interpretation of the Fall, which is sometimes called the historical/literal interpretation, subscribes to a literal Adam and Eve who were in a literal paradise in which they were in fellowship with God. By disobeying God's command to eat of the tree of the knowledge of good and evil, this first couple violated their relationship with God and fell into a state of condemnation and bondage to sin. This fallen state was passed on to all of Adam and Eve's descendants.

This interpretation usually takes two versions. In one version, the Fall of Adam and Eve is responsible for all the death and suffering throughout creation. In a second version, the Fall affected only Adam and Eve and their descendants and did not directly affect the rest of creation.

The first version is highly implausible on two grounds. To begin with, it is committed to young-Earth creationism, since if one believes in an old Earth then clearly death and suffering had been around long before Adam and Eve. Second, this version runs into problems when we consider animal death and suffering. Much of the death and suffering in the world is a result of the way creatures are constructed. It is not the result of some corruption of the creature's original design. The tiger, for instance, has instincts, teeth, and a digestive system intricately well designed to catch and eat prey; various bacteria and viruses are well constructed to cause illness and sickness; and grass is constructed to grow and then die in order to make room for other grass. Thus, this version implies that the Fall somehow reconstructed, or redesigned, various organisms on Earth. But, the only way this could have happened is through some intelligence. One is thus left with claiming either: (1) that some evil power reconstructed the organisms, in which case God would no longer be the creator of present-day animals and plants; (2) that God redesigned the organisms; or (3) that God created some "redesign program" that got activated by the Fall.

Clearly claim (1) is unacceptable. Thus, one is left with the claim (2) or (3), which, however, are not much better than (1) since they end up hypothesizing a second re-creation, either by God or through the redesign program, of animals and plants after the creation recounted in Genesis 1 and 2. Such a hypothesis has no basis in Scripture and runs contrary to any natural reading of Genesis 1 and 2: Genesis 1, for instance, clearly indicates that God created the creatures we have today before the Fall, not in response to the Fall.

To avoid these problems, advocates of a literal Adam and Eve often claim that the Fall affected only Adam and Eve and their descendants and did not directly affect the rest of creation. According to one version of this view, Adam and Eve were supernaturally protected from illness, suffering, and death by their perfect relationship with God. Because of the Fall, however, they and their descendants became subject to these things.

Even though this second version is more plausible than the first, it also runs into severe problems insofar as it ascribes to a literal reading of Genesis 2–4, which is what typically motivates its advocates. Besides the textual implausibilies in interpreting Genesis 2–4 literally, as recounted above, there are serious scientific problems with taking this approach. The major problem is that the anthropological evidence we have overwhelmingly points to the worldwide existence of modern humans for at least 40,000 years. These "humans" were culturally fairly advanced, as advanced as many tribal societies throughout the world: as Davis Young remarks, "they buried their dead in ritualistic ways indicative of religious impulses and possibly some conception of an afterlife, engaged in toolmaking, and produced cave art and a variety of beautiful art objects." They also used fire, produced ornamentation, and made simple musical instruments, such as bone flutes.[25] Furthermore, the evidence that the humans who did these things existed for at least 40,000 years does not rely on a single method of dating, but on a whole multiplicity of methods: for example, Carbon-14, potassium/argon dating, Uranium track dating, amino acid racemization, paleomagnetic, electron spin, thermonuclesis, and methods involving looking at the plant and animal life contemporaneous with the fossils. Moreover, it is based on a large number of fossil finds.[26] The only way around this evidence seems to be to adopt a young-Earth creationist position. Yet, as even such leading defenders of young-Earth creationism such as Paul Nelson and John Mark Reynolds admit, "Natural science at the moment seems to overwhelmingly point to an old cosmos."[27]

If we interpret Genesis literally, then it would be very implausible to push the time of Adam and Eve to 40,000 years. Although even literalists accept that the genealogies in Genesis have gaps in them, few find it plausible to stretch them much beyond 10,000 B.C. For instance, Gleason Archer, who defends Genesis 2–4 as literal history, claims that "However the statistics of Genesis 5 [and the genealogies in general] may be handled, they can hardly end up with a date

25. See Davis Young, "The Antiquity and Unity of the Human Race Revisited," *Christian Scholars Review* 24.4 (May 1995): 390, 395.

26. See Young, "Antiquity and Unity." Also see James P. Hurd, "Hominids in the Garden?" in this volume. Actual examples of this abundance of fossils and different dating methods can be obtained by a search of a general science index under "Dating of hominid fossils."

27. Paul Nelson and John Mark Reynolds, "Young Earth Creationism," in *Three Views of Creation and Evolution*, ed. J. P. Moreland and John Mark Reynolds (Grand Rapids: Zondervan, 1999), p. 49.

for Adam much before 10,000 B.C."[28] Taken literally, the genealogy of Genesis implies that Adam and Eve, and their descendants, were farmers and lived in settlements. Genesis 4:4, for instance, refers to Abel as tending a flock, and Genesis 4:17 refers to Cain as building a city. The extensive archaeological and anthropological evidence we have, however, implies that humans did not start tending flocks and building settlements until around 10,000 B.C.[29] Thus, combined with these anthropological and archaeological data, a historically literal interpretation of the early chapters of Genesis implies that Adam and Eve could not have existed much earlier than 10,000 B.C. This means they could not have been the first humans, contrary to what a historical/literal interpretation seems to imply.

Davis Young presents an excellent review of the four major responses that those who wish to defend a literal view of Genesis could give to the above problem, and he concludes that they all face serious difficulties (though we do not have space to further discuss these issues).[30] In light of these difficulties, I think that we have very good, though not definitive, scientific reasons to reject a historical/literal interpretation of the early chapters of Genesis. Notice, however, that these difficulties have nothing to do with the theory of evolution *per se,* but merely the evidence from archaeology and anthropology.

Of course, despite these archaeological and anthropological findings, one could hold the view that there was a first couple, Adam and Eve, who were the common ancestors of all humans and who lived in a paradisal state before they fell, but then disassociate this belief from a literal interpretation of Genesis. Although such a view is certainly possible, it becomes largely unmotivated, at least apart from Church tradition. If Genesis is not taken literally, why should we feel a need to believe in a literal Adam and Eve? The only motivation that I can think of is associated with the doctrine of original sin and the related Pauline statements, which we dealt with above.

Moreover, unless one believes in some form of special creation of Adam and Eve — which does not fit well with the evidence for hominid evolution —

---

28. Gleason Archer, *The Encyclopedia of Bible Difficulties* (Grand Rapids: Zondervan, 1982), p. 64.

29. Young, "Antiquity and Unity."

30. Young, "Antiquity and Unity." One such response is to deny that Adam and Eve were the first humans and instead claim that they were merely "representative" humans. Among other problems, this view seems to conflict with the "plain" literal-historical reading of Genesis that this response is being advanced to save, particularly Gen. 3:20, which says that Eve was the "mother of all the living." (A related view in which Adam and Eve are seen as mythical humans that symbolically represent each human being is advanced by those who do not believe in a literal Adam and Eve, particularly by advocates of what I call the *existential* view discussed below.)

one runs into a further problem: namely, God's bringing these first humans into a paradisal state seems unmotivated. In the traditional young-Earth creationist account of Adam and Eve, one could make sense of why God would create them in such a state: God is a perfect God, and hence God would create a perfect world, including a perfect human couple in a perfect relationship with him. Within this scenario, the imperfections, suffering, and death of the world are the result of God's perfect gift of free will. Once one admits that humans evolved from ancestral hominids, however, then the scenario looks much different. God would have had to take creatures with imperfect physiologies, imperfect brain structures, and imperfect instincts, and somehow bring them into perfect fellowship with him, knowing full well that they would fall again in a short amount of time because of the frailty of their own nature. What purpose could God have in doing this? It seems unmotivated, some game that God plays with these first humans.[31]

Finally, this view runs into the following theological problem: If this fellowship was perfect, what could possibly be the motive for disobeying God? Thus, I conclude that although one could follow Church tradition and defend a literal Adam and Eve living in an original state of justice and holiness, it faces significant scriptural, theological, and scientific problems. Accordingly, we have good reason to look for an alternative.

31. One could attempt to reply to the above argument by adopting the increasingly popular "open view" of God which claims that God does not know with certainty the future free acts of human beings, and hence would not have known with certainty that Adam and Eve would fall. This reply, however, still runs into the further problem of why God allowed the sin of Adam and Eve to infect their descendants. The usual answer is that it was practically inevitable that humans would eventually fall, if not Adam and Eve, then one of their descendants. So, the only way God could have prevented humans from becoming fallen was continually to perform miracles to restore individuals to their unfallen state or not let them infect others, which would arguably have negative consequences for human community and mutual interdependence. This answer, however, reintroduces our original problem in a modified form: Why would God put humans into an uncorrupted state, knowing that it was practically inevitable that they would eventually fall?

One might wonder if the HI view runs into a similar problem by hypothesizing an original state of unclouded awareness of God. I would argue that it does not, since God's being present (immanent) with creation flows from God's relational nature. In the case of self-conscious creatures, this immanence would naturally involve them being aware of God, unless something intervenes to obscure that awareness. Thus, under the HI view, there is a clear theological motivation, flowing from God's nature, for God's bringing about this postulated state of unclouded moral and spiritual awareness among the first self-conscious hominids.

Historical/Quasi-Literal

The next view we will look at is what I will call the historical/quasi-literal view. Like the HI view, this view denies the existence of a literal Adam and Eve, but unlike the HI view, it still retains the traditional idea that humans fell from some sort of state of moral, spiritual, and intellectual integrity through an act of disobedience to God. C. S. Lewis, for instance, expresses this sort of view in what he calls a "Socratic myth," that is, a likely story.[32] According to Lewis, when hominids reached a certain state of development, God gave them the capacity for both self-consciousness and consciousness of God, while at the same time putting them in a paradisal state in which all their appetites were completely under their control, and in which they lived in complete harmony with one another and God. Eventually, however, one or more of these creatures decided to choose their own selves over God, to "call their selves their own."[33] Once this happened, they fell, their minds and hearts becoming darkened and alienated from God, and in the process losing control over their own appetites.

Although Lewis's view runs into fewer problems than the literal Adam and Eve view, it still runs into two of the same problems that the HI interpretation avoids. First, it runs into the problem of accounting for how human beings fell: if they were in such perfect relationship with God, how could they be tempted to turn away? Second, as explained in more detail when we critiqued the literal Adam and Eve view at the end of the last subsection, God's bringing these first humans into such a paradisal state knowing that they would inevitably fall seems unmotivated, a sort of game that God plays. The only advantage I can see of Lewis's interpretation over the HI view is that it is closer to the traditional view of Adam and Eve being created in a moral, spiritual, and intellectual rectitude.

Finally, although this is not necessarily a problem, Lewis's account involves more of an act of special creation than he suggests. The reason is that a linguistic community seems to be essential to human self-consciousness and free will. But, since a particular language is something that one learns from one's ancestors, either that language would have had to slowly evolve — which would imply a slow evolution of self-consciousness, contrary to what Lewis presupposes — or God would have had specially to teach the first humans some particular language, which would involve a major act of special creation.

32. C. S. Lewis, *The Problem of Pain* (New York: Macmillan, 1962), ch. 5, particularly pp. 77-85.

33. Lewis, *Problem of Pain*, p. 80.

Ideal Interpretation

As in the HI view, this interpretation sees the Genesis story as representative of an ideal for which we ought to strive. However, our "fallen state" is more the result of our evolutionary heritage than the result of free choice. The evolutionary process left humans in a state of incompleteness, with various impulses — such as aggression — that we must learn to transcend or control.

This view fits the best with process theology and traditional liberal theology, which typically embraced some sort of evolutionary optimism. Taken as a *complete* interpretation of the doctrine of original sin, this view, I believe, fails both to take sufficiently seriously the depth of our bondage to sin as assumed in Scripture and to include the social, communal, and historical dimension of sin as part of the doctrine.

Existential Interpretation

Under this interpretation, Adam and Eve are symbolic figures that represent every man and woman. (Indeed, as mentioned previously, the Hebrew word for Adam simply means human being, thus rendering plausible the idea that Adam and Eve represent "everyperson.") The Genesis story and the doctrine of original sin are about the existential choice each of us faces of God over self as we come to self-consciousness. As Langdon Gilkey explains, this is the view adopted within much contemporary theology. Original sin — which is defined as our estrangement and alienation from God — is seen as what inevitably happens to each of us when our "self forms itself, when the self, through its own freedom and choice of itself, constitutes its own existence."[34] This choice, which we continually make each day of our lives, is one in which we ultimately place ourselves at the center of existence, in which we depend on ourselves instead of God. This is the Fall, and is something that happens again and again every day as we constitute our own self-existence.

Although this view is certainly insightful, as is existential philosophy which provides a large part of its philosophical underpinnings, as a *complete* account of original sin it runs into the same problem as the last interpretation in that it fails explicitly to include the historical and social dimension of sin as part of its doctrine. Further, as explained above, I do not believe it fits as well as

34. Langdon Gilkey, "Protestant Views of Sin," in *The Human Condition in the Jewish and Christian Traditions,* ed. Frederick Greenspahn (Hoboken, N.J.: KTAV; Denver: Center for Jewish Studies at the University of Denver, 1986), p. 159.

the HI interpretation with the biblical texts pertaining to original sin, such as Romans 1, Romans 5, and Genesis 2–3.

Biological Interpretation

The biological interpretation sees original sin as nothing more than biologically inherited propensities, such as aggression and selfishness, that help the individual or one's kinship group survive but typically do not promote the flourishing of the larger community. Essentially, under this view, the doctrine of original sin, the Genesis story, and the various statements in the epistles tell us nothing more than what science tells us.[35] Advocates of this view often assume that we are purely biological and physical beings. Hence science, not theology, becomes the primary place to look to understand the nature and origin of human beings.

There are at least four major objections to this view. First, I believe a strong case can be made for thinking that human beings are more than merely physical creatures. Such qualities as consciousness are difficult to explain on merely physical grounds.[36] Second, this view tends to reduce evil merely to our acting on biological impulses, ignoring the particularly serious forms of evil that are made possible by our own self-awareness and transcendence — evils such as idolatry of self, viewing other people as mere objects, and the like. Many present-day Christians and other religious believers agree with this criticism: they will argue that events of the 20th century, such as the Holocaust, show that the roots of evil go very deep, well beyond our biological nature.

Third, within this understanding, the voices of theology, Scripture, and Church tradition are practically ignored, becoming simply a sort of fifth wheel. Instead, it is the purported findings of science that are claimed to provide us with the correct understanding of human nature and the human condition.

---

35. This view of original sin is fairly common. For example, theologian Phil Hefner suggests a version of this view that the "concept and the fall and original sin may well be considered mythic renditions of this biologically grounded sense of discrepancy [between the requirements of culture and our genes]" (*The Human Factor: Evolution, Culture, and Religion* [Minneapolis: Fortress, 1993], p. 132). For two other examples of this view see philosopher Patricia Williams's article, "Sociobiology and Original Sin," *Zygon* 35.4 (December 2000), and relevant sections of philosopher Michael Ruse's book, *Can a Darwinian Be a Christian? The Relationship Between Science and Religion* (Cambridge: Cambridge University Press, 2001).

36. Much has been written of the problem that consciousness presents for physicalism. One good recent book is David Chalmers, *The Conscious Mind: In Search of a Fundamental Theory* (New York: Oxford University Press, 1996).

The only role theology plays is to give a name — original sin — to what science discovers. Specifically, this view ignores those Scriptures on which the doctrine of original sin has been traditionally based, such as Romans 5 and Genesis 2–4, which provide a clear link between human bondage to sin and the free choice of our ancestors.

Finally, as theologian Langdon Gilkey has pointed out with regard to similar views held by liberal Protestantism,[37] this sort of view tends to minimize the necessity of atonement: if evil is simply the result of instincts and dispositions bred in us by the evolutionary process, human beings can be perfected through proper social or genetic engineering. A bloody death on the cross certainly does not seem as necessary. Of course, advocates of this interpretation could respond that Christ's atonement and the related work of sanctification by the Holy Spirit give us the power to transcend, overcome, or transform these instincts and dispositions. Even with this response, however, Christianity will be put into a losing competition with science: wouldn't neurology and related disciplines eventually offer a surer and better means of dealing with these otherwise negative instincts and dispositions, such as aggression? If our problem is biological, then a biological solution seems most appropriate, not a religious solution. The vitality of religions in general, not just Christianity, depends on the claim that the human problem is at least in part "spiritual," not merely physical or cultural. (Nonetheless, the spiritual might very well be interwoven with both the cultural and the physical, just as the cultural is interwoven with the physical.)

Despite these problems with the biological interpretation, it could plausibly be thought of as providing a component of original sin. My objection to the biological account is that it reduces original sin to certain inherited biological traits.

A Theological Postlude

Above, I have sketched the basics of the HI view of original sin and have indicated why I believe that it is more adequate than the major alternative views that we have examined. Here, I want to briefly indicate how it fits into an entire theology that takes evolution seriously.

The view of evolution I propose is what I will call *theistically guided* evolution. I define theistically guided evolution as the view that all life on Earth is the result of the evolutionary process ("descent with modification"), but in var-

37. Gilkey, "Protestant Views of Sin," p. 163.

ious places God guided or influenced this process. God could guide the evolutionary process by mutating some gamete or even adding new information to the gametes, thereby resulting in one organism giving rise to significantly different offspring.[38] Since in this view God works in and through the natural process of reproduction, the offspring could be said to be both the product of the natural operation of the world and a creation of God. The extent to which God guides the process, and the extent to which the evolutionary process is a result of unguided chance plus natural selection, however, remains an open question.[39]

Theistically guided evolution is part of a more general view in which God *typically* works incarnationally *within* the natural world to bring it to fulfill-

38. I prefer to think of God's guiding the evolutionary process in a nonmechanical way, a sort of nurturing or brooding over the evolutionary process as God is said to brood over the waters in Gen. 1:2. (For a sophisticated account of how God could have guided the evolutionary process, see Robert Russell, "Special Providence and Genetic Mutation: A New Defense of Theistic Evolution," in this volume.)

39. I should note that I consider it an open question as to whether God's guidance of the evolutionary process is detectable, having never seen a good argument against this idea. Thus, at least in this sense, the view I sketch above is sympathetic toward the so-called intelligent design movement, the central claim of which is that some sort of intelligent guidance is detectable in the evolutionary process. My primary theological motivation for postulating that God guides the evolutionary process is that it puts God into a deeper interrelationship with creation while still leaving room for creation to act on its own. Accordingly, it fits better with the image of a relational God, as suggested by the doctrine of the Trinity. Further, it paints a picture of a God who is a nurturing but not overbearing parent with respect to creation, which I believe conforms better to the biblical witness. The other view, in which life is left to develop by means of unguided chance plus natural selection, tends to portray God as a great engineer who after the act of creation abandons the world to its own devices.

The view of theistically guided evolution that I am advocating also seems to be the best explanation of the scientific evidence: unlike the other major positions, it accounts for both the evidence for macroevolution, such as presented in this volume, and the seemingly impressive arguments against the adequacy of unguided chance plus natural selection as the primary driving force of evolution. For a fairly good overview of many of the scientific arguments for some sort of guidance of the evolutionary process, see David Ray Griffin, *Religion and Scientific Naturalism: Overcoming the Conflicts* (Albany: State University of New York, 2000), ch. 8, specifically pp. 265-92. One of the most impressive arguments against the adequacy of unguided evolution, I believe, is the argument that unguided naturalistic evolution cannot explain human consciousness or our capacity for highly abstract theoretical reasoning. This argument has been advocated by both atheists and theists. See, for instance, Thomas Nagel, *The Last Word* (New York: Oxford University Press, 1997), pp. 130-43; Alvin Plantinga, *Warrant and Proper Function* (Oxford: Oxford University Press, 1993), ch. 12; and Paul Davies, "The Intelligibility of Nature," in *Quantum Cosmology and the Laws of Nature: Scientific Perspectives on Divine Action*, 2nd ed., ed. Robert John Russell, Nancey Murphy, and C. J. Isham (Berkeley, Calif.: The Center for Theology and the Natural Sciences, 1993), pp. 149-64.

ment, instead of working by externally imposing form and design on the world as postulated by various scenarios involving some type of special creation. In effect, this view takes the Christian doctrine of the Incarnation as indicative of the general way in which God redemptively works within all creation. God enters into the material matrix — the Word becomes flesh — and from the inside brings it to fulfillment.

Now, the New Testament implies that the fulfillment of creation is one in which God is all in all, in which God is in some sense fully present within matter. Many New Testament Scriptures speak of this ultimate fulfillment of creation. Romans 8:18-23, for example, tells us that the whole creation will be set free from its bondage to decay and share in the glorious liberty of the children of God. Similarly, other Scriptures speak of God's ultimate purpose being directed toward the redemption of all creation: In Ephesians 1:10, this ultimate purpose is to "gather all things in him [Christ], both in heaven and earth"; in Ephesians 4:10 it is for Christ to "fill all things"; in Colossians 1:20 it is to "reconcile to himself all things, whether on earth or in heaven"; and finally, in 1 Corinthians 15:28 it is for God to be "all in all." What I am suggesting here is that just as from the beginning matter had the potentiality to be conscious, or at least embody consciousness, so matter has the potentiality of carrying or being infused with the divine life in a much deeper and more complete way than it is now, though we cannot at present see how this will occur (just as we cannot yet see how matter can embody consciousness).

From this perspective, one can see God's ultimate purpose being that the material cosmos becomes a full participant in the divine life. Following standard Eastern Orthodox theology, this complete participation of humans and creation in the divine life could be understood as participation in what the Orthodox called the "energies" of God in contrast to the essence of God.[40] For the Orthodox, the energies of God refer to the life of God — that is, "God in his activity and self-manifestation"[41] — whereas the essence of God refers to God's innermost self, which is forever inaccessible to us. Using this distinction, Orthodox theologians claim to be able to affirm the eventual complete participation of redeemed humanity and creation in the divine life, while at the same time excluding "any pantheistic identification between God and creation."[42]

God's ultimate purpose being this full participation does not mean that evolution necessarily needs to be linear. As we know from the fossil record, evo-

40. See, for instance, Vladimir Lossky, *The Mystical Theology of the Eastern Church* (Crestwood, N.Y.: St. Vladimir's Seminary Press, 1976), pp. 74-75, 97-101, 133-34.
41. Bishop Killistos Ware, *The Orthodox Way,* rev. ed. (Crestwood, N.Y.: St. Vladimir's Seminary Press, 1976), p. 22.
42. Ware, *The Orthodox Way,* p. 23.

lution is more like a giant bush, with the human line being one small twig. At first this might make the process of evolution look purposeless, and the evolution of human beings a lucky accident, as Harvard paleontologist Stephen J. Gould has claimed.[43] The existence of all these other branches, along with the many that have died off, appears purposeless only if we claim that God's sole purpose was the eventual evolution of human beings. But, there is no necessary reason to restrict God's purpose to us. In fact, even though humans can be considered the "highpoint" of creation and the avenue through which it will be redeemed (e.g, see Rom. 8:21), the above Scriptures make clear that God's purposes involve *all* of creation.[44]

It should also be noted that this idea of God working within creation provides a theory of inspiration of Scripture according to which God worked incarnationally through the literature and concepts of the Hebrew culture, with the end result being that some of their writings became the vehicle of divine revelation. This theory was already implicitly behind our account Genesis 1–11 and is fairly common among biblical scholars. It was well articulated, I believe, by C. S. Lewis, for seemingly independent reasons based on his profound knowledge and appreciation of literature. According to Lewis,

> The Scriptures proceed not by conversion of God's word into literature but by the taking up of a literature to be the vehicle of God's word. . . . Thus something originally merely natural — the kind of myth that is found among the nations — will have been raised by God above itself, qualified by Him and compelled by Him to serve purposes which of itself it would not have served. Generalizing this, I take it that the whole Old Testament con-

43. For example, see Stephen Jay Gould, *Life's Grandeur* (London: Jonathan Cape, 1996).

44. This perspective also helps, I believe, with the question of the redemptive status of highly evolved hominids that are clearly not human, such as *Neanderthals* and *Homo erectus*. Recent genetic evidence strongly indicates that Neanderthals were not human (see David Wilcox, "Finding Adam: The Genetics of Human Origins," in this volume). Nonetheless, they had a larger brain than humans, and they used tools and probably fire, and seem to have buried their dead, indicating religious beliefs. The existence of such beings — which have a form of sentience somewhere between current non-human primates and humans — really presses the case, I believe, for including all of God's creation in God's redemptive plan. Otherwise, it looks as though God abandons creation. Further, once we adopt this perspective, the meaning of human existence is put into a different light. This world is not simply a testing ground for us to make a decision for or against God. Rather, I suggest, our purpose is to have "dominion" over all creation in the sense that Jesus gives to this idea: that is, those who are in authority are servants of all. Humans are called to be servants of each other and creation, and thereby be the agents of the redemption of all creation (Rom. 8:21). Perhaps Adam and Eve's tending the Garden of Eden could be thought of as an image of this sort of servanthood. Yet, they chose control, instead of servanthood, when they ate of the knowledge of good and evil, and this was the Fall.

sists of the same sort of material as any other literature — chronicle . . . poems, moral and political diatribes, romances, and what not; but all taken into the service of God's word. Not all, I suppose, in the same way. There are prophets who write with the clearest awareness that Divine compulsion is upon them. . . . There are poets like those in the *Song of Songs* who probably never dreamed of any but a secular and natural purpose in what they composed. . . . On all of these I suppose a Divine Pressure. . . . The human qualities of the raw materials show through. Naivety, error, contradiction, even (as in the cursing Psalms) wickedness are not removed. The total result is not "the Word of God" in the sense that every passage, in itself, gives impeccable science or history. It carries the Word of God.[45]

Lewis then goes on to say that we might not like this method of inspiring Scripture but that we must be very careful not to impose on God what we think is best, or our preconceived ideas of how God must have done it. Rather, he claims, we must look to the form and content of Scripture itself to determine how it was inspired. Similarly, I would argue, we must not impose on God preconceived ideas about how we think God should work in the world, but rather look both to nature and to Scripture.

This idea of God's working within creation also makes sense of the doctrine of the atonement. According to the doctrine of the atonement, it is through Christ's life, death, and resurrection that we are saved from sin and reconciled to God. In the view of atonement I develop elsewhere — which has close affinities with the views of several of the early Greek fathers of the Church, views that were later developed through the centuries by the Eastern Orthodox Church — salvation consists of fully sharing the life of Christ, as implied by Jesus' analogy of the vine and the branches in John 15.[46] Because of the incarnation, this life is both fully divine and fully human; and because of the cross, it is fully in solidarity with the depths of human brokenness, sin, alienation, mortality, and the like. Because of its fully human component, and because it is in full solidarity with the depths of our life situation, we can participate in it. As Paul indicates in Romans 6, by participating in this life we are redeemed from sin and reconciled to God and freed from spiritual bondage and darkness. Thus, the effect of original sin is reversed. I call this theory the

45. C. S. Lewis, *Reflections on the Psalms* (New York: Harcourt, Brace, Jovanovich, 1958), pp. 111-12, 116.

46. For a development and defense of this theory, see part II of my "Girard and Atonement: An Incarnational Theory of Mimetic Participation," in *Violence Renounced: Rene Giraud, Biblical Studies, and Peacemaking*, ed. Willard Swartley (New York: Herald/Pandora, 2000).

Incarnational Theory of Atonement, and defend it as being scripturally, morally, and theologically sound.

Moreover, this incarnational way of God working in the world also fits with the way in which God works as revealed on the cross and in the kenosis hymn of Philippians 2:5-11: God does not work by external force from the outside, but from the inside through a process of self-emptying love.[47] In fact, I would suggest, insofar as creation has sentience, Christ has been sharing the sufferings of creation since the foundation of the world.[48] God has never been an absentee father. The crucifixion is simply the culmination of this process. Finally, this idea of God's working incarnationally within the material matrix makes sense of God's continuing work in the Church and in history in general. For instance, God uses weak and frail human beings to carry the Christian gospel, and God appears to work within history largely by inspiring human beings to great moral and spiritual endeavors.

In sum, the idea of God's working incarnationally within the material cosmos provides an overarching idea that coherently unites many elements of Christian theology and disparate things we know about the world: it sheds light on the significance of the incarnation, eschatology, the nature of inspiration of Scripture, the doctrine of atonement, the cross of Christ, and how God works in human history. The HI interpretation of original sin simply provides one part of the story regarding how God has worked and continues to work incarnationally in the world.

47. See George Murphy, "Christology, Evolution, and the Cross," in this volume.

48. Indeed, this could be thought of as the deeper meaning of Rev. 13:8, which under the "nonpredestinarian" translation states that Christ was slain from the foundation of the world.

21 Evolution, Cognitive Neuroscience, and the Soul

WARREN S. BROWN

Both evolutionary biology and cognitive neuroscience raise important issues regarding a traditional Christian understanding of the person. Particularly problematic is dualism — the view that persons are bodies inhabited by nonmaterial souls. With respect to evolution, it is not altogether clear where and when, during the long span of evolution, *Homo sapiens* would have acquired a nonsubstantial soul. Regarding neuroscience, brain research has increasingly shown that capacities once thought to be in the realm of the soul are related to (or caused by) the neurophysiological process of the brain.

Yet, for most of the two millennia of the Christian faith, the concept of a soul has played a very important and meaningful role. The soul has been thought to be the source of important aspects of human uniqueness: consciousness, rationality, free will, and spirituality. It is the soul that is corrupted by sin and is the target of redemption. The soul is viewed as the point of interaction with God, and the soul seems necessary in Christian thought about eternal life. These concepts that have been attached to the soul contain core truths that are critical to a Christian understanding of personhood. Any attempt to redefine human nature and remodel Christian anthropology in the light of evolution or the results of modern neuroscience research must not lose sight of important aspects of personhood that have traditionally been vested in the concept of the human soul.

In this chapter, I will describe the nature of persons in a way that I believe does justice to the essential elements of the Christian understanding of personhood and, at the same time, is not inconsistent with basic evolutionary and brain science. First, I will define an alternative to body/soul dualism, called *nonreductive physicalism,* which allows better integration of evolution and the sciences of human nature with Christian faith. I will also attempt to reestablish within nonreductive physicalism an understanding of humanness that is as rich as that previously carried by the concept of a soul. I will suggest how "soulishness" can emerge from the capacities of a complex neural processor without having to presume the existence of a nonmaterial soul. Finally, I will discuss human soulishness within the context of evolutionary progression.

Body and Soul, or a Soulish Body?

Monism offers an alternative to body/soul (or body/mind) dualism.[1] This position holds that humans are one and only one substance. One version of monism, called *Idealism,* believes that only the mental (or spiritual) is real and the physical is a construct of the mind. An alternative version of monism (and the version I wish to discuss) is *physicalism,* in which humans are considered to be physical beings with mental functions and spiritual capacities. However, physicalism has typically been associated with *reductive materialism* and *determinism,* which are repugnant to a Christian view of persons. Reductive materialism and determinism, together, maintain that human mental life and conscious agency can be reduced to (are *nothing but*) the operation of cellular and chemical processes that are ultimately determined by the laws of physics. In this view, all of the causal forces that affect human thought and behavior occur at the level of biochemistry and physics.

In *Whatever Happened to the Soul? Scientific and Theological Portraits of Human Nature,*[2] my colleagues and I explored the possibility of maintaining, within both science and Christian theology, an alternative version of physicalism: *nonreductive physicalism.* This position admits the fundamental biological nature of humans (physicalism) but asserts that there are nonreductive properties of mind. Thus, conscious decisions and will are real phenomena that are effective in exerting a top-down[3] (or whole-part) causal influence on the ongoing processes of the brain's control of behavior. Furthermore, from this point of view, soul (or soulishness) is an aspect of physical existence, not an additional immaterial essence. Humans *are* bodies — they do not *have* bodies; they *are* souls — they do not *have* souls.

Within Christian theology, the position of nonreductive physicalism

---

1. Monism is also an alternative to any form of tripartism that considers human nature to be composed of three distinct parts: body, soul, and spirit; or body, mind, and soul.

2. Warren S. Brown, Nancey Murphy, and Newton H. Malony, eds., *Whatever Happened to the Soul? Scientific and Theological Portraits of Human Nature* (Minneapolis: Fortress, 1998).

3. "Top-down" causal influences are effects of thought, a higher-level, whole-brain process (top), on the lower-level neurophysiological processes (bottom) that allow thought to occur.

would not deny the fundamental distinction between material creation and an immaterial, spiritual Creator — a form of material/nonmaterial dualism. However, nonreductive physicalism suggests that human persons are creatures that are entirely nested within God's physical creation. The line that separates the material and the immaterial does not divide the human person into parts.

Neuroscience and the "Soul"

Rapid advances in the study of the human brain within neuroscience, neuropsychology, and clinical neurology are making it increasingly hard to find a realm of human thought, decision, action, or experience that is not the product of, or very strongly influenced by, the activity of identifiable neural systems. Thus, there seems to be a rapidly diminishing pool of human capacities and experiences that have not yet been found to be influenced by neural activity and that might be reserved for the activity of a dualist soul. In fact, I would maintain that the concept of a separate, immaterial soul is trivial (i.e., unnecessary) with respect to understanding human life and experience unless it can be shown to have a separate and identifiable realm of agency, that is, to do something with respect to thought or behavior that is independent of what the brain does. If all of our thoughts, actions, and experiences exist within the activity of our nervous systems, then of what value is the concept of soul as a separate entity?

There are some obvious examples of damage to specific brain areas or other dysfunctions of the nervous system that have strong impact on experiences of the self that we have traditionally identified as the soul. I will mention just a few of these:

- *Free will:* How much free will is experienced by an acutely psychotic schizophrenic who kills another person in a paranoid delusional state; a person with obsessive-compulsive disorder who cannot resist the compulsion to engage in certain behavioral rituals; or an individual seeing space aliens while hallucinating on drugs? In each case a neurochemical imbalance or structural defect of the brain has created a malfunction of the nervous system that results in a very strong and nearly uncontrollable bias on the experiences and actions of the individual. How do we understand such biological infringement on free will if free will is considered a property of a nonmaterial soul? Might not free will be better understood as a property of the nervous system, capable of being short-circuited to greater or lesser degree by neurological dysfunction?

- *Sin, guilt, righteousness, and ethical behavior:* A long history of neurological case studies and research, including important recent work by Antonio Damasio,[4] has documented the diminished capacity of an individual with damage to particular parts of the frontal lobes of the brain (i.e., the orbital frontal cortex) to appropriately regulate one's own behavior. This problem occurs even when intellect is unaltered and the person retains the ability to verbally describe appropriate actions in the abstract. Often this disregulation of behavior results in an inability to abide by norms for socially acceptable or moral behavior. Such individuals may violate social conventions, laws, ethical standards, or the rules of courtesy, civility, and regard for the benefit of others. Marriages, family relationships, jobs, social standing, economic stability, and legal/criminal status are at risk in many individuals with this form of frontal lobe brain damage. If one considers outward righteousness to be a product of the human soul, then this disturbance of behavioral modulation and regulation must give one pause.

- *Peak spiritual experiences:* Most modern persons, Christian or non-Christian, identify as most uniquely spiritual, and thus most likely to be manifestations of the soul, experiences of religious ecstasy and awe — those moments when one feels most transcendent or overwhelmed by the feeling of divine presence. However, there is a significant literature in neurology that suggests that in some rare cases of individuals with temporal lobe epileptic seizures, such experiences can result from abnormal neural activity in structures of the temporal lobes and limbic system. While the actual incidence of religious experience associated with temporal lobe seizures is controversial, such cases clearly exist.[5] There are two conditions that are likely to be necessary for this neurological phenomenon to occur: (1) a specific form of temporal lobe seizure activity, and (2) personal experiences or social context that predispose the person to religious interpretations of unusual experiences. Nevertheless, in these persons experiences of religious awe, ecstasy, or ominous presence appear to be a product of their seizures. Thus, if strong religious experiences can be linked to certain forms of brain activity, how do we understand normal spiritual experiences? Do we interpret spiritual experiences as a way the brain can function (normally or abnormally), or as manifestations of an immaterial soul?

---

4. Antonio Damasio, *Descartes' Error: Emotion, Reason, and the Human Brain* (New York: Putnam, 1994).

5. An interesting literary example of a person with religious experiences resulting from seizures appears in the account of the seizures of Prince Myshkin in Dostoyevsky's *The Idiot.*

• *The experience and expression of love:* A critical commandment for the Christian is to love one another. But even this experience is susceptible to infringement from brain damage. *Capgras Syndrome* is a disorder of the experience of familiarity and regard for close friends and family. In these rare cases, damage to particular brain areas can result in a disorder characterized by the individual's conviction that close and familiar *persons* are not *real*, but are "doubles" and imposters. A family member, when encountered, may be visually recognized in such a way as to say, "That person looks like my wife." However, the person with Capgras Syndrome does not experience an accompanying feeling of familiarity and deep personal significance associated with the visual experience. Therefore, the patient presumes that the person in question must be an imposter — "not really my wife." At least subjectively, a critical aspect of our love for one another is the experience of familiarity and relatedness based on an extensive past history with these significant others. But Capgras Syndrome indicates that these feelings can be dissociated from visual recognition by a dysfunction of the brain. Therefore, the experience of loving another person is an activity of our physical selves, able to be disturbed by neurological damage. Thus, love of neighbor cannot be relegated to the purview of an immaterial soul.

An important caveat must stand with the preceding description of the infringement of disorders of the nervous system on soulish human experience. The neuroscience encroachment into the properties of the soul is not complete. There is still much of our human subjective and soulish experience that has not yet been demonstrated to have neural correlates, nor have the neural systems involved in most complex human experiences been completely described. There remain many mysteries. However, the infringement of neuroscience explanations on attributes and experiences traditionally assigned to the soul is an accelerating trend. What is more, the neurosciences have strongly influenced the modern understanding of the person. Thus, information from the study of human neurophysiology cannot be ignored. It must be considered in any Christian understanding of human nature.

In addition, the information accumulating regarding the neurology of higher human mental functions and experiences does not necessarily imply *reductionism* — as if our conscious experiences are nothing but a by-product of the operation of neural subsystems and therefore entirely determined by biological and physical laws. Donald MacKay termed such reductionist views as "nothing-buttery." "According to this view," MacKay writes, "only where physical explanation was impossible could any other account be taken seriously in its own right. Otherwise, the whole thing could be explained away as 'nothing but' the mindless motion of molecules."[6]

Nonreductive physicalism maintains that, while higher-level human capacities (e.g., thinking and deciding) are dependent on lower-level neural processes, the higher processes are, nevertheless, causal in their own right. New causal properties *emerge* from the *complex interactive operation* of the entire brain (represented in our thinking, deciding, and experiencing) that cannot be entirely accounted for by mapping the operation of various contributing neural systems. Human mental activity such as making a decision or imaginative problem solving cannot be entirely accounted for by descriptions of the activity of single neurons, small groups of neurons, or single brain structures. Thus, the demonstration that certain neural functions are important to a particular high-level human ability or experience should not be misunderstood as meaning that the mental property itself is nothing more than the operation of this subgroup of neurons. Rather, it must be understood as a demonstration that the brain, as it interacts with the environment, is the source of this mental activity, and that the brain area in question plays an important contributing role. The highest forms of mental ability are a product of the interactions created in a very complex system of neural activity involving most of the brain.

Soulishness and Relatedness

Considering the very large amount of current information on neural correlates of the highest forms of human mental experience, what, then, has become of the soul? In what ways are humans unique? How do we recognize the *Image of God* within a physically embodied person?

The view that I began to develop in *Whatever Happened to the Soul?* is that the critical feature of a biblical portrait of persons is the capacity for deep and rich experiences of *personal relatedness*.[7] I therefore argued that soulishness arises in humankind out of three dimensions of relatedness:

1. The qualitative and quantitative differences between human and nonhu-

6. Donald M. MacKay, *Human Science and Human Dignity* (Downers Grove, Ill.: InterVarsity, 1979), p. 27.

7. There has been a long tradition of considering rationality to be both most uniquely human and the definitive property of the soul. I have rejected this formulation since at least most forms of human rationality can be instantiated in artificial intelligence systems that are nevertheless strikingly nonhuman. Personal relatedness would require not only rationality, but also tacit-intuitive forms of intelligence, as well as emotional experiences and appreciations.

man *interindividual* relatedness. Differences of depth, scope, complexity, and range in time, space, and topic.

2. The subjective *(intrapersonal)* process of self-relatedness and self-representation.
3. The capacity for, and experiences of, *relatedness to God.*

Most, if not all, of the critical properties that have been subsumed within the Christian concept of a soul are captured in the concept of *personal relatedness,* particularly if one admits (as does the Christian) the possibility of relatedness to God. The soulishness of persons is called forth by God in his offer of relatedness. From the perspective of the biblical narrative, humans become unique through God's bestowal of a unique form of personal relatedness on humankind, not by being implanted with an immaterial soul. Our soulishness is also established and enriched by our deepest and most significant interhuman relationships. We become persons and "souls" as we experience ourselves within a relational network of God and other human beings. Finally, *spirituality* in this formulation would refer to the state of a physical human person being in a relationship with God, who is both spirit and person. Thus, although there are multiple ways that the Greek words translated "soul" and "spirit" *(psyche* and *pneuma)* are used in the Bible, I believe that much of what is being referred to can be captured by the capacity and experiences of personal relatedness in a way that does not require dualism (or tripartism).

Thus, from both physicalist and evolutionary perspectives, "soul" is an *emergent property* of interpersonal and intrapersonal relatedness. Soulishness emerges within three critical interpersonal exchanges: (1) in the depth and sophistication of an individual's relatedness to others; (2) in the state of (and experiences of) being related *to* by a human community; and (3) in God's sovereign act of extending relationship to humankind. This last aspect of relatedness — God's offer of relatedness — is the foundational source of dignity as a value attribution of humankind, and "soul" as a functional property of human nature.

This relational view of the uniqueness of humankind and of soulishness is not entirely novel and is not without proponents in theology. For example, H. Richard Niebuhr argues for the fundamentally social nature of the self.[8] Similarly, Arnold Come proposes a nondualist understanding of humankind in which the essence of human "soul" comes from the God-man relationship. Come states:

> It should be clear by now that in defining human "soul" we are not seeking some elusive, immaterial substance which is distinct from body even while

8. H. Richard Niebuhr, *The Responsible Self* (New York: Harper, 1963).

in a body. Rather, we are trying to isolate the uniqueness of that configuration of life we call "human," which is integrally fleshly or somatic. What are its unique characteristics, powers, capacities, and form which make it a genus of life unlike all others? This uniqueness of life is what the "soul" of man consists of. The Christian understanding of human life . . . derives from that God-man relationship.[9]

In a similar fashion, the difference between being a physical human *individual* and being a *person* (i.e., one who in my terms embodies soulishness) was described by theologian Jürgen Moltmann in a recent lecture at Fuller Theological Seminary in a way that is very similar to the concept of soulishness-as-relatedness that I am espousing. Moltman writes:

> An individual, like an atom, is literally that ultimate element of indivisibility. An ultimate element of indivisibility, however, has no relationships, and also cannot communicate. . . . If an individual has no relationships, then he also has no characteristics and no name. He is unrecognizable, and does not even know himself. By contrast, a person is the individual human being in the resonant field of the relationships of I-you-we, I-myself, I-it. Within this network of relationships, the person becomes the subject of giving and taking, hearing and doing, experiencing and touching, perceiving and responding. . . . The "person" emerges through the call of God.[10]

Some Implications of Soulishness as Relatedness

Counting personal relatedness as the basis of soulishness has important implications that must be mentioned but that can be only briefly discussed within the confines of this chapter. First, it is not hard to convince oneself that humans have dramatically enhanced capacities for personal relatedness. However, if soulishness is (only) a matter of the ability of each person to relate to others, then certain implications would follow:

- Persons with diminished relational capacity would be at risk for diminished soulishness (e.g., an autistic individual). As thoroughly embedded as we all are in a dualist conception of the soul, "diminished soulishness"

9. Arnold B. Come, *Human Spirit and Holy Spirit* (Philadelphia: Westminster, 1959), pp. 59-60.

10. Jürgen Moltmann, "Christianity and the Values of Modernity and the Western World," a lecture presented at Fuller Theological Seminary, April 1996.

sounds like an unacceptable potential outcome of this theory. Certain individuals might be denied a form of humanness because of their lack of normal levels of the ability to sustain interpersonal relationships. The ethical implications of considering any individual "less human" would clearly be unconscionable. However, considering the entire scope of relatedness more deeply, a compelling Christian ethic can be realized, as described below.

- Animals with greater relational ability (e.g., linguistically competent chimps) would have a modicum of soulishness. Certainly, the relational ability of at least one Bonobo (Pigmy Chimp) named Kanzi (described by Sue Savage-Rumbaugh and Roger Levin[11] and recounted in the section on Language, below) gives the strong impression of an animal with at least a small quantity of soulishness. Since Christian scripture reserves an important place in God's creation for humankind but otherwise provides little description of the theological status of the members of the animal kingdom, the concept of animal soulishness cannot be a source of major concern to Christians. Nevertheless, according to Arnold Come, "The Hebrew would have been nonplused to be confronted with the question of popular debate a generation ago, 'Do animals have souls?' For him, 'the animal world . . . is a swarm of living souls who fill the earth' (Gen. 1:20-21, 24 . . .)."[12]

- An intelligent relational robot might also have a modicum of soulishness. It is my opinion that a *truly* relational robot will exist only in science fiction. One limitation inherent is that true empathy between a human and a robot would be impossible, given the differences between embodiment within microcircuits versus biology. For example, how could the emotional experience of a person be adequately appreciated by an intelligent robotic system that does not itself blush, sweat, or experience changes in heart rate and blood pressure, important physical events that signal the nature of our emotions?[13] Nevertheless, at this initial level of consideration of the implication of soulishness-as-relatedness, the idea cannot be totally ignored.

---

11. Sue Savage-Rumbaugh and Roger Levin, *Kanzi: The Ape at the Brink of the Human Mind* (New York: Wiley, 1994).

12. Come, *Human Spirit and Holy Spirit*, p. 57.

13. The point about embodiment within microcircuits ruling out human-robot empathy I borrow from a talk by Harvard theologian Harvey Cox given at the conference entitled "Identity, Formation, Dignity: The Impact of Artificial Intelligence and Cognitive Science upon Jewish and Christian Understanding of Personhood," at Massachusetts Institute of Technology, April 1998.

In the description above, I suggested that soulishness also arises in the state of (and experiences of) being related *to* by a human community. Our deeply individualist concept of what it means to be human finds it easy to presume that each individual's relatedness must be entirely dependent only on his or her own capacities. From this point of view, my soulishness would be exclusively dependent on my ability to relate to others. However, when we consider the possibilities more thoroughly, we realize that equally important to our experience of interpersonal relatedness is the fact that others relate to us. We both give and receive relatedness.

In fact, relatedness need not be symmetric. It can be sustained within asymmetric interactions in which one party provides most of the relational activity and ability. For example, both an infant and senile older adult suffering with Alzheimer's disease have limited relational abilities. However, if a more relationally competent individual (for example the parent of an infant, or the spouse of an individual with Alzheimer's disease) makes an active effort to engage the infant or senile adult (through eye contact, vocalization, touching, facial expressions, etc.) a strong relational response is elicited and relatedness established. We need not limit and confine the possibilities for personal relatedness and soulishness to the capacities of a particular individual.

Therefore, within the context of this less individualist understanding of relatedness, we can revisit the points made above:

- If human dignity and soulishness can also arise as an interpersonally competent community relates *to* an individual, then soulishness can be maintained in a person with diminished relational capacity by nesting that person within a relationally competent and caring community. Thus, each community carries the *ethical responsibility* for the soulishness of all persons within its reach, and particularly for those of lesser capacity. For a powerful example of how deep relatedness can be asymmetrically sustained with a disabled person with profoundly limited communication, the reader is referred to Henri Nouwen's book *Adam*.[14]
- Within this wider understanding of relatedness, linguistically and relationally competent chimps or robots would experience soulishness only if they were granted relational status within a relational community. In the case of the chimpanzee Kanzi (mentioned above and described in detail below), a degree of relational status was granted to Kanzi by his human teachers and keepers. Admission to relational status within a human community and the willingness to extend relationality *asymmetrically*

14. Henri J. M. Nouwen, *Adam: God's Beloved* (Maryknoll, N.Y.: Orbis, 1997).

was the primary event in Kanzi's development of unusual linguistic capacities, as well as the degree of personal relatedness that he manifested. A modicum of soulishness seemed to have been elicited, even in this chimp, by a significant amount of relatedness extended from the available human community.

Terrence Deacon, in the conclusion of his book on the co-evolution of language and the brain, suggests the possibility of engendering soulishness in animals or robots based on intersubjective sharing:

> . . . as we have seen, the symbolic threshold is not intrinsic to the human-nonhuman difference. . . . This means that we are not the only species that could possess a 'pilgrim soul.' . . . It was a Darwinian accident, or miracle, of nature that this ability arose once and persisted for so long, but it has provided each of us with the opportunity to participate in bringing new 'souls' into the world, not by procreation, but by allowing our own symbolic selves to be shared by other human beings, and perhaps by other animals, or perhaps eventually by artifacts of our own creation.[15]

Finally, I described soulishness as arising also from God's sovereign choice to be in relationship to humankind. This last aspect of relatedness is the primary source of dignity as a value attribution, and "soul" as a functional property of human nature. Humans become souls not by the presence of a unique additional substance (an immaterial soul) but primarily by a relationship with God. In fact, God's relationship to humankind is the ultimate form of asymmetric relatedness: An omnipotent and loving God has chosen to be in relationship to the race of *Homo sapiens* who are part of his physical creation — creatures with relational capacities that pale into insignificance in comparison with his. So, also, the soulishness of chimps and robots would ultimately be dependent upon the gift of relatedness from the Creator of all things.

The Emergence of Soul

I have been maintaining that the soulishness of humans arises out of the experiences of personal relatedness, and that the capacity for personal relatedness is an emergent property evolving out of the neurocognitive capacities necessary for establishing, maintaining, and enriching relatedness. An *emergent function*

15. Terrence W. Deacon, *The Symbolic Species: The Co-Evolution of Language and the Brain* (New York: Norton, 1997), pp. 454-55.

is a mode of operation of a complex system that cannot be fully accounted for by close scrutiny of processes at lower levels, although it is dependent on the operation of lower levels. New mental (and relational) capacities emerge from the *interplay* of many lower-level capacities and, thus, the mental capacities do not exist at the lower levels. As these higher-level system operations emerge, they exert top-down (or whole-part) causal influences on the operation of lower-level systems. Complex system interactions create their own rules of operation and their own forms of causal influence that are not epiphenomenal.

It is this top-down property that makes it possible for physicalism to be *nonreductive.* However, as Donald MacKay has pointed out, the meaning of top-down is not that "the mind controls the brain"[16]; rather, mental properties are efficacious in responding to the environment in ways that cannot be accounted for by the operations of specific brain modules or neural subsystems. These actions of the mind on the environment can be online, creating immediate action, or offline, representing possibilities for action within symbolic mental scenarios.[17] For example, as soon as evolving brains became complex enough to imagine a complex scenario of a future possible behavior, consider the likely consequences of the imagined behavior, and implicitly evaluate the outcome as good or bad, then a form of conscious agency had emerged. Imagining and evaluating hypothetical behavioral scenarios continuously reprograms the organism's future response probabilities.

Thus, higher human cognitive capacities (such as language, a theory of mind, episodic memory, self-consciousness, imagination of the future, creativity, and complex problem-solving) emerge out of an evolutionarily expanding *neurobiological system* interacting with a developing human culture. Personal relatedness is an emergent property of the interaction of these critical *human cognitive capacities* as they are used *interpersonally.*

Finally, soulishness is a quality of being that emerges from the deepest experiences of *personal relatedness* (most particularly, a relationship with God).

Human Capacities That Evolved to Serve Relatedness

While all human mental properties appear to be continuous with precursors in primates, there is nevertheless a significant cognitive gap between primates and

---

16. Donald M. MacKay, *Behind the Eye* (Oxford: Blackwell, 1991), pp. 132-33.

17. Terrance Deacon (*Symbolic Species*, ch. 14) makes a strong case for the emergence of self-control and a form of free will based on the ability of humans to symbolize and mentally process future possibilities for behavior.

humans. What follows are brief descriptions of some of the cognitive capacities that are sufficiently more advanced in humans as to be important in any description of human nature, and critical to the emergence of soulishness.

Language

Perhaps the greatest chasm between the mental life of the most intelligent non-human primates and that of human beings lies in the use of language in communication and mental representation. However, the apparent size of the chasm has been moderately reduced by the extensive work done over the last twenty years in attempting to teach great apes a language system. The research on ape language has revealed much not previously known about the capacity of apes to communicate using an abstract system of symbols or gestures (including the ability of some to understand human speech). Nevertheless, the linguistic performance of apes is limited and dependent on the availability of the support of a human linguistic community.

I mentioned earlier the remarkable language capacity of the chimpanzee, Kanzi, described in the work of Sue Savage-Rumbaugh and Roger Levin.[18] As an infant Kanzi was a passive participant in various unsuccessful attempts to teach language to his mother. When finally allowed to express himself via the language system that was being taught to his mother, Kanzi seemed to know spontaneously how to communicate via the symbols. He had already developed an unusual (for a chimpanzee) general language processing capacity. Most remarkable was Kanzi's eventual grasp of spoken English. Kanzi was capable of understanding a wide variety of spoken sentence types (thirteen in all), including sentences with embedded phrases. Kanzi responded correctly on 74 percent of 660 novel sentences, showing "sensitivity to word order as well as to the semantic and syntactic cues that signaled when to ignore word order and when to attend to it."[19] This capacity was comparable to that of a normal 2½-year-old human. Impressed by the remarkable capacities of Kanzi, Duane Rumbaugh suggests that "apes have vaulted the language barrier."[20]

However, this research also suggests that language does not emerge spontaneously in apes but is dependent for its development on the support of a human linguistic community. Apes in the wild develop no more than a contextu-

18. Savage-Rumbaugh and Levin, *Kanzi.*
19. Savage-Rumbaugh and Levin, *Kanzi.*
20. Duane Rumbaugh, "Primate Language and Cognition: Common Ground," *Social Research* 62 (1995): 711-30.

ally and emotionally modulated set of vocal signals. Adolescent or adult apes specifically trained by human researchers can learn to use symbols or gestures to communicate with humans in a manner that suggests some linguistic properties. Kanzi, raised from birth in an environment with extensive exposure to human language, developed a capacity to understand language that was not measurably different from that of a normal 2½-year-old human, although language expression was more limited.

While neither personal relatedness nor our soulful experiences can be reduced to nothing more than the operation of linguistic processes, human relatedness is clearly rooted in linguistic capacities. Thus, possession of a significantly enhanced language capacity endows humans with dimensions of relatedness not within the realm of possibility for nonhuman primates. This is not to imply that primates, or other animals, are not relational in important ways. Certainly Savage-Rumbaugh and Levin describe a strong sense of relatedness between themselves as experimenters and Kanzi.[21] However, with the very limited language capacity of chimps come limitations in the depth and richness of chimp-chimp relatedness, and a very significant asymmetry in human-chimp relatedness.

Metacognition and a Theory of Mind

As important as language is to the emergence of personal relatedness, there are other cognitive abilities that are significantly enhanced in humans and must be considered. Among the important additional contributors to relatedness are *metacognitive skills,* particularly the possession of a reasonably valid "theory of mind." Metacognition is "thinking about thinking" — the conscious awareness of the workings of one's own mental processes. "Theory of mind" is the ability to accurately attribute mental states to other people, that is, being aware of the mental processes of others. Theory of mind is captured in statements such as, "I think she thinks" or "I think she thinks that he thinks."

As with language, a form of theory of mind appears to be present in the great apes (but not lesser monkeys). While research is ongoing, there nevertheless appears to be a large gap between the ape form of theory of mind and that possessed by humans. Behavioral observations of higher apes suggest some ability to represent the state of mind of another individual in terms of what that individual must know or be able to perceive. Perhaps apes have a proto-theory of mind, similar in kind to that of the human but of lesser power and complexity, akin to the metacognitive ability of a young child.

21. Savage-Rumbaugh and Levin, *Kanzi.*

The importance of a theory of mind to human relatedness can be appreciated by considering Asperger's Syndrome, that is, autism in an individual with normal I.Q.[22] This syndrome manifests itself by a severe impairment in reciprocal social interactions, including lack of appreciation of social cues, a failure to completely grasp nonverbal interpersonal communication, speech and language problems, and a stereotyped way of imposing routines on all or most all aspects of life. Many of the symptoms of Asperger's Syndrome that involve interpersonal interactions can be understood as a deficit in understanding the cognitive processes and mental life of other individuals, and a consequent failure of normal relatedness and empathy. Thus, individuals with Asperger's Syndrome have been thought to have an underlying deficit in the metacognitive skill of a theory of mind.[23] The relational disabilities experienced by individuals with Asperger's Syndrome make it clear that a theory of mind makes a critical contribution to personal relatedness.

The sense of "self" can also be understood as an aspect of a metacognitive theory of mind. To be able to think about one's own thinking, deciding, and doing is to have a mental representation of the self as a center of conscious activity. I previously speculated that self-relatedness was an aspect of our soulishness. Self-representation and the ability to think about our own thinking are important to self-relatedness. Thus, metacognitive ability and a theory of mind are involved in extending our relatedness both to others and to our selves.

Episodic Memory

Episodic memory is our conscious historical memory of past events, persons, times, and places — memories that retain some record of the specifics of time and place. Together these memories form our autobiographical knowledge, providing us with a sense of continuous historical personal identity, including a record of important events in our interpersonal and community relationships. Relatedness to other persons depends on both the experiences of relatedness to others at a particular moment and the sense of the continuity of that related-

22. Lorna Wing, "The Continuum of Autistic Characteristics," in *Diagnosis and Assessment in Autism*, ed. E. Schopler and G. B. Mesivob (New York: Plenum, 1988), pp. 91-111. See also Sally Ozonoff, Sally J. Robers, and Bruce F. Pennington, "Asperger's Syndrome: Evidence of an Empirical Distinction from High-Functioning Autism," *Journal of Child Psychology and Psychiatry* 32 (1991): 1107-22.

23. Dermont M. Bowler, "'Theory of Mind' in Asperger's Syndrome," *Journal of Child Psychology and Psychiatry* 33 (1992): 877-93.

ness, which is based in memory of specific instances in the past that involved the same individuals. A personal narrative memory is also an important contributor to the experience of being a unique center of conscious activity and agency and, therefore, to the subjective experience of relatedness to one's self.

Although it is difficult to imagine life without the ability to store autobiographical memories, there are cases in the neuropsychological literature that suggest the consequences of a deficient episodic memory. The classic case of anterograde amnesia (loss of the ability to form new episodic memories) is H.M.[24] Due to bilateral damage to important structures of the limbic system of the brain, H.M. lost the ability to form new conscious, episodic memories. If you met H.M. and carried on a short conversation with him, then walked out of the room for a few minutes, then returned again, H.M. would express no knowledge of the previous meeting. Any new information that passes out of his immediate memory is lost forever to conscious recall. Thus, H.M. is trapped within a narrow window of the memories of immediately preceding events, a window no wider than the amount of information he can keep consciously in mind at one time. Memories formed prior to the onset of H.M.'s brain pathology are easily recalled, but all events occurring during the intervening years are permanently lost.

In an expression that reflects the pathos of a person without memory of the recent past, Brenda Milner quotes H.M. as saying, "Every day is alone in itself, whatever enjoyment I've had, and whatever sorrow I've had. . . . Right now, I'm wondering 'Have I done or said anything amiss?' You see, at this moment everything looks clear to me, but what happened just before? That's what worries me. It's like waking from a dream; I just don't remember."[25] The consequences of such memory impairment to interpersonal relationships are well described by Larry Squire with regard to a similar case of anterograde amnesia (case N.A.): "He has no close friends. His socializing is limited by his difficulty in keeping a topic of conversation in mind and in carrying over the substance of social contacts from one occasion to another."[26] In summary, a personal, autobiographical (episodic) memory forms the basis of a continuous sense of personal identity and adds a critical retrospective dimension to our relationships with others.

24. B. Milner, S. Corkin, and H.-L. Teuber, "Further Analysis of the Hippocampal Amnesic Syndrome: 14-year Follow up Study of H.M.," *Neuropsychologia* 6 (1968): 215-34.

25. B. Milner, "Memory and the Temporal Regions of the Brain," in *Biology of Memory*, ed. K. H. Pribram and D. E. Broadbent (New York: Academic, 1970), p. 37.

26. As quoted in Milner, "Memory and the Temporal Regions of the Brain," p. 178.

Conscious Top-Down Agency and a Future Orientation

Top-down agency refers to the ability to modulate one's behavior in relationship to conscious thoughts and intentions. In other words, the phenomena at the top of the hierarchy of cognitive activity that we experience as conscious thought are not epiphenomenal, that is, mirages passively formed by the workings of a physically determined neural system that give us the mistaken impression that our subjective experiences of thinking and deciding actually cause our behavior. Rather, our thoughts and decisions influence our immediate and future thoughts and behavior.

The cognitive revolution of the last half-century has reestablished within the realm of scientific study the idea of conscious mental states and intrasubjective phenomena. The primary influence in this revolution has been an information-processing model of cognition in which various processing modules can be identified that intervene between the stimulus world and the pattern of behavioral responses. Important in the cognitive revolution has been the concept of top-down influences. The concept has been worked out most clearly in the realm of perception, where it has been recognized that perception of sensory information is influenced by both the nature of the stimulus itself (bottom-up) and the expectancy regarding the stimulus set up in the mind of the individual (top-down).[27] Extrapolated from top-down phenomena in perception has been the concept that higher-level conscious processes of attention, expectancy, intention, and planning are also effective causal processes that are influential in the future operations of lower-level neurocognitive systems and modules.

A *future orientation* is meant to denote the ability to run a conscious mental simulation or scenario of future possibilities for the actions of oneself and others, and to evaluate these scenarios. Evaluating potential future scenarios is tantamount to making decisions now with regard to desirable potential future behaviors. In this way, the behavioral output of a conscious human agent is determined not only by the immediate stimulus environment, but by evaluation of the contingencies represented in images and ideas of potential future states, events, and actions symbolically represented in our mind/brain.[28] Ability to regulate behavior via future-oriented conscious processing has many implications for interhuman relatedness. Both culture and the moral and ethical values it engenders in its members presume a consciousness of the future, and the

---

27. For example, see Margaret Matlin, *Cognition,* 3rd ed. (Fort Worth: Harcourt Brace, 1994), pp. 29, 37-40.
28. Deacon, *Symbolic Species.*

ability to imagine and evaluate the consequences of various actions. The processes of top-down conscious behavioral regulation and modulation and of reprogramming the brain for future behavior via evaluation of imagined scenarios are processes that would contribute to the development of moral character.

Emotional Feedback from Thoughts and Plans

Any discussion of human personal relatedness that does not consider emotions is obviously incomplete. We judge the qualities of our interpersonal (and intrapersonal) relatedness almost exclusively by what we sense in our affections and emotions. Toward others we "feel" love, friendship, a spirit of cooperativeness, like and dislike, hatred, disgust, sympathy, and care. Toward ourselves we might "feel" joy, bliss, contentment, fear, anxiety, and depression.

Damasio[29] has made a compelling case for the rationality, intelligence, and tacit knowledge[30] posited in our learned emotional reactions. The prospective mental scenarios mentioned above are evaluated primarily by the emotional reactions created in us when we imagine potential future events. The images or ideas that constitute thinking about a future possibility automatically elicit evaluative emotional responses. Normally we decide to do one thing versus another due more to these emotional reactions than to any conscious rational analyses we might produce. What is more, these emotionally guided decisions are generally socially correct; that is, they encode whatever social wisdom we have learned. Our emotional reactions inform us (many times unconsciously) of things we know but may not be able to formulate in rational discourse or conscious mental images. Thus, our tacit knowledge is communicated to awareness via our emotional responses.

The consequences of a deficit in the elicitation of such visceral, emotional reactions to our thoughts and plans are illustrated by individuals with damage to the orbital frontal area of the cerebral cortex (described previously). According to Damasio, the critical feature of the behavioral and social deficits of these patients is the decoupling of the process of thinking through options for action (running mental scenarios) and the elicitation of experience-based anticipa-

---

29. Damasio, *Descartes' Error.*

30. Tacit knowledge is the knowledge of the world of which we are usually not directly conscious, and which cannot adequately be expressed in words. Our knowledge of the meaning of the body language and facial expressions of others would be one example of tacit knowledge. We can be conscious of our general impression of another's body language and facial expressions, but usually we are not conscious of the specifics of the very complex pattern of cues that gave us the particular impression.

tory evaluative emotional responses that make themselves known through the autonomic reactivity of the entire body.

With respect to our understanding of the neurocognitive factors that have an impact on personal relatedness, Damasio describes the dire consequences on social behavior in the absence of a dynamic interaction between frontal cortex and emotional brain systems. In conversation, patients with orbital frontal brain damage may seem rational. However, their rational thought processes have little impact on their bodily emotional reactions, and, thus, bodily feedback cannot serve to modulate planning for actual behavior. Consequently, when life forces them to make important choices, they choose to act in ways that are capricious and socially maladaptive. The power of language, an understanding of the minds of others, a rich episodic memory, and the ability to formulate scenarios of alternative potential future events and situations all lose relevance to real-world decision making when cut off from the ability to elicit learned emotional reactions.

There is no reason to believe on the basis of either neuroanatomy or cognitive psychology that this "somatic marker"[31] system is itself substantially different in humans from that of other primates. Thus, what is unique about human mental systems and human behavior is the power of the cognitive processes that interact with the emotional evaluative system. It is the complexity and sophistication of the information that is evaluated, rather than the affective response system itself, that characterizes human social behavior. However, what is clear from cases of orbital frontal brain damage is that higher cognitive systems are not adequate to meet the demands of daily life if they are cut off from their ability to trigger relevant emotions. Disengagement of cognition from emotional modulation has dire consequences for the quality of personal relatedness.

The Evolutionary Trajectory toward Soulishness

How might these mental abilities that are so important for personal relatedness have evolved? If the process by which God created humankind was an evolutionary progression, was it a ruthless process of the selfish preservation of genes governed by survival of the fittest? Might other forces have played a part? What created the trajectory of evolutionary development that has resulted in human soulishness?

For the neo-Darwinist, the mechanisms that account for evolutionary

---

31. Damasio, *Descartes' Error.*

change are random mutation of genes and natural selection. Natural selection implies that the individual organism in which a particular mutation arises must survive at least long enough for procreation in order for the mutation to be passed along to future generations. If the mutation makes the individual more capable of survival, then procreation is more likely to occur. One of the problems in the evolution of behavior that has prompted much discussion over the last few decades is how *altruism* might have survived natural selection. Altruism implies one organism doing what is more beneficial for the survival of another at the expense of itself. Wouldn't any gene mutation that enhanced tendencies to altruism be systematically eliminated? To solve this problem, evolutionary theory has developed the concepts of *kin selection* and *reciprocal altruism*. Kin selection suggests that altruism toward kin would at least make more likely the survival of one's family, who are likely to share some of one's own genetic makeup. Reciprocal altruism is a mutual-help "deal" struck between two nonrelated individuals. "I'll scratch your back if you'll scratch mine." Despite these concepts, it is still somewhat hard to fathom how altruism came to be if the *only* rule is gene propagation through survival of the fittest individual (i.e., the individual carrying a new gene mutation) and the implied nonsurvival or nonprocreation of other individuals with their potentially competitive genes.

Although the concepts of kin selection and reciprocal altruism may solve the theoretical problem, this formulation seems strained and unsatisfactory in that altruism is a trait that apparently needed to await a period of evolutionary process before it could appear, in that it would not have occurred until some higher level of complexity and sophistication of organisms had been reached. For example, maternal protective behavior is thought to have emerged first, then altruism. Thus, evolution of a capacity for personal relatedness would be a considerable stretch for evolutionary theory, although probably not a theoretical impossibility.

A new concept, suggested recently by Robert Wright,[32] has important implications for considering the evolutionary emergence of personal relatedness and human soulishness. Wright borrows on game theory to suggest that an additional fundamental principle or law of evolutionary change is that biological life is a nonzero-sum game. A zero-sum game is a game where the outcomes for two participants are inversely related: if I win, you must lose, and if you win, I must lose — "winner takes all." A nonzero-sum game is one in which, to a greater or lesser degree, the interests of the participants overlap so that what is good for me is also good for you, and what is bad for me is also bad for you. In the world of sports and recreation, tennis is a zero-sum game, while two people

---

32. Robert Wright, *Nonzero: The Logic of Human Destiny* (New York: Pantheon, 2000).

mountain climbing together is a nonzero-sum game. Wright thus argues that natural selection operates not so much by the ruthless zero-sum process of "I survive at your expense," as by the nonzero-sum process of "cooperation means we both are more likely to survive."

According to Wright, the nonzero-sum dynamic has "crucially shaped the unfolding of life on earth."[33] The outcome of the fundamental dynamic of non-zero is an evolutionary trajectory toward increasing complexity, both biologically and culturally. Nonzero causes cells to survive better in the cooperative patterns of multi-cell creatures; and multi-cell creatures to realize the advantages of cooperative specialization; and groups of organisms and animals to develop patterns of group behavior; and *Homo sapiens* to develop a culture. With regard to culture, Wright concludes, "Ever since the late stone age, social evolution has amounted to an expansion and elaboration of interdependence, as nonzero-sum games have been played over greater and greater distances, among more and more people."[34] Nonzero provides the dynamic evolutionary force for the ultimate development of the mental and cultural capacity for deep, meaningful, and soulish forms of interpersonal relatedness. The emergence of the capacity for personal relatedness is an inevitable outcome of nonzero-sum evolutionary "games."

One of the primary motivations of reductionist forms of physicalism is to formulate an understanding of human and biological life that can be entirely accounted for (at least in principle) by the fundamental laws of physics. Thus, psychology can be accounted for by neurobiology; and neurobiology, by cellular biology; and cellular biology, by genetics; and genetics, by biochemistry; and so forth, down to the level of subatomic physics. But what if there are other laws, laws of organization and cooperation, such as nonzero-sumness, that escape description at the level of genetics, biochemistry, or physics? On the basis of the discipline of game theory, Wright proposes just such a nonreductive law.

Wright argues that the existence of nonzero is evidence that evolution has an inevitable direction toward increasing complexity of organisms, necessarily resulting in complex, sentient, and (in my words) relational creatures like humankind. According to the concept of nonzero, the progress of evolution has been influenced by a fundamental principle of the survival value of cooperative effort. This principle would make it inevitable that creatures would become more and more complex. This trajectory toward cooperation and complexity would necessarily result in complex relational creatures like humans. Once the neural/mental capacities of early humankind reached a level to sustain culture,

33. Robert Wright, "Nonzero," in 005.2000.01.14 at www.metanexus.net.
34. Wright, "Nonzero."

culture would itself be driven to increasing complexity by the same rules of nonzero-sumness. To put it theologically, God's intent to create humankind (i.e., creatures capable of personal relatedness and soulishness) was encoded in the universe within the fundamental law that survival benefits accrue from co-operation, and what is good for one is generally good for all. Although not promoting a theological position, Wright speculates that "this directionality provides at least some evidence that the evolutionary process is subordinate to a larger purpose — a 'higher' purpose, you might say."[35]

Finally, one critical problem with reductionist versions of physicalism is the objectional ethic one must derive from a cosmos in which all the determinative laws are at the subatomic level. What support does the commandment to "Love your neighbor as yourself" have within a world in which all causal influences exist at the level of physics? Yet, this law of love has potent support in a world with macro-level laws of operation such as nonzero-sumness.

A Matter of Semantics?

In closing, let me suggest some room for difference of opinion among Christians on these issues. Once we confront and accept the fundamental dependence of consciousness, free will, a narrative memory, moral/ethical behavior, the awesome experiences of divine presence, and so forth, on the operation of our nervous systems, then the choice to speak of "the soul" or "soulishness" is a matter of semantics and preference. I have argued that soulishness is a human attribute that has emerged from complex brain processes, but that it is a property of humanness that cannot be reduced to the operation of lower-level neural systems. However, because soulishness is emergent, operating by its own causal forces, does this make soulishness a nonmaterial thing? Or, is this emergent, nonreductive soulishness of humankind a functional description of a physical system because it is a property of complexly interactive neural processing?

Given the tendency that we all have to think of abstract nouns as if they referred to separable and discrete physical things, and given two millennia of dualist thought-habits within Christianity, I am of the opinion that considering persons to be soulish physical beings (rather than physical beings with emergent souls) is more helpful to our continuing understanding of the place of humankind within God's physical and biological creation. It also provides a helpful frame of reference for considering the developmental process by which humans evolved.

35. Robert Wright, "Nonzero 2," in 007.2000.01.21 at www.metanexus.net.

Remembering God's People

GEORGE L. MURPHY

One of the gifts for which we give thanks to God is our ancestors in the faith, those who have followed Christ in previous generations and who are for us examples of God's grace and models for the Christian life. Martyrs, missionaries, Church leaders, theologians, and monastics have been honored throughout Christian history. But it is not only Christians concerned with distinctively "religious" matters who should be remembered. All Christians have a "vocation," a call to serve God in the work that they do in daily life in the world. The memory of those who have been faithful in their callings, sometimes against great difficulties, can encourage those who do similar work today.

This is especially important for those who are called to scientific work. Believers throughout the centuries who have studied the natural world in the confidence that they were learning about the wonders of God's creation show that there need not be "warfare" between science and theology. Their example can encourage young people today who have scientific interests and abilities but who may have been given the impression that there is some incompatibility between honest investigation of nature and Christian faith.

There is no lack of Christians who might be remembered for work in pure and applied sciences, and it is possible to list only a few names. We can begin in the New Testament with Luke the physician. Hildegard of Bingen, a 12th-century builder and abbess of a monastery with deep interests in music, natural history, and medicine, and Robert Grosseteste, a Bishop of Lincoln who wrote commentaries on Aristotle's *Physics* and a book of his own on optics, are two medieval figures worthy of mention.

We cannot ignore Nicolaus Copernicus, who in the 16th century introduced the heliocentric model of the solar system that marked the beginning of modern science. Blaise Pascal, a brilliant mathematician who did important work in hydrostatics, devoted the latter part of his short life to apologetics and other reli-

Blaise Pascal

James Clerk Maxwell

Michael Faraday

Henrietta Leavitt

Scientists who made great contributions to their disciplines as expressions of their Christian calling: (A) Blaise Pascal, frontispiece, Viscount St. Cyres, New York E. P. Dutton & Co., 1910, courtesy AIP Emilio Segre Visual Archives, E. Scott Barr Collection; (B) James Clerk Maxwell, engraving from a photograph in the possession of Sir Henry Roscoe, courtesy AIP Emilo Segre Visual Archives; (C) Michael Faraday, painted by H. W. Pickersgill, Esq., R.A., engraved by J. Cochran, courtesy AIP Emilo Segre Visual Archives, and (D) Henrietta Leavitt, AIP Emilo Segre Visual Archives, E. Scott Barr Collection.

gious concerns. In the 18th century the prolific work of the Swiss Leonhard Euler made an impact on virtually every branch of pure and applied mathematics.

Two British scientists of the 19th century, Michael Faraday and James Clerk Maxwell, were both deeply committed Christians. Their work is the basis for the classical understanding of electricity and magnetism. The publication of Maxwell's equations of electromagnetism in 1865 coincided with the presentation by the Moravian monk Gregor Mendel of the results of experiments that gave the first insight into a scientific understanding of genetics.

Henrietta Leavitt made a crucial contribution to the discovery of the expansion of the universe by finding the relationship between period and luminosity for Cepheid variable stars that made it possible to use them to measure distances to other galaxies.

To turn from the realm of the very large to that of the very small: Arthur Compton won a Nobel Prize in physics for his work on X-rays that demonstrated the reality of radiation quanta. (He also served for fourteen years as General Chairman of the Laymen's Missionary Movement.) And Pierre Teilhard de Chardin, a Jesuit priest and paleontologist, was concerned throughout his life with the integration of the evolutionary view provided by science with a Christian understanding of God's purpose for creation.

These men and women have been instruments through which God has shown us, in different ways and in varying degrees, the splendors and the subtleties of creation. Their lives are examples of the perseverance of faith in the face of suffering, disappointment, and opposition. They are reminders to scientists today that their work is part of the human task of caring for creation, and not just a matter of gaining professional prestige or making money. And they are witnesses to all people that — in the words from the 111th Psalm which were placed over the great door of the Cavendish Laboratory at Cambridge — "Great are the works of the LORD, studied by all who delight in them."

We give thanks for Christians in science and for all God's faithful people of every time and every place in the Prayer of the Day for All Saints:

> Almighty God, whose people are knit together in one holy Church, the body of Christ our Lord: Grant us grace to follow your blessed saints in lives of faith and commitment, and to know the inexpressible joys you have prepared for those who love you; through your Son, Jesus Christ our Lord, who lives and reigns with you and the Holy Spirit, one God, now and forever. Amen.

> *Lutheran Book of Worship*
> (Minneapolis: Augsburg, 1978), p. 36

Contributors

KEITH B. MILLER
Department of Geology
Kansas State University

EDWARD B. DAVIS
History of Science Department
Messiah College

DAVID CAMPBELL
Department of Biological Sciences
University of Alabama

DEBORAH B. HAARSMA
Astronomy & Physics Department
Calvin College

LOREN HAARSMA
Department of Physics
Calvin College

DAVID L. WILCOX
Department of Biology
Eastern College

ROBIN COLLINS
Department of Religion
Messiah College

WARREN S. BROWN JR.
Fuller Graduate School of
    Psychology
Department of Psychiatry &
    Biobehavioral Science
UCLA School of Medicine

CONRAD HYERS
Chair of Religion, retired
Gustavus Adolphus College

MARK A. NOLL
McManis Professor of Christian
    Thought
Wheaton College

DAVID N. LIVINGSTONE
Professor of Geography &
    Intellectual History
Queens University of Belfast

JENNIFER WISEMAN
Physics & Astronomy Department
Johns Hopkins University

JEFFREY K. GREENBERG
Department of Geology &
    Environmental Science
Wheaton College

JAMES P. HURD
Department of Anthropology/
   Sociology
Bethel College

TERRY M. GRAY
Chemistry Department
Colorado State University

HOWARD J. VAN TILL
Professor of Physics & Astronomy,
   emeritus
Calvin College

ROBERT J. RUSSELL
Director
The Center for Theology and the
   Natural Sciences

GEORGE L. MURPHY
St. Paul's Episcopal Church, Akron
   Ohio, and
Trinity Lutheran Seminary

LAURIE J. BRAATEN
Division of Christian Religion and
   Philosophy
Judson College

JOHN C. MUNDAY, JR.
President, Avantrex Communications
Formerly Professor of Natural
   Sciences
Regent University